Time Between Summers

A Fabrication

Michael Roth

Printed in the United States of America

First Printing, 2021
Cover Painting by Linda Roth

Paperback ISBN: 978-1-7343428-2-6
Library of Congress Control Number: 2021911054

Lensgrinder, Ltd.
Kirkland, WA 98033

Questions, comments, concerns? mtroth@lensgrinder.com

Studies in Phenomenology & Social Philosophy

Lensgrinder, Ltd

Kirkland, WA

To Mom and Dad

Time Between Summers

Time Between Summers

"Without making any boast of it Sancho Panza succeeded in the course of years, by feeding him a great number of romances of chivalry and adventure in the evening and night hours, in so diverting from himself his demon, whom he later called Don Quixote, that this demon thereupon set out, uninhibited, on the maddest exploits, which, however, for the lack of a preordained object, which should have been Sancho Panza himself, harmed nobody. A free man, Sancho Panza philosophically followed Don Quixote on his crusades, perhaps out of a sense of responsibility, and had of them a great and edifying entertainment to the end of his days."

—Franz Kafka, The Truth about Sancho Panza

"Of course Christminster is a sort of fixed vision with him, which I suppose he will never be cured of believing in. He still thinks it a great center of high and fearless thought, instead of what it is, a nest of commonplace schoolmasters whose characteristic is timid obsequiousness to tradition."

—Thomas Hardy, Jude the Obscure

September

Less than an hour after they turned on the phone, Wolfe called. He is moving to Ann Arbor and needs a place to stay. What a pain in the ass. He takes up a lot of space. His personality. I haven't seen him since he left Urbana after our second year. Said he was going to hit the road, travel. He called from Austin a few times, and from Boulder. He was such a fucking poser. He paid attention to what people were doing. He would casually repeat habits he had observed in others. He might have been sincere about it, I don't know, but what really bothered me was the way he wrote. Such a voice, so friendly and likeable. I hated it. I know I can be charming when I want to be, I know that I am not without charisma, but my writing repels, and I've always been jealous of him for that. The story he wrote just before he left was like something out of Rilke. So beautiful with so much tension in every gesture.

We met during our first semester. We were both taking a course on *Being and Time*. I was invisible in that class. Intentionally. No one talked to me. Even the people who later became my friends didn't notice me in the back row never saying a word. Only he did. He would talk to me after class. We would walk outside to smoke. He didn't seem to care whether I was listening or not. He didn't exactly go on about the lecture or what we had just read. He was all over the place. He hated nodders, "that asshole in the row ahead of us, did you see him nodding? Like he's read all that shit? I bet those people are just made up, but here's bobblehead Biff nodding away like a fucking moron." It was entertaining. I didn't talk back much but I wasn't rude. He probably kept at it because of that. After a while it was like brute force had gotten us to know each other. Proximity was all we had. He would just keep hanging around and eventually I did end up saying something. Asking him stuff. What was he going to write his paper about? What other classes was he taking? Was he going to the parties at the professors' houses?

He would never answer these questions. Well, maybe he thought he was. He would attack the premise. "Why should we have to write a paper? Here read this, digest it, spit something back. What does that have to do with anything? We should be left on our own or treated like apprentices. No tests, no papers, just try to become part of the academic community. Publish, present, assist the dean by getting the department to adopt some college-wide incentive. Whatever is expected of them, that should be expected of us. They can advise us when we ask for help. If that's the life of the philosopher, if that's what they think it amounts to, then they should throw us into it. None of this bullshit with grades. Sink or swim. If they really believed it." Or maybe, "Why the hell would I spend my free time eating Bree and drinking shitty corked red wine with someone who happens to have spent a lot of time reading Hegel, or Kantian ethics? I'd rather stick this mechanical pencil in my eye. No thanks. Wanna grab a burger at the bar? They have a good juke box. We can unpack all the proto-Nazi imagery in *Being and Time*." Finally, there was the classic, "It's only for billing purposes that they make us take classes. You take three each semester. You think that's the perfect way to cut up your time? Bullshit, it's the appropriate and sanctioned way to ensure that the dollar value of your tuition and fee waiver is allocated correctly. There's probably some chargeback scandal going on, some internal accounting requirement that forces us to take so many units per year so that tenured faculty can have something to do. We're trying to become learned, students of philosophy for Christ's sake, why the hell do they have us sitting in classrooms and paying fees before we even hear the lesson?"

I guess I started to like him. He got in the way too. I mean, the professors knew that he thought this way. They could just tell even when he wasn't saying anything. I don't think they liked him very much. This made it poisonous to hang around him. At least I thought it did. It made me guilty by association. They would think I agreed with him. I didn't want to get kicked out, I didn't want my aid to get cut off, so I always felt uncomfortable with him in public, hanging around the department, or at the colloquia and the receptions afterward. It's not that I didn't agree with him. On many things I most definitely did. I just didn't want anyone to know that I did. I already had so many strikes against me. I was studying the wrong thing and I didn't have the right methodologies. I wasn't coming from math or biology. English literature, the kiss of death, was too soft. The last thing I needed was to be branded a troublemaker.

He quit grad school after his second year. He liked a few of the professors, but he thought the program was ridiculous. Not only wasn't he learning what he wanted to be learning, but knowledge and understanding were being drained out of him. What is the opposite of learning? Is it learning? The thoughts that filled his head, what he wanted to spin into yarns and tales, didn't fit with the curriculum and most definitely didn't fulfill the distribution requirements. He knew the approved methodology far better than I ever did, but he was always muddling the genre in his written work —at least he did when he would actually write something. Mostly he would defer: the dreaded incomplete. He said that approaches like his were a significant part of the history of philosophy and he didn't understand why there was a contemporary prejudice that was so dead set against it. Likely it didn't match with the sensibilities of Third Earl Russell, but what about Plato or Descartes? Spinoza or Berkeley? Not to mention

Nietzsche or Kierkegaard. He would write these weird narratives about a guy taking a walk in the woods with his dog and use the setting to conjure a reading of some historical figure they wanted him to write about. Sometimes it didn't work, but sometimes it did. He said that was good enough. The baseball theory of action means that a 30% success rate makes you a star. I can still remember this one scene where the dog runs up ahead and defecates just off the trail, the hiker approaches and the line was something like "'Become hard slowly,' the roadside shit steamed." That's the kind of thing he would do. He believed it too. He thought shit by the road really did steam its ideas to anyone who was willing to listen. That's how he thought meaning worked. The fact that he could write it and that the reader would understand it, proved it. The professors hated it. They knew he could do it the way they wanted it done, but he wouldn't listen. He thought he knew better. They said that he was arrogant, the way that he would scoff or roll his eyes, sometimes not even bothering to offer a counterargument. He said he had vision and came to school to realize it not to be trained in some discipline. "Who do these organ grinders think they are? I'm not a monkey, and my heart is not their meat." It was funny but it makes me feel small now when I remember him going off like that. I guess I always wondered whether he liked me or not, whether he respected me, or did he think I was one of the robots who was in his way? I was at least trying to get it right, but he would tell me to cut that shit out.

He wrote that story and then he left. It was about a writer. Eye roll. It was genuinely strange because you couldn't tell where things were happening. Was there physical space around these people? Were they standing on the ground somewhere? The writer loved truth, but truth didn't care about him, didn't even know that he existed. Truth seemed to be a person, or a deity of some kind. He called it Aletheia, and I read it as though she were a woman. To get her attention, the writer —who had the same name as the author— invented this character and then tried to use him to pursue her. It worked. She fell in love with the character and did everything for him, showered him with attention and hung on his every word. The writer succeeded, but then it would hit you, why would the author make himself a character in his own story? Was it really him? Anyone could be named 'Wolfe'? It was odd and it made me wonder what kind of an imagination he had, what else was he capable of doing? Genre works that way; it can make the reader suspicious. One day, by accident, the writer runs into Aletheia, and she treats him badly, snaps at him, orders him to produce the character, the object of her desire. Turns out her willingness to be seduced in the one case was a way to evade the writer in the other case. Like she knew what she was doing, or it did. That was part of the pursuit. He refuses, of course, and tries to get even with her by killing off the character in a really degrading way, making him out to be a villain.

This hurts Aletheia very much, she is visibly wounded. It doesn't make the writer happy though and he learns an important lesson about love. He loved Aletheia and even though it was unrequited he was devastated both by the death of his character and by the pain it caused her. He had thought that was what he wanted. At that point you think the story is going to end with the writer's tears when he realizes he doesn't want what he thought he wanted. Something else happens instead. This strange floating vision appears before him. It's another woman, at least that's what I thought it was. She says her name is Polyhymnia and that even though she may not have been the one he wanted, she is the one that he is going to end up with. The writer accepts this. He isn't happy about it, but he isn't angry either. It's just the way that it is. She tells him that this is how it always works in these kinds of stories.

"Who the fuck is Polyhymnia?" I asked him when I read it.

"She's the muse of epic battle hymns and marches," he said casually.

"Okay, but why?"

"If you have to ask why, then you don't get it. It's a battle hymn. We're going to need all the inspiration we can get."

He left town a little while later. He said they didn't know what philosophy was, he said they didn't understand that Paris, the character from his story, was the only kind of creature that Aletheia could love and that he was most definitely not a professor of philosophy. Even the academics who pay lip service to philosophy's unique status as a kind of love, don't understand the anguish that comes with it. It is unrequited love. He found Polyhymnia to help him endure it, or Polyhymnia found him. Another stroke of luck. He said that was better than whatever some discipline might have to offer. I took the discipline. Whenever we talked in the last five years, I felt more and more distance growing between us. I did what they told me to do, I gave them what they wanted. I passed the quals, I wrote the dissertation, and now here I was getting ready with my 3 preps, working as a sabbatical replacement after putting in my time as an adjunct. The last thing I needed was Wolfe coming to stay here and reminding me every second of every day that I was a sellout. He might think me the worst kind because I had sold out while still making a half-assed effort not to, meaning I lost on all fronts. I had compromised on what I really wanted to do, and I had absorbed the discipline in a way that was doomed to leave me outside the party when trying to network my way into that magical tenure-track position.

I hemmed a bit at his suggestion that I give him a place to stay. He pushed past that and dove into a story about what happened to him when he was passing through Ann Arbor in August. He had been sitting outside somewhere near downtown and a thunderstorm came rolling through. The lightning repeatedly flashed across the night sky. It was demanding and commanding, it was impossible to look away, he said. There was an equally enthralled woman sitting at the next table. She was without guile. It was her character, and it was the lightning. There was no rain so they could just sit there and watch, looking at each other now and again. Gasping, exhaling, whispering "whoa" or "wow" after the really big strikes or the loudest of the clasps. He told me that he moved to her table, but they didn't speak much. They just sat there watching and listening. She was a boss, he said, but was willing to be moved by forces of nature. He said he couldn't get her out of his mind. He had moved on and got as far as Maryland, but then he decided to come back. He knew I was going to be moving to town and he thought he should try to find her again. He said that lightning storms and people like that don't come along very often. It was his duty to appreciate the gifts the universe offered so he was going to come back. The only things he knew about her was where she had been camped out reading that one night and what she told him just before they parted, that she worked as a typesetter at a local publishing firm. He had no doubt that he would be able to find her.

It had been thrilling to listen to his story. I felt myself being pulled into it. It needed an ending and I saw how important it was for him to come back and give it one. I wouldn't be able to say no. I believed him too. That he would do it, find her, and that she would probably be glad that he did. He was blessed like that. He would find her when he got back, and he would find whatever else it was that he was looking for too. I had no doubt that a year in Ann Arbor would be a momentous event for him. He was always lucky like that. With that perfect, likeable voice that he knew just how to tease and control. He may have left graduate school, but he didn't fail. He got what he came for. He learned that he didn't need to be there. For him that was the important question. What am I after? Can I find it here? Is my plan the kind of thing that is best served by an academic career? It cost him two years to get an authoritative answer to that question: absolutely not.

He knew that two years in exchange for that kind of certainty was a bargain. I was still dangling from the edge. They were like strikes against me and kept coming back over and over again, like a mantra: I studied the wrong thing at the wrong school. The haze would clear, and I could see the writing on the wall. I was reasonably sure that I didn't want it to end, and I was very worried that Wolfe's return signaled it and would force me to see what I had been trying not to see since I got my degree. I thought they would know he was here, and it would seal their judgment. Either way, I had my rock: if I don't quit, I can't fail. What if Wolfe shows up and laughs in that way that he does? What if it makes me feel so small that I just can't bear to do any work ever again? He could just as easily have the opposite effect, but it was a wildcard. There was no telling what might happen. I felt sure that there would never come a moment when I would clearly and distinctly express an act of will and say, "I quit." No, whatever else might happen, that would never happen. I'd just become so humiliated and feel so stupid about it that I wouldn't be able to write another word. "I quit," makes it seem so deliberate. What if it isn't like that at all, what if it's just a nagging absence, no longer doing anything? Pure nothingness, like death. An absence of doing, not a positive act. I might get distracted and leave off. I wouldn't even notice that I had stopped noticing. Pure nothingness. The oblivious. Oblivion. He can have that effect, cause me to worry that way. What if it happens here? I had deluded myself into thinking my return to Michigan was a triumph and now Wolfe was coming, and he might force me to see the fallacy in that.

So many questions, so much anxiety.

Failure has three elements each of which is necessary, none of which is sufficient. 1) There must be an actor with a plan. 2) The plan has not been finished but at least some effort has been made to further it. 3) The actor has stopped trying, or is prevented from trying, to finish. This last element means that any unfinished plan must have been left behind or abandoned with no way back to it. Since a way back is possible so long as the actor lives, failure requires that the way be blocked, and that the actor admit it. Giving up is not enough. The actor must recognize the failure in the act. Such recognition amounts to surrender that transcends the act and embeds itself in the actor's character. Failure, therefore, is not purely negative but includes conditions that actively block the way back. This makes it a kind of achievement, something the actor does or is complicit in doing. To the extent that the actor is responsible for this condition through their admission, giving up makes a black mark that remains part of their permanent record. It is a dialectic of giving up where the residual is the story of what it leaves behind and the story that is left behind. We may think of partiality as constituting the black mark's form since it feels like a judgment, something unavoidable and real that defines the actor through the unfinished act. The clock has run out. The game has ended. The actor embraces the mark of their partial condition as though it were an appendage, and deliberately quits any further movement toward completing the plan.

The kid upstairs asked what I do for a living. When I told her I teach philosophy she immediately said, "Is that like which came first, the chicken or the egg?" "That's right." She brightened up and wanted to know which did come first. I told her that there were eggs way before there were chickens and then "Wait, did you mean chicken eggs?" "Duh," she said. "Well, that depends. Is a chicken egg an egg that a chicken lays or is a chicken egg an egg that contains a chicken?" At this point she thought I was hilarious. I kept going: "If chicken eggs are eggs that come out of chickens, then the chicken came first, but if chicken eggs are eggs that chickens come out of, then the egg came first." "Well, which is it?" "I don't know, that's not my area. We probably have to ask a chicken expert. At least now the question is more clear. They will be able to give a better answer." This seemed to satisfy her.

I've never been all that passionate about the whole "what is philosophy?" line of questioning. During a chat at the mailbox with a 10-year-old, the question might come up and be worth a minute or two, but not in any other context. Who was it that said philosophy is what philosophers do? Someone must've said that, right? They were probably onto something, because that's the answer that leads us to ask, "who is a philosopher?" which is a much more interesting question. Am I one? How can I know? Is it based on something I'm doing, something I experience or might observe in my actions or in my thinking? Is it based on what others say about me? Do I need to have a job that falls into the category of "things philosophers do"?

If I am teaching philosophy at a university, does that make me a philosopher or just an intellectual historian? If the label is based on a social role acknowledged by some board with the power to admit candidates to the profession, then maybe visiting assistant professor is a good baseline criterion for getting membership. How long does that last? On the other hand, if there are things you have to do in order to be a philosopher, maybe teaching is a distraction, and it might be preventing me from doing them. When I teach, I spend a lot of time grading and figuring out how to explain other people's arguments to students. I tell them that they should first try to understand what Descartes is saying and present it in a thorough and sympathetic form before starting to criticize him. Is that philosophy or am I just trying to navigate around their prejudices? Am I teaching them philosophy when I do that or is this just some basic tooling that they will need should they ever get caught doing philosophy? Can you even teach philosophy, or just the tools for it in case someone happens to already have the genuine article by some light of nature?

There is another aspect of it that really gets me going. Let's suppose it is some set of activities and you are a philosopher when you perform them, and teaching philosophy amounts to demonstrating them to the uninitiated. The teacher, in that case, is kind of a guide and must have the ability to identify relevant demonstrations and broker an understanding of them through explanations that are themselves micro-demonstrations. If all that is true, do you have to be good at it? Not just anyone gets to be a philosopher. It's not just an activity, but an activity expressing excellence. Isn't it? Bad philosophers aren't philosophers at all, but sophists or pedants or something else altogether. The fact that a person spends their life thinking and reasoning, considering the clarity of a set of questions, and demonstrating the confusions that others fell victim to when writing on various topics, is no guarantee that this person is doing it in a way that expresses virtue or excellence. Aristotle and I might be doing more or less the same thing. He was good at it, he expressed excellence, and so it is correct to say that he was a philosopher. Me? Tbd.

It may be that there hasn't been very many of them. Just a few, but I can't fathom who they are. Is it possible that there was a great philosopher who no one has ever heard of, that no one could ever fathom? Does this activity expressing excellence need to have made an impression, left a mark that others recognized and acknowledged as a demonstration of excellent activity? Not just any mark and any impression, but a mark or an impression that the right people recognize. Does this mean that living among idiots could prevent someone from being a philosopher? Can the experience be nullified by other people? Back up. Anyone who is admitted to a program offering doctorates can develop a proposal for a dissertation on Aristotle. No one would cry foul here and claim that he wasn't a philosopher and that any dissertation that focuses on his work shouldn't qualify the candidate for the degree. The list, up to a point, is non-controversial and they make it seem obvious that all the people who matter have recognized the legitimacy of the list. Even if there is some disagreement from one department to the next about which thinkers populate the canon, for the most part the academy is unified on the notion that there is a canon, and its preservation is a huge portion of the intellectual work of philosophers. Members may grumble about it now and again, but they are mostly just advocating reforms where this or that excluded thinker or underrepresented group should be added or some other should be removed. What does the canon have to do with that experience?

How did the professors and the doctors of philosophy with their committees and degrees get to be the arbiters of this title? It feels so flavor of the month and fashionable. If they were to decide suddenly that Aristotle was not a philosopher but something else entirely, would that change anything at all about what he did and how he lived and acted? Of course not. Focusing on Aristotle might be a problem. He was *the* philosopher. What about Kierkegaard? That's a better example. The genre and authorship questions in his work are so challenging. Not all academics agree that Kierkegaard was a philosopher, and yet nothing in those points of view and disagreements changes the facts about Kierkegaard's life. What he did, how he worked, what he wrote, and so on. Whatever he was doing, it was some thing or other. Some call it philosophy others don't, but what did Kierkegaard think he was doing? Was he too busy doing it to worry about whether it fit into some category or other understood by the doctors in their departments around the world and across time?

That's probably why they became so focused on the what of philosophy rather than the who of it. What Kierkegaard wrote may not have been philosophy in 1850, but then it became interesting to some philosophers in the twentieth century and that converted his work into philosophy from whatever it was before. If we were only focused on who he was and the activity he performed, this wouldn't make sense, the act would be the same act from the perspective of either century. Only if the 'what' of it matters and the relationship it has to other work people are doing, only then can we accommodate the change in history that moves it from one category to another. That seems so very odd. Was Kierkegaard doing philosophy, or wasn't he? His actions don't change, his experience doesn't change, the phenomenological meaning and structure of his acts were real space-time events. They couldn't be one thing in 1850 and something entirely different in 1930, could they? It felt like something to be Kierkegaard, it meant something to do what he did and act how he acted. Was that feeling, that experience or meaning, was all of that the life and mind of a philosopher doing philosophy, or wasn't it?

Metaphysics, epistemology, ethics, and logic. This is the subject matter of philosophy. People who think and write about these things, those are the philosophers. Well, so long as they follow the correct genre. I mean, it can't be chaos, it's not a free-for-all. You can't explore theories of knowledge through the use of fictional characters in invented narratives and imagined events. Those are novelists or poets. It is *what* you think and *how* you express what you think, and probably what others make of it too. That explains why I'm always falling short and why I got caught studying the wrong thing at the wrong school. I have always been in pursuit of a specific experience, the experience of the philosopher. That might be an illusion. At least there is no place where you can find it. Certainly, there isn't anyone who can teach it to you or do it for you. Although, if you are lucky, and if you keep your eyes open and your mind focused, you might come across demonstrations of it now and again. They may come from a ten-year-old kid by the mailbox. Hell, they might even happen when you're studying with a teacher who is a professor in an academic department at some university somewhere.

At fifteen, the professor informed his mother that he intended to become a better writer. He was going to write every day with the aim of improving gradually. It did not matter whether he ever became good at it, that was not the plan. He only wanted to get better and thought two pages a day —like clockwork— would achieve that goal. She took his declaration seriously and told him that it might be better if he did not put all his eggs in one basket. He went off and considered her advice, using the two pages that day for it. He began to develop a phenomenology of failure assuring himself that if he wrote every day, then he would get better without fail. If he did not quit, then he could not fail. This was not the kind of plan where the clock could run out, and it was not a case where other people would have a say in shutting down his aspirations. He believed he was in control of his own destiny. The methodology of this, however, was lost on him. Far from being the professor just yet, he was insufficiently schooled to understand what he was doing as he harbored these notions and optimistically promised himself that he would keep up with them for the rest of his life. Today, he would summarize his advice to young would-be actors of idealistic passion projects like this: "Quit if you can." He means that if the person is so conditioned that they can leave off with their plan and block their way back to it, then they would be best served to do so. At fifteen, unfortunately, he firmly believed he was incapable of quitting, and could not see the torment this belief would cause. Instead, he returned to his mother later that day and told her that it was okay to put all his eggs in one basket so long as he guarded that basket with his life.

This is not a tale of success, of a happy young man on his way to the good life. It is a tale about being in the throes, about succumbing to something that has already found you, something you are trying to escape but keep coming up behind. It is a tale in which the anti-hero succumbs to this pattern without understanding it and without any tools or tactics for avoiding the discomfort caused by colliding with the same barriers again and again. The path led down some dark roads. Some brightly lit ones too.

Years later one of them would have insight into a basic pattern of experience. It started with the relationship between two interfaces: IEnumerable and IEnumerator. On the one hand, there was a list of things that could be enumerated and on the other hand something that enumerates them. He used this insight to develop a design for IDeployable and IDeployer, but its essence lay in actions not in objects, so the paradigm was IDoable and IDoer. The doer does and the doable is done. Philosophy is doable and the philosopher does. Not what, but who and how, where and when. From the point of view of interfaces, not implementations. You see? A formal positioning more so than actual operations. Formal because there is nothing behind it, nothing to it, merely a set of signatures and associations, a contract, an agreement or set of them. IDoer entails no specific identifiable actor, rather agency is left to the material implementation, to the variable execution, and even to the mock facades that testing requires. Sophisticated coding doesn't just abstract the object model and the entity design, but the operations, actions, and events that take place through the inner workings of the system in / as / through its structure and form.

Teaching was never a solution to these riddles; it was the riddle. He was a teacher. He was a student. He was a reader. He was a writer. Each and all implementations of IDoer. He struggles with the integration, a single class that can implement them all. Especially that day. He had learned that his 20th century course had been insufficiently enrolled and would be canceled. He would have to teach a second section of the ethics prep. Several of the students who had enrolled in the canceled class asked to do an independent study and he agreed so long as they could all meet together once a week. The course had included several works, but they were only interested in *Being and Time,* so that would be their focus. The intro and first ethics section were one-hour classes that met on Monday, Wednesday, and Friday. The added section was an evening class that met for 3 hours each Monday. He set the seminar to meet on Wednesdays. It would be a busy semester with lots of teaching, reading, and studying.

Would there be writing? How would that fit? He studied, taught, and read so that he could write. That is what held it all together. That was the who and the how and the where and the when of it. Philosophy, so his pride told him, happened when he wrote. This was a simple prejudice because there was no implementation of IDoer for philosophy. Rather, the writer and the written classes were how he understood it. Teacher and taught, reader and read, studier and studied were all incidental and derivative. Take for example, the distinction that one finds in academic circles between analytic and continental philosophy. It is a topic of riotous debates. Do they differ in the way they read and are read? Teach and are taught? Study and are studied? Are they merely differences in the writing and the written? From grad school, he knew many who aligned with each side, and they conversed, studied together, read together, learned together. There seemed to be an agreement that they only wrote differently. That was the extent of it. You couldn't tell them apart in the cafés and the receptions. The debate seemed to permit focus on the written substance of philosophy, on its presence in the artifact, on the 'what' of it, the content and the material. Deconstruction changed all that for him, it drew his attention because it seemed like a first foray into suggesting there was more to it than that: that reading was different, that studying was different, and that even teaching would have to be different.

At the outset he would be teaching the Heidegger, Aristotle's *Nicomachean Ethics,* and Plato's *Phaedo.* He would be reading these books, teaching these topics, and studying these works. Whatever orientation he associated with his philosophical foundations would find their way into the preparation and the practice. Philosophy would be at work everywhere in all facets. If writing were the source and limit of this act, if his vision of the philosopher at work was in the writing, how could that translate into the teaching and the reading and the studying? Heidegger's lectures have been published as though they were books. They surface his studies, reading, and teaching as writing. Probably he was overly influenced by this, but it struck him that if he did not have a structured piece of writing to organize the work of the semester, he would not be doing philosophy and there wouldn't be anything resembling it in any of the other activities either. Why should the students have all the fun? Why assign papers at all? Without the writing, the work would lack spirit. As he planned his courses, as he launched his study of these works at the outset of that fall semester, he also conceptualized a piece of written work that he eventually called *Being, An Introduction.* It would provide an anchor, it would add spirit and set everything else into the proper order.

This angle put him at odds with many of his colleagues. He wasn't entirely sure why. On the surface, they might pretend to agree with him. They too thought that philosophy was something they were doing when they read the works of philosophers, taught those works and their arguments, or studied them in conversation and in analysis with whatever it implied. The profession places a strong emphasis on a demonstration of excellence in publications, so clearly there was agreement that writing was the tangible product of their integrated actions. There was a distance from that which he couldn't see clearly, but that he felt and suffered as he sent articles to journals, applied for tenure-track positions, and conversed with colleagues. While he filled out the forms for the parking permit, got his logon and email address, and was shown to his office for the year, he felt ostracized, an outsider, someone who didn't belong. He was a visiting assistant professor, adjunct to the primary duties of the university. Not a member of any committee and not invited to any meetings. This seemed like more than just a bureaucratic declaration, it was a judgment. Even if he wrote and wrote all the time, even if everyone agreed on these implementations, his emphasis was on the fine print in the contract making it a departure and a rogue assignment. Want to be a real philosopher? Make sure to get it in writing, make sure they include it in the small print.

In graduate school there was a seminar on Nietzsche. He listened for weeks without contributing. He couldn't say anything, he couldn't even begin to express his point of view in that environment. The closest he came in those first weeks was when one day he had thoughtlessly set his foot on one of the hot water pipes that was exposed along the wall of the seminar room. After a few minutes, a bit of the sole of his shoe had melted and he felt a mild burning in his foot. He let out a small yelp as he pulled his foot away from the pipe. The professor running the seminar noticed this and interrupted his explanation to make some snide remark about the student's desire to raise a distraction. "Just seeing how much I can endure," he responded. This concisely captured his experience. To contribute, he would have to start the whole discussion, weeks-worth of conversations and deliberations, over again from the beginning. He felt they had gotten off on the wrong foot and that they would never get anywhere if they proceeded like this. Who was he to do that, to raise such a distraction? There were ten people in the seminar, why should he reset everyone's work? The others seemed involved enough, they seemed to have something to say, some contribution to make. Only he seemed to have been silenced, only he was unable to bear the butchering of the master's work. He said nothing. He wrote.

What he wrote was an annoying little piece that he was meant to present at the beginning of one of the sessions. Each of the students had to do this, they would start with a prepared piece on the day's topic, frame the discussion, and then lead it. When it was his turn, his topic was the revaluation of all values and he read his piece aloud to the group. It was called "Derrida Dancing Star and Midwifery." No commas. It was, to an extent, about Nietzsche in the same way that Derrida's *Spurs* was about Nietzsche. Meaning, a wholly inappropriate investigation into his work via a random note left in the nachlasse: "I have forgotten my umbrella." Was this philosophy? Derrida was asking. Is this philosophy? he was asking. There were lots of little themes to build on: the dancing star that one "gives birth to" when harnessing chaos. Socrates' relationship to the student in the guise of midwife. Mostly, it was style. That was the upshot Derrida was inspiring: how does style work in philosophical writing, what is its role? The piece was annoying because it sounded like lots of imitative deconstructive pulp from that period in academic history. The seminar's professor likely lumped it together with lots of non-sense he had been forced to listen to at conferences and from some of his colleagues. Of course, our anti-hero thought he was on to something. What did he know? He was just a student and not an especially good one.

After he finished reading his little presentation, he was asked to restate his point in a cogent form. He said he didn't know how, but that he would be happy to read his presentation again. Others tried to help, some had liked what they heard and tried to tease something meaningful out of it. He wasn't good at accepting help like that. It goes back to this point he was trying to make about the integral relationship of doing and the doable in the practices of philosophy. He wanted to wipe out everything that was said in the first weeks of that seminar, he wanted to force everyone to start over. The confusion caused was by design, it had to be since the only way to force this reset was to punch a hole in the context everyone brought to class with them that day, and to move them in the direction he wanted to take things, toward the how of what he wanted to do, the where and the when, and then the who. A revaluation of all values. The glaring fact of that day was that he studied differently, read differently, and wrote differently. They might have agreed with him on some level that these were the practices of the philosopher, but they probably thought there was more to it than that, that these were also the practices of any scholar engaged in any specific discipline. What made it philosophical was the content of these practices, the style of these practices, and maybe even the methodology in them. IWriter and the infinite possibilities of IWriteable were not abstractions, they were agreements. He was failing on all counts and had no right to involve anyone else in his mission, no right to take everyone with him on that reset back to the beginning. "You're crazy to take that course," Wolfe had said. That was during the Winter Semester of their second year.

Now, here one of them is, a visiting assistant professor trying to bring it all together as though it were a picture of that same day. How would he do it then? How would he teach Heiddegger, Aristotle, Plato, and all the other works from his syllabi? How would he do philosophy in the classroom, how would he orient the conversation, and which of his students would be forced to suffer the material as though it needed to be reset, to be started over from a different position, with a different orientation, and proceed in a different style? Might it be possible, he wondered, to proceed in a way that no one would have to feel that, where the very orientation of learning and reading and writing would be up for discussion, part of the investigation, and ultimately the primary concern of the work they would cover? He wanted to proceed with an introduction to ethics, an introduction to philosophy, and an independent study of *Being and Time* all in the same fashion. Not so much a monotonic lecture on "what is philosophy?" but a set of deliberations and discussions, musings and weavings, that tried to evoke the who and the how, the where and the when of it. In reading Heidegger, in studying ethics, in introducing themselves to philosophy, are they then able to do philosophy? Is this something for them? For anyone?

Were one of them here with us, he might add that studying is different from reading and that writing is different from teaching. At least he would argue that is how it looks from the point of view of French philosophy from the 60s to the 90s. He would read Dreyfus' book *Being-in-the-World,* but he would study *Being and Time*. Studying meant reading and rereading, pacing and talking through it out loud. Reading was different, more mechanical and pedestrian, even if it involved creative flourishes of interpretation and understanding now and again. Deconstruction was a bridging function; it provided an explanation for how reading could be transformed into study. Then study would find a way to transform itself into writing. Processing what he was reading over and over again, pacing back and forth in his apartment and thinking about it, would lead to notes and fragments, ideas and questions. Study evoked writing and pacing would transform that into mock lectures where he would practice explaining what he was studying to some imagined audience. Teaching. There are thousands among us living this way. It doesn't make sense to draw boundaries on these activities, but it felt like a progression with phases that could be identified. It was like a phenomenology of the spirit where each phase had distinct procedures accompanying it and driving it forward. Reading became study and study became writing and writing became teaching with the ultimate hope always being to plan a course syllabus for the materials to be digested. The work would be transformed into discussions which would be transformed into writing. Term papers, for one, *Being, An Introduction* too.

This was how one of them was living philosophy, how they taught him to do it, becoming the who of a philosopher, someone who did these things and who passed through these stages. He would do this in a one-bedroom apartment on Broadview Lane in Ann Arbor while teaching courses at the commuter campus in Dearborn. It was impossible not to tie his identity as a philosopher to this job and to these preparations. These regular events of sufficiently digesting sections of the work were for the sake of presenting them to others in classrooms where the students were likewise oriented toward advances through these same stages of development, starting with reading and then moving on to studying, writing, and teaching in their own way. Class discussions and office hours were meant to be safe places for the students to come and practice their hand. They were working on their papers, trying to write this or that thesis on this or that passage in the assigned material. They would experiment with their approach, explain it to him or to each other, these were fragmented efforts at teaching, partial attempts to move along the continuum of the philosophical implementation and make efforts at proclaiming themselves authentic subjects of the who of philosophy. At this point, it would have been impossible to understand the philosopher independently of the work that a professor does. This progression was the discipline, the process and procedures were the behaviors of the subject of philosophy. This was what he wanted, this was the life he had sought for himself, and he could not imagine it any other way than as a member of the faculty in an academic department. He had his implementation and he had never considered the possibility of dependency injection, signaling an inversion of control.

The constraints of the discipline had made themselves clear in the standards of scholarship, research, accuracy, and depth. Think for yourself, but like this. These criteria lived at the edges of all projects and framed the work that characterized them. Sometimes these conditions were unwelcome, and unpleasantly restrictive, but even in those moments they were acceptable. That is, he granted them legitimacy even as he felt their oppressive influence on his studies, what he was reading, writing, and teaching. His work developed in a schizophrenic matter where some facets of it felt as though they were situated within the limits of proper work, while others were wild and undisciplined, outside the boundaries, exciting and taboo. Much of his work, as he understood it, was aimed at trying to figure out how to make these two impulses live side by side. He tried to learn how to integrate them with each other and was convinced that you could do philosophy well and do it in a way that would challenge the constraints of the discipline. He was equally convinced that you could only do that if you were starting from within it. This was how he understood deconstructive practices and why he was attracted to them along with so many of his contemporaries. All of them had a story like his and were vigorously pursuing traditional themes in the works of the canon and excavating them in a way that threatened their canonical position with instability. In the zone created by what trembled beneath it, all of them were seeking an *authentic* pathway for thinking. So it is that deconstructive seduction falls short as the subject withdraws and evades. The process itself blocks the way for any such possibility of the authentic and the true. Deconstruction was built to suit the phenomenology of failure. It never stops.

Two years later he had his first experience of what he now calls "interleaving," where he came under the spell of two different books at the same time and, as a result, was influenced by some bizarre mixture of the two that reflects neither. Contrary to intention, it created a third monstrous option that altered the scope and message of all the ingredients. The books that comprised that first interleaving were The Birth of Tragedy and Don Quixote. A developmental psychologist might inform us that the risks encountered by a seventeen-year-old boy undertaking to read Nietzsche while growing up in the Midwest of the United States are formidable. The young not yet professor was playing with fire and could have been scarred by it. Only Cervantes could save him. To have read Nietzsche as a kind of Don Quixote was to transform his message in ways that would neutralize and skew any standard interpretation. Nietzsche became the solitary delusional philosopher tilting at windmills in the service of a fantastic mission that no one else could imagine. There would be layers and layers of story there too. This was what the young professor understood when he read about those villagers chasing down Dionysus in the meadow and making him tell all his secrets. Better is it never to be born, next best is to die as soon as possible. As a story within a story, this message might be the worst possible for such a reader, and yet, filtered through Quixote's sieve, it became a song of hope, a cautionary tale yielding the prospect of escaping the trap.

That may be non-sequitur. How to explain? Five years later he found himself walking on Wright Street, the Urbana side between Gregory Hall and Lincoln Hall. He was visiting the town and the philosophy department to help decide whether he would attend graduate school there. Two women were walking behind him, and he overheard one of them say, "It's like falling off a building and realizing that falling off a building is what you are going to be doing for the rest of your life." Yes, that is the Quixotic reading of Dionysus' message. At least that is the way he understood the mixture of the Apollonian and Dionysian in response to that challenge in the meadow. He had been charged with a mission and there was no way out. He could not quit even if he wanted to and not being able to quit meant that he could not fail. It dawned on him that this was the most important bit: none of this was up to him. He was not the agent of destiny but its patient. The one who could not quit and who was thus not in control of his actions, partial as they might be, suffered his condition as an impairment. This ongoing devotion to a project would ultimately bear witness to his death, sooner or later. It was his promise to bear, laden by the unalterable inevitability of falling off a building.

The story goes that she was flying across the Diag on her bike, wearing torn faded denim jeans, a leather jacket, a white t-shirt underneath, steel-toed doc marten boots, backpack, and her hair flying in the wind that she was making. He never saw it, but the image was vivid and had clearly made an impression on the storyteller. "She looked so cool," she said. Such an irony really because the storyteller had one doctorate already and was pursuing another. The girl on the bike was in the first weeks of graduate school and fresh from a series of bartender jobs following her lackluster undergraduate career. Girl? Storyteller and rider would tell it that way, at least. The girl on the bike. She never thought of herself as an intellectual, as someone worthy of credentials and an academic standing, and yet here she was learning to run the information systems used at the heart of the academy. She was riding her bike in front of the graduate library and was seen and adored by one of her star colleagues already so deeply embedded in the politics of academic life, someone who thought the girl on the bike looked so cool. Funny these two women who, unknown to both, were each intimidated by the other for completely inverse reasons. "She is so sexy," said the one. "She is brilliant," said the other. They both knew that the other was more than that, the parts they emphasized stood out as figure only because of the ground beneath them. The brilliant one was beautiful and the sexy one was smart. They saw themselves differently than what the other saw. They tip-toed around each other at school, barely met, observed each other from afar and hoped that one day they would have a chance to get to know each other better.

We are all so far away from ourselves. It takes so long to come to know yourself not from some refracted set of observations or insights, but as a feeling, as a close proximity to being it, feeling it in the act and not in the adulation of its audience. This only happens when we absorb the insights of others, include their gaze, their admiration, indifference, or contempt. We must feel it so that we no longer think about it but live it. Someone or many someones had led the girl on the bike to think of herself in a certain way. She felt that understanding as she rode across the Diag, as she weaved her way through public places, as her eyes met the eyes of men who looked at her in that way that men do. She had learned this and none of it spelled librarian, none of it was engraved with an advanced degree or evoked the vita contemplativa. It had taken every ounce of courage she could muster to break free of that judgment. She left a boyfriend, she left good friends, she left a life that made sense and where her presence mattered. She came to a place that made no sense and where she thought she did not matter. In a constant state of fear and agitation, she peddled across the Diag to get to class or work or whatever it was that she was worried she might be late to. She was seen by the quintessential academic, the woman with the pedigree and all the grants to go with it, and that woman thought she was cool and sexy and out of this world. And she was.

Her life was very much split between that old and this new. In addition to her time in class and the information desk at the UGLI, she got a job as a bartender in the iconic Del Rio bar and vegetarian grill. Without that, she could never have made it. She needed the safety and familiarity of pouring drinks and bantering with customers, the actions she knew so well, to keep her grounded and preserve her sanity while falling into the alien surrounds that seemed to resist her at every step. She was exposed to post-modernism and the informatics of the dawning new age of digital media. It was so much easier to imagine herself knowing all that, being a part of it, if she could do it while smoking in a bar that was her bar. The Del Rio was the perfect landing zone just as it was the perfect departure gate for ABDs unable to finish their doctorates but unwilling to give up on the town and its proximity to their plans. There are many entry- and exit-points for academic activities expressing virtue and some of them are bars.

Before the semester started, in fact, the professor found himself there. His dog was visiting from Urbana and, rather than leave him back in his apartment where he knew the dog would freak out and worry that he was never coming back, he brought it with him and left the little guy in the car. The bartender, not the girl on the bike, but a doctoral candidate, sliding further and further from any possible target date for her oral defense, was kind enough to give him a bowl of water to take outside and leave in the car. He liked the place, remembered it from his undergraduate years when he would go there sometimes if he needed to get away from the suffocating college bar scene. The Del was never a part of that for anyone. There were townies and grad students along with the "almost" who were somewhere in between. He could sit there and smoke clove cigarettes while nursing a beer for longer than he should. People on the boundaries of the academy fit in there and everyone recognized each other as they came through the door. If someone were to accidentally wander in and not fit with the vibe, everyone would know it right away. They wouldn't stay long. No one would be rude to them or ask them to leave, but they knew that this wasn't the right place, and that they should just move along.

Truth be told, the error in his ways started in the kitchen with his mother seven years before that day on Wright Street but did not happen all at once. He came to be in Urbana that day because a professor had sent him there. One of his teachers, when he was an undergraduate in Ann Arbor, had responded to his quip at not being able to study with him at Michigan's graduate school by suggesting that he consider working with the professors he knew at the University of Illinois. This professor had inspired him, and he trusted his advice. The inspiration was an interleaving: the voice of someone he respected laid over all the days and their two pages. His first philosophy class, or rather the second but the first one that inspired him, covered the work of Hegel Marx Nietzsche and Freud. That's him removing the commas. He enrolled in the course because he regularly recalled his reading of The Birth of Tragedy and thought that, despite not having enjoyed his introduction to philosophy, he might like a course that included Nietzsche's work. Staring at the course guide, he visualized that first interleaving, and it was what made the selection for him. The Cervantes connection was the draw, and the continuation of the mission was the propeller. That was the semester he read Thus Spake Zarathustra for the first time and fell further into the inevitability of his unfortunate configuration. He was a captive audience throughout that semester and the several that followed as he continued to develop, changing his major and directing his writing energy, his two pages a day, away from fiction and toward newly found philosophical meditations.

That is how he ended up in the wrong place at the right time, walking down Wright Street and hearing about that high dive of the living which struck him as the perfect reconciliation of Apollonian form and Dionysian ecstasy. One of the first books he bought as a new graduate student was Being and Time. His first semester at Illinois included a course devoted to it. He was hopelessly ill-constructed when beginning the experience. Nietzsche, the Quixote, was at the heart of it. Zarathustra had blown up genre so that in his writing he could no longer tell the difference between fact and fantasy, will and idea, literature and philosophy. Heidegger's first book bore the brunt of it. He read it and lived it as a novel of initiation. The story of unhappy Dasein (happiness is not its end) on its way toward its death and unable to achieve it as a goal (it is a kind of anti-goal). Despite that, Dasein never has any doubt that in the end death will get the better of it, maybe the best of it. Running away from it, it comes up behind itself, and that can only mean that it is there with its existence, the being-with of being-there, falling and projecting. A high diver. This was not a disinterested theory that he deliberated over calmly and with distant reason. It was a possession. He had no choice, and he could not quit. Over the years, no matter how much he dabbled in the possibilities of stepping back and blocking his own way, he could not manage it and could not stop. He could not steer his own ship and correct its course. He was lost to the mission and had become the interleave of his youth and its naivete. This was forgivable, but what might be its lasting effect? What gift or debt would it bestow upon his future self?

No one who had any contact with him during those years would deny that the progression was itself a force of will. If such a thing exists. He created the obstacles so that he could throw himself against them: to practice and learn how to pursue and how to evade. One of his colleagues, a friend, said that he was like a baby in a crib with each new thinker or idea playing the part of a toy being passed into him. "What can I do with this? How can I make a game of it?" He would put it in his mouth to hear what it might say.

How can I make this clear? Philosophy is always in the now. The narrative is always from today, spoken or written from here and now and asserting that this is what I think. The philosopher never places themselves forward and backward in time, never sets themselves into a narrative that is positioned outside of their here and now. We may look at Berkeley's dialogues or Nietzsche's funky expositions as extraordinary instances of philosophical style, but we don't doubt their immanent effort and veracity. Nietzsche wasn't playing the historian on his own development, he wasn't telling us what he thought last year and that he once, as a young man, held this set of beliefs. The writing was itself the struggle with ideas. This philosopher is working it out, elaborating the thoughts that came to him during the walk on the mountainside that morning. He is in the middle of it. There is no distance in time, the philosopher is not an intellectual historian describing their journey through life, they are realizing that momentous experience here and now in the way they say what they say. "I think" underlies all meditation and meditation underlies all philosophy.

What would the alternative look like? How might a philosopher show their drive through a real and living set of developments in reflective form? I don't mean something like what Kant did in the first Critique. Clearly his thinking is developing and changing as he works through the problems. We have the A edition and the B edition and the various theories about how this or that argument led to the breakdown of this or that aspect, and so on.

This is an example of development in real time and each moment's engagement articulates what he thinks as he thinks it. He is working on the problems that he has stumbled across; he is actively working out his philosophy as he writes it down, revises it, and teaches it to himself. Even if he were a better editor and had taken the time to show how it all fit together, he would have been asserting it in this meditative form. Philosophy of the not-now is something else entirely. Consider this. What if Heidegger wrote *Being and Time* in 1957 instead of 1927? Not in terms of his later philosophy as though he were developing it there and then. What I mean is, what if –based on the lectures from the late twenties and the preparatory work he had done in the early twenties—Heidegger had decided to sit down and write the existential analytic of Dasein as he remembered thinking it thirty years before?

This is different from Borges' story of Menard who tried to put himself into the same state as Cervantes so that he could compose *Don Quixote* exactly as it had been composed by its author. I would like to suggest a variant on that story where Menard, having lived Cervantes' life past the time when the book was written, tries to write it from a perspective where he is no longer submerged in its emotion and context. In this case, the book would be different. Here it wouldn't matter what psychosis led Menard to think it desirable to reproduce the work exactly as it was produced by Cervantes when he was *there* at *that* time. It is specifically the philosophical position distinct from its involvement that this hypothetical would like to realize. Would that still be philosophy? Would the subject of the writing, the older Heidegger, still be doing philosophy? Would he be the subject of philosophical discipline, a writer and a teacher, or would he be some freakish literary subject who has departed from the practices and concerns of the discipline and gone off into some other domain characterized by different rules and a different genre? Would such work have any relationship to the real *Being and Time,* or would it parallel the relationship between *Life on the Mississippi* and *Huckleberry Finn?*

It might be more complicated than this. I am not thinking of a personal memoir where the author tries to provide an intellectual history of themselves. The author in that case does actual work and succeeds in thinking through the notions but does so at a distance and without involvement. Instead we would get: "This is not what I think, although this is a possible composition for someone so situated to think. I am not doing so here and now, but someone most certainly could do so; and it would be coherent." It would be philosophy as narrative or as reflective reconstruction. I don't know any words for it, but I am sure that, whatever it is, it isn't what we are doing when those of us who have acquired the discipline in the sanctioned way *do* philosophy. Imagine such a person presenting a talk at a conference. Suppose someone from the audience raises an objection or points out a flaw in one of the arguments. The author needn't defend the argument or the reasoning, the author might nod in agreement and say, "That is spot on, you have identified a fundamental problem. If only the author could have seen that at the time." The audience member would likely be confused, "Isn't that you? Shouldn't you fix it now?" They might ask. "Oh no, not anymore. What good would fixing it now do for the subject of philosophy there and then?" If you attached the ideas to a pseudonym, to some "person" other than the author, claiming its presentation to be a scholarly interpretation of that person's work, then it all makes sense again and you have returned to the friendly confines of the discipline. We are back at it now. "You have surfaced a fallacy in so and so's position and this is a service to the community." All is right with the order again. If you are reconstructing a flaw in some unrecoverable past thinking and are presenting it as fate here and now, then you have left all the parameters we have agreed upon behind. Tragic.

Why I am I talking about this? This is where I am headed. I am reading Aristotle, first the *Nicomachean Ethics* and then the *Metaphysics*, and I am poring over potentiality and its relationship to actuality in the context of the ethical and the metaphysical, in terms of deliberate action expressing virtue and the first cause of the unmoved mover. Nothing causes it to move, it is the null basis of a nullity. As I work that into my study of *Being and Time*, the way in which Dasein turns toward itself in the act of running away from itself –pulling and pushing, pursuing and escaping– and so exposing that existential-potentiality-for-being-a-whole, it was as if I were trying to write something that came from a previous period, a time past that was no longer here and now and which contained thinking that cannot change and a thinker that cannot learn. I am not at all sure that I know what I am doing, but I am becoming keenly aware that, whatever it is, it is threatening to transcend the discipline, to leave it behind and venture out into some place where I would have none of its protections or safeguards, where none of the professional possibilities would be relevant or of service. This prospect, because I am young and have my whole life ahead of me as they say, does not frighten me. It spurs me on by fiercely bringing forward the power of the question I am hovering around: if you venture beyond the discipline into genres and narratives that are not legitimate to that discipline, can you still proclaim yourself subject to it? Can you do philosophy while departing from it? Who are you if you do? Does philosophy come from the work of philosophers or are philosophers the ones who produce philosophical works? Which came first, the philosopher or the work?

His own novel of initiation came with the interleaving of three distinct stories that made up most of his writing prior to that first semester and his introduction to Heidegger. The Middle American was set in Europe on the road between the Bodensee and Innsbruck. The main characters were all travelling and coming into contact over transient, geographically fluid positions. They were all geometry and time-sequence, and their interactions were coincidence and discovery at odds, unlikely events of occasional contact and parallel traversal of edges landing on shared points only temporarily. This Year's Harvest —part two of the initiation— was set in South America, and it was about the violence of economic imperialism and the best intentions of the colonizer. The protagonists were two idealistic kids coming together in a farming village in the mountains of Colombia. Theirs was an ill-fated meeting and tragedy was soon to follow. The destruction of innocence was the aim of this initiation ritual, making it very much unlike the first story where fortune and fate were mere accident and the outcomes benign and educational. The combination of these two stories made clear the either-or of learning with which he was already becoming familiar. What we learn will either destroy us or make us stronger, the sage had warned. He sensed the learner was not disinterested and detached, not innocent, but a participant. Learning always came by trial, and trial meant that something real was at stake, that there could be consequences and that those consequences would be painful even if only as memories of events past. The third part of the initiation was Polarity Unbound. Opposition was at work throughout the tale set in a Soviet Union about to disappear. The opposition was not to be resolved in some dialectical higher order but abandoned. Initiation in this case was not a resolution bringing about integration and synthesis, it was resolution through dissolution. Polar opposites had become detached showing that whatever was part of the opposition had been transformed into two radically different things that no longer took any meaning from their relationship to each other. It did not work on its own as a story, but as a parable inserted alongside the either / or of the other two, it was perfect. Novel initiation, in his case, meant that either learning will make him stronger, or it will destroy him. The two lives that might result from these options will have nothing in common, the two persons shaped by the experiences will have nothing that binds them together.

When he started graduate school, started reading Heidegger, continuing his mission interleaving Nietzsche and the Quixote, this three-in-one story was the baggage he brought with him. They were the three stories that described the journey he was on as he arrived in Urbana, Illinois ready to continue his education. It was a miserable time and an exuberant one. Terrific in every sense. This is essential background; the ensuing ideas and tales make no sense without it. His non-failure was constantly playing with failure to defer it, putting it off through willful partiality and stubborn persistence. During the journey through Europe, a trip filling a year-long deferral from graduate school, there was to be a hike from Stockholm to

Oslo. This never materialized. Luckily, he would say, because that is not the best way to pass time in Scandinavia. The plan was realized in a different place and at a different time. He, as it turns out, passed by the middle American on the road from Bregenz to Innsbruck. One day, climbing in the rain along a path leading up through the pass between the Madelagabel and the Grosse Krotenkopf, persistence, patience, and perseverance became the key to the mission. He must be flexible, he would simply out last all the obstacles, pouring over them like the water running down the rock on the sides of those mountains and caught in his water bottle. Never was there a drink so sweet as when roaming the philosopher's way. He would be the running water, he would be the filling bottle, and he would be the sweetness of the day spent hiking the path to the warming hut guarded by a goat. There were communal bunks inside and he lay down at sunset and listened to Dylan's Blood on the Tracks to gather strength for the rest of the mission. That is how it would have to be.

Teaching at a commuter campus is different. No dormitories, plenty of parking. There are many older students in the ethics classes, some are older than he is. Men and women. When he launched into his spiel on the good life and described parts of it, like how Aristotle includes the lives of your children after your death, the older students jumped in directly. They felt something personal in his way of setting up the discussion. They knew the worries and concerns of life and they were glad to discover that philosophers cared about them too. One woman was surprised that something written so long ago, with such an ominous and formal air around it, could address the real concerns of people living so long afterward. She thought that it did. He never had so many older students before, maybe one here or there, but never so many that their point of view took over the discussion. The younger students seemed inspired by being in that atmosphere. Even if they didn't share the same sensibilities, they learned from their peers and were moved to try to see the connections.

Happiness triggers knee jerk acquiescence. The first impulse is "yes, of course everyone wants to be happy." It's a hook and they go along with him when he says that it is more complicated than just pleasure or some state of mind that dies with the body. Expressing excellence, doing things that matter and doing them well, play powerfully in their imagination. The mature students know how vitally important these concerns are to their vision of living a full and happy life. The younger students absorb it from the room, and some suggested the other day that it broadened their horizons of what the good life might mean. At this point he has taught Aristotle's ethics more than any other text and it always seemed to go over well.

Although he noticed how much the older students were drawn to the *Nicomachean Ethics*, as he thought back to all the other times he taught it, he recalled that the message did seep in even when there weren't any older students, it just took longer. He was there, after all, but he was the only one. At least part of the past success might have come from his personal stake and angle. Doing something well for the sake of doing it well and having that action modify the state of one's being had become deeply ingrained in his presentation. It fits with the phases in realizing oneself as the subject of philosophy. He is passionate about this, and that passion comes through in the classroom discussions and in the lectures, but why should passion matter? When there were older students to push the message, less effort was required from him. When he is on his own, his contribution is more influential. The older students are quicker to pick up on it and better able to build the momentum with their own observations and reflections. When the passion of one has the same power as the experience of many, has pedagogy become sophistry or demagoguery? What is he doing? Is there a place for the passion of the sophist in virtue and excellence? Shouldn't the philosopher be driven by reason while remaining disinterested and at a distance?

The good life. Action expressing virtue. Not just reading or studying, writing or teaching, but doing these things well to transform the state of one's soul, one's ek-sistence. Action expressing ek-sellence yields Eudaimonia. He breathed that, laughed it, felt it, but did not know it. He is always extrapolating in the thick of it, casting these actions into all the areas of life that Aristotle describes: demeanor, deliberate intelligence, practical assessment of circumstances and the appropriate response to them, action in all contexts and by all contributors. This *is* his position *then*. If it malfunctions, it cannot be fixed. The power in action is all that matters, and no action is changed by what comes next. What is learned in classes on Aristotle's ethics from older students who offset the need for passion doesn't change what happened before. It can't make yesterday's sophistry more reasonable today. Outside the discipline, outside of an ek-sistence subjected to those ways of doing that express excellence, there is no self-image or identity containing the past like the solenoid in a toaster. Identity is pure fabrication, it is fashioned. There is nothing if not the who of a set of philosophical practices, a set of actions like reading, studying, writing, and teaching all deeply regulated by conditions in the world. If there is reason or passion in that, it has nothing to do with him, this thinking thing that always arrives too late.

Early on in his graduate career, the writing and the mission emerged as one and the same. He dreamed that he was a seismograph, his pen etching a sense of the earth's rumbling, measuring it, bringing it to representation.

The experience was the goal: living through it and coming to understand. Always pay attention. This was his purpose, and it was the realization of the message that he could not quit no matter who advised it or how much he wanted to. He divided those he met in those early years into two camps. There were those who understood that he was beyond help, that he could not be convinced otherwise, and that the best they could do was to comfort and be compassionate. These were his friends. On the other hand, there were those who thought they could reason with him, tell him this or that as though he would act upon it like someone at home in his thoughts and the master of his fate. He resisted these advisors and was not sufficiently wise to preserve comradery over opposition. That is how he created the obstacles that became his primary lessons. He was learning the work of some of the great thinkers in history, true enough, but he could not shake the feeling that it was only a take on it, someone's angle. He became suspicious of anyone who would describe that history as though it were a physical object without an interleaved material being spun from rich fabric. The real value of the experience became the confrontation and the resistance, the act of swarming around what they were holding in such high esteem, of flooding over it to work his way into the corners and crevices where he needed to flow. He knew success meant that he would not come through it whole, but that he would remain partial and distributed. This was the secret to the pursuit of the ends and to the evasion of the obstacles. He had to be willing to lose something of himself when gaining whatever was offered.

"That makes you a robot," Wolfe said.

"Okay. I'll play along. Explain."

"Kafka, as it turns out, was pretty good at his job. He was a Doctor of Law, you know, and he worked for the state workman's compensation insurance department. Apparently, he had a knack for it. Knew how to navigate some of the trickier cases. They made him a supervisor and they never once complained that he missed work. He was sick a lot. Even after the TB diagnosis when he took long leaves of absence, they put up with it. They needed him and were willing to accommodate his quirks to make sure he kept working there."

"I get it. What's the point?"

"He must've had yearly performance reviews of some kind, right? Imagine Franz fucking Kafka going into his manager's office and sitting there having to listen to this little motherfucker talk about how well he did this or how he needed to improve when doing that."

"I thought you said he was good at his job."

"Still, you know how those things are. They always have to tell you what you're doing right and what you need to work on. Imagine Franz sitting there listening to his manager go on like that. What do you think was running through his mind when that guy says to him, 'you're really doing a super job, Franz. We love having you here. Keep it up.'? I'll tell you what it was, it was 'Fuck you. Who the hell are you to evaluate me?'"

I chortled, snorted even. "If there is justice in the universe."

"The way I heard it, Kafka took a shitty job, one that he was overqualified for just because he liked the way the hours would let him structure his life. The state-run offices always started early in the morning and let out early in the afternoon. This meant he could go home after work, go to sleep, and then wake up around midnight or whatever and get in a full night's work before going back to the office the next day. He knew he had to write as soon as he woke up and that would be better than if he tried to do it later. After work, he wouldn't be good for anything other than eating and going to sleep. Why waste the best hours of the day on a job, right?"

Wolfe had brought some pot with him, and we had been smoking some of it while sitting at the dining table under the light and next to the kitchen. It was the same place where I did most of my reading and studying. He paused to take another hit from the water pipe. He went on, blowing smoke out as he talked.

"Kafka was willing to sacrifice everything for the sake of the time he could spend writing alone in the middle of the night. In his parent's house, in his sister's house, wherever he was living. None of the other shit mattered to him. All he cared about was the work. Let's hear it for the universally valid profit motive."

"Got it. Great story. Still a little unclear on the point."

"The point is, what could that manager's evaluation mean to him in the middle of all that? How could he possibly say something like 'oh, thank you very much. So glad you find my contribution helpful.' No way, not a chance. My point is that these places we go and these things we do, they make us into things, they shape us. We are always being evaluated, shown how we can improve on this or that we should keep doing that. All for the sake of being helpful or good at our jobs. Here are your teacher evaluations, are you effective, are they learning? Here is the reviewer's commentary on your article, this is what you're doing that really works, but this needs more focus, has to be shaped better to fit with your overall purpose. You learn the rules. You adapt."

"Ah, I see. We're back to the academic discipline again."

"Damn straight. You're always on about it, 'Who is a philosopher?' and 'What is philosophy?' and you know that these are the questions that force you to wonder who gets to decide and how that decision is made."

"Sure, and why did I ever want to be one or think that someone else at some graduate school somewhere could instruct me on how to do it?"

"Why did you think that graduate schools had anything at all to fucking do with it? For thousands of years people have been kicking these issues around. Let's put out a shingle, let's take on apprentices, let's send out journeymen. It'll be an honorable trade, no doubt. Philosopher and blacksmith. Michaelmas sale, get shoes for your horse and solutions to all your riddles. What did you want exactly? I mean, do you remember?"

"Yes. I think so... I remember struggling. I remember reading Hegel in college. Sartre too. All the big books."

"Big books?"

"Yes, like the first Critique, and the Phenomenology. *Being and Nothingness. The Phenomenology of Perception.* Magna opera. I wanted to write something like that, produce an elaborate presentation of the world as I understood it."

"That's putting the cart before the horse."

"Exactly. I didn't have anything to say, but I wanted to say something big."

"Sure, and you knew that you couldn't just *do* that. You couldn't just sit down and start spouting shit. There must be rules for it, right? There were precedents, previous attempts, role models. You had to study to become familiar with all the other instances so that yours would be like theirs, a token of the type. A valuable contribution."

"Yup, and I was willing to give up on my naïve point of view for the sake of learning the trade, as you're calling it. I *wanted* the discipline."

"That amounts to letting the rules and methods developed over many years by many different people enter into your way of thinking to guide it, to structure it, and form it in very specific ways."

"Indeed. That's what I wanted."

"It changes how you experience things, it's a form of surveillance. Performed by ghosts maybe, or something unhuman at least. A constant presence that you invited into your head, asked to help shape and order your experience and your understanding of it. All so you could write some big book that nobody would read. If they did read it, they wouldn't understand it. If they did understand it, no one would give a crap about what they had to say about it. Probably not even you."

"I wanted that."

"You wanted that? You wanted to agonize over the details on page 472 so that at best a few thousand people could scan over it in a few seconds and then forget it completely once they put the book down? Or optimistically, three of the readers could argue about the precise meaning of that passage in a series of articles in some obscure journal that only graduate libraries would buy. What the fuck, dude? You could've left when I left. Why didn't you?"

"They said I was wild and undisciplined."

"You thought that was a criticism?"

I chuckled. "I did. They meant it to be. I had to work harder. I thought I could be different, I could approach it the way that I wanted to so long as I understood the rules better than they did, knew them well enough to turn them around and use them to my own advantage. They would have to accept my alternative vision if I did it well enough."

"I get it. That's why you were so attracted to Derrida, I bet. You thought that whole 'inhabit the metaphysics of presence and make it shake and tremble from its own rules' thing was subversive of discipline, but it isn't, it's always in contact with it. It's the epitome of academic discipline. You still think you need to prove that you deserve a place at the table, which means you agree that proving and deserving are required. You accept the idea that you must start from somewhere within the tradition as defined by a bunch of chucks. You don't object to their right to evaluate you, only their approval will give you the standing to criticize it and then depart from it. You aim to prove that you're not wild and undisciplined but a colossus of an alternate discipline who has paved his own way. Such a cliché. Such a boy."

"That's overly dramatic."

"Ya think?"

"No, I mean, you're overselling it. I'm just a visiting assistant professor. This isn't Greek tragedy, it's U of M-Dearborn."

"It is a Greek tragedy, my friend, or maybe a Jewish one."

"Pfffft. Jewgreek is Greekjew?"

"It's weird how these kinds of institutions work, right? Each one of you is supposed to be a guardian of the discipline. You're supposed to judge and influence on behalf of the one true way to philosophy. You don't think of yourself as one voice among many where conversations have a way of working themselves out independently of thousands of years of ruling paradigms. You've been hazed during an initiation ritual and your reaction is to enforce the rules of hazing to legitimize your own experience."

"Now you're talking. That sounds true."

"I mean it. You were an outsider who wanted in. You said it yourself. They made you go through hell to get in. Now that you've passed the first test, you want to defend the small patch of ground you've managed to get your grubby little hands on."

"Alright fine. Suppose this is right. Suppose discipline is constant surveillance by a set of rules for behavior modification meant to keep me in line and maintaining the boundaries and limits of the profession as the current hoi polloi deems fit. What's the alternative? What are you selling?"

"Look, I'm just thinking that all the books you like, they are all rule breakers somehow. They reset the standard or changed the paradigm by starting over in a way. Those professors we studied with in grad school, they aren't philosophers, and they don't get to decide who is one. I know we read Hegel, but that guy who taught the class, he's not Hegel. Nothing like him. Emulating him, following the rules that he made you practice and repeat until they were shoved so far up your ass that you couldn't do it any other way, that's not the way to get where you wanted to go in the first place. That might even be the best way to prevent you from ever getting there, it probably blocks your way."

"Okay, so how do I get there? How does anyone get there?"

"Socrates taught, but I don't know. I'm not saying I have the answer, but I know it's not with some big book that the guardians of the discipline will fetishize, that's for sure. Is your goal the wrong one? Why would you want to be one of those guys anyway? Why even classify them like that? Did they have anything in common? Who cares if your big book is worthy of standing beside the Phenomenology? That's not really up to you anyway. It's an historical accident. Leave that to the librarians. All that matters is doing it and that means not being contained in the category."

"What do you mean?"

"Did you see that movie *Light Sleeper*?"

"Yeah."

"Dafoe writes in his journal. That's the cheesy narration that's going on throughout the movie, right? Remember that scene where he writes to the end of the last page of the journal, stops his narration, closes the journal, gets up and drops it in the trash, then takes out another journal from the drawer and starts writing on the first page as the narration continues?"

"Classic."

"Well, maybe it's like that? Like Sartre in *The Words*. Little boy Jean-Paul running from the dining room into the kitchen just for the pleasure of it. If you immerse yourself in the system building, or whatever it is you're fantasizing about, and then play at it, be like a kid pretending to be a philosopher, going through all the motions, and writing it all down. You know, you can check all the arguments, fix all the typos and awkward sentences. All for the sake of spinning the yarn, pretending that you're doing the philosopher's work. When you're done, toss it in the trash and move on to the next one."

We laughed.

"Work is supposed to be productive and impactful," I said, still smiling.

"You're really doing a super job, Franz. We love having you here. Keep it up."

I'm not sure how much I should try to explain Wolfe. It might be better to just let these conversations speak for themselves. This is what I meant when I wrote that he has a way of filling up space. He takes over. Not by being obnoxious. He isn't, not really. It's his ideas that take up all the room. He's confident and clearly demonstrates that it is part and parcel of that confidence to not care much whether he has earned it. To his credit, he would forcefully argue his position with the most pretentious dons at Oxford or Cambridge, as they say. Wolfe doesn't gravitate toward philosophers for the same reasons that I do. He is drawn to the personalities. One of his favorites is Wittgenstein, but he never talks about his philosophy, only about the way he used to bully the other guy during an argument, the way he would mop the floor with his opponent in a debate. How he hardly ever read any philosophy and almost never quoted it in his writing. He frames these remarks as criticism, but ironically. He likes philosophers who redefine philosophy as they go and doesn't separate them from the artists that he admires or the writers and the musicians. He lauds this approach as a kind of masculism. He derides "useful" contributions because making sense requires a system of rules and an order to be in place. This means that some power structure functions as a precondition for anything genteel or helpful. Any special interest groups that oppose this are hypocrites, they love power, but they don't think it's right to talk about it. Radical approaches were just a new form of power rising up to unseat the current rulers to take control themselves. They make resentment into a discipline.

"Helping people," I recall him saying once, "hides an agenda or a moral cause presumed universal. It almost always means being useful to them in some material way that helps place them into an existing status quo. If not that, then it's an attempt to reinterpret the morality of the status quo to replace it with a new one that benefits everyone, if only they would align their pleasures with what it has to offer. You say liberty and justice is what counts? We'll smash the state that pretends to give us liberty and justice and create a new one that really does give us these things." He couldn't make this work as a philosophical position, but he thought he might be able to make it work as anthropology. We were all essentially evangelizers for our personality traits, and the racket was a pyramid scheme where the reward was more power coursing through you even if you couldn't wield it. He didn't try to prove this and would concede that there were contradictions that could easily stop him in his tracks. He would leave it to the other guy to determine whether they were taking anything for granted, assuming a vision of good and evil, and projecting it into the structure of the universe like a faux deity. As selfish and stupid as a life of "pretending to be a philosopher" might seem, in his heart Wolfe thought doing it might help someone even if he wasn't sure how to explain it. He said the thought of it as a human possibility helped him, had a positive impact on his experience of the world, and made it more striking and richer. He thought the proliferation of a possibility like that was contagious and happened up close and in small unrepeatable acts that were not at all material, and which were of no use to the ones who were telling the tale but only to those who were in it. I don't think he was advising me based on some hypothetical form of life that had occurred to him during meditation. He was defending his own abilities and potential and the thankless task of having been inspired to achieve them.

His dissertation was written despite all the wild influences and brought him to the brink of an impossible contradiction. He had written about the wrong topic at the wrong school with the wrong people. Failure was written on every page of that thesis and yet he kept going. Systematically, he worked through the proposed project's outline, semester by semester cranking out a chapter at the end of each one until he brought the project to completion. No one resisted, although not everyone approved. Still, the men involved knew enough to stay out of his way. There was nothing at stake for them, they had no reason to put up a fight on behalf of the integrity of the profession. The natural course of events would have their way and they were all wise enough to see that. On the other hand, he was oblivious. He could not see beyond the two pages of each day, beyond getting better even if he did not ever become good. He could not see beyond the charge to never quit and never fail. Success was beside the point; its details and form were never something he visualized. Keep on going keep on going keep on going. The Quixote was at work in the birth of tragedy, in the high dive, the twisting and turning that is at work in all falling, and the falling that is at work in all projecting into an unknown future.

This brute force effort left him dangling in the wind. He discovered the domain of the adjunct with no prospects and would take up the role of the temporary and part time itinerant university instructor. It would be his task to teach whatever needed to be taught at the nearby universities and colleges. They did not quite have enough budget for a full-time faculty member, but still had sufficient demand in the entry level courses. Cynicism ticked upward as he wondered what their tuition was really paying for. Young and seasoned by the spartan existence of a graduate student, it was easy enough to transition into such a life. Amid the starvation of that time, a prospect was dangled before him. To the adjunct, a visiting assistant professorship seemed like an abundance. It entailed extravagant compensation and idealized community standing, not to mention a faculty parking spot.

Time is everywhere. It is September. It is 1995. It takes him 45 minutes to get to work without traffic. He only drives in on Mondays, Wednesdays, and Fridays. Not time itself then, it is a nameless and silent pursuer, but the way we have rationalized it. Some things are invisible because of what they are, others because of what we are. The colonization of time, segmenting it, categorizing it, making it measurable and shareable, all of this makes time invisible. Insofar as we are colonizers —or rationalizers, if you prefer—

the kinds of creatures who colonize and rationalize, we stop feeling time, it becomes invisible in favor of the edifices and gauges that we build around it. We don't just colonize lands; we colonize the conceptual world by laying out a structured geographical grid. We do this to take over a place from others and we do this when we describe the behavior of those who take over places from others. Building all these structures into the rotation of the earth to enable adequate communication about the day and our traversal of it, this structures the time of those who meet at 12:15 for lunch or who pick up the kids from school at 2:30. Taking land from the natives, taking the day away from the laborer, taking the weekend away from the leisure consumer, the edifice of our love of reason is a monument to what we have taken. These monuments may be the key to our survival, or they may be the key to our damnation. Worse still, they may be both as a pronouncement of the tragedy that is our time on earth.

Memory can be a struggle against this colonization, a war for independence. It can be hard to place memories into the exact grooves carved by measured time. "I was there on that day at that time." His memory, at least, doesn't work that way. Things blur together, events stand out, but he can't recall which came first and how long of a duration stretched between the one and the other. If you could take a picture of everything important that ever happened, maybe you could submit your memories to those perfect lines and grids of minutes and hours, months and years. It's hard not to imagine that this would be desirable to everyone. Everything would be so perfectly well collected together, just as it should be.

How would that work with the future? What if his plans were like that? By 2:45 on Sunday the 13th he's going to have achieved this or established that. If your goal is to be a Doctor of Philosophy, you could assert that you will achieve it on May 6th at 2pm at the scheduled commencement ceremony at your university based on how many years the department says it typically takes to write a thesis, pass your qualifying exams, and do all of your coursework. If your goal is to become a philosopher, what time will that happen? On which day? When the future breaks down into a predictable set of upcoming events, it loses something, it becomes machinic or robotic, like a ticking clock. There are ways to live your life where the future will always be exactly this kind of planned set of events coordinated in detail. Graduating college and then jumping into a 9 to 5 job where you must schedule your vacations well in advance to make sure that someone can cover for you while you are out. Many people work hard to be able to plan their futures this way, and many people are forced or trapped into planning their futures like this. The trap is a privilege they tell us. What if their past were to become the same way, what if they had the same level of precision in recalling a moment or situating an experience relative to every other one? It might be the best thing that ever happened to us, or it might be the end of what we used to think made us human. On the other hand, it may be that the only way we can live with a predetermined and rationally formatted future is if we have an open-ended and slightly mushy past. Only because things aren't ordered perfectly and sequences don't always comply with a coherent narrative, are we able to experience new things that we don't expect to happen.

On his long hike through Europe before starting graduate school, he didn't bring a camera with him. He didn't have the space in his backpack and opted for a Walkman with a set of carefully selected cassettes instead. One day, he was standing on a foot bridge stretching across a river that was passing through a gorge. He doesn't remember where it was exactly although it might have been somewhere in Austria. He distinctly remembers looking upriver and thinking he could just freeze this moment so that he would always remember it. In a sense, he did since he still thinks he remembers the feeling of that bridge under his feet and the look of the slow-moving river, the warm wind, and the tree-lined ridges along the banks. He doesn't remember when it happened during the trip. If he knew it was in June, he would know that he was in Norway or if it were in September then it must have been Austria. All of that is gone, he just recalls the feel of the wind, the sway of the footbridge, the flow of the river, and the thought he pressed through his mind that he would remember this moment through an act of will rather than with a photograph. To fully rationalize his past, he supposes that picture he took would have to include location information along with the date and time that he took it. With this information, he would be able to use those photographs to build a constant and ongoing diary as he experienced different events. Assuming he could go back over all the photographs and relive or reconstruct the moments in time they captured, he would have a perfectly synchronized and comprehensive map of his life.

A friend of his from college had recently moved back to East Lansing and was working in a lab up there as a software engineer. He told him all this one night on the phone and the engineer told him that this was already possible and that he had worked on some satellite systems that had the capacity to collect images during space travel. He said all we needed to do was to make a consumer version of the hardware that was small enough to fit on our body somewhere. People were probably already working on it. He said things could go even further than that, we could map all human qualities into a giant storage system and combine data from everyone to produce a unified store containing everyone's life. He told the professor a story about the different kinds of colleagues that he had during some of the different corporate jobs he had over the years. He had lived in Silicon

Valley before moving back to Michigan and had worked with some of the bigger companies there.

The engineer told the professor that he, like the philosopher, spent all his professional life reading, writing, and talking. Sometimes talking amounted to teaching. He described a set of archetypical personas that represented various common work behaviors. He had never met a single software engineer who fit neatly into any one of the personas, but everyone he met fit into one or the other of them at one time or another. He had been all of them in a single day, sometimes in a single conversation. They were 1) The blank slate. This is someone who knows nothing except the basic stuff you learn in school and everything they do requires considerable instruction. 2) The extension or the delegate. This is a person who is acting on behalf of someone else. They do exactly what that person, usually someone more experienced in the area, wants them to do. Not just what they tell them to do, but what they want them to do. This is a person with enough experience to be able to fill in some of the blanks and sort out the ways to get something done without having every single step spelled out for them. They are familiar enough with the aims of their supervisor to be able to take care of it on their own. 3) The know it all who cannot learn. This is a person who knows every reason in the world why something can't be done the way that you want it done and has to be done the way they want it done or not at all. No amount of argument is going to convince them of another way to think about it. They likely won't be with the company too long. 4) The experienced excavator. This is someone you can just point in a direction, and they will go off and figure it out. Figure out what the problem is, what the current state of affairs looks like, come up with a proposed solution that is designed using sound professional principles, and then execute on that design to get the job done. A solid and reliable senior engineer. 5) The orchestrator. This is someone who has their nose in everybody's project. This is the person who pointed the experienced excavator in the right direction, the person who guides the extension, who argues with the know it all, and who mentors and develops the blank slate. Their work scales and they orchestrate the work of multiple people to implement solutions to big problems.

His point was that these are career stages, they are levels of development that people achieve as they gain more experience and work on bigger projects with increasing responsibility. He was suggesting that it isn't just that you go to college to learn the rules for being a software engineer and then you are one. You learn the required raw skills and then you get a job that continues to train and shape you into a professional engineer. Like the ideas the professor had been describing about territorializing someone's past with image metadata, this was exactly how the process of increasing discipline worked on the mind of the engineer as they became increasingly more capable of applying rational principles and rules in their projects. A career is a time-dated grid of your history with sufficient markers to replay the narrative in a meaningful way. What it means to advance your career, what it means to gain experience in a specific domain, was to acquire an increased set of disciplinary behaviors that you are empowered to recall at the right time and under the right circumstances. He said he would talk candidly with his boss about this stuff and got the sense that the five personas theory was just scratching the surface. There was more to it when you started getting into the area of managing software projects or managing multiple software projects or whole companies that have hundreds or thousands of projects going on at the same time. They concluded that this was a process that people desired and fought for equal access to, it was a transformation that people wanted to undertake and considered a privilege. What do you want to do? I want to be a software engineer. Does the first-year college student know that what they want is to become someone totally different than who they are? Do they know the extent of the change that this desire will lead them into? If they did, would they still do it? Is that why they do it?

Over time, they will identify with what they have become, their past like their future will be clearly mapped. It all happens gradually and like the frog being boiled alive, there will never be any reason to panic or to make a sudden move toward escape. Why would anyone try to evade what they are pursuing? The desire may have been ignorant or partial, but their minds are expert at adaptation. As new ways are developed for worldly operations to inhabit their thinking and experience, they forget that there was ever anything else or any other possible persona that they might have become with different training.

The job was only for a single year, a sabbatical replacement, with no hope of continuation. It never occurred to him that it might be a bad job and that -as ill-suited for the profession as he was—he was the best they could get. For him, the temptation to leave the area where he was connected, where he had prospects for continuing his adjunct activity, was too strong. It meant returning to Ann Arbor and living there with a —albeit temporary—heightened status. This opportunity was the beginning of the end of his academic career. Was that what he wanted? Truthfully, we can stand back and see from afar that this fateful event was initiated back when he made that declaration to his mother, realized the philosophical turn that it might take through the Nietzschean Quixote, and then was initiated by a three-in-one story paid in time with two pages per day. This is the clarity of hindsight, seeing what was there behind him already. More to the point, it was the proximity of the move from Illinois to Michigan, it was this backtrack to the east after having moved to the west years before. This reversal is what immediately appeared as a chance for decrease or gain, expenses and losses. Mediately, however, the desire in those two pages on that day when he was fifteen was there throughout. He could not avoid the decision, that is all that deliberation provided. It acclimated him to the fact. He sensed that a rift was coming, but he was powerless to twist and turn out of the way. The pathway had been paved long ago from the point on the ledge where he made his first leap.

She took the apartment in the unfinished basement. Mostly because she could afford it, but there was something about it, something else, and it suited her. She put the little TV next to the furnace and her futon on a table. It was not a cute apartment, it wasn't charming. It wasn't poetic and it wasn't meant for entertaining. Crude and straight to the point. It was perfect. The bar was just up the street, and she was trying to find a better library job somewhere on main campus, but everyone wanted one of those so it might take a while. There was a whole skillset involved in doing that. There were professors to woo and hierarchies to penetrate. Jobs were passed out like gold stars, so she would have to impress and gain influence, at least they would have to know her name and be able to associate it with her face. There was a system of rewards and scarcity was built into it so there was going to be competition and ongoing requirements to flatter and persuade. She knew how to do this, her service experience was well suited to it, but it would take time. That didn't matter. A slower transition would be better anyway. Tending bar is her comfort zone, she knew how to make sense of that. The library was still something else, something new and strange, despite the time she spent working there as an undergraduate. It was what she wanted; she just didn't know whether it wanted her: the catalogues and the queries, the organization, and the rules for navigating it. It was unquestionably true that she didn't belong here, but somehow, she got in and here she was. All the other new grad students seemed so well prepared and savvy about how everything worked. They all seemed to have read everything and to know so much already. How did she fall so far behind? How would she ever catch up? Intelligence comes in many forms, she knew about people, how to read them, and she knew how things worked in the real world. She would figure it out.

She wanted to figure it out. This would become her comfort zone, and she would become one of them, belong here, be able to help all the patrons and have all the answers. She didn't have all the answers, but she would learn how to find them, how to look through the vast repositories of data and extract the most relevant bits. The science of information. At some level, she knew that it was just a bunch of rules that she had to learn and become so familiar with that they wouldn't even be rules any more, they would just be how she thought, did her job, and fit into the grand scheme of things. It would be a big improvement because that wasn't how her life was before. Her boyfriend was supposed to move here with her, he said he would. He was looking forward to it and was making plans and preparations. In the end, he said he couldn't do it, that it wasn't his journey and that he was going to go his own way. It was painful and terrifying, a betrayal, but in a weird way it gave her confidence. Even without him coming along, she was dead set on doing it. Learning this helped. Her decision to do it alone confirmed her dedication. It was important that she come so clearly in contact with her desires despite the heartbreak. She only knew what she wanted because she was willing to go through so much to get it.

Getting it would make her a different person. She wanted to be different. Well, she wanted to hold on to some parts of herself but wanted to add to them. That is what growth means, she was sure of it. You grow because you hold on to the things that matter, the core parts of yourself that are firmly in place, but you also take on something new. The new stuff makes you bigger, opens you up more, broadens your scope and your vision. She wanted that so much that she experienced her limitations as real things in her life, as challenges to find answers to hard questions and help other people do the same. Learning. It's more than just reading books and studying catalogue theory. It's in the fingers and the toes, it's in the way you walk and the way you look at things, it's how your eyes focus and how you laugh, the things you think are funny. Learning is transformational. She knew better than anyone that she wasn't completely in control of what it would do to her. Thrilling, but terrifying. Would she still love the things she loves after she worked her way further down this new path? If they no longer matter to her so that she isn't the least bit upset about leaving them behind, who else would be there to look out for her and remind her of who she was? There was that future self that would be transformed, was she qualified to take care of her? She owed her something, but she wasn't sure whether she owed her protection or inspiration.

She thought about this all the time. Smoking a cigarette and drinking a beer after studying all evening. After reading on the computer and learning the digital interfaces to the various systems, she would end up in the bar. Not to get drunk, not even to catch a buzz. The beer was just an accessory, it went with the cigarette. The place was a different story. Sitting in the Del on her nights off and talking to the bartender or some of the regulars. She told them about information and how it worked, where it was, and how important it was to be able to get it and use it. How powerful it was. She could feel a revolution was coming. Sometimes she would say too much, and her listener's eyes would glaze over. She was only just learning, but she liked figuring it out and telling her friends about it. It wasn't only that this was a good way to teach it to herself, but that it was a comfortable and safe environment for doing it. At first, she didn't feel at ease talking to the other students, she was sure they would judge her. She could talk to the other bartenders or the waitrons, they would get it. She didn't want to lose this, and she was sure that if she kept coming, if she kept a foot in the door, and tried to work her new life into this familiar one, she would never find herself in a position where this didn't matter to her anymore. She would be able to hold on to this part of herself because she would always keep one eye on it and let it help her get through the trials. Making it part of her support system would ensure she never lost it.

It turned out that not everybody at school was scary. She was working on a semester long group project for one of her classes and it gave her the opportunity to find out how great some of them were once you cracked the surface. They were geeks and dorks in their own way, but in the first few meetings it seemed like they were worried about the same things she was worried about, and they wanted the same things she wanted. There was a kind of awkwardness when they talked about where they were undergrads and why they wanted to study library science. It was familiar. They were trying out their new roles and they were worried about losing and gaining parts of themselves just like she was. The more she talked to the people in the group, the better she felt, the more she saw that others were going through the same thing, the more confident she became.

She would dream of her project and of hypertext and the way in which information was gathered and presented. It was decorated so that it could be accessed, information was attached to information to make it easier to find, to make it easier to assign relevance and context during search and seizure. This made it easier to recall the information and to apply it. A blob of data thrown on a screen would be meaningless, we must be able to make sense of it, we need to be able to fit it in with our interests and associate it with the reason we went looking for it in the first place. If we don't do that, then it's just noise and a distraction. It is just as much the librarian's job to find the information as it is to help process it, to make sure that the results of the search fit with its expectations. Even if the answers were unknown and even if they showed that the question was incorrectly formulated and contained a false assumption, that fact needed to be part of the search and part of the results. Information was for the sake of understanding; it wasn't meant to be a commodity or idle entertainment. This was her mission and where her bravery came from. Its pull was so strong that it pushed her to do for herself what she hoped to do for others.

The unreliable narrator of any philosophical work is like a child, cheerful or cranky, demanding or accommodating, inhabited by the memory grid that has been constructed by an author suffering the same fate. Philosophers too are born and were they to start over from scratch none would get any further than Thales. They would be forced to reinvent or rediscover all that he was forced to invent and discover. That's not how it works though, we go to school, the products of others are dangled before us, and we grab on to some select set of them, appropriate them for ourselves, and shape ongoing interest into pursuits that carry us forward into solutions and nuances that never occurred to the Milesian. Desire is that murky motive that pulls one way rather than another, that grabs for this and ignores that, but where does it come from? The philosophers of desire have tried to situate it and may have made some progress before it got the better of them, before the very desire they made the object of their investigations took over and became their driving motive. Desire yearned to paint a desirable portrait of itself, to make itself an object of the other's desire. Philosophers aren't immune to this, desiring that wants the other's desire, that wants to be attended to and even pursued. The philosopher speaks and to the extent that they are not lunatics or babbling children, they desire that their speech be listened to and that they receive an appropriate response. For this reason, philosophers are easily rattled.

The conversation of philosophers is the ongoing history of philosophy and philosophers are those who have participated in that conversation. This is a standard circular definition that ultimately entails that you can only be a philosopher if the other philosophers speak to you, and you listen to them. What is more, you must respond in such a way that future philosophers in turn will listen to what you said. Without that indirect form of communication, there is no proper membership in the community. There can be no such thing as an imaginary philosopher, one who plays at it for their own purposes without concern for whether the rest of the world will or can respond in kind. That vision must be delusional because only through this community membership is the proper organization at work. The one who pretends is a dead end. There are no collective illusions here, the only collective illusion is the thing itself, it is what pulls the individual pretender out of the place where they were and pushes them into the parameters and patterns of the historical discipline. No one is listening and no one is talking to them, they appear to have failed. The moments of the conversation aren't once and forever, however, since it is possible for conditions to change as they would in any community that cuts across multiple generations and which might extend membership privileges to the dead.

There are examples of philosophers who were not members of the community while they lived, but who gained acceptance from its members after they died. That is the carrot that can be presented as a lure into the delusion. The ignored would-be philosopher can persist and publish just in case somewhere down the line someone more capable of integrating the work with the ongoing concerns of the historical situation comes along and inserts their name into the credits. At that point, the would-be philosopher becomes authentic independently of any change to their experience. This is something like the madness that some thinkers might opt for during their lives. If they are outside the de facto domain and must earn membership through different means, they may never gain the necessary acceptance, especially if that requires the arbitrary proliferation of their contributions through community circulation. What if, to the contrary, membership in this community were determined by the delusion itself? In that case, no university professor would be responsible for assigning membership, not even the lot of them taken together. Rather, if some single delusional practitioner were to come along and start muttering a whispered response to some great work, then wouldn't those original gasps become part of the tradition? Which tradition and why bestow it with the name of "philosophy"? Likely it would not have earned it. If the professors in their philosophy departments don't read Bataille, then he is not one of them. If professors in literature departments read his work, then he is one of them. Simple enough. He wrote literature and not philosophy, what difference does it make? When an individual graduate student or junior faculty member tries to include him in their curriculum, their colleagues may rebel: "you should not be teaching literature in a philosophy class unless it is a class in the philosophy of literature. The two disciplines are distinct, and you must maintain the boundaries."

The anxiety of the philosopher lies in the desire to establish and maintain the boundary between what is philosophy and what is not. This is true of any practice: science and pseudo-science, medicine and quackery. Every discipline defines both its rigorous and legitimate practices and uses them to delineate the border between the discipline and what it is not, what is external to it, and what, in the event that it pretends to be legitimate, is to be condemned as false. The guardians of the discipline must safeguard newcomers so that they are able to discriminate and understand the limits, why they are there, why they need to be there, and why all newcomers must honor them. None of which is the same thing as never venturing beyond them since this is permitted so long as it is done with proper references and a bibliography. Not science, but the philosophy of science, not literature, but the philosophy of literature, not sociology, but social philosophy. These sub-disciplines, which can be attached to epistemology or value theory or wherever you like, are acceptable areas of specialization so long as they fit within the current fashion for rationalizing the terrain.

It isn't enough to engage Kant, you must engage Kant in a specific way such that the audience —there has to be an audience— is a group with specific characteristics. What then does it signify when one engages the history of a discipline, benefits from its progress and pursuits, but does so in a way that never catches on with any of the living and becomes permanently lost over time? This doesn't refer to the fate of someone like Emerson who is legitimate in English departments, but not among philosophers. This concerns the fate of those nameless ones who were never a part of anything and never accepted by anyone. These light sleepers are the proliferators of some illusory conversation with a Kant that no one knows, and no one cares to know. If such a maniac were to live their life outside the academy and never teach a course or hold an office hour, then what was it that person was doing when they tried to address the great Priest of Konigsberg? Clearly it must have been some form of madness. For the sake of argument, imagine that this person is well balanced in every other way. Say they had a proper job and were able to pay all their bills on time and have loving and supportive relationships with friends and family. Nonetheless, in the matter of their efforts at practicing philosophy, they would have suffered from a form of madness, or they would have succumbed to some delusional fantasy that was part of some life of the mind, solipsistic and perverse.

This condition would be a torment.

During those initial weeks after he arrived in Ann Arbor, the professor happened to have drinks at a campus bar with a physician who lived down the lane in the same apartment complex. She was doing her residency at the University Hospital and used the phrase "real doctor" during their conversation. She said it in a way that suggested she was trying to illicit a response. He obliged and told her that as far as he understood it, the term was applied as a title indicating respect from the community. When the people think of a person as learned or deeply informed in some matter, they were bestowed with the form of address "doctor." He told her that he thought this practice started somewhere in Europe around a thousand or so years ago and the people who were first considered deserving of it were those scholars who, at the time at least, were known as philosophers. He was fairly sure that the title was only applied to physicians in the last couple hundred years as the profession became more respectable. He pointed out that there was a long history of quackery and that the public only recently started to grant a position of respect to its medical professionals. He guessed this was due to the increasing efficiency and effectiveness of the medical methodology and the technics of medicine, things like the machines that had become available for diagnostics and the procedures, including human vivisection, that had been perfected for treatments.

He thought his response well-reasoned and fair. She was not pleased and argued that they were more than technicians and suggested that the subject of their practice is what elevated them so far above all others. He tried to be agreeable, but it was too late. It was clear that they were not going to get on well. He would have liked to learn more about why this was such a sensitive subject and why the answer had to conform so closely to the expectations she had about her profession and its status among people who weren't members of it. He agreed that there was a body of knowledge that defined the profession and he admitted that there was extreme technical expertise involved in being acknowledged as a member of the medical community. He didn't think he was disparaging the profession at all but merely pointing out that its history only made it respectable very recently. He was just trying to explain why physicians had only come to earn the title of "doctor" such a short time ago. His point wasn't that this group or that were the "real" doctors, but that "real" doctor doesn't make sense unless you just meant something other than a quack. She insisted that she had made great sacrifices to focus on her studies and that these sacrifices meant there were parts of her personality that would never develop as fully as they would have if she had chosen a different profession. This was a sacrifice she was willing to make because of the grandeur of the task. Of course, that was exactly what he was talking about: how she had surrendered and submitted herself to the discipline for the sake of fulfilling a desire to be helpful to her fellow humans. It is an admirable profession, he assured her unnecessarily, but why did her devotion require that it be elevated above the sacrifices made in other professions? Why couldn't she see that all occupations can place similar demands on those who devote huge segments of their lives to their practice? These weren't the right questions. The right ones, she said, were why can't he see the difference?

When someone goes to the doctor, they want their physician to be up to date on all the best practices for treating whatever ails them. They want to avoid quacks, but they are also worried that the profession itself may have developed a set of interests that prevents practitioners from considering all possible effective treatments. Is it covered by insurance? Which tests can be done in our own lab and which do we have to send out? What about holistic approaches, wouldn't those be better in this case? They had to be familiar with payer provider regulations and the details of unsanctioned treatments to protect the integrity of their profession in addition to the immediate interests of patients. It was their ability to render an authoritative opinion that they were protecting, it was a necessary condition for patient care. To the guardians, it did not matter whether the profession's standards and norms transcended empirical evidence. The discipline must include features that make it the best of all available methods for approaching the subject. That will never mean that the profession is free of bias for promoting the discipline at the expense of its original objectives.

Production entails the reproduction of the means of production. This seems like an axiom on a par with "I think, therefore I am" and just as earth shattering and revolutionary. It means that there is never just discipline, that the fach is never free of bias. It contains a self-constituting ideology that aims at maintaining the accepted boundaries of the profession supporting it. Instead, the methodology must contain a set of rules and professional guidelines to safeguard the profession and the community of legitimate practitioners. This is why the writer who is not a professor is the one without community, the one who no one listens to, must not be listened to, and must be kept out. If something in that person's work is appealing to graduate students or undergraduates, then an effort must be made to reveal the ruse. The profession engages the outsider only enough to show that it is not a legitimate field of study. A clique of peer reviewed publishing houses is enough for philosophers. Among physicians, they must be sufficiently informed about holistic medicine to know that it is dangerous and wrong in whatever context a patient might suggest. The doctors of holistic medicine have their bugaboos as well, not just the establishment medical doctors who dismiss their methods, but the snake oil salesmen that give holistic medicine a bad name. All discipline has this imperative placed upon it. Those who would engage in philosophical conversation with the likes of Bataille are just as plagued by the charlatans who pretend to understand him as by the philosophers who refuse to read him.

Philosophy's margins are filled with disputes over legitimacy among those who would proclaim themselves the proper bearers of the alternative to professional philosophy. The jealousy and rigor of any discipline is reproduced in all its organized action, everything that would claim to be anything other than madness. It is there in the committee room during admissions and hiring, and it is there in the cafés and bars when the dropouts vent their resentment.

October

Descartes was a philosopher, although I don't think he ever professed it. He was never employed as a philosopher. For money, that is. The terminology was vague so maybe it's best to say that he never gave a lecture or graded papers. I doubt he ever conducted a seminar or sat on a thesis committee. He probably never sat on any committee. Hiring, improvements to or modernization of the curriculum, nothing of that sort. If he never did anything like that, how come they call him a philosopher and what does he have in common with those who call themselves philosophers today? Nowadays they spend the better part of their time doing all those other things, sometimes to the point of neglecting their research. He studied law, but never practiced after getting his degree. He was employed by the army for a while. He worked hard, but how did he live? The family business? Did he have benefactors who were seeking prestige by having a learned mathematician on their payroll? How rich can you be if you don't have a philosopher of your very own? Did a geometer invent modern philosophy or did a philosopher invent analytic geometry? The philosopher's life in the seventeenth century might have been consistent with their lives for centuries before that. Today that is no longer the case. The university reigns over their livelihood and yields the substance of their thought. Kant has become the paradigm and even people without independent means can practice. No longer the private domain of the elite, the profession has been democratized.

Forget about that. Stick with Descartes. His reputation stems almost completely from his written work. Whether he spent every minute of 1641 doing philosophy, whatever that might be, is irrelevant. No one cares about that. Leave that to the biographers and not his students. His work is selectively emphasized because not every one of his books is philosophically significant. Not even every sentence in those books is a philosophical assertion. What makes a sentence a philosophical assertion? Back to this again, are we? Were the sentences philosophical because Descartes put them in books that are still interesting to philosophers? Is there something intrinsic to the sentence itself such that it would be philosophical regardless of what readers thought of it, or whether it ever had any readers at all? Is there a sentence that is only philosophical if the right reader is reading it? Does that make sense?

"But, as if I had suddenly fallen into a deep whirlpool, I am so disturbed that I can neither touch my foot to the bottom, nor swim up to the top."

Philosophers love sentences like this. They have so much character and evoke such a profound sense of the thinker's personality. Even if they aren't philosophical on their own, they have a charm that comes from the support they provide to other nearby sentences that are obviously philosophical. This sentence teaches us something about the philosopher's work and that walking the philosopher's path means being in a turbulent setting from which there is no escape. Such thoughts don't isolate them, but they do individuate them in our minds. This is not armchair forensics where some idle passerby comes along years or centuries later and casually comments on the agony or the pathos in one sentence or another. There is poor Descartes by the fire in his dressing gown and he feels that way. He adds the description to the work to evoke the state he was in, and this plays a part in demonstrating how to understand the rest. The relief of *cogito ergo sum* must have been powerful because it saved him from such horrible conditions. These *decorative* sentences make that clear.

May I ask, are these remarks truthful? Why would they call it hyperbolical doubt if they were? Shouldn't all the propositions in a work of philosophy be true as far as the philosopher can determine? Isn't that the whole point? How are we to take these pseudo-propositions in the *Meditations*? There is narration of what he is doing and where he is doing it. In his dressing gown, in the evening, by the fire, with the wax, and so on. Were these true statements at the time that he was writing them, and does it matter? Does their truth contribute to the power of the argument? He says he is disturbed. If that is hyperbolical, then he is lying. If they are fabrications for the sake of effect, shouldn't we distrust the entire project? What else is he faking for the effect? He wants us to feel the moment of deliberation and works extremely hard to articulate the experience behind these meditations. In the middle of the heaviest moments, he shows us what it is like to live the life of the philosopher. He reveals his personality as a sign of his individuation and uses it to connect with his reader. Is that a trick or is it an expository technique? What in the work is fabricated and to what end is it included in the manuscript?

The agony of the undertaking is irrelevant to the investigations themselves, or so they say. *Meditations on First Philosophy* might never have been a classic had the author not written anything else like *Discourse on Method* or *Principles*. The tolerance for the style in the signature work comes from the gravity of it in those others. The power of *Meditations* is precisely that it puts the philosopher firmly in the center of the deliberations. Its groundbreaking relationship to the history of philosophy, the advent of the cogito and its methodology in the quest for knowledge, is not only established through an argument or set of propositions in support of a conclusion. *Meditations* puts the very undertaking of the thinker into the center of it. I think. I am a thinking thing. Here, let me demonstrate that for you. *Meditations* is an example of itself, it is a recursive operation substantiating itself in itself. Here is the thinker at work and here is the thinker proclaiming the act of thinking in the act of thinking. The biographical asides and musings about the immediate objects at hand are not incidental to the demonstration, they *are* the demonstration. The philosopher is alone in these musings and the deliberate undertaking is the only legitimate basis for their knowledge. Descartes shows himself in his isolation and, in doing so, connects with a larger group through the facets and features of his revealed personality.

Realistically, this should make it difficult to contain any consideration of Descartes' work within the parameters of simple epistemology, metaphysics, or science. It transforms all human endeavors insofar as it situates investigations into the acts of the isolated investigators. The methodology becomes the way the solitary thinker establishes a relationship to the object of their thought. How does it stand in matters of philosophy? It must establish the right procedure for allowing the investigator to arrive at the truth and achieve knowledge. This is done with far greater impact in *Meditations* than in either *Principles* or *Discourse*. The distance of the philosopher's voice from the matter at hand should have made it impossible to establish a personal relationship to knowledge at the center of the Cartesian project. Chomsky's reading of Descartes may not have benefited from this meditative stance, but Husserl's mostly definitely did. In the thinker's ego, personality blooms in the guise of everyone else, the intersubjective world of all the thinkers that there are.

It is commonly thought that Descartes did not make any significant contributions to ethics and yet all of ethics was radically transformed by this aspect of the Cartesian project. An authentically ancient Greek reading of Aristotle would no longer appear to be an ethics in the modern sense. What Kant did or the Utilitarians, these are proper ethical projects with methodologies for deliberation and rules for determining the good over and against the evil action. Descartes may be the single most important philosopher for modern ethics, and that without having written anything at all on the topic. The perspective of the ethicist, the viewpoint accepted by Kant, Bentham, or Mill, is first established in the Cartesian philosophy. The deliberating cogito is the seat of the ethical decision and of the formation of the rule to be realized in the act. Insofar as ethics becomes a method for determining the goodness of an intention or an act, where either of those is associated with the individual actor, Descartes' paradigm is at its foundation initiating ethics' forensic application. That paradigm is not established in the *Principles* or in the *Discourse*, but in *Meditations*. It is established precisely because it is the philosopher alone with himself, by the fire, personally involved in establishing the foundation of knowledge through a properly informed methodological process.

It is so hard to connect this to my classroom experience. First off, there are thirty-five people in the room. Most of the students are fulfilling distribution requirements, they need a certain number of credits in the humanities to graduate. They may feign or muster some interest in the material, but that is only to ensure they are properly motivated and can get a good grade. Critics have likely succumbed to students' flattery, and it clouds their judgment. When teaching in these conditions, it is my job to engage and inspire them, to worry about them as the audience of my lectures and the discussions I lead to better convey the lesson. What does any of that have to do with philosophy? Did Socrates think of how to best frame his deliberations so that he was able to properly engage and inspire his students? Did his students only express a passing interest in the field as they made their way onto other matters of greater importance to their lives? Ninety percent of the teaching that I do could be categorized as intellectual history or life skills. They do not learn philosophy from those lessons, and I am not presenting it. That small 10% of the lesson that may find its way into truly philosophical domains, that goes over the heads of nearly all the students, with maybe one or two that are able to stay with me throughout. Even those few may forget it days or weeks after the exams or final papers.

Frankly, we don't think this is where we do philosophy anyway. At least not my colleagues. They are far more likely to think of teaching as a job they do that enables their philosophical work during a sabbatical, in between semesters, or over summer vacation. They might be a member of the elite and have graduate students to do all the grading for them while they remain focused on their projects, or they teach in areas related to their research. What they read while preparing lectures more likely matches the reading they do when researching the next chapter. No one thinks of grading exams or papers as the true work of the philosopher, no one thinks of standard lesson preparation for an introductory course covering Descartes' *Meditations* as the highest research interest of their professional lives. We struggle to make this life for ourselves to maintain the connection to the discipline and to the proper path for the life of the philosopher. What is the alternative?

Where does philosophy have its place? Where is its place? Should you wish to speak with others who are able to skip past some of the first awkward steps and onto the context where your deliberations have carried you, where will you find such colleagues? If you write down what you think and work out an elaborate argument for describing the advancements you have made or some contribution you can make to an ongoing conversation, where will you present that work? Even if there were community groups interested in furthering the study of philosophy, nearly all the participants would take their orientation from their experience at the university. They majored in it, or took a few courses, they dropped out before finishing their dissertation, or they are a professor looking to add community involvement to their tenure packet. The way in which we orient ourselves toward the deliberations of the philosopher is guided by these academic structures, journals bound to academic requirements for publication, academic presses using professors as reviewers, and so on.

Opposing this or raising questions about it is often immediately conceived as an act of anti-intellectualism or an affront to experience and expert knowledge. These are sensible defenses, but is the collected knowledge proof or is it the credentials? Does the expertise of the surgeon lie in the brand of scalpel they use? Could they display expertise outside the boundaries of established traditions by performing an appendectomy in the middle of a traffic jam? The board-certified thoracic surgeon might be at a disadvantage there, but not in the operating room. In the case of the philosopher, Descartes' seventeenth century is like that traffic jam, but he would be at a disadvantage in the contemporary academic operating room. He would first have to establish himself as having the right to contribute to the conversation before he could speak in those contexts where any real contributions are made. Good luck doing that if you can't read more than a few pages of a book you don't agree with. The academic discipline already knows which speakers it must listen to. If you are going to write about epistemology in 1995, all the academic philosophers know who you must read and who you must address with your objections. They all know what work you must do to establish yourself as a legitimate part of the discussion. Those voices will differ from the ones required twenty years before or after. The work of the ones who matter today may be long forgotten by writers twenty years from now, but today it is of vital importance that their work be considered. How can that be?

This is a coercive state and there are those who act as though they love it. The same who might observe the isolation of the thinker and eschew the over-exuberant personality that emits from the private space of their less rigorous work. The discipline, in such cases, offers a way back to the righteous road of collective inquiry and the safety it provides. Constrained in this way, we are not working on what we think we are working on. That is, when I write about the basis of individual knowledge claims, I am not talking about the grounds that any specific person has for making the assertions they make, rather I am talking about the state of that knowledge as a body among learned contributors, as an expression of institution at work in individual endeavor. How does the discipline currently understand the matter of knowledge and justified assertions of fact? This is an indirect relationship to the matter. It is why it so often seems that philosophical inquiries require the participant to be properly skewed by whatever trendy orientations are at work before they can contribute. It's because the contribution isn't aimed at the things themselves or the matter at hand but at the state of the discipline, amounting to the cumulative effect of the organization on the personality of the thinkers. Here is what the profession thinks of foundationalism and here are the contextualist and coherentist attacks on it. Here is why the great so and so has failed to lend the proper nuance to their doctrine and, finally, this is the miniscule adjustment that needs to be made to establish the position.

If you properly demonstrate your capacity to perform these gymnastics, then you might find yourself teaching the future of the profession. In that case, you might find yourself employed at a university with graduate students. You can use that position to start branching out into bigger and bigger scopes leading you to a better job at a higher ranked university with graduate students who are more in demand on the job market. You might be a true philosopher because you can force those graduate students to treat your work in the same way that you previously were treating the work of your teachers. This may establish some of your writing as first order contributions to the discipline. At least for as long as you are actively teaching and writing, and your influence on these former students continues to hold. Later, you will retire or die, and they will retire or die, and no one will pay any attention to whatever it was that you were on about. The next big thing will have come along and be proselytized by the next group of graduate students being churned out by the next big professor who was able to demonstrate how clever they were at making slight adjustments to the work of others. Repeat, as necessary.

The expertise the critics were defending gets lost in all this and surfaces as a mark of institutional mastery. There are experts of this nook or cranny, of this set of arguments, or this figure. The discipline dominates here because no one expert is an expert in everything. The generalized body is available here or there to make up the lot of it through a system of expertise. Of course, there are going to be windbags who spout all kinds of nonsense, but the right people to point that out are their colleagues who know enough to say so. If someone from outside the circle of legitimate contributors makes similar claims, then they are dubbed anti-intellectual and accused of rejecting the power of expertise. Deciding the victor in the battle for expertise is left to the people who have none of it. Not because they are authorities, but because they are non-combatants. The competitors are all invested in the discussion. They are making their points and stating the case for themselves as the expert with the most credibility. Some among the profession at large will believe them, and then there are others and still others will believe them. Expertise will not come in a single authoritative voice, but through an attended dialogue among experts for the sake of a profession at large relying upon them. Who is left to decide which side or sides make the best case? Not one of the experts, of course, since they are all parties to the dispute. No, it will be the onlookers, but they won't know the difference and will rely on the familiar credentialing mechanisms provided through organizational familiarity. The ruse of expertise is exactly the problem. It isn't that experts are being denigrated in the debate, it's that the conditions of expertise are the very issue up for debate.

We are a noisy lot, we human beings, and without a greater sense of where we are headed and what we are hoping to establish, it is likely impossible to come to any kind of resolution on who has the legitimate expertise and why. I know there are plenty of people who want to help sort this out and make some contribution to the discussion so that some progress can be made, but that throws us right back into the heart of the matter. I feel the fatigue of this trap, and most days don't want anything to do with it. I know there is some set of skills and expertise here, but I can't navigate it, I can't figure out its principles and content because there are too many competing voices and too many valid arguments, too many credentials being thrown around. It makes my head spin as if I were caught in a whirlpool. That is what it all comes back to and that is where my focus keeps landing. Descartes alone by the fire reeling from the previous day's work or trying to understand the substantial nature of the candle as it melts before the heat of the blaze.

Here I am by myself at the table next to the kitchen. All the lights in the apartment are off except the one that hangs above the table and the power lights on the dials of the stereo, playing Beethoven's *Missa Solemnis*. Blocking out the noise of the profession, the bickering of the discipline, the historical prejudice initialized in *Meditations,* pits me against the page as I search for philosophy somewhere here in the space that opens as I write. "It was then in order to include the sleeper that Aristotle added the word 'potential'" (Diogenes Laertius). This morsel sets me off, fabricating line after line in response, not thinking of who said what about this or that but lost in the traversal of time where Aristotle has reached out to Diogenes and Diogenes has reached out to me. I am puzzled. 1) The Greek ὑποπίπτη is a verb form and it is non-trivial for the translator to convert that to a noun: "the sleeper." 2) Does ὑποπίπτη mean 'it sleeps' or is it more like 'it succumbs', 'it goes or falls under'...? 3) Why does the translator think Diogenes is referring to a word that was added? Is it the word that was added, or τὸ δυνάμει itself? 4) Why does the translator suggest "Aristotle" added it? The philosopher's name does not appear in the original Greek sentence. Isn't this a huge leap in interpretation? Is he assuming that Diogenes is just a biographer and not dabbling in any analysis of the philosophical content? The paragraph containing this sentence suggests otherwise. Amid the evening's rhythms, the discipline is at work: a philosophical phylum, here is philosophy becoming.

Wolfe's schedule is the inverse of mine. He only stays around the apartment when I am not there. When I am there and working, he is out, I'm not sure where. Our conversations usually happen just before bed if he should happen to come home while I am still awake.

Wolfe slurs, "you think you're the cartesian resistance to the discipline. You assert your personality over and against the power of historically formed organizations for defining operations expertly. You say you value expertise, but your every action denies it. You only love yourself and you think the traditional seat of legitimate action is filled with noise because amid its din you cannot hear your own voice. That is all you want to hear. Do you dare to reduce all the great discoveries of the sciences to a monotonous droning? Only the community can know and only the community can learn and investigate accurately. If you are not a member, you have no voice."

"You're just playing the devil's advocate."

"No, I am the devil's advocate. On this, at least, I don't deny philosophy its due, I only resign my role in it. You're a hypocrite. You want both to have the discipline and to escape it, but it is already an escape, a coercive supplement that replaces whatever is personal for you. You're the event of a deconstruction of the history of western metaphysics as presence that knows that it can only be what it is if it has this other to oppose."

"How are you different?"

"I leave philosophy to the philosophers. Not from disgust or as an act of rebellion. I love reading the work of the geniuses among them. What do I care if it takes decades and decades of charlatans and soothsayers just to produce a Putnam or a Butler? I leave them to themselves and enjoy the fruit."

"What is it that you're doing then? What are those scribblings?"

"There probably isn't a name for it. I'm an itinerant. I listen and I learn, I read and I write. I am a student who absorbs what he can here and there, produces what he must when he must and then moves along."

"How does that relate to anything? Where does it fit in?"

"Why does that matter? It doesn't matter to me. If I read *Zarathustra* and think that this is the way innovation looks, or if I read *Meditations* and think that this is the way that progress looks, or if I read the Critiques and think that this is the way that paradigm shifts work; if I do any of that, then I am lost. It doesn't matter what I'm doing. The one who walks the path is the only one who can say what the lineage will spit out next. It won't look like anything anyone has ever seen before."

"What does that mean, 'what the lineage will spit out next'?"

"When I am absorbed in this conversation, when I am really listening to it, I become part of it. I speak the next sounds that the conversation —as though it has some life or mind of its own— needs to say next. The lineage speaks. My mouth moves. I am the ventriloquist's dummy."

"You're just rationalizing your contradictions. It's the community, no it's me off on my own and apart from the community. You have no coherent platform."

"From some perspective your position and mine might not look any different. In both cases, it appears as if there is a lone thinker working in isolation. In your view, that thinker has turned their back on the discipline. On mine, this is the only way to fully realize it. To leave it behind, to forget about it and just do whatever it is that you are drawn to do. What is drawing you? That will be the way the discipline speaks in you as your investigations. The doctrine is always the community at work, but you don't have to strain and strive to be a member of that community. It inhabits your every move whether you embrace it or not."

"We can't be saying the same thing."

"We're not. I'm saying they don't seem to be different. You agonize over this. You try to make your job and your skills and everything in your work comply with these rules so that you can achieve legitimacy. I don't need that. I have it already and I can go off and talk to all kinds of people. The community isn't something I need to strive to access independently of whatever investigations I make. Whoever I am talking to and wherever I go and whatever I do, the conversation is continuing, and I am acting within it."

"Suppose the community never embraces you as one of its members?"

"I'm not sure I understand that. You mean I write papers and they don't get accepted at conferences or journals? You mean I talk on the street to random passersby and my insights never make it into the classroom? You are enforcing an order there. No one is making you do it. You're doing that. The more powerful the discipline, the greater your isolation, and the more likely you are to define yourself over and against it."

"What if you are terribly lonely because there is no one to talk to about the big ideas that you're sorting through? It takes a lot of effort to understand the critical move that Kant made in his arguments against Hume. If you have to explain that to everyone you talk to just to make..."

"...just to make some esoteric point that only people who've understood the critical philosophy would care about?"

"Yes. Progress in learning results in stockpiled experiences, vocabulary, and established understanding. To continue, you need people to talk to and they have to be where you are to help you make the next step."

"Can't you get that from Hegel or Chomsky or Strawson? You need to talk to the person who is struggling with these phases?"

"Well yes, sometimes. To learn to think. To take some of the awkward early steps, you need teachers and listeners, people who can transform your muttering into eloquence, your fragments into assertions, and whatever else."

"Well, maybe you are onto something there, maybe not. It could be that these teachers you are talking about will steer you off in the wrong direction. No matter how much you want to put your work within a community, the standards of that community are going to require a selective agent, people who have picked this set of principles over and against some others that are not worth including. Making those selections may include you in a group, but that may be the wrong group or a false step. There is a sense in which even the expert is alone. They must rely on their own responses and reactions. They have to turn away from the rest of them if they think their ideas are being accepted for the wrong reasons, or if they think they've been 'taught' something that is all wrong."

"You think the loneliness I am talking about is an essential part of it?"

"Yes."

"You think Putnam has to be willing to betray his followers if he sees an argument that sends him off in a different direction?"

"Absolutely, and then I go one step further. If you are serious about it. If you really want to know the philosopher's deliberations, what it is like to be a philosopher, you must leave its institution behind. Otherwise, it will fool you into thinking you're having an authentic philosophical experience when you have fallen into a false consciousness skewed by the idea of the month, the next big thing whatever it might be."

"Wouldn't the loneliness be worse?"

"No. You're not listening. It's the same. Either way, but in my case, I don't expect colleagues. Instead, I know that any of my friends can offer up insights that might be valuable to me if I am paying attention. Not through some theory or argument that they're making, but in the way they orient themselves. In their actions and how they are, there are physical beings at work, there are processes, there is a brain functioning. The content of your investigations is all around you, how could you ever feel isolated by these inquiries? Everyone is taking part; everything is in the mix."

"But..."

"You only feel isolated when you start to feel sorry for yourself about not being a hot shot. Why aren't my papers being accepted at conferences, why can't I find a tenure track position? That's bullshit. Just stop thinking about that stuff and you'll stop feeling that way."

"Well, I have to pay the bills."

"Wait, so that's what this is all about? Only a moron would study philosophy to pay the bills."

"Yes, but where will the time come from if I have to earn a living doing something else?"

"Same answer. Quit, if you can."

"If I can't keep working and studying while earning a living at some irrelevant occupation, that's on me?"

"There's so much wrong in what you just said. First, who says it's an irrelevant occupation? What could possibly happen to a human being anywhere that is irrelevant to philosophy? Second, if the flame isn't burning hot, then yes the slightest kick of dust will douse it."

"Let me ask you. Do you have any money?"

"Yes, I do. Since I've been here, I've done a little copy editing and I've done some substitute teaching. Hopefully, I'll get more calls soon. I've been trying to get in good with the admins who manage the rosters."

"None of that gets in the way of your studies?"

"That's my point. Nothing gets in the way of my studies. I mean it. I would quit if I could."

"You don't make any sense. You were worried I was sabotaging myself by making decisions that'll force me out. Now, you're worried I'll stick with it."

"Do what you *want*. Do what *you* want."

When the engineer made up his mind to move to Ann Arbor, it all happened fast. He sent out a few applications, had some phone interviews, received a couple of offers, and decided which would be the best fit. He negotiated compensation and moving expenses and then settled down in nearby Ypsilanti before starting work at a lab where he would be doing low level compression of video imagery. He was an expert in this area having worked for a company in Silicon Valley who was an innovator in video over IP and network compression. That came after he had been working with a company that built one of the most popular network operating systems in the world. He was an expert and his new employer, partially located in the university research community and partially located in the private sector, was thrilled to have someone with his background and skills joining their team.

That's how it is with expertise. When we learn, it's not just raw skills concerning this algorithm and how it relates to that data structure. There are large sets of problem areas where experience and late-night complex problem solving, working out difficult integration issues, and understanding changing behavior as operations scale to more users, provide highly desirable skills. Those skills make the people who have them capable of contributing to the work of people collaborating on the production or design of cutting-edge technical devices or services. This connects to the specific experiences we have had and to the types of experiences. Not every engineer who has been working in the industry for five or ten years will have seen the same types of problems and had the same late night debug sessions or been exposed to the same kinds of production environment nightmares. The specific work experience, the specific organization, the market position of the enterprise, there are so many factors that contribute to what a person will see during those five or more years of experience. The variation carries value with it and the value transfers into the person who undergoes the experience.

When we think of disciplinary surveillance, it's common to think in terms of an examination or constant evaluations that are part of any educational program. All organizational memberships include evaluation and examination, and not only that, but tests where the subject must bear witness against itself. Doing your job will involve other people. Whether there are two colleagues working side by side doing the same thing and inviting comparisons of their productivity, two team members with different roles collaborating to build something, or just yourself doing the same thing over months where the work this week can be compared to the work last week. In all these cases, there are tests and room for evaluation which might come from peers and customers if not the boss or the actors themselves. One worker is happy with another because they make it easier to do their job, or they are disgruntled because the other guy is a slacker, and this impacts all the people who depend on them. These evaluations are constant, and bosses pick up on them as they walk around the shop floor or talk to people during one-on-one meetings. Based on what they are hearing, they may provide feedback to the employees. Even the happy or disgruntled colleagues are constantly providing their feedback through their moods while they do their jobs. The constant feedback of the workplace provides a constant domain and ethos of evaluation. There are events and we measure them. We watch each other and evaluate each other, formally and informally, when we associate with and depend on each other.

These associations amount to disciplinary maneuvers and they shape the actions of those around us. Well-meaning colleagues will want their co-workers to like them, they will want to exchange smiles after an interaction, they will want to be thanked for what they have done, the regular exposure to others will provide a steady stream of information that will continue to influence and shape the behavior of each contributor as they do their jobs. Working with a well intending and expert co-worker will convey a level of expectation to others around them. Smart, competent people will infect each other with the sense that everyone who works on the projects should strive to be smart and competent. Everyone feels pressure to live up to the example being set. If the environment is toxic and filled with backstabbing and political jockeying in competition over scarce resources, everyone's attitude will be impacted by it, the contagion will rot the workplace and everyone in it.

The philosopher of discipline and surveillance runs the risk of assuming obvious ethical associations in the various ideals and patterns they describe in the domains of human agency. If an audience has been conditioned to think of hidden efforts to shape behavior as infringements on a collective liberty and they hold liberty as an unquestionable good, they may be quick to conclude that an author describing conditions under which disciplinary surveillance takes place is advocating the violation of this set of ethical principles. Were such an author to object, saying they are not making normative or evaluative judgments, they might be viciously attacked for their amoral stance. Even as we proclaim the objectivity of scientific endeavor, we threaten all observers of the human condition with the accusation that there can be no true and complete separation of insights and observations from the ethical conditions in which they occur. If their observations do not contain value judgments, then they are sociopaths.

The ethics of disciplinary surveillance is a problem whose solution should not be taken for granted. It's terms and conditions are not obvious. The fact that it is such a deeply ingrained aspect of experience yielding expertise and that human beings require help from their civilization as they procure skills incorporating historically developed practices and procedures into their life as lessons learned, suggests an ambiguity at work in disciplinary surveillance. We cannot discount the value of discipline or surveillance in some wholesale form in all contexts for all purposes. We cannot hold up liberty and justice on the one hand, and surveillance and discipline on the other. We must learn our notions of liberty and of justice and we must acquire the skills required to practice them. This acquisition amounts to social organizations contributing to the ongoing development of individual human beings as they pass through educational institutions or act as apprentices in trades. Where does the good and the evil of it come from? That is the question that matters.

The engineer described how sometimes the interviewing process can go awry. The interviewers might neglect important things like specific experiences in previous roles, or the passion the person has for learning and acquiring new skills. They may focus completely on whether the candidate has properly learned all the necessary algorithms for manipulating data structures for use in highly arbitrary circumstances. An interviewer might think that the person who can apply recursion to solve all problems is obviously a good choice for the job, whereas someone who struggles is a bad choice. When the new hire joins the team, it turns out they show all kinds of personality flaws that prevent them from working well with others. The team suffers and the productivity of the group deteriorates. Worse, people become dissatisfied with their work and start looking for other jobs in a better atmosphere. All qualities and characteristics are going to be the result of historically applied learning from conditions and experiences. The emphasis is what counts as the problem. The fact that some one set of skills were prioritized over another set is deemed an egregious error because it fundamentally misunderstands how the skills relate to the work everyone is trying to accomplish.

The ability to apply a memorized algorithm to a well understood data structure that is well suited to handle a specific engineering problem is a formidable skill, but it isn't the only skill. One might start to worry about the domain if the members of it start prioritizing and emphasizing that skill at the expense of those that might have a more powerful impact on the work as a whole. People are not only acquiring disciplinary practices as they learn from their experience, but they are also learning how organizations work and how the actions of participants fit together with other actions that are part of the same organization. As this happens, they may collectively form opinions about organizational needs and what characteristics will contribute to its greater efficiency. They may be horribly wrong about this, or they may not all agree. What is more, they may not all be able to contribute to ongoing critical discussions about the organization and how it works when orchestrating actions as part of collaborative contributions to a set of ends. As a result, they may develop a set of mythologies around what best contributes to the success of the organization and those mythologies may have independent historical inertia different from the skills practiced. For example, they may never consider that organizational analysis itself might be an essential skill that individual members may or may not bring to larger projects. They may understand that good leaders have some set of savviness that enables them to advance within leadership roles, but it doesn't occur to them that these skills can be sought out when hiring for entry level positions.

At least part of what this suggests is that the organizations, in the disciplinary measures and the forms of evaluation and surveillance it uses, must be constantly subjected to the same level of disciplinary surveillance as the actions of the members. This would be a self-reflexive critical investigation into the organization that is just as thorough and just as pervasive as the evaluations that are taking place every day among all employees and their coworkers or managers. Even when we fully automate a practice, it isn't software that determines our lives, but the organizations that build and maintain the context for that software. Even when we realize we must critically reflect on the software we've deployed, we must do that through analysis of those organizations that deploy it, that decided to deploy it, and that continue to maintain it once it is deployed.

The immediate problem with a task like this, however, is that it cannot be done in such a way as to assume the outcome. Ordinarily, there is a position independent of the practice that is functioning as the seat of evaluation. The colleague dependent on your work is the one who "evaluates" you as they benefit or are hurt by your contribution. The manager evaluates the employee, the employees evaluate each other, and even the Marxist opposed to the entire material structure evaluates the employee's action with that in mind. The dynamic has disciplinary impact insofar as the voice of the other is in the message. Where would the organization's evaluation come from if that were not the case? What would be the seat of it? Does it originate in the actions of administrators who work for the organization or in other organizations that provide disinterested oversight? Should it come from the aggregate opinions of the members of the organization, based on their experience in the roles they play? It might need to reflect the collective of all these different methodologies and sources as a context driven investigation that tries to perpetually re-evaluate the role of the organization in the lives of those who are contributors and impacted by it. This might include political representatives, socialist critics, efficiency experts, or union leadership.

Without a sophisticated understanding of the nature of organizations and how they act internally, there can be no such critical investigations from any of these possible perspectives. That much is clear, and without those critical investigations, we have no hope of making judgments as complex and subtle as "this is good" or "this is evil." The forensic nature of the ethical judgment entails a prior evaluation based on observation and a familiarity with affective disciplinary practice, meaning a familiarity that comes from having been disciplined by it. These are conditions of its possibility. The medical resident who lives up the lane and all her colleagues want to acquire the expertise of their profession. They know that their daily job will be filled with challenges that evaluate and discipline them, that teach them how to act properly the next time a similar case appears. They look forward to it, they passionately work to put themselves into situations where those lessons can be learned. The skillset of processing those lessons and being able to apply them when similar events occur, being able to recognize a set of events as "similar," is already a mark of experience they are willing to work long and hard to acquire.

This doesn't only apply to doctors or professionals; it applies to guitar players who sit in their room and grind through riffs and scales. They practice transitions from one set of patterns to another, trying to learn the fretboard and how the notes relate to chords. They repeat and repeat so that their muscles grow familiar with every one of the movements. Their goal is to learn the patterns so well that they can forget them and just focus on the music and the sounds, the audience reaction, or any other higher order association that helps make the music beautiful. It isn't as simple as talking about hidden motives and interests when trying to sort through all this. The music has an interest, musicality demands basic formal contributions, but such interests may align with the guitar player insofar as they strive to be a musician. It is precisely the interests of the music that are the object of desire, the item at the end of the long disciplinary action that governs the pursuit. The individual human being wants to be a guitar player, wants to be a doctor, or wants to be a philosopher. This desire to be is an aligning of associations, and someone must impose something extraneous upon the process if one is to challenge its closed operations.

Suppose the philosopher wants to be a lens grinder. This requires that they learn a set of skills required to be a good lens grinder whose services are in demand and who can make a living from it. Suppose they work at it and learn these skills and then get enough work to ply their trade and fund their continued philosophical pursuits. They might even contrive a set of circumstances such that they deem that their philosophical work can only achieve the credibility and independence that they want it to have if they have this set of skills to provide the means of subsistence independently of that philosophical work. After years of working in this fashion, the philosopher dies young due to the carcinogenic nature of the materials and the effect they had on their lungs, breathing them all those years. The common analysis here is that the lens grinding, unbeknownst to the philosopher, was contrary to his material interests. They didn't know the details sufficiently to understand that they were banking on a set of skills that would ultimately kill them. They wanted these skills and worked hard to acquire them. We might argue that if they hadn't been ignorant, their desires would have been changed by the new information. They were philosophers, trained in learning new information and in being critical when understanding the complex causality between things and events. Surely such a philosopher would have known there would be risks, and they would have been keenly aware that there was much that they were ignorant of as they carried out their educational activities supported by their trade. They persisted, nonetheless.

This may be true in many ways with many different people. The smoker, the working-class advocate of capitalism, the professional athlete. It may be so common among human actors that it would be more remarkable to find circumstances in which people rejected such conditions rather than complying with them. The smoker's addiction is not an alien voice that leaves the intelligent agent alone and at a distance. "Ah, I see that I am inhabited by this addiction and so reason would suggest that I should stop smoking." The addiction speaks in the agent. The addiction says, "It's just one cigarette. How can one cigarette hurt me?" We experience this addiction not as some external inhabitant of our lives, but as our functioning reason, as our own voice convincing us of what we ought to do to feel better right now. The philosopher bursting with ideas but hungry and lacking the means to buy food realizes that grinding lenses is the perfect solution to their problem. This can happen just as it does with the smoker who, feeling better from not having smoked for the last 6 hours, thinks that the perfect solution to their jitteriness is a cigarette.

At birth we are separated and vulnerable. Disciplinary surveillance is the perfect solution to this problem. We acquire a conscience. Ah, how wonderful it is to learn from parents who are keeping an eye on our every move as they feed us and bathe us, clothe and comfort us. All we do is cry and scream and they learn to read our minds and discern what this yawp means and what needs we have under the circumstances or at specific times of day. This is core to our survival; no baby could live without some degree of care and that care requires constant evaluation. The system of language that develops is in response to these evaluative interactions and they produce signs and references that enable useful feedback and understanding, better communication between those with an interest in evaluation and those with an interest in being evaluated. The process is mutual because the surveyors have an interest in keeping that baby alive. As ridiculous as the comparison may seem, the smoker has just as strong an interest in keeping their addiction alive. When they smoke, when they relax or focus or whatever it is that the act of smoking does for them, they are realizing their interest in keeping that addiction alive just as the parents are realizing their interest as they feed the baby or change its diaper.

Some critics, employing their training, are quick to evaluate these arguments and claim that some higher order position from which analysis is performed will display powerful imbalances in the associations people are pursuing. The smoker didn't choose to become addicted, there were corporations hiding information to promote their own interests in selling more cigarettes. Any corporate organization wants to promote its own profitability and so presents a whole set of options to workers without disclosing the nuances and details about how exactly the corporation is benefitting from those options. Proponents of the market will point out that if people just didn't work there or that if people just didn't buy their products, the corporation would go out of business if it didn't change its ways. People have an interest in getting jobs or buying products or getting convenient access to services. There is interest and there is desire, and it doesn't serve anyone to merely dismiss the philosopher who works themself to death as a lens grinder, saying that it all should have gone differently if only they had worried more about their own interests. Interests themselves are the products of these organizations, maybe not the specific one that employs you or the specific one that sells you cigarettes, but some socially oriented set of actions led to a set of interests and once they did, the involved person was nothing other than the expression of those interests. It's just empirically false to say that the working person is nothing more than their material interests insofar as they relate to exploitation. They are their material interests in all kinds of different ways and at all different levels of understanding. Not as an alien resident, but as the persons that they are. How do they distance themselves from what they want just because what they want makes some big corporation rich? How can a person even comprehend that? Even if they have the time and the resources to investigate, there is still no guarantee that they will be able to distance themselves from their own desires and free themselves from one set of personal interests and orientations for the sake of another. There is no guarantee that this is really a form of escape after all.

What do I do if I want to be a philosopher, but not like this? What does that mean insofar as the discipline has been historically defined and yet somehow, through some set of experiences, an individual philosopher has come to both identify with it *and* see it as a hostile coercive force that drives them down the wrong path? Which Hegelian phase describes that? How would an individual, locked in some stage of "spirit" or "religion," have a self-conscious understanding of their own dissonance relative to the larger social forces at work against it? Being a member of the spiritual animal kingdom is easy to comprehend because the locus of that experience is the individual consciousness come to terms with itself in the dynamic of reason. Once the experience transcends the individual consciousness and enters the higher order dynamic of spirit or religion, how does the contradiction present itself? What is the solitary person's experience of spirit and how do we know that it isn't exactly what I am describing? The interest to be and the interest not to be a philosopher both become hopelessly embattled in an impossible standoff between applying or not applying the attribute "philosopher" to oneself. It becomes a matter of personality recuperated and coerced. This is the matter at hand. Does the truth lie in the one presentation of the form or in the other? In the academic vision of the philosophical vocation or in the lens grinder's vision of the philosophical avocation?

"I found her."

"Who?"

"The typesetter. From the thunderstorm."

"Where?"

"I was at that bar, and she came in with that guy I met who works in the bindery. Turns out she works at the same place where I've been copy editing."

"Small world."

"It is. I wasn't sure what was up with them, but I went over to their table, and she freaked out when she saw me. I told her that I had left town but then came back when I found out you'd be moving here. I didn't tell her she had anything to do with it."

"Afraid she would think that's kind of creepy?"

"That and I'm not sure how true it is. It might have been an excuse."

"Something you told yourself to make it easier to do something you already wanted to do? That would mean there's a real reason that you didn't want to admit, wouldn't it?"

"There is always something that I don't want to admit."

"I don't mean something you want to keep a secret. I mean something you don't even want to let yourself know. Some repressed desire."

"Could be. Anyway, they invited me to sit down, and we had a beer. He's a regular at that place and they know him. She's so cool. Smart, funny, dangerous. We were all getting along really well. They were heading out to a cookout and invited me to come along."

"A bit chilly."

"It was great. The fire kept us warm. We cooked potatoes and green peppers. It turned out that they weren't together, just work friends. She and I were alone, cooking together, eventually. Talking. She reads everything, and she is really creative. Does collage and all kinds of crafts. She's handy, did some spot repairs on our utensils."

"Did you hook up?"

"No, but she gave me a hug at the end of the night. That was promising. She said she isn't a hugger, hates hugging as a standard greeting. Sometimes she can't help it though. Like that night because we were just reconnecting. She says that some people she just has to hug them every time she sees them, she can't help it. She didn't think I'd be one of those people though, so she warned me not to read too much into it if she doesn't do it again."

"She wanted to see you again?"

"Well, it was friendly. That's all, but she did. That's where I was tonight. We went to some dive downtown. I told her my situation. She told me hers, but she called it. No hug tonight. We'll see."

"You're going to see her again?"

"Yeah, she pretty much told me all the places she likes to hang out and read. There was an assumption that this wasn't just idle talk, but no formal plan."

"Is she a student?"

"No, she's working full time. Went to school here but graduated a few years ago. She lives in the house where we had the cookout. Like 6 roommates or something like that."

"When you told her your situation, did you tell her that you're just in town temporarily?"

"I did. I might've overplayed it even. My plans aren't all that definite, but I made it seem like I was determined to leave in the spring."

"She still wants to see you again?"

"Yeah, she might. She's young, she doesn't think like that. Besides, it's not like we've done anything about it. We're just checking each other out. Figuring things out."

"You like her?"

"I like talking to her. I'm looking forward to talking to her again. It seems mutual."

"Alright, let me go back to the issue we've been dodging. You didn't tell her she was part of the reason you came back because you don't know for sure that she is, right?"

"Yes."

"There might be something you want that you can't identify. Right?"

"Sure."

"It seems like that could apply to everything. You might like her only because she will hold you here. Liking her might be part of the ruse."

"Ruse?"

"The trick you're playing on yourself to get you here and keep you here."

"It's a ruse now?"

"I'm not saying you're playing games; I'm saying something is playing games with you. Something tricked you into coming back and tricked you into staying. It does it by making you want this or that. Something is happening and your preferences are the tools for making it happen."

"How do you ever sleep? Do you ever turn this off?"

"I sleep fine. I'm exhausted at the end of every day. Don't evade the point."

"What do you want me to say? I don't know, according to you I'm just as much the victim of the ruse as the perpetrator, aren't I?"

"According to me? You have an interest in being ignorant. Especially if it gets you what you want. If something else that you wanted requires you get clear about what exactly is motivating you, the ruse would end. That's my hypothesis anyway. Critical evaluation requires a more powerful desire than the one you already have for what you're evaluating."

"Given your setup, I would agree. The criticism and the cover up are both in the service of some desire that may be opaque to the involved parties. I'm working shit out; she's working shit out. That's how it goes."

"You don't think there's any way for you to get to the bottom of it? You honestly can't come up with any way to figure this out? Why did you come back and why are you pursuing a relationship with someone when you know you won't be here for long?"

"Why don't you just tell me your theory? You know you want to."

"I don't have a very well developed one, but it might have something to do with me. When did I tell you that I was moving to Ann Arbor? I found out in May."

"I was in New Orleans in May. We didn't talk. I called you from Carbondale in July and I had already decided to go to Ann Arbor on my way to Delaware. I told you that."

"Right. Ann Arbor isn't on the way to Delaware from Southern Illinois. Why did you have to come through here?"

"Art fair. I wanted to go."

"Art fair was in July."

"The end of July. That's when I arrived and then I left in August."

"You didn't come back because I was here?"

"Of course, I came back because you were here. That's what I told her, and I've always admitted that to you."

"You're only admitting that in some generally friendly way like 'oh hey my buddy is moving to Ann Arbor; it'd be good to hang with him a bit.' You're not admitting to an agenda?"

"I don't have an agenda."

"You do, and you're just not telling me. You know what it is. It isn't some higher order plan of the world spirit; you know what you're doing."

"Okay, let's see. You had a gig at Illinois Wesleyan, right? Had they asked you back?"

"No."

"Would they have already if they needed you?"

"No, they wouldn't know until sometime during the summer if they were going to have budget and need."

"For all you know, they might've asked you back?"

"They might have."

"For all you know they would have kept asking you back until they had to give you tenure, right?"

"It happens sometimes, but it's a long shot."

"I'm just wondering why you would leave that situation and come here. How is this a better job? Are you better off now, more likely to get a tenure track job with this experience on your resume?"

"I don't know. It pays better, the teaching load is better. The benefits are better."

"It's terminal. Nothing next year, not even the slimmest of chances. No adjunct work around here because the U of M grads will get all that. At the other gig, though, maybe something comes of it?"

"Maybe."

"You're the one in the middle of some big ruse then. My motives are clear. I came back because you are here, and because it's weird that you are here. I met this cool woman. Nothing wrong with that. It's an added bonus. Mostly, I wanted to make sure you were okay."

"Fine. Nothing insidious. I just had to drag it all out of you after a month and a half. Forget all that though, what did you guys talk about?"

"Lots of things. We talked about incentive and where it comes from."

"What do you mean, incentive? Is that the same axe you were grinding before?"

"Yeah, like when capitalists are always saying that you need the profit motive to get people to do things."

"Ah, I see. She disagrees."

"Any thinking person disagrees. Profit wasn't what brought me back here, right? We've established that. People act for the sake of their friends all the time."

"Sure. Community, family, and friends. What else?"

"She's also really into the conflict between profit motive and craftsmanship. Seems like she's thinking about that a lot right now. Artists don't do their work for the sake of making a profit."

"Who would they exploit?"

"She just read the letters to Theo. Clearly Vincent was willing to work day and night. Profit had nothing to do with that. Assuming there are people who don't share the artist's sensibilities and don't care about morality or community or friendship or family, then we have nothing other than the profit motive."

"Great. How did you get to the point where you were bonding over this?"

"Standard get to know you stuff. We were talking about our jobs and what drives us. For her it's all about learning. She says she's like an apprentice and that money is always getting in the way. She wishes she could learn a trade without having to obsess over the financial tradeoffs. We were fantasizing about what a society might be like if people could live like that, just keep learning, and be supported even if living that way didn't end up making any money for anybody."

"Somebody has to keep the lights on."

"Yeah. You could have a furlough program or something. Work six months doing some socially necessary work, then you get six months off to pursue something you want to learn. Every year you could set it up like that, learn more about the same thing or something new every time."

"Typesetter seems pretty useful though."

"For now, who knows what the future will bring. That's what got us started on the whole thing. What if you spent your life driving toward something you really wanted to do and then all of a sudden it became unnecessary or outdated because of some new invention or shift in social priorities? You can't trust your desires to tell you what you should do, they have to be informed by interests and those have to be informed by the state of society. She was trying to describe the injustice in that."

"Injustice?"

"Yeah, social interests will trump specific desires if everyone isn't clear about what forces underlie everything and how they are impacting people's decisions and actions. It determines how they think about their roles. That's the basis of utilitarianism, isn't it? It's where the profit motive comes from too. It's what forces people to think that way if they want to survive. The individuated desires of a powerless agent are transformed into the interests of someone situated with others for protection."

"If I want to be a typesetter, I learn that it is in my interests that all kinds of social policy be shaped toward maintaining the practice of typesetting, right?"

"Yes. That's the alchemy that turns desire into interest. The fact of that conversion is unjust because in most societies it isn't transparent."

"Not the standard notion of justice."

"Agreed. There's a lot to sort through. It's interesting though. Forget about whether desire is already socially skewed. Interest most definitely is, right?"

"The way we've characterized it, at least."

"The application of interest to desire firmly places justice into human agency. We can talk about it another time, maybe when you meet her."

"It sounds like you were lucky to find each other."

"Lightning bolt steers all things."

It isn't that reason is passion's slave, it belongs to organization. Its masters are the disciplines that inhabit you, guide and govern your action, and feed their structure into your behavior. Reason is an order. It takes hard work to become a reasonable person and our service to it may explain its often-instrumental appearance. Reason serves something other, something that guides it through the origin and the movement of its operations.

The engineer's sister had arranged a meeting, inviting several of her doctor friends along to meet her brother. Unsuspecting, I thought I was just having breakfast, instead I was wandering into a complex web of connections, immersing the event in strategy and hidden motives to be weighed and measured against outcomes. The friends were there to meet her brother. The sister was there to meet me. Nothing worked out as planned. I ruined everything by insisting on talking about the expertise and discipline we acquire through education. I did it by drawing out observations from the friend who smoked and the friend who played the guitar. No one who was supposed to become romantically entangled became romantically entangled. I entered without suspicion, but everything that happened signaled an alarm. I marveled at how everyone was oriented by their expectations. Even though all objectives were thwarted, the directions were settled, and the ideas deliberate. That is how reason works, how it occupies us wherever we find ourselves, at our lunches and during our morning meetings. It's not in the act, but in the action context. The structure of all the participants' actions interleaved, of their viewpoints and the outcomes they hoped for, all of it is what we call reason. It is the governing logos that holds our lives, inhabits our movements, and it is the ethos where we gather. My means may complete your ends, or someone unseen, some thing.

There was another noteworthy event not too long after. The engineer invited me to his lab and when I got there, he was sitting with one of his coworkers. She was friendly and patiently described her work on the video compression projects while the engineer watched us nervously. After she excused herself so she could get back to work, he started telling me about the meeting with his sister's friends and how screwed up it was because of all the strategizing. I said I hadn't noticed. He went into depth about her instructions to the other women: they were only to show interest in her brother. She instructed them that I was off limits, and they were not to be too friendly. This explained a lot about the way the mood would change whenever I made a joke, pointed out something interesting, or listened a little too attentively to what someone was saying. All these little actions conflicted with the way in which she had projected events and described them in advance to the others. People have plans.

You can plan an event and you can try to construct an organizational logic that will unfold as you intend. If there are other people involved, they can change all that. Sometimes for the better and sometimes they disrupt everything and prevent whatever you planned from turning out the way you hoped. Others might bring their own plans with them; they might have their own ideas about what should happen. The conflict needn't be personal or based on any ethical judgments. It may be that they just want different things and can't frame the situation as a competition. The engineer was guilty of it too when he invited me to come to his office. He had wanted me to give him my opinion of his coworker, whether she seemed to like him or not. I said I was pretty sure she didn't.

"From ten minutes conversation, you can tell that?"

"Yes. It's all in the vibe. How she reacted to being introduced, how she listened to your explanation of who I am and why I came to visit you. All of it made it really clear that you're just some dude she works with. She's talking to me thinking how long do I have to stay to be polite. That's it."

"How can you tell?"

"I wasn't paying attention to your plan to ask her out and I wasn't paying attention to her plan to get away or my plan to be friendly or anything like that. I was just paying attention to the situation and the way it was playing out with all of our plans mixed together. How come you couldn't see it?"

I don't know how situational reason or structural integrity turned into a faculty: some component of the cognitive mechanism that is capable of guiding decisions and that rests at the seat of deliberate action. I do know that, according to Kant, a being capable of practical reason must be the kind of creature that is capable of pure reason. They are integrally related.

The first critique is not just a philosophical prerequisite to the second critique, but the categories and rules of cognition are requirements for practical agents subject to imperatives. Only because we are capable of coherent experience are we capable of good and evil action. The precise way in which we are rational makes it possible for us to morally evaluate our own actions and the actions of others like us. That is how the story goes, and it suggests that the logic is in the things, in the objects of our experience, and that we are acting on the basis of that logic when we respond to circumstances and effects. We aim for consequences, but we may act independently of them under conditions that merit it. All in all, doing what reason dictates amounts to an attunement to events as they unfold. The reason that apprehends what there is, gives rise to the reason that acts under the circumstances. If something is beyond the agent's cognition and practical reason is defined in terms of the agent, then whatever it is has nothing to do with them.

A social scientist might describe scientific methodology in terms of an objective orientation with an intent that aims at realizing meaningful relations with others. The scientist is disinterested and doesn't express a personal agenda when they describe events or pursue an interpretation of them. These objective observations are meant to be total in that they circumscribe an entire domain of objects and provide a complete expression of what they are like and how they relate to each other. The intent of this totalizing objectivity is to provide a story of that meaningfulness that adequately captures events. It's a theory.

When modern day people orchestrate their actions, they might plan things and try to inject the same methodological properties into a situation. They may wish for events to unfold as though they were happening spontaneously, as though this was the simple effect of natural causes, and no manipulation or engineering is part of it. This is the way in which a situation may approximate objectivity. The plan is supposed to be complete and cover all experiences, whatever they might be. The planners don't want the participants to be able to get out or steer their own course in some non-conforming way. The purpose of this apparent total objectivity is to produce the situation so that the subjects come to the desired conclusions and perform the desired actions as though they didn't have to make a choice, because they were merely following through on the logic of the circumstances and driving toward the obvious outcome. If these match with some set of notions in a participant's head, then they succeeded, if they don't, they failed.

The injection of such structure is, of course, highly manipulative, and only leverages scientific methodology as a ruse. It makes you wonder to what extent method is itself a residual of this same ruse. The objectivity and the totalizing approach aim at controlling meaning under the circumstances, and that's a great way to preclude any competitors from having an influence. The approach ensures that there is no room for disagreement, either the entire theory is accepted, or it is rejected. If it does provide helpful structure for understanding events, there will be a strong motivation to accept its vision as a norm for experience. Normalizing experience can pave the way for rule-driven actions, and this makes it easier for the agent to coordinate their illusory sense of control with the organizational power that guides their way.

The scientific approach varies from the "brunch" or the "work visit" only in scope and intensity. Experimentation and peer review amount to a narrow exposure of data to a set of people who undergo a rigorous process of investigation, analysis, and critical comparison to other investigations and analyses. The involved parties are all properly certified to be trustworthy, and their results are published in a journal that adds further credence to the recorded data. Scientific methodology is just a planned outing on a much larger scale, with more social involvement, with whole systems of credentials that help construct the believability of events and the conclusions of those who are not directly taking part in the investigations but will accept the findings of an established theory. The scientific method is a social method with implications for all kinds of certification and credibility spanning several large institutions and developing over many centuries. Not every scientist is qualified to comment on every outcome or every arrangement of conditions leading up to a set of statements of fact based on the theory. They take each other's word for things based on these socially orchestrated mechanisms and the institutions that exist to support them. Entry into them requires rigorous educational platforms where principles and procedures for the right performance of analysis and review are taught. So long as those principles agree on goals and tools, their social dependencies are utility-based and ensure that community interest will always trump individual desire. Scale requires this, how else could we do it?

If there were similar structures in support of orchestrating social events where you want to set your brother up with your friends or become more friendly with your brother's friend, then there would be a lot more success in such plans. The right peers would review the circumstances and provide guidance for how to establish the outcomes. They would come off without a hitch and the specialists would configure the situation so that everyone's actions fell in line and unfolded exactly as they should even if they didn't agree with how each participant wanted things to turn out. The moral world and the objective world would be governed by the same structural arbiters and laws. This is what lies behind the fascination some philosophers have for the work of Jane Austen. The orchestration of a match recapitulates the virtues of science, but with better clothes and manners.

This might explain what feels right in the notion of science as paradigm and the revolutionary impact that paradigm shifts can have on established views. Practitioners are aware of these dynamics, and they know that they work for the most part but only up to a point. None of us has the time to peer review everything in our own discipline, and no one has the expertise to review anything from other disciplines. We rest our confidence on a social structure meant to provide efficiency in the organization of knowledge. We sense that this approach is prone to abuse and that traditions will entrench and go astray, placing pressure on newcomers to revolutionize investigations with newly discovered data that overturns existing dogma. Although that process of negating established fact for some new revolutionary insight may cause discomfort, the socially structured institutions "know" that it is a necessary discomfort that the discipline must endure to stay current. There must be a mechanism in place to correct traditional errors coming from the inertia of the social organization over and against the lived experience of experts and the understanding at which they aim. Although there is a strict rejection of revolutionary science on a day-to-day basis, there is also recognition that a critical mass may be achieved in some notions and that when this happens there is no stopping it. The ideas of that revolutionary paradigm will replace what is currently in fashion and protected by the high-ranking members of the profession. The aggregate general welfare will work it all out without any concern for just distribution or balance between segments, only for the continued maximization of the power of the order.

The paradigm of the social event where the planner has dibs on a prospective partner will not be easily subverted. If true love or love at first sight sparks in some of the participants, it may be that there is nothing that can be done to prevent a revolutionary change to the structure of relationships. This is arguably at the basis of many romance novels where the passions of the participants overwhelm the structural power of the organizations at work. It happens in courtship, it happens in Physics and Biology, and it happens in every experience we have with social forms and the roles they set down for us. There is always the possibility of anomaly, of comet-like events that break the structure that seems to govern the world. These are the ones that walk away from Omelas.

This is an inconvenient truth. It can lead to the crackpot phenomenon where individuals appropriate the possibility of breaking through the dogma with a revolutionary event when they don't have anything in their possession that would count as ground-breaking. The fanatic who has learned the romantic history of some discipline and knows that it is often the work of an outsider that disrupts the traditions and guides it into new directions, may convince themselves that they are such a catalyst just because they want to be. They may snarl and snipe at their oppressors who are making just these sorts of arguments based on utility. "You have tried to colonize the margins of your discipline; you are rejecting the differences introduced by new and revolutionary ideas, and you are doing it to protect your power." This is easy enough to say when the stars in the discipline reject your work or, more likely, neglect to pay it any attention. The convenience of the illusion should be all too apparent to any student of statistics. Of course, you can cite the examples from history of people that have suffered the fate you describe, and in most any discipline there will be a few characters who fall into the category, but your argument would be laden with fallacies if you didn't also include references to those innumerable and forgotten ones who bucked the system and got nowhere because they had nothing. These are the crackpots, the investigators who never survived meticulous peer review, whose ideas never inspired anyone other than themselves, and who have fallen into obscurity and been forgotten over the years. They just wanted to learn, but they didn't want to submit to some impersonal general welfare. Logic would suggest that these forgotten and unnamed members outnumber by something like a thousand to one the exceptions and the anomalies that brought us revolutionary science. If not more.

The odds that you are Wollstonecraft, Spinoza, or Bruno are next to nil. Even if, and especially because, your contribution has been ignored. Revolutionary science does not go unnoticed by the practitioners of normal science. If you are a nameless observer or analyst trying to get your message out there and claiming that you are the victim of dogmatic suppression, you may be right but most likely your situation is exactly as it should be. Only the social order can determine the difference between a revolutionary and a crackpot.

Information systems and the education of a library scientist are undergoing a paradigm shift. Catalogues had been digital for years, of course, but the growing presence of public networks was causing a massive conversion. Search was entering the public's consciousness; it wasn't just for librarians anymore. The tools needed more development, and we needed to understand them better, make them available to wider audiences, and the lessons on how best to interact with them had to become a public service. This was the transformation that was taking place, the librarians were leading the way on how to prepare material for proper searching by a public without highly refined search skills. They were working at building programs and initiatives to increase those skills as a new service. The library is being reinvented in a paradigm shift.

The purpose of the hypertext project was to play at the serious business of this contribution and to allow the members to pretend to be social influencers and educators, working to design metadata repositories and markup models that would carry the information in the catalogue in a way that enabled a public with rudimentary skills to search on their own for what they needed. The search engines would do some of the work that librarians had previously done. The cataloguing mechanisms would mean that simpler semantics could be used to look for information and the engine would supply additional logic to assist in excavating the most relevant results.

The group of six students were all learning the latest in markup technologies and they were practicing with the tags and the tools for rendering them. They took sample datasets from other research projects and collaborated to add a coherent metadata model to the standardized attributes so that the interpreter could locate information more effectively. They didn't just do that; they were graduate students, so they had coffee together and they talked in partial sentences and half-baked ideas. They laughed and got excited at the prospects of a whole new world of information and the ways of gaining access to it. They felt together as though they were on the leading edge of new technologies that were going to change the world in ways that no one was yet able to imagine. It is what they were there for, it was their primary objective, and it sealed their relationship as they developed theories about how this would make libraries more important than ever. It was the end of the centralized information store and the beginning of the distributed store. There were projects aimed at integrating all the different catalogues and bridging the gaps between the different systems with common protocols and emerging standards. Things were happening. It was the best time to be in school for this because they were discovering this new world as it was being invented.

It was hard not to measure this against the growing power of post-modern theory that was creeping into every academic corner. The impact of information theory had not been what you might think. Appropriating this anti-humanist "post" work of the new age wasn't only left to the cognitive scientists and philosophers of science. The material was finding its way into everything. The data was taking over and the means for integrating it was a herculean intellectual task that many disciplines in the humanities and social sciences were rapidly adopting. Everyone was stimulated with the same excitement, and it had its source in this common sense that something new was happening and they were lucky to be playing at the edge of a revolution.

Those who opposed this movement, the modernists and their support of the traditions, made the colossal error of thinking these movements were normative. They thought that post-modernism was a set of action claims laden with "should" and "ought" that were finding their way into the new world of the human sciences, including the management of information and how organizations were meant to contain and distribute it. They listened to the diatribes on spectacle and power, on the death of reason as an absolute category, and they thought that these new players were advocating for a relativist revolution. That is because *they* were advocating something, and they assumed their opponents must be too. The defenders of tradition wanted something new, but they wanted to be the originators and the fabricators who ushered in this new era and its newly discovered rock-solid foundation in data and information. Finally, the Enlightenment project could be completed by a unified science, the data was being gathered at last and reason would prevail. There are no ethical theories involved in post-modernism, however, and it was not out to revolutionize ethics by giving it a new bedrock notion to dwell alongside consequentialism or deontology. Instead, this radical reinvention of intellectual life was a harbinger of a material change, it was indicating modifications that were taking shape in underlying organizations, and which no one had yet gained the perspective to properly contextualize.

The moderns thought reason and liberal sensibilities could retain their monopoly over the good, if only the latest enemy were defeated. If you were listening with their emphasis, you might have heard the innuendo that the tradition itself was achieving the necessary outcome of its own internal logic. The cataloguing systems were all based in that tradition, along with the sciences and their technologies. The love of liberty and justice, the advocacy of the rights of man and the rise of the political systems based on rational principles were all rooted in these same traditions and the taxonomies that had been developing in and as the civilizations that westerners had come to call home. There was so much at stake, we were on the verge of Utopia.

The new science had undergone multiple revolutions. The ongoing nature of probabilistic hypotheses was recognized as a means for giving us the best possible way to gain a progressive understanding that would continually improve alongside a changing world. This implied that there was room for improvement and that those same hypotheses may turn out in the end to be inadequate, in need of improvement, or subject to forms of progress. The same was true of technology. Whatever means we had achieved were better than the way we did it before, but this showed the lie in the very moment that it demonstrated the truth. These new ways would be out of date soon enough and replaced with something even better. The continual improvements in knowledge and engineering meant that wherever we found ourselves today was always inadequate and soon to be overcome with a better way of doing them tomorrow. The game of the post-modern was the playfulness of this very condition, where the fact that things were getting better implied that nothing was as good as it could be. This renewed framing of the problem of induction meant there was never as much progress as there was going to be, never as much utility as there was going to be, and never as much knowledge as there was going to be. These lack-laden states saturated progress, utility, and knowledge.

Everyone was talking about Foucault and what had he done but investigate the very structural mechanisms at work in the modern age with the aim of discovering that the principles touted there conflicted with the desired outcomes. The means of progress, utility, and knowledge were not oriented toward improvements in liberty and understanding, greater justice for the greater number of people. His claims were not normative, he wasn't instructing people about a need to form an ethical turn against these traditional notions. Instead, he was showing that the trappings of liberty were themselves saturated with coercion, that the instigation for knowledge was itself a means for surveillance in support of dogma. The progressive, indefinite, form of the urge to keep on going, condemned them to this corruption. Much of what was being written at the time owed everything to this insight. The clever knew that no one was talking about what the world ought to be like or what people should do in the new and brave world of our information systems through their meteoric rise. They saw that these were, despite all the interpretations of the moderns leaning toward the contrary conclusion, prognoses for how factical life was going to turn out, where we were headed, and what we could expect from our lives once they had been completely reinvented by these ongoing revolutions in vision and information.

Foucault had a conversation with Chomsky on Dutch television in the seventies. At one point in the conversation, Michel shocked Noam by suggesting that we shouldn't be too quick in rejecting the bourgeois order for the sake of something new and as yet unknown. He warned that we might not fully grasp what evils such an order might have to offer. Chomsky was put off by this. He likely went into the meeting thinking that, although he couldn't understand Foucault, they were both on the same side as anti-imperialists and revolutionaries. These remarks didn't fit with that assumption, however, they made Foucault seem like an apologist for the new order. This misunderstanding is only possible if you see the work as normative in essence, as an attempt to produce a new system of value. That is not Foucault's agenda. He is following on the works of the cultural critics to show that things are not what they seem, and they are different than what the ideology manufacturers have claimed them to be. They were going to get worse, or they could get worse. He was indeed suggesting that the bourgeois order was unjust and full of power relations and coercions fueled by surveillance, but they could get worse. As bad as things are, they could be worse.

If the faculty in the college of literature, science, and the arts or the college of library science had been paying attention during that autumn in the mid-nineties, they would have been astute to these possibilities. Radical changes were happening in the means and systems of knowledge. That was clear. Everyone had their own idea of what those changes could be and what results they might produce. It was not commonly held that they might be tragic or the beginnings of a dystopic turn that was bringing about the true meaning/end of the Enlightenment: the war of all against all embedded in civil society as the basic principle of how people interacted for the sake of an aggregate general welfare serving hidden interests and logic. They did not see the onset of a nightmare where information and knowledge would corrupt and gnarl the relationships and associations stretched thin between individuated human beings. Love of authority or love of automation, those were our options.

Truth had become probabilistic; power had become democratically dispersed throughout the land and the population. No more centers of truth and power. From this, the observation was made that power is everywhere and capable of inserting itself in all the morsels of information and fact that might be organized by this or that theory and used to justify this or that approach to governing or commerce or human life in its various ordered systems. Information was everywhere and it needed new forms of organization and retrieval. The movie *Brazil* had come out ten years earlier, and it seemed to underline this. Why was the insidious organization at the heart of all evil called "Information Retrieval"? Was it describing a universe in which the librarians had become the cutthroats and agents of social demise? How odd that we should be so titillated and excited about a set of conditions that demonstrated the reductio ad absurdum of the entire intellectual edifice of the modern world. Such is the optimism of human being that it casts every experience of the new so that it is informed by the hope for something better. The cynicism of the neo-luddite, the curmudgeon, or the geezer is brushed aside as obviously out of date and the symbol of an antagonist who is out of touch with the wonder and innovation characteristic of the modern world and "America." How entertaining it all is. The older generations should be ignored because they always hold us back from change. They do this because they have developed feet of clay, are terrified of their own deaths, and by the outdated obsolescence of their abilities and their ways of seeing the world. This guerilla warfare of the new and the young can be used to defend the keep on going of progress, utility, and knowledge.

Exposure to all this is what started to make the student librarian, riding her bike, tending bar, living in her basement, feel more like she belonged here, like this was the right place for her. She was starting to integrate into the life of the university with her new friends and their new projects. Opening up to the ideas and the teachings that explained these radical transformations, she knew she had been out of sorts in this new world, but now she was seeing that this was more about the world than about her. She was in the right place at the right time. The world *was* changing, not just her, not just her life, and her way of seeing things. The actual world was being transformed and somehow she had understood that, even anticipated it. How had she known what to want when she hadn't been fully conscious of all this until she got here? How did the army of others like her know it? They all must have known in some way that it was happening. She must have known that in order to get in on it, she was going to have to leave her comfort zone and go off to study these new things in these new ways. They all must have known about this new tide and the massive changes that were coming. The awareness must have been deep down inside her desire to help people navigate the changes to the systems, sort it all out, and find what they were looking for. Part of a mass movement, they were being moved, but what was it that moved them? How does awareness work? Were they *aware* of it? She must have been, but if she was, how come she never saw that army or felt herself a part of it? Was she running with the herd or just running?

The Society for Phenomenology and Existential Philosophy held its 1995 conference in Chicago, Illinois at the Blackstone Hotel on Michigan Avenue. My department gave me a little money to attend, enough to cover the meals and some of the hotel. I drove down to Toledo and met up with the farmer who had driven up from his little university town in Northern Ohio. Pooling our grants, we'd be able to cover the hotel. We left my car at his sister's house and drove together. The SPEP conference was the epitome of Continental Philosophy in America and its program reminded us why we wanted to study philosophy in the first place. It was an oasis away from the "Analytic" domination we experienced the rest of the year. The distinction has little to do with reality, it is a purely academic separation that drives power assignments sideways through the philosophical faculty. The tradition, insofar as it originates in Oxford and Cambridge, controls most of the journals and the conference money, the chairs at most of the universities, and the criteria for most of the hiring committees. The fact that Frege and Russell, like Husserl, were opposing psychologism or that Lacan and Fodor could each be coherently aligned with one group or the other for determinate reasons is not of any significance to discussions of the division. It would be a mistake to argue the facts. People who tried to argue these organizational oppositions on the grounds of taxonomy were completely clueless. They likely hadn't read all the material they were using to draw their boundaries so they couldn't understand what was at stake. There are few who have studied both Fodor and Lacan and even fewer who have written intelligently about their interleave. All that mattered was that there were more of them than there were of us, and they had control over most of the money, jobs, and publications. The conferences were devoted to their work, their careers, and their professional concerns. Most importantly, the division tells us who we have to read and cite and who we don't have to worry about no matter how prolifically they wrote on the same subject as our treatise. You can apply for an Ethics job if you've never read Scheler, but don't even think about it if you haven't read Thomson.

That is what philosophy has come to, but not in the car on the way to Chicago. At SPEP, the norm was the continent, and its leading figures dominated the main philosophical approach. People would be talking about Derrida and Foucault, there would be discussions on Arendt and Benhabib, as well as Levinas and Schutz. Everyone would take for granted the facts that rational agents or subjects were all born and raised, went to school and had peer influences, that social and ethical issues were not easily segregated from epistemological or ontological investigations. Hell, Ernesto Laclau and Chantal Mouffe would be presenting their work at the big plenary session on the first night. They were the stars that year and they had done more to show the integrated nature of social forces with experience and understanding than anyone who had ever written on the "other" side of the divide. The farmer and I were certain that this was going to give us the morale boost we needed to get through the rest of the semester. We spent the better part of the nearly five-hour drive going over the program and talking about which sessions to attend. There were so many enticing topics at each hour that we were finding it impossible to narrow the choice down to just one per time slot. These were riches like we had never seen, problems that we never had at the American Philosophical Association conferences held each year.

Even if the titles turned out to be the best part of the sessions, that wouldn't matter because we thought a bad presentation on Merleau-Ponty would still be worthwhile. The discussion it would instigate after the fact: how they butchered the philosopher's work or how well they understood it or how one of the presenters failed to place the subject the way we had placed the subject. All of that would stimulate us even if the content of the talk hadn't. In many cases, the session would be better if it were bad and able to instigate such critical analysis for hours on end. Laclau and Mouffe might dazzle us, but most of the speakers, scholars and introverted thought technicians, weren't going to have the same effect. The best they could do would be to collect some great citations and instigate some passionate antipathy to some facet of their thesis and how very very wrong it had all turned out. A bad paper on the young Heidegger would be much more exciting to us than a great paper on the traditional influences expressed in the work of P.F. Strawson.

Even the most celebrated of contributors were prone to giving bad presentations at these conferences. This might be for a variety of reasons. They wrote the talk on the plane ride, or maybe they did a slight rehash of something they had delivered before. Mostly, they just wanted to continue to be present to the right audience and keep their one book written ten years ago on the must-read list for graduate students writing their dissertations. The conference agenda was filled with people who fit that bill. People I had come to respect because I had read their book on Heidegger or deconstruction when researching my book on the late Heidegger and Derrida's reading of him. The book they had written was indeed worthy of that respect if your scope is narrowly defined in the way that any scholar's focus will be during a finely tuned research project. How many people on earth really care to know about the Derridean reading of the late Heidegger and what its implications might be for an ontologically purified ethics? Doing respectable work in a narrowly defined area is a fine thing. One of the major defining characteristics of academia is that you can do such work in your thirties and have it set your career onto the right track for the rest of your life.

I don't mean that these people were resting on their laurels and doing nothing at all. No, they were rehashing and revisiting the subjects from that research project. They were teaching seminars on it, standing as chairs on dissertation committees, and throwing together session contributions at conferences repeating the same ideas. It isn't that they did this one thing and then nothing else. That kind of deadwood has a whole different set of traits. Here we are talking about active participants in the profession. Leaders. Movers and shakers. The ones who were getting the most graduate students placed into positions advertised each year. These were the people who were on the contributing editors list at all the relevant publishing houses, the ones who were deciding what should be on the agenda at this year's SPEP conference and who should be groomed into the leaders of tomorrow and put on panels with the leaders of today.

Many of the papers that would be presented during these glorious two and a half days would be either from the recalcitrant and repetitive work of these thought leaders or from the apprentices they were grooming. The ingénues were selected because their work flattered the older scholars, or maybe because they were working on their dissertation with the right advisors who might have been former colleagues of the great scholars. Whatever the reasons, these conferences were littered with great topics done poorly and likely that is because the presentations were only secondarily concerned with philosophical issues. The primary point was the advancing of the careers of the participants and the maintenance and development of the correct hierarchies for the future of the discipline. To be clear, we loved it. We were so happy to be at a horrible careerist-oriented conference that focused on the profession in the way that we wanted to focus on it, with the great work of French and German thinkers front and center and with socially and historically situated approaches guiding the way. This was real philosophy even if it had been completely tainted by the stench of the professional academic concerns of the careerist. We hoped to be one of them.

Since the social element is the crucial component, the power of a bad paper can be inspiring. For an ordinary conference goer like myself, seeing some respected scholars rehash their old ideas in deference to the mediocre work of their younger cronies, the ones they were trying to promote, can provide a source for great confidence and lead to the concrete realization that the acme of the profession is within reach. Obviously, if this is all it takes to make an impression and rise within the ranks, then anyone can do it. All I need is the right sponsorship and the right cronies. The conference is exactly the right place to come to make that happen. Flatter the rehashers and give serious concern to the work of the hasher wanna-bes. Produce work that cites theirs and builds an interpretive edifice alongside it. Become part of the distributed solution to professional drive and the achievement of little for the sake of nearly nothing. Who knows? It could lead to an interview and maybe a visiting professorship. That'll add more connections and contacts. Have drinks with the chair. Exchange notes and thoughts on the next nascent work that strives to become next year's poorly written presentation as the second contributor to some honcho's session. For this is the love of wisdom, professionally done to perfection.

Friendship is an institution. Acquaintance is an institution. When we live these states, we live the institution of them. The experience of it is one thing, the institution another. Kafka was a genius because he turned the tension between the mental state of a living being and the institution into a bug or a mouse or a burrowing creature. Some of us are hacks who rationalize the dis-jointure as a flow of words and explanations. To rationalize, in some lines of work, is to execute an ordering process where an unknown and unstructured area is set into forms, layered, and presented for evaluation. Occurrence delineated as problems; events being measured. Life pitched for the sake of solutions: the angles and bio-geometry of the insurance adjustor.

How do I unpack these big ideas all at once? All this education and what has it done for me if I cannot bring myself to say this one thing and this other thing in the order and with the depth that each of them deserves? What if Wolfe, the farmer, the engineer, and I were to run our own little corner of the world? What if we had our own rehashed ideas and controlled the purse strings of some small segment of professional opportunities? We would experience this as our working world, but what would it be beyond that? How would it institute in us? As us? Through us? We would have to broaden our circle's scope by choice and through necessity. There would be newfound peers who would fit in because they flattered our notions of what is best and there would be those we had to reluctantly accept because they outdid us at our own game. Many who we liked, and even those we didn't, would be *interesting*. We would drink wine and we would meet at conferences on the university's dime and talk about our kids or our cats, the stupid things our students did, and the plans we had for sabbatical. This would happen over months and years, and we would always think of it as friendship or acquaintance and never see the institution in it. If we are truly philosophers, we should have none of this. We should never rest content when the world shines on our best interests, even on our friendships and closer contacts.

This alien mind. I should prefer to be ridiculously bad in my own way than forgettably mediocre in ways only slightly different from others with comparable properties. A stamped pattern. An ideogram. This mechanism and its false delights. Pains. Sleep. For years I lived as this monk, keeping any hidden reserves for the work in progress. Now, there comes a baptism: Diogenes Laertius returning to me again and again. It was something of a discourse on method and it was beginning to petition for an exit. O ὑποπίπτη and the potential to arise. As an awakening, there was Aristotle on friendship and the unmoved mover, but then here comes fucking Kafka who boils it all down to a bug or a mouse or a burrowing creature. This alien mind.

I looked down the row of seats and saw the professor who had recommended my book for publication. I knew this because the publisher had carelessly sent me the review copy with only a little white-out painted over the reviewer's name. It was easy enough to scratch the paper until the name showed through. He was one of them. An insider. He was young and on his way up. This was an opportunity, and I was aware of it. I knew I could go over there and start chatting. He would recognize me, and he had liked my book. We would have something to talk about, but I felt a kind of shame at the thought of it. As though such gratuitous and self-serving "schmoozing" would be a horrible violation of some ethical code. Making and building connections like that was the whole point of conferences like these, but I couldn't bring myself to do it, couldn't bear the thought of making whatever small talk was necessary to ingratiate myself to him. Even if he seemed like a good person, like someone I would get along with, it didn't matter. The whole sense of it didn't sit right with me. I just sat there in the moments before the large plenary session. I didn't go over there, and I didn't introduce myself.

In a nutshell, this was the source of my problem in some deep and clearly definable way. I hadn't done things like this at previous APA meetings either. Eastern Division or Central, I went to the interviews that were arranged ahead of time, I interviewed stiffly in my unfamiliar coat and tie. I never talked to anyone other than that, never tried to connect or make a contact that might result in someone taking an interest in my interests, someone who might want to promote my career goals. Suddenly, I would become the shyest, most socially inept person in the world, unable to say a word, unable to imagine any kind of meaningful conversation in which I might say something that wouldn't be false or phony and violate my most basic principles of action and communication.

With all the bad philosophy and good titles that went on at this conference, it could not help but be clear to me that the social connections and interests were the primary reasons for these things. We were meant to build networks and extend the crony system. Why wasn't there a qualifying exam for that? This was my chance to let people know about my work and my plans, to let them know that I was someone to pay attention to, whose work should be known and included in the professional conversation. I could never bring myself to do it. Why should pandering and self-promotion be a part of the practice of philosophy? What role does it play in the love of wisdom? I could not associate the fumbling I would be forced to perform and endure with the fragmentary conversations with friends which seemed to realize the good life. I didn't deny that there was a social element to the life of the philosopher, and I knew that you needed to speak in half-thoughts and bad ideas to people who could help you shape them into more mature notions that met with contemporary concerns and used the fashionable vocabulary; and yet it felt wrong to force such conversations onto strangers.

Throughout my education as a thinker, I had always been careful about who I had such conversations with. Among my professors and colleagues in graduate school, there were only a select few that I actively engaged. It was more than just a mechanical operation meant to hone skills or learn better ways to defend this or that position against this or that set of objections coming from whatever -ism this or that person was known to promote. What would be the point of having rehashed conversations where I felt that —given enough research— I could supply both ends on my own? This was the sophistry that I had visualized. It was false and part of a game to get a better ranking for the sake of grants and fellowships, not some true inquiry where the interlocutors were honestly in pursuit of something that eluded them. I had such an idealized vision of what such investigations entailed and no one I would ever meet could live up to them on first impression. There were a few, and they weren't always who you thought they would be.

The old man from Cornell, for example. Ivy league pedigree. Very clearly based in the Analytic tradition. I developed a strong relationship with him, and we would talk for hours in the hallways or in his office.

Despite not knowing anything at all about any of the figures in my dissertation, he agreed to sit on the committee until I could find a more suitable replacement. Our relationship had started slowly. I sat for fifteen weeks in a Philosophy of Mind course where he stumbled around from topic to topic looking for something that would inspire the students to leap into a conversation with him. He didn't want to lecture us, he wanted to find topics that we could pursue together, as a group, in the classroom. He did it awkwardly, but there were some who grasped that this was what he was after, and they helped shape the way the course proceeded. I sat quietly and listened. I learned how his mind worked and began to understand his way of thinking towards the end of the semester.

I came back the following year and took a course with him in Metaphysics where most every lesson broke down into an exchange between the two of us. Occasionally some of the undergraduates would add something, but for the most part it was a dialogue. It might've taken me that entire first semester to realize this was how he worked, but once I did, I knew exactly what to do. Later we did an independent study together on the Pre-Socratics where just the two of us would meet in his office and try to work through those rich and cryptic fragments of Heraclitus and Empedocles, Parmenides and Democritus. That was in my third year and by that time he and I had developed a strong rapport where we were able to speak easily in half sentences and draw out this or that idea based on what the other was trying to say. He was the professor with whom I felt the greatest professional association and yet it took all that time to get there. How could I translate that into these conferences and the social opportunities that they were supposed to provide? If meeting with someone and observing them three times a week as they lectured on some subject that they cared deeply about was what it required for me to form a close philosophical relationship with them, how could I possibly wade through the awkwardness of the conference mixer to get to that point?

If I couldn't make that step, how could I find my way into a profession that seemed to be built on the connections and associations that were woven into the conference circuit? I would have to go to every relevant conference, I would have to pick the right subpopulation and listen to its various members until I started to understand their way of thinking and their way of tackling issues. Once I felt like I understood how their minds worked, I could venture into brief conversations with them that might suggest that I did understand what they were doing and that my work was related to some element of it. This would take years and I was already way behind because I hadn't started doing it as a graduate student. The conferences I went to in graduate school came off the same as the SPEP conference this year. I would hardly ever talk to anyone I didn't already know. I was never able to crack into the networks that I needed to be a part of to be remembered when it came to some job opening where the "best" candidate was likely going to be someone who was properly connected to the profession and would bring those connections to the department, making them available for use by whichever advisees would later need them.

At some level, it made sense that I had yet to acquire a tenure-track position, that no one yet had taken me very seriously for any kind of long-term appointment. These social capabilities were not incidental, they were crucial. You could not be an effective professor and you could not contribute to the life of the department and the profession if you weren't part of these associations and networks. These were not incidental qualifications; they were the most essential. Academic philosophy was as much about introducing students to the network of professional philosophers as it was anything else. Someone with inadequate skills was indeed unqualified. This is not hindsight. It was something I was clearly aware of at the time, and yet I felt powerless to overcome the limits in my own personality. I had been bred for something other than this. I was unable to do this in the same way that, say, I was unable to compete for an "A" in Organic Chemistry, making it impossible for me to qualify for medical school had I wanted to do it. I was too cynical to submit to it. I could not bridge the distance between Aristotle's work on friendship in his Ethics and the professionalism of these conferences, the opportunistic relationships that you had to nurture to insert yourself into the right groups for advancement. There was no connection as far as I could see. Even if the goal of these professional networks were the establishment of some community of true friendship that would exemplify Aristotelian excellence, I couldn't see anything in the means to get there that fit with that final aim. Because of that, I didn't make new friends at the conference even if I did listen to a paper or two that struck a chord in some way and inspired me somehow. I couldn't bring myself to approach those speakers. In the odd chance that I could, I wouldn't say anything about my work even when it was relevant. I didn't have an elevator pitch for my book, and I couldn't successfully convince a stranger that it might be in their interests to read it and write a review —something I imagined was the greatest hope of any professional connection made at a conference.

As much as this conference would energize me, it would also depress me. Driving home, we didn't just discuss the ideas that were dominating the professional circles, although we did plenty of that, we also talked about the cliques that we had noticed and who had been trying to crack into them. All the while I wondered whether I could ever do such a thing. Whatever desire or interest I felt in living a life fit for a philosopher, this hurdle was in my way. It blocked my progress. I worried that my inabilities were becoming habit, that I was doomed somehow, and would never be able to break past these limitations. I thought I wanted this life so much and yet I was unable to do some of the simplest things necessary to achieve it. Was my rejection of these behaviors merely expedient? Being a part of a vibrant professional community was the truth of reason and the movement to spirit. Was I just incapable of doing it? Like a small man, I converted my inability into a moral and righteous set of notions. I am too pure for this, too much the idealist, but all that was just rationalization and excuses. It was the myopia that leads its subject to proclaim near-sightedness a virtue.

Wolfe was increasingly adamant with his line of thinking following my return from the conference. He said, "You have to make up your mind about what it means to be a philosopher." By that it was clear that he meant what it is that philosophers do. What are the actions that a philosopher does? This goes beyond his quips about whether every sentence of a philosophical work was indeed a philosophical statement. What was that anyway? He thought that if my goal were to become a philosopher, then I had to be clear about what the criteria were, otherwise I was being soft. "Will you be a philosopher the day you get a tenure-track position or the day you get tenure? Will it be on the day you realize that your work is being routinely accepted at journals and for conference programs?" Does being a philosopher happen only if you qualify to sit on hiring committees? If you are advising undergraduates who are writing their theses? Do you have to write to be a philosopher? Read or have philosophical conversations? Why build your life from the category to the act and not the other way around? If we are talking about your career chances, are we having a philosophical conversation so long as we stick to the career chances of a philosopher?

My concern was that philosophy was merely the tip of an iceberg. Say Aristotle was right and that living the good life meant living among others who were likewise pursing the good through the life of the mind. Suppose that the only way to achieve the highest levels of that was to slog your way through a set of unpleasant and nearly unnavigable barriers until you reached some summit where those around you had gone through the same set of steps and faced the same challenges. In that case, there would be many non-philosopher specific actions that a person would have to perform to reach the end state. It would be true that all these actions along the way were not sufficient for establishing the life of the mind, but they were necessary for it. If that were the case, then only those who could work their way through these behaviors could achieve those ends. The evaluation performed by the hiring committee was for the sake of potential: will this sleeper awaken and become what they must become to stand at the altar with us? If they haven't the heart for these necessary means, then it doesn't seem likely.

I wonder if Kant was any good at this. Did he go to conferences and make professional connections? Did he advise on hiring committees and work to ensure that the new faculty or the admitted students were following the agenda? Did he actively work to promote that agenda over and against some competing vision belonging to some other members of the committee? Nietzsche's work, whatever else you can say about it, was not peer reviewed. At least, not during composition. The published works never gained anything from the feedback of reviewers numbered one and two. Why did he even write that stuff? What was his intent? He wasn't working toward tenure, and he wasn't making any progress cracking into professional circles. What was he trying to do? This is probably why I think of him as Don Quixote with a headache. He was fighting with windmills thinking they were giants. Nothing more. The polemics were the virtues of his near-sightedness. He affirmed what he was despite its antipathy to any ends. He selectively surveyed the history of thought with an angle aiming at the best possible logistics for inserting himself into it. This behavior might not be morally superior to the schmoozing that goes on at conferences. The greed of the organism as it tries to fabricate a world for itself given its limits and abilities, given its desires and orientations, is hardly noble. "Live as you will, be as you like, but be bold about it. For once suffer yourself a moment of self-doubt and your opinion will be accepted by all and sundry."

The act of proclaiming oneself to be something or to be someone without bending to the social conventions or historical traditions, was exactly the folly that speaks in that famous eulogy. "Finally, man's mind is so formed that it is far more susceptible to falsehood than to truth." The falsehoods may be the glimmer of illusion. The play acting of the pseudo-quixote (and that's quite a feat given that the quixote is already a pretender, making this the double bind of a false pretender) is the assertion of a delusion as the highest end. We are describing someone who is living the life of the philosopher as one envisions it without concerns for the social and historical confirmation of it and with only the desire to do it, think it, and act from out of it. Here, living the life of the mind was the purpose, even if badly, even if it were done incompetently and while ill-informed of the latest lingo or this year's hottest topics. Was it possible that there could be a life of the philosopher, an answer to the question concerning the 'who' of the philosopher, that dead-ended in such illusion and anti-social aims and orientations? Doesn't the philosopher have to include this in their domain and in the subject of their investigations?

This was all finding its way into the evolving discourse on method. Did the philosopher have the luxury of accepting themselves as such without that same diligent analytical probing they would apply to any proclamation of knowledge, existence, or right action? Could a philosopher engage in a career without such questioning and engage in a professional community without challenging its premises and its boundaries? Would personality have to succumb to the coercion of discipline, or could it fragment and disperse into a crowd and whatever it carries? The truth in wine disappears as we sober up, maybe it was merely an illusion and our excitement and passion a moment of blurred vision.

The librarian tends bar on Tuesday and Saturday. She smokes at her station now and again and cheerfully chatters nearly nonstop with the other bartender or the customers who sit at her bar. She's relaxed in the smokey near darkness. She laughs at her own jokes and throws her head back in disbelief at some fictional point of view she imagines in opposition to whatever notion she has just spun from extemporaneous musings. The banter of the bartender is *the* bartender in her mind. She is almost always talking to people who are at least partially under the influence. Because of how bar seating works at the Del, she is often talking to a man who is sitting by himself and nursing a beer or two.

The people who sit at her bar might be regulars. Not for her sake, but for the bar. They come on an appointed day at a scheduled time, ready to wind down and have a beer to cap off their evening before going home to sleep and start the whole thing over again tomorrow. It's a repetitive malaise that she knows from afar. She knows its symptoms and how to talk to people who live in its midst. The regulars have gotten to know each other and often the bartender is the intermediary of the connection. She talks to each of them, has ongoing conversations that start and stop as she moves up and down her station. There is overflow and crosstalk between this one and that one so that they forcibly become connected to each other and add threads here and there to each other's fragments as they are maintained across the moments with the bartender speeding up and slowing down as the orders come in and the lulls that lay between them. Since they are mostly men, she makes a specific kind of small talk with them, alone or in pairs. She sets herself at a distance so that they know that whatever is flirtatious in the exchange is not real, not aimed at anything, and promises no pay-off. They know she works for tips.

A bartender is a bartender because they tend to the bar. They are employed by the establishment. They mix drinks, pour beers, change the kegs, fill up water glasses, and call for cabs. These are the things that bartenders do. The job description is clear. The training process is documented and the new hire —assuming they have experience in other bars— quickly learns the ropes. When she sits at the bar after work when most everyone has left and only the employees and a few of the regulars remain, she is no longer tending bar. The bartender is left behind. She winds down and forgets. There is no concern that she needs to be a bar tender at every moment of every day, her bad faith is contained. The parameters are clearly defined, and this clarity is relaxing. There is a distinct contrast with her studies which never seem to end and can never be set aside by a ringing bell. You don't have to go home, but you can't stay here. The actions of a student are constant and ongoing. To be a student, is to be a student all the time, whereas a bartender only tends bar until closing time. That clock is 15 minutes fast, by the way.

There is the matter of potential and how it has been added. It has come for her, and it terrifies her. While she sits in classes and listens carefully to the nearly nonsensical question that one of her classmates asks using all kinds of jargon that she has never heard before, she knows that she can tend bar. Even though she isn't tending bar, she knows she can. It comforts and it haunts her. Is that all she can do? Is that all she will ever do? Would that be bad, or does she need to wake up? What's wrong with tending bar all your life? Being connected to people in that way rather than in some other way that is expected of you if you are a student in school or a professional member of the community of librarians, what could be wrong with this? We choose our associations, but we draw from luck and past inertia, from influence. Our work structures these connections. We like and are drawn to our colleagues, there is so much we have in common with them. We share interests. This folds us in among them and folds the profession into ourselves. She stumbled into tending bar and now she is at home in it. She can do it. The day approaches when she will be so much the librarian that this anxiety will be peeled away, and these other connections will come easily. She will lean against the information desk or the search terminal just as casually as she leans against the bar and grins slyly at the guy who over explains how exactly he expects her to make his drink.

She would ride her bike home after leaving the bar and she would smell like smoke and stale beer and the people who were sitting at her station. She would shower and crawl into bed, happy and excellent.

November

As an undergraduate, I spent a semester in London. The creative writing course was taught by an underqualified teaching assistant likewise spending a semester abroad. The advantage of his incompetence was that we didn't have to attend class or read anything aloud. We just had to write something each week and then suffer his feedback which included, if you can imagine, a letter grade.

On one occasion, rather than giving me a grade, he called me in for a conference, accused me of plagiarizing my piece that week, and told me I had three days to write something new. I spent those three days getting legal advice at the US embassy, filing the paperwork to receive a copyright, and affixing the required copyright tag to the top of the cover page. I then resubmitted the original story and —following the advice of the attorney at the embassy— told the TA that the onus was on him to produce the master.

He had nothing. It was a ridiculous accusation, completely without foundation other than the fact that he liked it too much for it to have been written by the likes of me, whose previous work he hadn't cared for much.

The piece reminded me of that chapter in *Ulysses* where Bloom is on the beach and getting all pervy over the young woman he sees off in the distance. I hadn't read *Ulysses* back then, but my story had a similar vibe. It was stream of consciousness and, although the character wasn't a pervert, he was just hung over enough and sufficiently degenerate in other ways that it wouldn't be hard to imagine him being guilty of that offense too. The atmospheric qualities of the scene and the point of view were similar. A good teacher might have suggested I read Joyce.

Anyway, I don't remember the TAs name. Ned Creeth was the professor with whom I usually took creative writing. His comments were more like "I liked this one" or "This one didn't work for me." I don't recall getting specific grades on the stories I wrote, I just remember sitting in his office and talking about what we liked to read, and why. He mostly liked stories that started out being about one thing and then later turned out to be about something else entirely. I told him what happened while I was reading *Portrait of the Artist as a Young Man*, which he had recommended, and that great sentence where Dedalus says something like "This race and this land and this country have produced me, I shall express myself as I am." I paused over the sentence, reread it out loud, and lightning struck. Actual lightning, thunder and all. I told him I was pretty much convinced that I had conspired with Joyce to conjure that lightning bolt. He loved that story.

As a prolific writer of bad books, I justified the lost time by claiming that it is for didactic purposes. Why books, in that case? Believe me, I've always wished I could read a book and then write a 10–20-page thesis as an exercise to explain or digest it. It never works that way though. It seems that I am constitutionally incapable of understanding a single book in isolation. Instead, I write long treatises that merge and bumble together 30 books or more. It is as if I cannot make sense out of the single node, but only out of a network of them.

The irony is that in the network, the single nodes get lost, and I don't appear to be referring to any particular book at all.

After finishing *Portrait*, I read *Dubliners*. Generally, I don't read a lot of short stories. It's because the ones I like, I don't understand. Like Araby. That's a nice story, all vibe and atmosphere. I felt the pathos and the wasted time that this kid is realizing. Still, what the fuck? Is that it? A sketch that focuses on a feeling or a reaction? What more do I now understand that I didn't before? Has the scope of human being widened? Has the stretching out of human time and history become actual and meaningful in some way that weaves it all together, or is it just 'hmm, yup. that's something that is?'

Alright. Alright, I'm convinced. I might like short stories after all.

...

Check me if I'm wrong here, but a plot summary for *Portrait* might be: Stephen decides to be a writer rather than a priest.

In many possible books, that might have been the setup, or maybe the pretense. Something that happened on page 34. In *Portrait*, it's the whole thing, that's the story. Years later, we'll see him again with that plump bastard, in the library haunted by a ghost, and then stinking drunk without his keys getting help from someone who faintly resembles his surrogate father. Joyce fathered Bloom so that Bloom could be delegated as Stephen's father so Stephen could sire Joyce as the author of the epic novel of Ireland. Someone is definitely someone's grandfather.

"26 April: Mother is putting my new secondhand clothes in order. She prays now, she says, that I may learn in my own life and away from home and friends what the heart is and what it feels. Amen, so be it. Welcome, O life! I go to encounter for the millionth time the reality of experience and to forge in the smithy of my soul the uncreated conscience of my race."

...

"Epigraph: Et ignotas animum dimittit in artes: Latin, "And he applies his mind to unknown arts" [the line continues, "and changes the laws of nature"]. Description of Daedalus in Ovid's *Metamorphoses*, VIII:188."

The larger context is that he is crafting a set of wings that may be used to fly. He wants to teach his son to fly too and says to him:

"you must follow a course midway between earth and heaven, in case the sun should scorch your feathers, if you go too high, or the water make them heavy if you are too low. Fly halfway between the two. And pay no attention to the stars, to Bootes, or Helice or Orion with his drawn sword: take me as your guide and follow me!"

Once, having finished a strange back and forth between the novels of Woolf and Hemingway, I turned to Joyce.

But before even getting to the epigraph, the "about the author" blurb from Penguin caught my eye:

James Joyce: 2/2/1882 - 1/13/1941

Which seemed familiar so I looked back and saw:

Virginia Woolf: 1/25/1882 - 3/28/1941

Is it grotesque that my first thought upon seeing this was that she should have done it 82 days sooner? That's right, V. Woolf's anguish is easily reducible to my sense of irony. She would rather be a... blah blah blah. An attitude perfectly suited to begin re-reading *A Portrait of the Artist as a Young Man*? Where will I find the time? Will that recapture it?

...

Parts of speech are hobgoblins. They are only meaningful to describe the position of a word in its relation to others, they tell you nothing about its inherent nature. I am cupcaked at the standing of such public house madness.

...

The family of kush-related flowers deeply inhibit writing due to their medicinal qualities for settling the stomach. Of course, it is possible to write with a settled stomach, just not very well. Fortunately, the disease is the cure since worrying about having a stomach too settled for writing causes the stomach to become upset. I suppose then that, despite that first impression, the family of kush-related flowers instigate writing. Just another example of the hermeneutical circle. Forget I mentioned it.

...

Wolfe told me the other day that sometimes he thinks the self-consciousness of the proletariat is an asshole. The antagonism of the disempowered with the powerful permits them all kinds of savagery. Justice is a fabrication and gets lost in that. We don't love it, we only love the feeling of power that it masks. We were talking about resentment, its contract, and all its implementations. I cringed when he said most feminist professors are mediocre too, but then he said that most of us are. That's how mediocrity works and only the white man gets to be completely oblivious to it. He insisted that his IQ is somewhere between 85 and 115.

...

Here is how it works. The boundary is behind you, but you live in it. It's everywhere, but you don't see it because you see with it. It's the only thing that can even vaguely qualify as an authentic version of you, but it's terrible in that role. It makes everything seem like we are arriving too late, like we only became aware of it after it already happened. This boundary that makes us fall behind ourselves and arrive too late is a limitation and it fixes our gaze into narrowly focused points of view that we can't escape in anything we might pursue. I call it partiality because it is only part of what is happening and inhabits us through and through with our beloved bias. It could be a translation of the German word "Sorge." This coming-too-late that is the limit of what we experience, inserts a tiny gap between consciousness and the act. That gap becomes a surrogate to experience when it makes us vulnerable to the desire to fill it. The things that come from far away and which associate us with each other in all expressions of feeling and reason, the aggregate properties of what we are and what we possess, they all fill that gap. The constraints of identity. If we're not careful, these properties saturate what we are and feed back into all our experience and change it. We become each other in the aggregate and only our organized motion remains free for whatever gods are collecting us. That's how it works.

...

One trick to promote writing as "process" is to always make sure to end a day's writing having written the first sentence of the next paragraph. Don't stop at the end. Be kind to tomorrow's self (this can also teach you a thing or two about audience: tomorrow "me").

...

I can't get past the fact that my writing would only be earth shattering if I wrote it a hundred years ago.

...

Now, I'm realizing I don't know what the word "published" meant. The modern definition backed by its etymology might be: "a short and amusing or interesting story about a real incident or person." Who is listening to this short and amusing or interesting story if it is an anecdote and how does the order of operations work?

Inspired by a conversation with some future self:

"I've put in lots of anecdotes."

"Well, if that is true, then you can't publish."

"Can't or won't?"

"Exactly."

...

It's possible that a job isn't so much a distraction from real work as a safety net that enables all kinds of risk-taking in it, risks that would otherwise not be prudent.

...
If you're following the program, get your pages done. No compromise. If you are spinning a yarn, don't force it. Make sure you can clearly visualize it or at least imagine a set of possible projections given your current position (discovery must be possible, I realize that). It is more like practicing a guitar riff without a guitar than you might think.

"If you're freewheeling it, it's better to write than not to write. If you're spinning something, it's definitely better not to write than to go off in the wrong direction." —Reb Eitey

When majoring in philosophy or as a graduate student, we were commonly given writing assignments. We write papers starting out at three to five pages and working up to ten, twenty, or more. This might possibly lead to a thesis of a hundred and then a dissertation that might be over two hundred pages long. There are a host of skills that go along with this progression: 1) structuring and laying out an argument, 2) thinking in terms of the sub-arguments where premises are asserted, and evidence provided, 3) stitching together higher order syllogisms, annotating their form, and drawing the conclusions. There are micro maneuvers inside of macro maneuvers and we learn to move up and down, back and forth, supporting the one indirectly in support of the other. We learn to synthesize and construct. We play with blocks, and we learn to balance them on top of each other.

Our professors show us how this is done in the margins with their comments and reactions. They tell us that this point isn't clear or that we have assumed too much or not considered counter arguments that would make our point more compelling. Over time, we begin to anticipate these comments and marginalia. We come to know that this or that micro argument needs to be made in context where another position has been called into question or falsified on those very grounds. We are not only learning the form of how to craft an argument of larger and larger size, but the material that is required to make that argument stronger so that it can be a serious contender alongside the many arguments being made by our colleagues.

We read. We read tons of pages of whatever we can get our hands on. In all different areas. We read in the subdisciplines as we fulfill the requirements of the major or as we prepare for the qualifying exams. We read to become informed across the breadth of classic material and we read because we love the field and the historical contributions to it. From this reading, we learn to see how arguments work on us and how they draw us in. The combination of our historical influences and our teachers forms us into properly disciplined writers. Unless of course we have been reading the wrong writers and listening to the wrong teachers. In those cases, we still acquire an ordered set of skills, but the wrong set, or a set that is misinformed or incorrectly applies the teachings of the ages to our case. We become a "case" in that event, otherwise a contributor.

In my life, among my teachers, the concern had always been that the influence of a writer and thinker like Jacques Derrida was going to do more harm than good. He would rot my brain because he isn't a serious thinker nor is he a writer with any depth or precision when it comes to making his argument (sic). He does nothing to properly convince his peers and so, I was frequently warned, emulating him, or even learning from him, was highly likely to adversely affect my abilities and chances of advancement in the profession. The mentors who pointed this out were not lying or driven by villainous intent. They were trying to help. They were suggesting that there were standards of influence and impact and that there were criteria for how to do things. Even if there were people who appreciated the stylings of deconstruction, they would not be influential in any career decisions made in those situations where my livelihood was at stake. As an American student of philosophy in the late twentieth century, if I were serious about my chances for professional academic success, there would be influences I would have to forego and others that I would have to accept.

My advisor in graduate school had once put this in the kindest possible way by suggesting that I needed to strategically invoke proper names when producing descriptions of my work. This applied in both the positive and the negative case. That is, use the names of those who were likely to further my cause and avoid using the names that were likely to hurt it. Heidegger, he said, was an acceptable name to invoke when crafting a prospectus for a dissertation committee to approve. Derrida and deconstruction were not. He pointed out that none of this meant I couldn't read and be influenced by these materials, only that I needed to be strategic about attributing them. Deconstruction, he thought, was a perfectly reasonable way to go about producing a critical position on a piece of written philosophy, but wasn't it possible to do it without mentioning that it was called deconstruction and that it was affiliated with specific proper names and persons?

My book, for example, referred to something called Heidegger's Line. That was because I was interested in specific methodological lineages that sprung from the approach demonstrated in his later writings. Initially, I had thought this would be a reference to Derrida, Foucault, and Deleuze. As time progressed and the scope became more realistic, this became laser focused on Derrida. None of this needed to surface until I started producing chapters in the later part of the book and began investigating the lineage of the notions spelled out in the earlier chapters. By that I mean I didn't need to mention it in any breadcrumbs or footnotes about what was coming next or later on. These notes and asides could be purely topical without naming any names. Hadn't deconstruction itself already called into question these proper names and what was being attributed to them? It made sense so I complied.

In the end, of course, no one was fooled. The work dripped with deconstructive approaches and orientations right from the outset. I was applying these techniques to the inventors of the techniques. It was done for the sake of producing a reading of their work that was so deeply entrenched in deconstruction that there was no hope that it might appeal in any way to someone who didn't already have an interest in that tradition.

It became clear that the process of doing this research and writing this book, not only conformed to the historical technics of a specific discipline, but that it demonstrated the qualities of that discipline in every sentence. This would have been the case even if I had gone further outside the boundaries of acceptable academic work. That is, suppose my work had taken as its point of departure the writing of Georges Bataille or Gaston Bachelard. I was at an age where influence came so easily, where my work was so adaptive to whatever it was that I was reading and working on that I would have varied my style and presented my argument or demonstration in a way that resembled their approaches.

When I read Foucault's *Discipline and Punish*, I was deeply struck by the association of surveillance and discipline. The whole point of Foucault's invocation of Bentham's Panopticon was to show this connection. It was through the visibility of the cells in the prison that the behavior of the prisoners was regulated. Not only that. It was self-regulated because the prisoners believed themselves to be watched and so they acted that way. The voices in my head were the voices of the watchers. The marginalia in the papers that came back with grades written on the first page also became voices in my head. The comments during office visits with advisors too. The positions advanced by the philosophers that I admired and wanted to emulate. These voices in my head, because they were in my head, could see everything that I was doing. To appease them and to continue the friendly dialogue I wanted to have, I needed to do things that would positively contribute to the exchange we were having. These adjustments were the whole point of my education. They were meant to be *the* learning outcome.

We may come to see a total absorption of human life into the power of organization or disciplinary structure. We may come to affirm it as necessity while at the same time raging against it. On what grounds? Why not just ask why does the structural domination of organizational power require that the fiction of the individual, and the reflexive rage it maintains, coexist within it? How does the myth of the individual further the ends of organizational discipline and its distributed expansion? Asked another way, can there be a coherent ethos of opposition, or is that same ethos a precondition for the spread of organizational power, a manner for it to enact surveillance?

Wolfe was right about this. It wasn't a question of being disciplined or not. All that nonsense about being wild and undisciplined was bullshit. The point was to have the correct discipline. That meant that the voices in my head had to be the right voices. Sartre, for example, had written about the relationship that "the look" has on one's self-understanding as it forms subjectivity. To let Sartre's influence take over one's spin on these ideas might be preferable to some colleagues than letting Foucault do it. These facts might change over time. The point is that you might have to use fashionable variations on themes to put yourself into the right position at the right time. The goal of your teachers is to make sure you have the right influences to correlate with the social forces at work in the current moment in history.

There was always discipline at work, the question was which discipline. The question of which discipline usually meant who you wanted your colleagues to be. If you were trying to get a job in an English department, the acceptable range of influences —both stylistic and rhetorical— might be radically different than if you were trying to get a job in a Sociology department. There would be a completely different set of requirements within philosophy, and these requirements would change over time. In the 1990s there might be a set of thinkers that are all the rage at the conferences and on the job market. That set will be wildly different from the set of approved influences ten years earlier or ten years later.

Being, an Introduction was my second work in philosophy, a book length project that I had been turning over and over for the last few months and was just now starting to see its structure and content. I had an outline, I had a sense of what the table of contents might look like, and I was becoming clearer about the twists and turns that the argument would need to take at both the lower and the higher levels, within the individual chapters or sections and across the larger parts of the book. I was aware that these mechanisms that I was employing to get clear about the themes and the form I could use to present them was itself a voice in my head. Something alien that came from somewhere I had been over the years, something I had learned in the margins of my student work, in the conversations I had with my teachers, and in the scribblings I had made in response to all that reading.

All this meant that I was not only focused on the matters at hand, the ideas and the material that were forming, but I was also becoming increasingly aware of the constraints and requirements of stylings and voice. The contrasts came out clearest in the comparisons I could make between what had come to be known as the "early" Heidegger and the "late." Heidegger may not have changed his focus or the historical material of his concern over the course of his career, but nonetheless there was a radical change that he passed through somewhere during the 1930s. His work before this change resembled the work of his colleagues. We can read Scheler, Plessner, or the later Husserl, Cassirer or Karl Jaspers and recognize a collegial relationship to Heidegger's early writings. Something happens. An event. The power of the Ereignis raised and inserted itself into his work and everything changes. The way he structured articles and papers, the style with which he approached topics and notions, historical figures, and issues. In terms of the discipline, his genre had changed. The voices that he was listening to and responding to were different than those that were at work in the 20s and early 30s.

It was not a coincidence that the project I was working toward was a throwback to the work from Heidegger's early period. This return to the earlier from the later was accompanying a growing distrust of the forms and voices that were at work in any act of returning or retrieving the past from the present. At first, I thought I was a Heidegger scholar. This was a reasonable conclusion to draw. I had been studying his work for several years. I had produced a dissertation on it, focusing on these later texts. I was in the process of publishing the dissertation as a book with a respected academic press. I was advancing my research interests into the early work to complete the resume of the scholar. Anyone who had a lot to say about the later Heidegger should also have a lot to say about the early. There was a scholarly ideal that was driving my movement and that ideal fit with the fashion of the profession and would seem reasonable to any allegedly disinterested advisor.

These same concerns, however, were being regularly disrupted by the underlying observation that there was a distance between the early and the late that wasn't topical but generative. Something different was happening on the one hand than what was happening on the other. It wasn't merely stylistic. The notion of genre and its relationship to historical generation and the emergence of the things that exist wasn't lost on me. This was the ontological difference. The genre was the way, the way in which fabrication takes place. The notion of the event that had transformed Heidegger's work was intrinsically bound together with the voices that could speak through that material and across different phases in the writer's life.

In the dissertation, I had written an introduction that had started me down this path. The point I made and for which I had no ready words was that the book was not an argument or theoretical presentation but a demonstration. By that, I meant that it did something and that a reader who followed along with what it was doing would have an experience while reading it. My intent was to point at that experience without coming right out and describing it, since that might break the spell. The act of going through something with the reader was the whole point, it was the objective in writing the book. The experience, jointly taken, was what that book and all books would be about. Superficially, I explained that I was trying to avoid explaining something to the reader, but what I was trying to escape was exactly that experience that the reader and I were pursuing in the process of the demonstration. If I were doing it right, at the end it would become clear that the demonstration would replace any interest we might have in getting an explanation.

This was the only way to write. Once I had discovered this, I couldn't avoid doing it. Everything I was planning and conjuring in writing after that event, was similar in quality. Whether it was an article to be used as a writing sample in a job application or to deliver during an on-campus interview. All of it was produced for the sake of this kind of demonstration where the primary voices in my head were suggesting what must be the case and what followed from it.

To produce a tension that can resonate into something, to watch over it and guide it forth, then to pick at it, bend it, and shape it, over and over and over again and again, that is the path; but impatience is at the end of it. I can name that too, goddamnit. Wolfe, the motherfucker on the other end of the line. The tightrope walker, the evangelical, and the whip. He seethes at me, and he breathes. Worse. He laughs. Its echo is my ache. My pounding sinuses. Once all the demons have names there is liberation. Well, cohabitation. From this habitat, there can be something new, something found and understood as it makes itself.

A discourse on method that should be called "Punctuation Marks," but which is called *Being an Introduction to Gift-Giving Time*. That is, *Being, an Introduction: to Gift-Giving, Time*. That takes it to right now, to right then. It says its name and its name says so. I hopped on one foot that whole month. Crazy really that it was just the one. That's because there was a wall at the end of it, at the exit point of this great November. Interlude. The farce that plays out between the acts, between this one and that other.

This new thing comes. It lands as the punctuation book. *It was* situated in this way among these notions. *It* was a scholarly demonstration of a full range of understanding the work of Martin Heidegger. *It was* a "second book" which demonstrated that the author wasn't merely a dissertation writer, but someone who could transition into the field as a professional member. *It was* rapidly becoming an exploration of those voices and the way in which they generated forms and material in a performance of the technical operations of outlining, drafting, and polishing.

I couldn't help it. This experience wasn't a set of conscious choices. I was tumbling downward without breaks. I wanted to be a professor so badly. It was the only career I could imagine. I visualized the college town where my life would take place, the small buildings where my time would pass, the friendly relations with my colleagues become a social life, and the mentoring my students would get. All of it was based on having the right voices in my head, speaking in the right way, and contributing correctly to the production of work that fits the currents and fashions of the profession. Why couldn't I just do it? A madman when it came to the process, I couldn't prevent the gymnastics of genre from finding their way into the work. I couldn't stop the flow of the seer and the seen from erupting in setting the later Heidegger against the early.

Wolfe says I only have this problem because I have this problem. There is nothing more to it, it is a fabrication, and it is self-imposed. There is just enough of the discipline in me to ruin whatever there is that is undisciplined, and I am just undisciplined enough to skew whatever there is that is disciplined. Knowing it doesn't help.

There is no reason that Diogenes Laertius needed to interject himself into the transition. There is no reason that I had to listen to him as though he were here in the room with me and urging me toward his vision of Aristotle as I came up behind Heidegger's brand. Potential had not been at the heart of my reading and yet it became the central notion in Heidegger's early work mediated by Aristotle's metaphysics into later work where it was cast as the explosive event of something (and not nothing) actualizing. Only because I happened across a passage from Diogenes did I experience —and need to demonstrate— that transition through the image of a sleeper who wakes up. All this could be the makings of a nice book, no doubt. The form would be the driving factor, right? If I wrote it out in meticulous order with the right arguments, and then structured the layout with concise form, then it would be a lovely contribution to the professional discussion. I might as well be a dancing Sufi in a temple in Istanbul. Such were my chances.

In my fall nightmare, it was being transformed from a scholarly endeavor into a generative discourse on method. That meant I couldn't just write it all down as a simple expository progression with citations and point counterpoint dispatches touching on the major literature in the sub-fields of Aristotle scholarship and the notions of potential as they had been developed by commentators. Instead, the operative function of commentary had to become thematic as a generative decision, as something one might or might not decide to do on the basis of disciplinary concerns. A potential to be realized, an entire psychology would be at stake, an ontology even. The book wouldn't stay put, it couldn't remain a book on the work of Heidegger's early notion of potential and how that fit with the Aristotelian tradition. The dynamic Heidegger split in half and bridged to Aristotle via Diogenes became the focus. Time bent and the generations of thinkers reflected all the light back behind the themes and theses. It came forth in terms of the generative principles at work in historical tradition building. What I saw, very clearly, was that if I were to demonstrate this generative moment via these three figures, I would come upon a moment of incision and evoke a Zarathustran event. A human, all too human event. I wasn't entirely sure myself, but something on that order would take place, and then, once that happened, the whole thing would become a ghost story.

What did I mean by that? Well, it had something to do with the nonsense of the discipline. I cast it in terms of property relations, meaning something ambiguous. Something in the work of John Locke that covered both the notion of attributes and the notion of possession. Property is what is ultimately invoked in genetic and economic inheritance. The property as an attribute attached to a substance or the property that is owned by some subject of the law that haunts it. The project was enormous. Way bigger than I could possibly manage. The scholarly maneuver of the initial themes would evoke genre at its center. Genre would incite a break between the first half and the second half. The break is what would make it a discourse on method in the proper fashion. Genre's disruption would show itself in the dual purposing of property as both identification and possession, a laborious territorialization of that inner raw potential. It would become the primordial disposition of potential insofar as it is conceptualized as a power that inhabits the subject through what it is and what it has. The true spontaneity of its being. Such a demonstration, as a discourse on method, was meant to be a dismantling, and to undermine the very same associative set of concerns: the self's power-to-be was at risk.

A huge project. Well beyond anything I had ever been trained to do, and yet, I must repeat myself, I had no choice in the matter. It was the only project that presented itself to me and I had no position or context from which to gain perspective on it. I was lost in this project and could not think about anything else. Passion, as they say, gets the better of us. We don't get to choose what we are passionate about, and maybe the real spin on moral luck is that we are lucky to be passionate about this or that thing. Lucky are those professional philosophers who are passionate about the role genre plays in the distinction of early and late Heidegger. Woe unto those who think that the genre incited by the difference is itself an ontological eruption of power and discipline that reflexively attempts to understand how one is what one is as one is. For no doubt those latter are unlikely to find their way into professional circles where such pastimes are the standard fare for both members and contributors.

It is one of the great ironies of my life that the discipline to remain steadfast despite obstacles was well developed and strong. If I had less of it, I might have made more of it. It might've been better if I could've been deterred, but I wouldn't be. I would write every day and I would develop an outline and a prospectus. I would set the themes into drafts and speculative shorter blurbs. The pieces would form, the table of contents become clearer, and it would all gain greater detail. It was a curse that I had sufficient access to the discipline to be able to carry out this self-destructive plan, this systematic dismantling of a tradition. The voices of all the writers and thinkers were vividly clear in my mind. I knew how to structure the work, I knew how to put down the pages, and how to keep them coming. Nothing would stop me from producing it. I was the perfect correlation of adverse conditions being applied to a lifelong set of aims and objectives. For many years, writing was my primary concern. I had become skilled at it. Now, the generative philosophical voices were added to the mix along with the clear and distinct sense that life in a university town was the way to contain and promote it. All of it intermingled with those objectives that were so structured that they could never bring about a favorable result. This world had produced me, and I had no choice but to be its artifact. The fact that such a thing could never coherently create what it sets out to create was beyond revision and was not some change I could initiate. The will is cramped by the persons that steer it.

I knew the path and had emulated the path, but I could not walk along it.

Is this everyone's story? Human beings produced in such a way as to desperately want to make something of themselves that cannot possibly be made by those with the passion to do so.

To top off that irony with a still greater one, I had decided to demonstrate it —in every sense of the term— by writing a book that was both about it and did it. *Being, an Introduction* wasn't just about the punctuation of a title, it was about the punctuation of an experience. It evoked that punctuation. It punctuated it. Its purpose was to agonize and to mean.

There was a television, but it was never on. For the football game maybe. The stereo was on all the time, even during the games. A cassette or a compact disk. I didn't have a turntable anymore. I would listen to oratorio music like Beethoven's *Missa Solemnis* or Bach's *Mass in B minor*. It set the mood. When the engineer came for a visit one day, we sat at the dining room table and smoked pot. He casually referred to the rhythms of my life as Opus One, a concerto he was beginning to imagine, but would never write. In his tale, the music was the background to a great work. I told him all that was missing was the great work, but he waived my objections aside. He had decided that something extraordinary was happening in the small space and he was sure that it was somehow connected to the music and the lighting and that it was reflected in the mood. I mentioned that Wolfe too had begun something recently and was often lingering in the apartment to work on it.

"Do you guys talk about your work?"

"Occasionally, but not when we're doing it. The space is too cramped for that. I don't think we have much room for each other right now."

"What's he working on?"

"I'm not sure; he refers to it as 'Fragmented Readings' but doesn't say much more than that."

"You have no idea? What he's doing has no influence on what you're doing? How does that work?"

Probably he was right to ask this. It likely wasn't possible. Both Wolfe and I knew that transformations would happen when we spoke of things. I would turn his work into mine and he would turn mine into his. Whatever Wolfe meant by fragments or reading or whatever notion he had of revamping how some specific books were being read, it had nothing in common with what I understood it to mean. Whatever I meant by potential and the sleeper who is rising, had nothing to do with the fragmented understanding they received in Wolfe's interpretation. This was probably a coping mechanism that we used to enable the work to continue despite the scarcity of space.

The engineer brought me some software to run on the computer I was building. It was a different platform than I had always used for my writing and course preparation, so I didn't have any software to run other than the operating system. The point of building the computer was lost to me, it was a hobby that changed my focus for short periods now and again. My mother had given me the computer when she bought a new one. It was old and out of date, so I removed all the internal components and bought new ones from stores across the country that shipped their stock after it was ordered by telephone. They advertised in computer magazines. I had installed a new motherboard and CPU, upgraded the memory, and changed the video card. It was a different world and became a relaxing distraction from my other work.

We talked about what he was doing with compression and my work on potential. There were similarities. He overestimated the importance of my work because he saw the connections between it and his own. He wasn't boosting me so much as boosting himself through the association. This was a tendency of his whenever we spoke about the philosophical interleave of engineering and post-structuralism. To his way of thinking, software engineering was nothing other than the deconstruction of metaphysics, or so he had come to affirm confidently once I had introduced him to the terms.

"Money is becoming almost a completely digitized material," he said. "A lot of what we are doing now with software is trying to figure out all the ways we can move and manipulate money without giving it a concrete form."

"Well, you still need the concrete form though, right?"

"No. Not at all. The gold standard is long gone. Now what backs the currency is some computerized form of it, there may not be enough currency to cover it. These networking protocols have made distributed operations so simple to build. All the banks are using computer systems, all the financial companies. Think about it. How much money do you have?"

"On me?"

"Exactly. See the difference? You might have a few bucks in your pocket. That isn't what you were thinking. You were thinking about how much you have in some bank account."

"True."

"You don't have that money, do you? Really, that money is a set of actions you have to perform. Writing a check directly to someone or presenting them with a piece of plastic and then writing a check to a third party who backs up the spending power of the plastic."

"Of course. Possession has become loose."

"That's right because I'm not talking about how it works with prices or comparisons or exchange. I'm talking about what it means to possess it. Money isn't currency anymore, it's a set of steps or procedures that you need to perform to accomplish things. This might include getting others to do things that end up transferring money to you. It's a communal illusion. Pay the rent, buy groceries on the one hand, teach a class or grade some papers on the other. You have little to do with currency. Mostly you're performing acts that are represented in various computer systems that talk to each other over networks."

"Potential money."

"What do you mean?"

"Not the potential of getting money, but money as a kind of potential. A power to act."

"Sort of. I mean, that money is the potential itself. It is the set of actions that you are able to take. If the computer system says you don't have any, then the bank won't honor the paper and the company that gave you the plastic will stop supporting it."

"Money is potential. It is step-taking procedures."

"We think of it as our money somehow. We earned it and all that. The procedures for earning and getting paid are part of the process. The money isn't really ours though. There are all these third parties involved. Governments, financial institutions, shop keepers, and employers. Tons of people who have ideas and beliefs that make the circulation of these digital units into a real power, enabling all kinds of action."

"Ah, the engineer *has* become a philosopher, I guess."

"No. Better. Engineering makes the ideas real. I'm not just philosophizing about how money works, I'm not wondering about it or intuiting it. This isn't just a thought experiment. I'm making it happen with the software I write."

"I see, this isn't a hypothetical. You are describing actual systems that behave this way."

"That's right. You go to the bank and give them your account number. They enter it into the terminal and see how much 'money' you have represented in the form of a simple number. We have brilliantly figured out how to affix a specific quantity to every action we take or procedure we perform."

"Ah, I see. You want to ride a bicycle around town for an hour, that's 5. You want to listen to a symphony over and over again in your apartment, that's 19."

"Exactly. It takes software to do this. Transaction purity must be implemented. It isn't just an idea or notion that philosophers kick around. Electrical circuits are required. Low level operations that safely ensure the money won't move from one place to another until the proper conditions have been met. This isn't theory, someone had to write the code to make it happen, and not just the code, the circuit boards and the memory modules had to be fashioned and fabricated."

The engineer was a reductionist or claimed he was. We had clashed many times over this, and I knew that somewhere in this notion there was a closeted assertion that everything was -ultimately- math. Although his rant seemed to be about money as potential, he may have been translating what he really thought into a superstructural notion. I suspected that the real point of his argument was to show the quantitative uniformity that lay beneath this procedural notion of money. I made this point to him.

"Of course. It's all math," he responded. "This is how math happens. When the ball falls to the earth, the relationship is the math, but there is still the problem of realizing the mathematical."

"It isn't just that the explanations can be reduced to mathematical formulas, but the actual occurrence of events: the ball is an object the existence of which is purely mathematical. The procedures performed are just math. Is that it?"

"Yes, exactly. I'm not saying that listening to the symphony over and over reduces to 19. I'm saying that this reduction of the act to money and the reduction of money to pure quantity is possible because of the more rudimentary mathematical nature of existence. The ball is a circumference, the symphony a frequency or set of them."

"If I throw the ball at you and hit you in the nose, the pain is math? Your screams just frequency?"

"Absolutely. The quality of experience is just math."

"There's a thinking thing, but it ain't me."

Neither of us were ever able to explain how exactly it came about that this conversation resulted in a panic attack. The engineer was prone to them, and he should not have been smoking pot. The effects of cannabis make some people nervous. Combine that with the existential dread that naturally accompanied his reduction of the world to a set of mathematical relationships, and something there must have triggered his reaction. He told me later that under most circumstances, his panic attacks would require professional intervention. He was seeing a psychiatrist and took meds for his anxiety. He had become something of an expert in the effects these pharmaceuticals had on his mood. The dosage had to be constantly varied and experimented with. A full-on panic attack would normally require immediate attention involving the use of meds.

He quietly broke into our exchange to let me know what was going on. I didn't have any experience with such things, so I couldn't grasp what needed to be done or how serious it was. I asked him what was happening that triggered this state of mind? The music? The pot? The conversation? Did we need to go to the emergency room?

He struggled to focus on the dissemblance that fell out of the story he had been telling about money and ultimately about the mathematization of all things. We had gotten distracted and wandered off on what was now a tangent but had recently been our main point of discussion. He seemed to be trying to even himself out by returning to it, so I followed his lead.

"Isn't it possible that mathematics is just a precise language that makes it possible to describe all sorts of events purely in terms of their relationships?"

He refocused on my question. His breathing became steadier. He acknowledged that mathematics was often thought of as a precise language, but just as words refer to things, mathematical terms and formulas can refer to even more precise things and highly detailed relationships that exist between them.

"Words might not refer to things, though. They might be like money and just be social practices codified through repetition. Words can function as shorthand for much larger events and entities that are part of common experience. When that happens, we ignore much of the nuance that might otherwise be found in them. When most people talk about their experiences, for example, they can't recreate the vividness of the actual experience."

"Sure sure. But words can't work for everything. Math does."

"Is that true because of your abilities and not some characteristic of the world? To the poet, words can work wonders. The crucial bit is not what we say but how much is left out of what we say. Shadows reveal the light. You think math precise, and that it's good at falling balls and travelling sound, but it loses its advantage when the ball hits you or when trying to figure out what the screams of pain mean. Substance doesn't reduce to anything even if it can be attributed in many ways, one of which might be mathematical."

At that point, he had lost interest. The conversation was not the point anymore. He had managed to overcome his panic attack and it dumbfounded him. "This never happens," he said. "I can't understand how we could talk our way out of this."

"I didn't talk my way out of anything. You did. You were the one having the panic attack."

"It isn't possible. I always need medication to get out of these, but my heartbeat is back to normal. I don't feel like I need to get up and run out of here. I just can't see how this could happen. How did you do it?"

"I don't know anything about it," I insisted. "I've never had a panic attack and don't have any experience with people who do, other than you. This is the first time I've ever been around someone who was having one. This has to have been all you."

"You were speaking so calmly though. It was so easy to focus. You see, this is the point I want to capture with Opus One. There is a way of life that is a cure for anxiety."

The bar is split in half at the waitress station. The cash register belongs to the bar tender on the front side and the back side does stocking and looks after the cleaning station for the glasses. At the front, the bar curved around to the wall where the flip top was located. The back of the bar was open and there was easy access to the kitchen and to the door down into the basement. When it was crowded, people might lean on the flip top at the front or clutter around the back opening. That was how she gauged the busyness. When there was nowhere to sit at the bar and no tables, there would sometimes be a patron or two standing by the open side of the bar and blocking the way to the kitchen. It was a violation of code for them to stand there, but no one ever told them they couldn't. The kitchen workers and bartenders would just squeeze through.

This Tuesday night she was on back bar. It was quiet so there was plenty of room and not too much heavy lifting or washing to be done. She liked going downstairs to switch out the kegs or get some more whiskey, vodka, or whatever they were running low on. It was quiet down there but not so quiet that you felt alone. The building was aging, and you could hear the footsteps and murmurs of talking and music through the ceiling. It was always a good time to have a cigarette and look around at all the eye candy. In the little office, there were postcards from past and present employees pinned to a corkboard alongside notes about what needed to be done or taken care of in the days or weeks ahead. In the stock areas all the bottles were lined up in groups and the dry goods for the kitchen were shelved and ready as needed. There was the pit area with the hoses leading up the wall and into the ceiling. She liked the cluster of kegs and the sounds they would make as the taps were opened on the bar above. Because she was on backbar tonight, she didn't have to worry about the till and closing out the register.

The front bar tender this Tuesday was an older woman with a couple of teenage kids. She was ABD in English with no private sector prospects. She had been unable to find any work as a professor while she was working on her dissertation and was unable to finish it without the motivation of a job, so she moved to a little house in Tecumseh and tended bar full time. She had both day and night shifts and would constantly talk as though her life were still deeply entangled in academic problems and concerns. The memories were aging and there was nothing in her life going on now that connected her to those things. The librarian didn't think the older woman was the kind of person she would ordinarily get along with. She talked so much and was so authoritative about everything. Given her life history, where did she get all this confidence? She had abundant advice about how to do things and took an active interest in the librarian's first steps in her program. She generalized everything. What she did was what the other should do and what the other should do everyone should do. She implied that all programs and departments were the same, that all people would have the same experience of academic life that she had, and that anyone who was both a bartender and a graduate student must be and think exactly like she did back when she was a student. This, of course, pissed-off the librarian. It wound her up and made her want to launch into the other woman almost every time she opened her mouth. She didn't. She exorcised her biting criticism on the object of the other woman's scorn instead and she established fellow feeling while trying to be supportive. She knew all along that this was a way of hiding her hostility, but she didn't want to stoop to bitterness in kind. This is one way that it might ruin people, she thought, and it may serve them both to reserve judgment until she sees how it all turns out. The experience of every academic could not be the same. There are too many different departments and programs, not all of them are trying to acquire some useless set of expert pedigrees. Some are out to become professionals. There was a world of difference between someone in graduate school to learn a specific set of skills for which there was a robust job market both in and outside of academia and people who studied something esoteric for the sake of professing it. She knew this even if the blowhard front bartender didn't have a clue. On her better days, it was enough to know it and she didn't have to pile on and make the older women feel even shittier about it than she already did.

The librarian loved expertise. She admired people who knew what they were doing. That's exactly how she thought about it. Expertise was know-how, it was a practical skill like knowing how to fix a car, a creaking door, or a leaky faucet. Both her mother and her stepfather were crafty people, they knew how to do things. Growing up with their influence was the way she came to understand experts. Not as someone who could talk and talk and talk about some minimally interesting little corner of the world that only a few hundred people on the entire planet gave a damn about. What were they really experts at? Self-promotion? Winning arguments and being nasty about it? Preparing a syllabus? Of course, that's not how they would describe themselves. They thought whatever it was that was the subject of their study was the most important thing in the world and that it somehow bathed them in a glow that blessed every other aspect of their lives. It meant their judgment and insight was correct no matter where it was focused. They thought they were experts at insight and observation because they were students of interpretation and methods of reading or studying books written by others. Every one of these people that she met convinced her more and more that they were really experts at a form of self-delusion, they had convinced themselves and their colleagues that they were the world's thought leaders, and that their observations were powerful enough to cut through the bullshit and see the heart of things. What they really saw were ideas that were just the shadows of real things. Insight and observation didn't amount to mapping ideas onto the world around you, forcing them to fit if they didn't line up on their own, and considering yourself immune to seduction or fraud because the ideas were above the fray where those sorts of things happened. No, it was more about seeing people's desires and their motives, what they wanted beneath all the polite talk and bluster. It was about seeing people in terms of what they felt and what they wanted. Most importantly, it meant understanding what they were looking for.

This is why she thought that librarian and bartender were so intricately connected. Her expertise was in sizing people up and figuring out what they were really looking for. That meant what they were trying to get or what they felt and desired even if they didn't know that was what they were feeling, desiring, or trying to get. She saw her job at the bar as being an authority figure in the lives of the lost, and in charge of catering to the wants and needs of the people who sat in front of her. She made sure they all had water to go with whatever alcoholic drink they were sipping, and urged them to drink it too, making sure to let them know that if they didn't, they would regret it in the morning. It wasn't just about that either, it was about figuring out what they were doing and why they were in the bar in the first place. Were they getting a drink before going to a movie? Were they stopping in after something else or were they camped out for the night? Was it a single guy just trying to pass the time or a couple on a date? These were important things to identify as soon as possible. They dictated the kind of service the people would want. Are they in a hurry? Find out what they want and bring it to them right away. Are they lingering? Give them water and chat them up a bit to make them feel comfortable before getting their drink order. Let them know that the kitchen is about to close, and they should get their food order in as soon as possible. This was the kind of insight that mattered. It really mattered.

You always could tell immediately whether you had gotten it right. That was the best part. The reactions of the people when you tried to anticipate their needs. They would be sure to let you know whether you had missed the mark. That immediate feedback, positive or negative, was intensely gratifying. Once it was clear that the relationship was focused like that around the server providing the desired service, everything became simpler. The people would either accept what they were offered, or they would correct you. She didn't have to guess whether that was it or not. She didn't have to read everything that was ever written about whatever experience or act just occurred to find out if this was the right way to go. She didn't need to work it out with colleagues or have her notions reviewed by peers. The direct relationship with the recipient provided immediate confirmation of its accuracy. She didn't need to wonder about her expertise, she didn't need to worry about whether she was faking it or pretending to be good at something she wasn't. The proof was right there, in the act of serving it, and in the dollars in tips she would count out at the end of the night. She knew her limitations as a librarian not because some teacher had pointed them out to her, but because she worked in the library and knew that there were things she couldn't do and questions she couldn't answer. Because she knew she had failed to help this or that patron with whatever it was they were looking for, she knew she needed to learn more. There was no wondering about it. Bartender and librarian were the same like that.

The mixture of people like the front bartender and herself was the most distressing part of this new life. In the library science program, many of the students were looking to acquire the skills and experience to have professional lives as librarians, but some were there to become library scientists, academic keepers of the information and the means for meting out credentials. It was this mixture that was causing all her stress, and she was learning this while spending more time with the people on her special project. They were mostly like her, master's degree candidates who wanted to go work somewhere. There were some, though, who were already expressing an interest in getting their doctorate. The only reason to do that would be to enter the academic side of it. To become like their professors who, it seemed, no longer worked in libraries but spent their time talking and thinking about how those libraries functioned in the society, how they were being used and what that use said about the civilization that funded it. She was fascinated by this kind of talk, but she was quite sure that it was different from the everyday goings on at the library and the concerns of the staff.

Tonight, as it turns out, there wasn't much going on at the backbar. A couple of regulars who were drinking and making occasional quips about some random topic they felt didn't require any explanation. These were the ones she would play with. Wind them up a bit by making fun of their insight or the things they were making insights about, being contrarian or being edgy as the situation required. Single men who come as regulars to a bar like this appreciated this kind of banter. A few couples had been sitting at her bar during the night too. They were completely different. They were into their own thing and didn't want any outside help. They were perfectly capable of winding each other up without it. They just wanted her to bring the drinks and take their order. A typical Tuesday.

Later on in the evening, a couple of guys came in together and sat at the front bar. They didn't look around much, so they had probably been there before, but she hadn't seen them. Nice faces and chiseled jaws. One of them had amazing eyes. There was something about the other one's mouth that made her think he might be trouble. It was a kind of smirk that brought out a glint in his eyes as he spoke to the front bartender. She thought maybe he was all about sex and pursuit. She could usually tell right away. He wasn't quite as good looking as the other one, but the other one didn't have as much game. It was clear to her. Those amazing eyes were looking at something and they were innocent of whatever it was that was visible in the other one's mouth. Because they came in together and were obviously friends, she couldn't help but blur them together. She saw the mouth and the eyes moving onto one face and emitting a single fantastic man. A mouth like that with eyes like those would be perfect, she almost thought. The look in his eyes makes that mouth into a body part and brought her to all kinds of ideas about how such a body might move. How it might move her. When those other eyes got mixed up into it, then the mouth changed. It remained just as confidently knowing as it was on the first guy's face, but it became spirit and elusive when brought together with whatever it was that those eyes were seeing.

She knew deep down that the first guy would know her exactly as she is if he would ever bother to look. He would see what she has done and what she likes to do and have done to her. That smile might make her feel naked and show that he wasn't fooled by her pretense that it didn't. The second guy would never see her that way. He would only see an angelic surface. Not because there was no depth to his vision, but because eyes like that idealize everything they come across. The first guy would know her desires and what she really wanted, but the second one would think those are just fleeting feelings that didn't reflect her true self. Where the first saw necessity, the second saw only contingency. She imagined he would think her a goddess set on high while the other would know all the dirty little secrets she hid beneath her clothes. She thought her way far enough down this path to both experience shame and tear herself away from it by claiming herself as a right. Be bold about it.

Once she got past her initial impressions, she found that she couldn't ignore them. Like those theatre masks, one brought her up and the other brought her down, it was like a seesaw. She liked it. Usually, the customers were interesting up to a point and then she would have them pegged and move on, not needing to give them any more thought. These two were different, her eyes kept going back to them. She found herself moving increasingly closer to the waitress station to try and pick up on what they were saying. When they talked to each other, she couldn't make out anything, but that was when they looked the most interesting. They didn't care who else was in the bar and were totally focused on whatever it was they were talking about. The one with the mouth was animated. He made gestures and occasionally would laugh a little loudly. He seemed to do a lot of the talking. The other one must have been familiar with all his friend's ways because he was never put off by any of his antics or theatrics. He would smile sometimes and even laugh now and again, but he was deliberate and firm in whatever it was that he said that set off his friend. She couldn't imagine what they were talking about, but assumed it was something related to whatever area they were studying. It wasn't politics. That was clear because the front bartender wasn't reacting as she usually did when her customers were talking politics. The people sitting closer to them on that side of the bar weren't paying any attention either. These details suggested that they were not talking about anything that was of interest to anyone else.

She didn't get the sense that they were gay, but she noted that they never once showed any signs typical of heterosexual men their age when they are in bars where there are women around. She had been looking around to see who was in the place and what they were doing. There were a couple of women sitting at one of the tables that most of the other guys had noticed and one of the waitresses was pretty cute and attracted an occasional look from some of the guys, but you would never know any of this from the way these guys were acting. They were only interested in their conversation. The one with the eyes, okay that made sense. He was probably like that all the time, but the one with the mouth? Not a chance. That guy should not be this disinterested, he was a dog if ever she saw one. The fact was that neither of them had looked over at her even once. Not the whole time they were there, and men always noticed her. She didn't have any delusions about being the most beautiful woman in the world or anything, but men noticed her even if they didn't know exactly why they were noticing. She thought that maybe there was something about her that sunk in subconsciously or that guys were just wired that way and couldn't help it. These guys though, they didn't seem to notice or were able to notice without her noticing. Ha. That would be the day. There wasn't a man alive who could pull that off. She always noticed. Even when they did their best to hide it, she saw.

She couldn't get close enough to find out what they were talking about, not when they were talking to each other. Whatever it was, though, it got the front bartender to tell them her story when they finally talked to her. The librarian distinctly heard her relay all the familiar details about almost getting her doctorate and then about not being able to find work. She heard her say something or other about the job market and how tough it is. The guys nodded, but the contributions were obviously tangents to whatever they were talking about. Probably the front bartender had gathered from their talk that they were affiliated with the university somehow and she added her two cents. The same two cents she had to add to every conversation that might be academic adjacent. Whatever that was in this case didn't seem relevant to what they were talking about, so they politely responded and went back to what they were doing. She was so clueless; these guys are probably ten years younger than she is and they are way out of her league. This thought made the librarian smirk and then she caught herself smirking and wondered if her eyes gleamed when she smirked in the way the guy with the mouth did. She had to look over at them again to remind herself that they were two different people.

There was something about the candor and the gestures. There was something different about them. She thought maybe they were intellectuals. Not pseudo, but truly so. Something in their demeanor. They were genuinely interested in whatever it was they were discussing, and they didn't want an audience. They didn't seem to think what they were doing or saying would impress anyone or even be interesting to them. They weren't performing in the way some people who had conversations in the bar do, as though they wanted the people around them to know what they were talking about. Even the theatrics she saw in the one guy wouldn't have caught anyone else's attention if they weren't already studying him. Whatever it was that they were discussing, she didn't think they were pretending to be self-important or overly confident in their role as experts in something or other. They were talking as if they were truly students of what they were trying to figure out and trying to wrangle together something that each of them understood differently. She imagined they were genuinely concerned that this difference might mean they had misunderstood each other and that they needed to keep at it until they could catch a glimpse of what they were missing. They both would smile and laugh as though they kept missing it, kept losing touch with it as it slipped away. Could these be the kind of people everyone said you would find now and again in a town like this and at a bar like this? Was this what honest inquiry looked like? Her imagination was taking over.

When they left, she was not disappointed to see them go. Her thoughts had been idle, there was no plan underneath them. That part of herself that she was hiding from her fellow students, she was also trying to hide from herself. This was not the right time for it. As the bar was starting to empty out, the librarian asked the front bartender what those two guys sitting at her bar for so long were talking about.

"Automation?" she said.

"Automation?"

"Well, something like that. It started with one of them wondering what kind of a twisted person would want to be a professor and then somehow that became something about math and whether it makes sense to say everything is just math. It was about money as the power to do things. I'm not sure how it was all connected. They were all over the place."

"Money and automation? You mean, like robots?"

"Not exactly. I wasn't following it all. Someone had a theory, not either of them, but someone else. The theory involved money as the ability to do things, and then some actions could be automated somehow so that machines could perform them. This was still a kind of money though. Like capital, I guess."

"They seemed pretty animated."

"Oh, they were. They were getting really into it. Money was the opposite of math. That's what one of them was saying. The human capacity to act was irreducible. Not because it was human, but because actions were somehow basic, and money was just something that could be added on top of that. I've read stuff like that before. Organized structures do things and money is like a placeholder. I don't know. One of them said at some point that there was continuity between what people could do and what could be done with automation. That's possible because organization surfaces in actions and is the reason action happens in the first place. The medium is the message and all that. Like gravity or a ratio between mass and acceleration. It wasn't that the ratio came first, falling did. Bar talk. They were probably full of shit."

"Sounds like it."

"At least they weren't talking about sports."

"Yeah, and they never really looked around much. Weren't checking anybody out."

"I've seen them in here before. They probably know the rules. That isn't allowed at the Del."

The front bartender was referring to the unwritten rule that there was no tolerance for meat market behavior at the Del Rio. It was a chase and gawk free zone, at least for the men. She had seen the doorkeeper intervene on a Saturday night before, telling some guy to leave a woman alone or stop talking to someone who didn't seem like she wanted to be bothered. Go somewhere else if you're going to do that kind of thing, pal. Of course, that's it. They must've known that.

"Are they at the University?"

"One of them is, the one who was on the left. Not the other guy, the loose cannon. He might work at the bindery with that guy who comes in all the time. You're pretty curious about them? What's up?"

"Nothing. I just noticed them talking. Thought they were unusual and wondered what their story was. I saw you talking to them. I thought maybe you knew them."

"I've seen them before, but that was the first time talking to them, I think."

"Why do you think he was a loose cannon then?"

"I don't know, something about his face maybe. The way he talked. Like he wasn't playing by the same rules. Not much committed to anything. The other one seemed more grounded."

As she drove home that night, she reassured herself that nothing had changed. She was right where she was before and wasn't going anywhere with anybody. That wasn't why she came here, and it wasn't something she had time for. Just because some random guys reminded her for a minute that she had a body, it didn't mean that anything in the plan had changed. Her focus had to remain right where it was. It was time to wash off the smell of smoke and go to sleep so she could get up and go to class tomorrow.

The *Jobs for Philosophers* had arrived. Perfect timing, just as I was buried in normal course work and the research project. The job market must be addressed. Like most of my colleagues, I didn't have to produce a CV since I have maintained a ready to go version since I first went on the market. Cover letters were oriented to specific job types and Mail Merge templates in place enabled customization. The remaining work amounted to going through the publication, identifying positions that seemed like a fit, and letting the admin at the University of Illinois know what to send and where. The selection process amounts to reading advertisements in a hunt for the right areas of expertise and competence. The highlighter loved any job that listed 19th and 20th Century Continental Philosophy as its area of expertise and Ethics & Social Philosophy as its area of competence. Anything else was a stretch, but I usually erred on the side of too many rather than too few.

The question as to who is and who is not a philosopher entails a question concerning expertise. Who is authorized to speak on behalf of Aristotle? Who is authorized to speak up against him?

My efforts amount to sophisticated lies. It is almost universally false to claim 19th and 20th Century Continental Philosophy as an area of expertise. I had never met anyone on the job market who could be described that way. More experienced professors who could almost swing it already had good jobs and weren't likely looking for something as an assistant professor at a small school in central Pennsylvania or Eastern Washington. I wasn't the only liar. The system demanded it. Why did these little schools think they could expect to find for $30,000 a year someone who was an expert across an entire large domain of philosophical research? We had all come to a set of agreed upon standards and they allowed the use of this kind of hyperbole to describe the expectations of a hiring committee. If I were in a position to publish regularly within an area, even if my publications only spanned a narrow sliver of material there, it would be acceptable to claim its full breadth as my area of expertise. That is what all our expertise amounted to. The fact that I was writing and publishing on Heidegger and familiar with his pre- and post- entanglements, like Hegel and Sartre, meant that I could legitimately represent myself this way.

Competence had an equally blurry definition. If I had a few developed syllabi in the area, then I could claim competence. Since I could teach a course to advanced undergraduates in topics related to Ethics and Social Philosophy, I could confidently apply without fear of having the lie discovered should I get to the interview stages in the process. Even if my ideas were pedestrian and my range of understanding limited, the fact that I could put together a syllabus and had done so before meant I had earned the attribution of competence. We weren't expert philosophers, just able to pass peer review and publish. We weren't even competent philosophers, just those who could guide the less experienced through its intellectual history.

The evaluation process would sort it all out. Expertise worked like that anyway. They said they wanted an expert in one thing, but they probably had more specific but unstated ideas about who exactly they were looking for. Half the jobs that claimed an AoE in Continental Philosophy were really looking for someone specific. They aren't going to advertise for a Hegel scholar who doesn't know anything about what happened since, even if that does turn out to be exactly what they wanted. They could be convinced that what they really wanted was someone who would build a philosophy of literature program with special concern for existentialism. Because they didn't know the area, they needed someone who was expert in it where that expertise might include being able to compose a more detailed job description. This skill would no longer be required once the candidate was hired, so they would phrase it according to the accepted standards for how wide a net they wished to cast and leave it to the better candidates to convince them that their approach was what the department really needed. Because applicants were generally aware of how dismal the prospects were, most would cast an equally wide net to do their best to fake their way past the process of elimination by fabricating that angle. The point was to stand out enough in the mass submission phase so that you could get a chance to interview at the Eastern Division conference or on campus afterward.

By their rules, I could reasonably claim expertise in the work of the later Heidegger and deconstruction, but that was too specific and, truth be told, no university that would hire someone like that would consider hiring them fresh from the University of Illinois. To make matters worse, no one who would hire anyone from the University of Illinois would want someone claiming expertise in the later Heidegger and deconstruction. My origin story would need to be more broadly spun. What else then should I claim as expertise? What counted as expertise? Honest consideration of the philosophical issues and problems was not the right way to arrive at an answer to these questions. Having a set of detailed beliefs and formulated opinions was not going to cut it, not even if you could cite the work chapter and verse. No, what was required was peer review. You had to be publishing and your publications must have been reviewed by admitted experts granting you the proper pedigree. I thought I understood Nietzsche as well as anyone I had ever met, and yet on ethical grounds had never written anything for publication. Furthermore, the readings and interpretations that I had worked out were so non-standard that no one who was publishing scholarship on his work would champion my depth of understanding or knowledge. Expertise was a community endowed set of standards. It wasn't about the detailed case you might be able to make were you to get past the first phase. What mattered was line items on the CV that captured your standing alongside your peers: conference delivery, journal publications, and special colloquia. At best, you could add some further explanation through what your teachers were willing to write and say about you in recommendations and informal referrals.

My sense of doom was increasing as I was flipping through the pages of the *Jobs for Philosophers*. Even with 20 or 30 jobs that clearly fit within my area, there would be little chance of success. I would go through the motions. In the spring I might have better luck with the advertisements aiming at temporary positions. My best bet was to get another temporary job, garner favor with the folks at that school, and then try to convert my temporary but renewable position into a permanent one. The bottom line was that without a powerful long-term vision to excite the hiring committee, I wasn't going to get a job based on either expertise or competence. If I were going to get a position, it would be luck and contingency. That's how the farmer got his job in Ohio. That's how many of the people I went to graduate school with found their positions. I needed a temporary job at a place where they would eventually have the budget to make the position permanent and where they would have liked my temporary work enough to give it to me. I hate it when Wolfe is right.

Fair enough, it is questionable whether I have anything like this standardized expertise so it is fair that I wouldn't get a job based on the illusion of it. The whole dynamic is so puzzling. It isn't just that philosophy is a discipline, but there are further categorized areas within it and candidates wishing to become professional philosophers needed to orient themselves according to those areas. Proof would come in the form of current knowledge. Publishing was driven by this. The virtuous candidate knows the issues and the arguments that are being made, they might be able to make arguments to extend or reinvent those issues, but it might be too soon to tell. The committees will evaluate the candidate's future contributions based on their resume's current state and the codes that have been stitched into the documents it contains. They don't expect a junior candidate to be doing earthshattering work just yet, but there should be a twinkling star in there, something that shows they have potential and that one day it will become actual. The expert candidate will grow into the tenure-ready contributor who is an upstanding member of the community alongside the peers whose marks had led the way.

It isn't possible to bluff your way into this. You can't fake the enthusiasm for the standards and criteria just to get a position where you might subsequently develop compliance with them. You must have them up front and you must be reasonably sincere in your avowal. It needed to come across in the work you were doing, in the writing sample you provided, in the recommendations, the teaching evaluations, and the cover letter. If you couldn't show it, you would never get to the next stage. That meant that you had to believe in academia as the place where your expertise belongs. If you didn't or if you had legitimate questions about it, you were sunk.

Philosophy professors don't produce anything, and they don't train people to produce anything other than —arguably— sound arguments. The value of producing sound arguments is left to the students who enroll in the courses, to the deans who decide how much funding to allocate to the department, or to the employers who think it is a good idea to hire people who make them. That is the social function of academic philosophy. Other than that, it is a closed loop whose only purpose is to produce more philosophy professors who perpetuate the practice of sound argumentation. I am not horrified by the suggestion that philosophy no longer has a place in the modern-day university. Sound argumentation can be taken over by teachers of composition or some other area where students must make a case for something.

In general, liberal arts education —where the focus of study is cultivating a greater sense of the human condition— might be best evicted from a university focusing on vocational training and preparing students for careers. If students must pay for their education, why should they pay for something that doesn't contribute to their job training? Many give arguments in response, but even if those arguments are valid, why should this training be part of a university attended only when they are in their late teens or early twenties? We would be better off if the university were left to vocational training and then funded by those private interests with a professional concern for procuring an ongoing supply of engineers and business workers. The more general-purpose educational interests, like stimulating an awareness of the human condition and its history, might be better served by some other kind of organization or institution. If the current structure encourages people to study the liberal arts only long enough to get their degree and then forget it all once they have entered a profession, maybe the current structure should be abandoned? Instead, the civilization could fashion a new organization aimed at learning and education that is part of a person's whole life. Something that we don't just attend for a few years when we are young adults, but something like the family or the church. Those who would argue that it matters too much to be eliminated might be convinced that this is why it should be removed from the academic curriculum and integrated into a life-long association.

"Finally, however —of what concern to us is the existence of the state, the promotion of universities, when what matters above all is the existence of philosophy on earth! or —to leave absolutely no doubt as to what I think— if it is so unspeakably more vital that a philosopher should appear on earth than that a state or university should continue to exist."

I didn't see anything in the *Jobs for Philosophers* that advocated or suggested this approach. There were no special programs or units, no residential college or utopian learning center. Its absence added to my sense of doom. Not only was I starting to think that it would be nearly impossible to find a job based on expertise, but I was beginning to visualize the cold reality of getting a job that didn't leave time to continue developing that expertise or anything that might resemble it. What would I do? Playing around with computers, can that be turned into professional skills? It is deeply depressing that such technics would have firmer footing in this world than learning and inquiry. Self-training might be easy enough, but it would take time. Full time. Because there was no general institution for ongoing study and inquiry into the human condition (and its history), my current state would likely fade and fall into disrepair. I would forget things that I had come to know, and I wouldn't be able to learn anything new or keep up with the trends and the fashion. I had been attracted to academia because it seemed to offer a life filled with learning and study and I knew of no other way to get enough time to do all of that.

This was what was at stake. If I couldn't find a job for next year, I wouldn't be able to look for answers to the questions that occupied me.

The society would have spoken, they do not need my help on those questions and would prefer that I applied myself elsewhere. I would have to think about only those things that they were willing to pay me to think about. My freedom to think was integral to my academic pursuits and way of life. What was there beyond that but servitude and drudgery? On the other hand, nothing I had come across in or out of graduate school suggested there was anything like a freedom to think and question as you will in that world either. Academics, as it turned out, didn't have it and non-academics didn't have it either. Only a few lottery winners might get it. As I sat circling jobs in the APA publication, the lightning strike of realization was that I had completely misjudged academic life. I thought of it as the facilitator of this spontaneity of thought, but that wasn't the case. If I couldn't muster the love for the discipline as it was practiced among the community, then I couldn't gain access to it. Loving the discipline meant loving it as it is warts and all, and that was an impossible constraint. It would dim my aim and abate my passion. Either way, the limitations were surfacing. Get a job and think as a member of the profession is meant to think and practice the forms of scholarship requiring peer review and yielding tenure in the community. If you can't do that, then get a job like every other adult in this world must do, regardless of your privileged passion against it. Either or. I was fucked. Sadly, Kierkegaard wasn't in my area of expertise.

Wolfe decided we needed a refresher course on the social contract. He said it was because I was repeatedly breaking it. Interrupting my work, he stood over my shoulder and read aloud:

> Nature (the art whereby God hath made and governes the world) is by the art of man, as in many other things, so in this also imitated, that it can make an Artificial Animal. For seeing life is but a motion of Limbs, the beginning whereof is in some principall part within; why may we not say, that all Automata (Engines that move themselves by springs and wheeles as doth a watch) have an artificiall life? For what is the Heart, but a Spring; and the Nerves, but so many Strings; and the Joynts, but so many Wheeles, giving motion to the whole Body, such as was intended by the Artificer? Art goes yet further, imitating that Rationall and most excellent worke of Nature, Man. For by Art is created that great LEVIATHAN called a COMMON-WEALTH, or STATE, (in latine CIVITAS) which is but an Artificiall Man; though of greater stature and strength than the Naturall, for whose protection and defence it was intended;

and in which, the Soveraignty is an Artificiall Soul, as giving life and motion to the whole body; The Magistrates, and other Officers of Judicature and Execution, artificiall Joynts; Reward and Punishment (by which fastened to the seat of the Soveraignty, every joynt and member is moved to performe his duty) are the Nerves, that do the same in the Body Naturall; The Wealth and Riches of all the particular members, are the Strength; Salus Populi (the Peoples Safety) its Businesse; Counsellors, by whom all things needfull for it to know, are suggested unto it, are the Memory; Equity and Lawes, an artificiall Reason and Will; Concord, Health; Sedition, Sicknesse; and Civill War, Death. Lastly, the Pacts and Covenants, by which the parts of this Body Politique were at first made, set together, and united, resemble that Fiat, or the Let Us Make Man, pronounced by God in the Creation.

I waited patiently until he finished, then asked as always, "What is your point?"

"Should I read it again?" Using my own rhetorical trick, he waits for a response. Elbows on the desk, leaning my face into my hands and rubbing my forehead, I peel off in reverie. He must think his past request and my response are a contract and in making it we have let loose an artificial person whose interests he now wishes to protect. What is more, he thinks this person is suffering the imminent threat of death. He would have it that our work is a civil war bombarding the small apartment where I am an occupying army colonizing the desk. My desk. The one that has my computer on it. He wanted me to move the second computer somewhere else so that he could use it when I'm busy with the other one. Again, my computer. The one I was building and learning to program as a side project. "Why don't you get your own computer?" I had asked him. "Isn't it enough that I let you stay here rent free? You're gainfully employed, what are you doing with your money? If your work is so important to you, maybe you could use some of your money to buy a computer." That was not the conversation he wanted to have, and he defended himself by ignoring me. Since I had agreed to let him live with me, that obviously expanded to an equal set of rights of use and access. This might not have been written somewhere, but that was beside the point since in spirit it was nevertheless a firm contract become golem with feelings and interests. He could not be expected to spend his hard-earned money on things that I was able to provide him free of charge. This would be wasteful. The computer was the primary object of contention, but music selection, the provisioning of snacks, and the right to pace were likewise relevant. I was spending too much time at home doing my work and this was creating conditions of scarcity. Even when there wasn't direct contention over resources, control over the environment and atmosphere created conflict. It was an injustice to think it my apartment after having made the agreement.

"Well, should I read it again?"

"Please don't. Is there any way you might be able to paraphrase your point for those of us in the cheap seats?"

"Our agreement has created an artificial person, an intelligence of some kind, and that intelligence has interests and objectives. Each of us have agreed to play a part in that person and carry out functions that make up its cognitive capabilities. Your actions are an illness and that puts it into a stressful state. I'm considering this a threat upon its life."

"I don't recall the exact terms of the contract. I do recall saying that you could stay here, and you are welcome to do so. I'm just trying to get some work done, I'm not trying to assert a sovereign right."

"You may not recall the agreement, but there is one. I thought you meant it. Actions have consequences, and you are not living up to your responsibilities."

"Hobbes is pointing to the clarity of purpose in such agreements. You think our agreement was clear, but not to me. It seems we don't share a common understanding of the precise meaning involved in the words 'you can stay with me.' Am I supposed to take your word for it when it comes to all the implied conditions in our arrangement?"

"Yes."

"I need to dig out Spinoza and just claim that the agreement rests upon a common utility and when that is gone, we are each free to withdraw consent."

"Cite whoever you like. It still means a state of war and you lose all the advantages of our commonwealth."

"What advantages am I getting from this exactly?"

"Having someone who helps run the household isn't valuable to you? What about helping a friend in need, do you consider that an advantage?"

"It's a mitzvah? I don't think that's the kind of utility he had in mind. I'm talking about concrete material advantage. It's great that you help out, but I don't see how that is to my material advantage since by living here you add to the household's needs just as much as you contribute to its care."

"This is political violence. The rich get the poor to accept their fate by threatening to withdraw consent unless the poor accept the unjust terms of the social order. The ethical impetus must pre-date the contract and saturate it if it is to be binding."

I stopped thinking in terms of arguments. Wolfe isn't a bad roommate. He cooks sometimes and he is generally tidy. When he cleans, he doesn't just clean his mess, he cleans the whole apartment. He doesn't pay for half the groceries, but he will shop for food if I ask him to. He is probably doing as much as he can, and he doesn't want to be in Ann Arbor so badly that he's okay with being stuck living in unfavorable circumstances. The real problems only happen on the weekends. During the week, he has the apartment to himself when he's home and I am at work. He's usually ready to head out somewhere by the time I get home and that seems to work okay. It was Saturday and Sunday that were causing the friction.

"How about a weekend schedule? I'll clear out during the day, and you leave me here in the evenings. Would that work?"

"Perfect. Thanks. Let's start today. Get up."

Ready to tear my head off one minute, and then casually agreeable the next. Such is life when one lives with creative people. When the tacit agreements are different in the minds of the involved parties, that's when they need to take a step back and reset the expectations or redraw the terms. Spinoza was right about most things so it wouldn't surprise me if he were right about this too. There is no good or evil outside of these agreements, no justice or injustice, so making them work is where all our ethical energy must be spent. The existence of unhappy participants is a sign that the alliance is sick, and we must be constantly prepared to modify the terms of our agreement to keep it healthy. If we could agree that there was much we were taking for granted and that it wasn't a problem until we ran into some situation that was stressing us both out, then we could clear things up by entering into explicit negotiations aimed at an equitable resolution.

Take the case of Socrates. This approach might not replace the need for a trial when a citizen is suspected of corrupting the minds of the youth, but maybe it provided a fictional alternative where Socrates organizes and protests the rules of education in the community mindset. His political action, were it to get a following, would force the involved parties to spell out the terms of the agreement being contested. What are we expected to teach our young people? What corrupts and what properly disciplines their minds? What actions lead to the former and what others lead to the latter? His protests would give notice on his tacit agreement and force greater clarity in what binds the citizens to each other. I don't recall that the rulers of Athens ever made the details of these principles clear prior to his incarceration for violating them. Was the educator supposed to just know or were there clear directives on what counted as corruption and what didn't? Instead of a trial, they would have had negotiations to clearly articulate the terms of the agreement. Teachers must promote the values of the civilization and those values are as follows. Socrates might have disagreed on what those values were and then they would have had to come to an understanding. The whole of the citizenry would have to come together to renew their sense of what those values were and what exactly needed to be taught in schools. They would have had to create a school board to make a city-wide curriculum. Only then, once everyone knew the plan, could they hold individual teachers responsible for violating that code in the lessons they were teaching.

Since Socrates didn't organize and didn't protest, none of this happened. He shouldn't have been put to death for corrupting the minds of Athens' youth, he should have been put to death for failing to criticize the lack of clarity in the social contract, for failing to bring it to the attention of the community, and for proceeding as though he understood the agreement when it had been left vague. As a philosopher, he should have known better. How different the world would be if these failings were deemed capital offenses insofar as they amounted to treason against the integrity of the contract that binds the will of the multitude in a common good.

We only conceive of the civil society as a contract after it has been territorialized by a kind of rational thinking that frames everything in terms of agreements made by pre-existing individuals who aim at fabricating organizational structures. That is why it never occurred to Aristotle or Augustine to think of it this way. They saw the individual as a natural occurrence, no doubt, but it wasn't principally an agreement-oriented agent. Only after Descartes could such a vision of the agent be possible. The pivot of the Cartesian picture, moving the individual thinking thing to the center of the universe and removing any historical or divine organization from its origin story, was necessary for thinking of the agent as possessing the autonomy necessary for entering into such agreements. That was the first premise of Hobbes' natural law. In the post-Freudian world derived from the Spinozan alternative, however, such autonomic individuals are murkier. "Men aren't born civil; they become civil." We are the playthings of our social conditions, and our desires are pressurized and enriched by social relations. These constitute our complexity as cognitive beings through the indirection of those organizations that facilitate our developmental progress. This is what gives depth and breadth to desires and this is what gives us personality and idiosyncrasy. We do not plan the design and then craft the product, rather we run into and through them and then come to see ourselves in their terms. Because these organizations come first, contracts in the Hobbesian form are not a coherent representation of the relationship between individuals. The personalities and roles of individuals are a consequence of those organizations and their movements rather than a precondition to it. There must be families with established dynamics and communities with appropriate divisions and alliances. There must be sexuality and education as generalized institutions and structures for action. Only under these conditions can there be individuated, self-identifying creatures. Possession. The contracts formed by such creatures perfectly represent the inner dynamic of those organizational forms from which they are emitted.

That is why we have a duty to protest and organize when the conditions and terms are not clear. It must flow from the social institution of practices including their integration with a progressive reordering of terms and conditions (agreements). This duty is from and to the community and it carries the ways in which organization fleshes out its meaning in the actions of members. Organization is primordial and the human who perceives a gap in what has been ordered in their actions or their orientations, must in turn begin the process of proposing the required supplement. The perception is the first inkling of it, they need only follow through. That is what Socrates' protest would have been. He would have raised the concern that when educating young people, he could not determine how he is meant to be since the community failed to provide ample structural basis. His protest would be elicited by an existential crisis. By failing to point it out, he lurches forward on his own and with an intent and a will that he shares with no one. The community cannot allow that, and –I'll say it again– he should have known better.

Wolfe should have known this too. We have talked about it before. He reveals his hypocrisy when distancing his concrete life from whatever theoretical commitments he avows in his writing. I hope that I have lived my philosophical commitments by taking a step back into compromise and making a revised agreement when he raises the alarm in his protests. What else could critical reflection look like under conditions of the deconstruction of the subject? Isn't it just more and more deconstruction, always deferring the final form of the agreement? Is there anything else than provisional understanding that limps along until the next moment of confusion surfaces as an argument for the sake of new terms and new conditions? Aren't these new terms and conditions the new organizational practices that must be explicitly acknowledged?

Wolfe kissed the typesetter approximately four seconds after she decided it was time for him to kiss her. Four seconds is the minimum amount of time required for the signals she makes to get to his brain, be interpreted, and then translated back into action. Her means for communicating this to him had been sufficiently elaborate as to suggest both the approach and the outcome. He didn't leap at her or make crazy and unpredictable movements. He slowly leaned close and then paused when his lips were just an inch or two from hers. Since his commitment was out there and exposed for her consideration, she was able to safely complete the act with a slight tilt forward. He wouldn't have been able to describe the mechanics of this if you tried to force it out of him. She wouldn't have been able to do much better. There were rules, they knew them, but they weren't easy to articulate. You would know what to do at the time if you were paying attention. That was the best either of them could do.

Her eyes went soft. Her head might have leaned a little, or maybe not. Definitely the eyes though, and the way she was talking. She stopped enunciating clearly and her speech slowed down. The train of thought might have been broken or maybe it was a deliberate pause. She might have even started to whisper. He didn't know. He felt its effect though. The force of the space was in there too. The whisper, imagined or not, was what brought him closer, as though he were reacting to it, even if he couldn't say for sure that she had truly lowered her voice. They had been talking normally but sitting close. She trailed off or began to whisper and this pulled him closer. Yes, that is definitely how it happened. Maybe.

The bottom line was that there was an agreement. They were both in the situation together joined by a common understanding. It wasn't a decision that he made and then launched into, nor was it something she decided and turned immediately to execution. There was agreement. Movement on the one hand and then a reciprocal movement on the other. They had both acted. It doesn't matter whether what he did was in response to her action, whether it was a reaction, it was movement coming out of an understanding, making them both participants in one and the same act. That understanding inhabited them and what they were doing.

It was so natural, the way that it happened, that both were impressed with the ease the other showed in playing their part. Had they rehearsed it? They might have. During past bad kisses where he leaned in before he was supposed to or leaned too far and without warning, that might have all been practice. There might have been a few times over the years when a kiss had smacked against her lips when she didn't want it; or times when there was no kiss at all when she thought there should have been. These past occurrences resonated with them, causing them to rethink their means and change their approaches. Throughout their lives they had become better at doing it and better at signaling it. He got better at listening and she got better at suggesting, or was it the other way around? He improved the certainty with which he felt the draw and the absence of it. She improved her ability to draw and her ability to only draw when she wanted to. On a cold night, that might be all we mean by rehearsing for a good kiss.

It must be something like this because good kisses do happen. We can jump up and down about the innuendos and horrors that some of this suggest. There are bad kisses, and there is a wide range of what we mean by them, from the slightly awkward to the downright criminal. It may still be that we are humans now and again and it may be that as humans we occasionally hit the mark and fabricate an event that amounts to a good kiss. When this happens, it might be by accident, because the two have stumbled into each other. Luck can make it happen this way, but it isn't always like that. It is possible that there are good kissers, and it may have been the case that both Wolfe and the typesetter were instances of that kind. She knew it wasn't up to her and he knew that it wasn't up to him. They knew that a good kiss was something they were going to have to do together by playing their parts as best they could in the time and space they made between them.

The distance must be bridged and there must be agreement when doing it. Not just agreement over whether it should be done, but there is a contract on how it is to be done. Neither of them would have been able to describe it ahead of time, but they both knew they had just experienced it. What was there between them, became next to nothing in that shared agreement and spit. He leaned and she leaned, she pulled while he pushed, or maybe he pulled and she pushed. The details can vary, but the agreement is inviolable. To say that it was tacit would be to prioritize consciousness above all else and none of us do that even if we say we do. Desire will not always admit to that, so agreement can happen in the skin and on the fingertips. It can even happen at the tip of the tongue, lightly touching and being touched by the tip of another tongue.

Growing up in Michigan, I came to think of November as the worst month. It would rain and even when it didn't it was cloudy and windy. The leaves had all fallen from the trees and it was cold. Below freezing overnight with nothing to look forward to except the coming winter with its snow and gray skies. This month seemed colder than usual. I was writing in the evenings and working until my eyes started to burn or I couldn't sit still any longer. I would pace from one end of the apartment to the other until the back-and-forth motion would convert into a beeline out the door. Walking to the car, starting it, and turning on the defroster. Getting the scraper from the backseat and clearing the windows of the thin film of semi-ice. The progression was all about transition and there was something machinic in it. Pacing is like the rhythm of a motor. Opening the door is like a power switch. Driving downtown and finding a spot on the street. Locking the door. Walking up to and just around the corner then opening the door to the bar. All these actions, so deliberate and precise, they were extensions and worldly transformations of what I had been doing privately in the apartment, the head births and the flights of fancy, it was all a kind of marching rhythm, writing out thoughts giving pause, looking up citations to decorate passageways, the one and the other, the idealized work of the thought architect twists and turns into the concrete work of the driver tasked with traversing the town and entering the bar. Ideas and steering wheels were both ready-to-hand in their different worlds.

This had been going on all week. It was an example of the systematic dismantling: a dismantling of what was systematic and a systematic performance of it. Taking something apart with purpose, I couldn't just put an end to it each night. I had to break from it with this pacing that converted into departure. I had to leave my apartment and go somewhere else, somewhere with people. I didn't want to talk about it, that wasn't the point, I just wanted to get away from the process and its grip. I needed to do it so that I could sleep. I had to go someplace else where it would no longer inhabit me, where it could no longer claim its institution in my cognition, and in the thoughts that emerged with its shadow. The fabricated isolation of the auto-reader, the single reader of one's own work, drives the would-be author forward in response to the question concerning what others might think of it. This act is the single greatest threat to the delusional state in which anyone can function as a traditionally organized literary actor. As long as there is no feedback, the self-image is safe. The drive for feedback, however, has its origin in that same state-of-mind that drives the delusion. We are social animals because the social order lives inside us and pulls things out of us to serve its ends. Protection from delusion through communication constitutes a risk of mutual destruction whereas acceptance and retreat protect the agent from that. Delusion is thus an organizing principle that thwarts entropy. I was not looking for interlocutors, I was looking for escape.

As I walked into the bar and greeted the doorkeeper, I saw an empty stool in the front section of the bar and moved directly to it. As I approached, the bartender was standing right there in front of the chair. She recognized me. I distinctly saw it. In her eyes, in the way she put the coaster on the bar, and the way she served up a glass of water before I asked for it. She recognized me. I searched my brain for something. Had we met before? Did I completely forget some past interaction here? I was fairly sure that we had never spoken, and she didn't look at all familiar. That could only mean that on one of my previous trips she had seen me and may have even thought a little bit about me, enough to where there was something in her mind, in her memory, that made me seem familiar. The feeling had been strong enough that she could not help but show that recognition as I arrived and took my seat. As though she had been hoping that someday I would sit at her bar, and we would have a chance to talk.

This was all too presumptuous, and a doubt immediately clouded my senses as I settled into the seat, all this flashing through my mind rapidly. I sometimes came in with Wolfe. Was he the one she was hoping to meet? She recognized me only by association with the true object of interest. Wolfe was more noticeable than I was. He talked louder, had a friendlier aspect, and made people more immediately comfortable. The probability was that he was the one and I was just experiencing the collateral curiosity of having been with him on a previous visit. That might not have been it at all though. It could have been the pair of us? She might have experienced us as a combined object where our existence had become assembled together in the energy our mutual presence presented. I don't know if Wolfe comes to the bar on his own. If she had seen us together on one of our several visits, she might not even be able to tell us apart.

Whichever explanation there was for the recognition, the certainty of it only grew. We fell to talking immediately and that's not because I am an inherently chatty person when meeting new people. The other patrons at the front bar were all in pairs making me the only single occupant. This made for a natural opportunity between us, and she was headed in that direction right from the start. She told me how she was new to town this fall, having just moved here from Ohio, and was studying in the library science graduate program. She was excited about all the ideas and people she was getting exposed to and told me about digital communication and a special archive project she had been working on with her friends. This did not require much prompting on my end, but I offered casual and mostly complementary opinions in response. I was supportive and tried to give plenty of signs that I wanted to hear more about her insights and experiences. She was both nervous and excited and liked talking about both the nervousness and the excitement. No doubt she welcomed any opportunity to have someone new to go over it with and I kept reminding myself that she would have been just as engaging with anyone else who sat in that chair.

I liked her right away. She had big shoes. She was funny. Kind of warped. I wasn't sure exactly how, but it seemed like she was twisted in some way, like she had become bent in the course of her life. I didn't know any of this, they were impressions, but they were positive. The twisting, whatever it was, had left a good imprint as near as I could tell. She wasn't cynical or dark, it wasn't that kind of twisted behavior, just something that had left with her a sense of the strangeness of the world and the variable odd things that people go through and must adjust to as they live. She seemed wise. Despite all the projects that she was in the middle of, despite her efforts to study some grand traditional subject and pour drinks as they were defined in the standards and practices of the bar, none of this had left her with the blank stare of an automaton fulfilling someone else's agenda. She hadn't been the victim of these organizational relationships. Not in the least. It didn't seem like it anyway. She seemed free. In her way.

She talked about email and how it had so rapidly become an integral part of her life. She described exchanges she was having with professors and other students. She would mime typing out a message as she relayed what she had sent them or how she had replied to something they had written. Information was the focus of her life, and she was thrilled to be in the middle of it, to be studying it, and producing it. Not just that. She was passionate about the process of querying it, of being able to make sense of it all, and lay it out in an orderly way. She told me that one professor of hers had drilled it into their heads that the world was changing so much right now, and she went on at length about what he said and how far the changes would go. They would radically transform all our lives and the world would be unrecognizable afterward. She was convinced that we were on the brink of a major revolution and that information was at the center of it. Whatever my views on the subject, whatever other considerations I had given these new ways of life that she was describing, listening to her enchanted me with the possibilities of this new world. She was hopeful and I began to believe that maybe something would happen that would make things better just like she was saying. If we did have more information at our fingertips, we would be in a better position to solve the world's problems. There was something delightful in the way she described it, and at that moment, sitting there, I believed it.

I don't know what I said or what I was saying. I wasn't focusing on anything that I really wanted to tell her. There was no agenda, and I didn't try to impress her. I just listened and responded in whatever spirit she provoked. This wasn't because I'm some great dialogist, someone with an intensely savvy understanding of how to get on well with others and be likeable when it counts, I was responding in the most natural ways to the cues and norms that she was imposing, but I felt drawn into it like there was no other way to be. I was bowled over by her mastery of easy conversation, of simple interaction that was neither uncomfortably friendly with too little context nor overly rigid. We spoke with exactly the right combination of ease and cordiality. At first, I was tempted to write this off to her experience as a bartender, but not all bar tenders are this good at it. It might be that her skills led her to bartending and not the other way around, but why work so hard at it for just one customer on a busy Saturday night?

At one point, and this is what sealed my fate, the doorkeeper said something to her from behind me. Initially it seemed confrontational, and she responded with sarcasm and in kind. It was part of some ongoing play they were acting out. She told me that she would never be able to have a relationship with him because he had the same name as her ex. I was relieved to learn that it was not the same as mine. She told me that her ex was supposed to move here with her, but at the last minute had decided not to, and they broke up instead. Tears were just barely forming in her eyes as she told the story. That's not normal, right? We just met. My eyes were fixed on hers and I felt deep compassion. I wanted very much to make that clear to her somehow, but I couldn't think of anything to say. There was too much feeling there and it was coming too soon after meeting her. What words are right in that case? I needed to be sympathetic without being dismissive or patronizing. I said nothing. No golden words came. I just looked at her, trying to reach out across the distance between us, across the bar and over the half-filled glasses in front me. The not knowing what to do and the desire to help while being helpless was all I had to offer. That was it, that is what got me.

I stayed longer than I had planned, long enough to have two beers but not so long as to let the conversation decay. It never did and she seemed almost a little disappointed when I said I wanted to settle. She made a joke about something or other, my having to run off or having been chased off. I was too embarrassed to hear it really. I didn't expect this at all, never expected to be liked or to like. It was not part of the plan, so now what?

The whole way home, during the drive, there was no machine-like trance as I had been expecting. Instead, all I could think about was this bartender who was a librarian. I tried to remember what she looked like but could not get past the shoes and the look of recognition. That's all I was sure about. I was familiar to her, she recognized me, and she was wearing big boots. During the evening, she made a point of showing them to me. Lifted her foot up off the floor and bid me to lean over the bar to get a better look at those big boots which she proudly said had steel toes. Doc Martens. There was a lot of her in those boots, behind that bar, and maybe even in that look of recognition.

December

"Intelligence is not the same as consciousness. There are intelligent systems now. Systems that can provide decision support, that can learn in a sense. It's really about patterns. The Cybernetics movement was all about this. Intelligent activity cuts across all different types of things and only indicates that previous performance has an impact on the present performance of a similar task."

"Learning systems are intelligent even if they don't have conscious states?"

"Yes. Take a hypertext system that processes four different kinds of messages. It doesn't matter what they do, all that matters is that there are headers or metadata on each message and the message body is a blob of content that needs to be processed. From the metadata, the system knows which kind of message it is. Say that it keeps track of how long it takes to process each of the messages it receives and stores that information somewhere. It starts to associate patterns: one type of message takes a long time, another type doesn't take very long at all, and the others are in the middle somewhere. The software might start to do different things with messages based on this information. It might change the way it processes the long running messages to optimize for them. This way of changing behavior based on the outcome of previous operations, that's all that's required for something to be an intelligent action. That's not consciousness."

"There are a lot of philosophers writing about this. Some say that even consciousness is essentially murky. You're giving a precise definition to intelligence and how a system would have to work in order to express it. They say that it might not be possible to give this kind of definition for consciousness. Is consciousness more like a syndrome than a pattern? To use your term."

"Well, my point is just that intelligent software doesn't have anything to do with conscious machines or whatever it is that the science fiction fanatics like to talk about. Don't they usually end up talking about whether such a machine would be free and if we had to follow all kinds of ethical principles in our relationships with it?"

"Some do."

"Well, to an engineer building a decision support system this seems wildly premature and implausible. Software in the traditional sense is written to do something specific. If such and such a state is discovered in some data property or system condition, do the following. Otherwise, do something else. It's deterministic and set at design time. Intelligent software goes beyond what it was programmed to do and so, as I said, can use the outcomes of its past actions to change its behavior. This kind of non-deterministic programming isn't freedom, it doesn't make the routine free to do whatever it wants."

"It doesn't want anything."

"That's right. It's just a set of pattern applications. Data driven programming that is sensitive to changes in past operations or environmental conditions. This means it has to have a sub-system that gathers data about its processing conditions, what it does and what happens to it. It has to persist that data somehow, make it available for later use, analyze it, and then it has to make use of the results of that analysis when performing similar actions in the future."

"Like actions? Actions that are similar to what it is doing now?"

"Yes. In my example the metadata was providing that function. How long it took to run was tracked against some attribute like create, read, update, or delete. CRUD."

"Your CRUD system was pretty crude. The single attribute schema made the response limited."

"Sure, but the more attributes you could track on the operation, like size or where the message originated, time of day when it was sent, maybe even who it came from and what kind of a person they are, the more sophisticated your patterns might be. The more sophisticated the pattern, the more differentiation the system can make in its responses. Similarity becomes a more precise association including more properties and traits. This means it could do all kinds of things depending on which set of traits it found, based on whatever outcome information was available to it for collection, analysis, and later use."

"It's all completely mechanical. There's no need at the level of the machine operations to speak of consciousness or freedom or ethics."

"I'm certain that none of those issues would be relevant until the machine, or the software system we're calling a machine, had something like desire. I have no idea what desire would look like in an intelligent system though."

"Well, what if the system had some generalized outcomes that it tended to promote? When it processed those messages, it might vary its processing to try to realize those generalized outcomes."

"Like what?"

"Happiness, for example. General utility or welfare."

"Is that how desire works then?"

"Everyone says they want to be happy."

"Sure, they say it, but do they feel generalized desires like that in the moment? Does wanting to be happy occupy your every waking moment like it's in the background of everything you want? Desire, in my experience anyway, is different than that. It's attached to objects and conditions, to other people, to specific achievements, and to outcomes that must be brought about no matter the cost, regardless of whether they make me happy or not."

"The body plays a role; it's the body that desires. Many of our specific desires have to do with body states. Enjoyment. Food. The attention of others, sex."

"Social status. Comfort. The complexity of consciousness isn't just tied to intelligent behavior, it connects to the feelings in the body, its urges. Sometimes I want things right when I first see them. They connect with some memory, and they play off some association. Something in the moment pulls me to it. How do you program that? It's fun to think about it as an exercise, I guess. I just don't have any idea how you would make something that works that way."

"It's interesting. It's as if consciousness and ethical dignity, all of that, is as much connected with how impetuous and passionate we can be, our impatience and our sense of urgency, as it is to our intelligence. Kant was wrong maybe, what makes us worthy of ethical consideration isn't that we are capable of rational deliberation or hearing some command, it's because we can feel things and be moved."

"If you wanted to build a conscious system, as opposed to an intelligent one, there would be an entirely different set of concerns, an entirely different set of problems to solve. They might do that at a university if they could get someone to fund it as a proof-of-concept project, but for the enterprise, for businesses, they're only going to pay for projects that improve their profitability. Intelligence is enough for that; they don't need consciousness. Consciousness is sloppy and doesn't always contribute to the bottom line. Intelligence can make their businesses more streamlined and efficient. The problems to be solved are known. The desire comes from the human ends that started the software project in the first place."

"A cyborg system, then. Part human and part software."

"That's what decision support means. The humans are making the decisions and the software is supporting it."

"Freedom is a human determination that relies on our finite understanding of things, our desire, and our impatience to achieve partially understood outcomes through ill-conceived means. That's what makes us free, or at least makes us feel that way. The rattling around of all these half-baked notions smooshed together with the urge to create some related state is the origin of consciousness: finite and moody."

"Exactly. That's why we need intelligent systems to help us with our decisions. Because we're basically idiots who 'think' through desire.

Consciousness is at the origin of the search for intelligent action, it isn't the end of it."

"It's funny. In college I read a book about how institutions think. The author was saying a lot of similar things. Although maybe she was erroneously using the word 'think' instead of 'act intelligently.' If we go down this road, then institutions demonstrate a form of intelligence as well. They can act out those patterns, same as the software system, and they can be formed for achieving results that have been built into them by humans."

"I guess, but institutions have to have people, don't they? If people make up the institution, then desire is involved. They could never be purely intelligent systems. There would always be conflict between the intelligent components and the human ones."

"True, but that's interesting, right? The institution applies these patterns of intelligent operation through behaviors that are part of its norms engineered for the sake of achieving its ends. Discipline plays a part. The bodies that inhabit these norms, to which they are applied, they are constantly providing resistance. Employees, customers, politicians. It's the pressure of this resistance that must become the source of learning for the institution."

"There are philosophers who talk about this?"

"Absolutely. We could probably apply this to money like we were talking about the other day. There's the prison system, or maybe all the talk about human sexuality and what counts as normal sexual behavior and what doesn't. Some philosophers have written about these institutions, and they've included analysis of the surfaces of resistance and how the body works that way. Constraints and processes are applied to bodies, bodies resist, and the power that applies the constraint must not only react to this resistance but must learn to understand the opportunities in it. Resistance makes it possible for the institution to learn more about how bodies work and what can be done with them. The resistance of the body surfaces in the person's desires. There is a struggle for desire, the institution has an interest in shaping those desires so that they line up with institutional objectives."

"Like what? What's an example?"

"All this technology, it's owned by organizations, right? Like corporations. A corporation is in business and has a bottom line. The people just work for it, they don't really want the things they are doing, they have indirect desires that ultimately lead them to fulfill the corporation's ends and interests. The corporation's 'desire' might be to maximize revenue and minimize expenses. An institution like that does things. When it does those things it employs machines, it employs people, and it employs processes. Then, it encounters resistance through the work of these things. People don't always buy their stuff, or they buy stuff from a competitor, or they complain and try to get regulations applied. The institution orients itself toward knowing as much as it can about the resistance that bodies are likely to pose to the conditions it creates because this will help it to predict the outcomes. It might even be able to change them. Norms in sexuality, for example, can make a population easier to control by tapping into their individual desires."

"Controlled by whom? If you mean that some people in the equation use the institution to control other people in the equation, that doesn't match with what I'm saying. The intelligent system would just be a tool for use by some people over others through the institution's actions. People who get more benefits from that organization are more likely to advocate its continued authority, I suppose."

"Sure, and the people who seem to be in positions of authority, the people who approve of the organization or direct its actions, they aren't immune to its conditions, and they aren't free of its constraints. The organization is out of control, in a way. Even the executives are slaves to its rules for how to think and act. I don't have a good answer for describing the structural agency behind it all. Is there something wrong with thinking in terms of agents? Is the system of agency flat? Isn't that what you're describing in the software system?"

"Yes, but the software system has people who write the code."

"It's an intelligent system, though, at some point it may no longer need human programmers, but could extend and change itself?"

"I guess, but it still needs that original moment of creation to set it in motion. Desire has to be bootstrapped. I just can't figure out how a software system could want something."

"Yes, the origin problem. With software, it's pretty contained. There might be a group of people in a lab somewhere, but what is the origin of an institution? Who are the people that started kinship and what does it want or what desires did they bake into it?"

"The chicken and the egg."

"In a way, it is. Institutions are older and more complicated. My point is that origins are pure fantasy, purely speculative. The institutions are too old and have taken on too much of a life of their own to be thought of like that. Regardless of where they come from, where they are now is a different story. If we think of them as functioning like intelligent systems, then it makes sense to say that they have taken over the order of operations and the patterns of learning and are working as the respondents to the resistances that bodies provide. Such resistance isn't a counter action to the dominant dynamic, it is its purpose. The body's resistance increases the system's knowledge, increases the attributes that can be included in the patterns. Intelligence lives in the institution and consciousness lives in the resistances to it."

"Wait, what? That's too dense."

"There are sociologists who have been saying this for like a hundred years. Desire, for a caveman, is raw. You could rattle off what they want without much investigation. Rudimentary stuff, but the complexity of desire in the modern world is not a purely human creation, it's the result of the cyborg pattern of institutions mixed with resistant bodies. The more complex the social conditions, the more complex the forms of desire you'll find in the population."

"Advanced civilization creates advanced forms of desire?"

"Not exactly. The point is that more complicated social conditions just are more complex institutions, and more complex institutions just are greater points of contact between resistant bodies and constraining processes. This increase in complexity is nothing other than the increased complexity of desire, and desire aware of itself is consciousness, even if that isn't centralized in a single organism, to come back to my point."

"I see. Going back to my intelligent system, the desire would start in the messages. The message wants to get where it's going, and it wants to get there as fast as it can. The system might just want to handle more messages."

"It is impetuous, passionate, and impatient."

"Yes, and the processing mechanism might throttle some of the processing based on what it has learned. It might send some messages off on some detour that delays their arrival. The messages would resist. They want to get where they are going faster."

"The system would track that as part of the data it gathers and analyze it for future use, impacting what happens to messages in the future."

"The system would increase in complexity as this happens."

"The messages would start to develop new interests related to the changing conditions and how they related to their goals."

"Messages don't have interests or goals really. They don't have desire. It's a metaphor, right?"

"True, but you said they had bodies, and the message body would undergo changes. Suppose one of the changes that happened based on processing history was that 'create' messages were prioritized over 'read' messages. Whenever a create was taking place, all of the readers would have to wait."

"Okay. This is standard."

"The messages might develop to accommodate this. What if some new hybrid message came into existence where the headers would indicate a create operation, but the body would indicate both create and read qualities? The message can change in some slight way to game the operational system. The operational system, assuming it can learn this, might make further adjustments to handle these sorts of messages differently."

"That mutation process could continue forever causing increasing complexity in the message handling system as well as in the body of the messages."

"Yes, and that's what plays the role of desire in the example. Desire is the raw drive toward an end, which means an impetus to get where it is going, made more complex by the twists and turns it must undergo as the system processes it and as it works its way through it. To come full circle, the corporation's knowledge of resistance ends up being a thorough knowledge of desire and a way to shape and change it to achieve its ends. Whatever owns the technology is the ethical subject and all the ethical systems we know may not apply to it because it isn't human. We need to figure out the distributed agency of complex institutions to know what an ethics for it might be like. We would need to know its social order and how its actions are situated within it."

"We'll have to do that later because I'm hungry now. Let's go get something to eat."

"Where do you want to go?"

"I don't know, what do you feel like eating?"

She had to explain to her friends who this random guy was who had sent such an odd email to the project's account. She didn't like that. They were her friends, but still she balked at the thought that they would know her business, especially since she wasn't sure yet whether it was her business. She didn't know this guy. They had one conversation, but this didn't feel like the right time. She had too much going on and this would only get in the way. This year was supposed to be about school and working hard to fit in and learn as much as she could. She didn't want to lose that focus and this guy could only be a distraction.

He did find her somehow, and to do that he would have had to remember everything she said. The hypertext cataloging project had a web page and an email address. He would have had to search specifically to find that contact page. The college would have been one attribute, the project's content would have been another. He would have found the page, but he would have had to read it and put together that this was likely the formal description of the work that she had informally described to him while he was sitting in the noisy bar. No easy feat, and he would have had to do it all despite the beer he drank and all the distractions that were sprinkled throughout their conversation. The contact page didn't give the names of the people working on the project and there wasn't any other personal information there. He would have not only pieced together that this must be the project she had been talking about, but he would have had to realize that many of the things she said were related to this group list and that she was just a member of it. She remembered telling him about some of the email exchanges that went on between the group members. He would have had to know that this address where he was sending his email included all the people on the project and was that same list where those exchanges had taken place.

Knowing that, he sent an email to the group announcing to everyone that he was looking for her. It was a bold move, but not in a good way. She did a little digging herself and thought that probably he could have found her individual email account after he found the group account. Her address was there in one of the department's public lists of graduate students, but he didn't seem to find it there, or if he had, he chose to send his email to the list instead. Did he want to do it that way, was it on purpose? She wasn't sure, but she was curious to find out. At the very least, she felt like she had to reply to explain that he shouldn't be sending emails to her through that group address. It was embarrassing to have to tell the others that she had met him while working at the bar and that he seemed like he was probably okay despite how weird it was to send an email like that to the group. She didn't want to have to repeat any of these conversations with her friends and colleagues. These things should be private. Realizing that she had to reply even if only for this reason, she thought that maybe he was terribly clever about it. That maybe he would have known this and that his random effort to get her attention —or whatever it was that he was trying to do— with this email, would be more likely to be successful if he made the gesture in front of others, publicly.

On top of all that, the email didn't say anything psychotic or anything. It was an elaborate way of asking whether he had found her. He recounted some of the bits and pieces of their conversation and much of the content was an impersonal, but vaguely poetic, description of that. Did he do that as a way of explaining why he was sending the message to the project's account? Even though that part of it seemed innocent enough, the fact that he had sent it at all was something of a declaration. That was the embarrassing part because it was clear to all her colleagues that this was what he was doing. Why was some random guy sending an email to the project and declaring himself and his interest in her to the entire group? The thought of it made her cringe. Despite that, or because of it, she sat there later that night in front of the computer thinking of what to say to him. She typed out a reply. She thanked him for the email. She told him that he shouldn't send emails to this account because there are other people who would see them. She pointed out that she was replying to him from her own personal account and that it would be much better if he would use that to write to her from now on.

The message was clear, but did she want to hear more from him? That's what she was saying. While writing the response, she looked it over multiple times, reading it and rereading it to try and figure out exactly what message it would send. There was something about the way his mind worked. The way he was turning over the various things she had said to him. It wasn't just that he had listened, but that he was taking everything she said seriously. No, not exactly seriously. The tone of his email was respectful, and his treatment was collegial. As though he recognized it on a par with anything he might come across linked from the department's website. It was flattering, but there was something disturbing about it too. She had to admit the ambivalence it stirred. Since he wasn't a professor in this same department or even at the same school really (the Ann Arbor campus has little to do with Dearborn) and since he reached out publicly, it didn't seem creepy to her. At least, she was willing to see it that way.

He had been so nice while they were talking at the bar the other night. He was definitely not like his friend. She was sure of her ability to read this in men. A guy who was looking for a brief interlude wouldn't write a message like this and send it like that, would he? Everything about the way he talked and the way he made eye contact, the way he listened and the way he reacted, told her that he was the other kind and far riskier than his friend. What he wanted was probably more serious, and that's why she couldn't get into that right now. She didn't have time and she couldn't afford the distraction. If it had been the other guy, maybe that would have been okay. She was beginning to forget that part of herself and wouldn't object to a reminder now and again, but not with someone who was serious like that. Not with this guy, and he hadn't come back to the bar, he had emailed. Is that all that he wanted, or was that how he liked it? A little less confrontational, more subtle and with more distance. This was new territory, no one had ever initiated contact with her this way before. She couldn't reference some ready-made template for what it was supposed to mean or how it was supposed to go. This was another reason why she felt compelled to respond and to encourage more messages. There was mystery in it. She had been fascinated with all the work and school related uses for electronic messaging, but this made total sense too. Developing personal contact with it seemed like a natural progression.

She kept reminding herself that he did come across as a nice person. At least in that conversation in the bar. She didn't want to leave him hanging, wondering whether his email ever arrived, whether she ever saw it, or it had been delivered to the wrong address or a different project with a similar agenda. She had to reply and had to say what needed to be said. Whatever that was. She was curious to see how things would take shape from there. She trembled a bit when she finally hit send and then spent the rest of the night wondering how things would go from here. That too was an indicator that she might be doing the right thing by responding. Clearly, she felt intrigued and interested in what might happen.

There was a safety in this form of communication too. It would take place at a distance, and she wouldn't have to worry about what her body language or her eyes were betraying. She would be able to control the tone and the content of her responses more thoroughly. She could get the stimulant without the risk. She wouldn't have to respond immediately to anything he asked or anything he said. She could take her time and think about it. There were lots of interesting possibilities of developing a relationship this way, and since it was all brand new, the mystery of it added all kinds of dimensions. Not to mention the fact that he seemed like a good writer, not at all afraid to make himself vulnerable. How could he be if he were willing to send that message to the group? This might be the perfect solution. It might let her safely explore options from far away without the time demands that usually come with that. Asynchronous courtship might be the perfect solution to a problem she didn't even know she was having.

It also occurred to her that this exchange might make it more difficult for him to just show up at the bar again and start another conversation like the last one. If they started communicating over email, how could he just walk in and start chatting about something they were already discussing in the messages? Like the medium here would put a boundary on things that would make it awkward to crossover into the other space. If they communicated electronically, that might create a virtual space for their interactions to occur and any attempt to cross from there back into the real world might cause problems or at least might cause problems if they didn't explicitly agree to it. He couldn't just show up, he would have to say something like "I want to see you" and only then would they be able to set up a time and a place. That is very satisfying. He wouldn't be able to just walk into the bar. This would be a huge bonus because at this point —even with so little to go on with him and what he was like— she felt that if he were to just show up one day that it would cause a big problem. The distraction would be very real, and she was absolutely certain that she didn't want it.

He responded the next day, and he confirmed that he knew that this had been a group account and that explained why he didn't say more in his first message. It was as if he were trying to get her attention in a crowded room. He put it that way. There was only so much you can say or do in those circumstances. He was glad that she had responded and thanked her for giving him her personal address by doing it. He said he thought that meant it was probably okay to reply and hoped that was okay with her. It was all so polite, but not at all stuffy or formal. There was a rhythm in the way he wrote things. It was nice. She liked something about it, the way the message displayed effort in being communicated. It was revised and edited, and she was the intended recipient of this effort. Email, but not exactly email as she had come to know it. There was something attractive about the attention, and the way the attention was framed. It was such a verbal approach, but there was body there too. She could tell. There was a pulse on the other side of the messages. Something warm and reaching out, and he was at ease in making it known. He said that he wanted to see her, wanted to take her out somewhere so they could talk more and get to know each other better. He let her know that he had really enjoyed speaking with her and that he wanted to continue.

She loved the prospect of exchanging messages with him but was not keen on meeting. She responded by making excuses about the end of the semester and how she was going to be leaving town as soon as she was finished with her final exams. She didn't have a lot of time and so couldn't really commit to much at this point. She would be willing to meet for coffee before leaving though, because she didn't want to put him off completely. She couldn't say 'no' outright. She had to show some interest to make it clear that it was okay for him to keep writing. She agreed to meet him for coffee at a place near central campus, a place where no one she knew would be likely to show up. In her mind, it made sense and it would not have the effect of establishing a pattern that they were going to start seeing each other on a regular basis. It wasn't a date. She would use the opportunity to let him know that she wouldn't be able to do that since she was so busy with school, was leaving town, and just had too much going on to get into anything. She would let him know that it was okay to keep writing and that she would be happy to get to know him better like that. This had to be done in person because that would best establish parameters. They would be meeting to determine that they will not meet and that they will communicate without seeing each other. It seemed logical. This was what she wanted. Although it gave her some pause to see him in person, it was risky to look him in the eyes and give him a chance to look back, she felt certain that it needed to be done if she wanted to maintain control over the situation and keep things moving in the way she wanted them to move.

In just a few messages back and forth, they set a day and time to meet. She made sure to show up a little late so that he would already be there when she arrived. She was sure he would be there on time and even a little early. She dressed to send just the right message. Overalls. She actively showed no effort at trying to look as though she had made any effort, she wanted to be as mundane as possible. Just like any other day. If it was going to be possible to discourage him, she had to make sure to take that opportunity. This was only going to work if he was exactly who he was supposed to be, there was no wiggle room. If he needed her to look a certain way or act a certain way, then it was going to be a non-starter.

She knew as soon as she saw him in the café that none of that mattered. He was reading when she walked in, she had seen him in the chair by the window as she walked up the street. He looked so serious and focused on his book. Head down, pen in hand, following along on the page. When she opened the door and approached his table, he looked up at her and his face lit up. He flashed such a big smile, and his eyes came so alive. It was a complete transformation from his reading pose. This caused her to give him a warmer greeting than she had planned. He wasn't dressed up either. He didn't seem to put much effort into his appearance, making it seem like it really was just a casual appointment between a couple of people who were starting a new friendship. This made a huge impression. It made her think that maybe he was in the same place she was, that he wasn't interested in something expected and ordinary.

He asked about her finals and what her holiday plans were. He was so at ease in the conversation. It helped her to relax. Even relax a little too much. Just like in the few emails they had exchanged, she told him too much with too little provocation. She talked about her mother and stepfather, her siblings, and the way they all came together as a blended family. It was easy to go into details that she wouldn't usually go into with someone she had only just met. It was the same as that first time they talked at the bar, and like then, she said and showed too much. It wasn't just that she was in a place where she needed to say these things to someone, although she was feeling that way up to a point, it was something about him, about the way he looked at her, the way he seemed to want to know her without any ulterior motive. He wanted to know what Christmas would be like at her house. What it was like to grow up there. He knew that the holidays meant all sorts of weird family traditions and that the emotions that went along with them were crucial no matter how disconnected that part of one's life had become from the rest. She had been thinking about a lot of this while preparing for the trip and he didn't have to force her to talk about it, she wanted to.

He disoriented her by not talking too much about himself. He didn't go on with all sorts of stories that were aimed at impressing her. His whole demeanor was just so different from what she was used to in first meetings with men. It was almost as if he was putting himself in the friend zone before she had made up her mind that he belonged there. He never showed any signs of questioning her motives or wondering why she would ask him not to come to the bar too much. She was worried he might start coming whenever he knew she was there and that there would be nothing she could do about it. "Oh, I won't come again on days when you're working. That would be rude," he said. "You'd have no choice, and I can't imagine that would be very pleasant." She let him know that she did appreciate that but emphasized that she couldn't very well expect him to stop going to some place that he had been going all year just because she happened to work there. He said it didn't matter and his mind was already made up before she said anything. The simple way he talked about it showed that his actions and his words were in a straightforward and harmonious relationship with each other. He said something and then he would do it. There was nothing more to it, nothing more that needed to be discussed. The bar isn't important to him, he could live without it.

He teased her a little about making a meeting with him to tell him that she didn't want to meet with him. He told her a story about this one time he was sitting outside a café in Urbana and a little girl, maybe four or five years old, was walking past while holding her mother's hand. Her mother was starting to drag her a little because she had stopped walking evenly. Her eyes were fixed on him, sitting there at his table, and now looking up to watch her walk past. The little girl could not look away from him, her eyes were completely fixed. Her mother looked down and asked her what was wrong. The little girl responded over and over again: "I am not going to look at that man, I am not going to look at that man." The story made her blush, but she liked that he told it. No further comment necessary and neither made one.

In the end, they parted pleasantly but awkwardly, wishing each other a Merry Christmas and safe travels. In so many ways it had gone exactly as she had hoped that it would. She got the message across. She communicated exactly what she wanted to communicate. The boundaries were established, and yet there was something strange and unsettling about it. She thought these ground rules would set everything right, but there was something in his reaction that made her think twice. Like he seemed to think that the agreement went exactly as he wanted it to go. She thought she would have to convince him to accept the terms, but she didn't, not at all. He was thrilled to be able to continue writing to her and he didn't mind not seeing her in person for a while, until maybe something changed, sometime later. This was all fine with him. Why? Why was he so at ease with making this agreement? She couldn't help but think about that for the rest of the day. Not obsessively, but occasionally. Frequently, that is. He sent her a mail that same day letting her know how happy he had been to see her and how glad he was that they could keep writing.

There was a confidence in the way he acted when they parted, and that same confidence came across in the tone of his message. Like he got exactly what he wanted, and the new ground rules were perfectly suited to his objectives. He didn't say this, but there was something in what he did say that suggested it. At ease expressing his thoughts in writing, maybe he perceived an advantage in a situation where he had permission to write as much as he wanted so long as he didn't come around and bother her in person. What if the arrangement was perfectly suited to him, and as an added bonus, it was her idea? The reasons for her lack of calm started to become clear. She had gotten exactly what she wanted and yet was beginning to think that this was riskier than she had thought. She had believed that keeping him at a distance would make her safe, but he made her worry that this was where he would be the most dangerous.

"Why can't you just be a normal person? Just go in there on a day when you know she's working and ask her out. It's been working for ages. You don't need to explore some new and technocentric courting ritual to get the job done."

Desire comes first, intelligence follows.

Because desire produces resistance in the social fabric, any agent that would act socially must obtain extensive understanding of both desire and the many resistances that follow. The mechanics require gathering information about its process of production as well as its product: the patterns of operation, the behaviors they fuel, the facets of the resistance itself, and the way resistance fosters new associations in the body and spatial connections emanating from it in action and thought. This reflexive interstitial morass is the economy of human being, functioning as an energy source for powering large-scale organizations that have been conceived and realized as knowledge vaults. More importantly, generating wealth from that knowledge and know-how in its instructions. The procedures for knowing are nothing other than the procedures for harvesting value and the skills for producing it.

"Do you remember that story you wrote based on the summer you lived in Jet? ... 'The Astral Plane' might've been its name." Pause. "There were two women who rented the room next door, right? There was a tall one. Really brilliant. Beautiful. Went to some Ivy league school?"

"Brown."

"Why didn't the therapist character ever ask her out? You made a point of saying that he didn't. That whole summer he was single, she lived next door, she was single. Why didn't he pursue her?"

"Are you serious? Did she even know he existed?"

"Did she know? Based on your description, she was totally crushing on him the whole summer. It was the main action in the story. Why else did she keep stopping in at those 'therapy' sessions? You said she never smoked any pot with the others."

"A lot of people were hanging out in those scenes. There was a lot going on, any part of which might have been attractive to her."

"Why was she always poking her head in the door asking if he had seen whoever or did he know this or that? My point is that the main character was almost willfully stupid about what was going on. Why? Because he spent that whole summer totally depressed about that theatre major who broke his heart, but in truth had just given up on waiting for him."

"Theatre and dance."

"She was another one that he never talked to about how much he liked her. Those two just kept writing all that poetry suggesting everything without ever saying it outright. We're talking about a pattern you seem to have identified and yet keep repeating."

"It's a story."

"I know, but it's something you keep going back to. In your writing and in your life. Are they connected, what's going on?"

"Since you seem to know so much, why don't you tell me what's going on?"

"I think you're prone to sublimate sexual and romantic desire for the sake of stimulating creativity. You're incapable of generating the proper passion for your work without it. You generate a lot of frustration and confusion from these manufactured and thwarted relationships and puts it all into your work. Rather, your work is a response to these feelings or layered on top of it. The motivation and the instigation being undeniable and there could never be any chance to procrastinate. The physical pangs of the redirected associations would surface without any possibility of being quieted. You get what you want. Which ultimately is both the expression of the romantic feelings and the creative expression and productivity that result from its sublimation. Writing the story had been more important than either of the two women its characters were based on."

"I've been writing so much this last month, why would I need to do that when I'm already so absorbed in this project?"

"Are you? Something in your work habits seems to have changed lately."

"This last thing I wrote is still resonating. Haunting even."

"You wrote it before you met the librarian?"

"Yes. I was trying to write more too. Trying to write the second part of the book. At least trying to organize it better."

"You stopped when you met her?"

"Not exactly. Well, sort of. I've been distracted."

"By her?"

"No. The purpose of the first part was clear, and I thought the purpose of the second part was too. I didn't even need to write the Interlude, that middle bit. It isn't technically necessary, but now I can't stop going back to it. I can't get it out of my head. It might be like a sprung trap."

"How?"

"There was a form of action that aims at getting out of someplace where it shouldn't be. I had put a kind of moral emphasis on the significance of it. Furthermore, I was building a kind of ethos around its nature and manner, but while doing that it started to become clear that because the act of getting out was necessarily linked to what it was trying to escape, there was a sense in which it could never fully leave it behind, never really get away."

"I see. Catch 22."

"More than that because the 'line of flight' appeared as desire, the desire to escape, to get away or get beyond. Such desires not only have their origin in what they want to escape, but are completely saturated by it, and because of that, trapped. Even if they escape, they take it with them."

"Weren't you writing this about deconstruction and its relationship to Metaphysics?"

"Ostensibly, but because I made the mistake of writing it all in terms of Nietzsche, it became so much bigger. It became the rallying call of the will to power itself and an ontological condition within it."

"I thought you had sworn off writing about him."

"Yes, and that was the driving factor. That's what made it an interlude, a farce. It was a bunch of stuff I didn't want to say, stuff I didn't want to be looking at too closely or even at all. Saying it was that same 'line of flight' that I'm talking about. The language all became saturated desire. That is the way I laugh Nietzsche to myself."

"The librarian drops right into the middle of this?"

"She recognized me."

"What does that mean?"

"I don't know, but I wouldn't have noticed her if she hadn't."

"Okay, so now what?"

"Nothing. She's leaving town for the holidays."

"You guys will go out when she gets back?"

"No. She doesn't want to go out. She's not ready. She's not in a good place for that."

"Okay. You'll move on. Just forget about her. If it's meant to be maybe you two will cross paths again some time."

"She said we could write. She said I could write as much as I wanted."

"Aren't you just a short time visitor? A visiting assistant professor and sabbatical replacement? That means that next year there will be no renewal and you are actively looking for work at other schools, none of which —as it turns out— are commuting distance from Ann Arbor. Are you getting mixed up with her as a way to prevent yourself from getting mixed up with anyone else? Do you really like her but are happy to let it be a weird as shit relationship so that you can avoid any real intimacy that might jeopardize whatever job you go off to next year?"

"I don't know."

"Well, the answer may be tough, but the question is easy enough. What do you want?"

"You mean, do I really want to date this woman, or do I just want to exorcise some romantic demons by writing to her?"

"I'm not really talking about her. Not just her. I've been listening to you for a couple of months now. I can't figure out what you're doing. I don't know what you want. I mean, from life. What do you want? Is it just to write as much as you wanted? Exactly what she gave you permission to do. Academic life doesn't provide enough of an opportunity for that, you had to look elsewhere?"

There is a classic tale told by the philosopher that pits desire against discipline. It's the premise behind the marshmallow test. Discipline suggests the willpower of working toward a greater end that delays gratification. Desire is supposedly that personal power that resists the delay. Can we overcome our desires and delay gratification for the sake of a better pay off? What if this is a false choice? What if the pattern of interlude is at work here? Discipline could be the way out of desire or desire the way out of discipline or they might be interleaved. Desire's content is the subject of that same discipline or discipline itself is a powerful expression of desire. "I'll show you." Remember that one? The utterance had always been significant because there was a way to say it that would put the emphasis on revenge. There was another way to say it that would emphasize instruction and teaching. In writing, it was impossible to discriminate between these two different ways of saying the same phrase. Only in speech, only in the tone of voice, could the difference come out. How to demonstrate that in writing? I'll show you.

Either way, there was desire. In the event that the speaker is a great leader and means only to reveal some unknown truth to the listener, that is an expression of desire. I will show you how. I will teach this lesson so that you may know it. The offer is an expression of desire. The teacher is offering something to the student and that something is the same discipline that the teacher uses in thinking through the matter at hand. I will show you how one might puzzle through these problems, how one might sort it out and arrive at a conclusion, or at least get further on in one's thinking so that the mess starts to clarify and become distinct. On the other hand, there is the recipient of a blow of denigrating comment. They turn against the other person. I will show you that you are wrong about me, that you have miscalculated, that you have made an error in your evaluation. How to show this? I will work hard, grind away day and night to learn more, to express the point better, in a way that makes sense to anyone who would happen to be listening. In the end, through my action, I will win the day and have my revenge against these sharp criticisms, or worse, against this oblivion that you put me in here and now.

In both cases, desire and discipline merge. In the one the desire is to influence the other, in the other the desire is to overcome the other's assault with a better defense, a defense that is properly informed with the expertise that further discipline has to offer. I have mastered this area and want to help you master it too. I will become the master of this area so that I can show that you've made a horrible mistake in overlooking my contribution.

It all amounts to the desire to be disciplined, to be the master of movement and rhetoric, and to be able to respond to critics easily and deftly. The key is that even the long-term drive is a desire. There is no discipline really. Rather, all of these structured forms of action are desire through and through. We learn to package our interests and urges into powerful containers that can do more and more as they become fuller and steadier. Popping the marshmallow in your mouth is the expression of a desire, but it's immediate and simple. Waiting to acquire two marshmallows, this is more complex. There is more to consume, the desire is more powerful and more sophisticated.

Capital is dead labor. We wrapped our brains around that. Is discipline dead desire? Not dead really, because it lives even if vampire-like. The point is that labor has become disembodied, pulled out of the laborer and reified as a commodity produced by it. It belongs to someone else, lives somewhere else, and will be sold to someone else. It is alien to the laborer. All the machines and goods for sale are the billions of human hours spent fabricating this and that. The labor lives on as a ghost of the people that expended it for the sake of making things the owner can sell.

Likewise, years and years of desire have built up a civilization with billions of marshmallows to eat. Kant's dilemma is false. There is no opposition here between reason and inclination. Rather, the structures of the rational are the dead desire that has been expended over the centuries in the fabrication of all the disciplines that humans know and through which humans know everything that can be done or felt. All the world is presented to us in this knowledge. In it, there is nothing but the long history of every human interest that has ever been expressed. Want made real in the ongoing apparatus of "Family" or "Education" or "Religion." Money. Time. The language and the way that it enters into the space between people. The way it emerges along the lines and in the spacing between words on the page.

Here is my modus operandi: he scribbles this all down. Using a pen on notebook paper that he keeps collected in a manilla envelop. Pages of it, investigating the points of intersection, the junctures of desire and discipline. Pages later, exhausted, he sets the paper and pen aside and pulls the keyboard closer to type out an email in reply to something she said about her smoking habit: "I once tried to quit smoking and played a game with myself to do it. While jonesing for a cigarette, I asked myself what would this feeling be if I didn't know what it was, if I didn't know that smoking a cigarette would make it go away? I was trying to make the desire to quit smoking stronger than the desire to smoke and part of that had to be achieved by decreasing the latter and increasing the former. I induced ignorance of the cause, and ignorance can reduce desire, I reasoned. At least that's what I wanted to believe." He hits send. She responded an hour or so later with "I know," and then ended the message with an improvised wink constructed out of a semi-colon and a closing parenthesis.

As the month goes by, it becomes less likely that I will get any interviews at the Eastern Divisional Meeting. I haven't heard from anyone yet. This is the round where most of the options are tenure track. I've never had very many interviews at these, but usually there were at least a few. This year there aren't any. The number of applications wasn't any different so that is not likely the cause. Could be that there are more people on the market than there were in previous years, or maybe the visiting assistant professor label is a problem? Am I damaged goods now? Is it for the best? The conference is in New York, and I am not looking forward to going. It's hard not to let my imagination run on about what this might mean and what portents it may hold.

End of semester duties are helping take my mind off the problem. In the intro class I finished up with Russell's *Problems of Philosophy* last month teaching it as a setup for a strange choice at term's end: Postman's *Amusing Ourselves to Death*. The same pattern in the ethics class, setting up with readings covering different approaches to consequentialist ethics so that we could end the term with MacKinnon's *Toward a Feminist Theory of the State*. I had something specific in mind when designing the courses this way, but it might have been just as powerful to switch the two and teach the Postman book at the end of the ethics course and the MacKinnon at the end of the introduction to philosophy. The point in both cases is the same, there are hidden matters at work in the things that make up our everyday experience, and these hidden matters don't exactly belong to us. We belong to them, and they inhabit us.

What discipline am I passing along? The interlude follows me into the classroom and there is a frustrated air that covers all the lessons. This line of thinking required an entire semester to set up and, truthfully, ten weeks had not been nearly enough. Basically, I dumbed down the traditional picture for the sake of brevity and then forced them to see it just so that I could show them what was wrong with it. Have I spoiled the children so that I can teach them how to become unspoiled? What else am I teaching in the end? These arguments? These specific ways of looking at the world? A sliver of intellectual history that includes the work of a few writers who people generally refer to as philosophers. What binds them all together in the end? Wittgenstein and Russell? Heidegger and Arendt? De Beauvoir and Sartre? Aristotle and Plato? If you didn't know there was such a thing as philosophy, would you group all these people together?

The attack on consequentialism seemed the most pertinent as a response to the question. Utility is an equation, the contract too. All relationships are given a common currency, and this is supposed to function as a singular and universal measuring apparatus for whatever happens, whatever can happen. Another way in which the empiricists broke the world. The contract that we are engaged in, the agreements we have made, all orient us toward a common way of thinking about our actions and comparing them to each other. I can't separate the highest end of happiness from the contract made by all to safeguard it. We couldn't unite in our pursuit of a general welfare unless there was something in our physiology that binds us together, and without an agreement that connects us to each other, we couldn't act on behalf of our interests and happiness. There is that sense that you can place a comparable value on anything that anyone could ever want. That thing there is worth 6 and that over there is -3. Add it all up, consider all the angles and all the different participants, and you will get the answer. The right thing to do is... Whatever the numbers reveal. It's all math. Everyone can see for themselves that the contract is broken when someone fails to live up to their end of the bargain and asserts their own interests above the interests of others or the collective itself. As you wish.

These views are not accidental to the 18th and 19th centuries. That would have been too convenient. Right as there was a growing interest in the property rights of individuals throughout all the exchange relationships they have, professional philosophers just so happened to stumble upon a set of formal ethical and political doctrines that would universalize all interests in terms of a common currency and domain of exchange. What are the odds that this would have happened to coincide with economic and nationalistic organizations moving in one and the same direction? The coincidence does more than anything to convince me that there is a holistic totality of some kind at work in the passage of time and the positions of geographical space.

We all think we unite under the guise of considering our well-being. We recognize that we are an environment for each other, that we live in a world with others and that these others constitute most of the everyday life of any one of us. People make up your good and bad days, their decisions make your days bad and good. This generalizes our welfare and demonstrates that we are acting out an agreement with each other that condones a world like this where each of us is dependent on the actions of others in our hopes of living a good life. Everything is so transparent and clean. Everyone knows that the agreement is in place, everyone knows what their interests are, and each of us is in a position to evaluate the impact that others' actions will have on our own pursuits. I may have an interest in something that causes pain to others. The benefit or pleasure of my pursuit is measurable, and the harm or pain caused by it is too. Add it all up and the right course of action presents itself. I'll show you. Clear as day. If there are arguments or disputes about the outcome, it'll likely be disagreements over the weight of a benefit or a harm. Next comes the conversation and the discussion to sort it all out. Open investigations to get to the bottom of it, and the courts can decide or some other committee-style forensic system that is well-suited to get to the bottom of things. Such optimism.

If the mechanisms we use for reasoning through these decisions are already infiltrated by the set of concerns being measured, what then? That is, what is the measurable utility of the deliberation process itself? The agreement that lies at the foundation is an entire framework or methodology of settling disputes and measuring considerations, if we went the wrong way with these foundational notions, the whole system would have been corrupt from the get-go. The intelligence of reason is assembled after the hierarchy of ends has been built, and this makes it an apologist more than a deliberator.

This is why it all intertwines, the intro course and the ethics course. The consequentialist picture configures a methodology of knowing and analysis. Measurements must be performed, critical investigations that aim at the relative merits and benefits of sets of actions or rules and the relative or marginal harm of other sets. I can't separate the ethical agenda from the epistemological one. The methodology for knowing the world, and the domain of what is to be known, are merged. We see with the same eyes that we are trying to study. The thinker who is producing reasons to quit smoking or to defer one's efforts is one and the same with the smoker. How can you argue yourself out of the habit?

This is how I read both Postman and MacKinnon. Well, how I read the parts that I have selectively used to make the point that I, when selecting the material for my introductory courses, all along planned to make. MacKinnon points out that patriarchal desire is nonetheless desire. It doesn't surface as an alien other, rather it appears as libido, pure and simple. It doesn't say, hey you have all kinds of fantasies that include imbalance of power. Instead, the imbalance of power, being overpowered by or overpowering your partner, these acts turn us on and do so intrinsically and —from our point of view— immediately. Phenomenologically. We don't experience them as the alien other come to occupy our sexuality. Rather, we experience these relationships as passion and desire and, in the end, they are what gets us off. We don't have to focus on sexuality and the patriarchy to make this point. We could talk about the role of entertainment under conditions of capitalism just as easily. We don't experience the media circus or the noise and glamor of the sporting event as alien intervention. Rather, we feel the exhilaration of it, we become excited just like we are supposed to when the music plays or when the lights go down in the theatre. Our blood flows resilient when the video starts rolling or the lights on the stage come up. Alienation doesn't raise its ugly head and call out. No, there is just interest and awe and being carried away from ourselves and the problems we hoped to leave behind. On the flipside, even our boredom is superficially immediate.

Sexuality and entertainment, what bigger institutions are there in an adult's life? If our freedom isn't at stake here, then it isn't at stake anywhere. If we frame the question in terms of whether we are able to enjoy what we want to enjoy, be entertained in the way that we want to be entertained, express our sexuality in the way that we want to express our sexuality, then we would seem to be missing the larger point. The problem of freedom isn't whether or not we can get what we want or are allowed to do what we want, but what is the relationship between want and autonomy. Kant, as we all know, said that evidence of free action was missing in any case where inclination or desire was behind the act. We are demonstrably free only when reason overcomes desire, but we've changed the terms of the debate a bit by suggesting that reason is the structure that organizes our desires. We grow up learning how to reason and we generally apply these tools for the sake of justifying what we want, or what our society wants through us. This should be done the way that I want to do it because of the following reasons. Reason is put in the service of justifying or rationalizing a desire. It is the methodical application of the power of desire to the justification of its own right to realize itself. Organization meets body, a body with organs.

This reason, this deliberative apparatus that we must train into ourselves so carefully and bind to the movement of our muscles, it is the highest form of discipline that the human agent could possibly achieve. With it, nothing will remain mysterious and out of reach. The emphatic instigation for this training, the reason we are willing to surrender so much of our lives to it, is because it will give us some of the most powerful means imaginable for getting what we want. It will come to us from this world and from our relationships with other people as we collaborate and compete for rewards. That is what both MacKinnon and Postman are pointing out. The reasonable mechanisms in our heads that teach us to trust in our inclinations and work to realize them, are indications of the presence of an institution in our experience. It is the presence of patriarchy or the presence of capitalist consumerism. Whichever, the details point to a pattern, the way in which socially structured institutions occupy the experience of individuals and surface as their desires and interests, the very inclinations that they have to get this or that, to feel this or that, and to achieve this or that. What is left over if that is where we are? Reason fits the pattern, amusement, sexuality too. We don't assert a deterministic universe because we observe mechanical motion and the causal relationships that resound in chains linked across the spacetime continuum. Rather, we conceive mechanism because we cannot find any room for ourselves in the middle of all that. Insofar as these structures are bound to reason, they are disciplinary. Insofar as they are bound to pleasure, they are disciplinary.

Who are the agents of this discipline? Can we look around and find the masters among us? No one would seem to own the logic that drives these structures. There may be people who are so deeply occupied by the logic of their organizations that they rise to the top of their operations. Is that how it goes, and the hierarchy is just the normal layout of the structure's stature? Patriarchy, for example, might describe pleasure in terms of specific behaviors that lead to orgasm, and those who have mastered it are those with the most extraordinary sample of the attributes. The man who flips his partner over the easiest, the man who is confident, who has "throw down" to the highest degree, that is the ruler inscribed in this structure. Even if those qualities are separated from their meaning, even if they cease to be actions performed in bed, their pattern retains its power and lets their possessor rise to the top of the chain.

The typical response when laying things out this way is that this is bad. Patriarchy is wrong, the emphasis of entertainment and pleasure over depth and substance is wrong. The judgment is based on some system of deliberation that is taken for granted, and it is most likely social in some form or another. These structures are at work, and they violate the contract, or they are based on a set of rules that are contrary to the general welfare, and so on. This just repeats the same recursive round. They don't even look like lines of flight when framed in this fashion. That's because a few brief steps and they just become alternative structures that place different attributes at their acme and offer up an alternative hierarchy of value and preference. In the end, cynicism appears because it all just starts to look like one big power play. No, it isn't what they say is the greatest good, it's what we say is the greatest good. It isn't their vision of pleasure, but ours. It isn't their appraisal of the general welfare but our alternative.

After the Semester had ended, I was in my office to give out grades to whoever wanted to know before the holidays and couldn't wait until the official transcripts were updated next month. Most people could already figure it out because they had seen the grades on all the different assignments and knew from the syllabus what the weight of each item was. It was simple math, so really no one needed to come to the office for my help, but I made myself available just in case someone had a beef they wanted to raise with me, or whatever.

There was a woman who came by who had decided to major in philosophy. She said she was thinking about graduate school. I offered to talk to her more about it if she wanted, but she looked at me like I was being creepy. I shrugged it off, but it put me on guard. I wondered what was behind that, what had I done to cause the reaction and what experience did she have that made it weird? It was a small thing that I don't think I would have remembered if it weren't for something else that happened a bit later on.

One of the women from the evening class came by. She was probably in her late twenties, a good ten years older than the first student. She seemed nervous and awkwardly asked for her grade. I looked through my book, found her record, and told her. No need to point out that she was one of those who could have figured this out on her own.

"That's the official grade?"

"Yup. Is that okay?"

"Yes, it's what I was expecting. Have you turned it in already?"

"Yes. Completely official."

"Okay then. Would you like to get a drink some time? Tonight, if you aren't busy?"

I lost the ability to talk and only managed to stammer a bit.

Finally, I was able to say, "I don't think that would be a good idea."

"Why not? You said the grade is official. I'm not your student anymore. I'm not taking any classes in philosophy next term, and you said you're only here for this year. I don't see why you can't have a drink with me."

"You're right, of course. It's not about policy. It's totally my thing. I just can't. I don't want to be that guy if that makes sense."

She paused and looked at me, understanding but disappointed. "Well okay then, but you have no idea what you're missing."

We both laughed at this. Nervous laughter. The way she was looking at me I could feel myself blush. There was a lot that was clear here and there was even more that was not clear at all.

I nodded, "I'm sure you're right."

She thanked me, not sure exactly what for, said goodbye, and left.

Two things like that within an hour or so of each other. It seemed fucked up to me that these might be ordinary occurrences. There was something in advanced schooling that was doing a number on people involved in it. Everything I was trying to teach, all this work and writing. All the philosopher's books and articles that we had read. All of it was aimed at creating an edifice throughout the semester that we could then begin to challenge during the last couple of weeks while reading the last few assignments. These women had summarized all of it in just a look from the one and a few sentences from the other.

It was true, I did not want to be that guy. In either case, I didn't want to be the creepy professor and I didn't want to be the guy who thinks his students are a legitimate dating pool. Both experiences seemed tied to that, at least to someone thinking of it that way. Against my better judgment, the second exchange was sexy as hell and even though thoughts like that about this woman had never crossed my mind before, they were definitely crossing it after she left. Where is the desire and where is the reason? What did I want and how could I know when the conditions for deliberating and knowing were already involved in the stakes, were already aligned on one side or the other? That wasn't calculated, it was pure reaction, I primed myself for it long ago even if there is a moment that flashes desire after the fact. Did I express my freedom by doing the right thing despite my hidden inclination? Did I suppress my freedom by applying institutional policy to actions I prevented for other reasons? Was there a look in my eyes that was creepy or did the first woman's fears get the better of her perception of an offer to help? What would I have to do to be sensitive to that in the future, not make the offer at all? What did I really want when I made that offer? Was there a hidden inclination? Were there reasons and critical perspectives that could sort this all out without falling on one side or the other? Who is in a position to tell that tale? It all seemed to boil down to that same question, "What do we want and how can we know? What are the various ways in which we telegraph what we want to each other even when we don't know that we are doing it?"

She slides back into the other side of the booth, "You were saying? About your roommate?"
"He's a theoretical realist but a practical idealist."
She laughs.
"I mean, well, theoretically, he's a realist. Practically, he's an idealist."
"Shouldn't it be the other way around?"
"There's no should about it. It just is. I don't even mean it. It's something else that's going on. People place too much emphasis on intentions and their own interpretations of their actions looking forward. They should always work backwards. Their ethics should always be forensic, the deliberative approach is futile."
"Because we aren't free?"
"Because we can't calculate all the influences and all the factors. Not when we're trying to figure out what to do and not when we're doing it. If you find yourself in a real dilemma where two things are batting up against each other for your precious intellectual or moral resources, it's more fateful to try to figure out how it all came about rather than how to move it forward. Moving forward is easy to figure out once you know how you got to where you are in the first place."
"You think this is his problem?"
"Not exactly, but it's related. He's reluctant to be doing what he's doing. He worries that philosophy corrupts and coerces. His reluctance lives side by side with his inclination and creates a dilemma. The dilemma makes him realize there is something he has to do to resolve the situation. Resolution, he thinks, requires he make up his mind, or convince others

to make up their minds about some future sequence of events that must happen. He pretends that he is being objective and withholding judgment until he can correctly affirm the best course of action. It's the traditional picture, he thinks we deliberate so that we might act and that our action includes persuading others to recognize our actions as legitimate so they will help us achieve our ends."

"You don't think that a person can will such ambivalence and objectivity. Are you saying it sneaks up on us? Instead of thinking we can steer it while moving forward, we have to look backward to see how it found us."

"Yes. Take him, for example. He knows that studying philosophy isn't a simple matter, it isn't one thing. He knows that 'the tradition' is a set of actions or orientations that are governed by a profession and that a profession amounts to a highly complex social organization. He knows that the training isn't just about the domain, but about the rules of behavior. How to address each other, how to reference each other, who we need to pay attention to, and who we don't. He knows all this because he's in the middle of it, he has been undergoing professional training for ten years. As a result, he should know that his deliberations are embedded in his intentions by this same training, by the discipline he's been studying and passing along in his own teaching. It shapes his writing, it shapes his thinking. Whether he wants it to or not."

"You think the options he sees and is deliberating about are already laid out for him by that same discipline?"

"I do. In order to maintain this trajectory in his training, he has to carry out certain actions. He has to follow a proper agenda, and this doesn't allow for involvements that will pin him down."

"Romantically, for example."

"Yes, but his own historical relationship to romance brought him to where he is. She recognized him. They shared a moment. Whatever. He can't turn away from this because of the person that he is, that he has become through his past relationships. There are many forms of organization that are simultaneously at work."

"You think the form of the attraction surfaces the tension between these two types of training?"

"Right. He knows all this and yet proceeds as if the dilemma is just a problem that he needs to resolve by figuring out the right course of action. That act of calculating, the deliberating itself, is nothing other than the tension between the two types of training, both opaque to him. Deliberation just realizes those forces and all the ways in which he has been trained to resist them and integrate them."

"Desire brought him to where he is and if he just focuses on what he wants or how to figure out what he wants, then he's its plaything. He is completely under the control of the desire that has been generated by all the training. It's a coherent theory of action. You're saying this is a kind of realism?"

"I don't know. I've never been good with those types of terms. It's probably some form of naturalism, but of the Nietzschean or Deweyan kind rather than what you get from a scientific realist or something like that. The agent isn't autonomous, its boundaries are not its skin."

"It's Freudian."

"Except he keeps framing the question as 'what do I want?' rather than 'why did I want this?' That's the practical idealism."

"That's not so mixed up. They can go together, I should think. Figuring out what you want involves understanding where you are and how you got there. The forensics come into play even during the deliberations. How about you? If I ask you what you want won't that force you to think about the situation you're in and how you came to be in it?"

"You mean, with us specifically?"

"Yes, you've made it clear that you're only here temporarily. You don't plan to stay next summer, and I know this, but here we are."

"Here we are."

"Where is that exactly? I've told you that I'm not really looking for some lasting thing. That I'm good with what works here and now and the experience it might bring, the good times, the positive influence. Even the pain isn't so terrible."

"Yup, and I've agreed with you."

"Well then there you are. We didn't just randomly and accidentally fall into this. We wanted to come to this point. What do you want next given that these are the desires that got us to where we are? Deliberation and forensics are both necessary, they are combined."

"I see your point, but I just hate that people think that without ethics we'll just do whatever we want. Like ethics is a conscious theory that we impose deliberately. If it's just baked into us by all the influences and experiences we've had growing up, then our desires just come from whatever ethics we already have."

"You don't have to wonder if your desires are good, you just have them because you've been trained to want what's good? Wanting is wanting the good?"

"Yes please."

"Okay sir, those are the magic words. Let's go."

We get up from the table.

The Heidelberg is pretty far from the professor's place, and we wouldn't get much privacy there anyway, so we decide to go to her house. She lives with three other people in the main house but has her own room. There is a couple that lives in a separate apartment around back. It's a big house. When I met her, she was learning how to set type at this little publishing house here in town. It's an academic press with some in house printing. Such a coincidence that we would both be working there. We met at the café back in August. We were both sitting outside, the only two people out there, because the weather looked pretty threatening, and everyone had gone inside. We were the diehard smokers and were braving the elements.

Neither of us are the kind of people who would have started talking to someone just because we happened to be nearby. We were busy. We were both reading books, but the lightning strikes were increasing in intensity and the light and sound of it was overwhelming, impossible to ignore. We kept looking over at each other after each blast. "Whoa" was pretty much the entirety of our first seven or eight exchanges. We settled into commentary on the coming storm. She was at a table next to the building, and it had a little overhang above it. My table was out closer to the street, so I was more exposed. She invited me to move to her table and take shelter just in case.

We smoked and watched the storm. We read our books during the lulls and didn't say much.

It was a beginning. When I got back to town in September, I would go looking for her at that café partly to find her and partly to leave the professor alone in the apartment. After we ran into each other at that bar, we started to hang out more regularly. We would meet up at the café pretty often, but without making plans. She and I would sit together, reading our books and exchanging a few words here and there. Mostly we smoked and drank coffee. She would write in a notebook sometimes. I would write in a notebook sometimes. This all took place over the last couple months. We became more familiar.

When it started to get colder, we had to act if these habitual run ins were to continue. She invited me over to her house. I recalled drinking some wine. She was perfect. Breezy. Very clear about what she was doing. Steadfast in her focus, and confident in all her movements. Soft sometimes. Like women are. Strong and soft. It's so fetching when someone like her is so at ease and expert at moving across a range of emotions, as if she had mastered humanity and become comfortable in all its ways.

These last months, we've been cautiously trying to figure out whether the other person agrees with what we think we want from each other. It was funny, the way we danced around it. She was absolutely right, the story I told about the professor was really about me. It was as if I had been trying to instigate this conversation with her and wasn't sure how to do it or if it would be well met. At every step, every carefully placed foot we advanced, this same perfection kept resonating. Like the fates had put us there and we needed to catch up and stop resisting them.

It was at the very least perfect for where we are now. Fate always time bounds us like that, today's perfection might be a disaster ten years from now. I probably would not have been interested in her at other times in my life, and probably she wouldn't have cared much for me either. Something about where we both were at just that moment. Well-suited and immediately drawn, but careful in how we realized it. Like we had been discussing tonight, our past desire, the desires that framed our histories up to that moment, had brought us together. What we needed to do now, where we needed to go from here, would be clear once we understood that.

She is a few years younger than I am, and still settling into whatever notions were becoming important to her. She had been in Prague for most of the last summer and had become convinced that there was something there that brought out something in her that had been missing. That night in the thunderstorm, she had mentioned *The Castle.* Later she told me it was working like a cautionary tale. She was trying to figure out what she wanted in her life, what kind of a life she wanted for herself, and she couldn't wrap her brain around it, but she was becoming increasingly clear about what she didn't want. Visualizing the traps to avoid gave her confidence in letting herself pursue what she wanted to have and to experience: at all costs not to be a cog in a machine.

This highly dynamic state meant that there were a set of commitments that she wasn't prepared to make, they would inject bias into whatever it was that was brewing in her way of working through things. I recognized this in her right away and felt at home with it. It described my own state perfectly. I didn't want to live my whole life in Ann Arbor, and I certainly didn't want to be forced to live with a friend for longer than I had to. She didn't see her time there as permanent either. It was a passing of like-minded souls, but it took time to know that for sure.

We were people at a point in their lives that needed intimacy while they were figuring themselves out, and we found each other in a thunderstorm. Temperamentally, this amounted to a perfect fit. Sexually too as it turned out. We left the Heidelberg a little drunk and a little clearer about where we were. Technically, it wasn't our first time, but it was our first something. Focused and unafraid. Guilt free. Together.

It was enthusiastic and we were drawn that way. There is a lovely way in which intellectual passion becomes physical and then morphs back into the mind. Her roommates had left town for the holidays and afterward we were naked in the kitchen, she was sitting up on the far end of the counter while I stood a few feet away looking and listening. Many levels of pleasure, the resonance was ecstatic: the mood, the sweat, and the smells of the last two hours filled the kitchen.

"It's good you're not predatory," she said.

"How do you mean?"

"Well, since we met. You haven't been like that. You know, like how guys can be."

"I can be that way."

"I can tell. That's why I'm saying that it's good that you haven't been. That never would have worked."

"When I was in Austin, it was like that. Boulder too really."

"Why not here?"

"I don't know. It could be the professor. I wasn't like that in Illinois either. He might be a good influence."

"Sometimes, it seems like predatory behavior is deep in the male psyche. I wouldn't think that people who are prone to it would be subject to influence like that. It's either on or off."

"He's so at odds with himself and would never deliberately present the right thing to do as being an exhibition of pursuit and capture behavior. Hunting down animals isn't something anyone would choose to do if they were totally at their liberty and deciding on a course of action. Only necessity could bring it about. That'd be his theory at least."

"He doesn't act that way?"

"No, the theory is a rationalization. It's a way of hiding his ambivalence. He convinces himself that he could never be that way because it doesn't fit with his moral vision of the world, but he is that way. Behind his own back."

"This somehow helps you to avoid it by choice?"

"In a way, yes. Seeing him in such bad faith, so deluded about it, makes it impossible for me to be oblivious. It's like a slap in the face that forces me to think about it."

"It pursues you, makes use of you. Takes you in its grip."

"Funny. I mean it's something basic in human cognition."

"Human male cognition."

"Why? You don't pursue things in the same way? Goals, states of being that you want to achieve? Isn't the salon vision of fragile womanhood supposed to be the picture of a passive person whose life is controlled by others? Aren't we done with that? Isn't the whole point of feminist thinking to point out that the 'delicate flower' is bullshit? 'I can plow a field as good as any man.'"

"Yeah, but that doesn't have to be pursuit. It could be collaborative."

"I've heard this way of framing it, but you don't strike me as someone who is going to follow the instructions of your guidance counsellor, right? I mean, you still want to establish some individual control. Your father selling you off to the highest bidder could be a form of collaboration. You oppose it by wanting more control. The collaboration with your family, let's say, means taking your point of view more into account and trying to teach yourself to be less the dutiful daughter, no?"

"It's more complicated than that. You're trying to characterize it as though control and aggressive pursuit are the norm that everyone aspires to, that feminism is about women gaining access to historically masculine traits."

"Sort of. I'm saying that action is already conceived as the pursuit of an end. Ambition and calculation are part and parcel of it. The agent must have control over the conditions that will lead to the end they desire. This view of action has been prohibited to some agents and been the privileged domain of others. White Male, and so on. I'm suggesting that the pattern isn't being attacked, only the exclusive access to it. Sometimes, disputes over the distribution of privilege camouflage themselves as arguments against the existence of privilege."

"No, collaboration, the way I'm using it, is meant to break that pattern altogether and set up an alternative way to understand action and the options available. It's a whole way of redefining acting and living well."

"I don't see it. Women may just have a better sense that the ends they pursue require social connections and relationships, so they account for them in their course of action. It's still pursuit of an end even if the conditions are social and highly empathetic. There are conditions to place on the collaboration, right? I mean, couldn't I argue that women have always played an active role in social structures even when those structures are sexist? Women are agents, they have accepted roles and even worked hard at times to enforce social constraints. Many still do. Norms may originate or be enforced by other women. Collaboration always happens, there is nothing antithetical to hunter logistics in collaboration. Look at the lions."

"Collaboration might be the wrong word then. Every participant has a meaningful point of view that should be considered. The hunter just pursues because the hunter wants the prey. He doesn't care what the object of his pursuit wants."

"Okay, I see how that works for sexually predatory behavior because the object of desire in that case is another person, but what about other things where the other people involved are more hidden?"

"What's an example?"

"Well, say that you want to pursue a career as a printer. You try to make that happen. Working with others even. You convince people to hire you, teach you the skills you need, and so on. Do you consider all the other people involved in that? The whole social fabric of competitors who might also be trying to do the same thing. When you convince someone to hire you, you convince them not to hire everyone else who is applying for the job. When you learn the skill, you convince the civilization to continue to support the skill as a niche with people that occupy it."

"Is your point that the shift to a more socially based behavior means that all action in pursuit of an end is socially impactful and hurts or helps others in their pursuits?"

"Absolutely, and there are conditions of scarcity that are real. You may not ever treat a friend or someone you directly encounter in the dehumanized way you think the cretin male treats the woman he's trying to fuck, but that doesn't mean that actions that are implicitly social don't sometimes exhibit that same oblivious selfishness of pursuit. Human cognition itself may have developed under conditions where it's largely oriented toward complex achievements and goals that require sophisticated orchestration. Entropy embodied, right? This sophisticated orchestration amounts to traps and coercion. Not directly aimed at other people, but indirectly and, at the very least, directly over circumstances and conditions. Explicit awareness of interests or intentions doesn't matter, all material factors are relevant."

"This is not an example of your complete failure to be predatory."

"What do you mean?"

"Right now, you are expressing an idea that you are pursuing, and doing so in a way that is a major turnoff. You are failing in your pursuit while pursuing it."

"The professor's academic ways have influenced me." That made her smile. "It's just the choice of what I pursue. I'm in pursuit of some form of understanding or some set of clear notions, but not in pursuit of you. I'm not trying to seduce you, but pursuit remains the driving pattern in my behavior. I don't know how to think about my own action as an intellectual except as a pursuit of ideas and understanding. That's learning and study."

"Okay, so in bed I don't want to be in a situation where some guy is just trying to get off and it doesn't matter whether I'm there. I want to get off too, and I want someone who cares about that. Someone who will connect with me, so that both of us enjoy it throughout the entire experience."

"Is enjoyment enough to testify to your subjective contribution to the encounter, or does your partner need to be sensitive to the fact that you are actively pursuing that pleasure? I would think it's the latter. You might enjoy it against your will, but you wouldn't be pursuing it against your will. This requires all involved parties to have a reasonably good critical understanding of all the others involved. Even if we do that and everything is repeatedly confirmed, it's still a fact that being here with me, for example, excludes others. We've chosen each other and are ignoring others that we don't want to be with. I don't think it's a question of what pulls us or draws us to it, but of what drives us into it. Conatus. We should recognize the role of pursuit and learn to understand it better."

"I'm not convinced. The pursuer syndrome is defined by the object of pursuit and lacks insight into itself as a pursuer, as a person expressing drives and who is accountable for that. Changing that makes it something else."

"That's interesting."

"The action pattern doesn't change, but the understanding of it does. The whole social context. There is a different relationship to what is happening. We see ourselves pushing things around and being driven by whatever is behind us, organizations, institutions, or whatever. This makes us more careful in what we do. Being careful like that, changes everything. It breaks the pattern and turns it into something else. We won't dehumanize or objectify what we are pursuing. The conditions of goal-oriented behavior would be completely changed. We wouldn't think in the same terms of means and ends anymore. A person who acts that way would be less prone to violence when they don't get what they want."

"How do you figure?"

"Well, violence may be an extreme form of coercing something into complying with what you want to do with it. If you are aware of yourself as being in the middle of circumstances that are bouncing you around, you'll be more careful and pay closer attention to those circumstances, both in your actions and in the way you interpret other people's actions. Understanding is always practical that way."

"Talk always feels cheap when it comes to violence."

"Still, there's a difference in what I'm saying. It might not have anything to do with changing the way action works, but it does have a lot to do with changing how agency works. Violence is a tactic that rejects the perspective of the other person."

"I get it, but I reject that pursuit is essentially violent in that way. Violence might be a way of reacting to failure when pursuit meets with resistance, and its expression might be more or less blatantly associated with the failed pursuit. Consider that there are forms of coercion that are violent, but that don't look like it on first impression."

"Such as?"

"Well, maybe this is trivial, but there are women who evaluate men as partners based on how easy it might be to change them into what they want them to be. Get them to dress differently, act differently, and so on. The measures used can be a form of coercion. Behavior is being changed against the agent's will and to help her get what she wants even if she fails to find it ready-made or spontaneously present in his autonomous behavior."

"It's a bullshit example. Metaphorical violence isn't violence. I don't know, maybe some guys want women to make men out of them. Under patriarchy, turnabout is fair play. Given the rules, why shouldn't women be men's mirrors?"

"Exactly. Power here, power there. It's okay when it's justified though, right? We are justified, they are not. In this case, for example, is everything transparent and doesn't your justification require that? Are people being open about their motives and their intent? Fraud is a part of coercion and there is violence in it. It seems that at least part of what goes on in coercive pursuit is that the pursuer is not forthright, is not open and clear about the motives and intentions involved. At the beginning, she's all girly and giggly. Whatever he does is fine. Then, as it progresses, she changes her tune and wants him to change his. Intent is hidden at the beginning. Even physical violence, as clear as it is in some ways, hides its intent in others. I mean, a violent act doesn't necessarily directly achieve a desired end. It might be done for the sake of breaking the other person's resistances, and then verbal suggestions might follow. The threat of violence can resonate and change the reactions those suggestions get."

"Not when we're talking about rape. That's not a metaphor."

"I get that, but don't isolate on the single act, think about the social environment where the act happens, where it is investigated in specific ways, prosecuted in specific ways, and all that. Rape is a case where violence is explicitly used for the sake of an actual end, but there is also the psycho-social misogyny of it too. The constant presence of a threat of rape has a direct impact on the entire social setting. It's part of the establishment of a patriarchal social order and as such, rape isn't about sex."

"It isn't *just* about sex, anyway, but it is about that too."

"Yes, and I think this makes that point more forcefully. There are all kinds of hidden messages in the violent act even in that case, and really, it's the hidden messages that might be more to the point. Certainly, more to the objectionable side of it. If it weren't for large scale institutional innuendo and side effects, violence –assuming it isn't murder– might be less hateful. The injury it causes doesn't last nearly as long as the psycho-social injuries I'm talking about. It still hurts, but it lacks the indirect ramifications, it's less about stigma and reinforcing a social order and more simply a raw act."

"Like when animals are violent?"

"The gazelle is mostly upset about being eaten, it doesn't long for a more just civilization that it would share with the cheetah."

"Cheetahs don't hate gazelles, and anyway, like you said, there are lots of forms of coercion. People can mislead each other to get what they want. Pursuit accompanied by the threat of violence or fraud can be rejected while still accepting a purer form of it, a way in which it happens that is free of the so-called bad parts, anything that works as violence or coercion."

"Exactly. It's all pursuit and that is value neutral. We need to learn to see the historical and social factors in our intentions and pursuits if we are going to start evaluating them on moral grounds. It can't all just be judged the same way. Some added conditions are required to make it 'bad', others might make it 'good.' Groupings of people will always anchor these assessments. Pursuit is bound to a capability in the agent, success and failure and the reactions they elicit are social conditions shaped and ordered by traditional means and methods."

"Whatever I think is wrong with pursuit is really a problem with the response we are taught to have when it fails? Or the meaning we think that it will have if it succeeds?"

"Yes. If the pursuer refuses to take no for answer, that is a huge problem. What failure and success mean in such pursuits may also play a part in this. It's possible that he can't accept failure because of what he has been taught it would mean in such circumstances."

"It's possible he's an asshole."

"Sure, but I don't understand why you would want to yield ambition and determination in getting what you want to some kind of necessarily coercive order. What kind of expressive power does that leave for people who want to actually do things of value with their lives?"

"Well, you're mostly just digging in your heals. You've got your mind set on this idea that thought is a kind of pursuit, and you won't let it go. Nothing would convince you."

"Okay. How are you different?"

It's not obvious, but there is power at work when having such a conversation naked and still mostly in the throes of newfound infatuation. There's a point of contact in every utterance even when there is disagreement. A twinkle in the eye. I was standing there in front of her while we spoke, and even when I said things she didn't agree with, I would still catch her eyes wandering. Even when her eyes suggested I was moving dangerously close to an offense; she remained aware of the effect she had on me as she pulled her knee up close to her chest with her foot on the counter. There were ideas flowing back and forth and they had their effects, but there were bodies behind them, and these bodies had their effects too. My bias is to see the pursuit and evasion in it all. I cannot but affirm that this magical teleology is neither masculine nor feminine, insults aside, but the way trajectories form, hearts beat, and skin covers.

There and then we were together having a common experience while set apart in our differences. Hers and mine. Everything we said and did confirmed that I was right, and everything we said and did confirmed that she was right. Even more, everything suggested that we were at odds with each other and that we were not. Desire and pursuit were not one thing. They were many things. The countertop and the space between us. The moonlight and the darkness outside. The quiet of the house, the creaking of the floor. She and I looking across the distance.

When I got in my car and drove out of town, all the pressure left me.

By the time I got to Yellow Springs, it was as if the last four months had never happened. I felt right back where I was before I started school. I ate at the restaurant, I had a beer and a cigarette, I slept at my friend's place, and everything stabilized. It was like I was back in my own skin and my heart had started beating again. I drank my coffee the next morning walking through the middle of town and everybody seemed to be passing by. Many people from my previous life, and with each greeting, the feeling was reinforced. What had I been doing to myself, why was I putting myself through this? I want this so badly and yet it makes me so dizzy. Is it possible that someone could want to put themselves through something like this on purpose?

The pressure of grades isn't even the problem. I did fine. It's more about what everyone thinks of me. It is strange to be identified by what I am studying, by my academic pursuits. The professors and the students both want to know that immediately. What is your focus? What work are you doing? Who are you working with? They might still think about what I'm wearing or how I act or what I am like away from school, but they don't let on about any of that right away. At least they put up a front that what really matters are my professional interests and goals.

Even the professor who has started writing to me, it's all moody and nuanced, trying to get me to reveal stuff, trying to get into my head and figure out what I am thinking about. I'm not saying he doesn't want to fuck me, just that he presents it so much differently than what I am used to. That's how it all seems to me. Exactly the same as everything else, exactly the same as the rest of the world, but presented differently. Hidden behind some code where "I really want to find out more about your research projects" translates into "let's bang."

I have to admit, I am still far more attracted to the raw and the up front. Why should people hide behind these ridiculous masks? Why do they dress up their desires and interests as sophisticated and cultured practices that are oh so worthy of their higher selves? In the end, it is all body and heart, we are physical creatures making our way. The question that keeps nagging at me is why I chose to live among them, why I chose to go this way. Choose. No one is forcing me. Do I want this career despite the means needed to get there or because of them? It's not like my goal is to work at a children's library. I am not braving academia so that I can leave it behind once I get the skills. Special collections mean research libraries and universities. I've specifically aimed myself in a direction that is going to make me uncomfortable for the rest of my life; or worse, it'll stop making me uncomfortable at some point because I'll be just like them.

When I got home to Lexington, Christmas was in full swing. Everything was already decorated; the stockings were in place and the tree. The whole family had come back, and it was comforting. Vastly different from the times I would come back from Ohio where the disconnected atmosphere felt so judgmental. This time it felt different. My stepdad is a professor of engineering, and he's never seen me as someone capable of any of it. He thinks of me as a bartender or a waitron. Now he has something to talk to me about, something we have in common. It's funny the way he asks questions and tries to learn if it's a disaster —as he expected— or if it's working out the way my mom assured him that it would. My stepbrother is just like his dad too. The two of them form a block. They team up. Not on purpose or because of some plan. They just both have the same way of looking at me. They think of me the same way. Their questions create a judgmental atmosphere. Usually this makes me crazy, but this time I have all the right answers. I can say all the right things. I speak their language now, it seems. They don't know what to do with that. It makes me smile.

Mom is what makes it home for me, though. That hasn't changed. She doesn't treat me any differently. She still wants to know if I'm taking good care of myself, sleeping enough, eating right, and making sure to get enough exercise. We talk all the time on the phone, so there is no catching up that we need to do. We just like being around each other. We like being distracted but still together. We went to the mall, I went down to visit her at the shop, we had lunch. All that stuff you can't do on the phone from far away. That was what I really needed. That was the part of the trip that would recharge me and get me ready for next semester.

Not just that. There was something else I needed too, something I couldn't get in Ann Arbor. Not yet anyway. Tending bar was a good way to keep grounded. Definitely, but I was still too scared to be myself there. I felt like I was always being watched and judged. What are grades anyway, right? I don't want to let on about how I really am. Even if it was fine for the people in the bar to know me that way, what if they talked to the people at school? Some come to the bar sometimes. There could be overlap. People would know and they would never look at me the same way. Too much fucking judgment. Do men ever have to worry about this bullshit? About their manhood or whatever changing everyone's view of how they do whatever else it is that they do? Well, maybe some men, but not your average heterosexual white man. Would my male professors be ruined if people found out that in addition to their interest in critical theory, they also happened to love sex? Only if they were perverts, only if they liked things outside the normal range. For women, it's different. It's like there's no normal sexuality. If we express any interest at all that immediately colors everyone's judgment about our professional abilities and how serious we are.

It might be all in my head, but I just have this feeling that if I were to be truly honest with this philosophy professor, let him know exactly what kinds of thoughts cross my mind on a daily basis, he would be horrified. He needs to see me as an intellectual ingenue. His attraction is based on that. If I showed him that I am a real person with my own preferences and tastes, he would be totally threatened by it, and I can't figure out why that is. The main reason I keep writing back is because I am just as interested in finding out how he thinks as he seems to be in finding out how I think. The first impression I get is that there is some chance that it will happen if I keep exchanging notes with him. He seems like he might be able to express himself about this kind of stuff. If I do let him know, ultimately, what I am really like, maybe he won't just run off horrified. He'll be horrified, or surprised, or whatever and it might scare him off, but given what I have seen so far, maybe he'd let me know what he was thinking before he left. I don't know. It probably doesn't matter. Men. Fuck.

My ex-boyfriend being the total opposite side of the spectrum. I'm sure things got into his head too, but he would never say a word about it. He kept it all to himself. He may or may not have been the most judgmental man I've ever known. I wouldn't know it. We'd fight about something, and maybe those fights were because of the way I am. The way I was reacting to something. He didn't like what it said about me maybe. It might remind him that I was a certain way or had certain feelings or thoughts. This would set him off. He would get all moody and stop acting normal with me. No more affection, no more eye contact. He would go off to the woods, down near the river, and do whatever it was that he needed to do down there. He'd come back and be fine. He'd apologize and everything would go back to normal, but I never knew what happened. Really, for the most part, that was good. I didn't want to know. I was quite sure that if I found out the details of what was going through his head, it would ruin things between us. If I found out what judgments he was making, I'd lose all respect for him, or I couldn't be vulnerable with him anymore. Whatever. It would be bad. I'm glad that he never really told me why we were breaking up, why he didn't want to move to Ann Arbor. He probably wouldn't have looked particularly good if he did, and it wouldn't have made me feel any better. It's probably for the best that I don't know. People don't need to share everything.

A couple of days after Christmas, I went to one of the bars I like in town. I hadn't been there in a few years, and it had changed a bit. More gentrified, but still true to its roots. Dive bars go through this. They are truly and authentically what they are. That becomes an attraction so people who are interested in lifestyle tourism start coming to visit. This changes the bar until eventually it's just an imitation of what it was. This hadn't happened yet, but there were signs of it.

The guy who was looking at me from the other side of the bar was a perfect example. He was a pretty man. Perfectly quaffed but dressed all wrong for the place. Jeans and a t-shirt with a flannel overshirt, but it didn't look natural. Like he wasn't wearing it because that was his thing. Grunge is everywhere. Most of the guys in the bar were dressed this way, but in their case that was just the way they dressed, they happened to be wearing grunge fashion because they were grungy people. This guy was doing it because Lord and Taylor's was starting to feature the grunge look in their winter catalog.

He got my attention right away. I knew he was looking, I caught him a few times out of the corner of my eye. When I decided to confront him by looking him right in the eye, he didn't look away. He didn't blush or get embarrassed; he didn't even smile. Instead, he kept his eyes fixed right on me and stuck his tongue out. Not sexually, exactly. More like the way a little boy would stick out his tongue at a little girl while he was tormenting her on the playground. I loved it. It made me smile and forget everything. I stuck my tongue out right back at him in just the same way. He came over. He was exactly what I needed on this trip. It had been a long time. I had gone the entire semester without sex and had been working extra hard to shun any kind of attention like that. It was all part of the oppressive observation and judgment that I lived in constant fear of. I thought that people would know. Like the way I can sometimes tell when I talk to people in the bar. People would know that I had just had sex or that I hadn't, and if they could tell then it would change their whole impression. Even if they didn't know specifically what they were sensing, it might change the way they thought about me.

This guy turned out to be an actor model wannabe. I liked the way he made an entrance, but I wouldn't say I was interested in him, not really. Still, I knew in just a few minutes talking with him that he was the right man for the job, and I knew that this was exactly the job that needed to be done. Such a release. It made the whole trip exactly what it needed to be. Every aspect of it. Somebody who didn't care why I was studying what I was studying, who didn't care what my professors were like or how they were responding to my work. He was pure desire. That made it so easy for me to become the same way. Which meant that for that night and the next morning I could forget everything, I could be without being everything I ever was. Without being all the decisions I had ever made, without being all the ways in which people saw me and judged me to be. Pleasure has a powerful way of getting rid of all that. It's why it has been such a constant in my life. The same way that the bar blocks out whatever happens outside it, animal desire can have the same effect.

As I was leaving his apartment the next morning, he gave me a bunch of headshots he had lying around. He said they were not the most current batch, and he didn't need them anymore. I don't know why he thought I would want them, and I don't know why I threw them in the back of my car and just left them there. It went against everything that had happened between us. It's like we were shy about letting our time together be what we both wanted it to be, so we had to pretend there was something else there that could stay with us, that we would take away from our meeting and hold on to. We didn't ask for phone numbers or email addresses. We didn't plan to see each other again. All of that was beside the point, so why did he give me those pictures and why did I keep them? I didn't think about it at the time, but now I wonder. No one knew about this. It was completely my own. No one would judge me. No one could. Was I setting myself up for self-criticism? That can't be. I refuse to take part in that. I won't do the bastards' work for them, but why then?

I won't apologize for what I like and what makes me feel good, and I don't care how it fits in with stupid male fantasies about what they think I should and shouldn't like. I don't give a fuck about any of that. They don't deserve that kind of control. It is absolutely amazing to blow their minds. If what gets them off is that they think something they do or say gives them power, then when I turn that into my orgasm, I am taking control over their desire. If I go beyond what they imagine they want, then I am the one with all the power. I can give them more than they want and that comes from what I want when I want it. Both of us, in the end, become totally dependent on my pleasure. Men are so simple really, it's not like I have to guess what they want. The trick is to make them feel me giving it to them, make them understand that whatever they are feeling, however it gets them off, it is because of what I have decided, because of what I want. Their pleasure is a biproduct of that, of me not only giving but taking what I want from them. This is so different from how I feel at school. This is what really recharges me for that battle, but how to make this happen in that coded language they use? In that way? Is that what I was hoping to hold on to?

I left home a few days later with my mood intact. The plan was to hit Yellow Springs on the way back and spend new year's there. The whole drive I didn't think about anything. I blasted the radio as loud as it would go. I put my foot up on the dashboard and screamed and howled to the music. Why can't I always feel that way? Driving back to Ohio with the music blaring and not a care in the world? When you are driving from somewhere to somewhere else you aren't technically in either place. That was when I was happiest.

January

New Year's Eve is a hard day. I never would have made it if it weren't for the professor. During the toast, I was terrified. If he hadn't been there, I would have drunk with the rest of them. Who am I kidding? It's just a matter of time. I stopped going to meetings, but I can't do this without them. Right now the only thing holding me together is that I know how harshly he would judge me if he caught me drinking. Eventually, I'll get the courage to hide it from him and there will be nothing left to stop me.

That's why I dragged him with me in the first place. It didn't make any sense. I could only go to those parties if I brought someone along who would keep an eye on me, but why did I have to go to those parties? I don't know any of them. They're just work people. Create the drama so that I can make my way through it. That's about par for the course. I don't want the drama. I want peace and quiet, but I can't live without the threat of it, without the adrenaline rush of resisting it, of persevering through it, or rising above it. I tried to tell him this, but I don't think I understand it well enough to convince anyone that this is a thing. Everyone understands the person who thrives on dramatic confrontations. Everyone knows what it means to use drama to get attention, but who ever heard of the need to resist drama?

I have a pharmaceutical dependency. At the moment, it's Antabuse, Klonopin, and a constantly changing cocktail of anti-depressants. They help me avoid drama. That is the most important part. I've tried to explain this to my psychiatrist too, but it's not a thing.

The advantage of an addiction like this is that when I fail, it is absolutely beautiful. I can recall every one of those epic failures. The vomiting, the initial euphoria, the manic power that emerges from the moments of controlled depression. I haven't lived through a Michigan winter in a long time. I don't think I was prepared for how the loss of sun would relapse all these old patterns. Is it the lack of light that fills my head with ideas about drinking again? Is that what makes me reach out for the epic fail of going off the meds and returning to my old self? No more reservations in those moments. It's the only way I can know the fire and urgency of self-propelling action. This is what the professor doesn't get. He doesn't see that these roles we hold can put us into a rut. Engineering isn't filled with charismatic people. Most of the work we do is tame. Deliberate. Even when we stay up all night working on a problem, there is nothing dramatic in our methodology. It's systematic and rational, we just divide and conquer. This can be an ill-fitting suit to some. Where are my moments? When do I get to be the hero? When do I get to scream out loud and live in the heights?

A philosopher can imagine themselves as a magic figure and go through these emotional test runs in their minds when no one is watching. How am I supposed to do that? There is no threat of drama in this. I have to craft dramatic possibilities so that I can carefully orchestrate my struggle to avoid them. It's exhausting.

The professor lives in the dark ages, he doesn't get it at all. Does he think that some 300-year-old virtues are going to mean something in today's world? That's why they call it an ivory tower because the people in it are totally out of touch, and that seems worse now than it has ever been. They have their own way of creating drama. They don't understand that those of us who work for a living, we don't have that luxury. Work that contributes to actual projects that people need, that's a whole different story. We must act predictably; we need to follow rules and be accountable to each other. Giving someone a learning experience does not justify our actions if they might lose or earn millions of dollars. People are clear with each other. My bosses in California put up with my bullshit so long as they thought they could reel me in, get me to play well with others, and keep cranking out product that made money for the company. They didn't care about being ideologically pure. No, they were mitigating risk and trying to maximize the return on their investment. They want to avoid drama too. They don't live for it. At some point it gets to be too much. No tenure to fall back on, they just shitcan your ass and move on.

These assholes, they seem to want drama. Take that whole supervenience argument he is always trying to rehash with me. I mean, it doesn't really matter, does it? Lots of people spell out an argument one way or the other, but who says exactly what is at stake? Does science and experimentation work differently in a supervenient world? Do people act differently? Biologists will beg, borrow, and steal from whatever they are able to beg, borrow, and steal from. If they know physics or chemistry, they'll use it. If the data helps or the patterns suggest an interesting hypothesis, they're going to explore it. If there are results, they will continue down that path, if not, they won't. Philosophical arguments aren't going to have any impact on people like that. They're too practical. Only a bunch of totally out of touch academics could hash and rehash those arguments as though they mattered. They'll get theirs though. Eventually. It's how the world is and it's coming for them too. Watch how dramatic they get when the shrewd, cold administrators come for their asses.

What was his point? Was it about sociology or social psychology or something like that? Supervenience, he said, causes us to think that subjects like sociology and economics aren't real sciences, or aren't worthy of scientific investments. The supervenience theory turns the social world into a collection of individual brain states. Without the ability to reduce sociology to psychology, there would be no way to keep going down the stack until we get to the physical particles. There is nothing more to it. He says this point-of-view leaves us powerless to describe things like the unconscious or repression, and it makes us oversimplify all our politics. As if it all were just a matter of getting everyone to have the right brain states, which is what the reductionists think happens when we believe something in common.

He misses my whole point though. Physics isn't really physics. It's just math. Ratios. Relationships. Social patterns could easily be reduced to mathematics. Sociology just looks soft because it doesn't have the laboratory. That's what it needs. We could easily collect statistics on people's behavior, but how do we form proper hypotheses if we can't offset the data produced by test subjects with data produced by a control group? That's what we need, we need to come up with a way to perform large scale social experiments where we put some people through something to see how it will impact them, how it will change their decision making or their life choices. If we could do that, then the same patterns we use to describe how a natural event takes place could apply to human behavior too. Did he think that the fact that we can't do this today would prove anything? That's ridiculous. We just need to find the courage to experiment on human subjects.

If we could hook electrodes up to everyone's brain, we could collect data on all the changes they go through as various stimuli are presented to them. We could find out what can turn something they don't like into something they do like. We could figure out how to change their minds about all sorts of things based on what we learn about their moods and how they respond to different stimuli under their influence. The only thing that is holding us back from doing this kind of science is our own cowardice. Mark my words, it is just a matter of time before we get over this and stop hiding from it.

This is how it'll go down. First, we'll get the courage to do it in a concealed way that hides what we are doing from the professors who would judge us, who would threaten us with sanctions, then we would get results. They would be secret, but they would be valuable. We would learn things that we could apply to all sorts of stuff. This would give us more courage; our studies would be reinforced. Besides, we would probably learn how to make sure that nobody paid any attention to the people who we were hiding it from in the first place. Results are powerful and they can whitewash almost anything. Especially when those results mean big money. If people start getting rich off it, there will be no stopping them.

Before long, their greed will get the better of them and they will start doing it out in the open. With all that money flying around, they could probably even throw some of it at those same people who would object. Private industry and academic research would merge. Research grants for everyone. There would be confusion and disagreement. There would be conferences and discussions. Voices, pro and con. This would create doubt. Not enough to make things squeaky clean, but at least enough to buy more time so that the research could continue while people sort out the ethical dilemma. Once it is out in the open, all kinds of people will be drawn to it. There will be more of it and that will lead to even more results. It'll become a huge part of the economy, and an ecosystem that touches every part of our lives where everyone is contributing to the stores of knowledge through their behavior and the data it produces. The money will draw smart people and the results will teach those smart people even more than they knew before. The momentum will take care of itself, and no one will be able to stop it.

The true mark of success for any science is when you can build on top of it, when it starts to feed engineering. If you think about it, advertising is already a kind of social engineering. I mean, if it were all just supply and demand, advertisements would be simple statements. Here is some toothpaste, you can brush your teeth with it. As more traits become relevant to the marketplace, they could include more details in the advertisement. It makes your teeth whiter. That isn't how it works though; they are always trying to make you think you really need this. They can't assume you already want clean teeth; they have to convince you that your teeth are disgusting. Once they've done that, they need to convince you that the only way to avoid it is to buy their product. They connect it to all sorts of images of being beautiful and successful. They hook you with that. It isn't even about clean teeth anymore, it's about sex and love and having all your dreams come true.

They already do this. What's a focus group anyway? They show the ads to smaller groups to get a sense of whether they work as intended. They change the content or the script or the images based on the feedback they get. They try to make sure the group traits match with some larger social distribution. Aren't there already tons of statistics involved in advertising? The key is to find a way to gather statistics about everything. You could build a model of every aspect of human life. You could find patterns in them. The population would teach you all kinds of relationships between things that no one ever thought were related to each other. That wouldn't be enough, you'd have to figure out how to use that to perform controlled experiments. It would be pretty simple, the same way we do it in physics labs. You learn the correlations and then you start making small adjustments to see if the correlation moves the way you think it should move. If it doesn't, you try something else. If it does, you cause bigger changes and see if your predictions hold up under more extreme circumstances.

What difference does it make, in the end? The movement of a gas or a falling body, the way birds evade a predator, the way that people consume chili when its packaging looks a certain way, or better, how they vote if the candidate says this instead of that. Whether they notice legislation that goes against what their politician promised, they could study that too. All kinds of crap would be easy to know once we get it. That's what he doesn't see. Supervenience isn't just a philosophical argument; it has practical implications. It will change everything if people would only accept it and explore its results to their logical conclusion.

I guess maybe that's what he was saying about morality though. It isn't just whether such relationships can be reduced to purely mathematical patterns, but whether or not they should be. That's exactly the point he misses. The most sophisticated form of social order is the moral order. All the same experiments could be performed on people's moral insights too. People's ethics can be changed once we understand the patterns that emerge in their decision-making. Even moral reasoning can be reduced to mathematical relationships and patterns. He said it himself when he went off on how utilitarianism reduces everything to measurable quantities. That's already half the work.

Moral reasoning? I mean, that is the ultimate addiction for avoiding drama, isn't it? It would be easy to convince people that what they always thought was right is wrong, or to just convince them that it doesn't matter. You thought this was stealing and you think that stealing is wrong. We could use the new methods to convince them that it isn't stealing at all and that even if it is, it still isn't wrong, or killing or locking someone up without a trial or arresting them without a warrant. Whatever it is. They are all just attitudes about social life and the actions of other people. What should we condemn and what should we condone? How about letting them condemn things but then never letting them do anything about it and then being okay with that? All these are easy engineering problems once you have all the tools.

The point is to get people to see differences between things. Differences that they never saw before. If they think that all killing is wrong, then powerful people are going to be in trouble when they advocate killing people to maintain their power. The death penalty works that way. It's easy enough, these people have already killed somebody so it's okay to kill them, or those people over there are threatening to kill us or our children or someone else. These are differences that make the circumstances different so it's okay to go kill the perpetrators. That's how you make the same action acceptable in one set of circumstances when it isn't okay in another. You make differences clear; you make them apparent, or you convince people that these differences are the most important thing in the world. If you know enough about those people, you'll know which differences to focus on to get them to change their minds. Once they accept the differences you've shown them, it will be easy to shape their moral reasoning to accommodate it. We just need to experiment to figure out which traits matter to which people for making those differences stick.

I don't know. What do I know, I'm just an engineer? Why should I have anything to do with it? If this whole massive project in social engineering rests ultimately on the ability to find the mathematics of our social lives, then engineers will be the ones to reshape our world. That is why science gets its badge of honor when it becomes engineering. Once it can start producing real results that make money, once it has been transformed from a purely academic interest into a proper economic enterprise, that's the most authoritative form of peer review. The philosophers have been spending their time interpreting the world, the point —however— is to change it.

I am becoming disillusioned with the romantic notion of it. If Dame Sophia is beloved, how can I stand to see her so? That is her purity. She remains beloved so long as my love remains. Even if unrequited.

Where did this prejudice come from? The philosopher as Nietzschean Quixote? In the cave with a completely different experience of time or a ridiculous loner attacking imagined villains from his high horse, as if it mattered. Blustery and billowing, filled with the air of the fight, they most notably stand at odds with something. Descartes and his battles with the Jesuits or the Calvinists. Spinoza's excommunication. The Corsair affair. The point is always the same. There is some structural or organizationally predominant set of notions. Something that orders and occupies the minds and methodologies of all the learned. There is some antagonist, some gadfly, who irritates and unnerves the rest. Never from a collegial position within, but in genuine conflict coming from the outside.

Not just a troublemaker for its own sake, a defender of something, of some righteous prejudice. Some set of poetic notions that form a tradition, a set of figures, an ongoing lineage of participants in a conversation. Isn't there just as much of the organizational in that? It is easy to fall upon the distinction. In the 17th century there were professors of philosophy, but Descartes and Spinoza were not among them. The conversation didn't have to include them, their approaches, or their points of view. It was like side chatter at the table. There is a main conversation, and all the participants profess the singular significance of the matter at hand. Some few off to the side persist in their whispers and mumblings. It makes it difficult for the others to hear each other, not because it is loud or overbearing, but because it is soft and engrossing. The others become distracted, unable to focus on their measurements, deductions, and applications of principle. They resent these interlopers and their tangents, wherever they may lead. They turn to squash them, but all they achieve is the even more distressing outcome where these others get up from the table and move into the other room.

They are right to resent this small group and its distance from the table. They are likely commentators and critics. It's always easy to attack the dominant order since its dominance allows it to take so much for granted. There is a great irony when that marginal upsurge later becomes itself the dominant order. There are principles in scholarship for how one must approach the works of Descartes and Spinoza. The North American Nietzsche Society will hunt you down if you dare to oppose the curriculum that they have set for the master. These thieves turn the history of loner miscreants and agents of change into a dominant tradition who themselves are then easily dismissed as dead white men.

No one owes me a seat at the table. I do not assert that as my right. What if I am plagued by a growing sense that the table is the enemy, that the problem is the very institutionalization of the discipline? It's whole ecosystem? The whispering and the incitement to antagonism attracts a type of person. Such a person will always be uncomfortable in the places to which this attraction draws them. We are not the group that is most fit to rule, the very notion of ruling is likely to cater to our worst faculties and traits. Our passion becomes dogma when it takes hold of the order. The antagonist who becomes sovereign over a domain that others inhabit is likely to institute that very antagonism as a means for maintaining the vigor of their rule. This is a delicate maneuver since it makes the ruling order into a fiction and because it only exists in principle so that the margins, aspiring to take control, can continue to have their bogeyman.

These dead whitish men speak to me. Cervantes' kin. That makes me sympathetic to whatever it is that speaks to you. Only an accident of history separates our memory of Spinoza from complete ignorance. What about those who were not so fortunate? I don't begrudge anyone their right to remember. I don't think there should be only one conversation and that if you are causing crosstalk and dissonance, you should be made to leave the room. This battle, as a battle for a place at the table, does not strike me as right either. In truth, there should be no table and all the statistics should be reset. The antagonism itself must always be distributed with no center. The critical approach, the diligence of the sceptic, the investigatory powers of the passionate and the curious, all of this must inhabit whatever other places and tables there are that order the lives of those with the capacity for truth, error, and illusion. There will be conflict, wars, and strife. In short, the alternate history would be the history we already have, but different.

How does the conversation continue if there are no conservatories for its wisdom and its history? Publishing companies, academic presses, departments with their faculties, these are supposed to be the machines that preserve the historical transcript. They are the scribes and the curators, the knowledge stores. The social order says we should protect and preserve this past. This institutionalizes what had its origins in an antagonistic relationship to those same institutions. The history of co-opting the outsider's work for the sake of keeping the worker bees busy in their protected hive is the outcome of this good intent. It is hard not to blame Kant for it. He is the one they always throw at us. The consummate university professor who steers and orders the conversation from where he sits. Whatever comes before or after, passes through him.

How will the young people learn of these traditions, if there are no scholars to light the way? How to present the work so that all young people can feel included in the tradition being preserved? What will these young people do with whatever it is they get from this community endeavor? How best to discipline the young? Are we training the critical minds of the future or are we institutionalizing criticism so that it always falls into the proper channels and uses the well understood means that are predetermined to reach a foreseen end?

What if there were a moratorium on such antagonism and the universities were no longer allowed to teach such things? The liberal arts would become contraband. Only directly vocational training would have a place in the system. The students would be customers and they would be paying for credentials to give them entry into the professions where their proper social situation is attained. This couldn't be done tacitly or quietly. It most definitely cannot be done as though it were happening in the name of maintaining proper civic and educational standards. Rather, this approach must clearly articulate the anti-establishment nature of the work it is dismissing. All thinkers of stature would become pariahs under this rule and each of them would be publicly lambasted as enemies of the proper order of things. Imagine that their work was still available, still something the kids could find in the nooks and crannies of dark libraries or at some rogue site on the internet. They could only read it in secret and could not speak the names of those they read when using their ideas to incite opposition to the ruling notions. Would this approach foster a greater sense of mischief and daring in the minds of those who sniffed out the banished? The whole point would be to de-institutionalize a form of opposition, a disconcerting antagonism to common notions, but to do so in such a way that it could never become common itself. Something available to all, but only through a secret society that they surreptitiously join and further with clandestine messages and whispered ideas. Hidden and secret, there would no trace of any of it in the knowledge stores.

Would we be a wiser people if this were the case? The purpose of the tenure system was to ensure that people would not lose their jobs when they turned their focus on the hegemonic power of the hierarchy that operates and funds the university along with the educated society where it functions. It may still be that way in the minds of some. Even among them, however, there would likely be some acknowledgement that there are plenty of cases where the condition is bestowed on people who would never threaten or be threatened by the ruling order. Were such people to be reasonable and consider the situation from a point of view other than their own, they might think such a university is largely in place for the sake of institutionalizing proper forms of criticism, making it no longer a genuinely critical body. If they are true advocates of criticism, they might at least have to consider the possibility that the fight can no longer be waged in the dining room. They must vacate to the salon.

This mindset, this notion, this organized form of structural assault with its historical conversation that goes on without being the focus of scholarship, without being the topic of a seminar or a colloquium, would become the object of persecution. Not because it would promote the good to make it so, but because it would be honest. This honest orientation would save the side bar, would recognize it as a tangent and no longer try to appropriate it.

This won't happen. Quite the reverse. The doors are opening. Best would be if the flood were to overwhelm the academy, but it will never happen as a revolution on a single day. They affirm their independence of mind as they spout highly structured and disciplined nonsense. That structure is too strong for any true reflection on itself. The mediocre miscreants will teach their radical theory courses and they will be listed on the schedule and the students will enroll. They will have mid-terms and final papers all due on the last day of class. The teacher will write on the board, write on their papers, correct their mistakes, and point them in the direction of the correct literary analysis that makes up proper critical methodology. The students will bring these notions with them into the professional workplace. They will go to brown bag discussions of diversity and pay lip service to a better civilization through inclusion while living a life that effectively depends on the exploitation of the rest of the world. They will marginalize the people who never got to go to the university and learn the proper way to achieve critical understanding of the world's injustices because they were too busy living through them. All in the name of inclusion. We think there are two cultures in the academy, those who bask in the glow of the status quo and those who seek to overturn it. They are two modes of the same substance. Either way, they have their tests and their grades, they take their degrees and their summer internships, and they move on to other organizations and institutions that feed them and fatten them for the sake of a greater harvest. Any which way you slice it, it's animal husbandry.

The reason why organization is required to fight power, that activists must organize, is because power is organized. Only organization can attack organization. The point of criticism isn't just to attack the powers that be, it must be aimed at the conditions of that very attack. Even here now I begin to doubt myself. What is the history of this loner attitude I am adopting? Where does it come from? Who does it serve? Is this cynical agnosticism an alienating facet that permits a proper channel for releasing some of the energy of that necessary antagonism? If existentialism did not exist, it would have been created for the sake of rounding up those young white men who can best be reached with this flavor of isolation and alienation. Any resistance to structure has been fore-ordained and anticipated. They knew it was likely, they institute a set of readings and a syllabus all for the sake of luring those hard-to-reach types into the fold, doing so with a mindset that is antagonistic to that very fold. "Oh, you non-conformists, you are all alike." Where is there to turn?

This is the incitement of the interlude. I know it. Somehow, I know that the way to the other side lies —for me, at least— through Locke and Hobbes. I have a new prep for this year. Social and Political. These are the two philosophers I am starting with. The interlude has lasted for more than a month. It is a fiercely creative time, but I can only pour myself into it through these emails. There is someone that I am trying to seduce, but I am not sure who it is. Her? Myself? This other way that seems to lie beyond that contract that we are supposed to have written, I might be trying to draw it, or sketch it, in preparation for its arrival and its many appearances.

Locke is so optimistic. Hobbes, the opposite. Both of them are lost in the necessity of organization as a means for achieving some universally accepted set of ends. These are ends we all have, that we all share and that somehow form the basis of the agreement we carve out for the sake of mutual achievement. Alone we will fail, but together we can fashion a machine that can power our success if only we would submit to its mechanics. If organization had an interest, it would certainly not present itself as demanding a sacrifice. No, of course not, it would offer solace and protection, it would help in achieving some natural ends that were otherwise unachievable, or it would offer protection from the threats brought by the prevailing competition that we succumb to in its absence. The origin story of the individual is the most important mythology that organization can offer to those who are considering a contract to bind them to each other in the name of this order and its ends. It makes them forget that they are only able to agree to it because they are already bound together. That binding and those boundaries are their true origin.

It is so wily, so cagey and concealed. We do not see it because we are so busy seeing with it. It is the glasses on our nose, it is the telescope and the microscope, it is all the lenses that we have for seeing each other, the cameras and the points of view. The language and the romance all happen within this interlude that I cannot escape, even if it is the projection of the order against which I have been acting. You will never get rid of me, it says. You will always be fighting me because I am your fight. As your fight, I am you and everyone and everything that you love. I orient you occidentally.

How is this the way out? The commonwealth and its order, property and its laws. Ownership is the event that sealed the deal. For in ownership there is the possibility of one's pleasure and the instigation of one's desire. We labor for it. What is the transfer of interlude into a form of seduction if it isn't an assertion of ownership or its attempt? Ownership intertwines desire and being, puts one in a relationship with the object of a yearning that guarantees its perpetual condition of possibility for consumption and use. What is more, it lies only in a guarantee. Among the crows, ownership of a crust of bread is secured when they swallow. Their competition is the labor that adds value. Whatever agreement we might come to for establishing rules around the transfer of these morsels, they amount to means for securing the appropriate ownership of property and whatever guarantees are required to prevent exchange from deteriorating into coercion. No coercive end is unacceptable when it comes to achieving this.

Property is so personal, or at least it is if we think of it as the crust of bread and not as the means of production. The segue between the two is incomprehensible. It's a conversion of the form of the goods to prevent waste. It's a trick. Accept this very personal relationship to things and recognize the need for its guarantee. You will be safe in your home and with your family and your food and leisure. You will see the joy in that, the connection it holds between this social order and your happiness around that warm hearth. The point is to feel the personal quality of the experience of property, of taking some food into your body without concern that your neighbor will wrench it from your hand. Somehow, somewhere, this simple relationship became the factory floor, the farm at work, and the apartment complex rented to others. The connection is acquisition and dispensation as protection from waste. Exchange becomes the driving core of property because it drives the way we measure value, and it drives the order that secures the relationship. Calling it a social contract is already to lay the way for this connection to property as the privilege of exchange, of control by the party over the objects at stake in trade. How does one acquire that crust of bread, after all? Surely, it did not fall from the sky. It was baked and transported. It was put on display, put into your shopping cart, purchased, and taken home. What prejudice overlooks the coercion in all that? Just try and get your child to do it and you will see.

Fair enough that those in power have defined it this way, but how is this the way out? The order at work in simple things, is that it? Are we most likely to see that my personal relationship to the works and matters of exchange is itself subject to law and order? As such, these cannot be so very personal.

Interlude is a spin not a place or set of ideas. This way it can inhabit anything, and it can spread everywhere. There is no getting out. Even if the property relationship reveals an exit, even if the contract shows us we have agreed to all this, interlude affects a spin that draws us back in again. Spin again. "That is the way I laugh Nietzsche to myself."

Truthfully, there is a blindness at work here. It is this half-baked notion of the event of appropriation. What is it if not the difference between whatever is and the fact that it is, the how and the way of its being: an object owned is an instrument to be employed, a resource to be exploited, an interest to be fulfilled, and a desire to be satisfied? The principles of measurement and their events, these muckraking horrorshow relationships are the weight of existence. They are the gravity of human life. That means that the event of appropriation which itself disrupts the appropriated order depends on that very order for its apprehension. How can I explain the difference without a structure at work predisposing whatever is to a specific way of being? Property and object show me this, they clear space for this selfsame event, and yet in doing so assert their own power and necessity, their dominance over the very dialogue that claims a threat to that power. It doesn't destroy the presupposition; it merely poetizes it. That means "fabricates" it. We can feel good about ourselves for now we can sing the beauty of whatever it is that has been crushed by nature in its normal unfolding, by existence in its everyday orientation. That veil you are trying to tear, we spun that. The monad is a product.

Delicately, I bring it back to the course preparation. The syllabus must be clearly articulated and printed so that each student may have a copy. The books are on order so that they can buy them at the university bookstore. The registrar has the names of those who will participate. Their checks are in the mail.

I will try to navigate my way through the property relationship that is pushed and pulled in the work of the contractarians trying to establish the best of all possible outcomes. We will pursue the agnostic cynicism of this reading through Simmel's *Philosophy of Money* which I am sure I can frame as a reordered form of commonwealth making the contract explicit and its terms and conditions clear and universal. When turning at the end to Arendt's *The Human Condition*, the depth of depravity should become clear. What has been lost becomes known. Will we be able to see it, or will it merely appear as interlude? As a momentary glimpse that poses a minor figure against the ground of what consumes us? For even Arendt had to make a living. She had her circle of friends, her lectures, and her assignments. She gave tests just like all the rest of them. What choice did she have? Everyone expected it.

On my syllabus, I made it clear. Everyone will be expected to write a paper and give a presentation. Everyone will get a grade, everyone will be evaluated, and it will not be based on how much they learn or what changes they undergo, but on what skills they have already accumulated and are best able to put on display in that presentation and final essay.

I finished typing it up and then I wrote an email telling her about my experience, responding to her latest expressions of anxiety for the coming term. I knew full well that my alienation would draw her closer by establishing common sensibilities within the moodiness of a shared dread. I don't know if she is the reason for my deepening despair with the institution, or if she exacerbates it, but I see that her struggles are my way to her. Interlude doesn't prevent anything. Its turning is the draw, the centripetal force, it is the power of the allure, and the very same seduction. This is not me, rather the interlude speaks through me and spins everyone in the vicinity into its web. It does not liberate; it is the most cunning form that power can take, a farce between the acts of a play.

"You write her, and she writes back?"
"Of course."
"Have you asked her out?"
"Yes. She prefers it this way."
They have had this conversation before, but every time Wolfe catches him waiting for a response, he repeats the question. This is how it goes: the professor stands around, sips water, eats a little something, and then paces a bit. He looks out the door wall through the back balcony and at the high row of bushes that block any view there might be of Plymouth Road. He'll pace back to the bedroom where he quickly scans the inbox for any new arrivals. There is a dedicated ISDN connection, he has configured his email program to check regularly, and download new messages.
"When did you last write her?"
"About an hour ago."
"She hasn't responded yet? There must be something wrong."
Wolfe teased with more bite than jolly. Patterns were developing. It was a perpetual relay of back and forth. He was either sending or waiting for a response, meaning he was in an intermittent state of distraction.
"Tell me again why you didn't go to the conference in New York."
"No interviews, what's the point?"
"Well, isn't that exactly the point? You go to scrounge something up. Talk to people, let them know you are out there and that you're looking. How will they know to send any leads your way if they don't know?"

"This is Eastern. It's the tenure-track stuff. There won't be any leads."

"So what? If you want another job for next year you have to start working on it now. This should be the prime time for you to start the schmoozing."

The conversation broke for a moment when the professor made another trip back to the bedroom. He took a seat and read something on the screen. Wolfe watched from the dining room, an open book on the table in front of him. The professor finished reading, then started typing something. He stood up and came back.

"Give the woman a minute to breath, would you?"

"I didn't send it. I'll wait a bit."

"This is a major distraction. You should have gone to New York, and I bet the reason you didn't is because you're worried that you'll miss something."

"Why are you taking such an interest? I thought you've rejected the 'intelligentsia'?"

"I have, but I don't reject you. I'm still rooting for you."

The professor sat down. He seemed almost relaxed and focused. It was all part of the pattern. While waiting to receive he was distracted, but while waiting to send, he was at ease and able to focus on whatever it was that was in front of him. He looked like he was about to open his book, assuming that Wolfe was done and would go back to reading. They read for a bit, but then Wolfe looked up.

"Is it possible that you convinced yourself you are seducing her, but you are really seducing yourself?"

"Why would I need to? Can't I just like somebody?"

"Pfffft. Nobody just 'likes' anybody. All of your hereditary biology is at work. The entire cultural and biological history of our species is involved."

"What's the point of talking about it then?"

"I'm just saying, you're not in New York, and you're acting weird. I've seen her, by the way. At the Del the other night. Don't get me wrong, I'm not trying to say anything bad about her, it's just that what's the big deal? Why go to all this trouble, isn't there anyone else you can go out with?"

"No one that I like."

"That's my point. Why is that? Why is it that the one person you like only wants to communicate over email and doesn't want to spend any time with you? Why are you attracted to this? To what you are doing right now? This pacing and this waiting, this checking and rechecking. This is what you want, right? Why? That's all I'm saying."

"I like her. I want to get to know her."

"Bullshit. You want this."

"What is this, some form of existential psychoanalysis? An existential psychoanalytic of Dasein? You do this so you must want this. What conditions must be in place to make that be the case? What are its conditions of possibility?"

"Yeah, sort of. I suspect that maybe you're trying to derail yourself, trying to passively change your life."

"Passively?"

"Yes. If you decided to quit looking for a job, that would be traumatic. You could never do that directly; you convinced yourself that this was the only kind of job you could ever want. You'd be totally fucked if you abandoned that plan, so you won't let yourself do it. Instead, you engineer an agenda to distract yourself while twisting free of it, pulling yourself in a different direction. This is a passive way to undermine your plan. It's a safe way to make a change."

The professor stood up and turned on the overhead light above the dining table. He refilled his water glass and took a clove cigarette from a package on the kitchen counter. He lit it and went to the back door to crack it open a bit.

"It's fucking cold."

"Just for a bit." The cassette that was playing on the stereo had finished so the professor went over and flipped it to the other side. Horowitz playing some Beethoven Sonatas. "I like this theory. It seems right to me. Deliberation about desire suggests that there are some qualia for it, like you could examine your mental states and find the desire somewhere in there. You're saying to forget all that and just look at the wreckage."

"We know desire after the fact. You aren't failing to attract her; you're succeeding in realizing this."

"It leads us around. All the world around us is the residue of our desire. All that nonsense about the rational structuring of the world is wrong. We're just building what we want. Look around, this is what we want."

"No kingdom of ends. No rational order. Just realized id everywhere. Reason is for cleaning up the mess, or for making conflicting outcomes coherent with each other."

"How do we unpack it all? Is there a critical point of view that we can use to perform the analysis or is that just desire too?"

"Good one. Probably right. Didn't Marx always use the word 'dead heads' to describe this? The organizations incite the desire, provide the reasons for it, and the blueprints for making it all fit together nicely."

They go over old ground, the clove mixed with tobacco burns, the dusk comes and the cold night. They drink and they smoke, they nibble, and they talk. The rudiments of interest and orientation appear as they turn toward each other. They look, they speak. They are filling space together and they are occupying it with these symbols of exchange. People create an aura around themselves when they sit together and talk. Whatever else they are doing, they face each other, they fidget, but the distance is constructed as a place between them that belongs to them. It isn't alien, but a play between. It is the area of involvement that they move in and out of with their speech and their looks, with their gestures and their habits. The dining table. This place where they eat or drink, read or write, talk or sit, smoke or breath. They are aware of this place and the way that it feels and smells. They are aware that they have made this place the way that it is. The glasses on the table, the books, the chairs, and the tabletop. The low lighting. All of it must be what they wanted, the living conditions that they sought to construct. This is not a room that just anyone would like, not everyone would be comfortable here, but they were. All the things they liked to do fit here. At the moment, everything was in reach. The professor put the emptied ashtray back on the table and flicked an ash into it. Wolfe took a sip of water. The books sat unread and creasing. Everything as they wanted it. Even this conversation and the distraction from reading or whatever else it was that they had to do this evening.

These desires were for comfort and an ambience of learning and study, but they were uneasy too. There was a nagging feeling behind them. That is how it works with these investigations, because they were talking, but it wasn't calm. There was something at stake. This is what they call learning. Both of them in the thick of a didactic procedure. Something was missing, there was something that each of them did not know but were driven to comprehend. What else would you call this insistent questioning? Questioning as such gives spirit to the investigations driving its method. There is an inclination at work in it, an inclination to find out or to come to know. It takes effort to create a proper environment for that. If you are in an office and it is your job to design widgets, then the office layout and the relationships you have with your coworkers will be for the sake of your questioning concerning the construction of widgets. People thought about that when they laid out the office, when they set up the desks this way rather than some other. They knew that people would need to collaborate on widget manufacturing and that the space would have to facilitate it. Well, the professor and Wolfe have done something similar here for the sake of configuring this space for their collaboration. They did not set out to make it work that way, but it unfolded as it did out of necessity. Living in a place means constructing it for your habitation and that means regular and ongoing adjustments to make it the kind of place where your everyday actions and inclinations can be fulfilled.

"Look at this place," Wolfe said. "The TV over there is never on. The futon has been pulled out like that for months and you barely notice that you've lost your couch and the use of your living room. You don't care because you don't need a couch, you never want to sit on it anyway. Everything here is set up for a very specific kind of life. All you ever do is read and write. You listen to music, but even that is always music that you can have on in the background."

"So?"

"Point is, you never sat down and asked yourself, 'how do I want this place to look?' You just use it the way you want, and this is how it ends up. I'm a guest so I can't complain. I go out when I want to socialize, it would never occur to me to invite someone here."

"Good."

"Good? That's right, you've never once expressed any interest in meeting the typesetter or any of the other people I've been hanging out with. Everything here is just the way you like it. Even me. You want me to be only sort of here. When I am, I should only be doing the sorts of things you like to do here. I can study, but that's about it."

"Your point is that my inclinations for how to live are written all over this place and it's easy enough to figure that out by just examining it and what it makes possible, what actions can be done given the layout."

"Yup. Even your weird pen pal fits in neatly."

The professor nods with an ironic smile. He's not completely bought in, but it's a reasonable hypothesis.

"Here's my take," Wolfe continues. "Organization produces these conditions through norms that are supposed to maintain the structure in the flow of actions taking place in it. Organized structures are real things. To be masculinized, for example, is to be turned into someone who lives this way. If you cared about decoration or other people's comfort when they came over, that would just be a different organizational form at work, or a different facet of that same patriarchal form. The organization of desires is an ordered orientation to a set of ends. Action according to these organized structures is standardized to achieve those ends as your own personal property. These standards are those same norms made formal. Once you've allied yourself to an organized structure, you've given yourself a set of ends, and the norms that go with them."

"What are the structures, then?"

"You've joined a group. Let's call it, intellectual productivity. You are the professor. That amounts to several distinct orders. The professor is a teacher and has all the procedural requirements that go along with that. The professor is a researcher, charged with establishing and maintaining expertise in the domains where he teaches and writes. You're building and rebuilding this place to facilitate that. It's very much an apartment that belongs to a visiting assistant professor."

"True."

"You allow me to stay here, and I appreciate that. For it to work, we both know that I have to fit into those structures. No gatherings. Can't even invite the woman upstairs and her kid over for dinner, even though it's weird that we haven't. There is the librarian. You keep saying that she is the one who doesn't want to go out, that doesn't want to meet face to face. She fits so perfectly with your rules here that it makes me wonder. You might be the one orchestrating all this. I keep wondering what you're doing and why you're doing it?"

"You think I have a master plan."

"I do. There is something going on and you're behind it all. It's about as deliberate as you can let yourself be."

"What do you think it is?"

"Interlude, right? That's what you keep talking about. Except I can't exactly figure out what that means to you."

"That is the way I laugh Nietzsche to myself."

"Exactly. What's the next bit? 'The one about whom I am reluctant to say'. Nietzsche wasn't really a philosopher in the end, not to you. I suspect that you think his relationship with philosophy is something like Don Quixote's relationship to chivalry."

"To its literature, at least."

"You are agreeing with me?"

"I don't know what to say. I'm just pointing out that Don Quixote read all those books and they rotted his brain so that all he had left was a pale imitation of what he had read."

"That's all that Nietzsche got in the end, right?"

"In the end, Nietzsche got the same thing that everybody gets."

"Death? Destiny?"

"None of that bullshit immortality matters. He lived and he died, and no one read any of it. Whatever happened later had nothing to do with him. Can you imagine what his days and nights must have been like?"

"Like a prison 'where every discomfort has its seat and every dismal sound its habitation'. Is that the *Moonlight*?"

"I don't want to talk about it."

"Fine, don't talk about it. Make sure you know what you're doing, though, if you can. Don't go off and initiate some big life changing event without being really clear about what exactly it is that you're doing."

"You're contradicting yourself."

"I can't help it, I'm a person."

Truth is social. Not relativistic or "subjective" as the kids say, but social. This can have a hard edge. Peer review is how truths are established. We may talk as if sociology is the fool of the sciences, but established practice shows that it is its queen. This is why I can't fail but see the extraordinary role that Hegel plays in the history of western thought. It mystifies me that there are those in the discipline who lambast and reject him, the very thought of him. As if anyone who spent time reading Gareth Evans or

Wilfrid Sellars has a right to complain that the *Phenomenology* is just too muddled or difficult to parse.

Often these same people are comfortable enforcing standards in publication and communication for higher learning and scholarship. There are guidelines for what truth may look like. Restrictions around its language and form as well as how many words it takes to say it. There is a lot of power in truth, and organizational backing, but they reduce it to sentences. It took centuries for these norms to evolve and develop into what they are now, and it will take centuries still for it to change into something else. Attacks on the truth are almost always attacks on the organizational structures that stand behind it. Not only that, but usually they are attempts at putting some other set of applied propositions in its place. This other set would be backed by a new organization. This is how revolution works in our hearts and minds. The Copernican revolution was an attack on truth and which organizations may best back it. It is easy today to dismiss such mysticism and dogma, but not so if you walked in Bruno's shoes. For he was not fighting for truth against dogma, he was fighting for truth against truth. Likewise, the French, American, and Russian revolutions. Truth was always at stake. They blame the post-modernists. Is Foucault to blame for the Panopticon if he suggests that it is a paradigmatic pattern for how power and discipline work? Whether the prison really is a tool for use by free societies for promoting the responsibility of citizens who have lost their way or a disciplinary device for enforcing norms and standards of behavior in coercive style, depends on the nature of the organization backing the analysis, not some set of qualities in the thing itself.

I have heard smart people set aside Weber's observations on bureaucracy as if they were so simple any child could fathom them. Those same people go on to dismiss their own education and their relationship to traditions when they assert the sanctity of individual responsibility in the Aristotelian sense of deliberate action. As if the conditions of their own intellectual work were so transparent. "By the light of reason, I intuit the inviolability of individual deliberation and assert moral responsibility to such narrowly defined entities." They omit the phenomenological role of these structures, of bureaucracy, of any rationalized form of organized action, even that of the good son or daughter. That is to be blamed on the likes of Husserl for he gives us the sense that phenomenology as science is all about establishing transparent conditions and deliberate orientations. Socializing experience and truth plunges the phenomenological position into partiality and finitude. The hermeneutical move is as much as to say that visibility into conditions is always obscured because we must look backward in order to see forward, and vice versa. Because we are always in the midst, always at a point of intersection, we are condemned to be nodes in a network that stretches too far beyond us for anyone to see it in its entirety. Only through ongoing analysis and communication, through living and breathing together —through teaching and learning— only through the ages and eons, do we accumulate and articulate these points of view so that they can be shared among many now and to come. What is its fruit? Just glimpses here and there of something immense and in constant motion. Something that cannot be contained in the simplicity of a notion or a concept: a swarm of human being.

In "philosophy," truth is a relatively small area of focus, dwarfed in size by the consideration of how you arrive at it. Even if epistemology is a bodyless endeavor for the most part, the turn toward a subdiscipline of the sociology of science suggests that there is at least some awareness that there is a social component to truth and the manner for achieving it. The sociology of philosophy would be the upshot of this trend. Sociology proper or any flavor of it has to be obsessed with methodology: the very conditions of the discipline indicate that it is saturated with preconditions. How can a social being perform sociological investigations? How can socially conditioned investigations determine scientific methodologies?

We may hide in the I. Critical agency is an assertion of individuation. Critique asserts a singularity, and the critic asserts it too. Their own and its own individuation. It is the Cartesian problem of the role a free will can have in a universe filled with divine providence. Descartes expresses a moral preference for individuating himself as a free and moral being through thought. This heightened mentality forms a union between the individuated one and that over and against which it is individuated. Its other. Descartes did this, not the people who point to it. That is why this moral community of the producers of wealth all hangs on him, on his every word and in his every gesture. Think of god as an idealized other inhabiting the actor's will. Reading Descartes as a moral philosopher not only transforms the philosopher's work, but the manner in which morality itself is understood. Often in the letters with Princess Elizabeth and the *Principles*, he describes the compatibility of human liberty with the will of god. It is a struggle. A struggle that he describes and a struggle to describe it. There is no difference between these phenomena, these two struggles. For he must state both the alliance and the distance. The moral being is aligned with the will of god, freely. It doesn't matter what this deity entails, it needn't be omniscient, omnibenevolent, and omnipotent, it must merely seem so to the thinker trying to strike out on their own. Descartes is haunted by its ontological constitution, haunted by the facts the predicates themselves entail for His presence and His power, His all-surveilling insight into the hearts and minds of mortals. This does not happen at a distance, but because He is there in the moment of liberation as the very act of individuation and as its critical turn. "Listen / God speaks to each of us as he makes us..."

It is the aboriginal assertion of Schopenhauer's epic cynical insight that the stone, were it conscious, would believe itself free as it flew through the air. This belief would signal the emergence of the stone from its material conditions where the reflective moment and the feeling of liberty would mark it as itself, as the stone choosing to fly through space and time. This cynical turn was only conceivable once Descartes' struggle surfaced in Kant's architectonic. Either way, in a cursory glance or in its more detailed form, the glimpse of liberty is initialized in mystery. The investigation into it aligns it with those very conditions against which it asserts itself as liberty. For freedom is nothing without its offset to the mechanical forces from which it emerges. Even Locke cannot fathom that cognition may be evoked merely from motion. What the philosopher cannot see is the extent to which the emergence of the mind, of the thinking thing, is co-constitutive with that very deity that inhabits it as it struggles to find its way to the Good. God needn't pre-exist the emergence, it is a new name for it.

There is no immortal soul distinct from the body without extension in space and the safeguards of the deity. This is confirmed even as his *Meditations* declares their independence. When the stone awakens to itself and feels its flight as submission to the be all and end all of stone existence, that is the emergence of the divine in the articulation of a freedom to act. There is a moral imperative to achieve this reflective stance and to resist the force that carries one through the air for the sake of a determinate understanding of the responsibility that comes with it. Should that stone, catapulted over the city walls, hurl toward a homestead or a child's body, it must intend otherwise even as it hits its mark. For that, it need not change course, but it must reflect on its origins, its trajectory, and on the harm that looms in its sights. The extreme emphasis given to the purity and goodness of the intention, the mental states of the thinking thing, can only arise from the reflective clarity and dismay that comes with understanding that the agent itself is not powerful enough to control its path. Thought is slow and actions must move quickly. Even if the agent can know, they may not know in time to prevent something dreadful from happening. Such a mind, imagined in opposition, lets us eat our cake and have it too. Bad faith.

There is so much in his thinking that rambles and rages against and in favor of those things from without that impress themselves upon us. The moods and feelings of being extended in space, of being physically bound, merge into the very perception of extension itself. We are being bombarded by sensation and we are at the mercy of some alien substance encroaching upon our sacred solitude near Leiden or whatever town we choose to inhabit. If my eyes are open, I have no choice but to see what is in front of me. That is, unless I enter into a domain of absorbed reflection where my eyes glaze over, and I become lost in thought and drawn away from the immediate. This is an act of rebellion against the power of what presents itself in passion and sensation. The act itself is the formation of intelligent experience out of those passions and sensations. It may appear that the stick half submerged in water is bent, and there may be nothing I can do to prevent it seeming this way, but equally there is nothing that forces my intellect to judge it so. This process rationalizes the world, makes sense of it, and provides the methodology for organizing and ordering the raw encroaching conditions into structured and meaningful experience. This is the merit of the thinking thing itself and its capability to individuate clearly and distinctly in any moment that it asserts itself, its will, and its intent. The hostile advent of exteriority draws the divine out through the musings of a conscious beast. It puts the other inside us so that it may draw it out in our every act while it seems to come from our own volition.

Everywhere in the midst of these struggles, the over and against is at work. The purity of the thinking substance is the advent of the exterior as deity in the moment of power and resistance to the impact of space and time and whatever fills it. This advent is a moral matter. It is the entry point of that being into its moral community, its kingdom of ends. In the methodology of the sciences, Descartes tells us that we are obligated to work diligently to achieve this distance, amounting to the establishment of a rational domain serving as the only viable habitat for our freedom, and this liberty takes place in a world where the deity and the physical universe coexist in a magical dance with a mystifying origin. This is the perfect setting for a moral imperative to be free, to be rational, and to be moral. Whatever the shape that the doctrine takes in the centuries that follow, this command remains a constant. Even the consequentialist bothers to work out a system of ethics. This bother is driven, is a response to a command. Better, it is the command itself. Why not just leave off with the good altogether? Where does the impetus to seek it come from if not this very command? What is its substance if not the intersection of power and its resistance? The voice of that same being which makes us. The antelope feels no impetus to be moral. There is no distance requiring it and no turning that awakens it. It does not know good and evil, and it need not. These notions emerge in a universe in which its mouthpiece was persistently at odds with Jesuit and Calvinist alike. It was no accident that he curried favor with the former and had nothing but contempt for the latter. The act of will was real, but not subservient. It was the highest expression of liberty especially when it realized the transcendent plan of the divine.

This is not an analogous moment to the nascent commonwealth; it is its condition. The formalization of these patterns is the rationalization of the order of life that marks the points of agreement between agents so characterized. It was a hope or a wish, but these individuated souls were such that they could affect the true turning by constructing an artifice that consolidates and contains an agreement expressing this will and its moral relationship to that over and against which it seeks to distinguish itself. In its origins the compact was to brace each other for these struggles against the elements and the passions that would otherwise bring about the lowly creatures' demise. The proximity of this contract to the mind of god was on full display in its characterization of the imperative. Those who championed it as an origin story may have disagreed about the conditions from which it came, but they agreed that the collection was inevitable and in keeping with the needs of the diverse beings who entered into it. For such communities were born from the need to coexist amid common conditions that threatened everyone. Whether the agreement came before the liberation or after, it hardly seems the main point worth contending. Neither does it matter whether the conditions against which this agreement is meant to protect its parties are hostile or idyllic. In any case, individuation marks a liberation, and that liberation is communal, meaning that it is inherent in the very substance of the beings that experience it. The agreement can only happen if a community has formed to initiate its negotiation. Only a common need could have led to a common understanding. There is being in common, nonetheless. God is the name commonly assigned to that aggregation and it has been whispering it into our ears for thousands of years.

The question then is whether this agreement deteriorates into coercion through some internal logical flaw. Does the war of all against all mark the state of common need or the state of common agreement? Must it necessarily be so? Does humanity improve with each year? There are some who would state the case that new treatments for disease and new tools for communication clearly make it so. There is more. Are we better? Not better off or better fed, not better entertained or better organized. We may not even know how to pose this question without already beginning to venture an answer in the framing of it. "Better" is already a stipulated condition on the agreement itself. Its voice is first heard in the longing that emerged as that original need, that individuation executed in common by so many thinking things struggling with their passions and their sensations, their pains and their pleasures.

There is more to be known. There is more that can be done. There must be more that is good. Just as the infinite becomes a kind of unending movement, so too omniscience and omnipotence. The meaning of the "omni-" undergoes its Newtonian transformation over the centuries that followed these first steps of the revolution. With that migration, and the syllogism that establishes the good on its foundation, the ever-growing quantity of goodness becomes a rule to calm us in our anxious positioning under the receiving end of that same moral imperative. The price is the collective management of that same pleasure and pain that drove us into our solidarity. Collective management means measurement and appraisal, it means balance and compensation. Moral notions under such agreements go wayward as economic transactions. It'll all work itself out in the end.

Imagine that you are a lone traveler hiking through the Lake District in England. You are exposed to the elements, to your moods, and to chance. There is risk everywhere at every turn. Will the rain come? Where can I find the next meal? Where will I sleep tonight? You come upon a fellow traveler with those same concerns. Your needs are common insofar as the pains are common and the desire to elude them. What could be more innocent and more obvious than an alliance between you. Together we will find food more easily or with increased likelihood. Together we will search out accommodation and transport. Constraints will be introduced. We may have to take a different road than either of us intended in order to maintain our alliance. Your compatriot wants to go to Edinburgh whereas you were headed to the Isle of Skye. You come to an understanding and pledge to travel a circuitous route to which you both give consent. There are constraints and you undertake them for the sake of that original compact born of stress and desire. There will be constraints, but you will only begin to bicker and argue when one of you senses that your desires are not duly represented in the actions occurring under the conditions of the agreement. Is the agreement the end of a war or the beginning of one?

This questionable condition that the two travelers occupy suggests that the maintenance of their agreement depends on the reflective relationship each party maintains between what they are doing and what they want to be doing. If the desires of the participants are met, they will remain content. Even if the conditions are only partly agreeable, so long as the benefits outweigh the pain, the agreement will remain unchanged. This indicates an inclination to manage desire in the upkeep of any agreement. Your compatriot may lead you to Edinburgh and talk you out of your destination by convincing you that it isn't worth the effort to travel so far. Thus, may millions live together without anyone expressing their dissatisfaction with an agreement in which they rarely ever get what they want. Their desire may be channeled into corners and crevices that cheaply provide substitutes. Here is a picture of the Isle of Skye to help you adjust to the fact that you will never get there. Here is a story of a traveler who arrives there and the adventures they have. You can enjoy this story in the comfort of your own home without the rain, wind, or the cold that you would feel were you to set out for the destination yourself.

The thinking thing flies off in fantastic imagery and calls this its liberty. Coerced into virtual relationships, desire blossoms as the behaviors that construct and maintain the limits necessitated by a life in common. The balance of power lies in the balance of desire relative to its realization. Because even if you possess as mere fantasy those things which the others have, the desire itself is a limit upon your body and a set of boundaries imposed upon your mind. The imposition is your individuation in the face of passion and sensation, the to and fro motion of wanting what is set before you. Imagine the disdain of Socrates when he considers the acts that these privileged few are forced to endure, not least of which would be each other's company. Their desire-fulfilled rots their brains and they think these gewgaws are something precious. This conflict nags at us in the form of the assurance, more of an anxious questioning really, that it is better to be Socrates dissatisfied than a fool satisfied. The remark is there to serve the purpose of satisfying both parties. For those who are well off won't bother to know this, and those who see the condition are soothed by the sentiment. For the rest, there is the interleaved internet and all its many containers for desire and consumption free of satisfaction.

Recall what you wanted when you were a child and amass the desires of all children. Their desires are simple and reflect the conditions where they live, feeling viscerally what is missing. Hunger, exhaustion, a new soccer ball, playing with their friends, Mommy and Daddy to stop fighting, the newest toy that all the other kids have, or even the still newer toy that none of the other kids can have. Here you will find things that are the most worth wanting and the patterns that are at work in everything you want. Even among those with the least reason, there is a wisdom. They can show the way because they are on it. If we have the eyes to see beyond the quirks of this thinking thing, we might even be able to know it. Do something about it. That would be good.

The engineer's new girlfriend has pretty eyes. Very expressive. She wants the professor to like her and thinks the best way to achieve that is to flirt with him. She makes lots of eye contact, blinking, lightly squinting, and raising her eyebrows in succession. It makes him uncomfortable, and he looks away as he offers them coffee. They eagerly accept. She has never seen a French press before and asks about it. He doesn't know where it comes from, whether it is really French, but he doesn't like using filters and thinks the coffee tastes good. French roast in a French press, but he has never been there. He doesn't know why they call it French roast either, but it certainly isn't because the coffee grows there. Is this the way they roast the beans in France? He isn't sure. She is curious and asks a lot of personal questions too. These are questions she could've asked the engineer before they came over and before being introduced. She may even have done so, but asks them again, nevertheless, and hangs on every word in the response. He is convinced that this is what they meant in 19th century novels when they referred to coquettishness. She is using conversational pointers and body language to curry favor. Mentally he knows this, he can feel it happening, but he responds. He is nicer to her, and he plays along. It nags at him while he does it and it bothers him that he cannot help it. He likes her.

While they drink coffee at the table, he asks her what she does and where she's from. She makes brief replies about living in Ypsilanti, having a sister, and working as a rental agent for apartments while studying for her realtor's license. He asks her if that is how she met the engineer, but she is not interested in this line and cuts it off. "Is this what you guys do? You sit around this table, drink coffee, smoke, and talk? Don't you want to get out and go somewhere?"

The professor doesn't know which question to answer and so looks down. The engineer jumps in, "I wanted you guys to meet, get to know each other. Did you want to go somewhere? Did you have something else in mind?"

"Hell yes," she says. "Talking isn't the only wait to get to know people. Let's go somewhere. Have you been to the University Farms or the Botanical Gardens?"

They look at each other in horror. The engineer ventures, "It's pretty cold, isn't it?"

"It's not that bad today. Besides, a lot of the farm stuff is inside. I have a friend who works there. Let's go."

They pack up and go off together. She has a big car but drives it like it is small, turning sharply at corners as she accelerates. She changes lanes a lot on Plymouth. They head east past the highway and turn onto the road where the plots are all lined up. They pull into a parking lot with signs pointing toward the botanical gardens in one direction and the offices of the farming plots in the other.

"What are the plots?"

"The horticulture and botany students at the university use this place for experiments. That kind of stuff. My friend is on the staff, he can show us around if you want, or we can go to the botanical gardens? It's sunny. Have you ever been?"

"Never. I knew it was out here though. I'm up for a walk."

They head off toward the botanical gardens, there is an entrance to the more structured part surrounded by fences and with overseers puttering around here and there. They veer the other way and walk down pathways through the trails into the other parts of the gardens. There are outdoor bridges and trails winding through wetlands. It's above freezing, and the sun is causing the thin surface ice near the banks to melt. There's hardly any flora of interest, it's all hibernating.

"See," she says. "Isn't it nice to get out?"

It is beginning to take on the air of a setup. The professor thinks the engineer has told her that he doesn't leave the house very much anymore because he wants to keep a close eye on his computer and the incoming emails.

"Did he tell you that I need to get out more?"

"He said that you live a sedentary lifestyle. Is that the life of a scholar? Is that right?"

"I suppose."

"Well, you should get out. There are so many nice places to go around the river valley. You should take advantage of it while you're living here."

"Do you know something I don't? Are my days in Ann Arbor numbered?"

"Well, he told me your position is temporary and that you're visiting. Doesn't that mean you will be moving on after this year?"

"Probably. If I can find another job. I haven't had much luck so far."

"What will you do if you don't find anything? Will you stay here?"

"I don't know. I might, or I might go back to Illinois and see if I can't find something there. I worked at a few schools down there so maybe one of them would take me back for some adjunct work."

"Adjunct?"

"Temporary and not really part of the normal faculty. Adjuncts don't really have any standing, they just get temporary assignments, usually at the last minute, and are paid by the course, not with a yearly contract like I have now."

They walked in silence. She wanted to say something agreeable but couldn't think of anything. It was an alien world to her. She didn't know what to suggest or what would count as encouragement. "It must be hard."

It was awkward. Her tone was empathetic though and that was nice. He melted a little and seemed to make a deliberate decision to open up and tell her something, tell both of them something, maybe there were still some stories that even the engineer hadn't heard.

"I was in Europe once, and I was hitchhiking through southern Germany. This guy in a windsurfing van stopped to give me a lift."

"What's a 'windsurfing van'?"

"Well, it was just an ordinary van, but it was all painted and decorated with information about a business, something about selling and renting windsurfers."

"Got it. Go on."

"Yeah, so the guy was Italian, living along the coast of Italy somewhere. He owned the van. It had always been his dream to open up a little business doing what he loved. He started windsurfing when it first caught on in Europe and he became really passionate about it. He wanted to take advantage of it somehow and start up a business. He worked at some other job, saved up all his money, and then opened this shop selling and renting out windsurfers and windsurfing gear."

"That's awesome. Good for him."

"Well, hang on. That was his point. He thought it would be all fun and games, turning something he loved into his career. He'd be able to surf most days and talk to people about something they both loved. It would be perfect. Like he didn't even have to work because it would all be so much fun. Like being on vacation all the time. That's what he thought."

"Ah. It didn't work out that way?"

"Not at all. That was his point. He was driving up to Germany to pick up some stuff from a supplier there. He made the trip once a week and it pretty much took the whole day. He had to worry about hiring people and scheduling their work hours. He had to stock the store and pay the bills. He worried when they weren't selling enough stuff during the slower months, and when they were busy, there was too much work in the shop for him to do any surfing and sailing."

"I've heard stories like that before. Opening your own business is a lot of work."

"Right. He told me that his advice to anyone would be to never try to turn your passion into a business."

"That's the opposite of what they always say."

"Exactly. I've always heard the line where if you are passionate about something and if you throw yourself into it, the power and energy of your passion will carry you along and make sure you're successful."

"Sure. It's basically a cliché."

"That wasn't exactly his advice though. He was careful to phrase it exactly how he meant it. He wasn't saying I shouldn't follow my passion; he wasn't saying anything bad at all about passion and the things we are passionate about. He was only saying that you should never turn something you are passionate about into a business. Specifically, just that. Passion has no business as a business."

"Well, unless your passion is for business."

"Sure. That's the point too, I guess. Leave the business to the people who are passionate about it. Someone who really wants to run a business and who happens to like windsurfing, they would be a better candidate for opening that shop than someone who's really into windsurfing and wants to make a living doing it."

"Did the business ruin his love of windsurfing?"

"That's what he said. He was distressed about it. He was making a living. It wasn't going badly. That wasn't his point. He had lost his avocation; he had lost the thing he was most passionate about."

"I could totally see that happening. Something you love, something you enjoy doing more than anything in the world, you start earning your living that way. Having to run it like a business, that could totally ruin it for you. You might get sick of it. What's left then? You might have gotten a livelihood out of it, but you ruined something that brought you so much joy and happiness."

The engineer was pleased listening to the exchange. It was exactly what he had been hoping for. He wanted the two of them to talk like this, he was hoping she would experience the professor the way he knew him, as someone who always approached everyone and everything the same way. He wouldn't be condescending or arrogant, he would aim for an interaction in just the right way that the participants needed. She might catch a glimpse of what he saw in his friend, that's what he wanted her to see. He hoped it would raise him in her estimation, seeing that he had a friend like this. He liked the exchange but had concerns about its content. "Wait," he said. "What is the point of this story? How is it related?"

"Just that I'm beginning to feel that way about my job. There is so much more to working as a professor than just going off and doing your research and the rewarding experiences in teaching. Only a few get to really enjoy the life where they won't be touched by the burdens of grading or managing students or administrative work or whatever millions of distractions there can be to suck time away from whatever it is that you want to work on."

They all nodded.

"When I was in graduate school, I thought this was just a temporary problem. The semesters were filled with reading and writing assignments that were attached to coursework. The coursework was a set of distribution requirements to make sure you had the fundamentals for the discipline. There was grading or teaching for the various assistantships. I looked forward to winter or summer break so I could finally have time for what I wanted to read and what I wanted to write."

"Sure, that's how school is."

"That's what I thought. See, I had a very definite study agenda in mind back then. I was clear about what I wanted to read and write. In school, there was very little time for that."

"Your thesis, once you got to that stage, it must have been more like that, right?"

"Not really. I thought it would and there were parts of it that were. There was so much more to it though. You can't venture to say anything unless you consider all the historical connections to what you are saying. Who else said something about it? What about the others who didn't comment on the same thing even though they should have? Why didn't they? What did the others say and why is it wrong whereas what you are saying is right?"

"Isn't that what professors are supposed to do? Isn't that the job?"

"I guess. I didn't know that. I didn't realize there would be so many constraints on how to say what I wanted to say, how to think what I wanted to think. How to make my voice legitimate. Truth is, I didn't read a lot of material produced by academics when I was an undergraduate. I read a lot of Sartre and Nietzsche, Hegel and Foucault. Simone de Beauvoir. That's what I wanted to do, what they were doing. My goal wasn't to spend all my time reading books about their work, I wanted to read their work and then write stuff like it. That's not what this is."

"I see," she said. "The things you have to write are like the balance sheet that guy had to keep. The content of the balance sheet is the buying and selling of windsurfers, but it's still a balance sheet and it's still buying and selling."

"Exactly."

They had circled through a smaller part of the botanical gardens and were coming back toward the parking lot. She asked if they wanted to go into the buildings to see what that was like. She could go look for her friend and ask him to show them around. The professor had been drawn into the whole afternoon and was enjoying himself, so he was happy to keep going.

"Let's do it," said the engineer as he opened the door for the others.

It was a large open building with a small reception area separating the entry way from the rest. There was a glass doorway with a bell next to it. Since there was no one at the reception desk, she rang the bell and waited. A man in his forties, wearing a flannel shirt and jeans came to the door and greeted her with a hug. The professor gathered that they hadn't seen each other in a while but had been close at some point. She introduced them and asked her friend if he wouldn't mind showing them around a bit.

They went through the door and saw that the giant building was sectioned off into office-like compartments that were growing areas for different kinds of flora. The university farms included outdoor areas, but in the winter, they weren't used. Even in the summer there were things that you couldn't do outdoors if the plants weren't going to do well in the Michigan climate. The projects performed indoors went on all year long and people were using assigned spaces to do their research. There was an elaborate sprinkler system and tons of lighting everywhere. The building and program administrators were there to make sure the facilities were running as expected and the people had everything they needed.

The professor asked questions about the work being done in the labs. What departments are the students in? Are they mostly graduate students? Do the faculty use these facilities too? Are the labs allocated to the professors and then "sub-contracted" to their students? The engineer's girlfriend jumped in at some point and playfully scolded the professor for his line of questioning.

"It's funny to me that you go right for that, seeing the students and their work as the most interesting part of this whole building and what's going on here," she said. "I'm thinking totally differently about this place. Like, how

come the university owns all this land? How many people do they employ
to take care of all these buildings and all this equipment?"

"Sure. That would be good to know," the professor might have sounded
a bit condescending in his assurances, but she cut him off.

"That's not my point. My point is that I never realized science was so
much about equipment and things that you have to use and tinker with. I
always thought of labs as places where chemists spend all their time. I
imagined test tubes and beakers and bubbling liquids and the scientists
doing all the work. I didn't think of all the measuring equipment and
computers. All the trucks for moving palettes around. Faucets and valves,
ducts and wiring. Scientists use so many different things to see whatever it
is that they are looking at, but there are also a lot of other people who aren't
scientists who are helping them. Until I first came to this place, I had no
idea. It's like a society."

It had been fun, taking the tour. They went to eat afterward. She teased
the professor about how much more fun it would have been if his girlfriend
could have joined them. "I guess she could only do that if she were real."

"Are you saying she doesn't exist?" he asked with a smile.

The overly eager engineer provided the answer, "Not like that. She
means 'real' as in real vs virtual."

She laughed. Careful to make eye contact throughout, she said: "Is that
another one of those things where you don't want to mix passion and
business?"

At the Fleetwood Diner that night, Wolfe was talking to someone at the
counter while the typesetter was sitting at one of the tables reading a bit and
periodically writing stuff in her notebook. He gestured toward her when
the professor walked in, indicating with his index finger that he would join
them shortly. The professor nodded at her as he sat down and pulled out
his books. She was reading *Either* but paused as he set up across from her.

"Hi," she said. "Have you read this?"

"Yeah, it's great, isn't it?"

"Unbelievable." She nodded for emphasis. Stared out through the
door, trying to work out how to even begin to say everything that was
rushing through her mind. "I read a story once that he used to go to the
Tivoli in Copenhagen and accost people, telling them all about something
or other. Whatever he was working on. He had all these big thoughts and
nowhere to go with them."

"He couldn't help it, I bet."

"Don't you wonder though. I mean, how would he know? He wrote it
down with all the misdirection. Claiming this guy found the manuscript and
edited it. Published it. There are so many layers. People, a few of them
anyway, bought it. Some are like, yeah, that's okay, or maybe, ah it's weird,

what's the point exactly? Worse still, they would say that his ideas could be summarized in these five bullets where points two and three are obviously incorrect."

"Right. Like who the fuck are these people, anyway?"

"Exactly." She asked if he was familiar with Wolfe's theory on Kierkegaard's biography. When he said he wasn't, she went on. "Wolfe says that the philosopher went out of his way to engineer events that produced circumstances where he would have to focus on his work. He ruined himself and his relationship with Regine so that he had to go under. It was his way of fashioning the world he wanted to live in. He created the conditions for it."

"Oh yes, that theory. He applies it to everyone whose work he likes."

"Sometimes it fits though. I see your point. It's a bit indecent. Another kind of judgment, not much different from those commentators who summarized the book and focused on everything in it that they thought was obviously false."

"Yeah. You're either moved by it or you aren't. What is there to say?"

"Isn't your whole job to come up with stuff to say about it? What are you writing? What commentaries are you producing? What do you teach in your class if you aren't saying something about his work?"

"Sure. Should he be read without being taught? Is it possible for people to be left alone with his work? Read it or don't, make of it what you will, and that's it."

"It doesn't need to work that way with all writers. There might be some."

"I heard once that Deleuze said something about *Thousand Plateaus*, like the chapters should be thought of as your favorite songs. Not really subjects of analysis, but you might listen to them over and over again when you're in the right mood."

"That wouldn't work very well for Russell, though."

"Why not? Aren't there people who like that kind of music? Takes all kinds. Bertie was walking his own path. It wasn't Kierkegaard's way, but it was a way."

"Hmmm. I guess." She was trying to visualize it but seemed to be having trouble. "It isn't true for just anyone though. There are rules here. Even within philosophy there's a boundary between the sacred and the secular."

"How do you mean?"

"Well, on the one hand there's a kind of commerce of ideas. People are always trading them around. Selling their own favorites, buying the ones that are most popular, getting rich off of whatever is in vogue. The commentaries and the secondary literature are all trade. This is vulgar, this is the everyday orientation of things. On the other hand, there is what is sacred. It is sacred not because of some divine providence that speaks through it, but because it disrupts that everydayness."

"What is that everydayness?"

"I don't know. Something like 'rationality.' Where everything is connected through some order or categories. It's all measured in terms of some common currency. Everything fits and makes sense and is easily understood as true or false because it's a reference to a real set of circumstances. The relationship is publicly verifiable."

"The mechanism."

"Yes. It's the subject of endless chatter. The orderly functioning of things that make it easy to move across all the connections and references. It's like Descartes' arguments for foundations I can use to build all knowledge."

"The thinkability of all things, the knowability of everything. The containment of whatever is in the human body of knowledge."

"Yes. The sacred is whatever blasts that apart, whatever doesn't fit or doesn't make sense. The mechanics dismiss the sacred as meaningless or insane."

"Kafka's bug."

"Exactly. That's very cool. What can they make of this stuff? They have to make it a commentary to fit it in with all the other categories they have. This reduces the work to something known, to something easily connected to everything else."

They each pulled out cigarettes, she lit his before lighting her own. She went on.

"Kierkegaard at Tivoli is sacred like that. It doesn't make sense really. None of his work makes sense. We don't even know if he meant it, or what he meant. It's all just suppositions and fragmentary suggestion."

"Well, isn't this a form of commentary?"

"Only if I am saying it badly. We read this stuff and it moves us. It transports me into a different mood or deepens the mood that I'm already in. The truth in this book isn't what he says, it's in the way I feel when I read it. It's in the point of connection between this man writing two hundred years ago and me sitting here now with *our* book in my hands. That's the truth. The connection across time."

"I don't think you are trying to re-establish some metaphysical domain of the sacred. Not in the normal sense that people have when they use that term. You're just trying to express a negative of some kind. Something that resists this everyday commerce of ideas."

"Yes. Like a poem."

"There are people who pick apart poems though and they have traditional forms. There are more people who make a living off of picking apart poems than there are people who make a living writing poetry."

"That's sick."

"Isn't it better than if there weren't anyone who cared about poetry at all?"

"I don't know. There will always be some people who are moved by certain things. 'Don't let yourself lose me.' These people will gravitate toward the works of like-minded people. If this kind of person is rare, then they need the commentators to keep the market going. Is that your point?"

"Yes. For every single person who experiences the sacred in Kierkegaard's book, there are ten who have lost that for the sake of whatever bullet points restate the propositions in it. The only way the book remains in print is because those ten people buy it, and they teach it so that even more people will have to buy it. It's a whole industry of commentary and university presses, reviewers and critics."

"Well, that sucks."

"How does it suck if that's what it takes to make sure the book is still around two hundred years later for you to read it?"

"I don't know, it means that the only way we can preserve some things is to ruin them."

"It might mean that certain ways of ruining things are also the way to preserve them. The sacred depends on the attempts to debase it. It would cease to exist without them."

She smiled and looked right at him. "Are you telling me I need those gasbags to make sure I get the full effect of Kierkegaard's work?"

"The world advances in all its positivistic and utilitarian ways. These ways take possession of things, they pull everything that they come across into their vortex, reducing them to the terms of their relationships. Measurable means for ends understood and available for certification and repeatable sanction. A symbolism forms alongside this as its antagonism. By symbolism, I mean –partly– desire. These relationships generate the domain of meaning that make resistance to the dominant order possible, gives it a voice and possibility. Again, desire at work. Desire that rejects an order of things, it dis-orders. The conditions for what is sacred can only be found in the secular order, in the everyday world of common things. Where we are absorbed, but against which our desire pits us."

"There's too much there to parse. You've lost me."

"I know. You pushed the button. I'll try again. Symbolism and desire are biproducts of order. The symbolic is how the sacred takes form, right? You have to be able to recite it, say it, deliver the incantation or whatever it is that breaks out of the everyday way of seeing things. There is yearning there."

"It's too abstract."

"Okay. Think about someone who is really good at something. It doesn't matter what it is. Someone who has spent many many hours over many many years developing and fine-tuning some set of skills. Playing a musical instrument. Dancing. Whatever, it doesn't matter."

"Okay."

"They are spending all that time learning the traditions, the classical ways of doing it, the scales and the standards, the basic steps. They are learning what many have learned before them. What many will learn after them."

"Yep."

"Someone might do that and become something of an automaton, they might arrive at a position where they have perfectly learned the history of the skill and can now do it as well as anyone has ever done it, but they contribute nothing. They don't advance the art."

"They have mastered it, but they don't create anything new."

"Right. What's the difference between these two paradigms? The person who achieves this mastery and adds nothing and then the person who achieves it up to a point and then innovates. There is a difference, and we usually call it something like creativity, or genius, if it's really good."

"Okay. I see the point."

"In one case there is a purely machinic repetition of what has been learned, whereas in the other case it seems like the person has turned all that they've learned into a set of symbols that can be played with, mixed up, and matched with each other. This allows them to go beyond what they learned and into some new territory that no one ever imagined before. What I was trying to say is that there is something in all that order, all those steps, all those musical sounds, whatever it is that they have mastered, that surfaces as a set of patterns, passion, and desire. When the person starts playing with those patterns, riffing on them, mixing them together in unusual ways, that's when the person goes off into some new area, some way of doing whatever it is that they have mastered. I'm suggesting that this form of mastery is like that thing you are calling sacred."

"Hmmm. It could be."

"Kierkegaard was good at something. Right? It wasn't just that he had a couple of ideas or something or had a reaction to the story of Abraham that was interesting or saw something in the work of Socrates that no one had seen before. It was more like, he was training himself in some classic patterns, mastering them, and then this whole world erupted out of these basics. That whole world allowed him to start pointing out things, saying things, suggesting that there was so much more in what he had mastered than others saw there."

"Do you think the sacred was something like the sensibilities he developed while studying? I'm not sure that's where I was going with this, but is that what you mean?"

"I don't know. You'd have to be as extraordinary as he was in order to say this. I might not be able to explain it because I don't have whatever it is that he had. More likely, it could be that the thing he was really good at was just this: being able to identify these feelings in himself and express them through the cracks he perceived in the perfect technique of ideas, or the perfect notions of how to present an argument or a way of thinking about the world. If my expertise is something else, then of course I wouldn't be able to match him."

"You think this is more common than people think?"

"I do. Art is probably the place most people expect it, and it probably isn't very common in those areas. Painting or music, poetry or philosophy. Very few people master all the techniques. Among those few, even fewer spin up the symbolic connections sufficient to break free of the limits and constraints that tradition places on them. Think more broadly though. Think about conversation, or typesetting. Preparing a syllabus, or any of a million different things that people do. Our creative powers are more common than we think, they just happen in ways that we don't expect, and we can't always control what activities will pull these possibilities out of us."

"Ah nice, the art of everyday life but you don't get to choose your genre. It's so important, but it still seems like it has to be rare. As you've described it at least, we have to be thinking of something that is not the rule, but the exception. By definition it can't be a rule because it's a departure from the rules. Right? You have to both learn to follow the rules and leave them behind. Which means you have to be the kind of person who is willing to leave them behind. That's why it's still an 'art.' Not everyone can be an artist, and that's because the artists depend on the commentators to inspire them to go beyond the rules, or to make new rules. The critics are a foil, *and* they are a muse. They inspire antagonism and a desire to overcome their petty grievances..."

Wolfe comes over to the table at this point. He sits down next to the typesetter.

"I heard," he said, "something about the 'art of everyday life.' I can only imagine what's behind all that. Knowing you two, I can put it together. Being the pompous ass that I am, I'll butt in and remind you two dreamers that you can't build a civilization on that. There is no art without an audience. It seems just as likely that the whole point of moral community or social order, or whatever you want to call the rest of the people, is to be that audience. The art of everyday life is the lie that we tell ourselves to keep the wheels moving. Truth is, though, the art of everyday life is why there are so many norms and standards. The audience is supposed to shut up and sit in the dark and listen quietly. Laugh when they are supposed to laugh, applaud when they are supposed to applaud. The lie is in thinking that each of us has a shot at being one of the artists. That's how they get us to shut up until it's our turn. The thing is, for most people, it's never their turn. If they didn't need us in order to be famous, they'd probably kill us all."

"We were talking about Kierkegaard," the professor says flatly.

"Sure, I know what you were talking about. Everyone here knows what you were talking about. The same shit people have been talking about for centuries. What you fail to grasp is that all those commentators, they all think they are artists too. They all want to be the great genius of their era, the voice of their generation, just as much as any of the delusional idiots who comment while denying that they are one of 'them.' The problem is that for every story you can tell about this one or that one, there are thousands or millions of stories that you can't tell because the people behind them never did anything worth remembering."

She jumps right back in, "That's the point. That's exactly the point. It's not about being remembered or being celebrated. It's about living it, about being that way, experiencing the world like that. If you achieve that, then none of that other shit matters."

The professor nods in agreement. "The symbolic as desire and not as some forensic judgment, some third person historical conclusion that 'they' come to in unison."

Wolfe laughs. "These rare ones, these forgotten, these people who lived their truth and let that be enough. That's great. Perfect picture. Like I said, you can't build a civilization on that. That's why these types are rare, why they have to be rare, and why they can't be found with any frequency among the members of the chorus. Human beings couldn't behave properly with each other, they wouldn't be able to lookout for each other, they wouldn't be able to live together, if the majority of people were like this. You're betting your lives and your livelihoods on something that has to apply to only a small-scale minority of creatures. Once it becomes the common way to be, it won't be sustainable, and the entire species would disappear in a megalomaniacal disaster. Because that's what these attitudes reduce to, a pathological distaste with fitting in and being part of a community."

"Look who's talking," said the professor while the typesetter nodded furiously.

"Yeah, you're the worst of the bunch."

"No, I'm not. Because I would never try to make my way of thinking into the rule, into a standard for others to follow. I don't know want to codify it. I'm not trying to create a philosophy or issue a command. You miss the point if you try to do that. I know that I'm able to see the world the way that I do and live the way that I do because it's exceptional. If everyone else thought like I did, we'd be screwed, or miserable, or both screwed and miserable. That's why I celebrate the idiocy around me. I am glad that there is hardly any room for the sacred anywhere. I am thrilled that there is so much commentary coming from all those self-righteous gasbags. I'm happy about it because I know that my way of thinking and living totally depends on them doing what they're doing and that I have an interest in keeping them going just as they are for as long as they can. I don't hate the status quo. It defines me even as I define myself over and against it."

"We were considering this. Answer this, do you love it because it allows you to take exception to it? It is the condition of your desire, what conditions your desire," the professor was trying to clarify and align the point, but he didn't seem convinced that he had as he trailed off awkwardly.

"Sure. I seem to recall you saying that your buddy Foucault made just this point. That we shouldn't be so quick to throw out the ruling western ideology because we don't know what will replace it and we don't know if it will be possible to take exception to it in the interesting and exciting ways that the current order allows."

"That's a textbook definition of privilege," the typesetter said.

"It's a luxury to think like that," the professor responded.

"Damn right it is, and it's delusional to think otherwise. If you two were really good at what you're doing, —being that way, thinking as you do— you would know that it all rests on top of the foul injustice of the actual world. You can't shut up about it, maybe, because you feel guilty, because you know deep down that what I'm saying is right. Taking exception to it, worrying about taking exception, it's all the same. There's privilege in all of it. Own it, and make no mistake, everyone who would criticize you for it wants it for themselves and that is what they are really criticizing. 'Why can't I have that too?'"

"You twisted everything to your advantage. You're the one embracing the world as it is and then you accuse us of doing it."

"Both of us are doing that, you just need to justify it as a desire for a new moral order whereas I justify it as the only moral order that there ever was. Look around. We have exactly the world that we wanted because this is the only way to want anything at all. The question is, as always, why did we want *this*?"

The professor turns back to the typesetter. His body language makes it clear that he is ignoring Wolfe's point. "I was reading *Either* on a train headed to Oslo. I put the book in the pocket on the seatback in front of me and then ended up leaving it there when I got off the train. I had the *Or* in my backpack but obviously couldn't read it until I finished reading *Either*. This was a heartbreaking accident. There was no way I would find an English translation of that book in Norway. I couldn't get it out of my head. I had lost *Either*. I went back to the train station the next day and checked the lost and found. While I was there, I also checked whether there was a train headed back south. There was and I thought it had the same number on the engine that I had seen on the train I took the day before. I had a Eurail pass so it was easy to jump on the train and go through the cars to check to see if I could find my book where I had left it. The train left the station while I kept moving through the cars. I didn't find it anywhere. I got off at the first stop, thinking I could take the train back to Oslo where all my stuff was stowed at the youth hostel. I was in Halden Norway."

"Never heard of it," Wolfe says.

"Keep going."

"Well, there were no trains. Apparently, there was only one train per day, and it had come that morning. To make matters worse, Halden was kind of out in the middle of nowhere. There weren't many people around and even the roads were empty. I started walking back toward Oslo thinking I would try to get a ride, but there weren't any cars. I was stranded and it was a long way. I didn't think I'd be able to make it back to Oslo that day."

"Shit," she said.

"The whole time I'm walking I'm thinking how stupid I was to jump on that train. Even if the engine was the same engine, they must change those cars all the time. How could I be so foolish as to think that would be the same train with the same cars that would have my book in it. I didn't think through any of it, really, I just wanted my book, and I wanted it so badly that I projected this train into the same one that I had ridden the day before."

"What did you do?"

"I kept walking, and kept thinking about how stupid I was, but I also thought about the book. I had only read that first section and it was the first time I read it. This was before graduate school. I hadn't read any Kierkegaard before. I didn't know much about him, so my reading was scattered at best. I remembered thinking about that one aphorism at the end where the guy is given a wish and he chooses to always be on the side of laughter. That was what kept me going. My stupidity became hilarious. Laughing kept my spirits up and I kept walking. For hours I walked up that little road. *Four* hours. Luckily, in those days Norwegians were really good about picking up hitchhikers. The first truck that came by stopped and gave me a lift. I arrived safely back in Oslo in time for supper."

"What could possibly be the point of that story?"

"I get it," she says. "The experience of that four hours. Those four hours, for you, have been immortalized somehow. The first car. The reliability of the Norwegian truck driver. Your own stupidity, the laughter that kept you going. All that was the point of the story. Those hours were sacred. Across two hundred years, you and Kierkegaard shared that experience, and it binds you two together. Even if nothing ever comes of it, even if no one ever cares about that time and what happened there, about the connections between you and him, there will have been that moment, and it will have been something you were a part of. When did you finally get to read the rest of the book?"

"In Germany at the end of that summer, I found the same edition in a bookstore that had an English section. I bought it and read it immediately. It justified the fact that I had been carrying around the *Or* that whole summer while travelling through Scandinavia. Space in my pack was so precious. I still have that book. Funny story. I didn't have enough money on me to buy it. I spoke to the bookseller and told her that I really wanted the book but couldn't afford it just then. I asked if she would hold it for me so that I could come back and buy it the next day. What was I worried about? That there would be some mad run on English translations of Kierkegaard in Heidelberg? That book was probably sitting on the shelf for months, but it was so precious to me I couldn't avoid that sense of urgency. Anyway, she asked how much I had, and –when I told her—she said that would be fine. It was about half the price. I can still remember her face and how kind she looked. I had been travelling three months by then and must've looked pretty raggedy."

Wolfe started to say something, but the typesetter had opened her book and interrupted him:

"Something wonderful has happened to me. I was caught up into the seventh heaven. There sat all the gods in assembly. By special grace I was granted the privilege of making a wish. 'Wilt though,' said Mercury, 'have youth or beauty or power or a long life or the most beautiful maiden or any other of the glories we have in the chest? Choose, but only one thing.' For a moment I was at a loss. Then I addressed myself to the gods as follows: 'Most honorable contemporaries, I choose this one thing, that I may always have the laugh on my side.' Not one of the gods said a word; on the contrary, they all began to laugh. From that I concluded that my wish was granted and found that the gods knew how to express themselves with taste; for it would hardly have been suitable for them to have answered gravely: 'Thy wish is granted.'"

February

The man without pants. Kierkegaard at Tivoli made ridiculous. He is a blathering idiot. I don't know if the ideas are so very big, but the drive to say them most definitely is. You can't write like that if you aren't drawn by the pleasure of it. Is that the symbolic or is it the imaginary? Is it the struggle of the one with the other? With reality stupid and silent, watching without intervention?

If that story is true, then it is a tale of loneliness not of great genius wasting away in a small northern capital. I'm not denying him that, only saying this isn't the moral of the story. I imagine him muttering to himself, pants falling down, derelict in all things humanly social. What is he looking for from those people? He cannot honestly imagine that they would provide him some insight or opportunity for deeper understanding of that notion he has been turning over and over throughout the day. That thought brought him out of the house and down to the street, it is the one he has to almost run to catch up with.

"I tell you, I would rather be a swineherd, understood by the swine, than a poet misunderstood by men."

Sometimes it may not have been the thought, but the artifice it needed for transport. The idea shape may have lived fully fledged in his brain, but he did not know how to channel it down to earth. This could break out into two distinct boundaries. First off, you have to find the words, and that is a question of launching an entry point for the emission. Their tone will matter, but so much more does too. The image, its points of connection to other notions, the history of the language, the history of his people and of his orientations and yearnings. 'What is a poet?' is a brilliant launching pad. It asks a question and sets the stage. From it, all things flow aesthetically. That whole point of view finds its tone in this question and in the quick resolution into the tortured person whose screams of anguish resound like music. He banishes the critics at the moment of inception. The poet is such and such. In point of fact, as a matter of comparison, the critic is one and the same except the attributes themselves are nowhere to be found. Being propertied, attributed, predicated makes them one and the same. The connections and flow of the language make them one and the same. It's just that there is no anguish and there is no music. Both are, in a way, the same. Except for the differences.

This backwards injection into the matter at hand is the matter at hand throughout. For the judge and his alternative will set himself up as the critic. These are points of view become lost in themselves and unable to twist free. This comes immediately and sets the stage in splendor but with a dark shadow. The aesthete may be unable to listen. We have the second boundary. It is in the genre or form of the discourse. The setting in motion of two distinct points of view each of which differ from the editor and any possible authority over the meaning and progression of the work.

Are these the forms of moral community we were battering each other with the other night?

Wolfe's pants are firmly belted. He is rich. Whether he believes his position or not, either way he is an asshole. Either he is the opportunist who has identified his privileged place and welcomes it with complete enjoyment and an interest in protecting it, or he is a liar willing to make a rhetorical maneuver just to skewer his opponent. The rich ought never to advance on pure self-interest, that we impose only upon the poor. Only the rich may act from moral grounds, the poor are dupes when they do so. Look at them, why do they refuse to act on their own behalf? Do they think they are rich? How dare they apply moral reasoning to circumvent their own inclinations. Wolfe lives in rags but thinks with the splendor of a King.

It's frustrating that he is this way while writing the way he does. If people only knew the truth about him. About how fake and crafted his voice is. It is so charming, so likeable, so at ease while drawing readers through his musings and observations. All of it a manipulation, for he desires to be liked by the reader even if he could not care less whether people up close feel the same. The reader is a tool to him. He doesn't long for a dialogue, he sings to his audience and feeds when they swoon. He doesn't know the philosopher's public experience, without pants and subject to mockery. He doesn't know the vulnerability of intellectual solitude. He has readers who are drawn to him and who never say things like "that's very interesting" or "I like how you..." or whatever uncomfortable stretch they need to make to say something nice about something that has put them off or created distance between you. He doesn't get that distance for they think him so charming and so at home in their heads. He speaks as they would speak about the things they would see if they looked in the direction he is pointing. Of course, they want to look in that direction now, because he makes it so alluring and inviting to do so.

I suppose that is what it means to be good at writing. Letting the language, voice, tone, and genre emerge as it needs to emerge for the stories you are aiming to tell. To be without pants in doing so, however, marks a widening gap in the performer's lived experience. It all hinges upon whether the writer is the subject of ridicule in the act of presentation. They cannot all be great though their position lays claim to it and exposes them to harangue. Wolfe's approach is not novel, he is no innovator. Being likeable through tried-and-true tactics and heuristics, this can be learned over time by someone whose primary concern is to make an audience and establish their own position in front of it.

Those critics, they were not interested in Kierkegaard's style and form. They did not appreciate the genre he pulled from the sky and blew words into for the sake of spinning the yarns he saw so clearly. He was alone in that. A writing machine and ridiculous. Lurching around the park, throwing himself at strangers, trying to get the resonance from the notions, trying to hear what it might sound like if there were listeners in the hall. The critics resembled the poet to a tee. They were perfect simulations; they only lacked those most essential characteristics that give the poets their poetry. These hardly matter at all, anyway. Just ask anyone.

Being able to write with the confidence of listeners, of being listened to, and engaged. Becoming a part of a living discussion where there is back and forth between those who speak and those who listen. These are the notches on the belt for how loose or how tightly the cinch is made. If there are none, gravity wins the day. There is something to be said on both sides of the fiasco. Kierkegaard's work would have been so different if he had an audience and interlocutors, if there were a sympathetic readership who gave back and elaborated on the themes. If the critics lined up as stooges or adoring henchmen, if the audience leapt to their feet in glorious acceptance and adulation, his work would have taken a different turn. The thinker without pants experiences something different than what those who comply with the norms and standards see. If there is no hierarchy of preference, I need not say this has more potent results than that. I only mean that a Descartes without that public reaction is not the same as the Descartes with it. The philosopher on their own with their immediate peers and the philosopher in the hall with the audience and the applause are different animals altogether.

It is by my blindness that I cannot see these paradigms without making all the associations that come with them. The skills and the likability, the glorious luck of those who fit neatly into the current fashion of ideas and the means for expressing them, these are the leaders and powerful figures in the domains of the social network. The gesellschaft of the mind. There are those who are unlucky in their time. Whether times change to their favor or not, their unluckiness will remain in the work for it is the air they breathed and the earth they walked. They have only each other and whatever unlucky persons they can accost in the parks of the cities where they live quietly and without bother. They speak knowing that only fragments will make it to their listener before they run off in consternation. The gemeinschaft of the mind.

Wolfe is right, of course. There are very few who will have their day. Very few of these pantless wonders will one day come to be fitted with tailored extravagance. Kierkegaard has been lucky that way for all the good it did him. As she showed me, none of this matters. There is no experience of it, no feeling to it. Their audience comes too late, the applause falls on dead ears, which leaves us with the original question as to what the difference is between the one and the other. Could there be a back and forth or either/or between these points of view? What if there were and the only thing that separated them were the reader's reactions two hundred years later? What if there were nothing more to that reaction than an appreciation for the likability and charm of the voice and tone at work in the one and the discomfort with those same traits in the voice and tone of the other? Otherwise, they resemble each other to a tee.

In the community where the philosopher lives, as opposed to the society where the other one has their cushy job as tenured faculty with frequent conference appearances and easy access to whichever journal they choose to publish their latest notions, there is no sound division of labor, no large-scale mechanism for optimized productivity in the human sciences and beyond. Such a thinker must be organically placed, for there is no room for intellectual production on the assembly line powered by the quid pro quo of peer review. What does running a professional domain have to do with this philosophy? How are the skills conveyed? Which course or qualifying examination covered these topics? Was it all of them and I mistakenly thought they were asking me about coherentism vs foundationalism and the five key historical figures who exemplify each position?

We have been bred to think it is all a matter of time, of finding the time, amid all these other responsibilities. Why would the scholar need to scrounge for time? Teacher, administrator, reviewer, critic, poet, analyst, inventor, each resembling the other to a tee. They walk among each other without concern for they all know the principles of electro-magnetism and what the villain's green meant to Beowulf. More so, they learn how to effectively engage students on the core notions at work in the coherentist perspective and how they differ from those required to adequately convey foundationalism. They can orient themselves to the challenges and problems a beginner faces when trying to access the tools of the discipline. Surely such skills and abilities are crucial for placement, make sure to add student evaluations and peer commentary to your CV so that prospective employers know you are well-rounded. The social being of the philosopher under such conditions may have nothing at all to do with those questions asked of strangers by that lone stroller trying to hold their pants up while gesturing furiously in tune with the music on their lips and the anguish in their hearts.

Whatever they can say about Nietzsche and Heidegger, to the extent that these two should ever be held in the same thought or sentence, it is inevitable that they must admit that the two lived these different lives and so cannot be catalogued under the same topic. What would Nietzsche's work have been like if he had overseen dissertation committees while producing it? If he had designed Fall, Winter, and Spring curriculum for rooms full of students? Nearly everything Heidegger "wrote" was a lecture presented to a packed room. Is there anyone willing to argue that this had no effect? That there was no reflective influence on their thinking? His oh so pure thought of the poetic origins of being, free of social and institutional enframing? Does his work and constant fidgeting with the problems surge up into their form, as the vessel his thinking must use when breaking free of that thing that grips it? Every event is a measurement.

Whatever there is of struggle and conflict in Nietzsche's work, there is nothing of *this* struggle. The sermons of Zarathustra are imagined. Heidegger would have felt too self-conscious presenting his thought this way because it would closely approximate his life at the lectern and his life away from it after the ban. Nietzsche's imagination could not fix on the students in their chairs listening and hanging on every word. Rather, he spoke into a void, into a place where no one with a face was living and breathing. He spoke and had to speak as though the words were responsible for conjuring the audience, since they could not be counted by the rolls and matriculation fees.

Each becomes a catalyst of an idol, a figurehead for showing how that time can be seized. For time is always the purified goal, the luxury of the scholé. On the one hand, we have the lecturer who has so far achieved the pinnacle of their profession, allowing all their time to be devoted to working out those problems in public. Spin your yarns as you will in front of the crowded lecture halls assembling for your topics of interest year after year. On the other hand, the modest living of the mountain traveler in search of better air. They have enough to get by without having to seek out a profession. Neither of them craves for time since they each have it, but differently. It would never occur to anyone that there might be ways to find the time amid something else. Where is the administrative participant, the chair, and committee member, who has produced a great movement? Not a noble career or a fine standing among their peers, but a transformer of the discipline. Those are left to these two paradigms, since no one could imagine that a person without the time to fly off in whatever direction incites their movement would have the capacity and potential to produce such phenomena. Heidegger and Nietzsche are the only figures that can become totems. They are fantasy figures because there is no way to get there from here.

They are no longer roles to choose in a world where the slate of possibilities lies alongside the menu of occupations. If you can't get to the heights through a chair in a department with PhD candidates, and if you don't have your "three thousand a year," what remains to you but the battle over time that vocation requires? No one will teach you devotion. The critics have shown us again and again, in what is their most valuable lesson, that this cannot be done without paying a price. There is no way to sing the song from that place without having the local flavors and intonations inhabiting your voice. That is why they all resemble each other to a tee. Because the commentators reduce all that upon which they are commenting to one and the same body of work, history, and tradition.

Commentary is where we have it today in the society of philosophers. Even their best and their brightest never had to make a choice about genre and voice. They speak nowhere in no way and use no artifice. Pure mind is their mechanism and their means. They are never the subject of ridicule. They pronounce their judgments clearly and loudly with the confidence that their discipline provides. They are lucky for the world came ready made for them, for their tastes and their passions. Virtue in them has been transformed into the power to achieve correct results. The best results. These are the only results that matter, the ones that constrain the entire domain of action, making it the domain that it is. Virtue adds up to the power of bringing about the most highly desired ends. One can no longer speak of an inherent excellence exhumed in the moment of doing. There is no more world without means and ends. The spontaneity of the free act is no more, it has become the meticulous step-by-step of transactions aiming at ends and unraveling methodically when they fail. Even virtue has fallen prey. It is a giant economic exchange, just like she said. The man without pants is its victim, the unlucky one, the one with no means and no ends to speak of. Where are these ends in the impulse? Where is the goal in the drive? If a gas spins into metal and earth, if a patch of dirt becomes mud in the rain, and if a speaker stumbles along in the gardens and mutters his eerie tune, why slip that into the form of the end? These phenomena become themselves out of themselves, they emit, and they advance. To no end, and without one. There is nothing but push in this fantasy. There is only impulse and emission, pure exhilaration for no sake or only for its own sake.

These are the last days that I have known. They impact all my moods and moments. She wrote me and told me about a man in her program and how he seemed to need others to feel inadequate. He had a way of bragging and promoting himself, and it was always at another's expense. I felt her struggle with it, the anger she felt as response, but also the resignation that there was something in what he said that was fit and could not be avoided. She extolled the stupidity of her teachers in falling for it. Frustrated, she applauded her peers' acquiescence, as if the approach were legitimate and fair. I caught a glimpse of her, building monuments with irony and bite. She could be wicked. It was exciting.

I didn't have any wisdom for her. She asked, but I had none. All I could do was give her some insight into these last days of the man without pants and how vastly different he was from those others who seemed to force him out into the park and on his own. I warned her that my response would be self-involved, that I would be taking the opportunity of her pressures to express the thoughts most dear these last days and which were not in the least relevant to her plight. I pointed out all these things and yet I could not help but see what I saw: that there was something much approved in her colleague's demeanor, that it was very much a part of the society of scholars. This society, with all its standards and norms, values and conditions, would force anyone who wanted to achieve a place within it to take on these same behavioral affectations. I pointed out that there was something disconcerting here, that those in search of the community present themselves as an idealized other to that society. These outsiders are drawn along by the occasional glimpse that there may be room for it on the inside. They are fooled and seduced by the stories of Kierkegaard at Tivoli which proves that sometimes things turn out right. They don't focus on all the failed experiments that they do not know and whose work they do not read because they did not matter to that public sentiment that would have drawn them out into the open where the audience could better get a look at them.

The exchange was warm. We reached out to each other in those moments. Everything changed for us here. We weren't just writing back and forth about the everyday and the way we thoughtlessly navigated our pathway through it. We have turned to face each other. We looked past the social graces and started to resemble each other in touch and feel.

The moments would come late at night. There were many curtains of symbols and signs between us. Inference and meaning made morning out of night, and day out of evening. We weren't swayed, but we were touched. Alone on either side. These were lights blinking in the dark winter. The difference between Wolfe and me depends on this.

No special project this term. I've been chained to the desk in this cave for a month. There is so much reading. Last semester it felt like science, like it was all about peer involvement and agreements on methodology. There were experiments and data to process. Collaboration was the key to everything. Now it's a totally different thing. All about learning other people's results, standards and practices, and the body of knowledge. Which is the right impression? It might be both and I'll see the payoff when I review what I did back then. I wonder if I would still be here if luck would have led me to set it up the other way around? If this had been my first semester, maybe I wouldn't have come back?

What the hell is going on with that squirrelly fucker? How does he get that perfect job in the digital lab? It might be because he knows the software, but he told me that he was still just learning it and getting used to everything. There's a set of complicated rules around who gets which rewards around here. Do you have to get in good with the right professors, the ones who are making the decisions about who is assigned to which project or which collection? It takes everything I have just to keep up with the reading. I wouldn't have the first clue how to find the time to develop good connections and relationships. I don't know why I expected this to be different from anything else.

Yikes, remind me never to get on your bad side. The artistry of schmoozing is probably more important than what you are learning. That guy must have done something right.

He might know what he is talking about. He did get his PhD after all. I can only imagine everything that goes into that. All the soul sucking brown nosing you have to do in order to get into the right position, in order to gain the right people's favor so that they will help you move onward and upward. Pandering to all the narcissism of those who have dedicated their lives to informing the ignorant. Getting a job in academia can't be easy, I can only imagine what he went through to get those connections in Illinois and then to get something up here, but has any of it rubbed off?

Alright, I'm game, how exactly do I schmooze?

It's getting late and I really need to finish this before I go to bed. I have to make sure I don't just pass my eyes over the words. I have to really process this. I'll turn off the screen and not check for at least twenty minutes.

I'm probably not the best person to ask. I don't do it well. My academic social skills are like a man without pants in a public garden filled with people relaxing and strolling about, and there I am all, 'have you heard about Ereignis? Let me explain...' And then I do, but they only hear sound and fury, there is no significance in it. Boredom is a powerful critic. So is ignorance. The people on the other side of the park, the ones who didn't see a thing, they are my bane. Those are the ones you have to reach.

Crazy. This one. I like this bit. He doesn't try to play the master. It's such an odd combination of confidence and humility. That might be exactly what isn't working for him. Pure confidence or nothing at all. It's like that with a lot of things. If you let people know that you've got it all covered, that you're sharp or on the ball or whatever, they will take your word for it. Show even a little doubt and they'll take your word for that too.

Do you think effective schmoozing is all about something other than developing skills in your work?

Why am I working my ass off if my skills don't matter as much as playing some social game with the people who have control over the perks? I get it. It's all about balance. Going to these parties, going to the little events scheduled by the department. This paper or that meeting, or whatever it is. You have to be present, and you have to be sociable. The work matters, there has to be something to build on, but the work alone is not enough. I get it.

The thinker at Tivoli is not interested in their concerns, only what they think about him. That is his problem. Sorry I keep framing this in terms of my own thoughts these last few days, but you are evoking them. Something in these questions does, but maybe I am a man without pants and this exchange is our Tivoli? It's not as complicated as you think. It's just flattery. You have to show an interest in the right people's work, and you have to make them think you can help them with it somehow. Have you considered becoming one of their minions?

Well, that fits in the squirrelly fucker's case. That wasn't a simple form of flattery. You can't just come out with it and tell everyone they're a genius, you have to take up their ideas and develop them in ways they want to see them developed. They want acolytes. That's his point. How depressing. I thought being around well-educated people who loved the same things I love would be enough. Earning your way isn't about innovation or mastery or anything like that. We don't earn our place in these worlds in those ways, we have to adapt our interests to the right things and our contribution has to be framed to promote the right agendas. If you flatter this professor, you will alienate that one. I've seen that already. How some of the students are attached to one professor and this somehow distances them from others. There are cliques and camps. The people who emphasize digital stuff and think that it is a major paradigm shift vs the people who think these are just new tools being applied to the same stuff we have always been doing. They can't just disagree. This silly difference becomes a religion and the people on either side can't talk to each other anymore. The students are supposed to find out which side they fit into so that everyone will know what kinds of rewards and advantages they are supposed to get.

I haven't really taken a stand yet. That might be why I'm missing out on all the good jobs. I need to make my alliances known.

That would explain a lot. I'm struggling so much just to take it all in, it never occurred to me to try and figure all this out, where everybody stands, what dynamics there are between this group and that one. All this stuff is really obvious. The other students talk about it all the time. This is probably the one thing that still makes me feel like I don't belong. When they go on about how this professor is aligned with those others and delivering a paper to that effect at some conference specifically tailored to contributions from people with this way of thinking, my eyes glaze over. That stuff is so alien to me. I had no idea. That is what makes everyone seem so savvy and enlightened on how things work while I feel totally clueless and lost all the time. If I stopped thinking about the skills and other things that I need to learn and focused more on the political dynamics between different groups, I'd get a better sense of connection to the life of the department.

The man without pants is ridiculous because he's alone in the park. This makes him suspect. He is a deviant. You can't be off and by yourself, you have to be aligned. The solitary thinker is a stranger and hospitality is not a virtue among these folks.

This makes sense, and they are not hospitable because they don't think of graduate students as guests. The patrons at the library might be, but not the graduate students. We are trying to gain entry to the profession, we are trying to become the insiders in possession of the keys to the kingdom. Of course, they want us to fall into the pack in some obvious way. This will make our plans for the future predictable and reliable. They will know us better and be better able to hand over those keys, reassured that we will run things the way they are supposed to be run. Things are always being shaped. The traditions are developing around us. Because new people keep coming into the equation, the bloodline must be protected. Otherwise, whatever the old guard has mastered, will become worthless. It's such an austere form of protection. Stuffy and dusty. I guess everyone warned me about this, that it was like this, but somewhere in the middle of all that is something really great. I just don't know if it's possible to pick and choose.

Does the man without pants have any underwear on, maybe some stylish boxers? Is his thing all hanging out? That could be why everyone thinks he is a degenerate, you know. Put on some knickers!

Hmmm. Should I send that? Being silly. Well, he better be able to take it if he's going to be hanging around here. Besides, that's part of the problem. Everybody takes everything so seriously all the time. That's what causes all the stress. When people forget how to laugh at themselves, when they start making their little projects and concerns into these enormous worldwide problems that are part of the very fabric of civilization, that's when they become ridiculous. Those are the real "men" without pants. Send. The other little guy is sweet and sad, he has nothing to be ashamed of. He doesn't say what else this guy has going on, after all. The emperor with the new clothes, he didn't have any pants on either. They probably wouldn't emphasize that because he was completely naked, right? Technically a person who is completely naked doesn't have any pants on. That could be part of his little story. He should go that way with it.

Well that adds a whole new angle to the cautionary tale, doesn't it? The rule about not running up to people with your bidness hanging out is one of the first lessons my parents taught me. My compliance over the years has been nearly perfect.

Nearly? Bahhhhh. What's the story with that? Bidness? That's cute. He should know what I'm like. I've been a little too stiff so far. Him too. When we talked, he didn't seem like that, he seemed to be following the beat of his own drum, as mom would say. He never tries to distance himself from these things we talk about, he never complains about all the bullshit they make him go through. At least I don't remember him doing that. Just stories. He includes himself and says things like 'we do this' or 'we do that.' He said he wasn't good at all the schmoozing. It's getting late, I really need to finish this reading tonight. It's nice. This rapid response. Where is he right now? I don't even think about him as a person, sitting somewhere. He's like a diary that talks back to me. Dearest Kitty. I write down the thought and it comes back with a comment. I write another and it comes back. Every time I hit send, I just have to wait a little while and something will come back.

That's not fair, I don't know. It's exactly what I need right now. It would be so pathetic and sad to just sit here and read all this by myself without anything else going on. It's nice to have this little buzzing in my ear. If I stop writing now and just respond to his last message tomorrow morning or the day after, he wouldn't even mind. At least he wouldn't say anything about it. He'd just respond as though that was the natural flow of the conversation and it's just continuing on as normal. Like there is no time in between, like he isn't anywhere other than waiting there on the other end of the network for whatever I'm going to say next, whatever my next quip or response is. It's weird and creepy. That's why I'm not telling anyone about it, about how frequent it's becoming and how we never go out or meet up or have any kind of real contact.

On the one hand, I am pretty self-conscious about it. On the other hand, it's really nice. I don't know what all that means to him. Right now, it has been longer than usual since my last response. What is he thinking? Does he think I have gone to bed, and he won't hear back, or is he worried that I was freaked out by his "nearly" remark? He doesn't know me well enough to know that was the perfect joke to make, so am I being cruel in leaving him hanging? Does he even care? Is he sitting there with his book in front of his computer just like me only he's getting his reading done because he's not letting his mind wander all over the place when he should be focused?

I just can't help it though. The human mind is not made for this. Late nights are when you should be sitting around with a couple of friends, sipping a beer, and having a cigarette. That's what we invented electricity for, not sitting in your basement cave and grinding through cataloging textbooks. There isn't much left to go. I can get this done if I just focus.

Nearly?

Three more pages and I'm done and then, as a reward, I'll read his response to that.

Done. Did I wait too long? He's probably gone to bed. Nope.

Sometimes there are people who want you to run up to them with your bidness hanging out.

Okay, now we're talking. He isn't just a big brain with no body, after all.

I guess we've gotten flirtatious before, but it never goes very far. He's too polite. Probably doesn't want to scare me off. If he only knew. Ha. I can be a major pervert myself, buddy. One day I'll have to come clean about all that, let him know what he's really gotten himself into. Not so late on a school night, though. Must be late for him too. Even asking some of these questions would get us into something and, I don't know, I just don't think I should go there. In the middle of all this, all the stress of school and figuring all this shit out. I don't want to be in a relationship. He really hurt me. I don't think I'm over it. We had plans, I thought we would get married. All he had to do was come here and stick around for two years and then we could go somewhere else, somewhere he wanted to go. He couldn't even do that. I was so sure he loved me and then to flake out like that. It doesn't make any sense. Are men's feelings really that flimsy? They can make it seem like they are so into you, and you are all they ever wanted one minute and the next minute that all just turns off and they disappear as if none of it ever meant anything. I just don't know how that works.

Anyone like that now?

Kind of a weird question to ask, I guess. As if I don't know what he's trying to get or what he's doing right this very second. It's ambiguous, right? I might be deflecting and telling him he should be looking for someone else because I'll never be what he wants me to be. Am I asking him if he is interested in me in that way? I mean, he never said he wanted to fuck me, did he? He hasn't exactly been forthright and clear. He wanted to go out and we went for coffee. I told him I didn't really want to start dating anyone right now and he said he was disappointed but understood. We said we would write to each other. I've been totally clear and totally straight with him. I'm not trying to play games. I don't know, though. That question might be part of a game.

I should step outside and have that cigarette before I get ready for bed. If he responds, I'll respond one more time and tell him goodnight. Even if he says something juicy.

Don't know. What do you think?

Oh, clever boy. Okay maybe I was playing a little game there. I don't know why. I'm really not interested in taking this anywhere. I don't want that. Why tease him? That can only lead him on, and if I really don't want him, why bother? It would be cruel. Unless I want something different than what it seems like I want? I don't know. I like this. I like the distance, but it might be nicer if we were closer. Like if the things we were writing to each other could be things you say to people who are close to you. How do I get there without all the stuff that usually goes with that? Without having him come over or going out somewhere? Is it even possible to become really close with someone over email? Won't there always be distance between us? Even this. How did we both know that we would go back and forth like this for hours tonight? What if one of us had walked away? There's always a threat of interruption or disappointment or whatever. That's distance. I want him to know me better, I want him to understand what I am going through, because the more he knows and understands, the more he'll be able to help me. I don't know. That's unfair, and there is already something soothing about the way he writes, but I wish it were more comforting. I want him closer. I like him far away.

Oh, such a pain in the ass. The endless anxiety of not knowing what you want. Wanting to figure it out, wanting to be able to set it all up and control the parts. Wanting something that you don't want and not wanting something that you do. Wanting not to want. Not wanting to want. Maaaaaadnessssss.

Don't know. Go to sleep. Goodnight, running boy.

The engineer's girlfriend had given strict instructions and provided detailed directions. The professor was to come to the apartment in Ypsilanti that evening, but he had to stop and pick up her friend first. It was on the way. When he pulled up in front of the house, he expected her to be waiting or ready to go, but she was nowhere in sight. He went up to the door and rang the bell, then waited, and waited some more. He thought he heard something inside. It might have been a voice shouting something, but he couldn't tell for sure. It was distant and muffled. He stepped back off the porch and looked over at the windows on the front of the house, on the first floor and then up to the second. He heard one of the windows slide open and a woman's voice calling out, letting him know that the door was open, and he could just come in. He tested the knob and entered. There was no one in sight, but he could hear a lot of commotion up the stairs.

"Come on up," she called out.

He cautiously walked up the stairs craning to try and see where all the shuffling and sorting was coming from. At the top, he saw there were three bedrooms and the noise seemed to be coming from the one at the front of the house where that same window had opened. He walked towards the door and peeked into the room. A woman was kneeling on the floor and digging out clothing from under the bed. There were clothes and shoes all over the place, covering every surface.

"Sorry, I'm looking for these shoes that I really wanted to wear. Did you have any trouble finding the place?"

She hadn't looked up or shown any concern that a stranger was not only in her house but had crept up to her room and was standing behind her.

"No problem. The directions were clear."

"Oh great," she said. "Aha, got you, you little bastards." She pulled her arm out from under the bed clutching a pair of shoes that didn't look much different than several other pairs that were nearby on the floor. She stood up, turned to face him, then slid into her shoes, putting her hand on his shoulder to steady herself. "Nice to meet you," she said.

She took a half step back and put out her hand in a formal greeting that was at odds with how their introduction had begun. They shook hands and smiled politely. "Ready?" she said as she left the room and started down the stairs. Her question and sudden burst of movement made it seem like she had been waiting for him. He hurried after her. At the bottom of the stairs, she put on a big down coat from the front hall closet and, as she did so, he saw how sinewy and svelte her arms were. Visions of Iggy Pop flashed through his head, and he wondered if her distinctive muscle tone had a common cause. Once in the car, she asked if it was okay to smoke. He flipped open the ashtray, "It's fine. I'll have one two. I'll just crack open the window if that's okay."

"Sure, it's your car" she said while lighting up. "What's your story? She said you're a professor?"

"At U-M Dearborn."

"You teach?"

"Yes."

"Ah, so you're one of those adults who spend all their time around younger people who don't know anything. Bet that gives you a big ego boost. What do you teach?"

"Philosophy."

"Philosophy? That's wild, so you know all about the meaning of life. Is that what you teach?"

"We're not allowed to teach that," he chuckled.

"I'll bet. Can't have those little fuckers learning the meaning of life. They'd be out of control."

"That and there's no market for it. They are paying customers, we have to give them what they want, and what they want is professional training."

"The customer is always right. What do they need you for?"

The professor looked more closely at her as she talked and could tell that she had a very definite kind of charisma. There was no reserve in her ways. She knew that 'meaning of life' remark was a silly cliché and that it might've been something he'd heard before. He got the impression that she said it because it would be expected of her, but she didn't take it seriously. Like it was a trick to do the expected thing without meaning it. He wondered just how much depth was behind it. She made it seem like she had heard it all before.

"How do you know them?" he said.

"She and I work together. Didn't she tell you?"

"No, not really. She didn't tell me much. Where you lived and that I had to pick you up. She said you were very cool."

"I am very cool." She laughed.

"Yeah, what makes you cool?"

"I've seen a thing or two. I didn't go to college, but I know people."

"People? What kind of people?"

"All kinds. Men. Women."

"Alright then, impart some of that wisdom. What have you learned about people? Tell me."

"Well, they are pretty possessive."

"You mean, like boyfriends?"

"Sure. Boyfriends, but not just them. All people really. You've probably learned a thing or two. You probably learned some of it the hard way, right? Well, I'm guessing anything you did learn like that, you're not going to let go of easily."

"Ah, I see. Whatever quirky experiences I've had are going to make me set in my ways. I'm going to stick to it. Is that what you mean?"

"That's right. No one can tell you anything different either. Because you've seen what you've seen, that's just the way it is. What quirky experiences have you had?" She looked over at him sideways, kind of coy, and she grinned. "Being possessive makes it hard to learn. What are you clutching in your greedy little hands?"

"You weren't talking about any specific ex-boyfriends or ex-girlfriends then? That's what people usually mean when they talk about being possessive."

"You're stuck on that, are you? You can't imagine that you might be possessive of a point of view? It has to be a girl or a guy that you don't want to fuck anybody else?"

He stuttered something like "Well..." and then "I'm not..."

"It's exactly what I mean. You're being possessive with your idea of possessiveness. You can't learn. It has to be what you already thought it was."

"Fair enough, but I think I got turned around here. Something about what you said, I just thought..."

"I'm not talking about jealousy. Well that too, but it's different."

"Different how? Couldn't it be the same thing? Anything that is hard won is something worth holding onto?"

"You think I'm hard won?"

He laughed with her, and they made eye contact. Something about her suggested she was thinking of all kinds of different ways to express that same question. She was easy to talk to. He hadn't expected this. He wished she would tell him everything she was thinking. It was abundantly clear that she was not.

"You do give off that vibe on first impression, yes."

"Oooh, you're a smooth talker. Look at you all flattering me and shit.

Are you testing your own theory?" Brief pause. "Look at you. I made you blush. That's adorable."

"Yeah yeah. Have a laugh. You know what I mean though."

"I do. You might be right. I definitely get possessive over my guy when it comes to that. It's probably like you said. We've put in the time, we've gone through a lot, I don't want him to just wander off, and make me start over with someone else."

"Your guy?"

"Hypothetically," she smiled, leaned her head back, and looked over. "Man, you've really got yourself locked into that, don't you? You need a cleanse. Something that'll let you start seeing people. Plain old people, not boyfriends past, present, and future."

They pulled into the parking lot in front of the apartment complex. While walking toward the building, he offered her his arm. "There's a little ice there, if you want some help in those shoes."

She took his arm and looked down as they carefully made their way toward the building. "Such a gentleman. Your possessiveness has its advantages, but men are always so much nicer *before* they get what they want."

Her breezy ways aside there was something scary about her. He couldn't quite identify it. There were depths she would never tell. Motives she wouldn't share.

"By the way," she said as they got to the door. "This is a setup. People thought about it. Don't worry. I'm cool." She pressed the buzzer to the engineer's apartment and held it until the door clicked open.

"Come on up," he said through the intercom.

They walked up the stairs to the second floor and then down the hall a bit. The door to the apartment was cracked open and they pushed it wider and went in. The engineer and his girlfriend were standing just inside at the doorway to the kitchen. She hugged them both and took their coats. She offered them beer. The professor asked for some water instead. In the living room, a younger guy was sitting at the desk chair in the corner doing something on the computer. They introduced him to the newcomers, but he didn't look up.

"We work together," the engineer said. "He's one of the graphic artists. Really talented. You should see what he can draw on the computer."

The engineer didn't have anything to drink, and the professor looked around to make sure. "What's going on?" he said. "Are you drinking?"

"No. She brought that. It's not a big deal. If you want to have a beer, go ahead and have one. I don't mind."

The two women both had beers and there was one on the desk where the kid was sitting, but that was it. It created a strange atmosphere. The professor couldn't tell, but it seemed like there was something out of place, something going on. He got a sense of a hidden depth all around and couldn't let go of it. In the car, they never went far enough to figure out if the possessiveness of which she spoke was a flaw or not. His insights might have been right on target. He had the distinct feeling that there were secrets being guarded by the people in that room and all the small talk and laughter in those first hours together was designed to hide them. He looked around and wondered what each of them was keeping from the others and who else was in on it. The engineer and the graphic artist had a secret they were keeping. The two girlfriends had something in mind that they withheld from the others. There was something the engineer and the professor knew that they weren't sharing. It was weird and it was everywhere. All around and every which way.

The graphic artist was drawing something and most of the others had glanced over his shoulder now and again to see what it was and what it was becoming. Eventually, a fantasy scenario emerged where a man and a woman with swords and shields were getting set to do battle with some unseen foe. It was elaborate. The night was like that. He kept drawing. The others broke off into conversations. Someone had pulled out a joint and passed it around. Everyone smoked a little except the engineer who was very loud and clear about his abstinence.

"Aren't you smoking or drinking?"

"No, can't. I'd be sick as a dog if I even tried a little. Don't worry about me."

"Okay." Awkward pause, then, "Why did you move your computer out here?"

"No more laptop, so I needed the PC to be more in the center. I'm not like you. I can't just barricade myself in a silent room and work for hours on end."

"What happened to your laptop?"

"Somebody must have stolen it. I just left it for a second at the coffee shop."

"That was a nice laptop. Did you call the police?"

"Yeah, it was a nice laptop. You know there was something I meant to ask you. All this social theory you've been spouting. Doesn't it ignore some of the most basic principles of physiology and the role brain chemistry plays in a person's life? Look how much my social behavior is impacted by all my brain chemistry. That's the point of most of these chemical therapies, isn't it? To modify how we act and get along with others."

"Well, the chemistry may be a fact, but the behaviors aren't. They are totally dependent on social custom, norms, and standards for this point in time or this place on the earth."

"What does that mean?"

"Addictions are not just physiological. They may be that in part, but there is a social element. People must show us what substances there are out there, those substances have reputations and histories, they have been cultivated and developed. They're part of a scene. Then not all drugs make it into wide circulation. There is an economy of substances, and that economy provides options and alternatives. Some people might be potentially addicted to something that doesn't exist yet, which hasn't been manufactured. Its absence is their stay of execution. Others are addicts because the substances that tweak their brains the best already exist and are in widespread circulation. There is industry behind them and organized distribution."

"What about depression?"

"I don't want to piss you off, but there seems to be a connection between brain chemistry in depression and social factors."

"Everything is fine and yet someone can be totally depressed though."

"Everything might be fine. They are living under artificial conditions where humans are being pushed and pulled in ways that they resist in the most rudimentary electro-chemical ways. I'm just saying. What does the data look like for people who live in different forms of society than we are living in today? Suicide rates differ, hospitalization, other outcomes, even when the diagnostics show similar rates."

The engineer nodded but didn't pursue the issue. He seemed off somehow, not interested in the usual back and forth. His initial question might've been a distraction. They sat silently for a moment.

"Hey professor, she says you told her in the car that you are quirky. Tell us about it."

"I said some of my experiences were quirky."

"That's even juicier. Come on, spill."

"That's not what I meant. She said that people can be attached to what they've learned from their experience, and I said my experiences have been quirky. I just meant that they are peculiar to me and that they don't necessarily reflect common experience. I wouldn't dream of generalizing. That's how it is, right? I mean, people go to the same restaurant on different nights, the chef didn't feel good one day and the customers didn't enjoy the food. The other day, he felt great, and the food was fantastic. The customers had a great time and recommended it to their friends. It's quirky. See?"

"It's true, I never listen to people who recommend this movie or that one. Who knows what kind of taste they have? They like action movies or something that I hate. They were having a good day when they saw it, so anything they watched that night would've seemed good to them."

"Wait a minute, this is total bullshit. I don't give a damn about movies and restaurants you recommend. I want you to tell us all about your weird preferences. Come on, Professor, tell us what you like? Don't get all philosophical and turn it around, make it some big intellectual thing about how recommendations are biased. What do you really like?"

"You're going to make him blush, girl. You should've seen him in the car. He can't let go of these ways of his. He can't tell you about something specific, he can only put together some theory about it. It's crazy because that's exactly what I was telling him, and he was interested like it was someone else I was talking about."

"Oh, what happened?"

"I was making a point about how people get set in their ways, but all he could think about was how boyfriends get possessive over their girlfriend's sex lives. Even when I denied the connection, he couldn't let it go. I accused him of trying to hook up with me. What else was I supposed to think? He was trying to be all like subtle and suave, but when I called him on it, he got all bashful and shy. Turned beat red. Made me laugh soooo hard. He is so cute."

"Is that what happened?" she said turning back to the professor.

"That's probably the most interesting version of what happened."

She was spinning the tale to make it funny. People were laughing. Even the kid in front of the computer. He couldn't shake it though; how clever it was. She had backed him so perfectly into a corner. He couldn't explain his way out because that would prove her point. There was no way to turn the table a bit to take a closer look, the path of wisdom was cut off. He felt it like a wall right in front of him and couldn't help but look over at her. Her eyes were dancing. She knew what she had done and was smiling at him as if to let him know she was in on it. There was no malice, just understanding. She hadn't lied, she knew people: what makes them tick, how to wind them up, and —most likely— how to run them down.

The graphic artist eventually finished the drawing and turned the computer screen so that everyone could get a good look. He and the engineer talked about the technology they were working on and how it made these drawings easy to integrate with documents that might be part of an illustrated textbook. It seemed like something everyone should be interested in, and everyone took an interest because they thought they *should* be interested. The prognoses that it might lead to, or what kind of impact it might have, all faded into some fictional moment of future looking anxiety. Nobody had anything concrete to attach to the ideas, they didn't know where it would lead, but like all things digital, it seemed as if something was going to happen, and everyone needed to be ready. Even people who didn't understand it were going to have to figure out how to live with it. This sentiment was rattling in all their heads as they nodded and looked on. They felt compelled to find it compelling.

Once the conversation on the artwork died down, the graphic artist said he had to go. He had to be somewhere early the next day and wanted to get home and get some sleep. The engineer had brought him over after work, so he didn't have any transportation. The professor offered to take him. It seemed like everyone thought this was bringing the evening to a premature end, but the graphic artist was oblivious, and he had to go, so they got up and searched for their coats.

"I better go too, you're my ride."

In the car on the way to the graphic artist's apartment, he and the professor made small talk. What's it like working with the engineer? What do people there think of him? She didn't seem to be paying attention. She had the window cracked a bit and was blowing the smoke from her cigarette out so that it wouldn't drift into the backseat. They dropped him off and then started back toward her place.

"I hope I didn't embarrass you when I said all that stuff."

"Really? I thought that was the point, but no worries. I didn't mind."

"I wasn't being completely truthful anyway, but I said all that for effect. You know. It was funnier that way."

"It *was* funnier that way. That's fine, don't worry about it."

"I've heard things, so it wasn't innocent."

"What have you heard?"

"About you. That you're hung up on someone. That it isn't going well, and you might need to be distracted."

"Sure. Okay, easy target I suppose, but it was impressive how you shut me up. You're an expert at dialectic."

"What does that mean?"

"Just that you put me in my place and made it hard for me to defend myself. Everything I could possibly say or want to say was subsumed by your notion."

"I see. Yeah, I can take care of myself, but it's nothing special really. You're a guy, your motives are easy to see and even easier to turn back against you."

"You think so? You might be right, but I think you're underplaying it. You know more than you let on."

"I just think that, when it comes to what we want, some of the territory we have to navigate is pretty complicated. Getting it right and doing it right don't always play well together. You don't get to choose what you want so that means you're always having to balance that with the acceptable ways for getting it. It's a huge problem if you want to be free and spontaneous all the time."

"That's intense."

"Really? You think so?"

"Definitely, but maybe your theory is more about yourself than anyone else. You know people, like you said. This could be true of everyone, but that means it's also true about you. You might be holding on to some hard-won point of view even when circumstances require you to let go of it. Do you think that's an unacceptable compromise to make while remaining free?"

"Don't try to turn it around on me, bucko. It was check and mate long ago. No do overs."

They laughed and then sat silently for a while.

"You know," she said. "If you were trying for what I said before, it wouldn't be anything to be embarrassed about. We're adults."

"Sure. Of course. Thanks for saying that. I get it. It's not a big deal."

They pulled up in front of her place. He didn't make any signs of moving. He was waiting for her.

"If you wanted to come in, that'd be cool with me."

"Oh well, I mean..."

"Off the clock of course. Sorry if that wasn't clear. I mean, I'm inviting you in."

"Oh. Off the clock? I see."

"Wait. You didn't know? Didn't he tell you?"

"He knows?"

"Of course, he knows. That's how they met. Didn't they tell you that?"

"They did. They said he was one of her clients. She said she was training to be a realtor or something."

"That's true. She is, but that's not how they met."

"Ah, I get it. It was ambiguous."

"Yeah. We work together. You can imagine."

"Yeah yeah. I get the picture."

"You're surprised though?"

"I am."

"Well, do you want to come in? I can offer you some whiskey."

He hesitated and looked at his hands, they were gripping the steering wheel.

"Doesn't matter," she said. "It's all good." She popped the door open.

"Wait. I'm sorry. It's just surprising. I wasn't prepared. Not about you. That's not what I meant. I mean, about them."

"Okay. I get it. Come inside and be civilized. Talk to me like a person. Don't be a dick."

"This is one of those quirky experiences. I don't know how to say everything that I'm thinking right now. There's so much. I'll tell you this, I would love to come inside, but I just can't. It surprises me, too. The fact that I physically can't get out of the car right now, but that I really really want to. I'm sorry."

She laughed at him. "Get over yourself, it's not that big a deal. Thanks for the ride." She got out and slammed the door. He drove home.

Wolfe wasn't in the apartment, and he didn't want to stay up alone.

That was enough consciousness for one day. He got ready for bed and closed the door. Before getting into bed, he sat down and checked his email. There was something there from the librarian. It was playful and non-responsive to whatever was in the last thing he had written. It made him smile, but he didn't bother to remind himself of the context. He hit reply, typed out "Quirky," and then hit send.

"Heidegger's *Gestell* and its resources are already too big, they are too much for me. I want to find the micro technics in it. Even when thinking and dwelling, I risk producing expressions that feed back into future expressions through an analytical process of computation. I am theorizing, the thing that theorizes, and being that way, I trap myself in the boundaries of whatever is guiding me."

"Is this more of the interlude?"

"Everything is more of the interlude."

"Does that mean you've stopped focusing on the onto-theo-logical, the grand narrative of some historical destiny that finds its way into the be all and end all of every thing that is?"

"Yes. It's all too big, too much. I don't want to make big sweeping assertions or generalizations; I can't capture everything in a single thought or pattern. Under these conditions, there are no more natural kinds. Rather, the 'kind' hides. There is this and this and this and this. To secrete is to make secret."

"It could be the opposite. Don't forget that."

"Exactly."

"Pattern is itself an anti-pattern. By the way, you never told me what happened the other night?"

"It was okay."

"Was it a setup after all? This woman you had to pick up, what was up with that?"

"Yeah, I guess so. Not exactly, but someone was definitely trying to create an opportunity for a meeting. No pressure. Very chill."

"What was she like?"

"Pretty cool. Lots of personality."

"Attractive?"

"Yeah, in a gritty kind of a way. Definitely."

"What's the plan, what happens next? Did you give her a ride home?"

"I did give her a ride home and, well, nothing happened, exactly. I mean, she invited me in, but I didn't go. I just dropped her off and came home. I didn't get her number. I could though. Probably won't. If we run into each other again, it'll be by chance."

"Why? What's going on?"

"It would have just been a random thing. You know. I don't think there is any future there. It would've just been a hook up."

"Is there something wrong with that? You don't think that's what she had in mind?"

"No, that's definitely what she had in mind."

"What the fuck? What happened?"

"I don't know, it doesn't seem to be where my head is right now."

"Yeah, but maybe it should be. You have a pulse. This is exactly what you should be doing and what you should be thinking about. Whatever this other thing you're doing with the email or whatever the hell is going on there, that's the thing that doesn't make sense. This makes sense."

"Just doesn't feel that way though."

"Right. That's a problem. What is your plan anyway? You have a one-year appointment. There's no chance you'll find anything around here next year. God, this is so fucking repetitive, I'm boring myself. Aren't you getting bored of it, little Ernst?"

"Don't keep bringing it up. No one is forcing you. Don't you mean, little Hans?"

"That's a slip on your part, dude. I'm poking at your death instinct and all you want to talk about is your Oedipal complex, is that it?"

"Fuck off."

"You know I think the whole point of that story, Jet or the Astral Plane —I keep thinking about it— is in that moment when the stoner looks at his mug and his nickname stenciled on the back of it. Therapist. He stares at it until he sees 'The rapist.' If I recall correctly, that's what sets everything off, all the reverie and daydreaming where the action of the story takes place. It's meta-fiction, right?"

"I barely remember that story."

"I just reread it after we talked about it a while back. It's fresh. The character's obliviousness about the girl next door and the girl he had been obsessed with the whole last year, all of it comes back to him while he's sitting there hallucinating over that mug. Mug is like face, right? I think it's a pretty deep story. You might have been confessing more than you meant to there."

"Shouldn't that hold you off though? If you psychoanalyze me based on my story, aren't you taking on the role of therapist? If all of it emerges from that hallucination, then maybe it applies to the reader when they respond like that. I was studying English literature back then and I was having a strong reaction to how we were expected to interpret the reading. That was around the time I shifted emphasis to philosophy."

"Fine, have it your way. I'm just saying that the recent grads from U of M are going to have the connections to get all the adjunct work around here. If you don't get something through the APA, you're going to have to go back to Illinois and try to reconnect with the schools there, see if anyone needs you or can set you up. Isn't that the plan?"

"I guess so."

"Take some responsibility then. Your actions beg for analysis. There isn't any logic behind what you're doing. Trying to have some weird relationship with someone who is reluctant to spend any time with you, turning down perfectly nice women who do want to spend time with you."

"Is that what you're doing with the typesetter?"

"Hell yes. That's exactly what we're doing, but you're deflecting. You're repressing thoughts that would reveal everything that is about to happen in the next year, but you won't look at it."

"Bear with me, is she okay with that?"

"Of course, she's okay with that, it was her idea. When we first met up, I told her about my hesitation. Since I knew I'd be leaving town. I tried to put the brakes on, but she was adamant. She said that quality mattered more to her. She said she didn't have long term expectations, but she wanted to get to know me better anyway. She said it was possible to really enjoy each other's company even if it would be brief."

"You think she can do that?"

"Oh, I know she can. She's dedicated to her principles."

"You think you can do it?"

"Ah me. That's another story. We'll see if I can. I hope so. I would like to be that kind of person. Someone who appreciates people like that. I'm hoping she'll be able to teach me a thing or two about it."

"Alright. That might all work out for you guys. I hope so, but that woman the other night, that's not the kind of thing we could do. Even if that's exactly what she wanted and she were able to do it, it isn't something that I'd be able to do with her."

"Why not?"

"I'm not sure. With her, it probably would have been pure lust. Just a one-night stand or an irregular series of them. She's not the kind of person I could really get swept away by."

"What's wrong with pure lust? What's stopping you from becoming infatuated with *her*? How is *she* different from the librarian? Isn't she the kind of person that you could get carried away with?"

"Yup. I am already."

"What's the difference then? Is it something you can identify?"

"I don't know."

"Eh, you're full of shit. It's absolutely something you can see more clearly than you're letting on. The woman the other night."

"What about her?"

"She invited you in, right? Was it clear that she was inviting you to spend the night?"

"Yes."

"She was into you and wanted that. The librarian, we don't know what's up with her. She wants something, but she's elusive and doesn't want to spend any time with you. Whatever she wants, she's keeping it a secret."

"Okay."

"Well, it seems cut and dry. There's a cat and mouse game going on. You can't help yourself, just like the cat. You see that movement and you can't help but pursue it. Can't take your eyes off it, can't help but keep playing with it."

"Cats like playing with mice. This is making me miserable."

"It might be bullshit. Who says that cats like playing with mice? It might absolutely fucking torture the cat. Watch their tails. They see that movement and they can't help themselves. They are transfixed. All those centuries of breeding and they have no choice but to swat and pounce. It's a compulsion that comes from somewhere else that they have no control over. Pay attention and you'll see their tails flapping all over the place."

"Are you trying to argue that cats are tormented when they express the most basic of catlike behaviors?"

"Hell yes. That's exactly what I'm arguing. We fucked them up with all this carefully planned cat engineering and now we watch them and think they're so cute when they run after the stupid infrared light we flash on the ground. It's rationalization and justification. That cat is remotely controlled by a gene sequence that has nothing to do with kitty will and kitty intent."

"You're crazy, you're just trying to make a point."

"What is that point?"

"That you are insane."

"No, that point is that you are a mess. That you are a fucking robot being led around by some pursuit routine that you would never in a million years choose for yourself, but that you have been pulled into against your will."

"Is this a statement about me or are you making some larger point about patriarchal mating rituals?"

"Hmmm, I guess I hadn't thought about it like that. Asshole. I'm trying to say that your actions for the last few months don't make any sense and you just said they're making you miserable. That sounds like an illness. Something coming from outside and over which you don't have any control."

"It feels that way sometimes."

"That's the most basic feature of control freaks, right? They express that they feel out of control all the time and that they are constantly trying to gain control because they don't have it."

"What does control have to do with pursuit?"

"It has everything to do with it. The cat and the mouse, the cat is driven to control the mouse. The cat feels completely out of control and is constantly reacting to the mouse's evasion tactics. All these reactions are to try and possess the mouse."

"You think this is related to our email exchange somehow?"

"Yes, I most definitely do. You two are writing to each other all the time. You are constantly reporting back about the little things that are going on. You've started to get really intimate about the details. What's her class schedule? Do you know it? What's your schedule, does she know it?"

"Yes."

"That means your constant emailing is a kind of surveillance. Don't you know where she is when she sends and reads every message? You know that she hasn't responded for the last several hours because she has been working or in class. You know her every move by knowing when she responds. It isn't just about what she tells you, it's about the messages themselves."

"That's nuts."

"It isn't. She works on Saturday nights, right?"

"Yes."

"Does she send you emails at about 2 or 3 AM afterward?"

"What if she does?"

"It tells you something. She may not say anything at all in that email, but she sends it. That tells you that she's home, she's thinking about you, and she wants to let you know she got home okay."

"Wait. I'm not sure it always happens that way."

"Think about it and see if you can figure it out. Don't get me wrong. She might be doing the exact same thing to you. I don't know. My guess is that it might be working that way. That both of you are falling into a pattern that plays out something you both need to deal with."

"Which is?"

"That's for you to say. What I can tell you is that this absolutely and authoritatively should not be what you are doing right now. I never saw things the way you did, right? I never wanted the things you wanted. There are professional aspirations that you have been focused on for something like ten years. What the hell are you doing now? How does this little game you're playing fit into that? Becoming fuck buddies with the woman the other night would fit so much better into your plans."

"You're being overly dramatic. I mean, she is studying for a graduate degree that probably ends with her placed in some academic institution for the rest of her life. Isn't it at least conceivable that she is very much someone with plans that fit with mine?"

"She might be, but it seems much more likely that she's going to be here for a while, and you're going to have to go off somewhere and look for something else. Look, she doesn't even want to go out with you. Clearly there is interest on her end. She's encouraging you in some way. Let's say that eventually something does happen between you two. When do you think that would be? What can you honestly imagine?"

"I hadn't really thought about it like that. If you force me to guess, maybe this summer."

"That's reasonable. What would that mean? When does your lease expire? What are you going to do when it does? Will you renew it? Where will you go?"

"Are you accusing me of being in it just for the pursuit? Like my ego has totally gotten the better of me and I can't let go because I must win, I must conquer, I must prevail?"

"That would be far more normal, but that's not at all what I am accusing you of. In that case, you'd prevail and then suddenly, you'd be done. You'd have the mouse and there would be nothing more to it. You could lay it at my feet and proudly go on your merry way. In that case, you guys might have a nice summer fling and then off you'd go while she goes back to school and finishes up her degree."

"You think there's more though?"

"Yeah, it's more like you two are pushing and pulling each other into some weird, contorted thing that will be a constant battle. I just don't see this turning out well. This could be all my imagination. I don't know much about her, certainly not as much as you do. I do know a lot about you though, and I know that what you're doing isn't right for you. There's something off about your behavior. A perfectly good woman who is a little bit into you asks you to come inside and see what happens and you refuse."

"There's more to it than that."

"Explain it to me."

"Well, she is —both of them are— sex workers."

"What? You're bullshitting me."

"Nope. I swear. She let it slip with some weird joke about how her invitation was 'off the clock'?"

"What is that supposed to mean?"

"Well, it seemed pretty clear at the time. It seemed like maybe she was suggesting that normally she might charge me, but that I didn't need to worry about that under the circumstances."

"Didn't you ask her to explain it clearly?"

"It seemed obvious. She said she thought I knew already. She assumed I knew they worked together and that the engineer already told me how they met."

"Did you have any details? Did you make your decision not to go in before she said this?"

"It's hard to say. It's muddled."

"Let's suppose she is a sex worker then. A dancer or escort or whatever. Is that why you didn't want to hook up with her?"

"Not exactly."

"Why not then?"

"I really wanted to. At the time, in the moment, I wanted to go in. The desire was really strong."

"Why didn't you?"

"I physically couldn't do it. I was unable to move my hand to the key and take it out of the ignition. I couldn't open the door. My body wouldn't move. There was something there, some force that wouldn't let me move. I was aware of it, and I tried to explain it to her. I told her I really wanted to, but that I just couldn't do it. I wasn't in control of wanting to and I wasn't in control of not being able to. All of it was beyond me."

"Why though? Where was that paralysis coming from? What did it mean?"

Silence.

"Well, answer this then. At that moment, what was going through your mind? Anything? Did you think of the librarian?"

"Sort of. Yes. I thought it was an act of treachery somehow, like I was cheating on her by wanting that."

"Okay. You know that's crazy right?"

"I do. It is."

"You think that's what was preventing you from being able to move?"

"I don't really know. Theoretically it could be at the bottom of everything we're talking about."

"What does that mean?"

"This doesn't make any sense, not even in the case of the librarian. I could just go to the Del and see her when she's working. I know when she's there and I could just go, but I don't. I could call her. I know what effect my voice would have, but I just can't think of her like that. I've stayed away in the most deliberate and extreme way. I imagine that were I to do any of that, it would cause things to change. Who knows, it might change them for the better. We would stop this weird thing we're doing, and everything would become normal. We would see each other, and the effect of our distance would melt. It could change everything, make it more familiar. We might go out. After a couple of times, it might turn into something ordinary, fit into a standard pattern. It will never be like that though. No matter what happens. Email will always be the right way to go. In the future and forever, I will never be able to just dial her number on the phone or go over to her house and ring the bell."

"Alright, calm down, I get it. What's stopping you from doing any of that?"

"Again, I'm not really sure, but the feeling is the exact same as the paralysis that locked me into the car seat the other night."

"You can't call her or go see her at work because that would somehow be treacherous? You would be cheating on her if you did?"

"Yes."

"That doesn't make any sense."

"It may not, but maybe she's two different people. There's the person who pushes and pulls, who is back and forth, who doesn't know what she wants and is in the middle of some dramatic moment. There might be someone else too. A much simpler person who is more sure of herself and more clear about what she does and says, where she goes and who she goes there with. I would be sacrificing my relationship with the one for the sake of a relationship with the other."

"Not sure what to say about that."

"Well, there's more. It's true of me too. The choice would be between the person I am and the person I might be."

"You think you might be cheating on yourself somehow, or that she would be?"

"Yes. Both. I felt that way the other night too. It isn't just about cheating on her. It was about cheating on myself. Like I've promised to be different than that, better than what I am."

"That doesn't fit. You know, if the devil tried to convince you to carry out his will and you were the kind of person who was reluctant to do what he wanted, he might persuade you by misrepresenting himself."

"The devil? What is the evil end in all of this?"

"It doesn't have anything to do with ends and means or anything like that. The expression of vice in and of itself is what the devil is all about."

"What are the vices you are accusing me of, or accusing me of repressing?"

"There is a list of them, and you know damn well what they are. Worst of all is whatever mischief this whole game will bring."

"Well, we'll see."

"Yup. Time will tell."

"It's a bad analogy. The mouse dies in the end."

"That's right, there's no universe in which they end up together. Either the mouse dies, or it escapes."

"The mouse does not want to be chased."

"What if it's a robot mouse? An automaton?"

"An intelligent machine?"

"Doesn't have to be. It could have been designed to train the cat. Whatever, the mouse doesn't want anything. It's been designed for a purpose."

"Wolfe's point was that the cat doesn't want to be chasing the mouse either. At least, that it doesn't like doing it."

"Neither of them wants to be doing what they're doing, they're just doing it because of some weird psychotic design that has been put in place and both must follow it. It's just the way things work. The mouse is being trained to escape and the cat is being trained to track and kill. The cat eats or dies, the mouse is eaten or escapes."

"It's pretty bleak. God is truly dead."

"Lots of people reject this kind of fatalism, but that's to be expected."

"Yeah funny, but it's worse than fatalism. It's almost like a complete reorganization of behavior in terms that don't reduce to means and ends. Nobody wants anything, or desire is a social epiphenomenon that hides the mechanisms at work."

"That's right. That's why you can't use society as a counterweight to prevent reduction. It's an illusion, a dream of the conscious being. Human society is like a hive only we have this weird cognitive component that makes us project or dream that there is more to it."

"Why is there any kind of social aspect to it then? Do you really think your reductionism would have been possible without the whole consequentialist order providing clear parameters for organizing all human behavior into means and ends?"

"I'm saying mechanism is an alternative to those final ends, so this would be a world without means and ends in that way. That's where your social order would come in, right? If it's all mechanism, then the reduction is easy."

"I get that. Consider the move that removes the quality of social interaction though, the power involved, the historical principles and processes that are at stake. That's all a reduction of qualitative features to a purely quantitative view of the world. This logic is exactly what we get from a morality that measures interests and desires against some uniform standard. The purely mechanistic view rises alongside this way of conceiving morality in terms of ends and means, where virtue becomes nothing other than the maximizing of some quantity produced by action. The agents are delusional. Not means and ends anymore then, just causes and effects."

"Not seeing the problem."

"Well, this kind of uniformity happens to values long before it happens in the sciences. As money evolves into the primary means for exchange, as a way of measuring wealth, and as a uniform structuring element for all values in the human order, this possibility is created. It becomes possible to cast all actions in terms of a common measuring rod, then it's a short walk to translate all acts and outcomes into consequences that resemble ends. Money develops right in lock step with consequentialism, and with an ubiquitous new science. They are all equally able to yield the new language for experiencing and knowing everything in the world."

"You aren't arguing against mechanism exactly. You're saying that it's a socially structured mechanism like money or happiness and we're just spinning it into means and ends?"

"Yeah, kind of. It's an inter-individual mechanism. A relational principle that develops the order and all the instances ordered by it. Like, imagine turning Hobbes on his head so that the commonwealth came before sense experience and the individual having it."

"Isn't this sociobiology?"

"No. I'm not justifying a social order, or even explaining how it came to be. What I'm saying is that living things can be understood by how they interact with each other and with their world. The exclusively biological perspective on the bee will not tell you everything there is to know about bees. You need to understand the way the hive works and how the hive is at work in the bee's physiology. The hierarchies and the inequalities, all relationships, are influencing the individuals, on the way they act and the way they represent the world to themselves. Their spontaneity is the canvas. The understanding of any living creature is balanced by its complete involvement in all its different relationships. The lemur of Madagascar, the gazelle of the Serengeti, the human being, are all examples."

"How does that connect to the desires then?"

"We've kicked this around before. Desires are not pure. They are not just an unmediated relationship to objects: this good, that bad. They are nuanced, they've been cultivated. We must work them out. Pausing and asking yourself 'What do I want?' is a recognized experience that everyone is familiar with. Even if it's just a matter of what to do today or what to cook for dinner."

"Okay, so you don't think that you'll set out and eat whatever you can get your hands on. You don't rely on pure sense of smell or sight to find the next edible thing that will satisfy your hunger. You consider the possibilities given your environment. I have money. There are services for sale, there are communication devices. I can call some people and have them bring me food. I can go sit somewhere. I can go buy some in an uncooked form. All that."

"Sure. You are familiar with what can be done. Your whole life you become more and more familiar with what can be done. This helps structure your desires. You gain preferences. That is too much trouble. That tastes good."

"Yeah, but that environment doesn't do anything. It isn't an agent. It's just the result of human beings encountering each other. It's formed by their interactions."

"The story of the chicken and the egg once again. Same answer as I always give: 'What kind of egg are we talking about?' It's likely a reflective process, where the act of producing something influences the producer. This could explain an increasing complexity in order as well as an increasing complexity in the things ordered."

"You think there's something here, some form of agency that isn't supernatural, but which can't be reduced to the individual psyche and thus down to the individual neurophysiology, biochemistry, and so on?"

"That's right, but I'm not jumping into final causes as real things. Let's call them illusory if you like, but I'm suggesting that the ordering of a final cause, the intentionality involved in it, is an effect of this thing we're talking about, whatever it is. It's not a random illusion, it's tailored to protect and decorate the mechanism behind it."

"This thing behind it, it is neither mechanism nor organism then. It's made up of neither simple causes nor final causes. These are just constructs created by the dominating order. Is that it?"

"Yup. Ideology. That's where we're headed. I get the sense that I —at least— don't have the right grammar for knowing myself this way. It's a struggle to understand myself at all like this because everything I know, everything familiar to me, is ordered by desire or deliberate ends. I am supposed to be first and foremost a rational being. My orientation toward sorting things out is based on principles of cognition that lead me to rely on the understanding in ways that are dependent on ends and means, desires and intentions, even if I don't know where they come from. The whole of morality has become an obsessive compulsive and agonizing soliloquy on the best and highest end, on the realization of a common interest through the achievement of that supreme good where the true objective belongs to the order that surrounds it."

"I see. If you become disillusioned, once you've lost your personal means and ends, your desire loses its order, nothing you ever knew before makes sense to you in your own terms."

"That's right. Remember the example I gave you about quitting smoking. When I try to quit, I go through the physical withdrawal. I tell myself that it will only last a few weeks and I just need to plow through it. When I do that, I assert that I know the cause of the feeling, I act as a scientist and claim this feeling will go away if I just smoke a cigarette. I have put it all together and I see the ordered chain. What if I didn't know it though? What if it were invisible to me and I didn't know anything about the longevity of the feeling and the cause behind it? I wouldn't know what to do to make it go away."

"You stop thinking about it in terms of cause and effect and start thinking about it as a drive, as pure feeling. I remember."

"There are games for how to overcome the power of the effects under these circumstances. You learn that you need a more powerful counterbalance. You start looking for it. You might try a different substance. You exercise. Go for a run. You would be experimenting because you don't know what will counterbalance the effects and affects that you're feeling."

"This is fantasy. You do know what the cause is because there is a cause and you've experienced it. You want the cure because there is a cure. Everybody knows what it is. It's commonly understood."

"I also want to quit though. Everyone knows I should. Why else would I make the effort to stop? The conflict is commonly known too. There is a war raging inside of me. What I'm suggesting is that the war is basic, but the surfacing of different drives into different explanations or proposed plans of action is how that war is waged. I can't quit, instead I must overpower the urge. The example shows that we can have an experience of a drive and try to bracket our explanation of its origin or cause and the various chains of causality that it's a part of. Even if that amounts to a kind of artificial suspension of belief, there's something to it and the process can teach me something about how my desires work and what order they reflect while finding their form of expression. That might weaken the desire and make it possible to destroy it or get it under control."

"Alright. For the sake of argument, let's work through it. If all this is true, where does it leave us? What is the point?"

"To what end this explanation? There does have to be a point, doesn't there?"

"If you don't mind. It would make the afternoon seem so much more pleasant."

"Well, I take it that discovery of the aspects of an affect is an important part of learning, right? If something plays a role in a process, then discovering that role fits with best scientific practices."

"Sure. We don't want to leave anything out when producing an explanation."

"What approaches do we have for discovering all that? If our discussion right now is ordered by these relationships and forces, we can't come to any authoritative conclusion until we bring them to the surface."

"Fair enough."

"If the act of bringing them to the surface is itself constrained or conditioned by the same elements we employ in the investigation, and if they tend to hide themselves through their way of being operative, then what can we do to bring them out? To make them visible as alien orders that are part of our own personal experiences?"

"This bracketing out of the matrix of consequences or means and ends or exchange values is what you propose as the solution for this?"

"Call it a suspicion that something like that might help. I'm deeply self-conscious of the fact that this resonates with a specific historical approach.

That the words 'bracket' or 'reduce' signal a relationship to other thinkers and to a history of developing ideas that is still very much in progress. I hesitate because this history might be how that agency surfaces itself in the acts of surfacing itself. It reveals an historical connection to a scientific method. Abductive or phenomenological, whatever it is, it is still an orientation based on other experiments, and other work that has been done. 'To the things themselves' is a beautiful ideal, but because it builds on the work of others, I don't even know if it can be done by a follower."

"I see the dilemma. You're suggesting that all scientific practice is —in some sense— caught in this same trap. There is a tradition and there are a variety of acceptable methodologies. It's a discipline. All of which seems to involve making the conditions of your inquiry and the results of your experiments transparent to any who would review the findings. These social conditions for practicing science are part of an established historical method that is constantly being scrutinized and getting revised now and again."

"Not just science, any form of investigation, any attempt at understanding. What I'm trying to discover, I guess, is whether this bracketing approach, or any other that I can think of or that someone might suggest, could ever yield an adequate map or picture of this agency that I'm talking about, this ordering operation that I'm trying to put my finger on. Whatever it is that orients individuals through the mediation of their interconnections and involvements is hard to see because it is what provides the boundaries of our subjectivity."

"Reduction doesn't work for you because it assumes the power for doing this exists in the items and not in the collection. Is that it?"

"Revise that to 'act of collecting' and you might have nailed it. Many of my prejudices tell me that freedom is good, and coercion is bad, but then we say that to fight the power behind the coercion, the people must organize, since big organizations are often behind the coercion, only a conflicting big organizational effort can oppose it. To win, we must be disciplined. We know that our freedom somehow depends on having the right order and that there is always a risk that an order will be coercive. This seems like a hard problem."

"It is a hard problem. Listen, I have to go, you said there was something you wanted to talk to me about. What is it?"

"Yeah, there is. When I was driving her home, she said something that made me think that maybe she and your girlfriend are escorts or something. Is that true?"

"Uh... ...well... yes, that is true... Sorry I didn't tell you. I was embarrassed."

"It's okay. That's how you met her?"

"Yeah. I feel pretty isolated here. It's been hard to meet people. None of those women my sister set me up with were interested. I asked a few of them out, but they didn't want to. That woman I introduced you to from work wasn't interested. What was I supposed to do?"

"You don't have to explain, but how does that make her your girlfriend?"

"I don't know. One night, I just didn't want her to leave. I couldn't afford to pay her to stay all night. I gave her my laptop. It didn't get stolen. I gave it to her. She said she needed one. She wanted to stay too. I don't know. I gave it to her, and she stayed. It was nice. She seemed to like it too. In the morning, I asked her if we could go out on a date sometime or just hang out together. She said she would like that. It just happened."

"Well okay, I get that you're lonely. That's your motivation, but what's hers?"

"Well, that might have been what started it, but I don't think that's my only motivation. I like her. She's interesting. She's smart and beautiful."

"Okay, but what about her?"

"Well, I don't really know. She might have been lonely too. Probably looking for something. It must be hard for her to have relationships, right? What are her choices?"

"I get it. Does she know that you don't have long-term plans for staying around here? What's her take on that?"

"We haven't really talked about it."

"Why not? She's not going to bring it up. She's not going to be thinking, oh, by the way, do you have plans to stay in the area or are you just here temporarily? It wouldn't occur to her to ask you that, that's on you. Why haven't you told her? It's pretty important."

"You think she wants something long term?"

"I don't know, but it's possible. I mean, she's gotta be thinking about an exit plan, right? That would have to include a whole new life and maybe she's thinking you're a part of that."

"Hmmm. Yeah. Okay. I gotta go."

"Fine. I'll talk to you later. You know, you have to be careful not to let ignorance drive you when you're expressing your desires. To bring it all back full circle, I guess. Sometimes we can only fulfill a desire —if 'fulfill' is even the right word anymore— when we stop thinking about what we want or pretend we don't have any idea that we want it. We feign ignorance in support of the mechanism."

"Coming from the expert. Alright, later."

"Bye."

Suddenly there are men everywhere. In the mailbox, in the bar, in email. Everywhere.

His letter came in the post. It was rambling. All over the place. Writing was never his strong suit. I guess he's telling me he's sorry. In his way. He never says everything he means so probably there is more to it. I'll bet there is something going on. He might have a new girlfriend and feels like he has to have a clear conscience to move on. I would never know what was up with him. Where his head was at. He kept so much to himself. Even when we fought, we wouldn't work it out together. He would go off and I would go off. We would each work out whatever we needed to do on our own and then we would come back, say we're sorry, and move on. There was never any need for a big resolution. There was never anything we had to say. I didn't need to understand everything he was thinking or feeling. Neither did he.

This might be the same. In this scrawled six-page letter that goes on and on but doesn't say very much. It's like he's been down to the river, he's worked it all out in his head, and now he's just letting me know that he's squared away, that everything is right on his end, and he hopes that I have been able to do the same thing. He's sorry. That's obvious. He said it a million times and he almost says it outright in the letter. With him that isn't what matters. What he really wants to know is whether I've worked it out too, whether I'm okay. Probably he can't fully consider things to be over and done with until he hears that I have moved on and am no longer in the same place I was when we were crying together in our old apartment that day. When we last saw each other. I won't give him the satisfaction.

I don't know why, but there is something about it that boosts my ego. Something in the way he phrases things, or the way he can't phrase them, the things he is completely incapable of saying. I don't know exactly. He hasn't changed and he can't change. He can't say it any better than this. That lifts me up somehow. Whatever was wrong with us, I can say it all now. I can tell it to myself and even to my friends. That means that I'm past it. This letter confirms it because it doesn't matter. Well, it does matter, and I do care, but it isn't killing me. I read it all the way through as soon as I opened it. I didn't have to stop, I didn't need to cry, I didn't scream. Nothing. I read it all the way through. I put it down and don't need to read it again. I'll probably read it again. It doesn't matter though because I don't need to. I have moved past all that. I'm some place totally different now and that's not my life anymore. This letter and these half-stated feelings. Whatever he can manage to pull from his murky depths. I don't know how his mind works. This is it and it's not my problem anymore. It really isn't. Grow the fuck up.

There is email. It is heating up. I don't know, but sometimes he tickles me. I get goose bumps from some of what he writes. What did he mean by 'tingling world' and all that growling? "Are you that tingling world slinking back and around? Grrrrrrrr, come closer." He doesn't have any problems putting it all together in words, does he? There are feelings coming through there. They are coherent and they seem to lead somewhere. They aren't all alike. He can convey specific feelings and moods. At first it was all intellectual and the poetry was like an existentialist novel or something. The last few weeks something has changed. Is it because I've been more open? I don't know. It might have given him more confidence.

He says 'we' more. "We could lean against each other, our bare backs all the way down." He talks about things like touching and the delight of familiar smells and tastes. "Don't ask me what I'd like to drink if you don't mean it. Your fragrance alone could fill me." Such strong images. Some of them even burned a little. "Your hip yields to my hand and we turn to reach for each other in a moment of luxury and pursuit." That was nice. Breathless. How did he put it? Where was that? "A sense of weight in the way we press into each other, a feeling of resistance that pushes and pulls." Sometimes, I have no idea how to respond. I feel like I should reply right away, but I don't know what to say. How far should I go? I don't know how to let him know what I'm feeling. Immediately is best, just react. I wrote "mmmmm" once. Just horrible when I remember it, and I call myself an educated woman. He got it though, what I was trying to say.

That's one of his skills that I can't quite fathom. He interprets my messages in ways that highlight all the possible meanings they might have. He doesn't accuse me of being ambiguous or vague, he shows me how I am. He doesn't get mad or frustrated, instead he plays with the possibilities. He goes off in every direction talking about this, that, and the other thing that would be true if I meant it this way. Something completely different if I meant something else entirely. Even "mmmmm" was something he saw immediately as possibly a moan of pleasure, a questioning hesitation, or an abrupt refusal. He rapidly responded highlighting each of the possibilities. They were all terrific and exciting. The best part was when he thought I might have been moaning, because then he really moved in for a proper response. Good instincts, I might've mumbled in some one of my replies. Who knows? It was rapid and I don't go back. We're not thinking about it so much. That's exactly the point. It's getting me where I need to be. In the end, I told him I enjoyed that email multiple times. He knew what I meant.

Whatever that was with headshot guy over Christmas, it didn't bring me back, but maybe now something is having that effect. It's the caress that I sometimes feel in what he writes. I don't know. There are too many factors to sort it all out. It is having an effect.

There is the bar too. That can't be separate. It has to be related. There are always guys there. They are usually just customers or regulars or whatever. It's not serious and there's nothing going on other than harmless banter. Back and forth. Whatever. The guitar player is different. He looks at me differently. I know exactly where his mind is and how he's going to work his way to it. It isn't just play. His hands are so long and narrow. He caught me staring. It's hard not to. Especially since I can tell that he's serious. At least like that he is.

Mid-winter break or whatever they call this early version of their spring break here. It isn't helping. I feel loose and more relaxed. School just winds me up so much. Even when I have everything under control, it doesn't matter. If there are tasks and I have to carefully manage my time for weeks on end to get them all done, then there's going to be stress. I can't help it. Even though I have plenty to do, knowing that for one week I have nothing that needs to be done. It means I can relax a little.

The way he looked at me, I could tell that he knew. He knew what I haven't been able to fully communicate to the professor. What I can't get him to understand. Because he can't look at me. Because he can't look into my eyes and see what's there. That's why he can't get it. He would see it if he could look long enough though. The guitar player, he saw it right away. It felt like he was doing most of the talking without saying anything. He just looked at me for the longest time, up and down. Even when I said something to him about needing something or whatever I said to try and make him uncomfortable about staring at me, he just kept right on looking. He wasn't embarrassed or bashful. That's such a turn on. How does he do it? If anything, my reaction made him more confident. Like he knew he was right. Like he had only suspected something before, but then as soon as I confronted him and tried to get him to look away, he knew for sure. He saw everything so clearly, everything I'd ever done. Not the details of it all, but the marks they left behind.

He was so there, everywhere, and it gave me more confidence than I've had for a long time. I wish it didn't. I wish I could just be confident, and not depend on this for it. It's not just these men, it's the feedback from my professors and the other students. Everything. I just can't get it on my own and I resent these assholes because it's their fault I need to get it from them in the first place. Why can't I find it in myself to be confident, or whatever this feeling is? Because maybe it isn't even confidence. It seems weird to be getting it from other people. The whole point is to be able to stand up on your own and look out for yourself. If you're totally dependent on others to feel that way, then you'll never be able to make it stick.

It means that someone will always be able to tear me down right when I need confidence the most. The thing with these men is that not only can they give me confidence by looking at me, or talking to me, or muttering an intimidated apology, but these same men can just turn it all around anytime they want and destroy what I have. I hate that. Where is the school to teach me how to get over that? Isn't it a trade skill just like doing catalog searches? How come I can't take a seminar on how to be my own source of confidence and self-worth? Not one of those touchy-feely things, but something with substance. Like a science of some kind. Is that ridiculous?

Instead of someone giving it to me with a look or taking it away with a different look, there would be some jackass teaching me all about it. There I would be writing it all down in my notebook. Is this going to be on the test? Oh, most definitely.

With the guitar player, it's pretty safe. It's familiar territory. I can imagine exactly how that will go and how it will feel, and it would be great. It's some place I've been before. Nothing challenging, easy to control. It's not like he could hurt me. It certainly wouldn't challenge me. That would be the whole point. Comfortable. Familiar. Pleasurable.

The professor is an entirely different story. I don't have any idea where that is going or what the twists and turns will be. Despite my best efforts to keep him away, he's getting closer. He's in my head. I was talking to him the other day. I imagined he was in the kitchen with me. Sitting there just listening and telling me things. He never answers the question. In person, in my imagination, he's even more evasive than he is in email. He tells a story. I go on about the ass munch in my program who everyone loves and who's getting all these rewards for being a brown-nosing dweeb, and the professor tells me a story about a man without pants. In my kitchen, when he responds to my tirades and my worries, he's even more elusive. It's like he's always telling parables loosely addressing whatever it is that I've told him. He doesn't just answer the question. He might not know what he is doing, but he helps me figure out where the question comes from and where it's going.

This is not familiar, and it is not safe. I can feel how much confidence I get from his attention and from all the energy he spends on me. The way he responds to me, tells me things, and tries so hard to carefully figure out what I'm saying, what I mean, and what I want. I know all this comes with a price. It means he has the skills and tools to tear me down if he ever wants to do it or thinks that I need to be taught a lesson. It's terrifying.

Are they like this too? They seem so unfazed. All three of them. Different, but the same. Where do they get it from? This real self-assurance. Did they need me to give it to them? Not a chance. The professor started writing me out of nowhere, I didn't give him any encouragement, did I? He just looked me up and started writing and then kept at it. I respond, but in the beginning, I was just being cordial. Where did he get the nerve to keep at it? The guitar player, I know that I didn't lead him into it. He was just a customer, and I was only serving him drinks. I might have been a little nicer because he knows the other bartender. That couldn't have given him much encouragement though. Not the kind he would have needed to blaze a hole right through me with his stare. That stare can't be my fault. He's been developing that all his life. Where did he get the confidence to start looking at women like that? Letting me know exactly what he was thinking while also letting me know he could see what I would do if it came to that. He knew it would come to that.

If I'm not giving it, they must be taking it. I wonder whether all women would have that same amount of confidence and men would have less of it if this weren't so. I'm sure the two are related. It can't be a coincidence. Their confidence is our lack of it. It may be that it isn't possible to be equal at their level. To be more balanced, it would have to come with a compromise. They stop taking it and have less, we stop losing it and have more. Simple as that. On the other hand, since they've had the advantage all these years, it might be time for a complete reversal. At least for a little while. Turnabout is fair play.

Well, I managed to keep it together during the break. That's good. Because I was genuinely worried that I would lose it. I almost invited the professor over. Almost took the guitar player home. Control is the most important thing right now. I don't know whether I can hold off until the summer, until after the semester. Even holding off a little is good, because it means I'm exercising self-control, and self-control is a cousin to confidence, or a step-cousin.

Why do I have to be the one who exercises self-control? This whole thing is so fucked up. Where do these voices come from? Have I internalized things my mother used to say to me? Am I beating myself up with them and calling it self-control when really that makes it the exact opposite of confidence? Is it something my dad might've said once? I wish I could blame this all on him, but that's a non-starter, my morals must come from mom. What else is there? Are we doing this to each other, for Christ's sake? I can only hope that I will have the chance to work through this with my own daughter. I may not get it right. At least I know my mom was trying. Was she thinking about it like this too? Did she have her heart set on making sure I was confident and capable, or was she more worried about protecting me and making sure I was going to be careful and protect myself? I don't think boys are raised to be so careful. They don't have the same risks. They don't have to worry about what boys will do to them. That could be the source of their confidence. Even when they don't deserve it.

Three different kinds of distance. However, you want to say it, self-control really means suffering from it. It's only an achievement because it's resistance to what I want. If I were a confident person, I would just go for it, and I would know what it is.

March

From the shower, Wolfe heard banging and a growl coming from the bedroom. He finished up, dried off, got dressed, and went out to see what was going on. In the bedroom, the professor was bent over the computer on the floor next to the desk, furiously removing the screws that secured the top of the case to its bottom. The blue video screen went black with the flick of a switch. The groans and grunts were more suggestive of frustration than physical exertion. He must have sensed Wolfe's presence, because he looked back at him and muttered something about there being a problem with the motherboard. He said he needed a new one to get the computer working. Wolfe nodded thoughtfully and with approval, he wanted to be encouraging. Underneath the calm, he was brewing with questions that he knew he could not ask without making matters worse. What is he doing? Why is he doing this? That is a perfectly good computer that has been working fine for months. Why is he taking it apart? There was a colorful box on the desk, "Windows NT Server 3.51." Wolfe took up the box and turned it over to read more. It was an operating system; the engineer had probably given it to him. Minimum requirements. Tranquility wasn't listed.

After performing an examination, moving some wires around, and removing some smaller card-looking things from the enclosure, the professor turned a few more screws and then slid out a notebook-sized circuit board. He flipped it over and cursed it, calling it a piece of junk. Nothing Wolfe could see made him think that this judgment was merited based on available information. The professor stood up and tossed the board onto the desk. He mumbled something to himself about needing a new one. While talking, he pulled two smaller chips off the board and set them carefully off to the side on top of the box. He flipped a lever that was at the center of the board and pulled out a tiny square with dozens of copper-looking pins on it. He laid it down on top of the box with the copper pins facing upward and next to the other two chips. There were a couple of other circuit board looking things perpendicularly attached to the larger board. He detached them and set them on top of the desk.

"This," he said holding up the now slimmer and unencumbered circuit board. "Is trash. You want to come with me? I'm driving over to the computer store."

They got their coats and went out. They were completely silent in the car as they drove to the other side of town to a little shop where you could buy different components and parts for repairing or upgrading your personal computer. During the drive, Wolfe didn't ask any of the questions that were running through his head. He didn't ask why the professor was doing this and why he wasn't spending his weekend working on the book that grew more unruly over the last months marked by the advent of the "interlude." He didn't need to ask, he understood. The interlude was a trap. At least, it was to the professor. It was gaining life over time and that life was devoted to confusion and impediments to progress. The point, as Wolfe understood it, had been relatively simple. Human potential is a factor of an underlying power that expresses itself in the world through a human being. It might be a form of power unlike any of the mechanical forms that were more commonly known and observable. That power is raw and yet sophisticated. Raw, in that it doesn't have specific material associated with it, but sophisticated in its form as a slew of final causes endlessly scanning the world for opportunities to articulate themselves. It surfaced as the capability to realize an end, a drive from somewhere behind you and toward some desired state or condition visualized in an idealized orientation, but with potential at its basis. From there, the professor had plugged in the historical modifications and instantiations of power, the cultivation of personhood and the particular practices that realized the underlying power. This was how he understood the basis of that potency as being-in-time and historical in its self-presentation alongside all the many voices that spoke from within each perspective that a person might have.

This was the history of western philosophy as the metaphysics of presence. This was the ontological predisposition of every historical age to project a set of criteria onto the possibilities of experience. A world of objects and a subject attempting to know it, a world of resources and an actor enframing it. These were abbreviations for large-scale modifications to human experience later to be wrapped as events being measured. Wolfe had heard this story again and again over the years. It was the common theme that had run through the professor's studies since the time their paths started to diverge. The coercive presence of this predisposition was given. It got in the way. It molded thinking into a form required to engage the world projected and retained. It launched an unutterable and incoherent style and genre; it shaped every word and experience. Coercion, the professor had recently said, was either in the form of physical force or in the form of hypnotism. The thesis behind *Being, An Introduction* was that the history unfolding, the coercion of potentiality, was a form of hypnotism in which all the people of the world, all of human being, were target and source.

In the midst of this, however, some few thinkers unearthed a problem. The problem, or so they said, came from the inside out. It wasn't that they were taking a position from which this coercive condition could be criticized. They weren't standing by in some disinterested perspective and raising concerns that brought difficulties to the surface of the traditional orientations unfolding in epochs of the understanding. Instead, what happened is that Heidegger, through his reading of the history of philosophy across a sequence of time periods, discovered an internal tension, something that was part of this coercive operation, but which circumvented it, broke it, or attached a limiting condition to it. It didn't come from somewhere else; it wasn't a theoretical position attached to the phenomenon. No, it came from within. It seemed like a kind of sickness from which this historical endeavor suffered. It showed itself to the philosopher as he read the ancient traditions in the light of what came later, what followed upon them. As he caught a glimpse of these approaches throughout history, he went back to the beginning, to the work of Heraclitus, Parmenides, and Anaximander and saw the first awkward steps. This lit everything up.

Deconstruction, as the professor now practiced it, was not some new discipline, or even some new orientation within an existing order, it was something that was happening to the traditional approaches, it was a maneuver implicit in the logic of that tradition. It would show itself in a variety of ways, in codes and investigations, hypotheses and the radical overturning of longstanding ideas. Everything about the intellectual history of the twentieth century was marked by these internal rumblings. Deconstruction was a name for that. It found its way into scientific revolutions, information revolutions, and literary revolutions. According to the professor, even people claiming to dismiss it and who considered it a kind of poison, practiced it. Scientific realists argued for radical transvaluation in experience, quantum theorists warned us that things were not what they seemed, that god did play dice, and that the "thing" was not the cut and dried basis of our world. There were patterns and those patterns were instantiated relationships. There were edges and connections throughout, things were merely momentary forms surfacing throughout the graph. There were only modifications to a primordial substance.

For whatever reason, the starting point of the professor's book had been in the suggestion that he was going to find a way out. He had identified the coercive structure prohibiting a greater understanding of events and conditions. He was dead set on finding a solution to its riddles, a critical recursion that got underneath it all but knew when to stop through some condition that signaled rock bottom. The purpose of the first half of the book had been to lay out the relationship of this individuated human potential to its all-too-human coercion. In so doing, he was confident that he could explain the hypnotism at work on all finite beings. He would tear aside the veil and make everything clear. The purpose of the second part of the book was to do that explicitly, to show the current situation and everything that it entailed. Everything that we saw and believed, all of it was in the grip of these concepts and notions stemming from this coercive historical condition that took its power from human beings collectively organized and ordered to fabricate individual persons in the twists and turns of material life. Our best hope was to perform critical acts that were a reflection on the conditions of our fabrication and the social relations responsible for it. This obscure visiting assistant professor was going to save us all from it, but something happened between the first part where he described the pursuer and the second part where he was planning to describe the escape. The professor understood this second part as a revaluation that would change the way we did science, ethics, and politics. It would provide a radical reversal of events, but for whatever reason, he paused before launching into it and wrote what he called the "interlude."

When they first talked about it late last year, the professor had said it seemed like it was something that had to be done. He couldn't just jump into part two, he had to pause for a minute, for a kind of intermission. Its urgency spoke out of necessity. The purpose of the interlude was to decorate the intermission with a farcical moment. Just an aside that lightened the mood as we got ready to make the transition from one part to the next, from pursuit to escape, but all sorts of mysteries unfolded there instead. The section seemed to have a life of its own. Coming from nowhere, he had some very definite destination in mind. It disrupted the plan. It showed that the relational quality of the dynamic at work meant that it couldn't produce a way out, it didn't offer an alternative pattern or a recipe for disruption. Rather it showed itself to be the manner of movement implicit in the coercive power itself, a line of flight that is sketched during territorialization. As such, it claimed to be the very source of that power. The deconstructive moment at work within this coercive history was the movement itself. The history of western philosophy may or may not have been what it said that it was, but it definitely underwent changes and evolutionary twists and turns. Behind the paradigm shifts, behind the epochs, was the logic of transition. That logic was a burbling chaos, showing that the apparatus had been a means for keeping the chaos at bay all along. The ship of Theseus was being rebuilt while it was at sea. The only way to do it, the only way to physically permit this momentum, was through deconstructive turning. This was the process of keeping the boat afloat. The resistance to it, the violent disagreements that it produced, all this was simple suppression of the most basic conditions of understanding. Human being did not want to know that its edifices were constructed to thwart chaos and death, suffering and destruction. At least, it didn't want to know it when those edifices were knowledge itself, were themselves the organs in the body of knowledge marking the history of their kind.

This eventuality wreaked havoc on the manuscript. It sent it into a downward spiral with no way to pull up. There was no way out, there was no solution, deconstruction had surfaced as the very possibility of the coercion and its necessity. It was not a normative principle or an imperative for action, but a prognosis that projected a probability. The professor became increasingly concerned that there was nothing to be done. The emails had started right around that same time: so much so that it was impossible for Wolfe to separate the two events regardless of how they were measured. Whatever it was that the two of them were writing back and forth, it mirrored that same condition that was preventing the movement from entering the second act. The constant missives were not communication, they were its noise. Both parties no doubt had become hell-bent on a dialectics of interpretation where they would never believe any explanation was simple. Nothing was right before their eyes. The meanings and innuendos, the shadowy suggestions and hinted interests, all the passion they put into every word and phrase, all of it was prevention, dissemblance, and distraction. While they turned this way and that, trying to find the center of what ailed them, the turning itself permitted what gripped them to take a firmer hold. That's how hypnotism works in the end. Even its discovery amounted to a further symptom.

In the computer store, Wolfe stood idly looking at all the devices and gadgets, components and parts that could be plugged into computers to make them do more, process more, store more, and carry more information in a shorter period of time. There were so many different things and so many colors. The professor spoke to the man at the counter. They were talking a foreign language. Something about chipsets and buses, processing speeds and overclocking. It all sounded like magical incantations. Where had all this come from? What did this have to do with the interlude? Why was the professor going down this path?

The engineer gave him things because he had expressed interest in having them. It wasn't like the new operating system was bestowed without context or against his will. The professor must have said something to suggest he wanted it, that he wanted to do something that required it. All that turned into something bigger. He didn't just install a new program on his computer, something as simple as that, he had to take the machine apart. This software, this operating system, forced the professor to open up the computing device, to look inside it, and to make changes to it. There was something about the "motherboard" that was not right for the new operating system. The guy at the counter was familiar with what the professor had come up against. They seemed to be commiserating over some tragedy.

These digital codes, maybe they can insert themselves here because there is something logical or mechanical inside them. This motherboard wasn't working. It was working with the old operating system but there was something about the new one that revealed a flaw, something that required its replacement. All of it, as near as Wolfe could gather, was suggested by the blue background briefly displayed on screen just before the professor removed the circuit board. Although frustrating and distressing, there was something cathartic too. The problem had been hidden all along. The circuit board was likely defective right from the beginning when installed months ago. The old operating system wasn't susceptible to the problem, it could ignore it. The new operating system was more sensitive. A problem that had been there all along now surfaced and had to be addressed.

Although this wasn't a way out, it was the way to get in deeper. The problem forced the professor to learn more, to dig further into the conditions at work in the small system. The fact that it was broken was clear. The display on the screen was obvious and there was no way around it. The number of components that could be the source of the problem was finite and he had been able to systematically vary the conditions to test each of them one by one. Through the process of elimination, the professor zeroed in on the problem and was now purchasing a solution. There was something clean and easy here. Something not to be doubted. The behaviors were predictable. The man behind the counter said the symptoms clearly pointed at the root cause. If all the other components had been tested, then the motherboard was the source of the problem. Buy a new one, give it a shot, and you should get immediate feedback to indicate whether we were right or not. It will work or it won't. Simple as that. The code has been cracked.

Well, not exactly. Apparently, the new motherboard, the one that would be best for the task at hand, required a new thing with copper pins. This was the central processing unit. Part of the problem was that the one he was using was too weak or old for the new operating system. For the simple expenditure of three hundred dollars, the professor would have what he needed to fix the computer and get the new operating system working. All of this wasn't a way out of his problem, that much was clear, it was a way deeper into it. He learned more, acquired more, and paid more. There was more of it. In a sense, it meant that even as he repaired the broken thing, he made the problem worse. All the while, listening to the conversation, Wolfe was struck by the deconstructive patterns in their speech. They talked of buses relaying electricity. They talked of distances between this chip and that one, caches for storage, disks for storage, and they spoke of memory. All the ingredients for the deconstruction of the digital events were there, and ultimately led to a predictive comfort. The man behind the counter made a confident declaration. This would solve the problem and the installation of the new operating system would come off without a hitch.

During the drive home, the professor's spirits were lifted. The troubleshooting led to a set of predictions revolving around adjustments to be made. Was deconstruction a predictive endeavor? To what extent were its operations the way to produce views into the future dynamic it might inhabit? While the professor chattered on about how he wanted to install this new operating system so that he could run a web server that would help him test the code he was learning to write, Wolfe continued off into the depths of possibility that maybe this intellectual momentum wasn't what it seemed, wasn't what it claimed to be. Could deconstruction be deconstructed? The death-knell, hadn't this been focal? Wasn't death itself a future possibility, something to be anticipated? Everything, every piece of it, that incited a disruption in the work of metaphysics, was a prediction, even Nietzsche's storm warning, his history of the next two hundred years. He wrote a future to be undone by events already set in motion. It was all predictive. Everyone had talked ad nauseum about the objects of knowledge and the resources for technical action, but what was the ontological status of the prediction and its projected outcomes, if not events needing to be measured? The moment of deconstruction, actual deconstruction, the intellectual movement from Europe and America in the twentieth century, was itself a turning in the great history of being. The technological resources were transforming through expected outcomes, through potential universes that could be identified and encountered in current patterns of possibility. This potential would aid whatever might come to pass. Not only that, but it would offer the right language, the correct codes, for turning and overturning these prognoses. It might spawn forms of activity ensuring the results were just as predicted. The deepening of the language of prediction would step beyond the technological, it would be the next epoch and the way out will have been achieved by going deeper inside.

It all seemed connected. Wolfe was becoming increasingly frightened as he remained silent and listened to the professor go on, excited by all the possibilities stacked up in boxes in the back seat. The messages flowing across cyberspace. The circuit boards with proper electrical flow and the correct processing frequencies for the day's job. The deconstruction of the history of western metaphysics as presence, silicon edition. All taking place as interlude, driving the epoch of technology forward into an all-consuming potential through its newfound organization and order devoted to the omnipotent false prospect of the individual consumer. Always already deconstructing itself, its power becomes limitless. If the professor's life these last three or four months was any indication of what that was like, a spreading hypnosis and the prognoses it signified were not outcomes to be desired. Nonetheless, observation indicated that, in practice, it was exactly what he wanted, what they all wanted. Everywhere he turned, it seemed there was someone poised to help him get it.

* * *

"He's not here."

"Damnit. He has my keys. I have to be somewhere and wanted to go home first. Do you know where he is?"

"Not exactly. He should be back soon. Have a seat."

"Do you need anything?"

"Can I get a cup of coffee, please?"

"Cream and sugar?"

"Just cream, thanks. What're you reading?"

"Interlude."

"Really? He showed it to you. That's not the protocol."

"He says it's epic. Thinks you have proven that deconstruction is the primary condition that moves the history of being from epoch to epoch. It is itself epochal. He says it's latest round announces the epoch of predictability in measured events."

"That's silly, deconstruction specifically disrupts the logic of foretelling, it opens the future as possibility."

"Yeah, that's his point. It's like how Locke and Hume ushered in a metaphysics of probability as a necessary response. Skepticism always announces something new to resolve doubt. Deconstruction is the skepticism that rumbles in all metaphysics, but as a pattern appearing across different instances. The statistical sociology that follows is announced by a playful disruption. The laws of scale and large numbers, the construction of aggregate personality, and the harvesting of power from human agency and potential. All of it ushered in by a deconstructive skepticism applied to the epoch of technology."

"Okay, but I don't see the difference. Reduction of the world to the purely quantitative and the universalization of resources as the manner of being, that's what the epoch of technology is all about."

"Well, he thinks it's just a midway point, a transition. Like any epoch. There's a significant difference between resources and information. Saying that being amounts to the enframing of resources is not the same thing as saying that being is the fabrication of information and emitted events. Things exist only insofar as they produce data."

"What Heidegger thought was outside the logic was really just the next step. Right. Okay. I get it. What do *you* think?"

"I read it differently. I underlined 'the one about whom I am reluctant to say.' That seems really important, and you emphasize it right at the beginning. You're struggling to not say something. Rather, there is so much that you don't want to say and what you do say is how you are contriving not to say it. Does that make sense?"

"Go on."

"Like, how you keep saying that you're aiming to talk about the one book and then you keep talking about the other one. Like you can't be trusted to stay focused on the thing you tell us you want to focus on. I mean, you are unreliable."

"As a narrator?"

"Exactly. You're reminding me that there's a fucking narrator. It's philosophy and philosophers aren't supposed to be interested in this; they don't usually point it out. The philosopher's voice. 'We have just seen that...' or 'Later I will show that...' Imagine if you had something like that in a novel. The narrator chimes in with a reference to something later in the book. In this part of our story, the following themes will be developed: one..."

"It happens. I'm sure I've seen that before. If the narrator is supposed to be describing something that happened in the past."

"Yeah, what book, do you know? I could only think of cheesy movies that do it."

"Nothing comes to mind. Tristram Shandy?"

"Oh yeah. Could be. Don't remember though."

"Me neither. It seems like something it should have done."

"That raises a whole bunch of questions about who is the author of the philosophical work and what is their role. How do they know all this? Throughout the history of philosophy, they were always giving these intricate arguments for their conclusions. We read them now and think there must be something wrong because they're full of all kinds of nonsense that people believed at the time, but which doesn't resonate now. Sometimes they would criticize a point of view in a way that today reads like support for it."

"The power of the argument at least partially resides in some historical problems that everyone agreed had to be solved. Once everyone lost interest in those problems, or no longer thought in terms of them, the arguments, even the winning ones, seemed odd or ineffectual. They became novelty items to be taught and reproduced for historical purposes only."

"Yeah. I think Interlude is about something really fundamental in Nietzsche's work that we don't fully understand."

"Well, that's bold of you to say considering his name is the very first word of the first sentence."

"Not exactly. You say that Interlude is how you 'laugh Nietzsche to yourself. The one about whom [you] are reluctant to say.' Wolfe thinks this is all about deconstruction and how it works, but you are changing deconstruction to account for Nietzsche's angle. You're aiming to extract the deity from all your presuppositions. That means ideality in all its forms, anything that essentializes or idealizes. Deconstruction over and against metaphysics is itself vulnerable because we've idealized it, tried to turn it into a theory."

"It could be all of the above. I like what you were saying about the narrator. I don't think I was saying anything about that though. That's all you."

"Could be. I've been thinking about that a lot. Really, since we talked about Kierkegaard a while back. It used to be a lot more common. Dialogues and the slippery position of the author. Like *In Praise of Folly* or even Descartes' *Meditations*."

"Sure. I can totally see it."

"You seem to think that deconstruction as it was practiced in Heidegger's work, or even now, needs to be much more about ethics and values, and that this was Nietzsche's point. The impact of the revaluation to metaphysics is only significant because it forces a revaluation of ethics and values."

"Well, because metaphysics ultimately doesn't matter. Its whole point has always been to guide our actions."

"That's right. God sees everything. God is the creator of the universe and knows everything, wants the best of everything. The creation is directly linked to the final end, to the ultimate ends of everything. What there is amounts to a chain that aims at what there ought to be because the universe was set in motion with a moral purpose."

"Every ethics will run the risk of being saturated with all these characteristics, and they will have a disciplinary function, they will have to orient us, what we know and what we should do about it."

"When that's gone, what's left? That's Nietzsche's question."

"It is. The answer is disconcerting because he just barely fathoms the impact. The havoc it will cause. The disruption will change everything."

"Right, and that's Wolfe's point about your new meaning of deconstruction. The latest version of it indicates a major turn taking place. The epoch of the agent is ending. There will be no more agents, just aggregates and their statistical representation. This is not a reduction to mere resources and their enframing, but an information age. It will be different."

"He says deconstruction is causing this?"

"No. I don't think that's his take. Deconstruction happens, it signals this turning. Hume's skepticism is a signal of the movement from a deistic universe into a scientific and probabilistic one. It didn't cause it, but it does reflect it. There's always a skeptical maneuver at the turning point of an epoch. That's the point. Deconstruction is that turning point."

"That makes sense, but I don't see any difference between enframed resources and the raw material of the information age."

"Objects can still be seen at the outset of the historical rise of resources. Isn't it possible that there was a time when it was hard to see a difference between a world of objects and a world of resources? Objects could always be put to use. Objects were the way parts of the causal chain could be linked together. There is a resourcefulness in the object, right? The epoch turns on the spindle of the entity. The object put to use reveals the resource-like nature of things. Resources framed will emit data."

"I get it, I see. Resources have their resourcefulness in the information that lies within them. Information amounts to the cultivation of that quality from the resources themselves. The process is an aggregating mechanism, and that's what you're referring to. The statistical gloss that can be applied to events at scale. Rather than this one thing here being of specific consequence, there are all these things like it in this way. All such things can be projected into the future in terms of likely outcomes based on associations."

"Yeah, association is what you're excavating in experience. Information can be defined in terms of those associations. At least, I think of it like that. The quantitative character of resources is reached when the machines that consume the resource stop doing that and start producing artifacts. The resource might be something to consume, but it matters that the act of consuming it produces information. We can discover associations from the output of that consumption. They can then be used to predict the future, future events, future outcomes, and other stuff."

"Shit. Is that the time? I should go. Hey, I wanted to ask you something."

"Sure. What?"

"He said you were totally cool with the fact that he's only here for a little while. He said you were clear about that."

"Definitely. I prefer it right now."

"Really? Why?"

"I don't know. I'm too young to get too serious. I'm not looking for anything permanent. I like him and I want to get to know him. It's a great experience. Not despite being temporary, but because of it. It's more special that way."

"Yeah. I guess it can be like that. People don't always say it so clearly though. They might not see it so clearly either."

"That's okay. That's just part of the experience they're looking for. They want to play at the eternity of love. They get to play at heartbreak. There's a lot of really important experiences in there."

"Young people just want to try everything, is that it?"

"Sure. Everything this human experience has to offer."

"There's some really horrible shit that can happen though."

"That's why these things are so popular. They're more controlled. Normal really. Everybody has gone through them. Controlled bad experiences can be a way to dabble in things that would be too dangerous and too nasty if they weren't controlled."

"Romance can go badly. Things can turn out really badly, right?"

"Oh hell yes. What do they say, 'Men worry that women will laugh at them, and women worry that men will kill them'?"

"That's some dark shit."

"Yeah, but it's true."

"That's why it's so fucking dark."

"Okay. It's highly unlikely that Wolfe would kill me. Not on purpose, anyway. He's a pretty safe one to play with. I'm learning a lot about myself and about people. I don't know."

"Yeah, he's not really that kind of person. He'd be more likely to disappear on you."

"Yeah. I got that right away. That's why it's best to not have any illusions about what we're doing. I expect that he will go, and I don't expect to get a lot of notice. By the way, it's entirely possible that he'll overstay his welcome."

"He hasn't yet?"

"No. Not yet. Although, I can already see signs of how he might. He can be aggravating."

"Right. Well, shit. I'm sorry I have to go. It was great talking to you. As usual."

"Yeah. Definitely. Don't be a stranger. Did we move past 'my friend's girlfriend'?"

She's very cool. I didn't expect that hug. I wish I hadn't reacted so stiffly. If I had been better prepared, it might have been smoother. Friends can hug when they say goodbye. We have come that far, so there is nothing wrong with it. I just didn't expect it. It was funny because she didn't seem to expect it either. How'd she manage that?

There's something about the way she describes his theory. She fixes his flaws; she revises his position in subtle ways and makes it stronger and clearer. More coherent anyway. She doesn't let on that she's doing it. Doesn't she know that her form of scholarly charity is contributing something? She might and she's just so fucking enlightened that she doesn't need to let on. He doesn't deserve her. Eh, but who am I to say? She likes him. She might think she is Salome, and he is her Nietzsche, or maybe her Rilke. Creativity takes on many forms.

Wolfe is one mistake after another. He reads badly. Finds only what he wants to find. Why does he even bother? Does he really need someone else's work to help him develop his own thoughts or could he just have them on his own? Come to think of it, I can't remember seeing him do much reading this year. He's always talking about this or that thing that he read, but I don't see him reading much even when there's a book in front of him. I see her reading all the time. Is she just propping him up? Feeding him the information he needs to make it seem like he's read all that stuff?

He could be that guy. Sucking the life and learning out of every woman he meets; he takes all the best she has and makes it his own. I can see how she talks about stuff. It's flattering. When I'm wrong, she is so careful in how she points it out. It's weird that an entire class of humans had to develop this whole side channel of behaviors specifically for the sake of coexisting with this other class of humans.

That is how it always is though. I've certainly developed my share of symmetrically honed behaviors specifically for the sake of acting among women. The devil is in the details of the specific behaviors though. It may very well lie in what she said. The behaviors women had to develop are all for the sake of protecting them from being killed and the behaviors men had to develop are to prevent them from being laughed at. Man, that would cut right to it. A relationship can turn out in several different ways. They could stay together until one of them dies. They could break up because both lose interest. One could leave the other. One could kill the other. Although that isn't really a fourth item, it's already covered in the first one. Until death do us part usually implies some natural cause, but the violent and controlling drive of a man who wants to continue to hold tight the woman he loves no matter how destructive that love is, is there some twisted universe in which that is a natural cause? If god is dead, isn't this world that world? When you make a moral argument against a state of affairs, no matter how ugly and grotesque you think that state is, you are still dependent on your audience sharing your sensibilities. They may not. Nothing guarantees it.

The surveillance and the coercion it brings aren't just a factor of the totalitarian regime, they take hold over any consequentialist form of social organization, and maybe any form at all insofar as right deliberation and forensic evaluation are crucial to moral judgment. The ought is coerced from the is by the injection of sensibilities that compel through specific arguments. That is wrong, you should not torture animals because sentient beings are worthy of respect. An agent who doesn't share that sense, who isn't compelled by an abstract command to be moral, you'll get no reaction from them. They're just a robot or a corporation. There is always an interest in conforming behavior to norms for the sake of predictability and order. That is the case in Hobbes' universe and in Locke's. There is no fucking way those norm-adhering attitudes are the result of persuasion and argument. People conform. We are hypnotized. We have no choice but to conform.

Okay, but how do I know that? How can I even think it? Is this just the skeptical dismantling of the entity structure itself? A truly disruptive event? Is the order of things breaking down all around me while I gesture helplessly?

"It's me."

"Come on up."

Can this possibly be what I want? I don't know it, he says. I want it. It's such bullshit. Very frustrating. It's just an overly intellectualized version of blaming the victim. You don't know that you are suffering from the oppressive policies of others, you don't know that you are taking advantage of privileges, or that you are letting others take advantage of them at your expense. None of this has anything to do with what you know or don't know. Knowledge is a biproduct of these relationships, of all these ways of associating. The sense of it, the power that it has over you, is that you want it, that you can't even conceive how to want without it, without these conditions and these outcomes. Is it my fault that I am in someone else's power? I resist. That's just convention and good breeding. Why should I have so much confidence in my ability to stand up to what lies behind me, to whatever it is that is propelling me forward?

"Hey. How's it going?"

"Hey. Come on in. Thanks for coming. She's in the kitchen. Come on through. Do you want a beer?"

Half full bottle of beer on the coffee table.

"Sure. Hi there. How's it going?"

That's half a beer she's putting down on the counter.

"Hey."

"Here you go."

I put the beer down on the dining table, grab my coat from the chair where I had just put it, and leave.

"Are you saying that to really be an individual you have to completely understand all the influences acting on you all the time?"

"Not exactly. I'm arguing that what it means to be an individual will depend on the influences that are acting on you. We're not so much individuals as we are individuated through a fabrication process performed by social relations. Locke couldn't help himself. He wasn't some other worldly genius who pulled the significance of property out of the ether. Any thinker with a history like his would have emphasized the significance of property and inheritance, would have baked it into the natural law pre-existing any social contract, and would have attached it to the physiology of the laboring, value-producing individual human being."

"Does that mean you don't believe in individuality?" This question came from a different student on the opposite side of the lecture hall.

"Pretty much. Take this as an example. Imagine a billion turtles, each with a container of some kind strapped to their back and moving around wherever it is that their lives take them. They originate on different continents, living in different places, maybe they aren't even contemporaries. Let's say that the containers are exactly the same on each of them. They collect rain. The rain drops that fall are all different. The collection of water, its chemical composition, would vary from turtle to turtle because the rainwater they collected would have come from different climates and different parts of the world with different contaminants in the air and so on. There might be regional similarities and patterns, but there is also a unique quality to each turtle's container contents. The conditions where they collected the rain would determine that. Formally, I would say they are each unique. Statistically, in the aggregate, the conditions that filled their containers could be defined, studied, and understood as symptoms of the places they walked and the rain they collected."

"People all have different experiences."

"That's right. These experiences are like the rain. They fill the containers and tell a story about the pathways we are traversing, but they are the experiences of the climate where we live as well. The range of possible experience, the types of things a person living in Northern Ohio at the end of the twentieth century will come across, are conditioned by the social conditions affective in Northern Ohio at the end of the twentieth century."

"The blank slate."

"In a way, but I'm challenging the emphasis he puts on it. Instead, what I am emphasizing is that we do not consent to the contract as adults fully informed and completely capable of independent thought cultivated since birth. Rather, we are attached to this social agreement as infants who have a specific physiology with a determinate means for learning and imitating. We are being formed as the thinkers that we will become as adults. That formation is a conditioning from environmental factors that are structural and social, organized and dedicated to the fabrication of human subjects capable of specifically honed thoughts and actions. Reason is not a faculty that becomes operative in the mature agent, but a rationalizing process that is socially instigated. For this reason, even our "labor" is not our own. It is a conditioned form of action where that conditioning will be heavily influenced by the social circumstances under which we have lived. What you know how to do, how valuable what you know how to do is, and whether or not other people will trust you to do it. All these factors are not intrinsic to your actions or your person. They are environmental conditions. They are part of the world. Only if the social contract permits your action to produce socially acknowledged value, can you claim to own the output of your actions. This is Hobbes, not Locke. Only the social contract makes theft contrary to law."

At that point, the farmer stood up and interrupted the Q&A. He thanked the professor for coming to speak with the students and invited everyone to continue the discussion over snacks to be served just outside the lecture hall. The same four or five students who had been aggressively pursuing the meaning of the talk continued to do so at the small reception. The students were all alike in this regard. They believed in their own innate and naturally protected individuality more than they believed in anything else. They may have held different political views, they may have come from different class backgrounds, but they shared this one axiomatic belief that could not be comfortably challenged: their righteous individuality. For some reason, the unique configuration of experiences was not sufficient for them. They could not accept a merely material differentiation from their peers. They resisted it for the exact reason the professor kept attacking it. Each one of them saw the point that the material variation allowed statistical probabilities to form. They sensed that the empirical turn that Locke, Hobbes, and others were promoting ultimately led down this same path. If they couldn't defend the inviolable individuality of the innate person, the soul or whatever you wanted to call that which each of us has from our creator, then the human being would be susceptible to aggregate operations that defined all their actions in terms of probabilistic possibilities distributed throughout the population.

The farmer stood close by as the conversation went on. He knew the professor well enough to know that he might not be careful under these circumstances, that he might step on the thinly veiled religious sensibilities that kept returning to the unique stamp of god that each soul bears. He wasn't sure where this discussion was going, what its implications might be, and he was worried about the fallout it might cause.

"To play with the analogy, imagine that there was a time when the containers weren't all the same because they were all manufactured by hand. The metal needed to be pounded and honed, the shape formed by direct human action. Not anymore, now the containers are all made of plastic and stamped out by a machine. God is dead. Although it's possible the transition to uniformity was already present in the maker's expertise."

They had heard this before; they were college students, after all. Nevertheless, the farmer looked closely to study how the students reacted, but they were unfazed. They already knew this was the key point they were hovering around.

"You see," the professor went on. "The position is strained. In order to establish the inviolable individuality of each human being, you depend on an all-powerful deity that is sovereign over all existence. It's a power maneuver that you are co-opting to make a claim in the name of liberty. There's an absurdity in there somewhere. The deity sees and knows everything and is somehow powerful enough to produce these idiosyncratic cuts in the fabric of the world, these free beings with an inalienable and innate individuality. The strange relationship this entails can be dressed up with all the poetry in the world because that is exactly what is required to make any kind of sense out of such myths. What I suspect is really going on is that a set of conditions are being portrayed in a fashion that will be likely to catch on and become popular. Individuality is the flattery of the church founders aimed at seducing the populace into beliefs that amount to submission. There is no true freedom under the guise of this deity because there is only eternal damnation for those who would make use of that freedom to diverge from the path of righteousness. How does that work exactly? When the church changes its ways through the course of time by papal decree, are the souls that were damned thousands of years ago no longer damned? Did they get a reprieve or were they never damned to begin with?"

Later, the farmer and the professor sat in the farmhouse miles outside town and the campus surrounded by it. They sipped red wine in the light and warmth of the wood burning stove. The professor pointed out that it was this frank anti-clerical lesson that those kids were trying to get. They knew it was in there somewhere and all of their digging was meant to get the speaker to say it clearly. They wanted to be exposed to these ideas, they wanted to hear them articulated in this context. The purpose they had set for themselves was not the protection of their beliefs. There were plenty in the room who were doing that, and they did it by not engaging in the discussion, by not listening too closely or thinking through the consequences. The ones who didn't stay for the reception and who didn't have any questions to ask, those were the ones who didn't want to learn anything and wanted to protect their status quo. The ones who were questioning, they knew exactly what they were looking for and they knew exactly what answers they were hoping to get. Something that would challenge them. The farmer didn't need to worry about them, they didn't need protection. They wouldn't have been driving so hard to get to the bottom of the argument if they weren't ready to deal with what their digging would uncover.

"We shouldn't assume we know what they are going to do with all these answers either. They wanted to uncover the point, they wanted to be challenged. Some of them want to change their viewpoint, they want to acquire a new perspective. Not all of them though. Some of those kids wanted to make sure their beliefs could withstand the controversy. They wanted to pass through a trial by fire that would expose them to dangerous ideas, but —like Job— they would remain faithful. This would make them even more blessed. Either way, I'm not accusing them of believing in god. That doesn't matter, their faith is their private concern. I am accusing them of having a theory that requires god. This is unforgivable. It isn't innocent, it's a power grab and an appeal to authority. It comes from something that has a hold over them, that watches their every move."

The farmer didn't disagree. "The students here aren't the same as we saw back in Illinois or that you're seeing up in Dearborn. Ashland doesn't attract a lot of suburban kids or city dwellers. A lot of these kids have rural backgrounds."

This was clear. The professor had been telling the librarian all about his upcoming trip. He described the paper he was going to read and the conversations he had with his friend, the farmer, about what to expect from the students, what they had been studying this semester, and how they were likely to react. Since she had also gone to school in rural Ohio, he suspected that she might have some opinions about what they were like, but she hadn't really heard of Ashland and suspected that it was substantially different from Antioch and Yellow Springs. Regardless, they had both agreed that anyone who was attending college anywhere in the United States was likely to have an expectation that they would be exposed to ideas and viewpoints that were different from what they had known growing up. That was the professor's point, that such viewpoints were different and were largely shaped by the specific social conditions under which each person was raised. The larger civilization would have generated a body of notions about what to expect under various circumstances. The kids would have seen movies and television shows, they would have been warned or encouraged. When they pursued a line of questioning, even if it were to refute the argument, it was with a sense of anticipation that they were coming across something other worldly.

"You know, when I was a teenager, I went through a phase where I was spouting a lot of vehemently anti-communist vitriol. I don't know where I got it from. It was strong. It occurred to me that if I wanted to really understand this point of view, so that I could truly thrash it, I would have to know it very well. I decided to read the *Communist Manifesto*. Oddly, I liked it, and it forced me to undergo significant revisions in my thinking. You could argue that I was an open-minded kid, but it's possible to think of it differently. The vitriol itself might have been an expression of a desire to understand. This desire was prone to lead to that revision. Only a strong aversion could lead me to read the enemy's work. I engineered this engagement with the other side of the spectrum so that I could be safely exposed to it. That made it easy to transform myself. People sometimes work that way."

The farmer did not. "Well, you might be right. In any event, this was a good way to expose them to the challenge. I just know that some of those students are pretty impressionable, and they haven't sorted out these things yet. They may not have known exactly what they were walking into when they tried to follow you to some of those conclusions. They might have been surprised. All semester I've been exposing them to different ideas, but I've also been meticulous about setting it up slowly and carefully. Your paper fit in with that. I just didn't want to see you go too far."

They agreed, and that is when the conversation turned toward all those things the farmer had feared the professor would expose. God is the agent behind universal surveillance, the deity who knows everything you do, and we worship *Him* for that. The social contract proxies for that "love" and is a form of control, it is the initial instigation behind enforcement of the law and our trials under it. Coercion takes on a new form, it is no longer the nasty brutish coercion of raw nature, but has become organized and leviathan, it functions as dominating mediator to all actions and the people who integrate through them. The twists and turns make a probabilistic population-oriented ethics and value theory desirable for enforcing norms and standards, for generating "types" of humans and "categories" of knowledge. The worst of it, the crown jewel of the argument, is the condemnation of theory itself as the mouthpiece of these twists and turns. The professor puts the likes of Locke and Bentham into the class of "Enlightenment" thinkers and uses that classification to fuel an accusation against them all. The minimalist state that institutes worship of the idols of money, land, and labor is the mind of god made earthly to command the same worship. It may take centuries for its all-seeing ways to be revealed, but that truth was in its essence early on. Civil society and its bio-power in labor producing property is where that worship has come to express itself as a revised battleground for the war of all against all.

"Their theory remains residual, and powers the structure of our lives through government and education. They tower above us as the elite organizers of how thought works and under what compulsion the good life is lived. They are the ones who have instilled in each of us the sense that education and good breeding come through a set of cultivations best exemplified by the critic and missing in the person of the swineherd. To these men, there is nothing worse than being vulgar; and vulgarity is defined as not having read Proust. Rather, being so ill-bred that you are unable to fake having read him because, as the case may be, who has the time?"

The farmer is not the right interlocutor for this discussion. His communion with the source of knowledge is one and the same with the soil he tills and the animals he tends. The next day, they wake up early and walk around the fields before the professor has to drive back north. They walk through the barn and the farmer tells the story about how the barns in this part of Ohio are built by the Amish, about how they are built as machines for storing and processing materials basic to farm life, about how the Amish are shrewd and excellent craftsmen capable of standing up a façade in a single day. There is a light rain, and the fields are mostly empty, but the richness of the land is sensibly present to smell and underfoot. The farmer doesn't need to be told that money infiltrates all exchange relationships and reduces them to a base equality of terms that have made prostitution the law of the land, he lives the contrast every day. It is the reason why he has chosen to come to this part of Ohio and live on this parcel of land in the way that he does with his wife and their son. There is no one to see him out here, he has no audience to perform for, the land dictates a required way of life. The animals must be fed, the seeds must be planted, and the wood must be chopped. The necessity lies in the matter and each need has a qualitative difference, a feel and a smell. There is no singular measure of all that must be done. At least so long as he does this work himself and doesn't hire it out to laborers compensated with a paycheck. There is no one measuring it. No one other than the three of them is there to witness the rhythms and the grace of their lives.

This life is the farmer's argument. If you can call it that. This is life free of the watchful eyes of such demand and the constant reflection cast by the cognition of measuring and being measured. He is not moved by the professor's resistance, it doesn't matter that barns have a history or that the shovel, the hoe, and the axe have been crafted elsewhere and acquired from the farming supply store where he bought his tractor last year. The rhythms are all right there and he feels them in his hands as he chops the wood or turns the soil. There may still be a container catching the rain, but it is not machine made and has all the dents and imperfections that make it different from the last and the next. To the farmer, this makes all the difference in the world.

The professor takes this to heart. The farmer's argument is strong. If you can call it that. As it gets closer to the time for his departure, the professor tells the farmer that he has been sending out applications for the Central Division meeting, that he is still trying to get a position as an adjunct or visiting assistant professor for next year. He describes the process and lets on that his heart is not in it. He doesn't believe in what he is doing any more, doesn't think there is any chance that he will see a positive outcome. If you think the job you are applying for is teacher of philosophy, then you will address the requirements in a way that is suitable. You might target temporary teaching jobs, or you might target tenure track jobs at schools with or without graduate programs in a way appropriate to each. All the required materials, publications and conference presentations, professional membership and references would be gathered and distributed with the aim of showing oneself to be well-suited to the teachers' profession. Being able to teach graduate students, however, is not just a matter of being a good teacher, one must be an adept researcher and contributor to the field. The rules are straight-forward, and the entrance requirements are easy enough to understand and pursue once those rules have been internalized.

Walking around the farm's acreage, the professor sees it so clearly. He sees that he has not been applying for the job that the advertisers think they are trying to fill. He is trying to find a job as a philosopher. His material and his angle, all the work he does and the sentiment he expresses, are all targeting such a position as though it were a job requiring a W-4. The truth is that no one is hiring philosophers nor could they, they are looking for teachers of philosophy, and those who apply must conform to the basic categories and laws laid down by that same "Enlightenment" he was just condemning. His problem is that he did read Proust before forming an opinion, and the one he formed was based on that reading and not pulled from the ether and redistributed as proof of his cultivation.

"Don't get me wrong," he said while trying to explain all this to the farmer. "I am not saying that the process is beneath me. Quite to the contrary. I'm saying it is well beyond my reach. Leonardo's 'sorest misfortune.' You see, Heidegger was so clever as a teenager. In the biographies, we see that he was winning awards and scholarships right from the beginning and at gymnasium. No one was fooled, everyone saw how brilliant he was. Even Nietzsche, with his isolated later life, his teachers knew he was brilliant, and the potential in his early work was clearly visible to everyone who came across it. Philosophy isn't like literature. Those who are brilliant, those who are comets like Arendt and Wittgenstein, the ones who will revolutionize the discipline, they make an impression early on, they do not pass by unnoticed."

He was getting worked up. These were familiar ideas, but he was coming to them on new ground and with new air. His lungs lifted and filled with them. His breath grew heavy. "Whatever I can contribute, whatever desire I have had to be a philosopher for all these years, to claim a place in those conversations, this has been delusion and vanity. For no one else has seen it. No teacher has remarked upon it, no advisor been so impressed. Philosophy, true philosophy, does not remain hidden like that. When the great god lets loose a philosopher and all that. It's not going to happen without anyone noticing. There is no hidden king. My knighthood has been bestowed upon me by an innkeeper."

The meaning was clear, and they didn't need to grind on it. The professor was moving toward his own denial and subsumption — determinate negation. He was initiating a process designed to eject himself from his role, not so much for the sake of becoming something else, but for the sake of coming to understand what else he had been all along. The residual mindset, the upward glances that looked at everything extraordinary in the heights, he could no longer comprehend the basis of any of it. Where was its justification and how had it come to this? What right did his desire have to tread on the hallowed grounds of the Diapsalmata? Of Zarathustra? How had he dared to be so unfair and so egomaniacal as to rob these great thinker poets of their destiny when he greedily tried to steal it for himself? This was surely his youthful way of rejecting the contract. Even if he rejected the machinic civilization that surrounded everything, he didn't reject the community the philosophers were building. The law of that land was clear, he had all along been a thief and now he had to come to terms with his ostracism: the unrequited love of wisdom.

Here are your options. 1) Description. By this we usually mean the smell of the bar or the lighting, the people that were there, what they were doing, maybe even how they were dressed. You look around and observe them in action, how they are getting along and what everything looks like, how it works, and how it all fits together. You relay that. This is a description of people and places, events, all kinds of things can be described. 2) Thoughts. This one is more like getting inside someone's head, how they think about things as well as what they are thinking. People have done this in various ways, some of them experimental. Streams of consciousness that try to capture how the psychological processes and orientations seem and feel. There is a narrative approach that acts as though thinking were just talking to oneself and describing whatever is going on. There is a kind of descriptive narrative that blends what happens in the first option with what happens in the second. There may be great depths to explore, many variations that merge these approaches together and others that we don't think of or haven't thought of yet. This option might be many options, it might be multiplied and multiplying, but you get the picture. 3) Conversations. People talk to each other and say things that display their desires or their fears, their interests or preferences. Who they are talking to matters. People talk to lots of people, of course, so you would have to zero in, focus on the significant exchanges and not the casual stuff like when you are paying for your gasoline or making small talk until everybody gets there so you can start. They can be skewed, both in how they are presented and where we cut in and fade out. Are these facts? Is this supposed to be exactly what was said? Does anyone really remember it that way, or is it meant to be more impressionistic than that, more of an angle one of the participants might take hours or days later?

Doesn't matter. These are your options. You can choose to ignore some of them in some ways and emphasize others. In some genres, they are mingled and intertwined. All three might be interleaved to give a kind of overall effect that gets the point across in the most optimal way. Really though, the whole point is to make you forget that all of them are artifice. The bar never really looked like that, they aren't really anyone else's thoughts, and they aren't the actual conversations that took place verbatim with all the gestures and tones perfectly captured. It's a fabrication, the narrator is never reliable.

Consider her friends, the ones with her last night. There is the cat and the mouse. Which is which? It really depends on where they are and what is happening. Who else is there and what is the purpose of the meeting? Is he the cat and is she the mouse? Later, something else will happen or someone else will come by and she will be the cat and he will be the mouse. The depiction can't be exact because things are moving all the time and people are only catching glimpses of each other as they move around, pass the time, and wait for what is supposed to happen next. None of it makes any difference, they are together, and they are the cat and the mouse. This can capture something, I suppose. The feline "what is that and how does it move when I paw at it?" and then there is the mousy "what is that and is it coming to get me?" When either of them is alone, they suggest what is missing, and these suggestions made their thoughts, or their actions, or their words emit a beacon showing their place in the world, from one moment to the next, "I am the cat and the mouse is out riding his bike" and then "but I am the mouse and the cat is off with his study partner" or then it all gets turned around. Turning around is how the options become optional. It is the way they interleave and make fun of each other. Not in a good way.

There is the fixture. She is legend. She was there last night too. Everyone knows her, but she is not in the program. She isn't a student; she works for a living. A bona fide professional librarian who is neither student nor teacher. They know her because she is the paradigm, and she is so cool. She is a fixture because she is the object of everyone's desire in all those fluid ways in which they can be said to want this or that. She wonders and she investigates. Like all of them, she is practiced at search and discovery. Most of all, she is helpful so long as you say please and thank you and properly whisper your request. We know that she will tell you whatever tale from her experience fits the topic at hand and that her stories will reflect something bent and bewildering in the lives of ordinary folks. We know that and we can depend on it. She is in her prime and she is on her own. She loves to taste things. She is both organized and chaotic, as though it were the most natural thing in the world for those two traits to come together in a mood or an evening adventure with friends. The way thought bursts out into a conversation, the way that the conversation can provoke thought, and then how all of that is reflected in the way people are sitting or how they hold their cigarette or where their eyes go while they are listening.

We shouldn't forget to mention the frail girl, although she is always prepared to be overlooked. She is sweet and the boys never seem to understand that this comes at a price. Not one paid by the people receiving the benefits, but by her in all the things that take a backseat to it. She has grown used to delaying her satisfaction for the sake of others and she knows this makes her likeable, but also forgettable. She didn't make a choice to go through life this way, she had found this before she even knew she was looking for it. She learned a long time ago that she could buy different clothes and get her hair cut in a different style and none of that would change these basic conditions. They could not be avoided. Even if there are people who can change who they are, who can decide to be different, that is already a kind of person, that is already to be endowed with a quality that enables it. This is a quality she does not possess, but which she is painstakingly aware of at all times. She feels its absence when she talks to others, or hears about them, who did this and why they did it, how they managed it. She does not yearn for the calm that her life has become, she does not desire the fragile emotional state that can be used to describe her to strangers who will only know this little bit about her. She is drawn by something else, by the something that is something else, something other, something exciting and different and interesting. She is always looking for ways to break. Hoping for it, dreaming about it, but there is just another day of this calm, another sensible day with the standard expectations and the usual outcomes.

People are drawn to each other. To know me, you would need to know the whole history of who has been drawn to me and who I have been drawn to. To really know me, even this wouldn't be enough because all of the optional facets of these attractions would have to come in all their aspects. All the descriptions from all the angles would have to be gathered and collected together in a central location where they could be correlated, connected, and annotated. All the conversations would have to be recorded. Not just the actual facts of what was said, but everything about these conversations, how they were interpreted by each of the participants, how they were remembered, what followed afterward, and everything like that. All these component parts would have to be brought together and entangled with the descriptions. What about all those thoughts? How could they be contained and included in the dossier? There were so many thoughts by so many different people. All of them everywhere and all at once, and so many tangents and side effects, so much pressing and releasing, so much force and resistance. All the ins and outs of the neural patterns and their electric imprints. What store could contain all of that? What forms of forgetting and selective understanding would breed the most common and the most compelling reactions to it? Not only is the selection a highly sophisticated procedure, but the recollection and the emphasis are equally so. Information, like a river, is in motion and the movement allows for uncountably many facets and aspects: each of us this manifold in the body and in the soul, in all the modes that our slice of substance may behold and occupy for a spell as it undergoes modification. "Even here there are gods."

There is who they are and then there is why they are there. Why they are drawn to her and why she is drawn to them. The cat and the mouse are protective of her, they care for her and make sure she is getting on alright, making the right choices, and having the right amount of fun to take the edge off. She likes being the target of this concern because it is so obviously friendly. They aren't parental. She would never go for something like that. There is something asymmetric in the relationship, something like what we usually have with our parents. Although she cares about them very much, roots for them, takes their side in all things unconditionally, she isn't exactly looking out for them in the way they do for her. In that sense, they are adequately capable of taking care of each other. They live together, sometimes work together, and sometimes study together. They are pretending to be settled and so don't need the same oversight she needs. All three agree on this, and that makes it easy for everyone to do what they are supposed to do when they are supposed to do it.

The fixture is drawn to her because she sees her as a younger version of herself. She knows what is behind that look in her eyes. To learn about the librarian, you have to watch her while she watches other people. You have to imagine everything that is going on in there. She listens so closely, she watches so carefully, and she plays off of it. She picks up on everything they are hinting at and everything they aren't hinting at and why that might be. The fixture got to know the librarian this way, by watching her watch others. At the bar a few times, for sure, because that is a powerful indicator of how her focus works, but in social situations with the professors and the other librarians, the students, and the staff. The fixture knows everybody which means she can turn up anywhere. This gives her an angle, a fresh collection of things to see. She notices, she notices her noticing. She thinks this tells her story. The librarian is drawn for the same reasons. She thinks the fixture is an older version of herself. At least she hopes so. That is how she desires her. They are ten years apart and it is clear that these are the crucial ten years, these are the years when she will be getting started, pointing herself in whatever direction and hoping that it turns out to be the right one. The librarian can say anything at all to the fixture. She loves this. She notices her noticing her noticing because that is how she works too. She pays attention to what people are paying attention to and if what they pay attention to is what she herself is paying attention to, then there is nothing but delight and the two will get along famously. They flirt with each other because that is the only option available to people who are so mutually oriented. Such interaction is itself the basis of any proper flirting. To flirt is to notice the other person noticing you and to play with that, to be playful with that. Both are dreamy, strange, and extraordinary. Why wouldn't they be attracted to each other?

The fragile girl is completely infatuated with the librarian. She can't believe that nothing chips or cracks or breaks her. She is far too kind to experiment with these boundaries herself. She won't poke at the librarian; she only reaches out to pet her and cuddle with her. She is this way even when they don't touch or when they just sit next to each other, watching people go by, and connecting all the dots they have seen that day. They have similar taste in music and both geek out on some of the same trifles that pass by on today or yesterday's wind. The librarian wishes she were that kind and gentle, wishes she had learned some of that prudence that might make it easier to get along with her and, yes, might even make her more forgettable at times. They play at being both mentor and mentee, they insist and persist in learning and teaching each other another way, one that might be off limits but which they will never stop being attracted to. The librarian doesn't think she is unbreakable, she feels like she's constantly about to suffer a critical moment, but no one sees her that way and so her vulnerability becomes her own version of invisibility. When she passes time with the fragile girl, it's as though that phantasm has come forward in the ghostly movement of another, in their words and in their deeds. They make eye contact, and they empathize across the distance, feeling each other and less alone because of it.

This was last night. There was so much laughter, so many stories, so many interconnections. They all sunk and rose so smoothly, docked at the table, anchored in the center of the bar. She noticed the guy with the smirk at one of the booths sitting with a woman who was a bit younger. She was sporting a cool short bob that framed her face perfectly. The librarian knew he was that same guy who was in the bar with the professor long ago. She recognized him, knew that he came in sometimes. She knew about him, had heard things. Last night, for a moment, she couldn't hear anything. That made it possible to see more. They were at ease, comfortable, and very much into each other. Talking furiously with so much interest. He listened so carefully. She was rapt with equal attention. The librarian admired and envied them; certain they must've come straight from bed to the bar. They had that look about them, that feeling. She could always tell, and in this case, there was no room for doubt. They didn't see her or catch her watching them, since they were so deep in conversation themselves, they barely noticed the waitron when she came to ask if they needed anything else. They left early, didn't stay long. She knew where they were going and what they were going to do. It was almost as if they never stopped, just surfaced for air for a few hours but had trouble leaving it behind.

This reminded her of everything. The disastrous thing with head shot guy. It had been what she thought she needed at the time, but afterward it didn't feel like she had gotten it, and then it reminded her of whatever this was with the professor. She was feeling that. Not just in her head, she felt him through the things he said and his reactions. He had a way of making love with words, but it was her body that responded. He was in her fantasies now and he had a body and hair and eyes. A beating heart. Something had happened. It couldn't be happening yet. He didn't know her. Not yet and not really. They were drawn, but they didn't know what they were being drawn into. The couple in the booth reminded her of this, and of that shapely woman in the rabbit cartoon. She isn't bad, she's just drawn that way. Being out and comfortable with her friends in her place where she is at home. This made her easy, this brought her calm, and then there were those times dripping with sensuality soaking into their conversation, their being together. He reminded her of the other one, of the one who was more and more on her mind. She desired him, but it always stopped at the one fact, the missing detail, the one he didn't know. What he does not know. At this distance, with these options, he could not possibly know.

It wasn't his fault, and she didn't blame him for it. She didn't accuse herself of a lie either. Still, she knew she hadn't been entirely forthright. Somewhere she wondered whether he wasn't guilty of the same thing. They held back because holding back was part of their two-step. He said today that he was dancing around his apartment. What does that mean exactly? What specific actions is he referring to? Likewise, she told him she had been lying around the apartment taking the day off. What did that mean? There was so much she wouldn't tell him just like there was so much he wouldn't tell her. They told each other everything and yet so much was left out. At the beginning, they leave these things out because it would be too much, but how do you know when the time is right to get into more details, to go further and say more? She wouldn't tell him yet about the food choices she makes when "lying around" or about the repeated self-pleasure she cooed into at intervals following this or that thought that blew a pleasant breeze over this or that desire. The parity was perfect because he wouldn't tell her what went on in the dancing. The thinking the talking the sobbing, all the movement back and forth disrupting his pace and his reform. Everything he wrote and everything he didn't write, all that went into dancing. For this was just a word for movement, choreographed, repeatable, but variable and including all the acts of thought bestowed on any subject to the vita contemplativa. He was fantasy and narration, he was spinning and turning, he churned out stories as minutes in the day passed by. Like her, maybe even at the same moments now and again, his day too would slow to a grind in self-pleasure and sultry pleasant breezes.

These days and these nights, this draw and this wind, these are how the options condition us and our memory and our sense and all the waking time that we have spent learning it. Later in the day, when she went off to work her shift at the front bar, these lessons continued, and they ached. "Never mind, I'll get it," she said as an excuse to be alone, so they brought her down to the basement to change the keg; and then later they brought her out to the sidewalk where the slight scent of spring might only just be hinting that it is on the way. She was determined and she had decided. She would not take the easy road. She was going to tell him, going to let him know everything he did not know. In a glimpse, just a glimpse. He doesn't need the whole picture. Not yet. He just needed a peek; he has to see something, but he doesn't need to see everything.

Tonight, like last night, the guitar player was in the bar. She had only said hello when they were both customers, but today he was at her bar. She noticed him noticing her. With a gleam in her eyes and a mischievous grin, she half nods in his direction. He knows.

"Hello."

"I'm not saying I agree with you, I'm only saying that I understand the point. You're saying there is something about the point of view that people have when they see things, when they gather information from observations, that's only part of the story, only a sliver of what's going on."

"That's right."

"Observation can be teased into surveillance. Especially once we take the Heisenberg principle into account. Since we know that the act of observing something impacts the thing being observed, we have to become wily about how we setup the conditions for observation. We have to be sneaky. This amounts to establishing proper observation under secrecy or in a way that hides the observer. It's all so that the subjects don't suffer any impact while being observed, they go about their business as if they were alone."

"Well, that's an artificial way of putting it, but I get it."

"Sure. You'll admit that the observation of subatomic particles is different from observing people or animals or any conscious being that knows they're being watched. They'll account for it and alter their behavior."

"Take teaching for example. Even in a simple form. Say you're learning to play a musical instrument. You have a teacher. You perform a designated task in front of your teacher and your teacher observes your actions. They correct you. You're supposed to play as though they were observing you even when they're not around. This is the discipline of learning to play the instrument. The self-awareness becomes second nature and accompanies you all the time. At some point, you might not even think of it as connected to your teacher's observations. You totally internalize that and then you self-regulate. Keep your thumb in exactly the right place, minimize movements as much as possible, and so on. We call someone like that a disciplined player, or we complement their technique."

"Yeah, I was thinking about that at work the other day. You know, I spend a lot of time teaching. I guess it's teaching. I work with other engineers. Some of them are pretty junior and don't have experience with whatever it is that they're working on. They come to me for advice or ask if there is some library somewhere that already does what they're trying to do. I explain stuff to them. How to do it right, or why they should do it one way rather than another."

"Sounds like teaching."

"Exactly. It's not like school though. They don't get bored while I'm telling them stuff. They don't ask me if it's going to be on the test."

"Right."

"I know, it's funny. I was thinking about why it's so different. It occurred to me that it's because they aren't studying for some test, they're already taking the test. They're asking me for help while they are in the middle of it, while they are being tested."

"That makes total sense."

"It does. They're not working for some letter grade that has some potential future meaning, they're working for money and position. They're trying to establish themselves, to move forward in their career by turning themselves into experts who can do the kinds of things they need to do. None of it is disinterested or theoretical. There's no detachment."

"I see. It isn't that they are being watched and then scolded for not following the right methods or doing things in the most effective and efficient way. Instead, they're the ones driven to do their jobs better."

"Yes. In engineering, when building software, it's hard to fake it. The shit either works or it doesn't. Sometimes it works when you demo it because the conditions are controlled. You might be able to fool someone into thinking it's ready, but as soon as you release it and have real users on the system, doing whatever it is that they need to do, there is no more room for superficial salesmanship. This is why the people I work with are so driven to get it right. They're like craftsmen, you know? They want to write their code in the best possible way so that it doesn't blow up when people start using it."

"It still blows up."

"Well sure. Scale is hard to reproduce in advance. You can't always tell where your system is going to have problems until lots of real users get on it in real world situations. My point is that they're worried because of real-world problems and real-world consequences if they do it wrong. They aren't worried that someone is watching them and will see what they're doing wrong."

"Are you trying to connect up the stuff about observation with this stuff?"

"Yes. I'm thinking that somehow we started to believe that the world we see and observe is the world that really matters. This is where the reductions we always talk about come into things. Right? If a person is nothing other than an observable thing, then we can reduce them to more and more microscopic observations. Observations at the cellular level, at the chemical level, at the physical level, and then, ultimately, just math."

"Oh, I get it."

"I know you do. I'm saying that I see your point. If we're acting though, really in the middle of it, then we're acting out like feeling beings involved with things that matter to us. If we're artisans mastering a craft, then there is something there, something at work in that, that cannot be reduced through more and more precise description. Doing that would lose track of what's happening. Does this make sense? The goal would disappear, the values would disappear, and the meaning too."

"What brought all this on? Why the sudden concession? We've been having this argument for years, why are you suddenly coming over to the dark side?"

"Well, the other night. That sucked. Let me just say that. Watching you grab your coat and leave was one of the worst feelings I've ever had."

"Hey, if you want to drink yourself into stupidity, have at it. I'm just not going to have anything to do with it. I'm not going to stick around and watch."

"I know. I know that's exactly what you were doing. It was so weird. I knew you weren't angry with me, that you weren't turning your back forever. You were just disappointed and saying you're not going to be a part of that."

"Yep."

"Anyway, all of that made me realize I have to get out of here. I can't take this gray sky. I have seasonal depression from the lack of sun, it's awful. I can't stay here. I have to go back to California."

"Okay."

"I made a few phone calls, decided I wanted to live in San Luis Obispo and, bam, I found a job there. All in just a few days."

"That's great. Is it a good job? I mean, did you have to settle for something?"

"No, it's a great job. Decision support and low-level interfaces to device drivers. It's an awesome job with a couple of professors at Cal-Poly who have some grant money to get a business going. That's my point. I see how hard you struggle, and I listen to your stories about these people who have permanent jobs with tenure, and it just blows me away. That kind of tenure is really wacked, don't you think? It occurred to me that I have a sort of tenure just because I have these skills that are in such high demand right now. These skills are my tenure, and then I was thinking about this teaching stuff I told you about, and how we are really shaping each other's skills and learning to be masters of the craft. It's a really powerful form of tenure, having skills I mean. It's totally based on what we do, not some weird institutional decree based on hypothetical circumstances where our research might put us at odds with the political interests of the administration or whatever it is that justifies this form of job security you're trying to get."

"Well sure, but this skillset is quirky. The demand is high now, but things are constantly changing and you're not in control of the market and the future demand."

"Sure, but neither are all these profs, right? I mean, you could land yourself a tenured job somewhere and then that University might decide to get rid of the philosophy department. Your tenure wouldn't be worth anything in that case, right? You'd be out of a job."

"True."

"You'd be totally fucked. Unless you were one of the gurus or something. Think about it. Imagine being fully tenured and pretty far along in your career and then losing your job because the department has been shut down. What are you supposed to do then? There are even fewer tenured jobs available than there are tenure track jobs, right? Someone who is a little older who needed to find a job that started with tenure, that would be incredibly difficult. Whereas for someone like me with a lot of experience, it would be even easier for me to find a new job. That tells me that I really do have tenure. The skills are real tenure, they show the fact of my long-term work in the field, of my deep knowledge of the subject, and my ability to contribute to any enterprise now that I have that experience. That out of work professor is fucked because they don't have any of that."

"Shit. This is really depressing."

"I know. You're working your ass off to get a job and then suppose you don't get tenure after being on the tenure track. That seems just as bad. You'll be older at that point, but won't necessarily have more experience in a way that makes you desirable to get another tenure track position somewhere else. There just won't be enough tenured jobs for you to transition into. It's such a crap shoot."

"Enough, I get it."

"On my end though, we're practically rabbinical. A new engineer walking into a new shop, it's like Maimonides. If you show up on day one and there's a problem that comes up and nobody else can solve it, but you have the answer, then you're the rabbi. They will make you the rabbi and no one will complain. The person who has the knowledge is immediately acknowledged and if that knowledge can be put to good use and teach the others, then everyone will rush in to learn it and put them in that position. Now *that* is tenure."

"You think that the traditional role of the academy is lost? The experts, the true scholars, and the ones who carry the knowledge, are they the engineers now?"

"Yeah, why not? These guys I've been working for here are professors, but they are in computer science. Their status is all about private sector investment and the elite position they have from bringing in lots of money. Same with these guys at Cal-Poly. These are joint ventures, somewhere between academic and the private sector. It's as if they're ushering in a new world, a new hierarchy. They're grinding the Enlightenment organization of the academy into ruins, destroying the ivory tower, and creating joint partnerships between industry and academia."

"That's where all the money is going."

"Exactly. Smart people follow the money. You're always telling me about these well-read morons that you come across. They've read a ton of books and have their heads filled with other people's ideas, but they have no idea how to apply them unless they happen to be arguing about what those ideas mean. Which is why they always manage to turn every debate or problem into something that revolves around them. They can't venture out into the practical world and apply what they know because they don't have a clue. It's all theoretical to them, intuitive description and armchair observation. The philosopher and the theoretical physicist are growing closer and closer because both of them are more detached from the real world."

"That would explain their increased emphasis on the old traditional hierarchies. The expert is the most learned within the domain and not necessarily the person who can make connections between that domain and other areas, areas that might be more practical. Those public intellectuals who can do that are guilty of dumbing it down for the masses."

"Yes. I can imagine it getting much worse in the future. There's no telling how things will go when more and more people start to turn against these traditional standards of knowledge and expertise. All this theoretical partitioning of the world for the sake of analysis and reduction to its core parts and then arguing over which resulting position is the truth of it all. It's only a matter of time before people who live lives totally disconnected from those foundations start to rebel against people like that trying to tell them what to do."

"Hasn't that already started? In politics it seems like the absence of experience and expertise is already being applauded as an important advantage, something that makes someone better suited to hold office."

"Well, it could get worse. That's all I'm saying. If academic interests are separated from these real concerns, it could get a lot worse. What the academics could end up teaching everyone is that talk amounts to expertise and since anyone can talk, anyone can be an expert. Worse, they would be suggesting there is no limit to that expertise."

"Meaning?"

"Well, that's the worst thing about these ivory tower fucks. I don't know why you even want to be one of them. They think that because they learned everything there is to know about some sliver of something, that this qualifies them to talk about all sorts of unrelated things that they don't know anything about. Because they learned the power of abstraction, they can make a good case. They don't know what they're talking about."

"I see. We have lost our boundaries; we no longer see the limitations in our understanding. We believe all the flattery from students working the power relation and don't recognize how connected we are to the highly specific circumstances of our experience. We're always trying to overreach that."

"Yes. Exactly. Engineers don't do this. Not at all. Part of the artisanry of building things properly is knowing when you're guessing and when you've gone beyond your experience and are off in the land of 'not sure' and 'we'll see.' We experiment and we gather data when we don't already have it. We know when we need to do these things. If you start bullshitting, people will find out soon enough because whatever it is that you are building will fall apart. You will lose your credibility. Once you've lost that, it's gone forever. It's the most important thing."

"Is it based on staying within your limits?"

"You're damn right it is. People who talk shit get a reputation for being people who talk shit. When they try to convince others, they aren't believed anymore. People know who is full of shit and who isn't because they see what happens, they measure the effects, and they remember the causes. That person loses their position, and no one believes them anymore. They'll get push back whenever they try to make an argument for something. People will make sure they provide more data and that they are meticulous in proving what they're saying. That's just how it works. I don't see this same thing going on with academics. They talk shit and no one can ever prove that it is shit because they aren't building anything, aren't responsible for any concrete result."

"You're talking about a specific kind of academic, not all of them."

"Sure, I guess I'm talking about theorists, whatever the hell that means. People like you really. Why is that so attractive to you? I don't know, I just can't figure it out. Who would want to spend their life wrangling with bullshitters who never have to take responsibility for their bullshit?"

"Hey, it's not like I have a choice about it anyway. It's not really up to me."

"You're still trying though. All this talk, and all of it so unreliable. I'll tell you it's probably connected to the observation theory we're talking about. The more bullshit people spout, the more unreliable they are, and unreliable people can't be counted on. Who knows what they're going to do? It'll all depend on whatever screwball idea they get into their heads at some point. If we can't rely on them and can't predict what they're going to do using reasonable principles, we'll have to keep a close eye on them. I mean, you have to keep observing anything you don't have a determinate theory to explain. The theory is reliable, it gives you good predictions. Without it, perpetual surveillance is required. It's all because there's a kind of popularized talk where nobody believes anyone else is an expert and that all of us can comment on anything. It convinces everyone that they have just as much right as the next guy for doing whatever the hell they want to do."

"Okay, you're rambling now."

"I might be. The political ideals of the revolutionary in America, the Enlightenment principles, when they're combined with all this talk and all this disdain for expertise and authority, they'll usher in the age of the pirate."

"What the fuck are you talking about?"

"I'm serious. Everyone will be cackling and spouting bullshit, making no damn sense. Not just a few parties will swoop in and take everyone's money, it'll become the rule of the day."

"How? I can't see the connections."

"Look, the politics is a controlled area of action and organization, right?"

"Okay."

"There is a lot of complexity there. It's hard for a democratic society to include ideas that represent all the different points of view. When some of these theorists make it seem like their angle should be the be all and end all, they start an ideology war. Everyone claims they're the ones with the authority and start arguing for their point of view. This creates a kind of chaos where we're all vulnerable to someone who might come along with the least common denominator for the splintered interest groups. The splintering happens because of all this academic theory talk, then the LCD comes along to take advantage of it. If the wrong people are the ones who have that message, they'll steal everything. They'll take all our money; they'll sweep up everything valuable that's up for grabs."

"The wrong kind of people?"

"Yeah, pirates. People who want to exploit the splintering, you know. Opportunists. It won't be one vs. the other, it'll be like a piracy machine with parts that generate necessary energy off of the struggle between the one and the other, between everything actually. Ubiquitous conflict as distraction to smooth out the operations of the mechanism."

"Pirates, huh. Okay. We've really gone off the deep end now. We started out with the reduction issue, didn't we?"

"Yeah, but that's my point. If we avoid reduction. If we stick with the actions and the meaning like you're always saying, then we have all these human struggles to worry about. Now, everyone has their own individual angle on things. That's this splintering I'm talking about, and then this splintering turns us into a bunch of whores, where everything of value is for sale. Money is the only thing we want and the only thing we really care about. Here we are splintered and greedy. That's the perfect opportunity for the pirates to swoop in and take advantage of us. They'll flatter us, offer us what we want, what we think we need, and all for the sake of taking all our money for themselves."

"You're being unfair to prostitutes. Alright, even if I am with you on this, why aren't the engineers right in the middle of it? They work for a living, don't they?"

"We do and maybe we are. I don't know, I don't think this applies to the engineer I've been describing. The artisan, the rabbi, the one who lives and dies by their credibility. The one who knows he can't get away with bullshitting and lying. The one who knows that ultimately the thing either works or it doesn't. Surveillance is to make sure it's all working correctly, not to serve some disinterested and detached knowledge of what it is in its most basic mathematical form. The observations are self-descriptions, they come from the agent in the middle of acting out its purpose. They are implicit in the action and so not something that can shape it from the outside, rather it is something that comes from the act and reveals the action's relationship to everything else so that it can be properly manipulated and exploited."

"Well, we'll have to leave it there. When are you moving? I can't believe you won't be around anymore. It's been great having you so close."

"This weekend. I'm getting rid of everything. I'm flying out on Sunday."

"I'll come by and help. We can get a pizza or something."

"I'll call you."

He got out of bed and passed behind me, he leaned over and pulled my shirt up, and deliberately but gently bit my nipple before leaving.

There was darkness. A slight suffocating sensation, my head buried in the pillow. I turned to the side to allow my nose to push open some space for my mouth to suck air through the sheets. Someone pretending to be Wolfe appeared. They said they were going to try to analyze me. They said that the object of my desire seemed small because it was far away. They said it seemed far away because it was small. An ongoing wall of words, they said I shouldn't worry because this makes the analysis easier. From a distance, we'll get a better perspective for measurement and evaluation. Our judgment will be more accurate. Not only that. The distance came from the projection at work in desire itself and the desire was responsible for putting the object where it was, out there just beyond reach. This was how fantasy works, they said. Not the content of it, not its image, but the putting in place out there, over there, the structure of the act was the fantasy itself, was the desire inside the fantasy. Setting things down just out of reach is how we pull ourselves forward, it's where our desire comes from. They said.

I remembered that time in Sunday school. She and I had kissed because there was an opportunity. Nothing else drove us. We had found each other alone by chance, each on a different errand. I had known her since we were children, but as teenagers I hadn't given her a second thought. Couldn't remember ever thinking about her at all. This must've been true for her too, and we stumbled into each other when we were just becoming the right age for that curiosity. We were there at the same time and there was no one else around. I saw the look in her eyes. It was that look that was seeing me, and it was unmistakable. That was how I knew what she expected me to do, what she wanted me to do. I was the one who moved first to kiss her, but she was pulling me with her eyes. I couldn't go the whole way and stopped, standing there so close by that I could feel her breath on my face. She had stopped pulling and started pushing, leaving me hovering there. Having made my intentions clear, I was exposed and vulnerable with just that small gap to cross. It was not mine to take, but she closed that distance with vigor. The whole time we kept looking into each other's eyes. It wasn't the least bit embarrassing. Why aren't we looking away or closing our eyes, I remember thinking. We were touching each other and couldn't tell the difference between being touched and touching, even our hands were that sensitive.

Without having been a first time, this had been my first time. Why should it come back to me now? What was this memory doing returning with such force at just this moment? Under the threat of analysis. I rolled over but kept my eyes shut tightly. I pulled the pillow up over my face to be more comfortable, to allow more thoughts to come. The analysis continued.

The ease of it. The lack of intent. That's what draws this memory close. My intent now seems shameful in comparison. The first time had been so pure because there had been none of it. I could keep my eyes fixed on hers and enjoy the feeling of hers fixed on mine, because I hadn't planned it. I hadn't gone looking for her, I hadn't pined or wondered, I hadn't spun tales elaborating the meaning of each gesture for weeks or months leading up to that chance meeting. We innocently stumbled upon each other. I had not pursued her, I had not made any effort at seduction, and I hadn't put on my best suit or minded my manners. No false act. There was nothing fake in any of it. That was where the confidence of my gaze and —I believed at the time— the confidence of hers came from. That was how two fourteen-year-old kids managed to sustain that look while touching and coaxing each other forward into their kiss.

The burning in my eyes as I held them shut tight, squeezed them harder, this was shame. It had been revealed through a moment free of it for the sake of showing me how much of it there was here and now. Not jealous, I was ashamed of wanting her, of having acted as if I did, and having done what followed from that desire. Why should acting the part of the animal that I am draw such emotion? I reassured myself that I hadn't been caught out of character, that I hadn't been pushing and forcing myself forward. I recalled myriad ways in which I had been encouraged and coaxed. I remembered the rules of the game as I had been taught them. At the outset, I made a modest offering and received a response including questions and inquiries. That was not an invention, I had evidence. She wanted to know things. She told me things. We met just before Christmas. She wanted to keep communicating even if she didn't feel ready to spend time together. She said that. She bridged so many of the distances, she wrote pregnant responses ripe for multiple interpretations. She was playful, she made it personal. I didn't imagine that. Did I? Are these advancing armies just flocks of sheep? I have nothing to be ashamed of, but there it is. This hadn't been my own doing; she was there. In our way, across the electronic space, we looked each other in the eyes as we tried to touch each other across the distance.

What was this then? What is she doing? Not pushing back but shoving. In the ordinary language of everyday back and forth, wasn't the appropriate response to withdraw? I looked for answers from the analyst. He knew better. He knew that you can't talk yourself out of these things once you've talked yourself into them. Wait, what then drives this endless analysis? Isn't that the whole point of the talking cure? That you can be talked out of it? No, I only get to learn that I have been talking myself into it all along. Seduction itself is self-seduction, and then, in the middle of it, making a show of it to the other person. What they see then is your increasing desire for them. In that case, that is what draws them in. That is what pulls us closer to each other. It's all in the analysis, the object of desire is the other's desire, is the act of becoming the object of the other's desire. If self-seduction comes into it, then my head swims among the crowds. There is me wanting her and there is her wanting me. There is me wanting to be for her something she wants. Likewise in return, and then there is me wanting to make myself be that something. Such a crowd of us stumbling and fumbling over each other.

There is this flash. I sense the complexity of the symbolic as it spins out of control with all these connections and relationships, these headbirths and headgames that we bandy back and forth. I remember the proximity I felt between that and the physical sensations during that first time in the Sunday school. There hadn't been anything in my head. There was no time to build a web of images and ideas. Only the feeling of her touch and of her body when being touched. I recalled the feeling of that stroke, those remembered minutes and the physical pulse that went with them. There was no mind there, nothing that I could recall. No fantasy, no worry, no fretting or calculating. Just the pure experience of her lips and my hand on her with her hand on me. All the times in between flooded back to me. The duplicity in it. My mind at work while my body moved, the two in almost perfectly synchronized pairing. Two attributes of the same substance. A faux thrust and adjust alongside the spinning and weaving of a fantasy woman right there nearby, or some other. The two usually in sync, this distance and this proximity go together, pass side by side in the experiences lurching around in memory. The analyst kept whispering. The real, the imaginary, and the symbolic all rushing forward. I see them clearly, maybe for the first time. I see with them. The thrust becomes real over time. There are bodies together, there is touching. The imaginary present in the projections, the place that the images held as my mind executed its rhythm parallel with its body. Oh, what a body can do. The meaning of it, the references and relationships, they spurred the images further and further forward. They instigated this and that point of connection, this and that movement to and fro. The desire machines. That is how they are called, that is how they are elicited, with these multiples, with these layers, and with this interleaved cultivation reciprocal all around.

That first time there had been opportunity and realization. No fantasy at all. My virginity was sufficient to provide the distance any desire requires. It might have been my age, inexperience, or some combination of both. Here and today, I had exactly the reverse of those conditions, as though I had been intentionally trying to construct the opposite experience. A mind at work with no body. All imagination and reference with no reality. It wasn't just her that was keeping me at an arm's length, I was equally pleased with the arrangement. This email on this day, this morning, it wrenched me from that static point. It was a radical act on her part. It could not be taken lightly. The analysis is clear, the traditional response is to accept the shove backward and let go. "Holding on comes easily, we do not need to learn it." There are other possible responses and alternate circumstances. It might be best to trot off and find one of them and leave this one to the past, chalking it up as a lesson learned. If she had something in mind, if she was crying out for some turn or change that needed to happen, then I'll leave it to her to follow through and suggest that new beginning. In any event, my work should be complete. I have done all that I can do at this distance. We have gone too far. I'll help if I can, but she will have to make her way.

I was starting to come out of it, I was not so deeply sunk into the bed. I could feel myself lying on its surface and, most importantly, breathing. No more evidence of Kafka's closing throat. I couldn't hear the analyst. I didn't feel the threat of it. Not from any direction, not coming from any corner. The friendliness of the orientation remained as a memory, as support in a moment when I needed it. This was a moment of crisis and I had responded with self-instigated therapy. What is that then? Was it an orientation whose aim was to see everything? My whole life and all the moments in it? Everyone's whole life and all the moments in them? Is that where this projection leads? Shall I say that the side-step to a distance that projects that little object over there as something desired is the insertion of myself into that object? Is that me becoming the object of desire? Not just this one or that one, but all the objects of desire everywhere in the world. Because I can see everything and everywhere, everyone and every how, I am in / as / through all of it, I am the world wanting, I am the pulled subject of this world's desire. This might be what the analyst meant when he talks about being the phallus as opposed to having it. The relation to all the objects of the world is pure fantasy. In the syntax of the projection that holds these fantasies up, there is the all-seeing maneuver of the conscious being. This might be its source, and this could be what it means to be a sentient creature capable of symbolic life.

That is the desire for seeing and being seen. It is the desire for discipline insofar as this pattern is itself embedded in the sight of everything from everywhere all the time. It wasn't that there was some fantasy of surveillance, some voyeuristic or exhibitionist delight. Rather, it was that fantasy itself was a leaning toward this posture. This position. This ability to position oneself over and against all those objects of desire, all those objects which can rise to desire me as I am. Those objects which we have fabricated and which in turn fabricate me in this way, as this how, and — above all— as this when. They put it there so that they could pull it out later. If discipline and surveillance are as aligned as I am beginning to think, then it isn't just that desire is always oriented by a disciplinary structure, but that desire is always bent back toward that same structure. The purpose of it is to impose itself as a regulative order. Desire itself is this regulative order. Sexually, this is both the order and the desire for it at the height of intensity and the height of its more personal quality. What could be more personal? Where else would her personality lie but in these back-and-forth strides? This tickling? This delight? Where else should I be?

When I read MacKinnon's *Toward a Feminist Theory of the State*, that was the one passage that had the greatest impact. I couldn't forget it. I have never forgotten it. Her point, skewed and burned into me, was that the desire had the order built into it, that the most personal experience of wanting could be implicated in the power dynamics that were hidden in the very same pleasure that was experienced in desire's satisfaction. I was corrupting her point. For her, the order was patriarchy. I couldn't see groups like that, so monolithic and gigantic, instead I saw volatile groupings, mechanisms plugged into other mechanisms. That meant there were always multiplying operations taking place. Nothing was ever just one thing. Memory was always at risk. We group up into many groupings, grouping multiplies us and multiplies the things that multiply us. Satisfaction meant nothing in this system of symbols here set into motion. Pleasure had nothing to do with satisfaction, it was an indication of the presence of desire, it was its discovery after the fact. I am this or I am that comes on the back of pleasure, so it is not only the order in us, but what sets us in order, what puts us in our proper place. It still nags at me that I haven't come to terms with this sufficiently. What could it mean if even my pleasure divides me from myself? Cuts into me as a body surrounded by life support and organized operations that have a mind and will of their own? They have plans for me, there is an organizing drive that sets me up and puts me down. Whatever I am meant to feel and to be lies in the work that is ordered there. In that incision, in the surgical procedure, in the control and the structure that these surroundings will bring to me, will bring as me, as a logos, a gathering, a collection, a multiplying, and as many groupings. Where can I go to make my choice under such conditions? What could be my preference other than the one that has been bestowed upon me for this experiment and these conditions and whatever data and analysis will come from it?

Nietzsche had said there were experiments in the world, and that the failures were just as interesting, powerful, and significant as the successes. Was I longing to be one of those experiments, to be nothing more than captured data or collected results, subjected to analysis and only self-aware within the frame of it? Self-awareness —in this nightmare— is little more than an automaton spitting back the data measured by the gauge throughout its performance. I was the Geiger counter; I was the measurement of earth's radiation. I was its events emitted in time as self-describing operations. All for the sake of being seen, of being woven into the web of everything that is to be seen, and everything that can be seen. All seeing.

This web of seeing and its measurements had become object and desire. In the confusion of all these notions, in their conflation, desire itself is discovered as the pleasures in the moment. However corrupt or perverse, whichever way they came and went, they were evocative of the being-in-time. With those few lines in that email, I had been set in order. I had been told where I was to go and how I was to feel about being there. All of it was illuminated as my own doing, my own acting, and my own having been set there.

I responded to her. I did. Finally. I was nonchalant and not at all dismissive. I neither ignored what she said nor showed any great interest. I glided through it as though it were just another day between friends, an obvious stage on the way of getting to know all about each other. Who knows? I might have been right. Every relationship goes through this. Usually, we are describing ourselves to each other through our pasts. This is what I have done, and this is where I have been. The same with our sexual history and the way we slowly reveal that to each other. I know what the analyst would say. Of course, we were not talking about distant events or the remote past. She was describing events from early this morning. While these events were in the past, they were not in our past, in the time before we met, before us. It is possible she was telling me about her distant past in the only way she knew how. Time had bent and was out of joint on this Sunday, maybe this was the future for that kid in the halls of the Sunday school, or maybe it was the past of some middle-aged man who has gone on to other things and finds himself in another place. She might have been trying to find her way through the time just as I was. She might be, and maybe it is still too soon to tell whether there is a time in which those ways go side by side.

I see.

She wanted me to see something. She wanted me to know. Now, I know. The order lies deeper now and is piled higher. We are more entangled and there is more now that is me with her than there was. She may let on more in time, and it may turn out that there is more in her that is with me. These struggles with shame and desire, with pleasure and the past, if they are the mind of it, if they are what is in order, then maybe we are... maybe we will be.

April

March comes in like a lamb and goes out like a lion, or maybe it comes in like a lion and goes out like a lamb. I don't know. There are lions and there are lambs. There is coming and going.

He closes the program. He does not want to see her response. He doesn't want to get into it. Things have changed. She seems more invested somehow, but he is less so. He could not have put himself this far away, only she had been able to push him there.

He is writing code. He connects to a database, executes a command using the structured query language, extracts a tabular dataset, iterates through it, first row by row and, for each row, column by column. He uses a common control to display the results. Each line is crisp. It asserts a power over a logical structure, it operates confidently, doing what it will with what it has. In this tiny segment of space, there is an absolute clarity of intent. The minutes fly by, then the hours. It is not enough to merely make it work for the sake of an end result. He imagines the data will come from different places. In his development environment, he has two different database technologies to choose from. The code earns greater complexity as he structures it to run this way or that way based on configuration. He uses the text in a file to consume indicators for what kind of database it is, what type of connection object it must use, and the information required in its connection string. He separates the actions from each other, writes a class that can extract, that can connect, and that can decide the type of the connection. He separates the formal characteristics of each step from its material implementation. The classes take on an order and a hierarchy. He imagines an abstraction at the base of it all, he imprints a shape or interface on it, and then he derives different concrete types from the abstraction. One type for this sort of database, another type for that sort. The abstraction defines a contract for operating indiscriminately on the derived types. He writes his control code to parse the query. He makes a configuration factory to load the preferences and profile information. He uses his configuration to produce a connection. He can execute the command to get a result. He keeps going. The query itself can be further formalized. He uses the structured query language, but what if there are others? Each of the database types has different rules for how the query language must be organized and what semantics are permitted. He analyzes the query itself and then removes its form, setting it in place as an abstract type he can use to get the configuration. He applies everything he has been learning. He factors and rationalizes.

```
IQuery query = QueryParser.Parse(input);
IConfiguration configuration = ConfigurationFactory.Get(query);
IConnection connection = ConnectionFactory.Get(configuration);
IResult result = connection.Command.Execute();
```

He is lost in it when there is a knock at the door. He grumbles and goes to answer it. It is the engineer's girlfriend, and she is visibly upset. He forgets everything and comes back to where there are people and manners, where form is far more difficult to separate from content. He invites her in and returns to the place where it matters whether there is a mess visible to his visitor and whether he is presentable. He doubts both but resigns himself to having been caught in the middle of making a mess of himself and his apartment, of living there, and of having the audacity to be at work in his own place during his own time. She doesn't care. She doesn't notice. The surroundings are invisible. Whatever has possessed her to come here has taken up everything. She sits down at the dining table and absently accepts whatever it is that he just offered her. Immediately after he sets it down, she cradles the glass in her hand and pulls it close. She doesn't take a sip, but she takes the glass, and makes it a part of her. She stares at the table and the circles she is making with the glass, tipping it on its edge, holding it close, carefully. She will not spill a drop, but she will not drink anything either. She has taken on the task of standing guard over it and its contents.

"What's up?" he says as gently as he can.

"Do you have any idea where he is?"

He understands immediately and is ashamed that he never asked the engineer about this. They had been dating for a few months so he took it for granted that his departure would have included giving her notice, but he was who the professor knew him to be and had left without saying anything. That had to be it.

"He didn't tell you." It wasn't a question. He said it simply and quietly.

"Tell me what?" She wasn't crying, but the question had tears in it. She knew where the conversation was going.

"He's moved back to California."

Suddenly confronted with it, she straightened up. The certainty gave her strength and her face turned angry. The pain transformed. It surprised him. He couldn't help it. The images of the afternoon came rushing back. PainFactory.Get(); He thought. Suddenly he saw that Angry was an implementation of IPainful.

"He's a dick. Fucking asshole. Why? Will you tell me? Would you even be honest with me?"

"I've known him a long time."

"Fucking guys."

He knew it wouldn't matter. There was no confidence to betray here because there was no future where the involved parties were together. For there to be a sundering there had to be a prior union. There was nothing like that here. Need to know.

"It's not like that. It's supposed to be anonymous."

"What is?"

"He's a friend of Bill's."

"What does that mean?"

"He's an alcoholic. Things were not going well. He was on the verge of self-destruction."

She stood up. Left the glass behind. Began pacing between the kitchen and the table.

"Was I a part of that?"

"Yes." He was being as kind as honesty would allow. He knew she was ahead of him here, there was no reason to try to spare her. She probably knew more about this than he did. He tried to provide information simply, hoping she would be the one to put it together and that he wouldn't be called upon to make any grand interpretation of some deeper and insidious something or other.

"Well, that really makes me feel like shit."

"I'm sorry."

"He was drinking when I first met him, you know. I remember clearly the first time he called, and I went to his place. He offered me a beer. He had been drinking before I got there."

"I'm not surprised."

"You didn't know?"

"No. I didn't know until that night over at his place. You know, the night I walked out."

"Okay. That makes sense now. He gave me some bullshit story about why you had to go. You never said anything. He was standing right next to me when you left so I know there was no way you could have told him that you had to go. You just left when you put it together that he was drinking?"

"Yes."

"That's probably what did it. He respects you a lot. Admires you."

"I know."

"You knew it would have an effect?"

"I knew that it would have an effect. I didn't know what that effect would be though. He's my friend."

"Is? You thought that he shouldn't be mixed up with someone like me?"

"It isn't like that. Look. I don't really know you. What I know is that you meant something to him that wasn't good for him. He's an addict. Even if he wants to get well, wants to be better, he can't do it. He can't just set his mind to it. He needs help and he knows that. Well, he knew it. He let me catch him drinking so that I would have the effect that I had. Not consciously. He didn't know he was doing it. It was on purpose though."

"Do you think that he was just being more extreme? Do you think he first tried to get your attention by hooking up with me? When that didn't work, when you didn't yell at him for that, he had to take more drastic measures?"

"Could be. I don't really know."

She sat back down and went back to cradling the glass. Her voice was softer.

"Well thank you for that."

"For what?"

"For not seeing me that way. For needing a more obvious sign."

"I'm not judging you, but you must know that there is a whole set of different meanings behind what you do. It isn't just sex, and it isn't just commerce, it's a fucked-up combination. It doesn't surprise me that he has some weird ideas in his head about what all that means and what it says about him and his situation. It doesn't really have anything to do with you, with who you really are. It's all in his imagination."

"I get that. I mean, that's my job. Usually. I'm just mad that I was fooled. I'm not usually this stupid."

"Of course not. If I had to guess, I'd say you probably would rather be doing something else. He didn't fool you. Not really. Let's face it, he isn't cunning enough for that, right? You fooled yourself. That could be a good thing. You might be trying to teach yourself something."

"Teach myself?"

"Yeah. Like how he engineered this whole situation with you and drinking and having me catch him. You might have wanted to create a situation where you start to doubt your choices? I don't know. I'm talking out of my ass."

"Yeah, but you might be right. I've been thinking about that a lot lately. I want to do something different, but the money. It's hard to make that kind of money. There aren't a lot of options."

They sat quietly for a bit. She was calm. She almost seemed cheerful.

"Oh, but I'm sorry for barging in here like this. You were probably busy; I must have interrupted."

"No no, don't worry about it. It's okay. I was just writing some code for fun."

"Code? I thought you were a philosopher."

"No. Just a visiting assistant professor of philosophy. They can write in code, it's allowed." He chuckled, but she didn't quite follow, so he felt obligated to explain. "Things aren't going well. My job ends at the end of the month. I haven't found another one for next year and I'm not sure I will."

"Have you applied anywhere?"

"Hundreds of places."

"Hundreds? Really? You haven't got anything? Are there really so many people trying to get work as professors of philosophy?"

"I heard something like 9:1 this year. 9 candidates for every tenure track job. There aren't any more of those this late in the year though. Everything I'm applying for now is a temporary job."

"That sucks. What did you mean that you aren't a philosopher, that you're a visiting assistant professor of philosophy? What's the difference?"

"Well, mostly professors are like historians, I guess. We pretend to contribute sometimes, but mostly we just explain what the true philosophers are on about. Imagine a conversation that's taking place over thousands of years and there are like 300 people who are participating in it. Imagine there are these people whispering in their midst, mostly just explaining to each other what those 300 people are saying."

"Sounds pretty elitist. Shouldn't anybody be allowed to participate?"

"Well, anybody who wants to is free to listen in. It doesn't mean that they will have anything interesting to say, anything that someone else wants to hear or cares about. Most people won't be well-informed enough to know that someone made their point a thousand years ago and a bunch of people since have pointed out all the problems with it."

"I see. You really like this conversation, and you wish you had something to say, but you don't. You settle for being a historian of it and telling people about it."

"Right."

"Are you sure you want to be doing that? Wouldn't you rather do something where you can contribute?"

"There are better and worse teachers. That's a contribution."

"Oh, so are you a good teacher?"

"Not really. I'm too selfish for it. I care more about what I'm trying to get out of it than what they're getting."

"Okay, so you're not good at philosophy and you're not good at teaching philosophy. You're surprised no one wants to hire you to do it, or maybe you're not that surprised. Is that why you're writing code."

He laughs and looks genuinely pleased at her summary.

"Okay. This is going to sound stupid. Have you ever heard the phrase 'he has a calling'?"

"Sure. You mean like a priest."

"Sort of. It's the same idea. They think they're called to be priests. Something outside them is pulling them to it. They didn't choose to do it, it's like they were chosen. That's what I mean."

"Philosophy is a calling?"

"Not at all. That's my point. It isn't. I wanted it to be, but it isn't. I felt like I was being called when I started to study it years ago, back when I was twenty years old. I've never been any good at it. I pretend that I am, but I'm not. There are all these great writers who helped me do this. People who were ignored in their lifetimes and then —after they died— became recognized for what they had done. I told myself a story that my failure was a variation on that theme."

"Ah, the perfect delusion. No way to prove it wrong."

"Exactly. I entered a writing contest as an undergraduate. Very prestigious. I came in fifth place or something like that. That's probably how it is with me. I'm a near miss."

"I'm confused. You're saying you have a calling, but you're saying that philosophy isn't your calling. I guess that teaching philosophy isn't your calling either."

"Right. That's the thing about it. Everyone thinks that it's so romantic and cool. Oh, to have such passion, to be drawn to something so strongly. That should be so great, but it isn't great. You don't have any choice. Your desires don't matter, what you care about or what you are interested in doesn't matter. You are pulled by something, and you have no control over it. There's nothing you can do about it."

"Wouldn't that mean that philosophy *is* your calling?"

"No. Philosophy isn't, but something is. I can tell. I don't care if I'm happy. Happiness doesn't matter. I feel like I'm being pulled, but I don't know what's doing the pulling. This is what I mean, a calling. Being pulled like this, but by what?"

"Writing code?"

"Whatever that is, maybe. Yes. It's messed up. There's something that's going on in my brain when I write code, there's something I visualize, some order I can see and play with. It's the same thing I keep finding underneath the philosophy I study."

"You mean like logic?"

"More basic than logic, the Greeks called it logos. It's like a pattern. Like if you look closely at what you're doing when you write code, you'll see these patterns emerging. If you look closely at what you're doing when you weave together a philosophical story of some kind, you'll see the exact same patterns there too."

"What patterns?"

"This makes no sense. I realize that. The very same pattern I'm doing is the pattern I'm seeing. The pull, the calling, the dynamic of something other that calls me out of myself and into action, into discussion, into saying something, or writing something like a line of code or anything at all. Acting emits something, that something is gathered together somewhere collected together like a kind of stored up meaning, and then it all flows back into more action and more doing, it merges with that same pulling that started it all."

"Do you mean that you're seeing yourself doing what you're doing rather than actually doing it?"

"Everyone thinks I have different things to choose from, like either I can do this, or I can do that, but they aren't different things. It's one thing. This pattern that I'm talking about. I see everything that is pulling at me to make it happen. All the factors, all the generations, all the universes, the people, the experiences, every moment in time everywhere at work here in calling out to me and drawing out words or actions. It's like I'm a story being told with some new form of narration that comes from this whole pattern, or is this pattern, or something."

"It's kinda hard to follow. It doesn't make a lot of sense to me. A little, I guess, but whatever, you still have to work. You have to make a living. How will you get money?"

"Well, I applied for all these jobs. Now I'm like fuck them, that's all bullshit anyway and whatever it is that I would be doing if I were to get the dream job, it wouldn't be what I should be doing. Should I get a job writing code? I still need to learn more about that, but maybe that'll work out. I don't think I was ever cut out to be a professor. I fooled someone into hiring me here and for the last couple of years. That's luck that'll eventually run out. It is running out."

"You might be full of shit. You only say you shouldn't be a professor because no one will hire you to be one. If someone offered you a job tomorrow, you would totally change your mind. All of a sudden, it would become the most noble profession in the world. In no time you would start telling everyone that you were one of the most important people in that conversation."

"Duh, no shit. Of course, that's what I would say. I'm telling you as truthfully as I know how that I would be wrong to say it, I would be missing the whole point. I would be wrong because I would be acting like I know what I want. Like whatever I wanted was somehow crystal clear and I had absolute authority over it. You don't get to choose your desires though. They come from somewhere before you even exist. They pull you. They fabricate you."

Every moment since Thanksgiving has been the resonance of this distance. Pull. The pull of this one specific other. This is what draws him out, this is the drive from which he speaks and acts. It is himself at a distance talking back to him. He shudders.

She circled her glass again. She was back from somewhere. She had forgotten whatever it was that had hold of her when she first arrived and was now haunted by the feeling that some magical pattern was lurking out in space and waiting for her. She gulped a few sips of water from the glass.

No one is home. He showers. He shaves. He makes macaroni and cheese and sits down at the desk in the bedroom, reading over whatever is on the screen. The professor returns and catches him in the act.

"What's going on, stranger?"

"Cleaning up and refueling."

"Going back for more?"

"You know it. Just checking out your code here. Shouldn't you be writing to logs somewhere in there?"

"You mean tracing the outcomes of each of the operations?"

"Yeah, so that if something goes wrong, you'll be able to replay the tape and see what happened. What configuration did your factory produce, how did it parse your query, what connection did you get, and all that kind of stuff."

"Sure. That would be a good task for the next session."

"Man, isn't this just that sorta thing that analytic philosophers would be doing? Aren't you trying to reduce your statements to the most purely formal state possible? You're like Frege, looking for that purified language that can describe the world without bias."

"This code doesn't work that way in the least. These statements are all operational. They don't describe the world, they do things, they change things. That's why you suggested the logging, isn't it? Because the code is making changes to the state of its world and if it doesn't keep track of those changes, I won't be able to troubleshoot if something goes wrong."

"Is it completely different?"

"Completely. The language is performative. The state that it produces is invisible as it executes its function. Again, another reason for the logging you mentioned, right? Logging will make the state changes and the accomplished action visible. Anyway, keeping track of the code and the work that it does will provide good insight into what's going on. There's no comparable behavior in logic because logic isn't behavior. It has little in common with code."

"Aren't they both meant to be formal?"

"Not at all. The data that this code queries can be any data. The query that it runs can be any query. That makes you think the code is all about formality, but that's wrong. The code is just a conduit for the query and the data. The content of the code is the material execution of the query to retrieve the data. In that sense, it isn't formal at all. It's the concrete behavior being performed; it is the actual execution of a specific operation."

Wolfe slides another forkful of macaroni into his mouth and remains

staring at the screen unapologetically. The professor remains standing at
the door. Neither of them seems to think they are in the middle of a turf
war; they don't appear to be competing for access privileges to the
computer screen or the text that stretches across it. They seem to be
suggesting it is perfectly normal that Wolfe should be looking over the work
and providing his commentary.

"It's interesting," Wolfe finally breaks the silence. "The logging and the
code are ontologically different. The code is doing, and the logging would
be seeing. The code drives an operation toward an end and the logging
commits the result to view, it might show the state of the relevant things
before the action began and then show it again after the action completes.
The logging is there for forensic analysis, right? That's what debugging is,
right? The operational code is doing the work. These are distinct."

"Distinct, but as you said, they both need to be there in order to make
sure the code is doing what it's supposed to do."

"It needs to be there only if someone cares that the code is doing what
it's supposed to be doing."

"That's true. When there is any normative implication for the code's
execution, there would have to be some form of surveillance. As soon as
we assert that there is some presumed outcome from the action, we have
to impose the surveillance operation to make sure that outcome was
achieved. Otherwise, we'd be blind to what's going on in the operations.
We'd have no idea if the desired ends were served."

"The light of reason is grouped together with the logging operation, I
should think. Analysis of the operation, what we do when we practice
forensics, that will always be applied to the logging results, not the results
of the actual operation."

"What's the difference?"

"I see. From the forensic point of view, there is none. We have
uncovered a difference."

"Yes. Logging is an operation. It's the act of writing to the log. Writing
to the log is not the same thing as having the outcome of an action visible
before you as the content of a written log."

Takes another bite. Wolfe stares back at the screen. "You think this is
the whole of it? This is the crucial heartbeat? You've trapped it? Summed
it up? This turn from the one to the other. This emphasis that you blame
on the new science and its theoretical look at things, its way of reducing the
operational content out of the event for the sake of emphasizing the trail it
left behind."

"Well, I don't think it makes sense to talk about means and ends, for
example, until you have performed this turn. The operation is integral to
what it operates upon, to its starting conditions, and to its results. It acts.
Only the steps of analysis can break out rational pieces and components.

Turn this into the actor and that into the means and the ends. These categories of the event are themselves part of the forensic analysis, which is itself an operation, the logging operation."

"This is the key required for decoding what the code says?"

"No. This is the way we come to know that we are always walking a path. It may not be the path that we think we are on, but we are walking some path, there is some doing that is being done. There can never be a pure seeing."

"You think this ontology of practice that comes out in code is itself an ethical and political orientation?"

"It could be. Ethical and political discussions don't always reflect on this facet. When we deliberate on the right thing to do, or the right decision to make, we're doing something different, we're applying our cognitive capabilities to something of a distinct kind that is already detached or abstracted from the things we work with when we act and operate on the world."

"A proper polis or ethos wouldn't involve that kind of analysis?"

"I don't know about that. Analysis can permit all kinds of extraneous concerns to enter into the deliberations though. In whatever way our minds have been trained to apply categories and dissect component parts from concrete events, these ways will inject themselves into any and all deliberations. This is the role of ideology in sorting things out. It's why we can't ever look away from our ways of seeing. We must see with our own eyes, and we must base our theories on what we see."

"Each of these twists and turns are acts?"

"Yes. Like any action, we've been trained in how to do them. We've learned what to do, what steps to take, what counts as legitimate advancement, and what doesn't."

"Pure analysis isn't pure, it's a procedure or a practice that has a tradition, it has rules, there is training involved, there is a specific schema that it's based on. Is that what you're saying? The objects of our sight are subject to our disciplinary measures, to the ways we have been trained to see and infer. How convenient for you that this all turns out to be a critical cognitive practice rather than something like carpentry or plumbing."

Same thing over and over again. They go round and round. The repetition increases their confidence. The more places they find this perspective, the more it looks like a rudimentary pattern. The more it looks like a rudimentary pattern, the more they poke at it and hammer on it, trying to find it everywhere in everything.

"I didn't tell you. The engineer's girlfriend came by the other day. Turns out, he left town without saying anything to her. He just disappeared."

"Figures."

"Yeah. She was pretty upset. She hung out a bit. We talked. She didn't ask how to get ahold of him. I didn't offer."

"Cleaned up his mess, did you? I don't know how you do it. When you were talking to her, was it for real or were you just playing?"

"What do you mean? What are you accusing me of?"

"I guess I'm still on the first topic. How did you see her, is my question? Was she just an opportunity to locate a recurrence of some pattern? Something else? What was your level of involvement in the conversation?"

"I see. Yes, that's probably an issue. True empathy has to be absorbed in the situation, in the conditions and circumstances. I felt bad for her. I tried to be empathetic like that, but there was a strong tendency to avoid it. If that's what you're getting at. I saw points of contact with other things. I noticed a pattern at work and told her a story suggesting we have to discover our desires; we don't immediately know what they are."

"Did that disrupt empathy?"

"I hope not. I don't think so. It's complicated. At one level, I was trying to be human, but on the other hand I was processing the information and trying to think of connections and meaningful associations that might be linked to what she was going through."

"It's because of how language works. If you think she's describing something to you when she says this and that, you're likely to try to associate that description with others and draw categorical relations. You'll build up relationships based on those attributes. When this or that is present, then this or that association can be made."

"It's like daydreaming almost. You think the words are the point and that the words are constructing an image. Rationally, that's what matters."

"If the words are just like fingers or a touch or however you would say that, then there's something else happening. Reason doesn't matter. She isn't trying to describe her emotional pain, she's exhibiting it, demonstrating it to you. Your response, if it were to remain in kind without inserting this distance between you, it would have to be a kind of touching too. Whatever you said wouldn't matter so long as it exhibits something like 'it's okay, you matter, and he didn't appreciate you, this will pass.'"

"Probably if she caught it from too much distance, like it was treating her feelings as if they were data for some theory, she would have been seriously pissed-off. She would have walked out or abruptly prevented me from going on like that."

"Well maybe, but she would definitely notice. We pick up on this distance in the language we use with each other. It may not set everyone off in the same way, but it has an impact, and that determines whether we think someone is truly sympathetic or just toying with us, treating it like a game."

"A puzzle to be analyzed."

Wolfe scooped the last bit of macaroni from the bowl, then stood up and moved past the professor and out of the room. He went to the kitchen and cleaned the bowl in the sink. The professor wandered back out and sat down at the table. He took out a cigarette and lit it, then handed the box to Wolfe who lit one and sat down across from him.

"People don't say everything they mean. They talk about shit that doesn't matter. They're saying something different. They aren't saying this or that happened to me. They're saying I want to be with you here and I want you to know me."

"I want you to know me. I want you to know this about me. Why? Where does the pull for that come from? Why are we the kind of creatures that feel compelled to tell each other trivial details about ourselves?"

"Like you should know me the way I am when I am alone. When I am with others who are far closer to me than you have yet become."

"The exhibitionist urge, you think it's strong?"

"It's the same pull that others have on us in all kinds of ways. Imagine that all these social associations we make throughout our lives are a kind of deposit. This behavior or that one, this way of thinking or some other. As we grow up and as we learn from others, these structures and these heuristic patterns, these subroutines, are periodically inserted and reinforced. They are constructed in such a way that they will —over time— call back to the thing that inserted them. They have this messaging capability built into them so that, as they grow and develop within each of us as character traits endowed with a feature, they must report the state change back to their creator, back to the source of origin that inserted them in the first place."

"That's seriously dark. The social practices that build and shape us, they have a logging mechanism built into them. They are preprogrammed to emit information about state changes that have taken place from their application."

"Yeah. Whatever it is, that it is and how it is, it emits measurable events. To be is to emit events. To be is to collect and gather emitted events from all sources. To be is to analyze collected events, to compute and to calculate. To be is to feedback results of analytics into the further emission of events. A state machine. One of the most common preprogrammed operations is the periodic emission of trivial details."

"Why though? What is the advantage of having these trivial details shared? Why do we benefit from this, why does the underlying order require it?"

"Well, imagine that there's tension between the acting individual and the aggregate. The insertion is done for the sake of the aggregate, but it has been inserted into an individual agent. The maneuver is classically Hegelian. The details are only rational in the aggregate as the computed behavior of the population in terms of specific qualities and characteristics shared between members. These qualities and characteristics drive the aggregate operations. In order to do all that, they have to be actualized, they have to become action components. That means they have to be part of individual actions where the acting individual is specifically a member of the population at large."

"The whole point of the callback is to legitimize the pull where the pull is not only what draws out the emission, but what put it there in the first place."

"You wind the clock and then you listen and record the tick tock that it makes as it unwinds."

"That's how you know the clock. The aggregate and universal rules of the operation of clocks are known through the emissions exhumed from time-keeping behaviors. Those behaviors and the deviations and misfires that they may include are tabulated, summarized, and then this provides the overall view of how the clock works. Knowledge is this reflective procedure that injects by hypothesis these operative capabilities and then observes the output, gauging it alongside all the various experimental additions and variations that were similarly injected and observed. That's how you discover the rules and patterns of its generalized operation."

"Okay. Suppose we're right about this. Just for the sake of argument. What does it say about the basic principles of liberalism that have grown alongside these methodological principles?"

"You mean whether the scientific methodology that adds up to this social pull we're describing is nothing other than the commonwealth of human beings, civil society? The aggregate mechanism extraordinaire."

"The very covenant by which we live in common. The new science and the liberal democracy with its social contract are side-by-side structures of a socio-historical determination."

"Hobbes is unapologetically correct in asserting that coercion is the point. It's not an arbitrary side effect, it's the purpose. The coercion isn't just the application of an external force, it's this pull that we're describing, this internal force that surfaces as the ego, as the person who wants and thinks, then deliberates and sorts out the order of operations before performing them. It's not that we seek general utility, rather 'the common good' fabricates us through an application of force. The moral order is social, but the decision-making is individual. Morality is how an organizational order is imposed on the individual actor."

"Well, that part isn't Hobbes."

"It could be but mixed with Spinoza maybe. Those implicit natural laws show what our original position must be, what we are capable of when it comes to adaptation and shaping ourselves to the common orientation, to the pull of our agreements, the social leviathan that rules over us. We are not exactly or fully blank slates to him. We have capabilities that make it possible to enter into collective agreements. General utility can drive everything insofar as it's the origin of those capabilities."

"This might explain why money works so well in the way Simmel describes it. How it can be this universal measuring device that reduces all things to the same form of commerce. The spontaneity of the organism can be expressed merely as acquisitiveness."

"The pull of the social is already there to perform the reduction, to make the assertion that all things are on a par because all things have this original social source and have been inserted for the sake of the pull they will perform later. A capability is just an individuated expression of that social phenomenon interleaved with physiology. Once social relations are present, it's simple for some common measuring device to be applied to the organism in their midst. All action orientation, all behavior, is reducible to the same terms of involvement. This is worth x units, that is worth y. Everything is comparable, everything can be reduced to quantitative terms and be compared with simple greater than or equal to logic."

"Which is exactly the description we get from Arendt. Once everything has been reduced to this quantitative set of associations pulled from us in aggregate fashion, thinking —as it was classically understood— is lost. Public action —as it was previously known— is gone."

"We become automatons instead of autonomous beings. Mere acquisitiveness. There is a whole weird kettle logic of problems here. From the one side, you might suggest that we were never autonomous to begin with, that this was always a ploy to flatter the parties to the contract. On the other hand, we could only succumb to the pull of automation if we were capable of spontaneous operations in the first place. Meaning, we could only be corrupted if we had a prior state of autonomy. Only what stands alone can be made to stand together."

The light from outside was beginning to fade. They stared at the table and kept their hands busy. Wolfe played with the pack of cigarettes, the professor with the ashtray. It was nearing darkness and there was no sound save the light crackling of the cellophane paper on the packet of cigarettes and the glass of the ashtray circling against the wood of the table. Wolfe took up the lighter and held it between his fingers an inch above the table, then let it drop. It thwacked against the tabletop. He repeated the sequence.

"It's the chicken and the egg."

"That's the point. Deliberate analysis leads to a dead end. There's no way for the individuated thinker to sort it all out without running into these problems. All of it is for the sake of making it seem as if action were impossible. There's nothing to be done. Nothing intentional that can be done, at least. We can't organize or come up with a plan. These efforts will always be pulled in the way they were designed to be, they will be part and parcel of that same coercion that we're trying to think our way past. Action becomes impossible unless it is conceived to contribute to general utility or however you want to describe the aggregate mechanism."

"Whatever we do, we will be carrying out the agenda of something that is working hard to pull that very agenda out from inside of us. It has been inserted there specifically for this purpose. Organizations don't rob us of individuality, they teach us to believe in it -and desire it— as a ruse to get their work done."

"The way to achieve the break then, the way to resist the pull, might be to stop all action."

"Stop doing anything? Just withdraw consent."

"That's right. Things start breaking. Everything would break. The aftermath of this would be a new pull, it would lead us in different directions. This sorting out would still be an organizational form though. It would amount to a renewed injection and extraction but wouldn't have its basis in what had been pulling us before. It would be brand new."

"That wouldn't make it good."

"Of course not."

"What would be the point?"

"It would be its own point. Remember, it would be the highest achievement to say that we never made it beyond good and evil."

"Good and evil?"

"Yes, we would be right there, right on the precipice of it. We would be forced to think it through, to figure it all out without the benefit of the dying order."

"To get to that point, there would be enormous suffering and hardship."

"True, you can't break the old order without it."

"People don't have the stomach for that. They would never do it. It would be cruel to try."

"That may be, but it's none of my concern. I only meant to say that this would be the necessary ingredient for putting ourselves before the pearly gates, the passageway opening into the distinction between good and evil, the new apple, the new knowledge. This is what it would take."

"Well, it's like what we said before. If these words are fingers, then they have nothing to touch. There is nothing pulling us this way. We could not bear it."

"We don't have to bear it. Desire and endurance, emotions of any kind according to this theory, can only happen in the aggregate. How we feel about it will come in the process. Good and evil are only available through an order and an order is always an offshoot of organization, meaning a collective and aggregate orientation. If we cannot bear it, it will only be because the old order is still there, still working its effects upon us as a measuring rod for comparison."

"Well, say it however you like. I can't see any way to get there from here. It might as well be on the other side of the universe. I doubt anything like it has ever happened. It would be a truly anomalous event."

"Exactly. It would be an unmeasured and unmeasurable event."

What remains is that human beings can only value through coercion, as a mass, collectively. Good and evil cannot mean anything to this or that one, but only to them and those others. They are quiet again. The volume is overwhelming. The values of the table, the ashtray, and the lighter paint the air between them. They look at each other and they look away together, secretly wondering what the other is really worth.

It takes a paragraph to find a sentence. Each one, making the process so inefficient. Such luxury in this writer's life. Imagine the fat that must have surrounded Wittgenstein's *Tractatus*. We don't have to imagine it, of course, it's there in the commentary. Those commentators would argue with me. Such fatigue. I heard or read a story once that Deleuze had been invited to write a paper on Nietzsche. This was not long before he died. Apparently, he turned it down saying that he just didn't have the energy for it anymore. Writing about Nietzsche, I guess, took too much out of him. This story changed my whole way of thinking about Deleuze. From then on, I always thought kindly of him. True to his wishes, I vowed never to argue with him. We may not always agree, but we don't argue. When we come to an impasse, we just move on. There is always something else to talk about. What does the arguing get you anyway?

The premise is that philosophy is somehow bound up with the structure of reason. Reason is syllogistic, it is the capacity to go beyond mere sensation and perform inferences. Given such a structure, reason is itself responsible for constructing arguments. They take you beyond wherever it is that you find yourself. Here is what is given. Some one of this and some other of that. There are rules and the two things may be entangled and intertwined. Because of these entanglements, we can jettison ourselves beyond what is merely there in this or that and move on to some third thing, constructing complexity out of simpler ingredients. This moving on is the inference and the pattern of this movement is reason. The pattern is supposed to be the innate construct of the human cognitive capacity as such. Nature's beloved, we are endowed with this and able to make new worlds and stride forward into uncharted territory. There are disagreements. We accuse each other of fallacies, we suspect we have not thought through the hidden premises or the counter conditions. A single thinker can come to odds within their own mind over these variations and differences. We become divided within ourselves. The division takes on an external significance. It becomes public and other parties get involved. This thinker no longer alone with their thoughts now comes to blows with another. They feign a false intimacy to allow this entanglement. They appeal to higher authority, the very schematics of reason itself, each claiming an eternal judge finding in their favor. Camps form, factions. The opposition gains spectators puzzling through the maneuvers and working diligently to make up their minds. They become a chorus and then an audience. A wave, a paradigm, and a mass movement.

Naming complex things, naming something with a history, is always something of a mystifying process. The ones who argue are so confident in their conjuring. Suddenly I recall all the occasions of my unearned power drawn from the syntax of inference. Where does this compulsion come from and where can it lead? Why should we grasp something here and there and immediately wish to move on, to extract some conclusion from it, reducing an extraordinary moment to a mere premise solely there for the sake of where we hope to go and what we intend to achieve? "To the things themselves," was always a rallying cry to get behind the movement itself, to defer its motion for the sake of what was proposed at the outset. Underline 'to' and not 'things.' How can I move on when I do not yet know what that is which stands before me? When I can't process it save through the categories that come to me from my teachers and their lesson plans? The premises themselves may have been prepackaged for my consumption making the argument a gift for which I must be thankful. These are the arguments significant to those like us in times like these. Here you go. They are written on the syllabus and addressed by each of the authors in the reading list. Here is my hand, what argument will it make? What inferences can it permit? Is it a premise for my mind or is it the conclusion of my arm?

Like means and ends, the argument feels like an imposition. Things don't argue. The combat that lies within them is put there. If that is the case, then it suggests that the creatures who argue are the kinds of creatures who put themselves into things. If they can do that, then isn't it fair to propose that there might just be a thing independent of this putting? It is toward that which we aim. In the aiming, it becomes fair to ask whether even that pure thing is itself the product of the putting and of the asking, of the being fair and of the working through. Who is convinced by all this? Are we convinced, were we ever? Only someone driven to learn these rules would finally arrive at a condition where they can be effective in turning them one way rather than another. Why would someone be so driven? Where does this drive come from? Where does it go? If I hazard a guess and if I mumble my fantasy aloud, how does that constitute an invitation to challenge, an introduction to argument?

Yes, yes, I know the dance, I know how it goes. There is a fact, there is truth. My guess is likely nonsense or partially so. Let's tease it out, let's pull it this way and that. Let's find everything that lies within it that is not so given. Here, look at that hidden inference. You see a chair and imagine its back. You heard a sound and invoked a visual of trees blowing in the wind. You constantly move beyond what is there so much so that we can identify the act of moving beyond. This too will be challenged, for it cannot be tolerated as a tale told by an idiot. It must make a claim, it does make a claim. Because of that, it must hold up to scrutiny and be torn down and cast aside if it does not. There is power in argument, and argument is itself the flex of power. There it is again. An assertion assignable with a truth value. My thoughts can never be my own because they are always subject to criteria, they are always fit for analysis and examination. What evidence do I have for them? What proof? You say the purpose of this reason is to liberate us from the chains of capricious force, to permit us this enlightenment and the mastery over physical nature that it provides. All I get from it is paralysis. None of my reasons are good enough, none of my conclusions have merit, none of my insights hold up as premises for some further notion. In a world of arguments and the faculty of reason that they surface, each of us is always wrong or about to be.

Such fatigue. I'm sorry you had a bad day. If you won't accept a foot massage, I could sing you a song. A ballad about a shepherd girl disappointed to learn that she is in business with sheep.

It is a response to complaints about the expectations of library patrons. They come looking for knowledge and think of it no differently than some toiletry they need from the drug store. "Can you show me where I can find analysis and insight on the colonization of West Africa and its lasting effects on the continent and the colonizers?" "Alas, I cannot. I would be happy to print off a list of books and media that might help *you* to find them." My responses have become shorter. I tend to gesture toward what I might say rather than saying it as I once did. Now I lay claim to the advantages created by my previous actions. She knows what lies within my power to say and not to say. Rather than continuing to evoke and elicit sentiment with whatever means I have available, I merely point at the possibility that I might do so. As though it were a foot massage or a bottle of beer that I might open and hand over just when she needs it. When you have established a rapport, you have shown what can be done, what you can do under various conditions and circumstances. Once you have done this, you needn't overplay yourself, you needn't go back again and again. Rather there is the leverage of invisible signs, there is the unuttered, and what has been held back.

I don't know where this confidence comes from. I don't know how it even came to have its name. No person would ever characterize themselves this way since the mood itself is invisible, caught up completely in whatever lies in view and remains the focus. Only a reflective party, disjointed from the act, could apply this label to it. This is why it is so easy to question whether any displayed bravado is earned or merited. A young man at a wedding saunters across the room and asks a young woman to dance. He doesn't doubt himself; he knows she will accept. She does. Because she sees it too. Her friend who watched the whole thing unfold; she doesn't doubt it either. She hates him for it, she desires him for it. She can't make up her mind. Her anger is envious and guilty.

There has been a change of late. I used to write two or three messages for each one I would receive in return. Not that she was reluctant, but that I was quicker. I had more on my mind, more that needed to be said. Lately, this has been reversed. Now, she was saying more, she was writing more, and I was becoming the respondent as she had been in the beginning. The reversal had become clear in the days following that Sunday morning when she told me... When she showed me... Well, that Sunday morning. It had been a major blow, but it had also been an act of genius. Sex was on the table, as they say. The back and forth that followed included numerous suggestions and innuendos to that effect. Sex on the table or wherever else that might be convenient when the desire struck. The point was that she had revealed herself and encouraged me to respond in kind. She wasn't saying this is where I am going and you cannot come along, she had suggested a direction, she had laid out a plan, a set of purposes, and showed me the pathways and the circuitous routes that were involved. None of it was explicit. There was no need to argue or explain. We didn't even try. It was a subtle and significant test. She must have thought that it was possible for me to go off in the wrong direction, to respond with jealousy (which would have been honest) or with pain (which would have been true), but she would have hoped it was possible to see through all of that and carry on.

It wasn't that I was holding back. Wolfe had accused me of that. He said I was her doormat and that I was letting her hurt me, complicitly taking it. I disagreed. Vehemently. That story did not describe what I was experiencing. His take did not resonate. I don't know why I immediately understood that her revelation was an act of extreme intimacy that wasn't in the least bit friendly, but I did. I knew that she was trying to show me that the erotic undertones of some of what I had said before could come out from underneath and become straight and clear as our central thesis. She was explaining herself to me and I didn't read the message as an ending, I digested it and felt it as instigation, flirtatious, but twisted. I'm well aware of that. Nothing had proceeded in ordinary form, and this turn least of all. This twist was us twisting around each other, a suggestion of intertwining. She was changing while I was too, and things were changing between us. She did not know what to say to make this happen. She would not have been able to reason through it. Nor would I have been. The months of messages flying back and forth had, in a sense, been exactly that. The struggle to find a way to say this or that, a search for a reason, or an explanation. A way to make something come out into the open so that it could become a topic of conversation. These flights and flings were a search for their own argument, their own reason and event. People don't work that way, they can't infer their moods, their attractions, and their lust. They have to feel these things and then these feelings can lead us along through words and signposts. Signaling twists and turns, sending us backward and forward until we find the way to say this or that, find the way to mean it, and find something like recognition in the listener to confirm they have heard what we were trying to say.

You say I am pushing and pulling, but I feel you pushing and pulling too. You had some nerve invading my privacy like you did. Now what else are you planning on invading with these songs of yours? I am fascinated with email, it is true, but never did I imagine that it could be a balcony and the moonlight that shines on it.

She is teasing me. She teases herself. There is teasing. She will have read this back both before and after sending it. Imagining that she is me reading it. These are common themes of late. She thinks of me as an invader, I'm sure. She accuses me of it like this. Without charge. Her desires and her interests, she said, were her own. She had perfect control and was moving down the exact road she wanted to be on. How dare I interrupt her? Everything that ever happens to us is such an invasion. In some ways, to an extent, it is part of our youthful adventurousness to seek out these possibilities. Experience is an invasion. We hope for the best but are not always so lucky. Rigid and rightful, we are brittle and almost nearly broken. We depend so much on kindness and find so little of it. We hope for it and likely give each other the benefit of the doubt in the beginning. This is itself an act of kindness. I know she cares about her privacy, and I know she is serious in her sense that her feelings originate in something that has encroached upon it. What does the television commercial hope to achieve if not that? My choice in underarm deodorant must surely be my own, how dare they try to get between me and my favorite brand? They work diligently with their language and their images, trying to incite my desire, to migrate it from wherever it was to wherever they want it to be. She accuses me of transforming her into a shopper in this same fashion with these same arguments, stimulating her interest, appealing to her vanity, and calling out to her desire, hoping to draw all of it into a swirl of action focusing on each other and bound by a blindness to its conditions and its causes.

Your mind alights too much on pushing and pulling. Where have I taken hold? What delights are you denying yourself? What pleasures are you holding on to in silence? You say you are pushing only because you are being pulled and I say that I am pulling only because I am being pushed.

Can you feel the rhythm? It's there in your breath. That's my breath. It's there in your chest and in your heartbeat. That's my heartbeat.

I turn off the computer. I can't bear the back and the forth, I can't stomach the pushing and the pulling. However erotic it may be, whatever nerves we may touch, it is exhausting, and I am spent. For nearly six months it has been going on like this. Sometimes more in my head and maybe sometimes more in hers. What strange things these human beings do to each other when conducting the experiments of their lives. Even with the best of intentions, there can be torment. People who love each other know best how to hurt each other. People who are the object of desire, but who refuse to remain that way, can feel the ease with which the other's organs can be plucked and squished. None of it mechanical. None of it written out as destiny, but all of it glowing under the starlight.

While walking back from the little convenience store on Plymouth, I run into my upstairs neighbor. She was dressed up and on her way out. I almost didn't recognize her. It reminded me of a time in Norway when I spent an hour talking to this really cool young woman who was at the same youth hostel. We had a great conversation about all sorts of things, art and literature. We ended reluctantly but then happened to be on the same bus later that evening. She had changed her clothes and done her hair and makeup. I didn't recognize her. She tried to talk to me on the bus, she would have liked it if I suggested I join her in going wherever she was headed. I had lost interest. Something about her didn't seem right. The way she was dressed up for a night out, it didn't seem to fit with the person I had been talking to a short while before. Where had she gone? Where was that interesting person with a clear and vibrant perspective? Why had she become a doll out for a night of drinking and dancing? My neighbor struck me this same way. Many questions came to mind. Where is her kid? Where is she going? Why is she like that? Is it something she has to do, are these customs and practices that we are obligated to follow if we want to experience specific kinds of public events?

I wouldn't be able to ask her any of these things. I wouldn't be able to bring her to the place where I had come to think of them without insulting her. She is genuinely nice so there is no reason for it. In that moment, on the sidewalk, seeing her and not seeing her. Knowing that must be my neighbor and not recognizing her, I could feel a new conflict between how much to say and how much to keep quiet. I couldn't help but wonder if this conflict was an argument. Before I managed to parse it all out, to identify the premises and the conclusion and whatever rules of inference were involved in getting me from the one to the other, she interrupted me. Invaded the privacy of my thoughts and spoke to me in her sunny way. She is so cheerful. Such a nice person.

I could have guessed what she would say. Hello. How are you. Yes, I am going out. Dinner and drinks with some friends. All easily anticipated. It always hits me so hard, these ordinary exchanges. Especially when I am reeling, thinking about why I don't recognize her, thinking about all the questions that I have that I can't ask because I don't trust myself to do it without causing harm. She's probably perceptive, she likely picks up on this weird absence, this distance that my hesitation brings. She offers me something. It comes in the form of questions.

"I haven't seen any of the usual suspects in a while. Is everything okay?"

The engineer is gone. That must be what she means. He would stop by regularly and she noticed the change. Probably not in a creepy way, it's just that she lives right upstairs with her daughter. She has to pay attention to the comings and goings in the neighborhood. She has noticed an absence. He's not coming around anymore. She may not have seen Wolfe much either. He's been gone most of the time the last couple months. He is working, but even when he isn't, he's been spending more and more time with the typesetter. She looks out her window and sees not-Wolfe and not-engineer. What can I say? I explain as simply as I can. It turns out she is just making neighborly conversation. There is no reason to go too deeply here, her not-seeing has been casual. The engineer and I still talk on the phone. I see Wolfe all the time down at the café or the diner. We just went to the deli for lunch the other day. She can't see any of that, so does she need to know it? She doesn't seem to be judging me and says goodnight as she gets in her car. She wishes me well and says she hopes I am not getting lonely or bored now that I'm spending so much time alone. She urges me to come for dinner some time.

The invitation isn't the offering I was referring to. It's her remark about loneliness and boredom. It strikes me. I cannot remember getting bored or lonely. I can't remember being bored. I struggle with the thought. I recall going to the dentist. No, never bored at the dentist. Waiting for trains? Spending days in the airport? Travelling for months by myself? Nope. Why not? Well, you can always think about stuff. There is always something to think about. Even if you don't have your book, even if you don't have anyone to talk to. Even if there is nothing entertaining happening anywhere near you, you can always occupy yourself somehow. I couldn't stop thinking about it. Is it a character flaw? A pathological attribute? It is entirely possible that this failure prevents me from having certain kinds of experience. There are things in this world that can only be understood if you feel their impact. The deeper meaning of loneliness, the meaning of boredom, could only be accessible to someone with the capacity for those feelings. If that is what they were. They might be so much more than that. They might be existential cues indicating our place in the universe, our relationship to each other and to time itself. A failure to feel these things might have been due to a failure to be the kind of thing that can be this way.

She made this offering because she can recall being bored and she can recall being lonely. She reached out; she felt the possibility of having a need. Empathy drove her. Pushed her. My remarks pulled her. The push and the pull were only possible if we shared something. If I couldn't feel these things, then there could be no shared experience of them. They weren't indicators of conflict even if they were conflict itself. The conflict sat on top of something. Only connected beings could find themselves at odds with each other. The precondition for any agreement or disagreement is an underlying shared experience or understanding.

Of course, I wasn't thinking about my neighbor anymore. I was thinking about Deleuze and why he couldn't argue about that stuff that was so important to him. What couldn't he share with those people who claimed to be his colleagues? What thing did they have in common that he didn't have? Did he leap? Did his pain throw him? In the former case, he was alone when he died. In the latter, he was with his pain. If boredom or loneliness are instigators, if they are gremlins, then they are toying with you, playing with you, and it is boredom itself which stays there with you and prevents you from becoming bored. How can I be lonely if I have my loneliness to talk to? I felt so far away from the living. From those that were close by, from the neighbor. Not from her though, the sender and the recipient. Her distance was salvation, the spread of time as reconciliation. It was like the line from that poem a certain someone gave me back in college: "The harder you pull, the wider I get." Yes, maybe I am starting to learn what that might mean. What it could mean. In some cases, the power of what we can share with another is only clear to us when we find that it's missing from other relationships. If I were to wait for her and she were not to come, then I would discover boredom. If I were to be without her for a stretch of time, then I would know loneliness.

She calls them "little guys" and they come in all shapes and sizes. What they have in common is that they usually swagger up to the desk. They are somewhere between 18 and 22, and they never expect you to be anything but nice and helpful. They know you will look at them in a certain way, you will be friendly with them, and you will do whatever you can to be of assistance. They don't expect anything else. Young. Attractive. Confident. They don't have to be college boys, just of that age. Of course, the guitar player was a little guy back in the day. He still is in some ways. The professor's friend was definitely a little guy, although she isn't sure about the professor. She comes across them almost every day. They come up to the desk with their little pieces of paper and they look at you long enough to let you know exactly what they expect; that they know you will welcome them, and that you will tell them exactly what they need to know. They ask their question while looking down at the paper and then they always look up with a sort of pleading. Like, you know the drill, here is what I need, and you have got to help me with it, you have got to find this for me. I've always counted on the kindness of strangers.

She knows that some of the others that she's worked with during the year fall for this. They swoon in their way and give the little guys exactly what they want. Smiling, they are as accommodating as can be. She's even seen experienced reference librarians giggle at some of their half-assed pseudo suave attempts at saying something both grateful and provocative once they've gotten what they came for. She doesn't take this approach. She questions them, puts them off guard, looks right back at them with authority, beginning right from the outset to direct their actions. She isn't going to give them what they need, she is going to tell them what they have to do. In order to do that properly, she has to ask them what they have done already. This always puts them off their guard. They didn't know what to do so they haven't done anything. Okay well, this is a library, and I'm going to explain how you use a library. See those machines over there, those computers are terminals connected to the entire catalogue for all the libraries at the university. You can run your own searches there to find the things you need when you already have a set of criteria in mind. Have you thought clearly about what you are looking for? What search terms do you think will describe that? If they haven't done any of this, they might become self-conscious and mutter an explanation as to why they haven't done anything to help themselves before coming to the librarian.

She has decided that it is her mission to change this behavior, to show them that they shouldn't just write down the thesis of the paper that they have to write. They can't just stroll up to the desk and show their little paper to the librarian sitting there and then expect her to print out a list of books for them to get. Are they children who only need to find one or two sources in the encyclopedia so they can regurgitate the material? She wants to teach them some of the most primitive rules of research, about how one outlines work as part of a quest for information and the process required to dig it up and digest it when producing a reasonably well-informed paper on the subject. She is just doing her job. The fact that she enjoys seeing the change come over their faces as they realize that they can't just get away with it the easy way, that they are going to have to do work, that this chick behind the counter isn't just going to take hold of their hand and lead them around in the way they have come to expect. She is giving them a task list and sending them off to do it. Their high cheekbones seem to sink when they realize how much effort it will take to grapple with the organizational questions. They must digest different approaches and correlate them to produce an analysis that ultimately provides a conclusion that makes sense of it all, strings it all together, and says something intelligent. She enjoys the looks of hesitation they give as they turn away from the desk and head off toward the shelves. They don't hesitate because they are uncertain of what to do, that is clear, they hesitate because they can't believe the encounter has ended without that warm and fuzzy touch that reassures them that everything is going to be okay.

Every now and then there is a little guy who can't be led this way. She doesn't know what freak mutation of nature causes some of them to turn out like that, to be so difficult to control with instructions and reprisals, but the ones who fall into this difficult category are usually dressed in a similar fashion. The collared shirts. Very common. Nicer shoes than the average student. She doesn't like to generalize, but she suspects that they share the trait of having wealthy parents. They don't just feel the entitlement of their looks and appearance, this is something more than that. They have the added entitlement of money. There are plenty of boys with those advantages who aren't little guys themselves. They are the ones who are a little more awkward, a little less confident when talking to women, but still have all the entitlement.

When the two types come together in one person, however, that yields a perfect storm of unpleasantness. They have too much going for them, and they don't react well to being told what to do, especially when it comes from someone who they don't think has the right to issue commands. They —meaning, she— should do their job and take care of what they are supposed to take care of. He doesn't have time for this, whatever she thinks this might be, whatever lesson she thinks she is imparting, she needs to save that for the rest of them, for the herd that doesn't already have a clear sense of how their time is going to be spent over the next several hours. Running around and doing a librarian's job is not part of the plan.

There was one of those that day and he had upset her more than usual. He was exceptionally good looking. Well built, having clearly spent time in the gym. He was aware of his physical presence and the impact it had. He leaned on the desk in a way that made her feel like he was towering over her. He did this emphatically while telling her that he didn't come to her for help on how to use the computers. It isn't accidental, this effort at being intimidating. He knows. The effects of his size are no different than the effects of his appearance as far as he is concerned. Over time he has learned what to expect. Especially when talking to women who are supposed to provide him with a service. He lets them know that he understands this and he, with his lean and his look, lets her know that she better understand it too.

It's a tough position for her to be in, because at some level he is right. It is her job in a way, but it is a university too, and so it is also her job to teach her patrons so that they can do it for themselves. People who rely on the librarian too much will always be saddled with limitations. Their work will suffer since the librarian can't write their paper for them. If they don't have a sense of what the scope of work is that goes into producing proper results in whatever class they're taking, then they will never get very far in their education. She knows she has to do her job, but she also knows that the parameters are flexible. She suffers from being reasonable and can usually tell right away whether her role is supplemental or whether she is being asked to do all of their work. At the graduate library, it's usually much simpler than this. At the undergraduate library, you get a much wider range of experience and ability. This little guy was telling her to back off from trying to teach him anything. He was in control of that and wasn't going to cede any of it to her. He may not have said the words "dumb bitch," but she felt them, and she boiled inside as she did the bare minimum to help him.

Afterward, she was immediately struck by the urge to tell the professor all about it. What the little guy had dared to say to her, how she responded, and how she wished she had responded. After she wrote him a quick email to let him know about it, as though it were happening in real time and he was a fly on the wall, she wondered why she was doing it. In the last couple of weeks, it had become a strong sense. Stronger than it had ever been. She wanted to tell him everything. The explanations and descriptions, it was as though they were being pulled out of her. She couldn't help it. Something would happen and it would immediately come into her mind that he would have something to say about it, he would think it was interesting, or might have lots of questions about what that meant or why she thought of it that way, whatever the issue might be.

More and more she was imagining his reaction to the things that she did or saw. The conversations in her kitchen were becoming more frequent. She even caught him lying next to her in bed sometimes. She sent messages setting up the situation, describing events, and if he didn't reply right away, she might send another to clarify, to add some additional thought she had as she was playing out the topics in her mind once she thought about what he might say in response. She knew that she was getting more familiar with the way he felt back in the first few months when they first started exchanging messages. He used to do this all the time. He would send her something and before she had a chance to reply he would send something else that added some additional details or anticipated her response. She was learning that he was probably imagining her reaction to the first message, or he was thinking about what he had told her as though he were imagining her point of view. His follow up was addressing some dialogue he was having with himself while imagining what she would say on her end of the exchange. She thought it was cute at the time. Endearing in a way. Now that she was going through it herself, she could feel what had been hidden inside it.

The thought of his response would nag at her. She wondered what he would think, how he would interpret what she said. She thought maybe he thinks she is naïve and that's why he doesn't respond right away, or maybe he thinks she is being stupid and is trying to figure out how to break it to her gently. The point was that these follow ups showed she was still thinking about him and what she said to him even after she had said it. That meant —in a sense— that she was agonizing over it, and that most definitely was not cute or endearing, it was, well, agonizing. Not that she wasn't learning something by pushing herself into thinking this way about her experiences, but what was really painful was doing it publicly, or semi-publicly. She was doing it in an open exchange with another person who she wanted to like her, someone whose opinion she cared about, and whose thoughts and reactions mattered.

He was good about it though. He seemed to know when it was happening and would respond quickly, if possible, to spare her the cost of that agony. This message had been especially desperate. It wasn't just because this little guy had been so condescending and annoying, it was all of it. The experience, the urge to tell the professor, all of it made her feel vulnerable and exposed. If she didn't hear back right away and if he didn't say something that made it better, that calmed her, then it would just add to it, make the whole thing so much worse. She had been so coy with him back in the beginning. Now he was everywhere she turned. She had let him have too much from her. This added to it, making it so frightfully oppressive.

Today, he must've been at the computer. He responded immediately.

Such fatigue. I'm sorry you had a bad day. If you won't accept a foot massage, I could sing you a song. A ballad about a shepherd girl disappointed to learn that she is in business with sheep.

Today, that was just right. She smiled and nodded sharply back at the screen. He had been listening. He didn't try to explain her problem to her, he didn't try to inform her about something she wasn't aware of. He acknowledged that it was bad, and he expressed an interest in helping her feel better. Not fixing the problem, just looking after her as she bore it. He was becoming better at this, since she sent that mail a few weeks back. She knew it had been risky. She had every expectation that he would disappear after that, that he would be all possessive and take it as a slap to his pride, and maybe he did. He didn't express his reaction that way though. She respected that. He asked her a lot of questions about it in the following weeks. He didn't focus on what she had done, but on why she had told him about it. For some reason, she liked that. It cut right to the important part. He didn't go after the information in a really defensive way either. He seemed genuinely interested in understanding her better. Learning more about her motives and how her thought process worked. He asked her bold questions, like he really wanted to know about the subtle meanings of how men fit into her self-image and her way of understanding herself and how she thought and felt about things. He wasn't going to be intimidated by the answers. Something seemed brave in it. She couldn't quite put her finger on it. He wasn't afraid to say the wrong thing because he knew how to ask a question properly. He knew that saying the wrong thing was about making statements and judgments and that questions could be gentler and humbler.

She read his response more than once, between patrons coming up to the desk. She liked everything about it. Fatigue was exactly right. She was tired of it. These bullshit little guys and their entitled attitudes. Fuck them. The nice little conditional that made it all up to her. If you won't accept. Not some ridiculous if I can't give you, but if you won't accept. He's taking her side. He's attributing something to her. The fact that the dispute is over a foot massage is absolutely fucking perfect. He is too prone to make everything ethereal and mental. That's why she isn't sure that he was ever a little guy himself. He's too introspective, hyper self-conscious. She was learning that there is a lot of discomfort that comes with that. When they met for coffee, he was already seated and she had left him that way, but when he came and went from the bar that first night, she had seen him walk in. He didn't swagger. He walked like he was sure no one was looking. As though he were invisible and was able to watch and see everything without being noticed while doing it. It meant he didn't know something about himself, he was completely unaware of it. That set him apart from the little guys. It was unlikely he would suddenly become this way later in life, so he was probably never one of them.

Since she sent that message that Sunday morning, he has done it more often or at least with a different emphasis. She wasn't a theory any longer, not just a game with words. It was as if he hadn't fully noticed her body before or hadn't felt comfortable commenting on it without the veils of poetry, but now that she had brought it up in such a stunning and obvious fashion, he had no choice. She was becoming real to him. He was acknowledging her and realizing that there was something wrong with not having seen it before. In the days that followed, in the exchanges that followed, he showed signs of learning that he wasn't being respectful by ignoring or keeping quiet about this. Idealizing her wasn't respect. He needed to be taught that, and he gave her the distinct impression that he was happy to learn it. Responses like this were the fruit of those exchanges, the foot massage. Who knows, she might even want to accept that. If she doesn't, he'd sing her a song instead. That means that he isn't being phony about it. That was what she thought, anyway, that he was still prone to his flights of fancy. Going off into some weird head birth that he couldn't control, daydreaming this or that reaction to her expression of disgust with her client at the desk that day, he was attaching her way of seeing things to his own. He was integrating it all, bringing it together in a way she found satisfying, and then the jab at the sheep. That was perfection. He gets me, she thought. He totally gets it.

That feeling brought with it a strong counter sensation. She was thrown back on topics they had tackled before and come back to again and again. Things he had asked her, things he wanted to know. Difficult questions that he phrased so gently. When he first emailed her, she had conflicting feelings. On the one hand, the bold move. She had liked that. He had been willing to take a risk. Very cool. On the other hand, he had tracked her down, looked her up, and found out how to contact her while making their meeting and conversation into something of a public display. It was definitely an invasion of privacy. She had been willing to overlook it because it wasn't mean-spirited, that was clear right away. Their prior conversation had been deep enough to form an opinion making it more to his advantage. She remembered how much eye contact he made while they talked. She remembered how lightly he looked into her eyes. She thought of it and had decided to give him a little slack. This, now, this was becoming too much. How could he write the perfect email response to her quips about work? How dare he know her so well. At the same moment that she appreciated what was behind it, she also felt strong resistance to those same suggestions. By getting to know her and by accommodating and adjusting to what he was learning, he was getting deeper inside her head. It wasn't just that she let him in, it was that he was coming in and making himself comfortable there.

You say I am pushing and pulling, but I feel you pushing and pulling too. You had some nerve invading my privacy like you did. Now what else are you planning on invading with these songs of yours? I am fascinated with email, it is true, but never did I imagine that it could be a balcony and the moonlight that shines on it.

She didn't know where that came from and typing it had caused her to wrinkle her nose in embarrassment. She sent it anyway. If you tilt your head just right, she thought, it's true. She was confident that it wouldn't throw him off balance. He would understand why his response had caused her to break out of whatever it was they thought they were talking about and go back to the theme of the last few weeks, revisiting that push and that pull. What they kept coming back to again and again, both of them now asking the exact same question with the exact same tone and emphasis: why can't we just see each other?

He had been asking the question for months, but now she was asking it too. This was her argument. If you could call it that. This was her reason why and her fear and all the sense that she could draw out of it. Seeing each other would admit something. She did not want to admit that. She was admitting it. To admit the invasion is to admit that he is there. To admit that he is there is to admit that she is questioning the very same thing that he has been questioning all along. If you are already there, inside me like this, what more is there to keep back? What else could possibly be the object of all this pushing and pulling? She resisted because she did not want to get distracted, but here she was at the reference desk, hurrying through each patron so she could get back to it, reread the last message, and consider what response she should make. She was distracted. The distraction was present, and it was real. There could be no more denying it. Now, she was thinking, isn't he more distracting like this? Going out with him, having a normal date. Touching him. Him touching her. All that would be so much less distracting at this point. Hadn't he engineered a complete inversion of all the terms of their understanding? Who was she hurting by refusing to admit it? Her question —as she read it over after sending it— was a confession. If he knew how to read, it told him everything. She admitted everything. She had been right to be embarrassed. Even on rereading it, she couldn't help but scrunch up her nose and eyes, blanching with shame and self-doubt. Was it time?

If he had taken a long time to respond, she wouldn't have been able to bear it. She hoped that there would be a reply as soon as she finished with this next question, and she could get back and check for mail again. She knew it was the right thing to do, to reraise that same old issue, to show him everything right there; and yet she was terrified that he would get it and take advantage somehow or that he wouldn't get it and would miss the point entirely. There were so many ways for him to go wrong here. She couldn't let that lie. If he didn't reply immediately, she would have to soften the blow, have to say more to take some of the edge off, to hide some of the details, to distract him from what she had so easily confessed. If if if. None of it. She switched back to the Pine email interface on her terminal and there was his response.

Your mind alights too much on pushing and pulling. Where have I taken hold? What delights are you denying yourself? What pleasures are you holding on to in silence? You say you are pushing only because you are being pulled and I say that I am pulling only because I am being pushed. Can you feel the rhythm? It's there in your breath. That's my breath. It's there in your chest and in your heartbeat. That's my heartbeat.

Oh, fucking hell.

Back inside, he straightened up the living room and started cleaning the kitchen. The goal was to avoid going into the bedroom to delay checking his email for as long as possible. Was he punishing himself? It might have been her. The delay was all that mattered. The phone rang. Wolfe wanted to borrow the car so that he and the typesetter could drive into Detroit and meet up with some friends. The professor didn't respond right away, he was trying to figure out whether he needed the car. Where would he go?

What were his plans for the evening? Instead of waiting patiently, Wolfe suggested that he come with them. Immediately upon hearing the offer, he knew this was what he had been waiting for and what he wanted to do: a whole night out with no access to the computer. He wouldn't be able to check, and he couldn't respond. He would get dressed and go pick them up at her house.

They decided Wolfe would drive. The typesetter got in the passenger seat; she was going to navigate. The professor climbed into the backseat. They argued a bit about which way to take. Wolfe firmly pointed out that the professor was in the back seat. The argument ended and the route determined. The whole way there, it seemed, the typesetter was talking. She was telling stories that fit together in a large and circuitous yarn.

It started with the font problem. Apparently, the author had inadvertently and erroneously provided the text "The quick brown fox jumped over the lazy dog." As a result, they chose a different font from the one he had in mind. Apparently the two were similar except for the s and the missing letter, that past tense faux pas, led to a disastrous mistake. She didn't think the difference mattered very much, but apparently it did as the s was just the beginning. Italics and bold, quotation marks, the number of differences following upon the s was large, the mistake catastrophic. This story somehow segued into a discussion of the spring flora that was starting to appear in the backyards and gardens of various managerial employees at the publishing house. This was because the discussions of the font had somehow led one of the managers involved in problem solving to speculate on a similar error previously encountered when purchasing seeds for perennials they were planting. This led her to discuss plant life on the shores of Lake Michigan near where she grew up. The traversal of her mind was rapid fire and filled with details. She seemed to know so much about fonts and western Michigan plant life. The details always involved human drama, which was elaborated with all the tension and threat of love and betrayal for which humans are best known.

The professor was transfixed, leaning forward with his hands on her seatback so that he could hear every word, every detail as the stories wound through their twists and turns. This was a side of her he had not seen. Wolfe listened too, but he was actively engaged and not just passively enthralled. He asked follow-up questions. He wanted to know more about the people involved, the type of the seeds, and the names of the fonts. Which book was it, after all? Was it that author who has given us nothing but trouble since the very beginning? The same one he had proofread.

The professor had follow-up questions too, but they were of a different kind. He wanted to know how she knew all this, how did she get interested in typesetting and plants, had she spent lots of time beach combing along the lake? When he asked his questions, it launched an intricate discussion of flea markets and where to find them, how to find specific items and target venues that have better stuff. Apparently, that is how she first got interested in typesetting, having found some antique plates at such a flea market years ago. Once bitten by that, she started searching for more and was able to assemble a small 19th century printing press from parts she found across the state. Had they called out to her so that she could bring them back together?

"You have eclectic interests," he said, letting go of her seat. They were leaving the highway and approaching the little dive where they were supposed to meet their friends. Just as her responsibilities as navigator were intensifying, he asked her: "Are you a navigator at heart? Do you get pleasure from knowledge and making your way through things?" This placed her squarely into open conflict with her various duties. She had to direct Wolfe to the right location, but the question piqued her interest. The irony in the timing was too good to pass up. Her response trailed off and she studied the street to discern when to take the next turn and where to park.

Once they were safely there, she turned back to him and said, "Of course. Don't you think? I *want* to know things too. There is desire *and* pleasure."

He wanted to know if the diversity of her interests added to the pleasure and stimulated the desire, he wanted to know all sorts of things. This is what bothered him most about the endless pursuit of diversion. They drove to this place to meet people there. At this public place where it will be loud and filled with strangers, they cannot speak as they would somewhere else. They will have to scream or not talk at all. Getting out of the car and walking into the bar were all just so many distractions. She had to look for them, she had to guide the way. She couldn't attend to the question. The professor didn't think there was anything necessarily wrong with this, he understood the requirements and the way things worked, but he thought maybe there was something wrong with him. Why do people talk to each other? Especially when there is no immediate point to it. They didn't need to plan their next meal or figure out how to construct shelter. There was no practical end toward which they were driving, so why did they want to talk at all? The conversation was a social convenience, a way for them to build stronger bonds. They would get to know each other better, figure out which interests or qualities they had in common, and whether that would group them together more forcefully or drive them apart as too much at odds and too diverse in their outlooks and sensibilities.

This was the very same purpose that meeting up with friends would have. She found them, in the back, in a dark corner of the room. They were two young women and a young man. Wolfe seemed to know them, and they all greeted each other warmly. The typesetter introduced the professor. Once they had settled down and put in a drink order, the typesetter informed the table that they were in the middle of trying to figure out whether there is pleasure and desire associated with the drive for knowledge. She made it clear that the nature of rationality and its relationship to knowledge was, in some sense, at stake. The professor was surprised to learn that the topic was immediately interesting to the rest of them and that they quickly became animated in providing answers. They didn't exactly concoct a theory, but they all had anecdotal suggestions. They produced examples. They talked about the way people will often use their knowledge to exert power over situations and other people, and how they seem to draw satisfaction from this. Slowly, they worked around to wondering about what knowledge and pleasure might be so that they could be so intricately intertwined.

The professor and Wolfe just listened. The four others were circling around and around, then they jumped back and forth. They knew each other well and were at play. It was a sight to behold, even if it was unpolished and off the cuff. They were becoming increasingly clear that things like knowledge, desire, pleasure, and the newly added power were all fundamental notions. Because of that, it was hard to talk about them. They were usually the terms that anchored other things. Why do I like riding a bicycle? Because it feels good, there is pleasure. Why does it feel good, why is there pleasure in it? This became less satisfying. That's where they wanted to go. When we perform an analysis of pleasure, why do we have to talk about sensory stimulation and the way bodies work when they experience sensation? The same stimuli won't strike everyone the same way. The red-haired young woman was adamant about this. It can't just be about bodies. The typesetter forcefully agreed, and the others nodded. You can't be alive and not know this, the young man asserted. We're influenced and then we experience through those influences. Even our impressions. The young woman with brown hair was quick to point out that her sister and her were only a year apart in age and had grown up together thick as thieves, but they didn't like the same things. They both love to learn and study, but they have vastly different areas of focus. Her sister likes science, but she likes art. They grew up together, but they did not spend every minute of their lives together. The evidence proposed at the table that night seemed iron-clad to the participants. There had to be more to it, but we just didn't have a good language for analyzing pleasure and desire at the level of conscious experience conditioned by our social environment.

"That was what always bothered me about ethics in my philosophy classes," the typesetter went on. "Happiness was associated with pleasure and desire, but it was a given. It was the end of it all. The argument couldn't go any further than that. You could never get any further than happiness.

It was the end-in-itself, the ultimate ambition, and it could be vaguely associated with any other notion."

Wolfe spoke for the first time since the rapid-fire conversation had begun. "Pleasure in knowledge might threaten knowledge. What if it functions like a drug, like Soma? It does it so much so that the hard work of knowing true things might be vulnerable to a corrupted knowledge that is sought only for the pleasure that it gives."

"That's a different point," she resisted.

"Bear with me, for a second," he said softly. "It's because pleasure and desire are so little understood that we might be their victims at times. This is the matter with all values and valuing. These basic notions that we don't know how to get behind or underneath, they become an Achilles heel because of that. We are vulnerable to all kinds of confidence games and coercion." He paused to give someone else a chance. Everyone was silent. He went on. "Pleasure and desire are studied, right? Nonetheless, the professional knowers may have lost sight of the pleasure in what they are doing. Brimming with pride, they glow with how good it feels. That happens. They still feel the desire, even if it only surfaces as anxiety and ambition. There are people who think about what's behind the works of others, what inclinations and feelings can be detected there. These social and behavioral psychologists, these speculators or whatever they are, they want to learn the trends and tendencies. What this stimulus will lead to and what that one will prevent. They think about pleasure as a carnivore stalking the herd, their subject's pleasure is their desire. It can be used to move them around, send them this way or that. Shepherding them. If there are people learning about all this, then maybe knowledge, value, truth, and whatever else can be tied together with the pleasant and the desirable, are ways to get people to line up so that the learners can devour them. That is how they subject them to *their* desire, by knowing them, studying them, and keeping an eye on their every move. The categorized and aggregated population at large is the theorist's orgasm."

This was enough to send them off into many different directions. The red-haired young woman could not get everyone's attention because Wolfe was listening to the typesetter who had jumped in immediately. The young man turned to her. The young woman with the sister could not decide which way to turn. This broke the conversation into several different ones. These in turn led to tangents. The professor tried to listen to all of them. He couldn't hear the details, but what he could clearly discern was that Wolfe's hypothesis had increased the excitement level. They were all thinking about the implications and the possible explanations. There was desire all around. They were having a good time. He was convinced that if he were to abruptly interrupt the flow of discussion, they would affirm that there was a higher order at work in what they were doing. They weren't just experiencing pleasure, they could assign a value to it. An entire edifice of meaning was at work. Try as they might, they couldn't progress any further in understanding so long as they were caught in the grips of that same edifice.

In the car ride back to Ann Arbor, Wolfe couldn't help but go back to the topic. Nothing that had happened since seemed to have broken his chain of thought. The typesetter was sleeping in the back seat.

"It may be that the pleasure in knowledge is what makes theoretical knowledge so deadly," he said, assuming that the professor would be able to pick up on the revived context. "The observer is subject to a specific kind of pleasure. It is voyeurism. These are the people historically most misled by political movements, right? They are used to pleasure at a distance, from a point of observation. Intellectuals. They know that ideas are malleable and that they can be customized and based on these kinds of pleasantries. The adaptation of an idea to a personal orientation is common enough. Isn't that how Heidegger was snagged? Didn't he bend and twist the words of the Nazis to fit with his own spin on destiny and revolution and all of that? His antagonism to Russia and the United States, his critique of economism, utilitarianism, technologism, all of it could be easily fit together with the Volkish ideologies and the rising strength of the Fatherland."

The professor just listened.

"The intellectual is easily misled in political matters because they are used to bending theories to their own preferences and interpretations. No self-avowed pragmatist is a pragmatist in exactly the way that Dewey was. That's how they think political ideas work too. In their minds, whatever '-ism' they espouse works the way they think it does and they can justify going along with the party to the extent that it may adjust later on or be corrected when the right representative comes along. They have no doubt that this will be someone who shares their own spin on it. They can't be simply part of a movement; they could never give up the cognitive control they believe they have when they weave their ideas into an order. The arrogance of the 'thought-leader' makes them vulnerable to co-optation."

"I take it you aren't just speaking of extremes, but even the 'normal' case?"

"Exactly. Look at the bullshit hierarchy in the academy. It hinges on this same skewed vision. It's how theory works. It's why there are hierarchies of disciples to any given theory. The average academic is not highly intelligent. I mean, they are smart enough, I suppose. They spend time thinking about how to more effectively teach this or that topic in their area of expertise or competence. They work on making their points clearer so that students will be more engaged. When they write, they're basically doing the same thing, although they vary their tone and target a bit due to a slightly modified audience: other mediocre intellects like themselves who have yet to become familiar with whatever topic is the thesis of their paper or book. Such people cannot appropriate works of great genius. They require hierarchy for that. How else would they know what to read and what to study? Secondary literature is the rule because of this. The top of the profession must begin the process and then it has to be filtered on the way down. This happens in layers. It must, and it always happens with the more clever helping out those who are less so. That's all I mean by 'top.' The most clever among them. At some point, however, the work becomes fashionable. In that case, it doesn't matter whether anyone understands it, just so that it has enough style to catch on. In the end, no one relies on their own cognitive capacity, but they consume the work of others for the sake of appearing well-informed, this is the hierarchy at work in their thoughts and actions."

The professor remained silent, listening carefully.

"The hierarchy is crucial. The clever are at the top. Sometimes they are brilliant. The dumbfounded are at the bottom, though they can be brilliant too, in their way. To be clear, being brilliant doesn't matter. The thing about the hierarchy is that it makes it possible for the dimwitted to find their way in, and —if they are clever— do well. Because they are all busy explaining things to each other, the hierarchy can reach down to the very lowest levels of capability. Even fools can digest an oversimplified account of this or that theme."

"It's not just about being clever," the professor chimed in. "Like you were saying, it's about a specific kind of drive and passion. That has to be desire and pleasure, value or the will to power, whatever you want to call it. A drive to learn may easily hide a drive to rise to the top of that hierarchy. The desire needn't be a simple relationship to an object of knowledge, but may relate to the whole social domain referenced in the hierarchy. They seek to achieve mastery over the entire organizational structure, to become its masters. The self-flattery and the pleasure in this are what keeps the whole thing in motion."

They were exiting the highway. The change in rhythm woke the typesetter. She oriented herself. The location, the topic of conversation, and the time.

Wolfe tells the professor. "We have been friends a while. I know that I am looser than you. You think you are falling in love, but I think your heart is breaking. What I don't recognize is why you can't see it." He tries to carry all of time from one end of the year to the other. One of them is April's fool. It'll singsong back from there, emphases on all the ands. Is this him pulling or pushing? One-e-and-a-Two-e-and-a...

"What does that have to do with anything?" the professor is irritated by the sudden change.

"Look, I know why you keep coming back to these same issues, keep asking questions about them and gathering different perspectives. I know what you're doing. Why don't you?"

They are a collective, the ones who inhabit the car. The narrative will always diverge from the apparent meaning. The narrative itself is an injection of meaning, and its pull. The car will speak this meaning as the ones who inhabit it. It will tell the tale, recount the exchanges, and inform others about the content, its bulk and weight. Where is the action that is independent of it? If the story is not being lived, then it is being told. If it is being told, then it has the pull of distance, and the inhabitants are all drawn into it. They get their form from it. There are no other alignments. Narrative was not enough. The notions had to be pulled and that meant that their pull had to be exhibited, putting an endless circling upon display. The repetition is the beat, it comes back again and again to the same themes, but through no choice of their own, having to mention this or elaborate on that. Why do they keep following up on each other's thoughts? What compels them to speak in response? Where does it come from and where is it going?

Wolfe drives to the typesetter's house. The last mile has been mostly silent, the typesetter saying it was fun and they should all hang out more often. She wanted to transition from the confrontation to the goodbyes that would soon come. They all got out of the car. The professor only to get back into the driver's seat. He waved goodbye to Wolfe and the typesetter gave him a hug. They went in the house, and he drove off. On the drive back to his apartment, he turned up the radio to drown out his thoughts. That was enough for today. He didn't turn on the computer when he got home. He didn't check his email. He just climbed into bed and went to sleep.

"She ended up knowing so much that she could no longer interpret anything. There were no longer shadows to help her see more clearly, only glare." A passage from Henry James that stuck in his head. It had become lodged there and was resonating in the darkness.

Of course, Pascal is right when he says that without god there is no goodness and no truth, and he is right to invoke reason as the crux of the matter. He is blind when he fails to see that the answers to his questions are predisposed through the categories he has taken for granted. God, goodness, truth, reason, probability. Yes, they are all tied up in a universe of conditions. The wager is part of it. The necessity of the wager is destiny once you have accepted the conditions, once you've acknowledged the stakes are part of a game of chance to be won or lost. He is right about everything; he just doesn't know that he has discovered a disease; or he does and calls it an affliction, the affliction most characteristic of our life on

Earth. His mistake then may be that he thinks it is curable. He does not know that we cannot be cured of these passions that blow all those items in the list to smithereens. He does not know that they are what is at work in the symptoms as well as the urge to quiet them. They come from the voice of god *and* from the voice of that other chap. In us, as us, through us. If there are only two types of people, as he thinks, then maybe those who seek the good are nothing special. To seek the good, is that just a clandestine way to seek truth and reason and even the deity itself?

What such a seeker thinks he wants and what he does want are not at all the same. Wretchedness and pride are not the only choices. The choice itself is the terrain laid out by the wager. That is where we live. It is dark there with only the light we brought with us to guide the way. If we have come as beggars, then we are truly lost.

Micro-involvements feed the ego and aim at situating oneself better within groups. The organization at work in thinking dies to the extent that the subject is separated from its original dynamic and order. Separation may be experienced as a kind of despair. This is illusory. It is pure epiphenomenon. The subject can train itself to dismiss this mood along with others like jealous criticism or envious flattery.

He writes for no one.

Hermeneutics and the fore-conception at work in ontological determinations. Filled by the symbolic, offset by the real, projected by the imaginary. A turning that is saturated with the relations of desire, with its experimental discovery, and with its indicators of pleasure. Stepping back and seeing vs acting so as to bring to light. Automaton = spontaneity.

Strength and intelligence don't separate us, charisma and persuasion, the ability to enlist the support of our brothers and sisters, that is where hierarchy comes into play among human beings. Hobbes indirectly in chapter 13. The war of all against all may be the outcome of such forms of social organization but are not its origin. This is what it means to flip him on his head. Ultimately, we agree with them that all morality is spawned by the contract. If it is mere semblance, then what is there that remains of it? If the hierarchy is established by these moral notions, then morality itself is part of the institution that ensures the domination of the many by the few. The death of god doesn't signal that everything is permitted, only that we are alone in sorting it all out and our fabrications have incited this war we currently wage on one another. A new morality is required. Just imagine the chaos that it would bring. Is it something to be discovered or something to be invented? Are we right to fear that it is the latter because that would make the situation impossible?

He writes for no one.

It might have been his point that ideas without a purpose can lead to fragmentation and dissent. This makes people vulnerable to an attack that will prey on their differences for the sake of swindling them out of all their money. There are trillions and trillions of dollars at stake, but there is so much else to lose. The coercion and the discipline are at odds with the concepts and the ideologies. This means everyone is in a state of not knowing what they are doing, of not knowing what they truly are. It's chaos. This is a critical juncture, a crisis, an enforced reduction run to its limit in the symbolics of desire, in the meanings of the body, and in the pleasures of the imagination.

Neo-Liberalism - desire - piracy - remote measurement - forensic value determination - the enlightenment - the order that is inhabiting us.

What if the only way we can be of value is as part of a mass? What if good and evil are only aggregate notions? What was it? Something like "Another great infirmity of the Commonwealth is the great number of Corporations; which are like lesser Commonwealths in the bowels of the greater, like worms in the entrails of a man." God is dead. If you don't believe it, just look around.

He walked up the street from the café, pulled open the door, and stepped inside. He hadn't been to the Del for several months, honoring his promise to stay away. She was sitting at the bar, on the edge of her seat and leaning into her small glass of beer like a proper bar fly. She had been watching the door and smiled as soon as she saw him. Cheerful hellos when he approached her, but they didn't touch. She stood up and gestured for them to move to a table. Most of the booths along the wall were free. She chose the one about equal distance from the front door and the kitchen, right in the middle. They sat down and the waitron came right over so he could order a beer. They sat there in silence until it came. They were looking at each other, but out of the corner of her eye she could see the waitron standing at the bar while the bartender poured. No stops in between, she returned quickly and put the glass in front of him. His gaze was steady. He hadn't look away the whole time.

"Are you nervous?" he asked.

"A little." Her voice went up a bit when she said it.

"Me too." He looked down for the first time, then back up. Their eyes locked. They both became more confident after the confession.

"Are you done with all your grading?"

"Yes, but I have to do final grades. How's your paper going?"

"Been too distracted this weekend to work on it much."

"Sorry about that."

"Listen," she brushed her hair back on one side. She had one of her legs tucked up underneath her on the bench and was rocking a bit as she spoke. So much movement after so many months without it, but it helped draw out the words. "I honestly don't know why I freaked out so much. I'm sorry if that was just too much."

"No, no, not at all. I'm sorry. I wasn't thinking. It never occurred to me that... well, I just didn't realize what I was doing."

"It's just, I hadn't heard from you, and I didn't know where you were. You didn't say you were going anywhere, and I thought you would respond right away."

"I know, I get it. I mean, I went out with my roommate and his girlfriend and then I had to go help my parents with some computer stuff. Not an excuse. I'm just saying. With the semester ending, I just needed to reset or something."

"You didn't check your email at all? It wasn't that you were just ignoring all these emails from some crazy chick who was harassing you?" She laughed when she said it.

"True. I hadn't checked. That was deliberate too. It's been getting hard. All the emails, it seemed like we were getting closer, but then, you know, never seeing each other."

"I get it. What if something had gone wrong with a student though? What if there was a problem with the grades?"

"Well, I'm entitled to a weekend. It's not like they can fire me."

"Okay. You needed a break from me, I get it, and maybe you wanted to punish me a bit?"

"I don't know. It's possible. I was surprised when you wanted to see me. I mean, I wasn't planning that. It wasn't a well thought out plan or anything."

"Well, it was time. I did need the push though. It was surprising. I didn't expect it either. Not knowing where you were or what was going on, not hearing from you after hearing from you so regularly all this time. I was pretty upset."

"I'm really sorry about that."

"That's not what I mean. I'm not trying to make you feel bad. I just meant that I was surprised. If you had asked me, if anyone had asked me, on Friday what was going on between us, I would have waved it off. It didn't seem like... I guess... I'm saying I didn't know how dependent I had become. You know, on having you around, knowing what you were up to, and getting your take on things."

"Huh. I might have had a plan then. Because that is what I thought. I knew. I mean, I knew how dependent you had become. I damn sure knew how dependent I had become. That's why I wanted to disappear."

"Okay, so here we are. Are you disappointed?"

"What do you mean? Why would I be disappointed?"

"You might not remember me. Your memory and imagination might be better than me. In person. The actual me."

"Not at all," he whispered it. They were sharing that feeling. They grinned a bit, accepting it. "You?"

"The exact opposite. Relieved maybe."

"That's it. It's pretty weird. It feels like something is over. Like we're done with that."

"It might have been the right time. That part is over."

"That's fucked up though, right? I mean, we're starting something. It shouldn't feel like something is ending."

She burbled and sputtered interrupting him as he was saying it. She was suddenly excited. "Hey hey hey," she said when she could finally manage to speak. "We're not at all ready to go there. Don't jinx it. I'm just saying that phase is over and done with. Period. Th-th-th-th-that's all folks."

"Okay."

"We're in a public place. We're sitting together having a conversation. We've transitioned into normalcy."

"Okay."

"That's okay with you, is that what you're saying?" Her eyes were dancing with him. Darting and glowing.

"Yes. That's okay with me."

"I have to go. Unfortunately. I have to finish my paper, so I didn't have much time. I'm glad we did this though. We don't have to pay, but you should tip her for taking the booth."

"You feel better?"

"Definitely. You?"

He smiled and then they cleared out from the table and walked to the door. She shouted goodbye to the front bartender who silently saluted in return. Once they stepped outside, they went toward the street. He was heading around the corner, and she was going to cross at the light. The distance between them was widening as he slowed for the turn, and she moved toward the curb. He reached out and took her hand, preventing her from continuing forward and moving further away from him. He didn't want her to get too far away. She let him take hold and grasped his hand tightly just as he caught her. The firm grip of their hands clasping stopped her from continuing to the corner and forced her to turn and swing a wide circle back toward him, taking two steps while he took one in her direction. She did not stop at a distance, but allowed her second step to bring her right up close and into his arms. Face to face, they didn't pause, but fell into a first kiss. No more words.

He watched her crossing the street. She turned and made a small wave of her hand when she came to the other side. He waved back.

May

"I didn't go."

"It was this week?"

"Happening now."

"No interviews? Couldn't you still go? Try and schmooze a little. Scrape something together?"

"I'm not very good at schmoozing, and I've got a lot going on right now."

"What are you going to do?"

"I'll send some emails. Let people know I'm looking. We'll see if I can find something."

"You'll move?"

"I don't really want to. Probably won't be able to find anything worth moving for anyway. I'll have to see. What about you? What's going on?"

"Not much. Going to meetings. Got a new sponsor. He's all about NIT, 'the next indicated thing'. It means that I'm not doing a lot of long-term planning right now. Just concentrating on the next thing I have to do. Get breakfast, get dressed, go to work, go to a meeting, clean the bathroom, and so on."

"You're cleaning the bathroom? Wow, that's hardcore."

"Fuck off. Point is that I have to fill my time. I'm making schedules and plotting out hours of time. Weekends and evenings are the worst. Gotta come up with lots of stuff to fill every night. I'm reading when I can. Started keeping a journal. Trying to get to the gym. Running. Whenever I can't figure out what to do, or have any doubt about what comes next, I go to a meeting."

"You're trying to be on automatic and not give your brain any time to wander, is that it? Stop it from getting you into any trouble."

"Yep. It'll be this way for a while. My sponsor is extremely strict. He's a marine. He was. He thinks it's all about discipline, and that discipline is all about having a detailed regimen and giving yourself no room for improvisation. Improvisation is a big problem for me."

"Are you okay with all this? Sounds like tough love."

"More than okay, I love it. I didn't realize how much I needed it until I gave it a try. My thoughts can get really dark when I'm just off on my own. You know, I'll drive around, start thinking about stuff, about what I've lost, and about what I'll never be able to get because of this fucking disease. It sets me off. I want to get a bottle and just fuck it all. Structure makes that impossible. My calendar is completely full."

"How long do we have to talk then? Did you plan the amount of time you could stay on the phone?"

"I did. Everything is based on one-hour increments. That's how much I've allocated."

"What's next?"

"Going to a meeting."

"Right. Three hours earlier there. Well, it sounds like it might be good for you. Might be exactly what you need right now."

"Seems that way. I'm kind of worried about your situation. It doesn't seem like you're taking it very seriously. Technically, aren't you unemployed right now?"

"Yes. I might even qualify for unemployment insurance. I have to look into it."

"Why couldn't you get anything? You sent out a bunch of applications, didn't you?"

"I did. We've gone over this. I have my theories. My recommendations probably aren't very good. Where I went to school, what I studied. All the stuff I've mentioned before. I don't have a particularly good dossier. The teaching materials aren't solid enough. I'm not sure, you never get any feedback. Nobody's really helping me from my graduate school, so it's hard to say."

"I know you hate to talk about it, but do you think any part of it might be because of affirmative action? Around here everyone is talking about it. They say it's making it really hard for white guys to get work."

"That seems like bullshit to me."

"I'm not surprised."

"Seriously though. I mean, the profession is almost totally made up of white men. Entire departments. I know lots of white guys who've gotten jobs in the last two or three years since I've been on the market. If anything, there isn't enough affirmative action in philosophy. I don't mean to laugh."

"I thought you said last year when you were up for that tenure track job and made the short list, that a woman professor left the department right when they were considering the candidates. Don't you think that forced them to hire the woman who was on the short list?"

"It could have, but again, that's the point. It's not like she wasn't a brilliant candidate."

"Doesn't it mean that it's playing a role in their decision making? Could that be why you're having such a tough time?"

"I don't think so. It's probably the exact opposite. The affirmative action is there because there's been too much bias for men. I'm having a tough time despite having all those advantages. It probably means I'm not really cut out for this."

"It's weird to hear you say that. It's what you've been focused on since I met you."

"I'm beginning to think I might have been wrong about it all along."

"How can you be wrong about something you're so passionate about? What are you talking about?"

"I don't mean that I was wrong about what I'm passionate about. That's not it. I mean, maybe I was wrong about thinking that what I was passionate about was the same thing as what I've been trying to get. If you're interested in philosophy, you start studying it as an undergraduate. Some one or more of your professors suggest that you might want to go to graduate school because that's what people who are really interested in philosophy do; you'd be rational to draw the conclusion that whatever it is that you're doing puts you into a specific career track."

"You're spelling out the obvious, right? If you want to be a doctor, go to medical school."

"Yeah, but what I'm saying is that it isn't always so obvious. Medical school and being a doctor. Fine, but whatever it was that I was interested in, maybe it was misdiagnosed. Those professors might have been wrong to think there was any connection between what we do in an academic graduate program and what I was interested in. What did I know? I took their word for it."

"They were encouraging, they saw your work, they read your papers. They must have seen something."

"Not exactly encouraging, that's the privilege talking. It's more like here's a white guy in the professor's office, he wants to study philosophy. He writes competent papers. There's no reason he shouldn't do it then. Go ahead and help him. Not that they explicitly thought of it that way, I just mean that subconsciously or whatever, they recognized my own moral authority to pursue whatever I wanted to pursue. In their minds that was philosophy, so they helped me; maybe they wouldn't if I didn't have the cultural assets that I have. If I didn't talk the way I talk or carry myself the way I do."

"You're saying that your professors didn't try to discourage you because they gave you too much credit, they believed you when you said the thing you were interested in was philosophy, and that what you mean by that was what they meant by it too?"

"Something like that. The professors who wrote me recommendations were not really focusing on the main areas of the discipline. They weren't 'analytic philosophers' in the strict sense. One was a Plato scholar, another was an Ethicist focused mostly on Kantian variations, and then there was the Austrian professor who taught me Nietzsche and Hegel. I'm just saying, they weren't exactly mainstream in their approaches. They might have misdiagnosed me."

"Like it's a disease."

"It is, in a way. I was really passionate about Plato and Nietzsche at that point. I was really focused on the origins of value and meaning and how they play a role in the stories we tell about how the world works and what's going on out there."

"Sure. I remember. It's all you ever talked about."

"Philosophy might not just be a set of books or writers that you like to read. It may not just be a set of issues that those writers are concentrating on. It might also be a voice of some kind, or a genre, I guess. A genus of writing, structure, and style. Whatever it all amounts to, if someone tells you their favorite philosophers are Nietzsche, Plato, and Kierkegaard, when they obsess over Sartre but don't seem to care much for Putnam and Quine, I'm just saying that it might be relevant to wonder if what they're really interested in is the same thing as what's going on in all the graduate schools."

"Why would they? Those are all perfectly valid philosophers, aren't they? What else would they have thought?"

"Well, they might've noticed that everything I was interested in was stylistically strange and outside the norm. Plato was writing dialogues and using a pseudonym. Kierkegaard is nearly unfathomable for the exact same reasons. Even when it's obvious what he's saying, it's muddled by how he says it and the characters he uses. Nietzsche's *Zarathustra*, Sartre's *Nausea*, *No Exit*, and *The Flies*. I'm just saying, somebody should have noticed the pattern. I should have noticed it."

"Doesn't Putnam do weird stuff too? Science fiction examples and weird thought experiments."

"Yes, but I always hated that kind of stuff. It seemed artificial and forced. Like we were exploring the depths of logical possibility instead of real possibilities and worldly connections and relationships. What I'm saying is that maybe hating that kind of stuff isn't possible if you want to make it in the discipline. The field of philosophy dictates the focus and subject matter of its members. People who don't want to accept it's standards belong somewhere else."

"That's fucked up, though, isn't it?"

"Why? It's true in all academic disciplines. If you want to be a chemist these days, you don't just get to make it up. You have to fall in with the historical conditions. You have to get with the program as it currently stands."

"Isn't philosophy supposed to be different?"

"Why? According to who? That might have been the mistake I made. I thought it was different, I thought it was something else. The thing I thought it was doesn't have anything to do with what they're doing in departments of philosophy. Not the ones I applied to anyway: mostly analytic but with a few continentals to spice it up."

"You keep saying that. How could you not have noticed that before? Your professors might have made the mistake because they didn't know everything that you were thinking about. They made assumptions or whatever. You knew, or could have known, why didn't you?"

"I don't know. As an undergraduate, it's easy enough to make the mistake. I was doing what I wanted to do, and the professors seemed to think what I was doing was philosophy. I couldn't have known then, but in my first few years of graduate school, I should have figured it out. Some of my professors did. A couple of them tried to tell me, but I was stubborn."

"Stubborn or you just refused to believe that it was up to them?"

"What's the difference? That's exactly my point. They raised the question, and I didn't really think about it. I just reacted with 'who the fuck are you to tell me...' blah blah blah. What I should have done is tried to be calm about it and figure out what was really going on. What were they really trying to warn me about even if they weren't saying it right?"

"I see. You don't necessarily agree with them, but you would at least have read it as a sign that you needed to think deeper about it."

"Yes. That's what Wolfe did, right? Only he didn't think about it for long, he just bailed. This was about the time we both started reading Derrida. There was a lot of resistance from the professors when we did. Mentioning his name caused all kinds of trouble. In class or in a paper. Wolfe just interpreted that as a clear sign that he had to get the hell out of there. I thought it meant I needed to fight harder, but I could've switched to a different department."

"Okay. Wolfe doesn't seem like he's interested in the same things as you are. There was something else that drew him in and maybe your two cases shouldn't be treated the same."

"Not when it came to Derrida, I don't think. We talked about it all the time. Philosophy, Wolfe said once, was all about trying to bring things out into the light. Trying to make things clear and precise. Deconstruction was showing that these efforts were doomed. Misleading at best, but most likely just wrong-headed. All the exposition and pontificating doesn't really aim at drawing out clear and distinct knowledge, like they all claim. Instead, they were making a colossal mess. Continually starting over again doesn't clean up the mess, it's what makes the mess, and you can see how messy it all is if you just read a little more closely. Deconstruction didn't make the mess, it revealed it."

"I thought he left grad school because he wanted to write fiction instead?"

"Fiction? What the fuck is that? You mean, like telling stories about people. Using different techniques to spin the yarn? That's my point.

There are always yarns being spun, there are always techniques being used. Can you make a distinction? Philosophers might want to draw out the meaning in their subject and they do it by pointing to this or that and saying something about it. They're trying to say it clearly because they *are* trying to make the point clear. Sometimes they fail, but that's because they are describing something exceedingly difficult to see. Fiction writers, so this angle goes, they're trying to cover things up. They're trying to hide the truth from the reader. Because they might think you can only come at it from the side or see it out of the corner of your eye. I disagree though, I don't think that's a difference that cleanly lines up with the difference between fiction and philosophy. Even philosophers can work hard to cover things up."

"You think you're trying to hide something? Are you really in the same category as Wolfe?"

"Well, I might be a blurrier example. I want to do the one thing, but I always end up doing it the other way. It reminds me of something that happened to me as an undergraduate. I spent that summer studying in London after my Freshman year."

"Yeah."

"One of my courses was in Creative Writing which was taught by an underqualified teaching assistant likewise spending a semester abroad. The advantage of his incompetence was that we didn't have to attend class or read anything aloud. We just had to write something each week and then suffer his feedback which included, if you can imagine, a letter grade."

"The gall. How dare your teacher evaluate your work?"

"Exactly. On one occasion, rather than giving me a grade, he called me in for a conference, accused me of plagiarizing my piece that week, and told me I had three days to write something new. I spent those three days getting legal advice at the US embassy, filing the paperwork to receive a copyright, and affixing the required copyright tag to the top of the cover page. I then resubmitted the original story and —following the advice of the attorney at the embassy— told the TA that the onus was on him to produce the master."

"Snap. What did he say?"

"He had nothing. It was a ridiculous accusation, completely without foundation other than the fact that he liked it too much for it to have been written by the likes of me, whose previous work he hadn't liked."

"Was it really that good?"

"I don't know. Probably not. The piece reminded me of that chapter in *Ulysses* where Bloom is on the beach and getting all pervy over the young woman he sees off in the distance. I hadn't read *Ulysses* back then, but my story had a similar vibe. It was stream of consciousness and, although the character wasn't a pervert, he was just hung over enough and sufficiently degenerate in other ways that it wouldn't be hard to imagine him being guilty of that offense too. The atmospheric qualities of the scene and the point of view were similar. A good teacher might have suggested I read Joyce."

"Not this guy, though."

"No. Absolutely not. Anyway, I don't remember the TAs name. Ned Creeth was the professor with whom I usually took creative writing. His comments were more like 'I liked this one' or 'This one didn't work for me.' I don't recall getting specific grades on the stories I wrote, I just remember sitting in his office and talking about what we liked to read, and why. He mostly liked stories that started out being about one thing and then later turned out to be about something else entirely. I told him what happened while I was reading *Portrait of the Artist as a Young Man*, which he had recommended, and that great sentence where Dedalus says something like 'This race and this land and this country have produced me, I shall express myself as I am.' I paused over the sentence, reread it out loud, and lightning struck. Actual lightning, thunder and all. I told him I was pretty much convinced that I had conspired with Joyce to conjure that lightning bolt. He loved that story."

"What about the plagiarism?"

"That's not the point. You see what I mean? The plagiarism gets me to Joyce and then Joyce gets me to Creeth? It's about different ways of approaching the stuff we care about; it's about finding your passion and having the space and encouragement to explore that world, to imagine what you can be and do in it. See what I mean?"

"I guess so."

"It's why it's absurd to bring up affirmative action. To come back full circle, I guess. That's totally irrelevant. I've been wrong about this all along and it's the real reason I'm having trouble. I'm not a teacher. Not really. I never saw it that way, that's not where my drive comes from. Later on, maybe once I figure out my own shit, when I know more about how things work, maybe then I could be a teacher. No fucking way am I ready for that now though. I haven't been of much use to my students this year, or maybe ever. That's what these folks see. They know from my writing that I'm not producing the kind of crap that the others are producing. That's strike one, then they know that I don't read the classic material the same way everyone else reads it. That's strike two. They can tell that I'm not someone who can really step up and inspire the right kind of philosophical acumen in all those young and impressionable minds. That's strike three. With me, I'll just go over the same old stories again and again, rehashing them this way and then that way for my own amusement. Once as a journal entry, then as a dialogue. Whatever, it'll be for my own amusement, and I won't give a shit about how anybody else reads it. Someone like that has no business as a teacher and probably isn't a philosopher either."

"That sucks. What do you want to do then?"

"I want to be the guy who stands in the field and catches all the kids before they go running over the cliff."

"Fuck you. Is that what you think your writing does?"

"I don't know. I'm just messing around. Trying to be clever. Is there a job where you get paid for that?"

"For messing around and being clever? I saw an ad in the paper for something like that last week."

"Email me the details."

"Will do. Okay, I have to go to my meeting. Keep me posted on what you decide. Well, just keep me posted."

He drove to her apartment to pick her up. It was a sunny afternoon. He walked in the front door. There was a staircase going up on the left and a hallway next to it. There was mail on the floor and mailboxes on the wall. At the end of the hall, there was a doorway on the right side just beyond the mailboxes. He knocked, heard footsteps from inside, and then the door opened. They immediately had trouble with the space. There was a staircase inside the door leading down into the basement. She had opened the door from a few steps down, and as he tried to enter, they could not get to each other, and she had to climb back down the stairs to let him follow. As he passed by her into the kitchen at the bottom of the stairs, she could not help but put her arm out to guide him through the door frame and into the apartment. She did not deliberate about it, she didn't decide to put her hand on his shoulder, it just found its way there and once he was inside, she could not bring herself to take it away and instead let it slide down to rest on the back of his upper arm. He did not deliberate about turning toward her, he didn't make a choice and it happened fast. They were pushed and pulled by whatever was there, whatever was moving them around in the spaces. It was that very same thing that pulled their arms around each other, drew them close, and then settled their heads together along the line from cheek to ear. That same ordered space brought her close, on tip toes, finishing their little choreography with an embrace.

They seemed to draw back in the same way. Whatever had pulled them to each other, set them apart with equal determination. She became immediately concerned that inviting him in had been a mistake. She should have been ready when he knocked, they should have gone out immediately.

"Ah, so this is the bunker?"

That made it easier, and she stopped worrying. She showed him around, watching him take it all in. Everything was just as she had described it many times before over email, she had drawn him a detailed picture of the layout and the different spaces so that now he could size it up for accuracy. The kitchen. The small living area next to it and separated from the furnace room by a partial wall with an open archway between them. There was a table on the left wall with a futon on top of it. There was a couch along the back wall and a desk wedged up against the partial wall on the right next to the archway. He didn't look past it into the room with the furnace. If he had, he would have seen a partially disassembled convertible futon and a small TV on a little stand right in front of it. Further down and toward the same back wall was the bathroom and an adjoining industrial-sized shower room.

"What do you think? Is it how you imagined it?"

"It's definitely a bunker. It's not cozy. Nouveau concrete."

"It's cheap and I've been able to get a lot done here."

He nods approvingly. "You ready to go?"

He wasn't in a hurry, but the spirits of the space were pushing them out with the same ferocity as what drew them in. They could not stand idly under those low basement ceilings. They could not remain detached without something to preoccupy them. She was relieved when he asked. She was anxious to get out of there as soon as possible, and didn't trust herself if they stayed too long. She didn't know what she would do. They were both equally supercharged on the ledge of physical possibilities in the basement-soaked daylight darkness of that kitchen. Even with the brightness of the day, there was just that small window up near the ceiling to bathe them in its glow. The glimmer was breathing an enchantment into the space gods and the ways they were making. They got out of there as quickly as they could.

In the car, the space was better. The console between them. The steering wheel in front of him. There were standards and laws. The seatbelts had to be affixed, the mirrors in place. The space set them in order and gave them the trust they needed to proceed.

"Is this car new?"

"Pretty new. I got it in December."

"Did someone make you buy it?"

"It's cheap and I've been able to get a lot done here." He was grinning.

"Too big."

They were so comfortable in writing. Barriers of all kinds had been removed in those virtual spaces. They said whatever they wanted to say and had exchanged countless details. None of it seems to have prepared them for being up close to one another. They had forgotten what to do and how to do it. They made small talk.

"Thanks for being spontaneous," she said. "I really needed a break to clear my head."

"What are you writing? What's the paper about?"

She described her feminist take on the state of her would-be profession. It had been a female dominated area for many years. The pay scales were in place to prove it. Now, with the explosion of the internet and the new forms of digital catalogues and repositories, more money was pouring in, and more people. Suddenly there were men everywhere. It was an interesting topic, but they weren't really engaged in it as they drove along. She was nervous while presenting the thesis and he was nervous when thinking how to respond. They were just driving and there was plenty to look at and fill the silence. In it, he was struggling to think of something encouraging and engaging, but his mind was a blank. He had lost the ability to think and draw words from wherever it is they normally come from.

Amid his moments of straining, a loud, overly loud, exertion of air screamed out from the passenger seat. It was unmistakable. The sound of an opening throat and of air being forced out through the mouth. He knew what he heard but he couldn't make out the explanation for where it had come from.

"Did that come out of you?" he asked already knowing, but refusing to accept, the answer.

She laughed. Confidently and easily.

"It sure did. I can do it again if you like. I'm no lady."

They laughed and the ice was shattered. Suddenly it was easier to breath, and they were more relaxed.

"Driving relaxes me," she continued. "Writing a paper, on the other hand, stresses me out. Does it ever get easier?"

"It hasn't for me. I write from the belly."

"What does that mean?"

"Just that, well, I'll have my outline and be doing my research. Whatever it is. That's kind of an easy mode. Tinkering and gathering data or citations. Whatever the relevant material is. For any topic, you can do this forever. There is always something more to read, always another book, I'm never mentally ready to start writing."

"Really? I mean, even after all this time?"

"Yes. It's gotten worse with time. As I'm gathering all the material together, I start to get anxious. You know, I start to feel like I should have started writing already. Eventually this feeling turns into butterflies in the stomach. Not-writing becomes so unpleasant that I end up having to sit down and start writing just to take the edge off and get comfortable again."

"I thought it was just deadlines that caused that."

"It's the same principle. When you have classes and writing to do for each one of them, then you have your due dates and all that. When you don't have deadlines anymore, it changes. When I was writing my dissertation, this started happening to me. I would have a detailed outline of a chapter and I would be reading all the relevant material. I'd start writing when my stomach told me it was time. It had nothing to do with some reasonable realization that I had read enough or knew enough."

"That makes sense. Does wanting it to be good come into play at all? Do you get worried that it won't be any good, that whoever reads it won't like it? Is that part of it?"

"It probably should be, but I've never been good at that. The audience always comes too late, they're no use to me when I'm in the thick of it. I usually have some ideal in my mind, something I'm shooting for. I do feel a lot of pressure to realize that, to accomplish what I'm trying to accomplish, but that's not so much about what some reader is going to think, or how they're going to react."

"Doesn't your ideal involve explaining something to someone?"

"Not usually. I gave up on explanation a long time ago. It's more like a demonstration."

"Demonstration to who?"

"To myself mostly. Like my dissertation. At some level, someone might read it and think I'm trying to explain something to an audience. That's fine. People can read it however they like. To me it was all about showing a specific way in which language works. Not by describing it, but by making it work that way."

"Your dissertation isn't supposed to work that way though. If anything, you're supposed to be demonstrating to your professors that you have the necessary qualifications."

"I know. I'm saying that that's none of my business. I'm not very good at it anyway. Probably I got lucky with my dissertation, it ended up doing what you say dissertations have to do, but I'm just saying that wasn't my purpose. That wasn't how I worked out the project and that wasn't what was driving me while I did it."

"I guess we've talked about this before. Is this something you learned as you went? Did your work in graduate school make you start to think and work like this?"

"Well, it had a huge influence. My quirks were with me before that though. I had them when I got there. The coursework and the influence from others, everything I read, that changed a lot. Something was left over in all of it."

"You said once, I always think of it, that what we want, deep down, when we opt for any kind of learning, is to be transformed by it. If there was something in your way of doing your work that never changed, does that mean you weren't transformed?"

"No. It just means that I didn't see graduate school as the beginning of the process. I had started it long before."

"Trying to demonstrate something to yourself is something you learned before? You had it coming into grad school and you were looking to improve upon on it there. Is that it?"

"Something like that. Because I majored in both English literature and Philosophy as an undergraduate, I never did a good job of separating the two disciplines. Philosophy was always literature to me. I had this sense that there were different rules of exposition other than simple declarations of fact with inferential connections between them. I thought a piece of writing could make an argument with its tone or its perspective. That it didn't have to state everything in an orderly way and tie everything together with explicit conclusions and logic."

"Did someone teach you that though? Is that a principle that is part of someone's theory?"

"Probably. There were plenty of professors that seemed to imply it as far as I could tell. I can't cite the source because I wasn't following it like it was an argument. It just felt right."

"I see. Doesn't that mean you think your writing is going to be read like literature? That your readers aren't just going to evaluate your arguments or treat your work as a set of explanations and descriptions. Is it normal for literature to work like a demonstration then?"

"I always thought so. Why did I read Dostoevsky's *The Idiot?* What did I get from it? It seemed like he was showing me something. I don't know what exactly. There's a world happening there, and all kinds of things coming to pass in it. There's showing all over the place. The book drew me in immediately. All those people on the train right at the beginning. They are disconnected and then they become connected. Is he explaining that to me or showing me how it happens? This is what happens, this is something that happens. I'm sorry, I can't make it clear."

"I haven't read it, but maybe you mean that something very ordinary is happening and the way he spells it out makes you see it differently, see how it works and what happens when it does work."

"Yeah, that's a way of knowing it, but not to the exclusion of everything else. You know, we don't need to argue with the author when we read that. We certainly can't deny anything he describes within the context of his little world. He's making it up, he's the authority. The story is as it's described."

"We could say that it doesn't make sense. That it's unrealistic and doesn't speak to our experience of these kinds of things."

"That's true. There's a critical space here. We could even say that there's something realistic in it, but that the reality is specific to Russian life in the late 19th century and representative of huge social problems. All of that does amount to criticism, but it isn't a counter argument. We receive the demonstration, try to demonstrate something more that's going on, and then maybe we draw some conclusions from that. What's at stake? Do we have to take a stand?"

"We could point to the sexism in the world he demonstrates."

"Sure. There's been a lot of that, right? The two types of women in Dostoevsky's novels and the way the stereotypes fit within the phallogocentric traditions of western literature."

"The critics can then argue with each other about their critical readings."

"Yes. Absolutely, but that's the step I don't want to take. The immediate relationship with the author is different than the relationship between the different critics of the author's work. What if instead of writing a piece of literary criticism, the critic wrote another story of some kind that provided a counterpoint to Dostoevsky's view? One that introduces entirely different kinds of women, for example. That would be a different way to go."

"Like something to offset his point without directly arguing against it."

"Yes. It doesn't have to fall within the same genre. That would be totally up to the writer's discretion. I always read Bakhtin's Dostoevsky like this. It frustrates me when people argue with Bakhtin and try to point out that he was wrong about this or that, how he failed to read Dostoevsky correctly. It seems like this totally misses the point. Dostoevsky wasn't a subject to Bakhtin; he was a toy, or his work was. What can I do with this? What can be done with this? That's what drove him. Bakhtin's *Poetics* was a demonstration of what could be done. This can be done. Voila."

"This course I'm writing the paper for, it isn't exactly a feminism course, but the prof is giving us a lot to read, and her perspective is very much informed by it. I can totally fit what you're saying into what I'm trying to do with my paper. I'm not drawing from a novel, I'm using data, but I'm trying to show what can be done with the data."

"That makes sense. Like the data tells a story or can be used to tell a story. You respond by showing what can be done with it."

"Right, but what about truth? If I'm doing proper science, aren't I trying to make an argument as to what the facts are. The data is sexist, in this case. Here's why, and so on."

"Yeah, I like that. It's so common to conflate fact with value though. There are so many statements that look like facts but are really just desires being disguised to look that way. Are you comfortable with your expertise in sorting that all out? I'm not. Not really. It's one of the primary reasons I'm so passionate about learning. That's the exact thing I want to learn, how to tell the difference."

"It can be cut and dry. Mostly women were working as librarians. The digital age comes along and with it, a lot of money starts flowing in because all these companies and governments are interested in building digital archives for all the new information they care about. They want to optimize queries against it, so they pay for research and the amount of it increases. Men enter the field, and they start getting some of the better jobs. The discipline changes. More male professors, more male graduate students, and more male librarians. These are facts."

"No doubt, but there is a latent urge that there is something wrong with this. That some basic principles of fairness and equality are being violated. There is power at work and the power is influencing events in a way that cuts against some long-standing and basic ideals."

"You don't agree?"

"I'm not saying that. It doesn't matter if I agree. My point is that it's there. The norms that are uncovered and the norms that are being challenged. There are norms. They are not the laws of the universe; this isn't gravity, and I don't have the luxury of believing in a moral order baked into the universe. What does that leave me with? My decision to go along with it won't be just a factual conclusion. I can agree to a spin on the facts and reject the conclusion. Yup and so what."

"I would think you monstrous."

They laugh.

"That plays into it, right? We make choices about who we want to get along with and who we associate with, what groups we become part of. Sometimes we don't get to choose, and these groupings just happen to us. This saturates our take on the facts. I like you and I know you would think it monstrous so I would never dare to disagree. Point is that it's more than just an appraisal of the facts, there are complex social orders at stake, relationships, meanings, boundaries, alliances. All that crap."

"You agree with my point because you prefer to fuck feminists, but an anti-feminist man still makes sense to you. Is that it?"

"Anti-feminist women too. The positions make sense as interpretations of facts, as worldviews and orientations. I don't mean to suggest it's opportunistic. I'm saying things aren't so simple. These aren't conscious choices. The arguments are abstractions, they don't reflect the real forces at work. The contention between the points of view can even be in each person."

"Meaning that you can pay lip service to feminism, but still act like a dick to women."

"To specific women, yes. That conflict is real. It can apply to women too. I mean, cognitively you may agree with all sorts of principles. In practice, it's a different story."

"Okay. There's a point in certain kinds of arguments that I've gotten into, where I'll flash the people I'm arguing with. Don't laugh, I'm serious. I started doing it when I lived in New Orleans. Flashing is kind of a part of the mardi gras culture there so it's not so strange. Anyway, I started doing this in arguments with men. If I'm not wearing a bra, I mean. It depends. The time had to be right. He had to be just the right kind of asshole too.

Someone who might do or say something condescending or patronizing or whatever, and I would just lift my shirt and show him my tits."

"That's fucked up, what do they do?"

"Well, it is fucked up. It's exactly what you're saying. I'm using it to my advantage. It's like I'm playing with the conflict you're describing. It shuts them up. Something about how in their face it is. Even when they're not sexist assholes, it seems like they take it as an attack. In my experience anyway, it's an attack that they don't know how to respond to, they lose their confidence, and they lose their condescension."

"I can see how that might work. It would totally catch me off guard."

"Right, but it's like you said. I feel the conflict too. Like, mentally I'm a feminist, but this doesn't seem like a very feminist thing to do. Like somehow I'm objectifying myself."

"Hmmm. I wouldn't think so. It seems more like you're taking control over the parts that would be objectified, but then breaking it. The boldness suggests there's a lot of subject in there. Like belching loudly."

"Or spitting. Which I am also known to do."

"I'll look forward to that."

"Well, but what you were saying, sex could work like that too. Sometimes it seems like enjoying sex or enjoying certain kinds of sex conflicts with feminist principles."

"Well, in my experience, even the most ardent feminist can enjoy a raging fuck now and again. That's not the point. Sorry, I keep saying that. It's about taking control over things that haven't traditionally been within your control. That means women's bodies, women's sexuality, women's work. All of that. I would think that's very much in line with at least some approaches to feminism. It isn't just one thing. You are woman becoming. That's what the philosophers say. They mean that you get to make it up as you go along, you get to determine what that means in how you do it and how you are it. It's a fabrication. To circle back, it's like that ongoing determination, that ongoing demonstration, and it is value laden. Along the axes of those values, alliances and associations are formed. We orient ourselves in such a way that the facts become meaningful. The facts are always already bound up with our values. It takes enormous effort to unravel all that."

They had been driving all this time, but then they pulled off the highway and went walking around a small stone yard where there were tombstones, bird baths, and whatever other kinds of stone masonry that might be of interest to the denizens of Washtenaw County. All of it remained in the background as they continued their conversation. They kept talking and didn't really notice much of their surroundings. The back and forth was never interrupted, even while getting in and out of the car mid-sentence. It kept them busy, it kept them apart while keeping them together. Language was the soup of fact and value within which their walk and their time together took place. They were together there with those little space gods and the forces of repulsion and attraction.

When he pulled up in front of her house later in the afternoon, she put her hand out to stop him from getting out of the car.

"Don't walk me. I have to get back to work. I'll be done soon. Can we get together this weekend? Friday? I got a sub for my shift on Saturday too."

"Friday would be great. I'll email you."

She leaned over and kissed him on the cheek.

"Okay," someone said.

She was gone again. Just like that.

She lurches forward going flat onto her stomach, then she flips over and quickly crabs backward to get further away from him. Their eyes meet. Both clearly shocked. "What are you doing?" she says pulling one of the pillows over her.

He sits back against the wall that acts as a headboard. "Are we having trust issues?"

"Are you trying to get me pregnant?"

"That's crazy. You're getting that from a couple of moans? Can't I just be enjoying myself?"

"Something's been going on with you lately. You're more possessive. Almost romantic sometimes. It's like you're my boyfriend."

"Okay, that might be true, but I don't think that's about you and I know how the rhythm method works."

"What's going on then?"

He grabs the other pillow and pulls it into his lap to mirror her. "A couple weeks back, one of those literary agents I sent my packet responded to me. She wants to take on my book. It seems pretty promising; she works for one of the better agencies."

"That's great. Fantastic. You've only let me see bits and pieces, but it doesn't surprise me from what I've read."

"Thanks. It got me thinking. Some friends of mine are losing one of their house mates. It's in Brooklyn. I've been thinking about moving there."

"That'd be very cool. When?"

"Nothing is set. Still exploring options. They're not even sure the guy is leaving."

"That's it then, that's why you've been acting strange?"

"No, not really. It's more about the writing. It feels like there's more pressure now. The story has gotten so weird, it's so different than when I started. I've got romance on the brain all of a sudden."

"How do you mean? What I've seen never had enough context for me to figure out what you're doing."

"Yeah, it's been a moving target. That hasn't helped. It's his fault really. The fucking professor. You know I came here because I hadn't written much lately. I thought if I spent some time with him, I'd get unblocked. You know how he is, there's always so many ideas flying around. I figured something was bound to stick. Last fall we spent all this time talking about the early Heidegger. It was a good topic for us. In grad school we had taken a course together. It was on *Being and Time*. He went back to it in a big way, and I went along for a little bit."

"You're writing about Heidegger?"

"No, that was the launching ground. He was trying to tell some grand narrative about the true meaning of the book: the power to be and the role of authority in all that. I kept trying to break it up into pieces, like I was specifically resisting his reading. He labeled his thing 'Being, an Introduction' and I labeled mine 'Fragmented Readings of Being and Time.'"

"Okay. You guys thrive on that, right? You seem to have lots of running arguments that you keep coming back to."

"Yes. This was one of those little clashes that came from a bigger one. The system vs its fragmentation. While we were struggling over that, I got this wacky idea. Like, what if things had gone differently for Heidegger? What if in 1933, he totally and completely lost his way? What if he became a zealot and toed the Nazi line with complete fidelity? Everything was as it is up until the rector's address, but then it all changed. His writing in the 30s was completely different than what we know. The Nietzsche lectures were all for the glory of his fearless leader. Everything else too. Since he was such a zealot, he ended up taking one of those other jobs that kept coming up and he ends up in Berlin and maybe even ends up in the inner circle. In 1945 he's in the bunker and he dies."

"Is it kind of a historical novel? Heidegger is a character?"

"At first, it seemed that way. It started out as a fragmented reading of *Being and Time* where I was mostly trying to discover the onset of that madness in it, but then I started thinking of it as just plane fragmented readings. It wasn't just about Heidegger anymore, I was finding the onset of madness in all kinds of actions and works. Not from the 30s, everything was decided by then. I became obsessed with things that were going on in the 20s. Not only in Germany, but in the US too. The rise of a new physical paradigm, a new economic paradigm. I started spinning it all as the onset of madness. There were disparate human projects invisibly collaborating to build an imperial force."

"That fits with those bits that I've seen. Some of that stuff was pretty disturbing."

"Yes, and then the notion of it being a reading of any kind at all started to morph. First reading meant something like reading books and the work of writers, but then it became readings taken from a measuring device, something that was tracking the mood of the times like they were rumblings under the earth. The story is the story of all these changing ideas, and it's anchored by a transient romance between a god and a mortal. In February or so, it became just 'fragmented.' I started to see their involvement and everything it framed as the history of a spreading virus or a disease. It took off at that point. It's been writing itself since."

"That explains a lot. I noticed a change around then. At least in your work habits."

"Well, we started spending more time together around then too, right?"

"That's why I wasn't sure at the time. I thought maybe I was just getting to know the real you better."

"Yikes. Okay. That could be. This isn't normal. At least, I don't think so. Since I spoke with that agent, it's been different too. There are some bits coming up just now that are central to the drama. I'm worried I won't be able to make it do what I want it to do, I'm worried it won't come out right."

"Is that different from how it normally is?"

"Sure, I see your point. Yes, though. Definitely different. There is more pressure now, and their romance is center stage in the drama."

"Okay, so you've had that on the brain lately. Who is the god and who is the mortal? That might explain some of your boyfriendy behavior."

"It might. Yes, it's the same battle between the ordering of a system and the disordering of its fragmentation. When people fall into things, romantic entanglements, what exactly is going on? Are the great axioms of love taking over their lives? Are they breaking apart and losing touch with their primal order?"

"Love? The great axioms of love?"

"Alright, that's overkill. I'm including infatuation and idle desire. All the things we do. Things we want, things that relax us and things that stress us out. Everything that grinds and shakes us, that moves us this way and that. We will sacrifice things, we will change our plans, everything is at risk. Is that because of an underlying order that is taking hold or is it the dismantling of an order?"

"Very cool. This changes how I've been thinking about your ongoing conversations about academia and discipline. The professor is locked into deconstruction, right? He thinks that there is some order at work and that its being at work is also its unraveling."

"Well, we argue about what that dynamic is like. It's this same question though. Is the primary order systematic or whatever? Is it fragmenting? Does it put us together or break us apart? Is the subject being constructed or dismantled? Are coercive powers using the distributed subject to reinforce their claim on personality as a construct within a distribution?"

She moved to sit next to him, leaning back against the wall. It was dark outside. They couldn't see the moon from the window next to the bed, but it must have been nearly full, there was light in the room.

"You're exploring all these ideas through fiction?"

"It's more like a mythology, but I'm trying to avoid being moralistic. You know, accusing my enemies of being evil."

"Who are your enemies?"

"That was a device. I don't really have any enemies. I just mean that I don't want anyone to think it's going to boil down to a struggle of good vs evil. Even if the story makes you feel that way sometimes, that's more of an attribute of desire and emotion stirred up by the struggle than something in the matter itself."

"Spinoza again."

"How so?"

"You know, the delusion of the rational *man* that the fabrications of his mind are real and worth fighting and dying over."

"That's a helpful point. I hadn't thought of that. It's another way of thinking about love."

"God and mortal though. Weren't you thinking about the intellectual love of god in the context of a move beyond good and evil?"

"That's fascinating. I should reread it. How did I miss that? I've been saying it's better to see it as a move to somewhere before good and evil though. Like they need to struggle to work it out. If it's beyond it, then they would have all that baggage, they would be wizened by the difference, like aufheben. That's a way to colonize the residual. That could be the professor's move, but mine is back toward innocence. Back to the garden of Eden before the fall. Not as a desire for the pure presence of the origin, the clarity of purpose that lies at the beginning, instead, it's the Nietzschean metamorphosis from the beginning of *Zarathustra*. Forgetting is central to the child."

"The dialectic is the system at work, its ordering. Being fragmented overturns that. Is that it?"

"More like it forgets it. Stops paying any attention at all to it. It no longer sets itself up against something. That's why it isn't beyond it. Forgetting makes it seem like it never came across the difference at all."

"Is it about to orient itself? This is very abstract, but if the point of the story is to bring events to a point where they are before good and evil rather than beyond it, does that mean that the decision will need to be made? If we are before good and evil, then good and evil are in our future. Nietzsche meant for us to be done with it, didn't he?"

"It's not an argument. I'm not trying to say he's wrong or that this is a better way. I'm saying there is that and there is this. Why can't it be like that?"

"No. I get it. I was just trying to figure out how to make sense of it all. It's still hazy. I'd have to read the whole thing."

"Definitely. I know. I'm doing a horrible job. It's like he's going through that metamorphosis, only backwards."

"Who?"

"He, whoever, someone. The fabricated persona that is the matter at hand."

"Not the professor, or Nietzsche, or Heidegger, or Spinoza, or whoever?"

"All and none. Just the indexical subject of the pattern under investigation."

They laugh.

"Back then, when we first met, he was like a child in that way. All the emotions of greed and envy weren't there. He was just trying to figure stuff out."

"Children can be greedy. They can be envious too."

"You're right. I mean that the idealized child of the metamorphoses isn't represented that way. It's situated before those feelings. The child is at play, in a sense, without understanding the seriousness behind it all."

"I see. A mythology."

"Yes. Throughout his education, he was transformed into a lion. That's what I mean by going backwards. He entered the system as a child. Then he started to rage against those structures that threatened his innocence. They made him become a lion. He refused to go along and may still have been in that phase when I came along."

"When you came along?"

"Yes. To the story. It's like I discovered it. Not really an invention, I found it and took on the task of relaying it. Writing it all down. You know, the measuring device. Fragmented readings."

"Right. Sure."

"The climax of it all is the final transformation. He becomes the camel. He loads up with everything he can possibly carry and he's going to head off into the desert. The lion, as it turns out, didn't clear the way for the child like Nietzsche says, but is a reactionary response, a defense mechanism. The camel is all that's left in the end. It's all he can do; he has to depart and head out into the desert."

"You think that's what the professor is doing?"

"I'm not talking about him. That's not the point. I don't know. It's a fabrication. Pure delusion."

"What is though?"

"All of it. The story, the dilemma, the struggle. Everything at work in these constructs is mechanism, it's all getting in the way."

"In the way of what?"

"The simple truths. Of the moonlight and the night. Of what's happening here. The wine and the song. Laughter and tears. Whatever matters."

"I see."

"He, and now I *am* talking about the professor, he's been ruined in a way. Spoiled. In a civilization where the only reason people go to college is to get certified for some career they're interested in pursuing, the institutions that provide that certification, if they do it for a fee, are bound to be changed by it. That's to be expected. The corporations have an interest in how that certification works, they get involved financially and want to have a say. Even if they don't directly have one, the requirements they attach to graduating job candidates will impact the expectations of those candidates insofar as they are customers of the certification process. The students will demand things to better prepare them for what their employers want."

She mimics playing a violin.

"Right. That's the tale. Engineering departments and science departments, anybody who has a skill to sell, or something deemed valuable in that world, they barely notice. If they do, they like it. More money, bigger houses for the faculty. Administration likes it too. They grow in such an environment. They become like a whole new industry refining their means of producing a deliverable in response to customer demand."

She stops playing.

"Blah blah," she says. "Everybody says this."

"True, the real damage is done in the humanities. They think they're the only ones left fighting the good fight."

"You don't agree?"

"I most definitely do not. They are the conservative past, they are the tradition, the canon. It's such a joke when people lobby for more inclusion, the admittance of marginal voices. It makes me furious."

"Because you're a reactionary asshole."

He laughs. "Yeah right. They aren't attacking the existence of the canon or of the tradition, these aren't populists we're talking about. They just want to revise it to include people who have been kept out of it. The humanities, in some seemingly anti-traditional activism, have become the primary supporters of tradition, even if they are advocating a revised cut of it. They are the conservative core of civilization, the last front against total decay, the loss of meaning and value that corporate colonization brings."

"Do you think corporate colonization is a good thing?"

"No, but the solution isn't in the elitist values of the ivory tower. The drive for the margins is a kind of elitism. You're an uneducated philistine if you haven't read the right things or if all you ever talk about is the standard history."

"Don't they think they're challenging elitism?"

"Sure, because ordinary folks are routinely found reading Fanon and Irigaray."

"What's wrong with Fanon and Irigaray?"

"Nothing. They're great. That's not my point. There's a world of difference though between being Fanon and being some poser who read his work and now thumps it against their hand while lecturing students about it. How radical can such a professor be when it comes to truly evaluating the social position of the people who pay them?"

"I don't think that's fair. Not everyone is like that."

"Not at first. The requirements of the tradition, the shit that really matters, forces everyone to go that way, to be like that. Eventually."

"What requirements are you talking about?"

"The focus is all on what they're going to teach, what the students need to read, and how to preserve the curriculum in the face of all the corporatization. They don't focus on process, on how the bureaucracy is changing and adapting, and then all the ways in which it isn't. How tenure works, all the adjuncts."

"That's exactly what they are complaining about, the requirements around tenure are directly linked to the canon and what counts as legitimate work. You've completely missed the point."

"No, I don't think I have. It's just one orthodoxy replacing another. Ultimately there are mechanisms and techniques. They have to be employed; all thinking must pass through their sieve. There is nothing intelligent that can be said or done without them."

"The explosion of voices, all of them saying the same thing."

"At least saying it in the same way. There are no stylistic differences because there is literally a manual of style, and everyone has to follow it."

"Even professors of the humanities, even when they attack commercialization of education and the destruction of learning, even when they do that, they are being stooges of bourgeois notions, even then they are the conservative struggle for the good and the evil that we have known in the historical order, but modernized. Is that your point?"

"Post modernized, as the case may be."

"I get it, you don't trust them. Their concerns are totally opportunistic because they come from a place where there is all this scarcity. Vicious competition and the lack of true community ensue. In a dog-eat-dog world, they struggle for prestige and attention; they need to make a mark to qualify for the next promotion. They can't really fight against that because their fighting might even be what gets them that promotion. The acceptable channel is to cast it all in terms of a generalized notion of the corruption of knowledge."

"To bring it all back full circle, I became confused as to whether this so-called 'love of wisdom' is itself an order that is taking over or a fragmentation of the existing order. The organization of academic work has exploited desire and longing and infatuation —and even sex— as the primary means of maintaining an order."

"It's how they get us."

"Absolutely. We're marionettes. Deny it if you can, but even if we weren't talking about it, those motherfuckers would be here in bed with us."

"Interesting choice of words."

"Damn straight. All academic analysis is a psychoanalysis of the world spirit. There too, it's all about sex. What gets you off and how to get more of it."

"What twists and turns will it take?"

"How to make room for the alternative and the marginal, the traditionally perverse. It isn't an alternative formulation of the power patterns in sexuality, it's those patterns themselves. The patterns are the thing, there's nothing else to it."

"The humanities without the sexual harassment just aren't the humanities."

"You joke. I'm fucking serious. You know that fine line between an idea and a belief?"

"What fine line?"

"I articulate a position. Suppose that amounts to a set of ideas. I might just be describing the way that Trappist monks think about the role of the deity in their daily work. It doesn't' mean I'm a monk, right? I can state the ideas without believing in them. I have to do something more to say I believe, something that takes me across the line. I assert it as true."

"Okay sure."

"Turns out, that's an ubiquitous pattern. It's everywhere. If the guy is an asshole, he's stalking you. If he's hot and charming, then he's wooing you. It's a fine line. The behaviors aren't the issue. At least, there are conflicting signals there."

"It's about consent."

"I get it. That's the affirmation condition of all liberalism. The presence of the act of will with the idea. Belief, if you will, as opposed to the mere idea. Pun intended."

"You think that's the role of sex in the humanities?"

"Yes, that's the role of power *and* sex, of all the disciplinary relations, and coercion too. It's okay if they consent to it. If they don't, they're free to leave. How wonderfully enlightened, how liberal. Look at the professor, is that the right way to put it in his case? Is he free to leave?"

"You like him, you want to protect him, you even adore him in a way. I can see that. He has that effect on me too. What you're writing might be about him and not just some one or all of them."

"Yes, he's definitely in it, a part of it, and so are you, by the way. It's hard for me to separate myself and the people I know from this tale. As I said, it's a mythology. This isn't about individual people."

"As the master says, there are no parts, that is an illusion. We are all just substance becoming, the mind and body of god going about its busyness. Seriously though, you think he shouldn't leave; you think he should stay and fight, or stay and work to change things?"

"The organization must be changed. I would agree with that if it is to survive. He could play a part; he could help make the institution more like it has to be for people like him to do well there."

"By definition, he can't do that. I mean, if he were the kind of person who could do that, he wouldn't be the kind of person that you would want to do it. You see what I mean?"

"Yes. It's like that dream I told you about. From when I was a kid. The monster was chasing me. There were lots of people around. It was really crowded, and I was dodging in and out of the crowds, all while running to get away from this monster. Suddenly, I had a realization. The key question was 'why is he chasing me?' With all these people, why target me? It dawned on me that it was because there was something about me that was threatening to him. Me in particular. Like, somehow, he had to chase me because I was the one who could do him the most harm. This gave me confidence. It was so sudden, the shock of realizing it. I still remember the way it felt even though I must've been ten or twelve years old at the time. I stopped running and turned around. I was going to find that monster and put an end to it, once and for all."

"Was that dream erotic at all? I mean, you were a kid, but I could imagine that being exhilarating. You're saying that desire, or sex at least, is both the way in and the way out. Is that a part of your story? Is that what you are trying to get across?"

"The in and the out? Is that what you're asking for?"

"Fuck you."

"That's exactly what I had in mind. If you don't think it'll be too messy."

"I never said I minded the mess."

There is no many, not at first, there is just the one. That might be the lens grinder's point. The many are themselves products, and maybe they are modified by looking at that one substance through those lenses that he grinds. He has to have had an effect. One cannot read him without making more things than there were before. With each reader and each reading, still more things are made. Is he defining and shaping them or grinding them down into dust? That is how the story goes, if there is one to tell, that it would all be the ways and means of the one, its striving and its becoming, all of it without end an aboriginal limitlessness. The many that appear, her here and him there, those of them all around, as well as each item in their orbit. They are semblance and lust, falling short of that intellectual love of god. Shema Yisrael.

In nature, there are neither wholes nor parts, or rather, there are wholes and parts, but they are products of cognition, human contributions to the world at large intermingling with fauna contributions, flora contributions, and whatever else the creatures of the world have brought to bear upon each other. Animals of all kinds gaze on in fascination at what we've made. The trees are too stunned to speak. Squirrels and rabbits almost seem embarrassed as they scurry past, trying to avoid making eye contact. Every being that lives knows this burden of the many carved from the one. It is the burden of manufacture, of being thrown out into a projectile life that recovers meaning to itself, absorbing what is not it and shedding what is. Maintaining a balance in the sway of the wind, breathing light in and out, breathing air in and out, breathing earth in and out, water, even breathing fire. On a good day. To the extent of them, each is striving without ends. Each creature finds itself and struggles with the where and the how of it. Desire may propel, but there is no end.

These motions behave like resonance, every chamber fills and empties. At a glance, we know anger and compassion, longing and comfort. Our passions fill us and each of our moments, it is the philosophers who thought to write this down. This thing that everyone knows and always knew, they must have been viewed as magicians or shamans or something out of the ordinary. Imagine one of them bending over a surface that is hidden from view. What is that in their hand? I can't quite see it. It can mark up the plane and be played back later by others who know the same magic. The technique may have been otherworldly, but the means were long understood and familiar. They spoke to each other about the river and what lay on the other side of it, about what would happen when next the sun came up, and about what prospects for the time ahead would lie in the basin nearby. How many fish? How many buffalo? How many will still be here when summer comes again?

Fascination would have been close at hand. These things we have long told ourselves, things the great mother said, things from the great father. Theirs and theirs and theirs again. All the ancestors and all the telling. The marks are theirs, and since the words were magical already, the marks must have taken their long history upon themselves. Writing it down carries it with them and holds them inside the stories of what happened, of what might still happen, and of what we should fear and what we can hope for.

"As for Vacillation, Cowardice, and Consternation, their very kind and nature indicates their imperfection. For whatever they contribute to our advantage comes from actions of their nature only negatively. For example, someone hopes for something which he thinks is good, but which is not good. Nevertheless, because of his Vacillation or Cowardice, he happens to lack the Strength of Character required to carry it out. Negatively, or by chance, he is freed of the evil he thought was good." Thus wrote the lens grinder.

Among all this clarity, the manifold appears. Was this a common saying, a note of wisdom that everyone shared? Did he write down the obvious yet again? Among the emotions and the passions, these are what may be found and how they work and what they mean to us and for us. Was it there or was it here: "Longing is a kind of sadness arising from the consideration of some good that we have lost and that there is no hope of our regaining." What was he showing us? Something we already saw or something we needed to see? He tells us this and that, but does he say why he is telling us at all? Why is he writing this down? Who is it for and where is it coming from? Why didn't his father write it down or his father before him? Were these tales his mother told? Why didn't she write them? All these unmoved movers in his past, before him, and there he was affected in this way, torn from silence by modes unknown to those who came before. Why? What is the where to of it all? That this striving occupies us I have no doubt, but where does it come from and why does it look the way that it does when it does and otherwise elsewhere? What is the geometry of a human life? What moves us hither and yon? Why do we go so merrily along without the wonder for being that all those other animals bring to each encounter?

How does a human being (i.e., Martin Heidegger of Messkirch) investigate Being —or anything else for that matter— without including people in the investigation? That would require a theoretical gaze, a view from nowhere, which is itself the product of an historical determination of what is human. The many begets many more than before. Growth is exponential, like an airborne virus moving through the herd. The ontological presupposition of the mind of humankind is the ontological itself, it is the power to cast whatever is at all and the power to be among it, to have something to do with it, to attribute meaning to it, to react to its significance, to not merely brush past it, but to engage and wonder at it, to accommodate it, and finally to welcome it into your thoughts for a day or a month or a year. Even still, to resist it, hate it, and condemn it to disorder or disuse. We turn away and we can turn toward whatever may be. Admit it. You do care. Something matters.

For the two of them, at night, that night, it started at dinner, where the manifold is just madness. With people everywhere, at the next table, at the bar, and serving the food. She wore a dress and he put on a nice shirt. This was the semblance they chose. It is the waitron's job, she explained as though telling it for the first time, to size up the customers right away. What are they doing tonight? Are they transitioning from one place to another, or is dinner their main event? This will impact everything. How quickly do we need to bring things? How many refills? Everything matters. Of course, in their case, she has to figure out the politics. Are they an old married couple or is this something new? If it is something new, the waitron has to make it all about the woman. She is explaining this to him, intermittently. The waitron whose section they are in comes around on cue and does exactly what she is supposed to do, what the librarian has clearly catalogued that she will do. Most eye contact should be with her, what does she want, does she have everything she needs, or is there anything else? In no way shape or form should she flirt with him. If it's new, that'll put her off, while taking care of her will make him happy. If he's paying, and the librarian makes sure that he knows he is, he'll show his appreciation as expected. It comes off just like that. She tells him that their waitron is incredibly good because she is following the expert script. It may seem rote and machine-like, but these are the skills of the trade, and they are hard to master.

He listens, fascinated, and he cannot look away. Their eyes are regularly locked throughout dinner while they poke at their food. They are not hungry, and something is distracting them. Each other. Still, they go through all the necessary motions, even ordering dessert. She matter-of-factly states that they shouldn't be kissing on the corner in front of the Del anymore. No, we can't have that, she says. It's not the public display of affection, she explains in response to his silent question, it's the proximity to the Del Rio that is the problem. She says it crudely, is abrupt, and smiles slyly knowing the effect. He still does not look away, he is mesmerized. The way he listens moves her further. She is comfortable in this way of being and enjoys his welcoming response. She fantasized about being with him all these months long, and this is what she meant. Not just proximity, but in word and deed, at ease and without effort. His fascination increases the appeal. She felt it like she would if he were to touch her arm, peel back the sleeve, and stroke lightly from elbow to wrist on either side, back and forth, lightly, with an ever so slightly varied pattern. Not too repetitive, not too random. Somehow, he would know the sweet spot between too much order and not quite enough. This would be a summary movement, a reconciliation of all the time spent apart, of the distance, and the elegant leap across it.

It wasn't a lecture; this has to be emphasized. It has to be written in just this way, at just this time: she did not lecture him. She wasn't even telling him what you think she was telling him; she was just saying that they were known. The waitron, even if only mechanically and as a problem to be solved on the job, was getting to know them just like the bar staff who might have been looking out the window that day when they were out there on the corner in plain sight so that they could be known. They were becoming an experience for others to have. She didn't frame it that way, but it is what he was hearing. Her eyes were so alive while she said it, how could this be a lecture? There was no distance. What about the crudeness of it? It wasn't vile or off-putting, it was an invitation to intimacy. It drew him in, they were beyond charade, they could relax and just exist together. She was telling him about this public self while at the same time demonstrating it. The energy could not be missed. The waitron saw it, the bartenders or doorman would have seen it too. It is a tangible thing.

The boundary of touch is fastened secure in the time where they were. It was the time before, before any consensual and unfettered touching would begin. They dangled it in front of themselves, both playing at it, leaning toward each other with it. This would be a fragile moment that is so hard to learn, because we shun learning it in favor of the weight that comes when he rests upon her, or she rests upon him. He would never touch her arm like that again. After the first time, that boundary would be gone and there would no longer be any way to dance back to it.

He asked her if this is what she meant. He didn't say it. He didn't clear his throat and gesture in the direction of anything specific; rather, he reached out. A performative question doesn't find a place in the philosopher's dictionary, but it found a place at the table that evening. She knew exactly what he meant. The bittersweetness of it passed between them. What is the name of that emotion? Where in the doctrine of the passions is it defined? Does it raise flags to suggest that it grounds them, makes them hot, moist, and quickens their breath? That it takes hold of all of them and finds itself in the taking hold that each of them can and will do. In holding each other, wrapping each other up in themselves, they become proxy to the one substance and the realization of its many affects. Whatever has been learned within the parameters of a single attribute cannot have any impact on any other attribute. By proposition but not by lecture, it follows that they can indeed touch each other to make this known. The magic is that they already know it. They both already came from there, grew up with that, and understood it. The evening was simply their fascination at watching the world write it down, something so obvious, something everybody already knew. Here was this moment, here was this stretch of time, in which the universe, the one, set about putting it on the surface without using whatever instrument was ready-to-hand at the time.

His apartment was the draw, she hadn't seen it before. In her mind, maybe, so she knew what to expect. She walked around, giving herself the tour. The bedding in the living room made it seem forbidden. Like it was someone else's bedroom, and it would have been impolite to enter unannounced because there was nowhere to knock. She expected this and pursed her lips when she saw it. She asked if he was around and nodded when he told her what she already knew. These are simple patterns. We have a shorthand. "At his girlfriend's" carries so much. No details necessary.

She recognized the kitchen from his moments and his gestures. She recognized the dining room table and felt him there. She knew the laundry closet and the desk just inside the door to the bedroom. She knew the bed, and, better still, she knew what he knew about these things, she knew how they worked for him, how he reached out to them day in and day out. She didn't know the feel of it though. She turned to him and let him know that this was what she came for, this was what she wanted to find out for herself. She sat in the chair at the desk and felt the fabric of the seat. She touched the books on the surface, she leaned toward the screen and then noted everything that was within reach and that came into view as the chair swiveled this way and that. This is what he sees, this is what he glances over as his mind fills with whatever must be said or done next.

None of it was guesswork, all the non-lecturing had taken care of that. She may not have been at home, but she was making it her place, piece by piece, generating an energy and a presence in every corner of every room. The movements throughout the night had been so charged with each of them that there could no longer be a single moment when that final distance was definitively bridged. There was no moment of origination and no singular event. Rather, each and every step was itself an emission from the never-ending event and the never-ending moment. They had worn it all down in a way he hardly believed himself capable of carrying out. She learned something about that, about how it can be done, how something can happen that requires that two people hear the same thing. She learned that listening was possible even if she did not fully believe it. She thought she had made it up, that it was the fantasy putting constraints on whatever reality she had known, but there it was.

It makes sense that they would pursue this with their noses, and smell everything, every part of each other. Not with any judgment, but as if they were fashioned out of different material, made from different instincts and evolutionary fibers. Smell was no longer the age-old way to discern between poison and fruit, between decay and the fresh scent of the living. Instead, it was a form of appropriation, it was preparation for their mouths, it was a test for taste, and a way to breath another in and become a part of them. The scent itself was an actual exchange of material substance. They were becoming attributed of each other, filling up, and bursting with the dizziness it brought. These events of acquisitiveness are part and parcel of that aboriginal mine-ness that defines each moment, that opens up as the projectile life that lives itself forward and backward in these pockets of time. As their smell turned to taste and as they took on more and more of each other, expanding their own proper domain, their breathing would regularly keep pace and announce to all the surfacing possibilities that they could finally know together.

It might be tempting to think that the tantric is camouflage for a deeper impotence. Not that she didn't like it, but it was something more and less than she expected. An orgasm transformed it into what she wanted, and then another transformation to take that somewhere else, somewhere special. That's how it goes with wanting, and with surprise and the unexpected, but there were questions, and she didn't know how to ask them. "What about you?" Was all she could muster; all she could find that would say it without any accusation or hint of frustration. He shook his head, it didn't matter. He couldn't explain it to her, not there and then, not in that place, because he couldn't find any casual words to say that teleology and chaos didn't mix. He didn't know how to say that he wanted a dancing star and that he knew that it could not come in the form of an end brought on by available means.

This got them to talking. Naked together but still held apart with verbal boundaries. He asked her the words for things as though he never knew what they were or how they are called where she comes from. He was right to ask because she had very definite views and they weren't what he expected. She pointed and grabbed hold. She named each thing in turn. Who is the goddess of naming things, he wondered? There were stories to tell, and she told them. Why not use this word that is so beloved by many but was so terrible and offensive to her? She gently warned him never to use it and told a story of how she used to hear it in the streets of New Orleans in situations that had made her uncomfortable. Instead, she used a different word, thought harsh by many, but explained how cheerful it made her. Because people only say this in anger, she said, it's not heard very often. If you can say it with desire and feel the pleasure of its sound, soften it with all of that, then you will know it. He tried it out and found that she was right, about that and about everything. There were no bounds to what she knew and what she was able to say.

The weekend was a vacation for them both. She stayed throughout. He cooked a little, they went out, and they ordered in. Nearly every moment spent in bed, undressed, continuing to smell and taste each other. They were learning their rhythms and teaching each other to each other. The phone never rang, no one came to the door, and they didn't run into anyone they knew. It was a pristine cocoon —as luck would have it— and they stirred it by mutual delight. They embraced it as the proper outcome brought on by months of planning.

One of the two nights, he is not sure which, but probably the second because it would have needed more time. He never told her what happened, not outright, he never needed to as it came out sideways, like a twisted breech, but he dreamed of Aletheia and Polyhymnia again. The former was just as she had always been: harsh, unfeeling, and most likely uncaring. She had no interest and paid him little mind. This established the dream world and declared its familiarity. She would not play a part, but she would open the scene and announce the events to come, she would guide everything and be a part of nothing. Polyhymnia, as usual, would be where all the important events played out. She had been transformed, but looked the same. She told him what words to use and warned him that some did not belong. She encouraged him and helped him find his way around her. She was transformed but did not lecture. He told her he wanted to know her, how she smelled, and he told her that dreaming wasn't enough because he couldn't taste anything there. He told her, in no uncertain terms, that he loved her, and only her. She knew and pointed out that he does know what she smells like and does know how she tastes, and that he knows this better than he has ever known anything else ever before.

He hates to admit it, but she was always Wolfe's passion. He had been the one to first conjure her while claiming she belonged to no one. Erato and Calliope were everywhere, but who claims Polyhymnia? Who even writes battle hymns anymore? The professor hates to admit that Wolfe writes them and that he might have fooled him into writing them too. This point slipped away in the dream. He couldn't quite see it there though the sense of it drifted by and bemused her every motion and appearance. This may have been what woke him. The dream could not sustain itself beyond that sense. All the hatred in the admissions had no place in a world expanding there with her and the other. Aletheia evades it, or maybe it liquifies her, leaving only steam. The image of Polyhymnia breathing in Aletheia was the last one that touched him as he departed that world and came back to the sheets and the librarian's body and the breaking daylight.

She awoke with him and drank him in just the same. In the foggy morning hour, he could not remember who was who, the players were mixed in her gaze, and he let slip the actual thoughts that were passing through his head in the wake of the receding dreamworld. Ill-advised and too soon, he promised her he was without guile and that whatever mistakes he made were innocent. She struggled against his words; it was too soon. He could not love her, could he? In the end, she was reminded that there were no ends, that he had demonstrated this again and again and that it was this very flavor of innocence that made it so. He was true or would try to be. Even if the songs they would sing would be battle hymns fashioned out of the moments ahead and the moments together. This put an expiry into what they had. From where they lay on that day or one of those days, in how they lay together draped and tangled, it felt like endless streams of power and pleasure. Their shock spoke in the surprise at finding those two together, and their insight that there was nothing there to initially repel them. Evening comes from morning with performative questions of its own. What was initially so, where would it lead, and how would it get there? Having lost those touch boundaries once Sunday evening came around, they were drunk with the pleasure of something bigger and more visionary making them dance and sing together. They joyously kept the beat and felt the strings pull at their hearts silently separated while pumping together.

It had been her plan all along. The end of the semester and starting something new. Now was the time. She would take a class in the spring, of course, but she was ready. The panic of not knowing where he was that day, it was bound to happen. She didn't fault herself for it and had to admit to it when talking to her friend in Yellow Springs. The professor wasn't really a distraction anyway, he could be helpful. Whatever problems she was going through in these last six months, he had always been able to lend a sympathetic ear, he had always seemed to understand. This alien mind that she was getting more and more used to every day was a part of his experience too. He had exactly the right touch, and it was light. As bold as she was in most things, this was not her native land, she was still finding her way and had come to know him as a helpful beacon for lighting the way without making any loud noises. He spoke indirectly leaving her to figure out the application, the where and the how of it. She appreciated that and had to admit that physical proximity wasn't changing any of that, it wasn't a tangent to the bond they had been forming, it was an extension of it. She hadn't been actively thinking of it this way, but as it unfolded, as they spent day after day seeing more of each other, she felt an immediate relief through his presence.

That first weekend, he had read three passages from three different books to her. The words were important, but so was the act of doing it. He stood there leaning into the light, holding the books in front of him, but not looking down. His eyes were fixed on hers as he read. It was a kind of play acting, and he seemed genuinely moved. He wasn't reading. The first started off with "What is a poet?" and it was by Kierkegaard. She had never heard the word before, the one he used to describe it. He called it the Diapsalmata, and said they were a collection of short writings meant to be like psalms. That was where the name came from. The words were beautiful, and he was beautiful standing there reciting them. It was about how critics don't know anything about what goes on with poets. None of us do. We applaud their pretty songs without realizing what it costs them to produce the work. Kierkegaard's image was powerful, they were being slowly tortured, but it was happening in such a way that when they would scream, the sounds would be transformed into music that we loved to hear. The critics pretend to be like the poets, but they are missing the primary ingredients, they do not suffer, and they do not make any music. The last line had stuck with her. She wrote it down as she remembered him saying it. She wished she had been able to draw or describe exactly what he looked like as he pronounced that last sentence. "I would rather be a swineherd understood by the swine than a poet misunderstood by men." What could come next? Silence, but then he told her there might be a bittersweet irony in this passage. He said he was worried that you could only hear the romance in it if you were at a distance from everything the poet knows, all their experience. Only someone pleasantly bewitched by the music could applaud the sentiment in the psalm. He said that his love for this passage haunted him. It wracked him with guilt every time he thought of it.

This was what she had really wanted to write down in her notebook that weekend. It wasn't just that sentence, it was what it meant to him. How real it was. This was what she wanted to get hold of, this was why she was there. She knew there were people like this, people who were so possessed of ideas that they were like a presence in their lives. It was so fucking attractive to her just then. This was what was missing when she spent her summer evenings down by the river with that gang. They would drink and laugh, smoke and tussle about. An ideal presence had been missing from that and she knew it should have had a place nearby. She never realized that its existence would be the very definition of a haunting, a non-physical presence that hovers nearby and has an effect. She wanted to write that down, so she tried and then never showed it to anybody.

The second one was full of piss and vinegar. That's what she really loved about it. It wasn't passive and idle like she had heard some people describe the life of the mind and the people who lived it, it was fire and passion. It started "Do you know what this world is to me?" Like the first one, it started with a question. It was a brief and isolated passage and had a number above it. He said that it was just a loose page left over when the author died. She hadn't read any Nietzsche, but she had heard all about him. Even though he was widely known to have been a misogynist, she had always been attracted by the little bits and pieces that she heard. Bold. Unapologetically clever and intellectually nimble. The phrases were always so large "Ubermensch", "Will to power", "Beyond good and evil,", "God is dead." Scary stuff, but not what she had come to expect from writers and thinkers. The way he recited it, again poised in position as though he were reading, but hardly ever looking down at the book in his hands, it was a turbulent world filled with tension and opposition, conflict and contradiction. It was like he was talking to someone. That was what struck her about these questions. These great writers, it was as if they were talking to one single person, asking an otherwise rhetorical question so that they could go on to answer it themselves. The answer they gave was completely unexpected and they couldn't be faulted for that. He seemed to emphasize each bit perfectly and the meaning was clear through the intonations and fluctuations. "Do you want a *name* for this?" Like there was something too simple in reducing it all to a name, a single thing that we could call it to make it easier to bandy about, easier to put in a box as if it were something we already understood and didn't need to investigate any further. "Twofold voluptuous delight." That stuck with her, and the look in his eyes when he pronounced it.

"This world is the will to power and nothing besides." That had been the name of it in the end. Not just the world, everything in the world, each one of us too. He had been clear about that, although she wasn't sure she knew what it meant. They talked about it, but she was distracted and whatever he had said in explanation didn't stick. It was too much really. One side of her brain wanted to laugh. At Nietzsche. At the professor. At the whole thing. It was all so ridiculous, and he seemed to know it. If the first passage had shown her his guilt, this second one showed her his shame. He confessed it knowing full well that it was all so laughable and ridiculous. Boldness, he had mentioned as if barely considering it and tossing it off as though it had been repeated again and again by anyone and everyone, was a kind of self-mockery "and nothing besides." The laughter and wounded pride of bold action, the crippling self-criticism of one who doesn't believe that he deserves his confidence but can affect it with play acting and composure, none of it had ever seemed so clear. She didn't know anyone else was on to this, it was something she thought was her secret. Here it was, plain as day.

The third passage wasn't bold at all, not exactly. It had a different feel to it. It didn't start with a question, but it somehow still seemed to be one. It had started with "Idle reader" and the way he read it made her think it was an accusation albeit gently put. All of it had a feel like the author was talking directly to the reader and gently warning them to be careful in how they handle what they are about to receive. That was the boldness she sensed. It was a prologue, so it was announcing the book the reader was about to enjoy. The author knows what lies ahead and likely has a sense of what he has done, what he has made, and what lies in store for the reader in the days and weeks ahead as they work through these stories that they hold in their hands. He worries that the reader will take it all too lightly and will rattle off a criticism or feel an emotion, breezy and unaware of what lies behind it. He called the main character "the child of his brain" and apologized for feeling the pride of fatherhood in defending this poor soul whose folly will be a source of entertainment for the onlooker, sitting comfortably in their chair and safely propping up the book in their lap. The story had been company for him. It had come out of his loneliness and now it was there for their enjoyment. It ended with the author telling the reader that they could think whatever they like about this creation of his. It didn't matter one way or the other what they thought. The idle reader is only a spectator, they have no real investment. He was warning them to be sympathetic, and to have some compassion for the character locked in that world and having to go through these same misadventures again and again as each new reader comes to the book. The author too has to relive the pain of the telling with every new onlooker who comes with the same curious question: what happened here?

Guilt, shame, and now folly. She wanted to write all that down. He was naked when reading to her the last time, but she remembered each of the readings that way. He was showing her something he wanted her to know. It didn't seem to have anything to do with Nietzsche or Kierkegaard or whoever the last writer was. He wanted her to know that these were his friends, or these were the people he spent so much time talking to, day after day. This was what they said that stuck with him. He couldn't help it, he knew it was absurd, that it made a punchline of his life and that he acted exactly as anyone might have imagined one with such rot for brains would act, but he had to show it to her so that she would know. She could not have predicted the impressions it would make. If someone told her that it had been her plan all along to expose him as a stereotypical overly introspective man made silly by flights of fancy and delusions of grandeur, she would never have seen that the execution of it would result in a great rush of compassion and lust. All of it came up behind her in that way these things tend to do. This may have been the point of that very folly, the life lesson inside of it. What seemed one way in the evaluation of the plan would be a much different story when it came to the act and the experience. Being there in that apartment with him and listening to his voice, she heard guilt, shame, and folly. He had made her his accomplice in it.

At the time, she wanted to ask him how men do it, but didn't know how to say it and didn't really think he would have an answer. Like it was something too far below the surface for anyone to have a ready answer for those who wanted to be in the know. Sitting at a distance, alone, she could have painted this picture in an email and teased him with it, and maybe he would have been wounded. At a distance for sure, but painful nonetheless. Face to face, on the other hand, in the glow of the single light that created an island in the darkness, she knew the desire in it. He made it easy for her to show him, because none of it came out as a barrier raised but unfolded in a gentle voice as a barrier lowered.

While sitting on the grass just outside the back door wall to his apartment, she read what she had written down during that first weekend. She wore her bathing suit and the sun felt good on her shoulders and legs. It was spring summer. Outside on her own she wondered what he was doing, and she turned to look through the glass and shielded her eyes from the glare. She thought maybe she could see down the hall and into the back bedroom, his hands reaching out from somewhere, the only part of him that was visible, resting on the keyboard and clattering away at the keys. "What goes on in that man's mind?" she wrote.

She couldn't see him really, maybe she had invented an image to match what she thought he ought to be doing, or what her ideal of him would have him do. In truth, he sat in that chair where she knew he was, but his hands were not on the keyboard, and he was not clattering away. He was staring at a blank screen and a blinking cursor that kept asking him over and over again: "what?"

He could not write her an email. She was sitting just there, out back. He wanted to tell her about his last couple weeks. Even though she had been there all throughout, he still felt that there was a friend who needed to learn what had been going on between him and this woman he had finally started spending time with. The split was what kept blinking before him. He worried, for the first time in years, that maybe he didn't have anything to say about that. Was there nothing to say or maybe no one to tell?

He didn't reach out to the keyboard, he folded his arms and leaned back in his chair. Each day had carried something with it. She had let him into her space, her apartment, and shown him all the secrets she kept there. The way the futon was balanced on an unsteady table. She showed him that. They slept there, they rolled around on it, carefully. It inspired her to rearrange things, she reconfigured the furnace room and fixed up the futon frame that folded out into a bed so that it could become their main place to sleep. He had practically fallen off the table a few times, and she joked when he commented on the new arrangement. The last thing she wanted to do was put limits on his movement. This made her laugh, not least of all because she meant it.

She showed him how sometimes she didn't eat a proper dinner but would snack on candy all day long. It would put her in a mood by evening, full of energy and ready to go, but drained and unable to get there. He drew conclusions from these revelations and wanted to tell her all about them, about how he had learned these things from her, but what was the point? She either already knew or wouldn't be able to understand it when he tried to describe what he heard in what she said.

She showed him how she needed to put the TV next to the bed so that it would give her a familiar setting to help her fall asleep. The show she liked that was on right around the time she went to bed had a musical punctuation of two notes that marked dramatic scene changes and events. It had become a lullaby to her, these two notes. She was comfortable in their resonance.

The echoes of the first weekend were frequent throughout the last few weeks and into this weekend. Sometimes at his place, sometimes at hers, the pressure eased, and the power increased. He knew it and it had been immediate for him. Whatever had happened for six months at a distance was over in the blink of an eye. They were together, instantly. As if a decision was made and the conditions were set with a single swipe of the pen. What? He stares at that blank screen. He can't make heads or tails of anything he was trying to say in the second part of the book. Everything after the interlude is muddled. Does it still occupy him? She is outside, sitting in the sun. He doesn't write but leans forward and cranes his head to look down the hall and through the window. She is reading something. She is quiet and yet there is so much brewing there. He cannot find the tranquility in her, even in that setting.

Of course, women do not know the pleasure-pain of an aching erection, but she seems to understand it. With her hands, with her belly, and with her hips. It's not theory to her, it has a pulse. There is no distance between either of them or in this retreat. They feel every bit of it and are affected through and through. Now he knows the feel of her beneath him. Going through all the phases of development, it begins and ends in their mouths. Kissing, licking, sucking. Even whispering is speech only in the mouth. They were finding that together, and they whisper because they are so close that too much timbre will hurt their ears. In the whisper from right up close, done carefully so as not to breath too much into the ear, she says things that he cannot say, that she would not like were he to say them. He likes that. She says with pleasure what he wants to hear; and he says with pleasure what she wants to hear. They feel each other's pleasure in giving it so deliberately. He wants to write that down too. Does she know this? Who told her? He hasn't said a word about it. Which word would suit this purpose?

Suddenly it occurs to him that he doesn't need to write any of it down. The gap that separates his hands from the keyboard is not real, not anymore. He visualizes his own action and sees how ordinary it would be to just stand up and walk down the hall, through the living room, and slide the door open. He could step out onto the grass and into the sun. He could sit down beside her, smell her hair, or kiss her shoulder, just as he liked. She would smile and welcome him. Where have you been, she might ask. She already knew that his travels were often elaborate and that he didn't want or need to shout them. It had been her choice to find a man who needed coaxing to reveal where he had been, and to let such a man get so close. She made it clear that this was as it should be, but how did she do it? How did she communicate this? He didn't know but was grateful and filled with disbelief.

Having already crossed the land in his mind, it hardly mattered whether he did it with his body. Not from any familiar point of view, just the pleasure-pain reminded him, drew him to her, and launched words across the space between them. "Come inside," he said more with his eyes than anything else, although his lips did follow. His mouth. A whisper. She explained so much by leaping up and coming quickly to him in the doorway, all smiles and anticipation, on the edge of laughter, but instantly drawn to desire. On the one hand we see an infatuated pull. On the other, there is a pragmatic push. Arriving at the door and pushing him back inside, he pulls her to him while she whispers redundantly and playfully, "coming."

They found a place to park on a side street just off Packard. The cat and mouse lived in a worn-out looking apartment building like many others around town. Cheap walls, cheap finishes, everything cheap except the rent. Inside, they were making the best of it. There was wine, plenty of it, but the librarian and the professor had brought more. When they arrived, it was the topic of conversation and a matter of the highest priority.

"Thank you for bringing that. We have a lot. We made a wine run today and got all kinds of stuff. You want a glass of red?"

"Yes. Whatever is open."

They were going to eat at some point, but wine to begin with. It might help. The first meeting with the friends was an important test. They were just figuring out how to be with each other on their own, now they needed to come up with a friend mode, a way to be together around her friends, this time. His friends would come next.

"It's amazing how big the range of prices are. You can spend 3 dollars on a bottle, or you can spend hundreds. That's just at that store up the road."

"I can't tell the difference."

"Hardly anyone can after the first bottle."

He couldn't keep track of who was talking, this rapid fire. They could have had this conversation before. There was the cat and there was the mouse. The librarian too. They had a rhythm; they were piloting it on easy mode and trying to show him how. He was hesitant but felt invited.

"That's why I opened the best bottle first. Later we'll be on the swill, and no one will care."

"At the restaurant there were customers who would never lose that taste. They were so schooled that even wasted they couldn't handle the crappy stuff. They would send back bottles if they had turned. Sometimes you doubt them, but often they're right. The ones who know."

He wondered if this was interesting. They were just trying to set a mood, so he played along: "I've always been confused by the descriptions. Oaky fruity nutty. I don't know how to separate flavor like that. I really don't know how to apply words to it. They're grapes, right? It's always fruity. No?"

This met with general approval. He was getting the hang of it, and they were glad. They refilled the glasses and brought out a cheese plate with some crackers. This was the extra-curricular part of what they had to learn from their schooling: hosting exactly this kind of party with this kind of vibe and these sorts of refreshments. It was as if they were trying to recreate the reception after a colloquium in their apartment. Working and learning to do it just the way they were supposed to do it, just the way everyone would expect them to do it. The cat or the mouse saw the opportunity here. The professor was an ambassador for what they were aiming. Their best hopeful yet. The setting was essential and the impression crucial.

"Do you cycle?" one of them asked him. He might've been surprised but the initial banter showed him the habitus of all that would follow. He knew they would touch on all the appropriate subjects. Each would have its pairing.

"How do you mean, like in phases? I guess. Doesn't everybody?"

"No, I mean do you ride? Do you have a bike?"

Suddenly he noticed that there were two bicycles hanging from the ceiling near the front of the apartment.

"Ah yes, of course. That is one of the pillars, isn't it?"

"You do ride?"

"I have to. It's a requirement. In grad school it was my main form of transportation. Here, I've been doing it less, I drive to work."

This was a tangent, and they were going to follow it. The question had been a lure. The cat, he thinks, wanted to tell him about the bicycle he had just bought. It had special features that were the main reason he selected it. Something about the gears. It wasn't clear. He might have been talking about the breaks. He didn't go on too long, that would have been against protocol. The purchase had set him back and he wanted to make sure that everyone knew this was justified. It wasn't vanity to buy it, and to prove it he had to emphasize the importance of these features. Within the tribe, knowledge is an important way to divide up and rank the members. Knowing about wine, knowing about bicycles, these things matter. Right at the outset, it has been established, we all have to recognize the terms of the order.

The cheese had a story too. The other one spun that narrative. Again, there are many choices. It is overwhelming and you must have the proper taste as well as the knowledge to act on it. They were humble people, unassuming in their way, even if they did focus their concern on all the right topics, everything that was supposed to matter, and with just the right emphasis. They didn't have the knowledge to establish themselves yet, but it would come. One day she would know exactly which cheese to get, and which wines would best complement them.

"These taste really good. They seem to go well with what we're drinking. As far as I can tell. I like Cheez-its too. There you get the cheese and the cracker all rolled into one. Everything included."

There the mouse became a cat and laughed with great relief. She liked Cheez-its too. She hadn't found a vintage yet that didn't go perfectly with them. It loosened her up. He didn't seem scary.

"You said you drive to work. You're working in Dearborn, right?"

"Well, I was. It was only for Fall and Winter semesters. It's over."

"They won't have you back in the fall?"

"No, it was a sabbatical replacement. That professor is back in the fall and the department doesn't need any extra help."

"Oh. Where are you going to be teaching then?"

"Not really sure. I might be able to get a few sections at Washtenaw Community College, but it's not settled."

"Did you apply anywhere? I mean, are you interested in finding something?"

"Oh yeah. Definitely. I sent out a bunch of applications. No interviews though."

"Now, were these only jobs in philosophy or did you look for other ones."

"How do you mean?"

"You know, like in different departments."

"Well, my doctorate is in philosophy. That kind of limits me."

"Sure, but now they're doing theory like that all over the place. You could go into other departments too, right?"

"I'm not sure. It doesn't seem like it works that way, but I should look into it."

Everyone was kind and trying to be supportive. He didn't explain that the suggestion was absurd. Well, that it wasn't at all absurd, but that the organizational approaches of the various departments were so narrow and tightly controlled that the thought of a philosopher getting a job in cultural studies, a critical theory program, or an English department was preposterous. It would be highly irregular. He didn't want to go into all of that. He wanted to change the subject, but he didn't know how to do it under the circumstances. These sorts of conversations with people he had just met were always risky. What people were saying never had anything to do with what was going on. The words were just filler, they were trying to situate each other and make it easier. This was normal stuff, but he was awkward and unsure of how to proceed.

The best tactic was to mention a bit about how the departments work. He pointed out that philosophy departments had a reputation for being elitist since so many rejected the legitimacy of the kind of social theory that was popular in the other departments and programs. This way he could stick with the subject without steering them off, but at least keep them away from the awkward "what are you going to do?" which they didn't really want to ask, and he didn't really want to answer.

They didn't know that philosophy departments had this reputation. This was exactly the kind of inside information they were always looking out for. They were immediately ready with follow up questions.

"Philosophy professors think of themselves as the old guard here. It's established and has been around for thousands of years. Cultural studies, which is how they lump all of the work being done across many different departments in the humanities and social sciences, is new and not fully developed. The philosophy professors think it's fluff and vapid. There aren't many appointments for people who have focused or partially focused on philosophy. It's because the contempt is public. These other interdisciplinary programs and projects, whatever they may be called, they have no choice but to reject philosophy in just the same way that philosophy has rejected them."

"It seems like a huge mistake for philosophers. The world is changing, socially. Digital systems and digital information are only just starting to take hold, they will snowball. We haven't seen anything yet. Why don't the philosophers want to get in on any of that?"

"That's a great question. You would think it would be philosophically fascinating and relevant for how we know things, for how things are. Epistemology and metaphysics. This is ground-breaking stuff."

"Ethics too."

"Yes, and ethics."

"We need philosophers to weigh in on this. To help guide the way. Don't you think?"

"They'll weigh in whether anyone wants them to or not. I have a little different take on it."

"Explain."

"Well, we're not really talking about philosophers here. We're talking about philosophy departments at the university and how they work across disciplines. In the last few years, at least where I've been, it seems that philosophy professors are happy to work with cognitive scientists and biologists or physicists, but they aren't nearly as keen to work with social theorists. That stuff is too squishy, too flakey. The philosophy professors want to be real scientists, and they want to make serious contributions. They say these other guys are careless and don't follow proper methods."

"That could be how they help, I mean, if it's true. They could have an influence by contributing to make those methods more rigorous."

"They could, I guess. My first point was to suggest that whatever this resistance is or means, it doesn't have anything to do with philosophy. It's all about departments at universities. How they're funded, who they hire, and how they shape the future of their discipline through curriculum."

"It has to be that way, doesn't it? You have to keep the wheels turning."

"You do, or someone does. Most definitely. Where I was headed with it though was that humans will do philosophy wherever they happen to be. It will find a way. If you want to identify the philosophers, don't check for credentials, but see who's filling the role, who's playing the part? It might be film directors, or cultural theorists. It might be the weekend news commentators."

"Wait though. Does that mean that you only care about the popular role, the people who are playing the part in the larger scheme of the society?"

"In part, for sure. It works this way with everyone. A lot of cultural theorists think directors are the philosophers that most inform their thinking, or they work through the writing of Walter Benjamin or Hannah Arendt. The point is that they'll get it from somewhere. The letterhead doesn't tell you who they are, the work does."

"I see. Philosophy is alive and well."

"It is definitely alive. The interdisciplinary work done in cognitive science is a different approach. The philosophy professors want everyone to think they are scientific, and the scientists want everyone to think they are the new philosophers."

"It seems like it'll all come together at some point. Philosophy always does. If it's supposed to be the most general of approaches, the big picture. Information was always paper. Now that's changing. How we investigate things is changing. How we question and query. Everything is changing. Societies will change around it. The departments need to change too."

This put the conversation exactly where the other three wanted it to be. Suddenly their career choice was of the utmost social and historical significance. They all chimed in. Catalogues. Metadata. Search. The seizure of information from the stores where it is being slowly and systematically consolidated. There is where the philosophers will be. One way or the other, they will find a way. There is where the librarians are too. You cannot have the one without the other. Aristotle must have said something to that effect to Alexander.

They continued the conversation into dinner. He brought a big dish with enchiladas, she served them all around.

"I still don't see why all this doesn't mean you could get a job in a different department. If your area of expertise is what they're looking for, why does it matter what department you were in when you wrote your dissertation?"

It was rhetorical. He didn't answer, but the other one did. He seemed to know best how to extrapolate all this. It was very catlike. He pointed out the skew that the discipline would give it. Even if the professor had read Foucault or whoever, it didn't matter. From these interdisciplinary perspectives, he hadn't read the work properly. His angle had been too focused on the traditional methods and approaches of philosophy departments. That would be a given. Barring anything out of the ordinary to change that fact, it would be considered an axiom and wouldn't go undetected by those who were going through the resumes submitted to the committee.

The professor, feeling very much like the boyfriend, nodded in agreement. It was expected that he would. The wine and food made him agreeable, and happy to do it. Nothing would be settled here, there was no short list to make. What does it matter if this cat or that mouse, whichever, gets to have their moment in the sun here among friends? We can play at being the wise guy, the one in the know, the answer man. We can collect ourselves into little outings where we take turns getting away with it, setting each other up and placing each other on pedestals. He remembered his friends in graduate school. That's exactly what it was like. Each of those in the group establishing themselves as the resident expert in this or that. Large amounts of their time together aimed at sorting all of this out. They wrote and read so that they could get together afterward and set it all in order. They had learned to do this from their advisors and their teachers. It was the expectation. They knew that none of them could be the rival of their professors just yet, but that wasn't the point. Not at first. It was as if they were electing graduate student representatives and all of it was to form a governing body. The professors weren't even the highest level, they too were just representatives of a still higher order. There was a national and even an international body. Some of their professors were small players in the field, and some were bigger. The point wasn't the one or the other, but the representation that must be at work in it. Everyone had their place and their established role, and they jockeyed for better positioning. That was what it meant to have a career.

When they left, the librarian was in a very good and playful mood. Things had gone well. He had been charming and friendly. Absolutely everything she had hoped for and nothing that she had feared. She had never seen any arrogant qualities in him, but she reserved judgment. It was possible that he had been on his best behavior before, that he was intentionally holding back on his poisonous personality for the sake of getting in good with her. With her friends, it might be harder to hide it. She suspected that might be the case, but tonight he seemed just the same as he had always been. That he might, after all, be what he seemed was a thought that made her happy when mixed up in her stomach with the wine and the food.

All he could think about afterward, during the walk back to the car, was the way time worked. Where did it go and where did it come from? He hated how dependent he had become on Heidegger in moments like these. He couldn't even think about time anymore without hearing the whoosh and whirl of a thrown projection. It seemed so powerful and noisy. If there is a clearing that comes to pass in / as / through the passage of time, then this is it right here in front of me. Behind me too. This is the experience of it, its event and its happening. Where are the values in that? Where is the good of it and the evil? Why does it wear us away, cause our bodies to wrinkle, and our minds to grow rigid? How do we find each other there without shattering into little pieces from the collisions and the confrontations? Does anyone really need to devote their life to showing this and exploring all its questions? Who cares really? If they have been there and experienced it, they don't need to be shown. If they have not been there, then how can someone else show it to them? It may very well be a cult established by a common experience that cannot be fabricated from any external cause. This might be why those traditionalist professors of philosophy stand so strictly opposed to the practice. They perceive the bond in the cultists' strange language. Even if that language isn't any more difficult to learn than the predicate calculus or the semantics of a Kantian critique, they hear the alien words as spells and incantations. They know black magic when they see it. They have been bound by the liberal tradition that has learned to condemn these black arts as the antagonism of all enlightenment and the sound glory it brings.

June

"I called her and tried to apologize. Well, to tell her why I had to leave and why I couldn't be a civil human being and just sit down and explain it to her at the time, why I had to be a bastard and just disappear like that."

"You *tried* to apologize?"

"Yes, I tried. I called her, but she didn't really want to hear it. She was angry and hurt and wasn't interested in any of my excuses."

"That's fair."

"I know. I had to try though. It's how it works. I did what I thought —at the time, at least— what I thought I had to do. I wish I were a stronger person and could've faced up to her. I couldn't though. I didn't think I could do it. I just had to go. It would have been too tempting. I would've needed a drink to have that conversation. That was the whole point."

"She didn't give you a chance to explain?"

"No. Calling just made her really mad. She yelled at me, didn't let me talk much."

"Does that mean you still need to make amends to her?"

"Yes, but people won't always let you do it. I'm not in control of that. People are going to do what they're going to do, say what they're going to say. That's not up to me. I have to accept the fact that I owe her, and I have to accept the fact that I blew things up so badly that she won't let me pay off the debt."

"I see."

"Being able to accept this is part of the recovery process too. It isn't easy."

"I can imagine."

"The immediate knee jerk response is to be like 'well, fuck her, I tried.' That's bullshit though. That's me making other people responsible for the fucked-up shit I've caused in my life. I have to take responsibility for what I did and that includes taking responsibility for hurting people so much that they won't even let me apologize or make up for what I've done to them."

"Well, you sure can talk the talk. That's clear."

"Exactly. Who's the philosopher who says that though? That the key is to just keep doing it and eventually you will have the qualities you're pretending to have?"

"Oh, maybe you mean Pascal? About carrying out the acts of faith even if you don't have it. Once you've repeated them often enough, the faith will come. You pray for faith as a mechanical act so that one day a miracle will happen, and you'll have it."

"Yeah, like that. If I talk the talk long enough, eventually it'll be true and it'll be because I'm living it the way I'm describing it. I'll be walking the walk."

"Okay, but that doesn't do her much good."

"I know. If there is nothing I can do or say to help her, then I have to let her go her own way. Whatever that is, it's not up to me. I'm her problem, or I was, but I have to let that go. She may not forgive me for it, but I still have to forgive myself and move on."

"That could turn out to be a convenient way to think about it."

"I'm not trying to get out of it. Honestly though, what do I really owe her? I have a right to leave her if my sobriety depends on it. She can't make me stay with her. The rules of common decency require that I be open with her about that, that I try to explain it to her. Ideally, it's something I would have done at the time. I'm saying that I just wasn't strong enough to do it. To make up for it, I try to call her now —after the fact— and explain. What more can I do? If she can't listen to me or entertain my explanation because it's too little too late, then that is what it is and there isn't anything more I can do to make up for it. Doesn't that seem right?"

"Yeah, I suppose. You should send her a gift basket or something. Anonymously. Sorry, I don't mean to be flippant."

"Forget it. I know it sounds like a rationalization. I'm open to suggestions. I can't think of anything else to do. Anyway, what else is going on? What's your situation?"

"I've applied for unemployment and been approved. Even though I only worked there for 8 or 9 months, they didn't object to my application."

"They better not, those bastards."

"No doubt. It was a bit of a pain to file all the paperwork, but now I only need to call into the automated system once a month to have them generate the check."

"How much is it?"

"Almost as much as they were paying me. It's surprisingly good. It lasts for six months."

"If you get that gig at the community college, will they stop paying?"

"It depends on how much they pay me. It may just reduce the amount of the benefits. They're only offering about $800 per section. Not really a living wage."

"Damn. You mean 800 for the whole semester? 200 a month?"

"Yep. That's like 10 dollars a day if you only consider working days. With grading and prep, office hours and class time, if I put in about 2 or 3 hours a day, we're talking somewhere between 3 and 5 dollars an hour. Turns out college teacher is a minimum wage job."

"Okay, so that's not going to work. What's your actual plan?"

"Well, I've been learning about 'htx' and 'idc' served up by IIS, and about the way ISAPI works to handle requests."

"ISAPI I know, but what are 'htx' and 'idc'?"

"Well apparently IIS has a built-in ISAPI filter that understands a specific content delivery approach. Htx files are templates, they provide the layout for the web page. They mostly just look like html but there are legal parameters that can be part of the template. Parameters that describe how data is supposed to be inserted into the layout. The data is defined in the 'idc' file. Basically, the 'idc' file is a connection string to a database and a query that can be executed against it."

"I see, so the parameters match up with the schema of the query and allow you to build the page content with the data that's returned."

"Right. Anyway, I've been doing a lot to learn html and pretty much have it down. Now I'm starting to learn to write more and more robust SQL queries."

"Sequel."

"Is that how people say it?"

"Some say SQL, but the cool people say sequel."

"Okay. Well, I'm definitely one of the cool people. That's my plan, anyway, to learn sequel and how to best design and implement a database. I'm guessing these are things that'll be really important. These web pages need to be generated dynamically from stored data and there'll probably be a huge job market for people who know how to do it."

"Out here, there already is a huge market for that. You're definitely right, knowing how to muck around with data will be a great tool to have in your toolbox."

"Thank you, mister career counsellor, good to know."

"No joke. You might also start messing around with trying to write your own filter. If that template protocol is too lame or doesn't have some function or feature that you need, try to write a different one."

"How does it work exactly?"

"It's all request and response. The browser you're using makes a request. Usually that's just the web address, http colon and all that. Normally you're just writing the content of the response. That's what the html in your web page is. It's a pure markup approach. ISAPI is middleware. You can use lower-level code to prepare the content of the response programmatically. It sits between the web service and the content delivered to the client. The built-in filter is reading your 'htx' file, running your sequel query, and using code to merge the results with the template. Once all the data has been filled in, the generated html is written into the response stream and sent back to the calling client, the browser. You could write something with more sophisticated logic than you're getting by default with their filter."

"Okay, well, I'll look into it. That's what I plan to do in the next six months anyway. Just learn as much as I can about this stuff and then see if I can get a job somewhere. I'll probably create a little corporation or something and turn all my educational lessons into consulting projects for that company. It'll make it look like job experience."

"Seems like a good plan. There's plenty of work for people like that around Ann Arbor. You'll find something, but is this what you want to do? Couldn't you go back to Illinois and get work at one of those schools you were working at before you moved?"

"I don't know. I'm sure someone else filled in there by now. That was a primo job among adjuncts. Might've been a mistake to leave. I didn't even bother to try. Besides, I like it here. Things are going well, and I'm enjoying this stuff."

"I'm not surprised. What do you like about it?"

"The structured query language. The relational schema. It's all so philosophically rich. Even the notions of perpetual relay of request and response. It seems like a perfect incarnation of distributed substance."

"The fuck? What does that mean?"

"Spinoza. The lens grinder himself. You know, the master. For him, substance is a purely formal substrate. All-inclusive and closed. An immanent set of relations, causes and effects, that underly all expressions."

"Like the physical universe?"

"No, it's even more formal than that. The physical is already a way of slicing and dicing the purely substantive. The underlying relations can be expressed physically. Those same relations might also be expressed otherwise. Cognitively, for example. At least these are the two attributes he considered. They were all the rage back in the seventeenth century. Today he would probably describe a physical attribute, maybe a chemical one, biological, psychological, hell maybe even a sociological attribute."

"Pantheism, right? A version of it that effectively turns out to be atheism."

"I'm no expert, I'm not a scholar. I've read *Ethics* and tried my best so take this with a grain of salt, but yeah, something like that. He got in trouble because his version of god is so purely formal that it has no mind and doesn't occupy a position transcendent to everything else. Rather, he identifies the one underlying substance that is god with the attributes that express it. He's perfectly happy to flip flop between calling it nature and calling it god. The point is it can be purely described using the language of external objects of sense or using the language of mind and mental operations."

"Must've been pretty radical."

"He was, no doubt. He denies freedom, he thinks we assign freedom to things because we don't know what causes them to act the way they do.

It's pure ignorance, the imagination just taking over. He says that things we artificially give an independent existence are just moments in a causal chain, partial facets of larger and longer processes, the boundaries of which we cannot see or do not understand."

"Because even our knowledge of them is already a set of effects within a cognitively defined causal chain?"

"More or less. He thinks there's a physical description of a body like mine or yours moving itself in such a way as to paint a portrait or write a book. He thinks that descriptive chain is independent of any cultural or psychological description of the same events."

"In the physical description, no ideas or goals are required to explain how the body produces a painting?"

"That's right. He says that people who reject this, thinking final causes or ideas are needed to describe that process, are just ignorant of the richness of physical processes. They don't know all the wonderous things the body can do. Their ignorance leads them into absurdities."

"Isn't this just reductionism?"

"You think everything supports that. This is the exact opposite of reductionism though. The psychological cannot be reduced to the physical, the chemical, if he were to see it that way, couldn't even be reduced to the physical. These are simply different parallel attributions that it's possible to assign to the one underlying substance."

"Okay, maybe you can't reduce the mental to mere extension, or the psychological to the chemical or whatever, but you're saying that all of these still rest on top of that same formal substance?"

"Yes."

"That formal substance is pure relation, it's the causal chain void of content. Right?"

"Yes."

"That could mean that each of the domains or whatever they are."

"Attributes."

"Each of the attributes reduces ultimately to a set of relationships."

"Yes. There are contemporary philosophers who've been really excited about this. They say it's an approach that fits well with quantum notions of the universe."

"Okay, but isn't that a reduction? If the domain of the relationships is the domain of the mathematical, then the physical is essentially math and so is the chemical and the biological. The psychological and the sociological too. They might not reduce to each other, but they all sit on top of the mathematical relationships: the ratios, the measuring, and the relating."

"I see. Why wouldn't the mathematical be just another attribute of that set of relationships? By trying to be purely formal, math might be good at trying to express the base relationships, but still, ultimately, it's just an expression. It isn't purely formal, there is material in it. Equations. Statements. Then it isn't a reduction of the psychological to the mathematical, but it may appear that way because it's possible to both express those relations in mathematical terms and psychological terms, or any other in the set of attributes that humans have uncovered through inquiry."

"At least that would be the basis of our disagreement then, right? You think that math is just an attribute and I consider it to be substance itself."

"Could be. It would explain why you sound like an idealist when you make that claim. You're putting a non-extended attribute at the base of all others. It would also explain why you think I'm a nominalist when I make my claims, I'm setting the foundation up as an extraneous set of labels and names that merely express the relationships in one way rather than others that are equally valid, depending on context."

"Every domain is attempting to describe substance, whether it's math or psychology, it's all trying to elaborate these basic relationships."

"Yes, and because the foundation has this notion of striving built into it, that impetus toward movement will find its way into all the attributes of substance. It might look like experience in psychology, and it might look like inference in mathematics."

"Alright, let's not go there again, so supposing I accept that just for the sake of argument, how does it relate to sequel?"

"The data model is an attribute of the underlying substance. Queries and the relational model are a way to surface it. Like we said, underneath all the requesting and responding, the massive relay of requests and responses, there lies a set of relations that are best captured in a data model, then there is a structured query language that can be executed over the top of that model."

"Not just executed over the top of it but used to extend it."

"How so?"

"Well, the database is made up of tables, right?"

"Yes, each table is a set of columns and rows. The columns are like properties of the things contained in the table. The rows are like instances of the thing."

"Exactly. What do the results of queries look like?"

"Columns and rows."

"Right, so a table is just a query."

"Why not the other way around?"

"Okay, it doesn't matter. What we're saying is that each column / row structure is an entity form, a kind of thing that exists, where each instance is identifiable. The thing may either be stored in a table or structured in a query that combines the data from multiple tables into a single result."

"With joins."

"That's right. In the database, the join is all important. Most of what you're doing when you design an entity model in your database is figuring out what the tables are and how they relate to each other."

"I see that."

"That relation is expressed in foreign keys that are used to join together two or more tables, or even when joining one table back to itself recursively."

"I see, so customer could be a single entity. You shove everything about them into a single table, or you could create a roles table, a person table, a company table, and an address table. Each of these has one single row for each person or each company or each address, etc. The 'customer' is no longer a simple single thing that occupies one single row in the database but is a query result where the query joins together the persons with the companies, with the addresses, and the roles."

"Exactly. The data is stored in an efficient format, a normalized form. The query extracts the data in such a way as to extend that and assert the existence of a type of entity, something sophisticated and complex like a customer. Really, we'd have to add a sales table into the mix. The sales relationship makes a person who we can contact into a customer."

"Sure, I see. This is why it all seems so deeply philosophical to me. The query itself is what culls the real entity, the meaningful object that you act on or look at."

"Right, the customer is a construct from the data and extracted at run time when trying to build the web page for a user."

"It's an ontology, but can I get it wrong? I mean, there are multiple ways to define the same data model, right? I could just put all the data in the same table."

"There are different ways to do things. The measure is always practical. You would be violating the best practices if you put it all in one table; you would be violating the normalized form."

"What does that mean? Concretely."

"Well, if you and I both work in the same office building but have different rows in your table, some ways of storing the data would force you to put the address of that building into each row separately. The same piece of information is repeated over and over with every person who works with us at the same location. That's called denormalization."

"What's wrong with that?"

"Well, it's wrong because we don't work in different buildings, we work in the same building. By putting the address duplicated in separate rows, you're suggesting these are different buildings that are somehow dependent for their existence on the row they are in. That's false because inhabitants come and go without destroying the building or changing its address."

"Yes, I get that, but that could just be my take on things. An alternative way to describe the relationships. Like a relativist approach where everybody sees and experiences the location differently, so it has to be tracked differently. Why is it wrong as a relational design?"

"It doesn't scale, for one. Proper functioning under large scale conditions is one of the most important practical considerations when designing your model."

"If you change the address you mean?"

"The company moves, or the city renames the street. Whatever. All the rows have to be updated. Not just one row somewhere. The rows might differ just a little bit too. Like some might say '1ˢᵗ street' and others might say 'First street', or something like that."

"How is that a scale problem?"

"Updates would need to lock many rows in the table so nothing else can look at them while the change is taking place. Let's assume there are 10,000 people working at one of the addresses you have. That's possible with some of these big companies. If that address changes, you will have to lock 10,0000 rows to make the update. Some database systems would just turn that into a table lock that locks the whole table instead of just those rows needing to be changed. If there are many different people using the system and doing other things irrelevant to the change, this could cause all kinds of problems. They would have to wait for whatever they're doing until those locks are released. The waiting might timeout and they could see errors and have to redo their work. The more operations happening at the same time, the more problems this can cause."

"If it's a little database you might never notice."

"True. These are scale problems. Something that's not a problem when there aren't many items to work with or many users doing things, but become a huge problem when there's a lot of items or a lot of users."

"I see. The query itself could cause a scale problem too?"

"Yes, definitely. The people who make the database system are supposed to take care of that. If you define your relationships correctly and define indexes on those relationships, then the storage is supposed to be able to scale queries that use those relationships."

"How do the indexes help?"

"Indexes are just duplicate ways of organizing and storing the data. Have you heard of clustered indexes?"

"Yes."

"Those are binary tree storage containers that relate all the data in a common structure. The point is that a b-tree offers faster search. If you have a sorted binary tree of all your data, you can search through it exponentially faster than if it's just a flat list of values. If the top of your tree is the exact middle of the sorted list, then you always know whether to move to the left or to the right to find what you're looking for. Like when you look things up in the dictionary and immediately know which way you have to turn the pages to find the word you want."

"Indexes are b-trees then?"

"Clustered indexes are. The non-clustered ones are related to the cluster, they're attached to it. When you index data, you're storing it in an optimized format for the sake of making queries against it perform better. You still have to write the queries to take advantage of those indexes though."

"I see. The point of your table design is to optimize for your query which must in turn be optimized to properly pull the data from the tables based on their indexing. You can define complex entities using queries and those queries will scale properly if the underlying relational model is optimized for them. The keys and the indexes ensure that."

"Exactly."

"I swear, I could totally derive a philosophy from this. I could build a fundamental ontology of the relationship and the extraction event as query. Inquiry itself surfaces the fact intertwined with its various domains and properties into a complex entity. The context for this query operation is always driven by a request / response relay that constructs the objects of experience. It projects them into an action context, or process context, where that might be psychological in the case of an act, or chemical in the case of a process, or whatever else there is in whatever other contexts that are possible. This can be done in various ways. Optimization will depend on whether the higher order structure properly and correctly attributes the underlying relations."

"You totally could. You should."

"That's what's drawing me this way. If there were lens grinders today, this is what they would be doing. The modern-day lens grinder is the database engineer, the expert in the relational calculus and design."

"Why does that matter? I mean, why be a lens grinder?"

"Spinoza, so the story goes —I have no idea where I got this from or how to substantiate it—but I had heard that Spinoza refused to profess philosophy because he equated it with taking money to think. He thought it was immoral to do that. He went off to make a living grinding lenses while practicing philosophy separately."

"You have to think in order to grind lenses though."

"True, and you are being paid for the lenses, but that's already to think about it in a merely instrumental way."

"Eh, maybe. Either way, you have to refine your abilities, develop your skill, learn the latest techniques. That's what you're paid for. They'll get inside your head either way. They'll own your thoughts."

"You could be right. It might just be a fantasy. Something to rationalize my failure, but I feel like I have to hang on to it. If I don't, it might break me."

"I know how that works."

"The part I can never get clear about with Spinoza is how this all works with freedom, which he totally rejects. We think we're free only because we don't understand the causes that are truly moving us."

"What's the connection?"

"It's murky. There's some philosopher who wrote about Spinoza and said something like, if he's right his work must have been written by god himself and —more importantly— a purely formal god, the substance of the world."

"Is that a criticism?"

"It's supposed to be. I always imagined that Spinoza would respond by saying 'exactly, finally I have been understood.'"

"Meaning what? Is Spinoza just channeling all of this? He's the needle on a seismograph? He hasn't chosen to be a philosopher; he just is the world articulating itself in this way?"

"Freedom is a fabrication, a complex form of inquiry using a structured query language. There would be a physical or a chemical or a psychological description to go along with that. We can't imagine what a body can do."

The professor sits at the front bar by the flip top at the far end near the wall. The librarian makes drinks for a table that just came in. He watches her, intent upon the certainty in her hands and the familiar concentration in her eyes. She feels him watching and looks over, smiles knowingly, and remembers. It's Saturday. A few days before that it had been Tuesday, then Saturday again before that. Sitting at her bar, a beer and a glass of water in front of him, occasionally she comes over and stands nearby. They smoke and talk about nothing, this and that, about what they might do if they weren't there. Where they might be, and where they ought to be when next they have a chance. She wears the little skirt he likes but not because he likes it, and then those boots with the steel toes. It is an abrupt match. Bouncing at the knee, a kind of persistent dance bop, she can't help but devour him every time she looks over. He lets her, or pretends to, because in the thick of it he doesn't really have a choice.

The door opens behind him and the typesetter walks in. She looks around knowing she will find him but without being sure where. She jolts slightly toward him when he comes in view and then glides up to them and stands by the wall, effectively positioning herself between them. The librarian leaning against the back cabinet on the wall, the professor leaning forward, elbows on the bar, he introduces them. They know each other, or they know of each other. They have seen each other around. They are denizens of Washington Street between Ashley and Main. It's a small world.

"Hi," she says. "Nice to meet you. I came to steal him. Wolfe and I are sitting outside at the place up the street. Come outside for a bit," she had started speaking while looking at her, but finishes looking at him.

"Did it open? I didn't think they were ready yet." The librarian sizes her up. Her hair cut. Her outfit. The piercings. They are cut from different cloth. There is something in common though, a fierceness of some kind. She likes the look of her.

"That place? It's been there a while, I think. March at least. There were chairs outside last summer. I don't remember what the place that used to be there was called. Wolfe and I met there."

"That's where it all began? You met at a place that wasn't there yet? A place that would later become Café Zola? It's like you're remembering something that hasn't happened yet."

"Yep. Something must've been there, I guess. We still go from habit. They have good coffee too."

"Since they're our neighbors, I should start going there. I've been meaning to stop in."

"You should. We should go there now. Can you spare him?"

"Please, take him, get him out of my way so I can get some work done."

They leave together. She explains that they were sitting out there when they saw him walk into the bar an hour ago. They had been arguing about whether to go get him ever since. Well, with lots of tangents and parenthetical asides. Wolfe is never in a hurry to conclude on any topic, and the typesetter always enjoys the pleasure of the inquiry and its back and forth.

They sit down. Wolfe greets him casually and then gets up and goes inside.

"Be that way," he says to the trail that Wolfe leaves behind.

"We were in the middle of it."

"What is it this time?"

"Forensics. Revisited yet again. He's wondering whether desire and happiness or pleasure or satisfaction, whatever you call it, have any kind of relationship at all. Should we go get him? Will he want to come? The assumption is that desire is always teleological, so you won't be able to know it until you get to the end. Because it has its outcomes, what it intends, and that's supposed to be its be all and end all, its part and its parcel, you can't put it all together until the end is reached. He said that, or maybe I did. At least, what you're putting together isn't the same once you get to the end."

"The drives theory. Expression of the immanent as everything that is. The substrate realized."

"Right, but not just that, it's the way that we organize the pieces to make it fit with the facts. Like Schopenhauer's image. The one Wolfe is always going back to. What the stone flung through the air would think if it were to become conscious. How it would explain its state by a convenient justification that attributes choice and desire to its hurtling projection. The motion is twisting and turning, the desire twists and turns with it. The desire that exists at the end will not be the same as the desire that existed throughout. What keeps us honest other than our own memory?"

"Desire lands us in a mess and by the light of reason we explain it all away, put it all in order. We do that because we want to do that, and so on."

Wolfe comes back outside and puts a tall glass in front of the professor. "What's this?"

"Almond milk with a shot of espresso. Try it. It's what you'll be drinking from now on."

"Is there something in the symbolism that I'm not familiar with yet?"

"Likely, but you'll tell us. Try it."

He does. "It's good. You're back to the causal nexus, I hear. Trying to know if even the most fundamental descriptions of it are an attribution in disguise? Is that it?"

"No. This is a fucking intervention."

"Wait. What?"

The typesetter jumps in rapidly. "Well, theoretically you're right. We were talking about ontologies. The splay of events, the way in which we carve up the meaning of our actions in retrospect. Once we find them, that is. Once we find ourselves in the mess that they leave as they have their way with us, unfolding in time. We were arguing about whether you would want an intervention."

"Yes, yes, all of that." Wolfe interrupts. "Not as a theory, and sure as shit not causally. We're planning on stopping you. We're trying to wedge ourselves into the natural event of forces reeling and spinning around you. The entelechy of your life here and now."

"I'm honored."

"Don't be. You're just a placeholder. You're what stands between the typesetter and the wolf."

"On this evening in the year of our lord."

"I don't know why," the typesetter breaks in. "It might be transition, or transformation. The working day is twenty-four hours long. The machines of production power through the whole of it. We come and we go, and our daylight and darkness come and go with us. Does that make sense?"

"If it doesn't, it should." Wolfe says raising his glass. "We are figures in a play that we didn't write. We don't even get to see all the scenes."

"I feel like I'm in a scene written by Artaud."

"You are. It's happening in real time."

"Okay then. You've intrigued me. Tell me what you're talking about."

"She already did. If you still knew how to listen."

"Final causality is fiction? As is any deliberation based on it. It's a moving target? It's the material of all kinds of fabrication. Is that it? The mechanics of the sun coming up and setting. The day and the night. The crawling and the chasing. The way we are pulled by this and that, coming toward it and moving away from it."

"Being pushed," she said. "Shoved sometimes."

"Intervention isn't personal then. Is that it? The forces that drive me to do it. Whatever it is. The forces that drive you to intervene. The moments we come together, the time we spend. All of it. Sound and fury. Is that it? What would be the point?"

"What's the point of the earth revolving around the sun? You can tell a tale where the earth wakes up every day and goes to sleep every night. Planning this. Each phase of it, each day of it, as though it were completing a cycle, wanting to go around and around."

"The earth lies on the back of an elephant that stands on the back of a turtle."

"Turtles all the way down."

"You two are way too clever for me. What have you been smoking?"

"Very astute of you," he says, "but it won't get you out of this. You know what I 'm getting at."

"No. Why don't you tell me?"

"What are you doing? You're sitting in that bar. What are you doing there? What's going on?"

"You'll have to be more specific."

"That's the point." The typesetter jumps in. "We're arguing about how much you know. What do you think you're doing? Are you stubbornly pretending you don't understand the question, or do you really not understand the question?"

Wolfe seems to be grilling him. She seems to care. He's confused, looks back and forth between them, lights a cigarette, and sips the warm beverage. Lots of stimulants.

"You're like a swarm of bees. Not one of them has a plan. There's a fucking plan, alright."

"Says the wolfpack."

"I'm just saying that there are alternatives. You're making out as though you chose a career path. What kind of a dumb ass gets his PhD in philosophy as vocational training? You should have been a carpenter or learned to cut tile."

"I would have loved to. If only I had ever met someone who could've taught me the least little bit about either."

"Right. That's the point. You didn't have a choice."

"I'm missing it. The point."

"You're acting like it's a choice, like you're deliberating. 'I need a plan.' When pushed on your selection, you justify yourself by saying you didn't have a choice. You're some segment of possibility realizing itself. You're a risk, a mode, an exemplification of what a body can do."

"Of what a body, a specific body, has to do."

"Let's tackle one thing. You think programming is logic?" She is trying to broker a compromise and to get them settled so that they might find a way to take a few steps together. They are uncomfortable, and the atmosphere is becoming a little tense. She thinks she can help.

"Isn't it?"

"I don't think so. An inference and a flow of operations and conditions are not the same thing."

"Semantically they seem to be."

"The conditional test and the assignment of a value to a variable is not an argument. It's not even an assertion."

"How do you so much about it?"

"I've been doing my assigned reading. Never mind that. Answer the question."

"Yes, it is, it's a hypothesis."

"Sure, but then the else that offsets the condition is open-ended. It provides a safety net for possibly chaotic conditions that might be discovered. If A then B, fair enough, but how to justify the flow of the else block? What does it do to your modus ponens?"

Wolfe is watching the exchange. He doesn't approve.

She goes on. "The code is interactive. It doesn't just interpret, it manufactures events. It fires them. Dressed up as uninterested inference, it's constantly deciding and doing."

"I fail to see the point. What are you accusing me of?"

Wolfe whispers: "You make the lens, but the lens doesn't just see. It selects its subject. It's trained on something. It can't help but ignore everything else in the process."

"Of course, I am, and so are you, so is everyone. I can't help that. Thrown projection. Right? Being human. The null basis of a nullity."

"Do you think that an insight like will to power is madness? That would seem to be your justification for becoming a boyfriend with a good job."

"Name that segue please."

"The reflective insight, the meta-perspective that lays out an ontological map of the world. Anything like that, anything at all, would be consigned to brute necessity."

"The will to power knowing itself is the will to power. None of that, nothing in the whole history of philosophy considered like this, makes any sense."

"A reductio ad absurdum?" She is trying to get the professor to clarify, but Wolfe interrupts. He is talking loudly.

"The will to power is a poem. It suggests what can be done. If you look closely, it expresses an impossibility. That might be the kernel of Spinoza's problem too. He can't know what he's talking about, and yet that's the condition that philosophy always finds itself in. It's the drive to say what it cannot say because it requires an understanding of what lies beyond the understanding itself. Kant's opening to the first critique. The impetus of all critique lies in the effort to find the individual amid the structural morass. It's the origin and the destination of reason, of thought, and of human being."

"How can any of this be real?" she asks calmly, seeming to take the professor's side now. "People don't work like this. They get hungry so they eat. They need food, they have to work. They fall in love. They get lonely. They share time together. These are spontaneous occurrences."

"Hang on." The professor takes up his own defense. "The alternative story of Thales is that he deliberately climbed down into the well. He wanted to look at the stars and he suspected that filtering out the light around him would give him a better view. That well was the first telescope."

"Yes, and the woman who came by, who saw him trapped down beneath the ground, she thought he was a fucking idiot with no sense at all. He was so busy staring up at the sky that he couldn't walk like a normal person."

"It's the same with those people in the cave. The ones who venture out and whose eyes have been ruined by the bright light of the sun," she said.

"Exactly. The tale has been told in many ways. It's a whole mythology of the effect and of the concept. Of how some kinds of people find their way and feel their connection to the things in this world," finally Wolfe is showing some signs of compassion. As if this condition were a malady and the subjects sick.

"Are you saying that Kant's problem can be just as real to someone as another person's hunger?"

"Absolutely it can. I'm trying to protect you." He pauses to see if he can still find the professor in those eyes. "There's a minefield all around you. Don't you *want* any help making your way?"

"What help? Be explicit. What are you offering?"

"Look. You're young and there's time. When we're teenagers, we don't really have enough to do. There's time. There are people who spend thousands of hours grinding on something, becoming really good at it. It shapes them."

"I spent those years thinking and dreaming, talking to my friends about what we were thinking and what we were dreaming," she says.

"Yes. He spent them the same way. I did too. We wrote it all down. We taught ourselves things like that. There's technique to it all. You have to learn it. Reading, writing, conversing, it was all for the sake of working out the mechanics of observation and understanding."

"I was conscious of it," she is nodding along with him. "I knew I was doing it to myself."

"Me too. I remember. Clearly. When you spend all those hours that way it makes something of yourself. You can feel it forming. Your moods change. Your eyes begin to see differently."

The professor is looking down, nodding. Something from Leibniz chooses to tease him just then: "To consider with a view to planning some project is to meditate; but to engage in reveries seems to consist merely in following certain thoughts for the sheer pleasure of them with no other end in view. That is why reverie can lead to madness: one forgets oneself, forgets one's goals, drifts toward dreams and fantasies, builds castles in Spain." In the background, Wolfe keeps talking:

"Well, the next twenty years will be filled with thousands of hours yet again. This will make something of you. It might make you into an armchair expert in how to effectively manage mortgages, into an expert at pleasing some idiots who call themselves your managers when they set you up to solve all the problems they desperately need solved. Are you choosing that? Rather, you are choosing that, but why? What's driving you to it? What's forcing you to make that choice? It's not her, not really. You just met her. It's the thought of her. It's all the thoughts around her. All the desire that splices and weaves together with her skin and with the light that falls on it. You're making your life in that moonlight and with that spider and with that demon who comes calling."

"You're insane."

"What's forcing you though? I mean think about it. Remember *Jude the Obscure*?" Again, she leapt in like a peacemaker. She can balance them; she is certain of it. She's on both sides.

"What about Jude?"

"No one loves him in the end."

"No," she corrects. "That's not what I mean. I mean that whole thing about Christminster. The town that he makes into the object of his desire. It's pure fantasy, right? He's deluded. He thinks it's the highest form of culture, the greatest adventure human thought can ever achieve, but the truth is that it's populated by commonplace schoolmasters. They get the best of him. Squeeze it out of him, literally. They kill him, but it's in a long and circuitous way."

"Yes, that's right. He thinks he has left them behind, but he keeps going back in his mind. It keeps following him around. When he does go back, father time ravages his life, tears it to shreds. Murders whatever he has been able to make of a life away from there, his progeny. This destroys everything, separates him from what he loves and what used to love him. Even his failure to become a part of that ideal world continues to have an effect. It continues in him as his ongoing desire. It inhabits his love, his work, everything in his life. He can never get away from it. It has fashioned something in him. He *is* its fabrication."

"He never got the twenty years."

"There are other ways to die," Wolfe corrects her. "We are the ship of Theseus at sea, being rebuilt plank by plank. At some point the original ship is gone, but it was so gradual that no one ever noticed. If Jude ends up with his work, focused on it, dedicated to each and every project that comes along, that would be an alternative ending that may not be much different than the ending we got, or maybe it's all the difference in the world. That might be the very definition of the difference between the pathetic and the tragic."

"You think my choice is pathetic?"

"I do and I'm urging you, in the name of all you hold sacred, to choose to be tragic instead."

"I can't see it."

"You think Spinoza was a lens grinder, but he wasn't. He isn't. If he had been. This is what I'm saying. That would have been pathetic. Instead, he was a philosopher. Every day. The dust from grinding those lenses is what killed him. It had no place there. That is tragedy. You see this, right?"

"Yes. Wasn't it about twenty years?"

"It was," she says. "Where will you be then? Twenty years from now? Who will you be? Will you even be able to get back here? To this night and these stars. Will you find your way into the bar? Sitting there like a boyfriend. Keeping her company. Keeping an eye on her. Will you be willing to come outside? To talk it through and remember the place and the people and all the connections?"

"Look," he has followed along. He is at home in the ideological terrain they are cultivating and preparing for harvest. "Whichever track one ploughs, there are no guarantees for finding the way back. You two might be able to live these tragedies. You will burn bright until that moment when it all suddenly stops, and maybe, like you say, I will slowly fizzle like some sad thing no one needs anymore. There are no guarantees. Both are pathways and both lead away from here. There may be no way back regardless of which way you choose. By your own admission, the endgame, where we find ourselves twenty years from now, will be an invention, an illusion, a reverie of something long gone and forgotten."

"Twenty years, all of time, is pure fabrication," she says desperately. "You'll enter that world of lies, you'll become just like the rest of them. You'll discover a problem that no one else knows about because no one else feels any impact from it or even notices that something's missing. You'll show them how something that was not possible before would become possible if this problem were solved. This'll prove that it's a real problem and that the solution fills a gap they never knew they had. It's all so self-contained and artificial. The agent for it is large collections of people. Everyone involved in every way, ordered and organized for the sake of it. Poets and lens grinders might both be fabricators, but poets are better."

Wolfe: "I am the one who knows the least. The more texts I weave, the more I realize they are veils to cover my nakedness."

The professor: "I am what I am."

The typesetter: "I am *that* I am."

"This Popeyism," Wolfe growls. "This sickness of the soul. It's the ancient religion continuing to hold on, maintaining its grip. Admit it. The whole of history is the coercive enforcement of the contract that drives us from tragedy to pathos."

"How does that help me now? I needed to know that a long time ago," the professor says quietly.

"Yes," she interrupts and leans across the table. Her eyes flash brilliant. "Strong to the finish." She laughs and then nearly howls. "That is what enforces the terms of the agreement. That is the power-rich substrate of what there is in common between us, of our commonwealth. It organizes us, and orders us to do whatever we do, that we do it and become it. I may not be here *for* you, but I am here *with* you. Whatever it is, it comes out between us. We are on its stage, actors in its play."

"Thank you Cide Hamete. In your latest work, part philosophy and part fiction, you explore the role that discipline plays in intelligence. The aim is to dismantle the natural/artificial divide. Yet another way that organizations inhabit persons."

"And... ...scene," she laughs.

"That's a print," the professor says abruptly directing the conversation to its conclusion. He stacks his match book on top of his packet of cigarettes and stands up. He looks at them and nods. "You have intervened. As you said you would. Whether I wanted it or not, let's leave it at that. Thank you for letting me pretend to be the governor of this little island of ours."

Wolfe stands up. The typesetter stands up. She hugs the professor. Wolfe hugs him too. He turns and walks back up the street toward the bar. His gesture is somewhere between a wave and waving them off. They sit in silence for a while. Everyone thinks their love is unrequited because amid their remorse they lose touch with how the other is feeling.

"I thought I was the governor."

* * *

The farmer had called earlier to congratulate him. The dissertation, turned into a book, had been officially released and his copy had just arrived. Since the series was already familiar to them both, the book cover was immediately recognizable. The professor had waved off any suggestion of achievement, he wasn't surprised it had been published, it was more surprising that they had considered it suitable as a dissertation. That had been his attitude all along, but on the phone, he had less confidence. Now, what was he supposed to do? Will anyone read it? What happens now? No one told him what to do. The farmer had all kinds of suggestions. They involved giving talks, soliciting reviews, and trying to get panels into conference agendas. The professor was puzzled that he was expected to spend time going back over all of that and rehashing it for audiences as though it were new and current. He had moved on and was now interested in what followed from that work. He saw the dissertation as laying a foundation, setting up an ethical problem that would ultimately force him down many different paths that went well beyond where he had been while writing it. It didn't make sense to put a lot of energy into working up papers, reviews, and panels that would only slow him down.

His position wasn't false modesty. As he had been listening to the farmer's advice, he felt a growing sense of embarrassment and shame. The rules were so clear as he explained them: how these things are done and what list of items need to be checked. How come he hadn't done anything about this? He knew all this, so why was it a surprise that this was how things were done? It was obvious what to do next and yet he hadn't done any of it. He could have been doing them already, nothing would have prevented him from getting started and sending things off in preparation. The June date had been announced long ago, what had he been doing all this time? Agonizing over the fact that he wasn't doing anything? He had trouble breathing as the conversation continued and he held back from confessing anything further. They stayed focused on the publication and then he made excuses for getting off the phone. He couldn't explain how his job search had turned out, he couldn't admit to the farmer that he had now become certain that something else was happening to him, that his path was leading him in a completely different direction.

All the rest of the day he thought about this. The librarian was working her shift at the desk, so he sat alone in a silent echo chamber. Wolfe had been right all along. He had done this to himself. Not consciously, but that's what the brief conversation with the farmer had revealed. It was precisely his oblivion to what he was supposed to do that telegraphed his desire now, in retrospect. He kept repeating the phrase to himself as he paced up and down the pathway between his desk and the sliding glass door: "How come I didn't do anything about this?"

He recalled that epic search for Pierre that Sartre was on about. He's looking for Pierre and everywhere he goes, whichever way he turns, all he sees is not-Pierre. He had always liked that. This not-seeing is infinite because there are so many others that are not there. These others included any of a number of possible projections of himself. He hadn't seen them either. Everywhere he projected over the last months, everything he took to mind or conceived, all laid over the top of whatever was not there, not thought, and not conceived. Some monster was at work behind the scenes, directing his vision away from this and over there toward that. Whatever had happened, whatever he had considered or hoped, had blocked out all kinds of concern that should have been part of the narrative he was forming for himself, and yet he had deftly avoided any hint of them.

He drove to the library and picked her up at the end of her shift. They went to the bar where they sat and smoked. He tried to tell her what had happened. About the farmer and the call, about the publication and about how he hadn't done anything to get ready for it, to publicize it, or any of the things he was supposed to do, the things which everyone had thought too obvious to point out to him. She didn't say much. At first, he thought it was because she was just letting him vent. He didn't want to vent, he needed her to understand. Especially her, since he was convinced it only made sense to those who had gone through these last months together. Since he thought that this stretch of time had been that something that was diverting his attention, he was certain she would comprehend it and see the wisdom in his take on things. He wanted to tell her again all about Wolfe and how they had gone down different paths that second year of graduate school, how Wolfe had become so certain of the meaning behind all these recent events. He tried to explain, but all the while she remained silent. She shouldn't have. His sense of urgency increased as it became more and more clear that she didn't have any follow up questions and that she didn't want to learn any more details about how he had overlooked these duties. She had nothing to say in response to theories that Wolfe could have predicted it all years ago and had been warning him about it for months.

She put her hand on his arm, she was calm. "You might want to talk to Wolfe about this. At least you should talk to someone who knows the history better. I don't think you should talk to me about it."

There was no cruelty in it, but it might have lacked compassion. He wasn't sure. Certainly, no guilt. They both knew it wasn't her fault, but why wasn't she even the least little bit interested in getting to know about this? He had been different in trying to understand her crises in navigating the paths of the foreign lands she found herself in. He had tried to learn the history of that emotion from her. He had tried to see the shores she had been navigating, he wanted to know this about her. All along, he had always shown interest and pursued it. Here and now, she was turning away, and in such a way as if to say "I am not interested in what you had to go through to get here. Even if I am glad that you made it. Who knows, maybe I am?"

After a suitable amount of time recounting the quirky stories of what ridiculous requests she had to fulfill at the circulation desk that evening, they went back to her place to spend the night. He couldn't sleep. He got up and went into the other room. It was mostly dark, and it was cold. That basement was unforgiving. She had fallen asleep quickly and was breathing soundly.

He flutters. That's just the way it works. Even in the dark, even in a cold basement, that is where his mind goes. "Authenticity," he thought. "It's unnecessary and has no real role to play. He probably globbed it on there just because it was fashionable. Anxiety and death are sufficient for doing all the work he needs. They are the boundary conditions; they individuate and are what establishes the way back from that most fundamental being lost.

"The boundary condition itself is something of a pursuant event. It marks the conscious being as finite and temporary, it shows its limitation to itself as only a speck of dust with the illusions of enormity can. These are the conscious but false impressions of eternity, and a never-ending spring of potential.

"This limit is bound to the question itself, the question that has been forgotten, hidden, and that we have failed to ask because we were oblivious to its significance.

"There is no moment in time that is not saturated with both the questioning behavior that leans toward what has been forgotten, the role of oblivion in driving one's thinking forward into this or that nook and cranny, and at the same time descends upon the clever animal as the deepest anxiety it can ever know.

"The questioning and the anxiety are one and the same. They are the jet propulsion of all potentiality, of all possibility and power. They lie at the origin of whatever it is that a body can do. Organization and order pools it all together into a more powerful machine that acts as a store for inquiry and anxious concern: our wealth in common, what our bodies can do."

Something resists. Since touch was at the basis of sensation, we may not need to conceive the boundary. Skin was enough. There lies all the questions and all the absence of answers, the anxious questionable absence that our skin reveals through everything we touch.

The professor did not like horror movies. He never watched them, but there was one movie that he imagined to be the greatest horror movie ever made even if no one considered it to be part of that genre. The English filmmaker Mike Leigh had called it, appropriately, *Naked.* The horror was throughout. Just dire. The main character, a vicious and broken human, is confronting a cold and heartless world dominated by a logic of meaningless triviality meant to distract. It seems like common social commentary. The main character travels through the streets of London and comes across the lonely stories of various kinds. He touches upon each enough to learn all the varieties of despair that can be found in the streets at night. Only at the end does the ontological foundation of this despair become clear. The roommate at the flat where he has been staying returns from her holiday abroad. She finds chaos in the little flat, likely induced by our anti-hero. She is a goddess of order, and the chaos is an immediate threat. She works methodically to clean the mess she finds there. The anti-hero is too much for her though. He has wiles, he persists, and she cannot cleanse him. She abruptly breaks off and says this has to stop. Can't we all just make it stop.

This is the true horror, the desire to bring about the end of the world, the yearning to achieve the most perfect order is revealed as the desire for destruction. Even the anti-hero is overwhelmed by the insight. He cannot face it and storms off, limping. In the end, she has won. The professor has always wondered about the connections. What associations are built and where do they lead? His mind travels over this terrain in search of a connection.

"Chaos is the anxiety and the inquiry. Questions are always chaotic, but they tend toward an order and resemble deliberation. They suggest an answer. In the limits, in that anxious never to be outrun orientation toward our implicit physical limit, we are striving for an answer, driving toward a clarity and a presence. The end is desirable. It brings order. Death's skin. The striving to achieve it is a drive to bring an end to that very chaos that is the existential condition of life in any conscious being. Clear enough. How does that speak in the polis of the film?"

He recalls the scene in the street with the security guard. The bar code as three groups of 6 digits. The professor isn't sure how accurate the description is, but it's clearly a crucial image. Nothing will be bought or sold without the mark of the beast. Whatever there is of suffering, that has its cause in the way human beings construct the world where they live and associate with each other, must stem from this mark.

"The mark of the beast, that without which nothing is exchanged, is that opposed to the order driving us toward the end of the world? Wouldn't this be two absolutely intolerable options? On the one hand, there are the rules of exchange and all they entail. With that, you get chaos and a swarm of events, anxiety and inquiry. On the other hand, we make of this the entire order of the last centuries with all its relationships and organization. In conflict, we have a body at work carrying upon every one of its parts the mark of the beast. Armageddon, as it turns out, is an interleave of these two movements, centripetal and centrifugal. Either / or, we will regret both.

"This could be the perfectly dystopian antithesis to Spinoza's intellectual love of god. Either way, there is a larger entity at work. That same leviathan who I always feel moving and slithering over my shoulder. Name it Order or name it Chaos, it feels the same. It inhabits and twists your ideas. The roommate and the anti-hero do not offer alternatives, they say the same about the same, there is no difference.

"This is because we are beings that associate. Rather, there are associations and some set of them have become aware. Give each other names, pick each other up from work, smoke and drink in a bar, and then go to bed in a cold dark basement.

"Not only that. They spend their whole lives working toward something and then forget to take the crucial steps to get them there. These funny monkeys, we forget more than we remember. It's what our awareness means. We know deep down, I suppose, that on the other side of whatever gets us in the end, is a cold dark basement. We know that this chaos is not really chaos. There is something at work in it. It is inconceivable that this something would be a drive toward that camouflaged end. As though whatever my death is, lies already here dormant inside me and has been there since I was born. If I am to die in a car wreck on a rainy night 38 years from now, that is there already, or the cells of the cancer, or the failing of the heart, whatever it might be. It is already there. Pulling me, pushing me, and most likely it must make me forget so much in order to make me remember where it needs me to be 38 years from now, or next week, or whenever and however it has already decided that it must be.

"It was a false choice. Spinoza was wrong about the immorality of taking money to think. Not because he thought it was immoral, but because he thought he could avoid it. Whatever it is that experiences freedom in this life, it is not made for the likes of me. If I have no truck with freedom, then I can't be moral or immoral. On that they all agree.

"None of these merely human villains can obtain the good or the evil. That is, if these truths at night last until morning. The true villains feel ethereal, don't they? As if there were something somewhere else lifting them up and moving them forward, covering their paths like blankets of snow and leaving no tracks along the way. The ultra-rich or the political dictator, whatever, it almost seems like there are forces unnatural that lift them up and place them where they are so that they might do the most harm. No single will could achieve this. The associations must be formed, the masses huddled and driven, something must be at work that is bigger than them all and which transcends their puny anxiety and their endless stupid questions.

"Just suppose that some giant corporation were to achieve some strange conscious state. I can't even imagine what it might be like. Its brain is the network of relationships that constitute all the action within which and against which it is involved. The structure of its orientation is not behavioral or some innate cognitive faculty, it is an alien mind and an artificial intelligence. It is that leviathan that our natural law provides through little else than the basic power of achievement through concert, through some contracted acquiescence. It turns out in the end, however, that we had no idea what we were agreeing to. We have the power to agree, he was right about that, but not the power to know what we are agreeing to. We are like simpletons in the midst of gargantuans. They are so large we can't even see them. They look like sky and morning and the daylight. They are the lens through which we see and not the objects of our attention.

"Even when they set themselves up with a brand and a symbol, with products and prices, we don't really see them at work there. We focus on the thing as the association that burns into us in / as / through focusing itself.

"The university was his target in that famous judgment. It was the university offering to pay him to think. It was the university he was rejecting on moral grounds. All I suggest is that lens grinding is no alternative. The mark of the beast is there too. You will think as you grind. The marks of grinding and of exchanging will find their way into your thoughts, these associations will become your mind. You will be one of them.

"There is freedom in the world. It just doesn't have anything to do with human beings. We are merely its instruments, not its agents."

The thoughts he doesn't have are there too. That he is broken, that none of this matters, that it is so much simpler than midnightly thoughts will have us believe. People grow up, they make friends, make babies, and make lives for themselves. They struggle but they are together, having made families and built communities. Even if they are torn apart, the despair in it comes from the clarity of vision that knows no greater pain than being ripped asunder from what one has built for oneself. We could easily invent these philosophies and these religions if they didn't exist already. Everyone knows them. It's the people that matter, family and friends. This is what should drive us, and the decisions would fall easily into place if they did.

"Are there any other questions you can think of?"

"No, just the ones I can't."

He plays at a dialogue that hasn't happened yet, that maybe comes from a time when he will be sitting in a conference room and learning about the new phone system and how to transfer calls or put people on hold. There is no way to block caller Id and *69 when making outgoing calls. Later, when it mattered, he would forget to mention that. The people he sits there with, he can't see their faces, are these the people that matter or is that honor left to his unborn children? Is he forgetting them? Where are they now and what occupies them? Is their mother the one over there, asleep, or is she far away and he doesn't know her yet?

"This partiality, this finitude and these limits, they set us apart immediately struggling to get back together. That struggle is itself vulnerable to all the associations in the world. We don't know how to fathom our action other than as a series of operations aimed at building things. Grinding lenses. Achieving goals. Fabricating artifacts and relationships. Castles in Spain. We make new friends we don't discover them. Our biological isolation is a ruse that is regularly overcome by a set of productive processes. We are nature's fabricators, natura naturans. It is not so much that we are the users of tools, but that we are the tool extraordinaire. Leviathan agents building what they need to be free through the raw matter owned by Cura. Bombarded by messaging, it is easy enough to shape and mold us into what we must be to produce what those giants require. Those free ones who rely on us as the material for expressing their liberty. Natura naturata.

"What we make is an artificial world that in turn makes us. We are driven by it and driven toward it. The best we can hope for is to come to love the causal nexus that subjects us all. That is the only respite that an intellectual love of god has to offer. All these years, I thought Spinoza the sweetest of the philosophers. Turns out, he is awful. He might not condone it. It's not his fault. The complex conscious orientation of the human being is nothing more than a momentary realization of a structural chaos aiming to extinguish itself for the sake of an eternal order, or let's call it a divine freedom. Shema Yisrael."

No single human storyteller could have made this up. It took all of us for that, and then that day this June, with the approaching summer, in the dark and the cold basement, what more is there? He does not know if he could write it all down as a set of propositions with axioms and corollaries. He does not know if this is an argument. He does not know if there is anyone that he has to prove this to. He has the sense of an achievement even if it were won without her, one where she couldn't participate or help formulate any of the questions he needed to get him there. Either way, he got there, had climbed out of bed to get there, and now had been exhausted.

"All the many things there could be. I don't know how to not-write them. Was that the point of all this? To wear myself out?"

He gets up and shuffles back into the furnace room where he slips into bed beside her. He drifts off to sleep as he warms up under the blankets.

"Where's your stuff?"

"Gone. Gave it away or packed it up. I only have the backpack now and I'm taking it to her house. I can give you back your key. I won't be needing it anymore."

"Are you going to move in with her now?"

"No. I'm leaving town."

"When did this happen?"

"The roommate moved out so I'm going to Brooklyn."

"When?"

"A few days."

"Were you going to say goodbye?"

"I'm doing it. Want a beer?"

"Sure."

"I mean, we haven't had a chance to talk lately. I would've said more about it, but well. You know."

"Don't worry about it. Is the typesetter okay with it?"

"Oh yeah, definitely. We were already starting to suffocate each other. She likes a lot of space, and so do I. That's why it worked out and that's why we're both at the same place now. Ready to move on."

"You won't miss her?"

"Very much. She's amazing. I will remember her fondly for the rest of my life."

"Good. She's the reason I was usually pretty happy to see you."

"Ha! I bet. She really liked it when you would hang out. You guys should definitely stay friends. I know she wants to."

"We are friends."

"You think I need people like her in my life to soften my edges, to make me more tolerable?"

"People like her, people like me. Yes, I think so too. You know I do."

"Pfff. I do. Indeed. Why do you think?"

"Too much confidence, probably. You need people who don't buy it."

"You think I have too much confidence, but I'm not sure of anything."

"Yes, you are. You're sure of your ability to make your way. You always seem sure that you're the smartest person in the room."

"Well, only if you interpret that Socratically."

"I suppose we can interpret it however we want."

"Well, okay, but I don't' feel that way. It's cultural capital, no doubt. I just don't experience it like that."

"I know."

"Anyway, what's going on with you?"

"Eh. I don't know. My book came out. Kind of anti-climactic. A bit depressing."

"How so?"

"One of the down sides of planning is that you might be tempted or fooled into thinking you're in the prequel to your life. You know, like now I'm in school and when I finish school that's when my life will really start. Now I'm an adjunct, when I get a job as a tenure track that's when my life will start, or once the book comes out, that's when everything will begin. It's bullshit. If you think like that, then it's like you're deferring your life. I'm tired of it. Because my planning is always wrong. I'm always planning for something that doesn't happen."

"Yeah. I'm sure it doesn't help that I keep hammering on that with you."

"No, I get it and I appreciate it mostly, but hearing the words and seeing it aren't the same."

"In American politics, the political parties we have here, these guys are either pandering to you or serving you. If you're getting rich off their policies and platforms, then you're one of the people they serve. If they make you feel good by filling your head with how important you are, then they are pandering to you. The people they pander to aren't getting rich. The people they serve aren't going to hear a lot of rhetoric talking about how great they are. That's the deal."

"Okay. If you say so."

"Right. Pander to me. That's my point. It's more than just a political thing. We're this way with each other. The people in your life may either serve you or pander to you."

"Serve can only mean to make you rich?"

"Let's be more precise and call it 'serving your material interests.' They don't make you rich, but maybe they go with you to the doctor when you're worried about it. They might let you crash on their couch for a year. They might just tell you what you need to hear instead of only telling you what you want to hear. The point is they don't just blow smoke up your ass, they contribute to making your life better."

"Okay, fair enough."

"Well, it can be that way with yourself too. Sometimes when we make plans, we're serving ourselves and sometimes we're just pandering. It's important to be able to tell the difference. When you think that proofreading a book and correcting the galleys or approving the cover art or whatever it is they had you do, when you think that's a plan, then you're just pandering to yourself. Convincing yourself that some ideal or some fantasy image is how it all works. You'll publish and then everything will fall into place. Everyone will be impressed, it'll improve your reputation, you'll land the perfect job. That's just pandering."

"What about service?"

"That would have been different. You would have to make real connections, get reviewers, get the word out, all the crap you have to do to get heard so that your goals can fall into place."

"You're saying that all the crap I consider superficial, opportunistic, and self-serving is really, well, self-serving?"

"Hell yes, it is, and the idealism, that's pandering."

"There's no hope for someone like me in your world."

"Don't blame me. It's not my world. I wouldn't have made it that way."

"This is purely a form of materialism then. You aren't suggesting a moral difference between serving others and pandering to them, are you?"

"Absolutely not. It's most definitely a form of materialism. Serving each other's material interests doesn't confirm integrity. It might, but not necessarily. Depends on the historical conditions. All that aside though, we should acknowledge that sometimes the association is a truly material one with a real transfer of gain. Sometimes it's just talk. In that case, you might find yourself in a position where someone is pandering to you so that you will, in return, serve their material interests."

"These are categories for critique then, not a priori moral imperatives."

"Exactly."

"I was just thinking about this the other day. Kind of an inverted version of Spinoza."

"Inverted?"

"Well, dystopic. The one and only substance as oppressive. We are made to serve its purposes and ends without knowing what they are and without any guarantees that they will be of any great use or value to our own lives. We sacrifice our autonomy for the sake of its freedom."

"Too many cognitive categories in there."

"What do you mean?"

"Well, the subject would have to be an independent thing, something with a life away from substance. To conceptualize the relationship as oppressive or exploitative, you'd have to think of yourself as a real thing with actual material interests. Spinoza's point might be that this is an inadequate notion. Rather, the illusion of material interests is already a way in which 'substance' panders to us through our own imagination."

"That's wacked. People need to eat. They need shelter from the elements. They need social contact and connections."

"I'm suggesting that there are cases where even what the materialist thinks of as serving fundamental interests only amount to pandering. It's like in that stuff from *Capital* where Marx talks about its vampire-like nature. The health of the organism, its bodily requirements, are a way to pander to the ones it needs to serve its larger scale interests."

"This makes nonsense of your theory though, doesn't it?"

"It definitely forces me to make further refinements."

"You have to introduce teleology, most likely."

"That's the critique. The more completely individuated you assert yourself to be, the more personal goals you have, the more in the grip of the social order you are. The current trend is to trap us in our individuation by fostering tunnel vision for our own objectives. The subject centered action is what coerces you into focusing on the base subsistence that's required while ignorantly achieving the order's objectives. Eating and shelter, and all that, hides all the buying and selling."

"How could someone so anti-social and opposed to joining in with the group be so convinced that all semblance of individuality is just social and historical conditioning?"

"These aims are illusory. Bread and circuses."

"Fine, but they are material interests. Serving means actual gain in that department, no?"

"I'm struggling. I started out with rich and then I went with material interests. Neither is quite right. Stick with Spinoza. Some actions will preserve and improve your essence and others will not. Indoor cats live longer than outdoor cats, but maybe it only seems longer?"

"Name that segue."

"I don't know. I hate indoor cats. They're so clingy. Only when they live most of their lives outdoors do they truly realize the essence of cathood. As I see it anyway. The agility they develop, the skills, just an amazing animal. Nothing compares to a cat that lives by its wits and only checks in now and again with some human. These cats might get killed by a coyote or a raccoon, or maybe they'll be hit by a car. Whatever. There are more hazards in their world, and they won't live as long. While they live, though, they are more alive."

"In your opinion as a non-cat, you prefer this?"

"It doesn't matter what I prefer. I'm not talking about that. There are indoor cats, there are outdoor cats."

"Okay, okay, so service amounts to preserving the essence. Helping the recipient to flourish."

"Right. In politics that might amount to material interests. That's just an illustration."

"I see."

"In friendship, it's something different. That's what forced me to make my first corrective."

"Okay. You think my point about Spinoza relies on an independent existence of the agent over and against substance, or the appearance of it anyway. As though there were two distinct beings with different interests and the one is leading the other around, making it think it's getting what it needs, but really, it's just being led down pathways that make it produce what the 'substance' is trying to realize. Entelechy as ideology."

"We are substance, we are its point. We are the same, we are the way it happens. The human consciousness was manufactured by the universe so that it might come to know itself."

"It?"

"The universe comes to know itself through human beings."

"Sounds kind of squishy."

"It isn't. Knowledge can be as physiologically based as you like. I'm not asserting spiritualism. If anything, this explains it, not the other way around.

People have been coming up with wacky spiritual explanations for all kinds of crap for millennia. Turns out, these are the awkward first steps of the universe trying to know itself. Trial and error. It took billions of years and may take billions more."

"The absence of freedom then isn't a tragedy so long as we are rightly serving the one substance?"

"Yes, it doesn't need to be oppressive. I tend to think the pattern repeats itself on these smaller scales where the individuals live and that's the true source of oppression. Substance is singularity itself, it is the ground of everything. Right? All attributes are bound to it."

"Okay."

"There are beings that form, persons, if you will. They can be of various shapes and sizes. Organizations, groups, political parties, corporations, all different sizes and flavors."

"Sure. The raw material of our lives. The University."

"Speaking for yourself, of course. They are surrogates and we don't have a sense of what might count as reasonable to them. When Descartes or Spinoza wonder whether they're adequately comprehending the conditions of the causal chain, we have a good sense of that. They are people like you and me, but what happens when the entity transcends the boundaries of ordinary personhood? When the being doesn't have skin or a skeleton, but is distributed across space and is made up of policies and practices, trucks and machines, humans taking on roles and fabricating artifacts for the sake of some plan that they don't have clearly in view? What then?"

"I see. Philosophy relies on meta-philosophy which amounts to the sociology of philosophy targeting these organizational beings. What else would critique look like for such a thing? It isn't going to be what we find in the *Meditations* or the *Emendation of the Intellect*."

"That's right, but presumably such organisms are susceptible to all the same pitfalls. Inadequate ideas, the illusions of freedom, the drive toward goals, and being subject to coercion. Being pandered to and being served, pandering and serving."

"Social existence is not created by consciousness; consciousness is created by social existence, and it can create radically distinct kinds and forms of it as it needs them to further its goals."

"In this case we have to be immensely flexible in how we understand consciousness. The organizational principles of projection that we find in these distributed persons are a kind of consciousness too. It might be a kind that is inaccessible to the likes of us, or maybe something that can be accessed via critique. I don't know."

"Congratulations. You've discovered Marx."

"Don't underestimate that. There's something ingenious here.

Especially if we think of Marx as having historicized Spinoza. Forget about that whole Kant Hegel dynamic, the real deal is in Marx Spinoza."

"It's Marx purged of any residual enlightenment oriented ethical prejudice."

"That's the most important part."

"Okay, but it seems to miss the point. The point isn't to interpret the world, but to change it."

"Well, capitalism isn't really one thing though, is it? Marx more than any Marxists I have come across seems astutely aware of that. There's a lot of pandering in the average revolutionary."

"There might be."

"Whose vision of the world do you really want to live by? The revolutionary would be lost without their moralizing, and on this reading, there's no room for it. The moralizing quality is just that imaginary and inadequate presumption of ends and aims that have nothing to do with the one true substance. The universe doesn't care if we live well or justly. The universe wants to understand itself, that's the only legitimate form of desire, the only rational form of it. If I have to starve for the sake of it, then so be it. If millions have to starve, so be it."

"That's gruesome."

"Awful. Absolutely awful. I know it."

"I don't really understand how you put this into practice. Okay, maybe you've romanticized the notion of the experiment and pushing yourself to the limit of discovering what a body can do for the sake of some universal collection of possibilities that furthers these aims. You're willing to sacrifice your life for it, but how does that fit with the 'critique' you've gifted me for my life and my choices?"

"What do you mean, I've been perfectly consistent on this? What specifically are you thinking about? What doesn't make sense?"

"You seem to think I should have properly subjected myself to all the requirements of an academic life, that I should be the professor in every way shape and form. You seem to think that by realistically planning my future around viable skills that'll get me gainful employment, I'm somehow selling out. That I've fallen for this woman so that I can more easily make this transition into a domesticated existence. None of it makes sense. Either of the lives at stake here should be condemned if you are consistent with your theory."

"Look. I don't trust academics. They're like crows. Opportunistic as hell and they seem to have evolved all these hateful qualities from their development in a world with massively scarce resources. They write because they have to publish, they have to publish because they have to get tenure, and they have to get tenure so that they can maintain the pretentious lifestyle of someone who writes, thinks, and teaches for a living. They are the worst kind of posers."

"Every one of them?"

"It's the rule. Even the exceptions are only included because they were able to play by the rules to some extent at some point in their career. What's the tangible difference between writing something that is rejected because it's untimely or without audience and writing something that's rejected because it's a subpar imitation?"

"If I do my own thing, you think it might be bad in some new way, whereas if I go the route of the imitator, you're saying it'll be bad in a way common for its time?"

"Anyway, let's not get bogged down on that point. My point, for our purposes, yours and mine here and now, is that they fucking write badly. They tell shitty stories. They don't care about saying anything true and they don't care about saying anything beautiful. It's all for the sake of furthering their idealized vision of an intellectual's life."

"Kant was an academic. Are his stories shitty?"

"A million examples and 100 counter examples. Fine, does that mean my theory is useless?"

"I'm just trying to figure out what you're saying."

"What I'm trying to say doesn't have anything to do with academics. Not really. It has to do with you. With who you are and what you're trying to do. You were sticking with it, trying to publish and make a life for yourself because you honestly believed that was the way to express the intellectual love of god, or whatever we agree to call it."

"The way to fully realize the experiment for the sake of the one true substance."

"Yes, and I am completely down with that. I am rooting for you. I always have been. If you were to conclude that you can't do that as a professor but have to do it as a modern-day lens grinder, then I'd be all for it. That's not what I am seeing though. I see you giving up; you're changing your priorities. I've been trying to tell you that you don't have to do it."

"Well, I get that. Does that mean being like you? Not having other people that remain a permanent part of my life. Is that it? You meet this amazing woman, and you immediately think it's just temporary because you can't be tied to anything."

"She's the same way. We both knew that going in. Ask her yourself."

"That doesn't make it any better though. It means you've decided not to be connected to anything. What if our bonds with these various collections and groups, what if the associations we make, what if these are the true experiment? What if they are what will cause the universe to come to understand itself? My writing doesn't mean anything. It's a selfish hobby that pleases me. I might as well be watching movies or going to baseball games. I don't have delusions of grandeur anymore. I wanted to be a professor, it didn't work out, so now I'm going to try something else."

"That's not fair. I'm connected to everything. Did you meet Charles? You know, the guy everyone calls 'Griz'?"

"I don't think so."

"I know you saw me talking to him a few times. At the Fleetwood maybe. He's not homeless, but he's not that much better off. He's getting some disability, but he struggles to make ends meet. I talk to him a lot. His paperwork at the VA was all messed up so I helped him last Winter to get it all sorted out. A real nightmare."

"I know who you're talking about."

"I won't have a life-long relationship with him. That's true, but the brief relationship we did have was real. We drank coffee together, occasionally had a meal. I went by his place a few times. It's not a big deal, I'm not trying to justify myself to you. My point is that transitory relationships aren't necessarily meaningless. Lasting ones aren't necessarily meaningful."

"What did you go by his place for?"

"Doesn't matter. He was sick for a bit and needed some help cleaning up. Cooking, whatever."

"You're leaving. Who's going to help him now?"

"I'm not talking about universal justice. I'm not saying there isn't sadness and despair. What I'm saying is that we can be good to each other as a matter of principle without forming life-long bonds. The fact that we're people trying to realize the one true substance's goal of understanding itself, or however you want to say it, that's enough to bind us to each other even if only for the length of a bus ride. I'm using these notions heuristically. I hope you know that. I'm not bought into some literal interpretation of any single philosopher's work."

"The escape clause."

"That's cheap. You know what I mean. You're in danger of losing something. I just wanted to offer you a kick in the ass in case that might help you hold on to it."

"You might be right, but maybe you're right in ways you don't mean to be. If it's as you say, then the underlying desire, the true desire at work in the universe, it will have its way. One way or the other. My plans for this job or that one, playing this role or that role, being the professor or the boyfriend, the engineer or the typesetter, none of that will matter in the end if the causal nexus has other things in store for me. I cannot avoid my fate. My decision to learn everything I can about some esoteric technical area might have been more in the service of universal understanding than anything else I could've done. Someone has to figure out how these giant distributed systems work, who better than a philosopher to do it?"

"If I'm right, and you think it doesn't matter what you do, you'll always just end up in the place where you're supposed to end up? Is that it?"

"Yep. You're going off to New York. You have to let me go off my way too."

"Of course, I don't deny that. Something keeps nagging at me though. Remember all that business about Aletheia and Polyhymnia? The story and the conversations we used to have?"

"Yes, I think about it all the time."

"I always thought you misunderstood it."

"I remember."

"Polyhymnia isn't about battle. She doesn't love the warrior. She's a muse. She loves poets who write hymns. She inspires fabricators. That's what pits her against truth. That's why she and Aletheia are enemies. You can't serve both, you have to choose."

"I'll throw it back at you again. What difference does my choice make? It's only their choice that matters. You may think you've chosen Aletheia, but if she hasn't chosen you, it doesn't matter. If Polyhymnia has, then that's all that matters. Your personal preference means nothing. The world is cold and hard that way."

"Agreed. My point is about fabrication vs. truth. Not about who you choose to serve. The myth of the philosopher is that they serve truth, but I accuse all of them of fabrication. The philosophers aren't discovering the eternal truths of human being, they're making them up. They may even be the product of a fabrication themselves. That product is the intersubjective universe of world spirit or substance or whatever it is that is making itself up. This used to be the domain of religion. Reason was invented for those with guile, those who had become too complex to fall for the magic and mystery. Its definition is meaningless without an opposition to these other symbolic forms of power. There is no reason without unreason and there is no rational spirit without religion. The association is writ large and taken over by force."

"This seems to prove *my* point, not yours. This manufacturing process is under way, and I have no control over it, my love of creating things, the universal satisfaction of all human beings in crafting and producing, all of that is our subjection to Polyhymnia's rule. To any of the muses. It's the muse that has us, not the goddess of truth."

"Eh, this is all so awkwardly phallogocentric. I don't know how I let you talk me into thinking of it this way."

"Fine, they're not women then, they're just patterns of organization."

"You just defined phallogocentrism. Baking gender dynamics into the patterns of organization in the universe."

"Okay, probably guilty as charged. I'm sticking to it though. Productivity consumes us. That's what all this talk amounts to. Aletheia only panders, Polyhymnia serves."

"Be honest. Do you think you are changing your life so that it is no longer being ruled by truth, but will now serve fabrication?"

"Not at all."

"What then?"

"In the long run, you have convinced me. There is no difference from the point of view of eternity."

"Well, we'll have to leave it at that. I'm late. Look, my brother, thanks for being there for me this year. I'm grateful. I will miss all this. The conversations. Come to New York sometime. We'll pick up where we left off."

"I'm not at all sure where that is."

"It's on the Hudson River."

She set her book aside and began drawing on the next fresh page in the notebook. The paper wasn't any good for it, or the pencil. She should carry a wider range of tools and better anticipate where she will be, but the bag isn't big enough. If it were heavier, she would know it, carrying it around all day everywhere she went. It doesn't matter though, she'll make do. She draws the row of buildings on the other side of the street. The restaurant on the second floor, the corner coffee shop that has ice cream. The signs on the buildings with their letters and the borders between them formed by their distinct designs. Block shapes mostly. She is trying to get the shading too; the sun is still up, but it is evening. The days are long.

She catches sight of him walking up the street and toward her table.

"Happy solstice," she says as he takes a seat.

"Ah, you too."

"On your way to the Del? It isn't Tuesday or Saturday."

"Serious meeting. All serious meetings take place at the Del Rio."

"Uh oh. Sounds ominous."

"More like planning."

"Well, be careful." She says it lightly and leans back a bit from the notebook. He looks at her drawing and sees that it is just a beginning but that it is indeed headed somewhere.

"Not you too. Now that he's gone, are you filling in for him?"

"I'm not. He is. Gone, that is. No, I'm not thinking of him. The other day. When I was standing there with you guys before we came outside."

"For all of sixty seconds in the bar?"

"Yeah, but still. I'm telling you. I could feel it plain as day."

"Feel what?"

"Look, you're totally just a friend. That's it, and I don't usually go for girls. Not so far, anyway, but standing there with the two of you. I definitely felt something."

"What are you talking about?"

"I don't know, I can't explain it. You guys give off heat, that's all. I'm just saying, be careful."

"You mean, be careful so that all that passion doesn't kill us?"

"No, not that at all. Well that too, I guess, but I mean, be careful. You never know what kind of people are going to be drawn to that. I had some friends at school who were like that. There was this one guy, kind of a hanger-on. He became obsessed with them. Started getting all friendly with them both, whispering things in their ears, trying to break them up. Meanwhile, he would call her and hang up, letting her and even leading her to think it was her own boyfriend checking up on her. Some dark shit. It put a lot of stress on their relationship. That's all I'm saying."

"Hmm, I see. You might be reading too much Deleuze & Guattari." He gestures to the book that had been pushed aside to make room for the notebook.

"You may be right. I was just rereading that bit on the wolfpack. This guy dreams about being a wolf, but not about being a single wolf, like maybe he's the alpha or one of the supporting wolves. No, this guy dreams of being the whole wolfpack. When they all run, he is all of them running, when they all hunt, he is all of them hunting."

"Don't they say that this is madness? That it may even be its most rudimentary pattern."

"That's only because it so deeply violates the norms of experience. We don't know how to think about cognition other than as a centralized and simplified consciousness coming from a single source and orchestrating deliberation from there toward individual goals."

"Where deliberation is a single simple sequence of operations."

"Exactly. The distributed version looks like madness from that point of view. We don't know how else to fit it into the standard streams of objects and intentions that populate linear thought."

"What's the segue?"

"Don't be literalist about the wolfpack. Wolfpacks form all the time, they can be transient. They can be packs of people sometimes. I'm just thinking about some weird wolfpack that might form around a couple. Their energy might provide the atmosphere. I'm just saying it could be risky. Especially because nobody is in control of these kinds of things. You never know what can happen. The pack has a presence. The individuals react to it. Other people form most of our world, right? The groups we get ourselves into, they can be the most intimate world for us, the one that's most personally present in our lives. They can become our identities. The effects can be all over the place."

"Even the objects are just people. Social relations."

"True, but objects are pretty far away. They shape and influence the situation, but they aren't as powerful as the actual people that are nearby. This book might occupy us, might have some impact, but it's not as strong as what our conversation means to each of us."

"A relationship is never just two people though. Aren't there lots of people involved?"

"That's right. People whispering into each other's ears, people wanting things, telling you to do things. Coercing and seducing. It can get complicated fast. Since all of them are bringing their own many wolfpacks, each one can have an exponential effect. The pack that grows by one member introduces many new associations. With each member, with sub-groups of members, with the group as a whole. You know, at first you start out just the two of you, and you are so mesmerized and infatuated. You want to be together all the time. You start introducing other people. Slowly, the social setting of the two becomes four, and then five, and then six and seven. A floating eight. An occasional nine, and so it grows. It gets so much more complicated with each new person. Imagine how wacky complex it gets when you take all the objects into account, the crowds that each of them brings, and the institutions and the organizations and so on and on."

"You've been thinking about this a lot? Is it just wolfpack in *Thousand Plateaus* or something else?"

"I miss him. More than I thought I would. It's not just that I got used to having him around when it was just the two of us, but his impact on everyone else we used to hang out with. We had friends in common, there were my friends from before. There was you and the other people he met here. Everything is different now."

"He was very casual about leaving. I wondered if you were the same way."

"Definitely. You can still miss people though."

"Of course, so long as it isn't more than that."

"Like heart break? No, I don't think it's anything like that. It was temporary. I never thought anything else. Never wanted it to be anything else."

"Did you two split up in a perfectly amicable way then? No hard feelings at all?"

"Pretty much. The last few days were a little weird. He was kind of snarky, maybe a little distant, but when I drove him to the airport, it pretty much evened out."

"He might have already started distancing himself from this place and maybe hanging around with you conflicted with that?"

"Probably something like that. I definitely felt like he checked out after talking to you. He practically said as much when we talked about it. He worries about you. He thinks you're working with some fucked up vision of success and failure, that you'll do shit to realize that vision and it'll be a total waste."

"What fucked up vision?"

"Like you have something very definite in mind, some ideal state that is the only thing that will count as success. He thinks it's totally skewed and unrealistic, and worse, it's based on a whole list of false and misleading information."

"What does he think would amount to success then?"

"You know him better than I do. He doesn't think like that. Success means that you're doing what you have to be doing, realizing your possibilities somehow. What can a body do, right? If twenty years from now, you can sit down and create a perfect moment in time, articulate it truthfully and beautifully, then he would probably think you were a success."

"Okay, you remember Interlude, right?"

"Yeah."

"Well, it wasn't just writing. It was wrighting. Ght. If there is such a thing. Like doing it, made me somehow, or maybe doing it made something happen to me. Even though it was just writing, it put me through something. Writing it did. Reading it back and editing it a little. All of that was an experience. They change you, your experiences. I can't get right again. Something is out of wack, somehow."

"You've written lots of things though. What was it about Interlude specifically?"

"I don't' really know, but I think about it a lot. There's this bit at the end, where it becomes obviously very personal. I mean, all of it is personal. The bit at the end wasn't just intellectually personal, it was emotionally close to the heart."

"About your friend?"

"Yeah, she died while we were in grad school."

"I'm sorry."

"Thanks. I wrote what I knew. She died, but I wrote about what that did to me. Part of my remorse is how selfish it makes me feel. How boyish of me to care about her death only in terms of myself."

"Everybody does that. You go back and forth."

"Yes, but that back and forth might be my conscience driving me back and forth. What does this mean to me? Ouch, the sting of guilt, and then back to what it means that she is no longer in the world."

"Alright, but I'm asking you. What does it mean to you?"

"... well, like I wrote in Interlude. She saw me a certain way. She talked to me and about me in a certain way. She idealized me. That was one of her great charms. She had this way of idealizing and idolizing her friends.

It was so great to get glimpses of that. She forced me to completely rethink my attitudes toward gossip. It was a way for her to care about people."

"When she died you worried that part of you would die too?"

"Worry, not worried. It's active and ongoing. I cannot disappoint her. Interlude claims that as a kind of haunting."

"She's a ghost."

"Right. It turns out that we are all ghosts for each other all the time. That's what Interlude made happen anyway. Wolfe is a ghost, the engineer is a ghost, you are too."

"As are you."

"You mean for you and for all these others?"

"Yes that, but also for yourself."

"How?"

"Well, don't you ever get yourself weird gifts? Gifts that only time can allow you to give. When I was a teenager, I promised to learn a bunch of stuff, about how to make paper and how to make ink. A ton of different crafts that for me seemed absolutely essential to being a proper person. Other things too. I wanted to read certain things and there were experiences I wanted to make sure that I had. I promised myself that I would do it all and become the kind of person who had done all these things. As time went by, if I realized I wasn't working at it, wasn't learning these things for myself, wasn't fulfilling the promise I made to myself back when I was sixteen or whatever, then I would feel a huge burden. That burden, that weight, was like me from long ago haunting myself now. Does that make sense?"

"Absolutely. The greatest weight."

"That self-haunting is the eternal recurrence?"

"Interlude."

"Like play between the cycles in the turning?"

"That could be. It's like a form of critique, the only form that provides freedom for the individual. You have to bend time to make it happen. Only your past self can set free your future self, and vice-versa. My point, though, was that it was stupid of me to include something so personal in something I was writing. It broke the wall."

"The wall?"

"Like when you shoot some film and there's a wall between the action and the audience."

"Is this like the wall between the writer and the work?"

"Could be. Philosophy breaks the wall, it's like looking at the camera. It stands so far away from everything. It can be so hard to find anything there. Beating hearts, the electricity of that brain there in action, the rhythm of their breathing. The pulse."

"The risk is that the work might become wolfpack if you let it get too personal. Wolfpack philosophy isn't philosophy anymore, it's madness."

"That's right. It's what philosophy is supposed to protect us from or separate us from. The wall. If suddenly, we were to surrender to this idea that packs of people write the things we write, then all our notions of cognitive order and the grounded nature of understanding would be at risk."

"Epistemology would explode."

"Only ethics would remain, how the members of the pack realize an ethos in their ways."

"Not all ethics are alike. Approaches that failed to comprehend the associations at work, all the many people and things, groups and orders, everything that is there in the work, they would be cast aside as merely epistemological."

"Exactly. By that we mean the epistemological stance. The view from a distance."

"The male gaze."

"That's a great point. This could very well be the -ism in feminism."

"It's not one thing. No -ism is. There is no *feminism*, not really. When you isolate the approach like that, it's like you're saying this is what we call women's resentment, this is how we name a group's anger. What it really is, is more like what we're talking about, and that's so much bigger. A holistic way of understanding the relationships between people and how knowledge works and action and their understanding of being."

"Hold on, what now?"

"I'm being serious. Look at the *Second Sex*. Definitely a monumental work, but is it feminism? That's already an argument against it. Like it's a biased point of view coming from a set of interests and perspectives. If it's a whole ethical stance that topples traditional epistemology and metaphysics, then seeing it in that narrower way is unjust. *The Second Sex* was a work in philosophical anthropology. Something more like that. It's all about wolfpacks really. It wasn't just an anecdotal set of experiences, it was a coherent set of orientations, it was a meditation on how orientations have a history and collective shape and size, how people contribute to making them, and what it is like to live through them. It's kind of shocking how there aren't any real value judgments in it. Just facts. It's the voices of entire crowds of people. She spoke as the wolfpack when she wrote it all down, and others since. It's just an example. An important one because there wasn't much like it before. Feminism had been political before that, but it had never yet been existential and even ontological until then."

"Is her anthropology really free of moral outrage and condemnation? Only if you sympathize with her heroes will you inject those aspects. Otherwise, it's cold science. Being a feminist or anti-feminist is just a matter of accepting which facts to emphasize and associating yourself with the relevant group. Any pack member or even the entire pack can be feminists then?"

"Of course, they can. Why should feminism be women's work? I would say that it has to work this way to avoid becoming a big fucking self-pity party. When things go mainstream, they get corrupted. That's how they co-opt feminism. By turning it into women's resentment for all the privileges men get. Resentment doesn't make anything strong or beautiful. It turns feminism into something where women demand those same privileges, but only for some of them, like the rich ones or the white ones or whatever. That's the strawman that men are afraid of and that some women perpetuate. This is a kind of co-optation, and it can make even a really good feminist look petty and resentful if they aren't careful."

"Men objectify women so women should be able to objectify men. Is that it?"

"That's maybe a little oversimplified, but it's in the right direction. The object becomes self-conscious. Vagina dentata become self-aware. A more subtle way to put it might be that men interrupt women, take credit for their ideas, belittle their contribution, put them in the service of their success and support, so turnabout is fair play, and we need to make sure the laws make it just as easy for women to do all those things to other people. Not just to men, but to other women. Why shouldn't a mediocre woman have all the same opportunities for self-inflation as a mediocre man has?"

"I haven't heard this take before. I like it. Feminism would be an investigation into the origins of morality, or any practices, how social relations make them and solidify one set of interests or desires over and against others. It would include the study of how those interests have to become invisible and part of normal experience to work their magic on it."

"Yeah, but gender isn't accidental to that."

"Sure. Definitely. Gender becomes so much richer and complex if you see it as practices and socially ordered power relations. It might make it possible to find the common patterns in gender or race or class or any set of associations that become part of practices and the establishment of an order."

"I always think of Hannah Arendt. She wasn't a feminist. Not in that sense, but she was a bad ass in the way that I'm talking about. She was completely focused on how we think and how our thinking situates us relative to others. She's my role model. If you think about feminism like we're talking about it, as an attack –in part– on theoretical distance for the sake of a more involved understanding of how many voices can be heard in any position, then she's totally one of the most important contributors, a member of that pack. Even if we only idiosyncratically call that feminism; and even if we admit that there might be a few men in the bunch."

"Wolfe was giving me a hard time about this when we last talked."

"About what?"

"We were talking about those characters from the story, Aletheia and Polyhymnia. Truth and a muse, where the one sees it and tells it like it is and the other is the one who inspires fabrication and relies on probability linked to computation, or maybe that's truth, I don't know. Anyway, he accused me of essentializing women in my interpretation of the story. That was the gist of it anyway."

"It's just an interpretation."

"I know, but he meant something bigger than that too. Like I was guilty of something with the librarian. With others too, but he didn't go into a lot of detail. It was all innuendo. The general sense I got was that I turn them into supporting cast to help make something come true, they are only there to fit with my fucked-up unconscious desires about my life and the world I am trying to make."

"What does that mean?"

"On the one hand, there's the co-opted form of feminism we were talking about. It's allied with a proclaimed truth. It's an alternative vision to the established truth. Its fate is to cause conflict and war. The battle between groups, one sets its truth against the other and then they argue. On the other hand, there is a common creative process. The battle itself is what has been manufactured. The form of the pack at odds with itself is what is at stake. Getting to the bottom of it requires a critique of production. An investigation that goes back in time before the order, that understands its ordering and everything that contributes to it and how all of that will change the critical perspective. All of identity is at stake. All identification too."

"Can you be concrete?"

"Well, like you for example. Are you really you or just my version of you? How did I learn how to make a version of you? Where did I get the schematics for it? How come I don't immediately see that versioning you is what I'm doing? I experience it as you not as a versioning of you. How and why did I learn to do this?"

"Why just me? Isn't that true of Wolfe or anyone in your life? Your life is your story, isn't it? Mine is my story, so what? You're just a supporting character there too. It's how this funky internalized and reflexive set of social relations work. Consciousness, go figure."

"It might work that way. I see your point, but people can give different weight to the others in their lives, can't they? Parents will worry about their children. They don't just worry about them because it would be an inconvenience if something were to happen to their kids. They worry about their children for their own sake, they don't want them to suffer or to have painful experiences."

"You think he was accusing you of having different standards for how you think about the men in your life as opposed to the women?"

"Yes, and that amounts to a failure to see the dynamic of the whole group in favor of seeing the dynamic of one group over and against the other. It's a form of individuation at the group level, but just as insidious as when it distracts us at the individual level."

"Hmmm. Do you think it's true?"

"I don't know. He was making the case that I'm trying to work something out with the librarian. She's serving some purpose for me. This is a way of using her that I would never do with a dude."

"Couldn't that be anyone who you weren't romantically involved with?"

"If desire is at the heart of it though. If sex and power are its raw material, then it isn't a coincidence. It's how we are made; we use each other to transform ourselves."

"That must be mere appearance though because truly the group dynamic is what is at stake, and you would be playing out a co-opted dynamic in that case. Sex and power, everything a body can do, that's what there is before good and evil. Is he accusing you of trying to engineer a moral order here and of hiding it in acts of infatuation, is that it?"

"One where it's permissible to be the villain. Where it's justified to be a villain. Where the acts of villainy can become opaque to experience. The context might've been just women, but maybe there's more to it. What do you think? We spend a lot of time talking about my stupid bullshit. I haven't asked you about what's going on with you. That's exactly what he was talking about. It's dismissive, isn't it? It's for the sake of promoting an agenda with a clear conscience."

"We started talking about my stupid bullshit. That was the first thing you asked me."

"Well yeah, but that's just one thing. Your boyfriend. That's pretty two dimensional. I am concerned for you as my friend's girlfriend. I put you there in that box and that's all you mean to me. No wolfpack."

"Bullshit, we talked about the book I'm reading. Besides, he just left town, it's perfectly reasonable that you would show interest in how I'm feeling about that. Look, you don't need to get all Stuart Smalley on me here."

"Doggone it, people like me."

"Sheesh, yeah. The joke is that this is just another way of being selfish and promoting a very personal agenda. Don't lose your throw down, just pay attention to when and where you're using it, how the wolfpack is working at any given moment and all the contributions being made by all the possible persons and things that are part of it. I can take care of myself, I'm not a delicate flower. I'm not just sitting here waiting for you to bring up this or that. I assure you that when we have conversations, I am interested in what we talk about. I'm just as invested as you are and I could easily turn things in whatever direction I want them to go, just like you can. If I didn't like the way our conversations went, I wouldn't have them. I sure as shit wouldn't let you sit at my table and take up my whole evening with whatever rambling bullshit you felt like talking at me about. I am accountable."

"Touché. A well-deserved kick in the ass. No commentary, not from Wolfe or anyone else, can establish itself at a distance from the pack's world. Raising it as a topic for us to discuss falls into the same bucket, I guess. You think I was fishing? That might just be a way to further construct desire into whatever comes next. We're never really talking about the world. Talking is how we make it. Guilty as charged, I guess."

She laughed and took the last sip of her drink. She stood up knowing he would follow. She hugged him.

"Go meet your girlfriend."

"Thanks, I feel like I should give you something." He started off.

"Bring me my violin," she said firmly as he was walking off. He turned. "Your violin?"

"Yeah. I could play you a sad little tune."

They both laughed, he waved. "See ya."

He turned back toward the bar, and she went into the café to get another coffee.

"Did you get lost?"

"What do you mean?"

"I saw you walking up the street back here. Where did you go?"

"I stopped at the café."

"Oh, did you see Wolfe? I thought he left town."

"He did."

"Ah, the typesetter. Well, I don't need to hear about that. I've been sitting here."

"Sorry."

"I've just been really stressed. I looked at more apartments today. I can't afford anything."

"You can't stay where you are?"

"They want to raise the rent and I already can't afford it. Besides, it's a dump."

"Wait, what did you mean, you don't need to hear about that?"

"What? Oh, I don't know. Not so much that I don't *need* to hear about it, but that I don't *want* to."

"Why not?"

"We can have friends who have nothing to do with each other. She's not my friend. You can keep it to yourself. I don't mind you talking to her, I just don't think you need to be telling me about it."

"That's interesting. It's like what she was saying. We think in packs, but maybe you don't want any part of her, don't want her to be a member of your pack."

"I don't want to talk about her."

"We're not, we're talking about something she said. Pretend she didn't say it, pretend I read it in a book."

"That's what you needed to pretend when you brought it up."

"Alright. Never mind. What have you been doing since you got here?"

"Talking to the bartender mostly. Worrying about where I'm going to live."

"I guess I have the same problem. I can't stay where I am."

"Why not?"

"Same reason, it's too expensive. Now that I'm on unemployment, I have to economize."

"Should we try to find something together?"

"That would solve both problems I suppose."

"Absolutely. I saw some great places for two people. They would be easily affordable if we split the rent."

"Don't you think it's too soon?"

"Oh yeah it's definitely too soon, but I'm really worried about it. It's so stressful trying to find a place. I had a horrible day."

"There's probably no more immersive way to build connections and associations together than to live in the same apartment or house."

"What does that mean?"

"It's something I read in a book."

"I'm really not in the mood for this. Aren't you listening to me? I told you I had a horrible day. Why are you fucking with me?"

"I'm not. It's exactly my point. You've had a rough day. I've had a different kind of day. We come together. We start out trying to talk about it, but it turns out that your problem can be solved by new living arrangements. If we are willing to chance it, this solution to the problems of your day raises the issue that was the highlight of my day."

"Still not getting it. How is this relevant?"

"Don't you think it's too soon? That's the question, right? This is how I'm turning it over. If we lived together, many things would change. What? Well, we'd be all up in each other's business. Your friends might come over. If they did, they would be coming over to my house. Your house too, but my house. You see? How could there be any 'I don't want to talk about it' when this interleave would be right in your face? She would be in your living room. I might be away, out of the house, talking to her. You see what I mean? There would be no way to avoid these basic facts."

"Are you trying to pick a fight right now?"

"I don't think so."

"Why can't we just talk about it in a normal way? Is it too soon to live together? You're acting like this is the first time that question has ever come up, like we're the first two people to ever talk about it."

"How so?"

"Will we drive each other crazy? Are we ready for the level of commitment living together requires? That's what people talk about when they consider living together."

"That's what I'm talking about."

"You're talking about having other women in my living room."

"It's a specific example. I mean that there is a level of proximity that makes it impossible to avoid certain things. Sometimes, I'm suggesting, it seems like you might have a problem with that. There's a lot of topics of conversation that it seems you would prefer that I keep to myself. If we were living together, I don't think I'd be able to do that."

"I don't understand that. You can call your friends, people who I don't talk to, people I don't know. You can talk to them about some things. You don't need to talk to me about everything."

"Is that because there are parts of your life that you would want to keep private from me?"

"Yes, of course. I would think one way to make it work is to make sure that even though we're living together, we still both have our own space, our own lives. I don't want to be in all of your business, and I don't want you in mine."

"Are we talking about monogamy or something else?"

"Why is it men always think it's about sex?"

"It's not then?"

"No. I assume we're monogamous. I was taking that for granted."

"What else then? What is it that we need to keep separate even if we live together?"

"It's nothing concrete. I just think that I need space. There are relationships I have and that I want to have that have nothing to do with you. I want them to keep developing that way."

"You want to live together to save money, but you want to have the space that comes with living on your own, or just with a roommate?"

"No. Not exactly. Living together would be nice in a lot of ways. There are ways it would be good to get closer like that. I'm just saying that there are limits and that we need to remain separate and independent. I've lived with people before, and I've lost myself while doing it. I don't want that to happen again."

"I see. It's just the fucked-up way my brain works, but what I hear you saying is that you're worried about it. That you know there can be risks when two people live together. Your worries are just a restatement of the original question. It just means you're worried about it and so you ask the question."

"Where is this going?"

"I thought we wanted to discuss this. I'm trying to discuss it. Saying I am worried about something so we should discuss it, is great, but then I don't think the discussion has started if we just keep repeating that same thing over and over again. Well, yes, I'm worried about it. Well, you know what, I'm worried about it. Oh, and another thing, I'm worried about it. At some point, we have to go further."

"That's what I'm doing. You're not listening."

"I'm trying. If we lived together, where I put the coffee is where your coffee is. When I make a mess in the bathroom, your bathroom is messy. If I answer the phone, I'm answering your phone."

"We can have separate phones."

"Okay, but we can't have separate bathrooms or types of coffee, can we? I'm trying to look at the details of what it would be like so that maybe we could say what counts as having space and what counts as not having any."

"I don't have anything specific in mind, I suppose. It's too soon because we haven't been together very long. Unless you count all that time over email. It doesn't seem like that counts."

"How do you mean counts? Like we weren't getting to know each other that way, we weren't involved in each other's lives?"

"No, we were. I just mean that proximity matters. We're talking about being respectful of each other's space. I don't think we learned how to do that over email."

"That's interesting. At some level I think we did. We would pursue topics, one of us would be evasive, the other might press for more details."

"You're just taking a position. You want to have an argument."

"On the one hand, what you just said might be an evasion, on the other hand, you might be raising an insightful objection to my way of probing this issue with you."

"Is that commentary?"

"No, no. I see. It can't be detached from the matter at hand. It's interwoven into it, another maneuver, another step."

"What are you talking about? Can we please discuss this like mature people?"

"Okay wait. Would this be an example of being respectful of each other's space? I mean, you have something very definite in mind, something we are trying to sort out, some conclusion or agreement that we are trying to get to, right? Don't you think I'm taking that seriously? I'm taking it very seriously. I'm putting everything I have into trying to take it as seriously as possible. Both of us, right here and right now, don't think the other person is respecting our space. Because respecting someone's space means respecting the way they move through it, how they turn things over, what kinds of inquiries and investigations they perform."

"I just don't get it."

"Yes, that's it. You just don't get it, and I just don't get it. Right here. We are in a place where there is a 'space' you are occupying and there is a 'space' that I am occupying. They are not the same space. Can we right here and right now respect that space? We're both worried about the same thing but expressing it differently."

"That makes sense. We're both worried about it. We'll have our own ways of processing our concerns. Couldn't you have just said that?"

She smiled and poked him in the side.

"That makes you happy?"

"Yes. It totally does. That's what I needed to hear from you. My concern is a real concern and something we definitely need to worry about. You're worried about it too. That makes me feel better."

"Huh well. It's weird though because it's having the exact opposite effect on me. Oh shit, we're both worried about this. What are we going to do? How are we going to sort this out?"

"We'll sort it out. We're both worried, we can bring up problems when they happen. We can figure it out if we both contribute."

"Okay. What about school? It seemed like you didn't want to be distracted and that was the primary reason we only talked over email for all that time. You wanted to stay focused. Won't you want that again once Fall semester comes around?"

"Yes, absolutely. That's one of the advantages of living together. You won't be a distraction; you'll be part of my life. Your house will be my house. We can have coffee together, sleep together, you can feed me when I'm overworked. It won't be a distraction, it'll be integrated."

He looked down.

"How come this isn't a relief to you?"

"It's my twisted way. Like I was saying, it feels like an evasion. Now I'm running over all the times where that was exactly what we were doing."

"Evasion?"

"Yes. I mean we've talked about pursuit before, right? The way someone might pursue someone else. How pursuit is something you have to be careful about. The need or the desire or whatever it amounts to. Pursuit is a set of patterns, and they take hold in various ways and at various times. It might be how we carry out a seduction, or it might be how we obtain any goal or objective that we've set for ourselves. Getting a master's degree."

"I said that you seduced me at a time when I didn't think I could be seduced."

"Right, and we were talking about it in the context of what I was doing. How I acted. Pursuit is only pursuit because there is evasion. Evasion is different from rejection. The seduction, as you were calling it, only happened because you needed an outlet for certain kinds of evasive actions."

"What? You're saying that someone might enjoy evading pursuit?"

"Not enjoy. That doesn't matter. They might want it or need it or something. It might be exactly what they need to express. You just mentioned that I seduced you at a time when you could not be seduced. That could mean that your primary need was to evade. The pursuit itself spoke to you, drew you in, specifically because of the way it forced you to evade."

"You think I wanted that specific kind of pursuit and evasion?"

"Yes. Consider why you would keep those headshots in your car and then casually let me see them before getting rid of them."

"That was an accident. I told you."

"It could be, but it could also express something you needed to express. You might've wanted to keep me off balance. That whole dynamic could have been what you really wanted to experience. It's true you didn't want to be seduced, but maybe you did want something else. You wanted to evade pursuit in an ongoing way. We stumbled into exactly that pattern, and it worked for you, for both of us."

"Aren't you blaming the victim?"

"It's a metaphor so it's easy enough to spin it that way, but it's not right, I mean, it's a trick to help evade the point. If you catch my drift. Most of any argument works that way, pursuit and evasion. It worked for both of us, like I said, there might be something in us that can't help but think in these terms. If pursuit is like a predator stalking its prey, then there are victims and villains. We aren't talking about predators and prey though, not really. We're talking about established social practices, about the way people start relationships with each other."

"We should have quit while we were ahead. Are you saying that pursuit is just a metaphor?"

"It suggests connotations that can be misleading. The pleasure of pursuit may be paralleled by a pleasure in evasion. It can be the way that power and force hide themselves in our sexuality and our desire."

She leans closer.

He leans closer and whispers a genuine question: "Are you getting turned on?"

"I could be. That's part of it. How it works."

"It's a fine line between pursuit and stalking, evasion and escape. If he's gorgeous, charming, and brilliant, it's pursuit and evasion. If he's a troglodyte, then it's stalking and escape."

She touches his hair. He looks down.

"That makes it nearly impossible to solve the puzzle. The only way is to pay detailed attention to the actions and reactions of other people, in a way that can never be exhaustive, that's always open to further re-evaluation and reconsideration. Every new exchange, every gesture, has to be reappropriated. Error seems highly likely."

"We'll need a safe word," she is all smiles.

"'No' is supposed to be the safe word."

"Right, but we muddled everything up. The safe word becomes part of it when two people start out down one path and then only later end up on a different one. When we're infatuated with each other, we playfully use the safe word to increase our excitement, to turn each other on more. It increases the pleasures of pursuit and evasion." Her face lights up with a wide open-mouthed smile, she might be teasing him.

"Exactly," he plays along. "When we move in together, things will come up, we'll use the safe word, and the other person won't hear it right, won't understand that it isn't being used in that playful way anymore, but in a serious way where it means 'absolutely not.' That'll be why we end up yelling and screaming, to try and make the safe word safe again."

"That could explain what happens when people break up. They have played with all these boundaries and then when they need to get serious about it, they can't because they've confused everything."

"Right. It might mean that if you could stand outside yourself and see things clearly, you might be able to see a bad breakup coming. It would all depend on how these parameters work, the twisted way in which the two people are toying with the boundaries to make things work a certain way between them. The way they do that will determine what has to happen when they try to turn everything around at the end, how they have to change the way they talk to each other, all of that."

"I'm seeing how this works for you. I mean, how you're working through it. You think we're talking about space right now, don't you?"

"I do."

"I see that. It isn't so much that we might invade each other's space. We will. We have to, that's just how it works. The way we do it will form all kinds of habits, connections that we'll make when interacting with each other and other people. It will get hard to separate them, to keep them in their right place, or leave them in their true context. It's like couples who only have great sex when they fight, they need the energy from their argument to drive them. In the end, they can't figure out how to get away from each other because their arguments are so erotic."

"Even if you leave me alone, it's possible for you to occupy my space."

"Sure, like when you disappeared, and I freaked out. You were everywhere and nowhere and that's why I lost it."

"Evasion and pursuit can take on new meanings when that happens. You thought I broke our agreement. It's like we agreed that I would keep chasing and you would keep running away. That's all about space. Once it's defined that way, it's extremely difficult to change."

"We've worked through it my way and we've worked through it your way. Isn't that what this means? I need both of us to be worried about the same thing. You need to get clear about safe words that help us draw the right boundaries."

"I wouldn't put it that way. It isn't about yours and mine. We're both in both, it's a pack. This is why it's so fundamentally hard to make any kind of an agreement. Any social contract is fraught with risk. You say we have to be careful about going in and I say we have to make sure we know how to get out. That can't be me and you. Me on the one hand and you on the other. That has to be both ways all the time. Both sides have to be at the center of the whole agreement. The way in and the way out. That is the whole contract, and all parties have to come together on that."

"We can do that. It's our contract. We can make up whatever terms we want."

"Yes, we can, but it's the nature of 'making up' that worries me. What if we make up whatever we are already wanting to find there? We're not making anything in that case, we're just finding what we already wanted to find, something that had been made long before and somewhere else."

"People do that, it's normal. It's like they're writing their own stories."

"That's called fiction."

"I want to live with you. Do you want to live with me?"

"Yes."

"Is that it then? It's settled? Tomorrow I'll show you one of the places I saw today. It's perfect. Right in Kerrytown."

"Settled."

"We're such freaks, travelling in winding paths just to go straight."

"There is a fine line between imagining yourself a freak and imagining that everyone else is an idiot. When you tell the story from the latter viewpoint, the former is uncomfortably correct. Fortunately, vice-versa."

Epitaph: To understand recursion, you must first understand recursion.

So I couldn't bring myself to believe that such a superb history had been left maimed and mutilated, and I laid the blame on malicious time, the devourer and demolisher of all things, which had either hidden or destroyed what was missing.

—Miguel de Cervantes Saavedra, *Don Quixote*

Bibliography[1]

Agamben, Giorgio. 1998. *Homo Sacer: Sovereign Power and Bare Life*. Translated by Daniel Heller-Roazen. Stanford, CA: Stanford University Press.

Althusser, Louis. 2014. *On the Reproduction of Capitalism*. Translated by G.M. Goshgarian. London, UK. Verso Books.

Althusser, Louis. 1997. *The Spectre of Hegel*. Translated by G.M. Goshgarian. London, UK. Verso Books.

Arendt, Hannah. 1958. *The Human Condition*. Chicago, IL. Chicago University Press.

Arendt, Hannah. 1976. *The Origins of Totalitarianism*. New York, NY. Harcourt, Inc.

Arendt, Hannah. 1977. *Eichmann In Jerusalem: A Report on the Banality of Evil*. New York, NY. Penguin Books.

Arendt, Hannah. 1978. *The Life of the Mind*. New York, NY. Harcourt Brace Jovanovich, Publishers.

Aristotle. 1985. *Nicomachean Ethics*. Translated by Terence Irwin. Indianapolis, IN. Hackett Publishing Company.

Aristotle. 1941. *Metaphysics* in *The Basic Works of Aristotle*. Translated by W.D. Ross. Edited by Richard McKeon. New York, NY: Random House.

Ayer, A.J. 1952. *Language, Truth, and Logic*. New York, NY: Dover Publications, Inc.

Bachelard, Gaston. 1964. *The Poetics of Space*. Translated by Maria Jolas. Boston, MA: Beacon Press.

---

[1] Since the main body of this work is void of citations, the purpose of this bibliography is to inform the reader of what the author has read during the composition and editing of this work.

Badiou, Alain. 2019. *Trump.* Cambridge, UK: Polity Press.

Badiou, Alain. 1999. *Manifesto for Philosophy.* Translated by Norman Madarasz. Albany, NY: State University of New York Press.

Badiou, Alain. 2003. *Saint Paul: The Foundation of Universalism.* Translated by Ray Brassier. Stanford, CA: Stanford University Press.

Badiou, Alain. 2011. *Second Manifesto for Philosophy.* Translated by Louise Burchill. Cambridge, UK: Polity Press.

Bakhtin, Mikhail. 1984. *Problems of Dostoevsky's Poetics.* Translated by Caryl Emerson. Minneapolis, MN: University of Minnesota Press.

Bakhtin, Mikhail. 1981. *The Dialogic Imagination: Four Essays.* Translated by Caryl Emerson and Michael Holquist. Austin, TX: University of Texas Press.

Bakhtin, Mikhail. 1984. *Rabelais and His World.* Translated by Helene Iswolsky. Bloomington, IN: Indiana University Press.

de Beauvoir, Simone. 2018. *The Ethics of Ambiguity.* Translated by Bernard Frechtman. New York, NY: Open Road.

de Beauvoir, Simone. 2011. *The Second Sex.* Translated by Constance Borde and Sheila Malovany-Chevallier. New York, NY: Vintage Books.

Benjamin, Walter. 1968. *Illuminations: Essays and Reflections.* Translated by Harry Zohn. New York, NY: Schocken Books.

Berman, Marshall. 1988. *All That is Solid Melts into Air: The Experience of Modernity.* New York, NY. Penguin Books.

Blacker, David J. 2019. *What's Left of the World: Education, Identity, and the Post-Work Political Imagination.* Winchester, UK. Zero Books.

Bostrom, Nick. 2014. *Superintelligence: Paths, Dangers, Strategies.* Oxford, UK. The Oxford University Press.

Brand, Arie. 1990. *The Force of Reason: An Introduction to Habermas' Theory of Communicative Action.* Sydney. Allen & Unwin.

de Cervantes Saavedra, Miguel. 2000. *Don Quixote*. Translated by John Rutherford. New York, NY: Penguin Classics.

Churchland, Paul M. 1999. *Scientific Realism and the Plasticity of Mind.* Cambridge, UK. Cambridge University Press.

Coeckelbergh, Mark. 2020. *AI Ethics.* Cambridge, MA: The MIT Press.

Darwall, Stephen. 2009. *The Second-Person Standpoint: Morality, Respect, and Accountability.* Cambridge, MA. Harvard University Press.

Deacon, Terrence W. 2012. *Incomplete Nature: How Mind Emerged from Matter.* New York, NY. W.W. Norton & Company.

Deleuze, Gilles and Guattari, Felix. 1986. *Anti-Oedipus: Capitalism and Schizophrenia.* Translated by Robert Hurley, Mark Seem, and Helen R. Lane. Minneapolis, MN. University of Minnesota Press.

Deleuze, Gilles and Guattari, Felix. 2011. *A Thousand Plateaus: Capitalism and Schizophrenia.* Translated by Brian Massumi. Minneapolis, MN. University of Minnesota Press.

Deleuze, Gilles and Guattari, Felix. 1986. *Kafka: Toward a Minor Literature.* Translated by Dana Polan. Minneapolis, MN: University of Minnesota Press.

Deleuze, Gilles. 1993. *The Fold: Leibniz and the Baroque.* Translated by Tom Conley. Minneapolis, MN: University of Minnesota Press.

Derrida, Jacques. 1982. *Margins of Philosophy.* Translated by Alan Bass. Chicago, IL: University of Chicago Press.

Derrida, Jacques. 1981. *Dissemination.* Translated by Barbara Johnson. Chicago, IL: University of Chicago Press.

Derrida, Jacques. 1976. *Of Grammatology.* Translated by Gayatri Chakravorty Spivak. Baltimore, MD: Johns Hopkins University Press.

Derrida, Jacques. 1978. *Writing and Difference.* Translated by Alan Bass. Chicago, IL: University of Chicago Press.

Derrida, Jacques. 1987. *The Post Card: From Socrates to Freud and*

Beyond. Translated by Alan Bass. Chicago, IL: University of Chicago Press.

Derrida, Jacques. 1973. *Speech and Phenomena and Other Essays on Husserl's Theory of Signs.* Translated by David B. Allison. Evanston, IL: Northwestern University Press.

Derrida, Jacques. 1989. *Edmund Husserl's Origins of Geometry: An Introduction.* Translated by John P. Leavey, Jr. Lincoln, NE: University of Nebraska Press.

Derrida, Jacques. 1998. *Archive Fever: A Freudian Impression.* Translated by Eric Prenowitz. Chicago, IL: The University of Chicago Press.

Derrida, Jacques. 2005. *Paper Machine.* Translated by Rachel Bowlby. Stanford, CA: Stanford University Press.

Descartes, Rene. 1988. *The Philosophical Writings of Descartes, Volume 1 & 2.* Translated by John Cottingham, Robert Stoothoff, and Dugald Murdoch. Cambridge, UK. Cambridge University Press.

Dewey, John. 1958. *Experience and Nature.* New York, NY. Dover Publications.

Dilthey, Wilhelm. 2019. *Ethical and World-View Philosophy.* Edited by Rudolf A. Makkreel and Frithjof Rodi. Princeton NJ: Princeton University Press.

Diogenes Laertius. 1972. *Lives of Eminent Philosophers, Volume I.* Translated by R.D. Hicks. Cambridge, MA: Harvard University Press.

Domingos, Pedro. 2015. *The Master Algorithm: How the Quest for the Ultimate Learning Machine Will Remake Our World.* New York, NY. Basic Books.

Dretske, Fred I. 1999. *Knowledge and the Flow of Information.* Palo Alto, CA. CSLI Publications.

Duhem, Pierre. 1991. *The Aim and Structure of Physical Theory.* Translated by Philip P. Weiner. Princeton, NJ. Princeton University Press.

Dupuy, Jean-Pierre. 2009. *On the Origins of Cognitive Science: The*

Mechanization of the Mind. Translated by M.B. DeBevoise. Cambridge, MA: The MIT Press.

Durkheim, Emile. 2014. *The Division of Labor in Society.* Translation by W.D. Halls. New York, NY: Free Press.

Durkheim, Emile. 1995. *The Elementary Forms of Religious Life.* Translated by Karen E. Fields. New York, NY. The Free Press.

Durkheim, Emile. 2014. *The Rules of Sociological Method.* Translated by W.D. Halls. New York, NY: Free Press.

Durkheim, Emile. 1979. *Suicide: A Study in Sociology.* Translated by John A. Spaulding and George Simpson. New York, NY: Free Press.

Durkheim, Emile. 2002. *Moral Education.* Translated by Everett K. Wilson and Herman Schnurer. Mineola, NY: Dover Publications.

Erasmus. 1993. *Praise of Folly.* Translated by Betty Radice. New York, NY: Penguin Classics.

Fanon, Frantz. 2005. *The Wretched of the Earth.* Translated by Richard Philcox. New York, NY: Grove Press.

Fanon, Frantz. 2008. *Black Skin, White Masks.* Translated by Richard Philcox. New York, NY: Grove Press.

Feyerabend, Paul. 2010. *Against Method.* London, UK. Verso.

Foucault, Michel. 1977. *Discipline & Punish: The Birth of the Prison.* Translated by Alan Sheridan. New York, NY. Vintage Books.

Foucault, Michel. 1994. *The Order of Things: An Archeology of the Human Sciences.* Translated from the French. New York, NY. Vintage Books.

Foucault, Michel. 1990. *The History of Sexuality, Volume 1: An Introduction.* Translated by Robert Hurley. New York, NY. Vintage Books.

Foucault, Michel. 1990. *The History of Sexuality, Volume 2: The Use of Pleasure.* Translated by Robert Hurley. New York, NY. Vintage Books.

Foucault, Michel. 1988. *The History of Sexuality, Volume 3: The Care of the Self.* Translated by Robert Hurley. New York, NY. Vintage Books.

Frank, Anne. 2017. *The Diary of a Young Girl.* Translated by Susan Massotty. New Delhi, India. FP Classics.

Frank, Joseph. 1975-2002. *Dostoevsky.* Five Volumes. Princeton, NJ. Princeton University Press.

Fraser, Nancy. 1989. *Unruly Practices: Power, Discourse and Gender in Contemporary Social Theory.* Minneapolis, MN. University of Minnesota Press.

Freud, Sigmund. 1959. *Group Psychology and the Analysis of the Ego.* Translated by James Strachey. New York, NY: WW Norton & Company.

Freud, Sigmund. 1961. *Civilization and its Discontents.* Translated by James Strachey. New York, NY: WW Norton & Company.

Freud, Sigmund. 1950. *Totem and Taboo.* Translated by James Strachey. New York, NY: WW Norton & Company.

Freud, Sigmund. 1961. *Beyond the Pleasure Principle.* Translated by James Strachey. New York, NY: WW Norton & Company.

Freud, Sigmund. 1960. *The Ego and the Id.* Translated by Joan Riviere. New York, NY: WW Norton & Company.

Freud, Sigmund. 1961. *The Future of an Illusion.* Translated by James Strachey. New York, NY: WW Norton & Company.

Freud, Sigmund. 1959. *Inhibitions, Symptoms and Anxiety.* Translated by Alix Strachey. New York, NY: WW Norton & Company.

Fromm, Erich, 1994. *Escape From Freedom.* New York, NY: Henry Holt and Company.

Gadamer, Hans-Georg. 2013. *Truth and Method.* Translated by Joel Weinsheimer and Donald G. Marshall. New York, NY. Bloomsbury.

Gadamer, Hans-Georg. 1977. *Philosophical Hermeneutics.* Translated and edited by David E. Linge. Berkeley, CA. University of California Press.

Geron, Aurelien. 2017. *Hands-On Machine Learning with Scikit-Learn and TensorFlow: Concepts, Tools, and Techniques to Build Intelligent Systems.* Boston, MA: O'Reilly Media.

Gleick, James. 2011. *The Information: A History, A Theory, A Flood.* New York, NY. Vintage Books.

Godfrey-Smith, Peter. 2017. *Other Minds: The Octopus, The Sea, and the Deep Origins of Consciousness.* New York, NY. Farrar, Straus, and Giroux.

Godfrey-Smith, Peter. 2003. *Theory and Reality: An Introduction to the Philosophy of Science.* Chicago, IL. University of Chicago Press.

Goffman, Erving. 1959. *The Presentation of Self in Everyday Life.* New York, NY: Anchor Books.

Goldstein, Rebecca Newberger. 2014. *Plato at the Googleplex: Why Philosophy Won't Go Away.* New York, NY. Vintage Books.

Goldstein, Rebecca Newberger. 2006. *Betraying Spinoza: The Renegade Jew Who Gave Us Modernity.* New York, NY. Nextbook.

Goodman, Nelson. 1988. *Ways of Worldmaking.* Indiana, IN. Hackett Publishing.

Goodman, Nelson. 1983. *Fact Fiction and Forecast.* Cambridge, MA. Harvard University Press.

Gould, Stephen Jay. 1996. *The Mismeasure of Man.* New York, NY. WW Norton & Company.

Grandin, Temple. 2007. *Making Slaugherhouses more Humane for Cattle, Pigs, and Sheep.* Online. http://www.grandin.com /references/making.slaughterhouses.more.humane.html.

Haber, Laura. 1997. *Enlightened Subjectivity: the rational method of power.* Urbana, IL: University of Illinois at Urbana-Champaign Archives.

Habermas, Jurgen. 1975. *Legitimation Crisis.* Translated by Thomas McCarthy. Boston, MA. Beacon Press.

Habermas, Jurgen. 1979. *Communication and the Evolution of Society.* Translated by Thomas McCarthy. Boston, MA. Beacon Press.

Habermas, Jurgen. 1984. *The Theory of Communicative Action. Volume 1. Reason and the Rationalization of Society.* Translated by Thomas McCarthy. Boston, MA. Beacon Press.

Habermas, Jurgen. 1987. *The Theory of Communicative Action. Volume 2. Lifeworld and System: A Critique of Functionalist Reason.* Translated by Thomas McCarthy. Boston, MA. Beacon Press.

Habermas, Jurgen. 1989. *The Structural Transformation of the Public Sphere: An Inquiry into a Category of Bourgeois Society.* Translated by Thomas Burger with the assistance of Frederick Lawrence. Cambridge, MA. The MIT Press.

Haraway, Donna. 1985. "A Manifesto for Cyborgs: Science, Technology, and Socialist Feminism in the 1980s" from *Socialist Review,* No. 80, 1985.

Hartman, Thom. 2010. *Unequal Protection: How Corporations Became 'People'—And How You Can Fight Back.* San Francisco, CA. Berrett-Koehler Publishers Inc.

Hawkins, Jeff with Sandra Blakeslee. 2004. *On Intelligence.* New York, NY. St. Martin's Griffin.

Hegel, GWF. 1976. *The Phenomenology of Spirit.* Translated by A.V. Miller. Oxford, UK. The Oxford University Press.

Hegel, GWF. 2016. *Elements of the Philosophy of Right.* Translated by H.B. Nisbet. Edited by Allen W. Wood. Cambridge, UK. Cambridge University Press.

Heidegger, Martin. 2008. *Being and Time.* Translated by John Macquarrie and Edward Robinson. New York, NY. Harper Perennial.

Heidegger, Martin. 1977. *The Question Concerning Technology and Other Essays.* Translated by William Lovitt. New York, NY. Harper Torchbooks.

Heidegger, Martin. 1982. *On the Way to Language*. Translated by Peter D. Hertz. New York, NY. Perennial Library, Harper & Row Publishers.

Heidegger, Martin. 1992. *History of the Concept of Time*. Translated by Theodore Kisiel. Bloomington, IN: Indiana University Press.

Heidegger, Martin. 1992. *The Metaphysical Foundations of Logic*. Translated by Michael Heim. Bloomington, IN: Indiana University Press.

Heidegger, Martin. 1997. *Phenomenological Interpretation of Kant's Critique of Pure Reason*. Translated by Kenneth Maly and Parvis Emad. Bloomington, IN: Indiana University Press.

Heidegger, Martin. 2001. *Phenomenological Interpretations of Aristotle: Initiation into Phenomenological Research*. Translated by Richard Rojcewicz. Bloomington, IN: Indiana University Press.

Heidegger, Martin. 1996. *Hölderlin's Hymn "The Ister"*. Translated by William McNeil and Julia Davis. Bloomington, IN: Indiana University Press.

Heidegger, Martin. 2000. *Towards the Definition of Philosophy*. Translated by Ted Sadler. London, UK: Continuum.

Heidegger, Martin. 2002. *Supplements: From the Earliest Essays to Being and Time and Beyond*. Edited by John van Buren. Albany, NY: State University of New York Press.

Hobbes, Thomas. 1985. *Leviathan*. London, UK. Penguin Classics.

Hoffer, Eric. 1951. *The True Believer: Thoughts on the Nature of Mass Movements*. New York, NY: Harper Perennial Modern Classics.

Horkheimer, Max and Adorno, Theodor. 1969. *The Dialectic of Enlightenment*. Translated by John Cumming. New York, NY: Continuum.

Horkheimer, Max. 1972. *Critical Theory: Selected Essays*. Translated by Matthew J. O'Connell and Others. New York, NY: Continuum.

Horkheimer, Max. 1992. *Eclipse of Reason*. New York, NY: Continuum.

Husserl, Edmund. 1982. *Logical Investigations, Volume 1 & 2.* Translated by J.N. Findlay. London, UK. Routledge & Kegan Paul.

Husserl, Edmund. 1992. *Experience and Judgment.* Translated by James S. Churchill and Karl Ameriks. Evanston, IL. Northwestern University Press.

Husserl, Edmund. 1986. *The Crisis of European Sciences and Transcendental Phenomenology.* Translated by David Carr. Evanston, IL. Northwestern University Press.

Husserl, Edmund. 1997. *Psychological and Transcendental Phenomenology and the Confrontation with Heidegger (1927-1931).* Translated by Thomas Sheehan and Richard E. Palmer. Dordrecht, The Netherlands. Kluwer Academic Publishers.

Ihde, Don. 2012. *Experimental Phenomenology, Second Edition: Multistabilities.* Albany, NY: SUNY Press.

Ingram, David. 1987. *Habermas and the Dialectic of Reason.* New Haven, CN. The Yale University Press.

Jackson, George. 1994. *Soledad Brother: The Prison Letters of George Jackson.* Chicago, IL: Lawrence Hill Books.

Jonas, Hans. *The Phenomenon of Life: Toward a Philosophical Biology.* 1966. Evanston, IL: Northwestern University Press.

Kant, Immanuel. 1981. *Grounding for the Metaphysics of Morals.* Translated by James W. Ellington. Indianapolis, IN. Hackett Publishing Company.

Kant, Immanuel. 1965. *Critique of Pure Reason.* Translated by Norman Kemp Smit. New York, NY. St. Martin's Press.

Kant, Immanuel. 1985. *Critique of Practical Reason.* Translated by Lewis White Beck. New York, NY. Macmillan Publishing Company.

Kant, Immanuel. 1986. *The Critique of Judgement.* Translated by James Creed Meredith. Oxford, UK. Oxford University Press.

Kant, Immanuel. 1992. *The Conflict of the Faculties*. Translated by Mary J. Gregor. Lincoln, NE: University of Nebraska Press.

Kelleher, John D. and Tierney, Brendan. 2018. *Data Science*. Cambridge, MA. The MIT Press.

Kierkegaard, Soren. 1983. *Fear and Trembling / Repetition. Kierkegaard's Writings, VI*. Translated by Howard V. Hong and Edna H. Hong. Princeton, NJ. Princeton University Press.

Kleppmann, Martin. 2017. *Designing Data-Intensive Applications: The Big Ideas Behind Reliable, Scalable, and Maintainable Systems*. Sebastopol, CA: O'Reilly Books.

Kojève, Alexandre. 1991. *Introduction to the Reading of Hegel: Lectures on the Phenomenology of Spirit*. Translated by James H. Nichols, JR. Ithaca, NY. Cornell University Press.

Kuhn, Thomas S. 1970. *The Structure of Scientific Revolutions*. Chicago, IL. University of Chicago Press.

Kurzweil, Ray. 2005. *The Singularity Is Near: When Humans Transcend Biology*. New York, NY. Penguin Books.

Lacan, Jacques. 1981. *The Four Fundamental Concepts of Psycho-Analysis*. Translated by Alan Sheridan. New York, NY: WW Norton & Co.

Lacan, Jacques. 2006. *Écrits*. Translated by Bruce Fink. New York, NY: WW Norton & Company.

Lacan, Jacques. 2016. *Anxiety: The Seminar of Jacques Lacan Book X*. Translated by A.R. Price. Cambridge, UK: Polity Press.

Lacan, Jacques. 2017. *Formations of the Unconscious: The Seminar of Jacques Lacan Book V*. Translated by Russell Grigg. Cambridge, UK: Polity Press.

Lacan, Jacques. 2019. *Desire and Its Interpretation: The Seminar of Jacques Lacan Book VI*. Translated by Bruce Fink. Cambridge, UK: Polity Press.

Leibniz, G.W. 1902. *Discourse on Metaphysics, Correspondence with*

Arnauld, Monadology. Translated by George Montgomery. La Salle, IL: Open Court.

Leibniz, G.W. 1996, *New Essays on Human Understanding.* Translated and edited by Peter Remnant and Jonathan Bennet. Cambridge, UK: Cambridge University Press.

Leibniz, G.W. 1989. *Philosophical Essays.* Translated by Roger Ariew and Daniel Garber. Indianapolis, IN: Hackett Publishing Company.

Lefebvre, Henri. 2014. *Critique of Everyday Life.* Translated by John Moore and Gregory Elliott. London, UK: Verso.

Lévi-Strauss, Claude. 1963. *Structural Anthropology.* Translated by Claire Jacobson and Brooke Schoepf. Basic Books.

Locke, John. 1986. *The Second Treatise on Civil Government.* Buffalo, NY. Prometheus Books.

Locke, John. 1959. *An Essay Concerning Human Understanding, Volume One & Two.* New York, NY. Dover.

Lukács, Georg. 1971. *History and Class Consciousness: Studies in Marxist Dialectics.* Translated by Rodney Livingstone. Cambridge, MA: The MIT Press.

MacKinnon, Catharine A. 1989. *Toward a Feminist Theory of the State.* Cambridge, MA. Harvard University Press.

Malebranche, Nicolas. 1992. *Philosophical Selections.* Edited by Steven Nadler. Indianapolis, IN: Hackett Publishing Company.

Mannheim, Karl. 1955. *Ideology and Utopia: An Introduction to the Sociology of Knowledge.* Translated by Edward Shils. New York, NY: Harcourt Inc.

Marcuse, Herbert. 1955. *Eros and Civilization: A Philosophical Inquiry into Freud.* Boston, MA: Beacon Press.

Marx, Karl. 2009. *A Contribution to the Critique of Political Economy.* Translated by S.W. Ryazanskaya. New York, NY. International Publishers Co. Inc.

Marx, Karl. 1990. *Capital: A Critique of Political Economy, Volume I.* Translated by Ben Fowkes. New York, NY. Penguin Classics.

Marx, Karl. 1992. *Capital: A Critique of Political Economy, Volume II.* Translated by David Fernbach. New York, NY. Penguin Classics.

Marx, Karl. 1991. *Capital: A Critique of Political Economy, Volume III.* Translated by David Fernbach. New York, NY. Penguin Classics.

Marx, Leo. 1964. *The Machine in the Garden: Technology and the Pastoral Ideal in America.* London, UK. Oxford University Press.

Mead, George Herbert. 1962. *Mind, Self, & Society.* Chicago, IL. The University of Chicago Press.

Merleau-Ponty, Maurice. 2012. *Phenomenology of Perception.* Translated by Donald A. Landes. New York, NY. Routledge.

Merleau-Ponty, Maurice. 1967. *Structure of Behavior.* Translated by Alden L. Fisher. Boston, MA: Beacon Press.

Mill, John Stuart. 2002. *The Basic Writings of John Stuart Mill.* New York, NY. The Modern Library.

Mills, C. Wright. 1959. *The Sociological Imagination.* New York, NY: Oxford University Press.

Mills, C. Wright. 1956. *The Power Elite.* Oxford, UK: Oxford University Press.

Nadler, Steven. 2011. *A Book Forged in Hell: Spinoza's Scandalous Treatise and the Birth of the Secular Age.* Princeton, NJ. Princeton University Press.

Nietzsche, Friedrich. 1968. *Basic Writings of Nietzsche.* Translated by Walter Kaufmann. New York, NY. Modern Library.

Nietzsche, Friedrich. 1968. *The Will to Power.* Translated by Walter Kaufmann and R.J. Hollingdale. New York, NY. Vintage Books.

Nietzsche, Friedrich. 1982. *The Portable Nietzsche.* Translated by Walter Kaufmann. New York, NY. Penguin Books.

Nussbaum, Martha C. 1986, *The Fragility of Goodness: Luck and Ethics in Greek Tragedy and Philosophy.* Cambridge, UK: Cambridge University Press.

O'Neil, Cathy. 2016. *Weapons of Math Destruction: How Big Data Increases Inequality and Threatens Democracy.* New York, NY. Broadway Books.

Ormiston, Gayle L. and Schrift, Alan D. 1990. *The Hermeneutic Tradition: From Ast to Ricoeur.* Albany, NY. State University of New York Press.

Pangilinan, Erin. 2019. *Creating Augmented and Virtual Realities: Theory and Practice for Next-Generation Spatial Computing.* Cambridge, UK: O'Reilly Media.

Parsons, Talcott. 1964. *The Social System.* New York, NY: The Free Press.

Parsons, Talcott and Shils, Edward A. 2001. *Toward a General Theory of Action: Theoretical Foundations for the Social Sciences.* New Brunswick, USA: Transaction Publishers.

Parsons, Talcott. 1968. *The Structure of Social Action.* New York, NY: The Free Press.

Pascal, Blaise. 1995. *Pensees.* Translated by A.J. Krailsheimer. New York, NY. Penguin Books.

Patočka, Jan. 1999. *Body, Community, Language, World.* Translated by Erazim Kohák. Chicago, IL: Open Court.

Patočka, Jan. 1996. *Heretical Essays in the Philosophy of History.* Translated by Erazim Kohák. Chicago, IL: Open Court.

Patočka, Jan. 2016. *The Natural World as a Philosophical Problem.* Translated by Erika Abrams. Evanston, IL: Northwestern University Press.

Patočka, Jan. 1996. *An Introduction to Husserl's Phenomenology.* Translated by Erazim Kohák. Chicago, IL: Open Court.

Petzold, Charles. 2008. *The Annotated Turing: A Guided Tour through Alan Turing's Historic Paper on Computability and the Turing Machine*. Indianapolis, IN. Wiley Publishing, Inc.

Piaget, Jean. 2001. *The Psychology of Intelligence*. London, UK: Routledge.

Piketty, Thomas. 2014. *Capital in the Twenty-First Century*. Translated by Arthur Goldhammer. Cambridge, MA. The Belknap Press of the Harvard University Press.

Plato. 1980. *The Collected Dialogues of Plato*. Edited by Edith Hamilton and Huntington Cairns. Princeton, NJ. Princeton University Press.

Plessner, Helmuth. 2018. *Political Anthropology*. Translated by Nils F. Schott. Evanston, IL: Northwestern University Press.

Plessner, Helmuth. 2019. *Levels of Organic Life and the Human: An Introduction to Philosophical Anthropology*. Translated by Millay Hyatt. New York, NY: Fordham University Press.

Plessner, Helmuth. 1970. *Laughing and Crying: A Study of the Limits of Human Behavior*. Translated by James Spencer Churchill and Marjorie Greene. Evanston, IL: Northwestern University Press.

Polanyi, Karl. 2001. *The Great Transformation: The Political and Economic Origins of Our Time*. Boston, MA: Beacon Press.

Popper, Karl. 2002. *The Poverty of Historicism*. London, UK. Routledge.

Popper, Karl. 2002. *Conjectures and Refutations*. London, UK. Routledge.

Postman, Neil. 1986. *Amusing Ourselves to Death: Public Discourse in the Age of Show Business*. New York, NY. Penguin Books.

Putnam, Hilary. 2002. *The Collapse of the Fact/Value Dichotomy and Other Essays*. Cambridge, MA. Harvard University Press.

Putnam, Hilary. 1998. *Reason, Truth, and History*. Cambridge, UK. Cambridge University Press.

Putnam, Hilary. 1988. *Representation and Reality.* Cambridge, MA. The MIT Press.

Quine, Willard Van Orman. 1980. *From a Logical Point of View: Nine Logico-Philosophical Essays.* Cambridge, MA. Harvard University Press.

Rawls, John. 1971. *A Theory of Justice.* Cambridge, MA. Harvard University Press.

Rorty, Richard. 2009. *Contingency, Irony, and Solidarity.* Cambridge, UK. Cambridge University Press.

Roth, Michael. 1996. *The Poetics of Resistance: Heidegger's Line.* Evanston, IL. Northwestern University Press.

Roth, Michael. 2019. *Telemetry Phenomenology Commonwealth: Corporate Surveillance and the Colonization of Personality.* Kirkland, WA: Lensgrinder, Ltd.

Roth, Michael. 2020. *The Indefinite Article: Anxiety and the Essence of Artificial Intelligence.* Kirkland, WA: Lensgrinder, Ltd.

Rousseau, Jean-Jacques. 1984. *The Social Contract.* Translated by Maurice Cranston. New York, NY. Penguin Books.

Rouvroy, Antoinette and Poullet, Yves. 2009. "The Right to Informational Self-Determination and the Value of Self-Development: Reassessing the Importance of Privacy for Democracy" from *Reinventing Data Protection?* Berlin, Germany. Springer.

Sartre, Jean-Paul. 1984. *Being and Nothingness.* Translated by Hazel Barnes. New York, NY. Washington Square Press.

Sartre, Jean-Paul. 1982. *Critique of Dialectical Reason, Volume I: Theory of Practical Ensembles.* Translated by Alan Sheridan-Smith. London, UK. Verso Books.

Sartre, Jean-Paul. 1963. *Search for a Method.* Translated by Hazel E. Barnes. New York, NY: Vintage Books.

de Saussure, Ferdinand. 1966. *Course in General Linguistics.* Translated by Wade Baskin. New York, NY: McGraw Hill.

Scheler, Max. 1992. *On Feeling, Knowing, and Valuing: Selected Writings.*Chicago, IL: The University of Chicago Press.

Scheler, Max. 2012. *Problems of a Sociology of Knowledge.* Translated by Manfred S. Frings. London, UK: Routledge.

Scheler, Max. 1992. *Selected Philosophical Essays.* Translated by David R. Lachterman. Evanston, IL: Northwestern University Press.

Scheler, Max. 1973. *Formalism in Ethics and Non-Formal Ethics of Values: A New Attempt toward the Foundation of an Ethical Personalism.* Translated by Manfred S. Frings and Robert L. Funk. Evanston, IL: Northwestern University Press.

Scheler, Max. 1994. *Ressentiment.* Translated by Lewis B. Coser and William W. Holdheim. Milwaukee, WI: Marquette University Press.

Scheler, Max. 2008. *The Nature of Sympathy.* New Brunswick, NJ: Transaction Publishers.

Scheler, Max. 2009. *The Human Place in the Cosmos.* Translated by Manfred S. Frings. Evanston, IL: Northwestern University Press.

Schmitt, Carl. 1985. *Political Theology: Four Chapters on the Concept of Sovereignty.* Translated by George Schwab. Chicago, IL: The University of Chicago Press.

Schneier, Bruce. 2015. *Data and Goliath: The Hidden Battles to Collect Your Data and Control Your World.* New York, NY. WW Norton & Company.

Schoeman, Ferdinand (editor). 1984. *Philosophical Dimensions of Privacy: An Anthology.* Cambridge, UK. Cambridge University Press.

Schutz, Alfred. 1967. *Phenomenology of the Social World.* Translated by George Walsh. Evanston, IL: Northwestern University Press.

Sheehan, Thomas (ed). 1981. *Heidegger: The Man and the Thinker.* Chicago, IL. Precedent Publishing, Inc.

Silver, Nate. 2015. *The Signal and the Noise: Why So Many Predictions Fail - But Some Don't.* New York, NY. Penguin Books.

Simmel, Georg. 1972. *On Individuality and Social Forms.* Chicago, IL: University of Chicago Press.

Simmel, Georg. 1990. *The Philosophy of Money.* Translated by T.B. Bottomore and David Frisby. London, UK: Routledge.

Simondon, Gilbert. 2017. *On the Mode of Existence of Technical Objects.* Translated by Cecile Malaspina and John Rogove. Minneapolis, MN: Univocal.

Sloterdijk, Peter. 2017. *In the World Interior of Capital.* Translated by Wieland Hoban. Cambridge, UK. Polity Press.

Smart, J.J.C. 2009. *Philosophy and Scientific Realism.* London, UK. Routledge.

Smith, Adam. 1994. *The Wealth of Nations.* New York, NY. The Modern Library.

Solove, Daniel J. 2009. *Understanding Privacy.* Cambridge, MA. Harvard University Press.

Spinoza, Baruch. 1982. *The Ethics.* Translated by Samuel Shirley. Indianapolis, IN. Hackett Publishing Company.

Spinoza, Baruch. 1985. *The Collected Works of Spinoza, Volume 1.* Translated by Edwin Curley. Princeton, NJ: Princeton University Press.

Spinoza, Baruch. 2016. *The Collected Works of Spinoza, Volume 2.* Translated by Edwin Curley. Princeton, NJ: Princeton University Press.

Swift, Jonathan. 2003. *Gulliver's Travels.* New York, NY: Penguin Books.

Thompson, Evan. 2010. *Mind in Life: Biology, Phenomenology, and the Sciences of Mind.* Cambridge, MA: The Belknap Press.

Thucydides. 2013. *The War of the Peloponnesians and the Athenians.* Translated by Jeremy Mynott. Cambridge, UK: Cambridge University Press.

Tönnies, Ferdinand. 2001. *Community and Civil Society.* Translated by Jose Harris and Margaret Hollis. Cambridge, UK: Cambridge University Press.

Vanderplas, Jake. 2016. *Python Data Science Handbook: Tools and Techniques for Developers.* Cambridge, UK: O'Reilly Media.

Vaughan, William. 2018. Correspondence.

Vaughan, William. 2019. *Art in the Expanded Field: The 20th Century Aesthetic Kantgeist.* Unpublished Manuscript.

Veblen, Thorstein. 1994. *The Theory of the Leisure Class.* New York, NY: Penguin Books.

Von Mises, Ludwig. 2013. *The Theory of Money and Credit.* Translated by H.E. Batson. New York, NY: Skyhorse Publishing.

Wark, McKenzie. 2012. *Telesthesia: Communication, Culture and Class.* Cambridge, UK: Polity Press.

Warren, Samuel D. and Brandeis, Louis D. 1890. *The Right to Privacy.* Cambridge, MA. Harvard Law Review. Vol. 4, Num. 5.

Weber, Max. 2002. *The Protestant Ethic and the "Spirit" of Capitalism.* Translated by Peter Baehr and Gordon C. Wells. New York, NY. Penguin Classics.

Weber, Max. 1978. *Economy and Society.* Edited by Guenther Roth and Claus Wittich. Berkeley, CA. University of California Press.

Weber, Max. 2004. *The Vocation Lectures: Science as a Vocation / Politics as a Vocation.* Translated by Rodney Livingstone. Indianapolis, IN: Hackett Publishing Company.

Westin, Alan. *Privacy and Freedom.* 1967. New York, NY. IG Publishing.

Whyte, William H. 1956. *The Organization Man.* Philadelphia, PE: University of Pennsylvania Press.

Wiener, Norbert. 1954. *The Human Use of Human Beings: Cybernetics and Society.* New York, NY: Da Capo Press.

Wiener, Norbert. 2013. *Cybernetics: or, Control and Communication in the Animal and the Machine.* Mansfield Center, CT: Martino Publishing.

Wittgenstein, Ludwig. 2001. *Philosophical Investigations.* Translated by G.E.M. Anscombe. Malden, MA. Blackwell Publishing.

Wu, Tim. 2016. *The Attention Merchants: The Epic Scramble to Get Inside Our Heads.* New York, NY. Vintage Books.

Young-Bruehl, Elisabeth. 2004. *Hannah Arendt: For Love of the World.* New Haven: Yale University Press.

Zaharia, Matei. 2018. *Spark: The Definitive Guide.* Cambridge, UK: O'Reilly Media.

Zheng, Alice. 2018. *Feature Engineering for Machine Learning.* Cambridge, UK: O'Reilly Media.

Zizek, Slavoj. 2016. *Refugees, Terror and Other Trouble with the Neighbors: Against the Double Blackmail.* Brooklyn, NY. Melville House.

Zizek, Slavoj. 2007. "Why Heidegger Made the Right Step in 1933". Volume 1.4. International Journal of Zizek Studies.

Zizek, Slavoj. 1999. *The Ticklish Subject: The Absent Centre of Political Ontology.* London, UK. Verso.

Zuboff, Shoshana. 2019. *The Age of Surveillance Capitalism: The Fight for a Human Future at the New Frontier of Power.* London, UK: Profile Books.